RECEPTIVE ECUM
TO CATH(

MW00807581

Receptive Ecumenism and the Call to Catholic Learning

Exploring a Way for Contemporary Ecumenism

Edited by

PAUL D. MURRAY

With the assistance of

LUCA BADINI-CONFALONIERI

OXFORD
UNIVERSITY PRESS

OXFORD
UNIVERSITY PRESS

Great Clarendon Street, Oxford OX2 6DP

Oxford University Press is a department of the University of Oxford.
It furthers the University's objective of excellence in research, scholarship,
and education by publishing worldwide in

Oxford New York

Auckland Cape Town Dar es Salaam Hong Kong Karachi
Kuala Lumpur Madrid Melbourne Mexico City Nairobi
New Delhi Shanghai Taipei Toronto

With offices in

Argentina Austria Brazil Chile Czech Republic France Greece
Guatemala Hungary Italy Japan Poland Portugal Singapore
South Korea Switzerland Thailand Turkey Ukraine Vietnam

Oxford is a registered trade mark of Oxford University Press
in the UK and in certain other countries

Published in the United States
by Oxford University Press Inc., New York

© Oxford University Press 2008

British Library Cataloguing in Publication Data

Data available

Library of Congress Cataloging in Publication Data

Data available

Typeset by SPI Publisher Services, Pondicherry, India
Digitally printed and bound in
Great Britain by
CPI Antony Rowe, Chippenham and Eastbourne

ISBN 978–0–19–921645–1 (Hbk.)
ISBN 978–0–19–958798–8 (Pbk.)

1 3 5 7 9 10 8 6 4 2

This work is dedicated with gratitude to

His Eminence Cardinal Walter Kasper,
President of the Pontifical Council for Promoting Christian Unity,
for his inspiration in the way of Receptive Ecumenism,
and to
Shelagh Mary Murray (1937–) and James Gerard Murray (1934–),
my parents, and first educators in the way of Catholic Learning.

May they each continue to grow into the fullness of the promise this Way holds.

Foreword

In January 2006, at Ushaw College near Durham, the city of St Cuthbert and St Bede, an international colloquium was held in my honour on the subject of Receptive Ecumenism. The colloquium was held in conjunction with Durham University's generous decision to confer on me an honorary doctorate, drawing attention to the important work of seeking reconciliation among all of Christ's disciples.

A briefing document circulated amongst participants helped to articulate what was meant by the phrase Receptive Ecumenism:

whilst the strategy espoused here is a mutual process in which each offers its own gifts as well as receiving from those of others, the primary emphasis is upon learning rather than teaching. That is, the ethic in this process of ecclesial learning, or Receptive Ecumenism, is one wherein each tradition takes responsibility for its own potential learning from others and is, in turn, willing to facilitate the learning of others as requested but without dictating terms and without making others' learning a precondition to attending to one's own.[1]

Following upon the Durham colloquium, the present volume is a further exploration of the theme of Receptive Ecumenism.

When I first saw the plan of the colloquium, I was surprised. Since I live in Rome I am accustomed to surprises. The main reason for my surprises is not Rome, but rather that ecumenism is itself full of surprises—leaving open for the moment whether they are always surprises of the Holy Spirit. But in this case the surprise was a good one. Ecumenists tend to be utopian, and often the wish is the father of their thoughts. When reality does not correspond to their thoughts, suddenly they become typical German Hegelians and speak of 'bad' reality, of an ecumenical winter, or, even worse, of a glacial period. By contrast, the approach of the Durham colloquium, and of this collection of essays, fortunately seems to be less continental, less Germanic and more British—that is, more realistic. It takes what might be regarded as the specifically Anglican approach of a *via media* and speaks of an intermediary ecumenical situation. I welcome this assessment and I am grateful for it. Though Hegel comes from the same Swabian tribe that I come from, there is one common feature between us Swabians and the British: exaggeration is not our job. We remain down to earth.

Ecumenism is linked with hope, but hope is fundamentally different from utopian ideas. Ecumenism is firmly founded in a central and fundamental reality: that is, the death and resurrection of our common Lord Jesus Christ. Therefore,

---

[1] For further, see Chapter 1: Murray, 'Receptive Ecumenism and Catholic Learning—Establishing the Agenda'.

hope will always be hope against hope. When we join Jesus' prayer on the eve of his death, 'that all may be one', when we pray in his name, then such a prayer has all the promises of the Gospel with it. Then there is no room for pessimism or scepticism. I am convinced: Christ's Spirit who initiated the ecumenical process will bring it to its fulfilment. But He will do it, when, where, and how He will. Hope therefore is linked with patience, which is the little sister of hope.

In the meantime, it is right that we ask what we can do in the present context. Joining Jesus' prayer means first of all spiritual ecumenism, which becomes practical in what Pope John Paul II defined as ecumenical dialogue—not only an exchange of ideas but an 'exchange of gifts'. This is an excellent definition, which repeats in new and fresh expressions what theologians following ancient patristic tradition of the still-undivided church called the reception process. With this theme we are therefore in good company.

The Second Vatican Council described the church as a pilgrim people, as a church which is on the way towards its eschatological fulfilment; that is, as a church that has to grow and to mature to the fullness of what it was from its very beginning and what it will be for ever. To be in dialogue, to listen to each other, and to learn from each other does not mean to become a new church but to become a spiritually renewed church. We do not want to meet at the lowest common denominator, we do not want to give up what was holy to our forefathers or to make short-sighted compromises. Through dialogue we will not lose anything which is worthy, but we will be enriched by the gifts of the others. To learn from each other can be the way the Spirit guides us in the whole truth.

Over the past four decades, bilateral commissions have produced texts which have invited closer relations and an increase in common mission and witness. But obstacles or complications have often emerged in the context of the reception of dialogue statements. Hence the potentially transforming effects of such statements on the ecclesial lives of the dialogue partners have been lessened. In asking what might be learned or received with integrity from other Christian traditions, the model of Receptive Ecumenism is attentive to practical steps which could be taken as a result of that learning. It is conducive to a bridging of theological discussions and ecclesial practice. This enterprise is thus a part of an 'ecumenism of life' which needs to accompany the 'ecumenism of truth' reflected in the dialogues.

My wish for this initiative is that it be marked by a spirit of patient listening and humble learning. I am convinced that it will contribute to a new start and hopefully also a new spring within the ecumenical movement.

Cardinal Walter Kasper
President of the Pontifical Council for Promoting Christian Unity
Rome

Preface

Paul D. Murray

Staff of the Department of Theology and Religion at Durham University and of St Cuthbert's Seminary, Ushaw College, in collaboration with colleagues in Australian, European, and North American institutions, have been engaged for a number of years now on a research project in Receptive Ecumenism and Catholic Learning. This has, in effect, constituted the first public activity of the Durham Centre for Catholic Studies.[1]

The fundamental concern lying behind the project might be summarized thus: too often in the ecumenical context the default instinct is to lead with some such question as: 'What do *our* various others first need to learn from *us* if we are to get ecumenically serious and make any real progress?' At one level this is an entirely natural question to ask: if we did not each find particular value in the various contexts in which we are located—if we did not find them contexts that mediate the call of God and that facilitate our deepened conversion into that call—then, presumably, we would cease to be located there. With this, essential to the ecumenical task, is a clear appreciation of the significantly different understandings of the nature and unity of the church that are operative across the Christian traditions. Leaving aside considerations of appropriateness of tone, it is this concern that lies behind the August 2000 Declaration of the Congregation for the Doctrine of the Faith, *Dominus Iesus*.[2] So, the problem perceived here with the question as to 'What *others* might fruitfully learn from *us?*', lies not so much with the question itself as with its potential overemphasis relative to other concerns, with the result that significant ecumenical learning comes too easily to be perceived as a responsibility solely for others rather than for oneself and one's own community. In this regard, the ease with which such a tendency can be at work within each and every Christian tradition needs to be honestly recognized.

In contrast, the fundamental principle within Receptive Ecumenism and Catholic Learning is that each tradition should focus first on the self-critical question: 'What can *we* learn, or *receive*, with integrity from *our* various others

---

[1] Emergent since early 2005, this Centre was formally established in October 2007 and launched in May 2008.

[2] Congregation for the Doctrine of the Faith, '*Dominus Iesus:* On the Unicity and Salvific Universality of Jesus Christ and the Church' (6 Aug. 2000) (London: CTS, 2000), also at <http://www.vatican.va/roman_curia/congregations/cfaith/documents/rc_con_cfaith_doc_20000806_dominus-iesus_en.html>; cf. Walter Kasper, 'The Current Situation in Ecumenical Theology', *That They May All Be One: The Call To Unity Today* (London: Burns & Oates, 2004), 15–16.

in order to facilitate our own growth together into deepened communion in Christ and the Spirit?' The driving assumption is that if all were to be asking and acting upon this question, even relatively independently of each other, then all would be moving, albeit somewhat unpredictably, and in such a fashion as might open up currently unforeseeable possibilities.

The project was originally envisaged as having four stages to it. First was a generative or conceptual–developmental stage, during which the guiding ideas and vision were articulated, and about thirty scholars and distinguished ecumenists and ecclesiastics representing a range of denominational commitments and theological expertise were invited to produce discussion documents, probing this thinking in relation to a variety of themes, contexts, perspectives, and analytical resources. Following this, there was to be a second, critical–constructive stage, during which the authors of the discussion papers would be brought together, along with other invited scholars, ecumenists, and ecclesiastics with varying expertise in the theological, pastoral, and social–scientific analysis of the church, to engage in sustained critical–constructive exploration of the thinking behind the project and initial papers. At the heart of this second stage was an international colloquium that took place from 12–17 January 2006 at Ushaw College, Durham, the Roman Catholic Seminary for the north of England, to mark the conferral by Durham University of the degree of Doctor of Divinity _honoris causa_ on His Eminence Cardinal Walter Kasper, in recognition of his outstanding contribution to contemporary Roman Catholic theology, and to ecumenical thought and practice in particular.[3] This second, critical–constructive stage— variously described by key participants as 'historic', 'groundbreaking', 'the most significant academic theological event in the UK in living memory', and as 'providing the much-needed fresh thinking and practical model that could be applied elsewhere'—was envisaged as leading into a third stage of refinement, further development, and formal articulation, leading to the writing of a major scholarly volume. The dual purpose of this volume would be: (a) to propose and test a fresh approach to ecumenical theology and practice—Receptive Ecumenism—fit for the exigencies of the contemporary situation, and (b) to illustrate and apply this approach, as befits the basic vision and ethos behind the project, to Roman Catholicism's own specific need as the host tradition for receptive ecumenical learning from other Christian traditions; hence the twin concepts—Receptive Ecumenism and Catholic Learning. The result is this present volume. Finally, it was envisaged that the project would culminate in a fourth stage of dissemination, seeking to draw attention to the work thus far completed and promoting its further uptake and application through further conferences, meetings with potential 'multipliers', public presentations, and popular-level articles.

---

[3] See Elena Curti and Michael Hirst, 'Amid the Cold, Signs of a Thaw', _The Tablet_ (21 Jan. 2006), 12–13; Pat Ashworth, 'Unity is Symphonic, Says Cardinal', _Church Times_ (20 Jan. 2006), 5.

In fact, however, the project has already spilled over into a very significant fifth stage, marking a further shift from the conceptual–analytical–theoretical register that is generally to the fore in this volume, to the directly practical and local in the shape of a three-year Regional Comparative Research Project in Receptive Ecumenism and the Local Church, involving the Roman Catholic Diocese of Hexham and Newcastle, the Northern Synod of the United Reformed Church, the Northern Baptist Association, the Methodist Districts of Darlington and Newcastle, the Northern Division of the Salvation Army, and the Anglican Dioceses of Durham and Newcastle. Intended as a particular local lens through which matters of universal ecclesial significance can be tested and taken forward, this further phase is unfolding as a collaborative interdisciplinary study of what each tradition might learn from the other participant traditions against three key trajectories: (1) governance and finance; (2) leadership and ministry; (3) learning and formation. This is but one example of the practical initiatives which have already been inspired by the thinking behind this intentionally programmatic volume. It is hoped that there will be many more. *Receptive Ecumenism and the Call to Catholic Learning: Exploring a Way for Contemporary Ecumenism* has both a past and, it is hoped, a continuing story of divers ecclesial enactments in service of the pedagogy of the church.

In this vein, what this volume is essentially about might best be expressed in terms of: (1) *the dreaming of dreams*; (2) *the testing of such dreams for their viability*; and (3) *the discerning together of what might either hinder or promote their embodied ecclesial realization*. These are the three voices, the three concerns, in which and in accordance with which the volume unfolds. We might refer to them respectively as *the poetic*, *the analytic*, and *the pragmatic*; or, alternatively, as *the imaginative–constructive*, the *critical–constructive*, and *the practical–organizational*. They might be held to be the three key voices in which all good ecclesial theology is performed,[4] which fits with the intention of this volume to model what committed, critical ecclesial theology of the highest scholarly standard should be like.

Of course, the placing of lead emphasis on the imaginative, the constructive, *the poetic*—the dreaming of dreams or, better, the having of dreams evoked in

---

[4] The identification of *the poetic*, *the analytic* and *the pragmatic* as the three key—and necessarily interrelated—voices of theology is resonant with John Henry Newman's reflections on the threefold office of the Church—priestly, prophetic, and kingly—as delineated in the 1877 preface to the third edition of *The Via Media of the Anglican Church* and the use to which Nicholas Lash has, in turn, put these reflections as three intertwined, all-pervasive aspects of authentic Christian living in relation to God. Where, for Newman, the priestly represents the devotional heart and soul of Church life, the prophetic represents its critical reason, or formal theological function, and the kingly represents its organizational reality and system of governance, its body politic. See Newman, *The Via Media of the Anglican Church*, 3rd edn. (London: Longmans, Green, & Co., 1877), p. xl; and Lash, *Easter in Ordinary: Reflections on Human Experience and the Knowledge of God* (London: SCM, 1988), 136–40; id., 'Life, Language and Organization: Aspects of the Theological Ministry', *Theology on Dover Beach* (London: DLT, 1979), 89–108; also Murray, 'Theology "Under the Lash": Theology as Idolatry-Critique in the Work of Nicholas Lash', in Stephen C. Barton (ed.), *Idolatry: False Worship in the Bible, Early Judaism and Christianity* (London: T. & T. Clark, 2007), 246–66.

us—does not neglect that the greater part of theological labour is carried out in considerably more sober mood than that might otherwise suggest. As is true also of the chapters printed here, the staple diet of intellectual work in the ecclesial context, as in any other, lies not in fantasy but in disciplined attention and critical scrutiny. The point in leading with the constructive, *the poetic*, is neither to diminish nor to marginalize such patient labours but to call out to centre-stage the real purpose for which ecclesial theologians ultimately pursue them, and this regardless of professional context—whether that of the secular academy, or ecclesial administration, or the denominationally founded institution.

Related to this, there is a sense in which we should be able to say of all intellectual labour that the real point of our disciplined attention is to learn to see more adequately what is the case precisely in order to be able to perceive more clearly what possibilities lie open for increased well-being.[5] If that is true of intellectual labour in general, it should certainly be true of all ecclesial intellectual labour which simply cannot be pursued for its own sake, without falling into idolatrous self-contradiction; any more than the church can properly understand itself as existing simply for its own sake. The authors of the chapters printed here are united in the conviction that whatever refined degree of eloquence and expertise we might develop in our particular areas of specialism and responsibility, the point of it is to enable the church to walk more discerningly into its future, out of which and towards which it exists, so that it might, in turn, better serve its task of illuminating the possibilities for created flourishing in God.

So, this dreaming of dreams is neither detached from reality nor does it stand as an end in itself. It presupposes both life in the church in all its historical specificity and a great deal of sustained patient labour of understanding and action, much of which is mediated to us through the work of others. It departs from such patient labour only in the sense that it takes off from it; not in the sense that it denies it. It is, we might say, what becomes possible when ecclesial intellectual activity 'grows wings'. Again, it presupposes its own provisionality, its own need for testing; and this not just at the level of ideas, theory, and concept, but also in relation to the embodied, institutional reality of ecclesial life. It is an exercise in what Nicholas M. Healy refers to as the need for a practical–prophetic ecclesiology.[6] Constructive ecclesial theology—ecclesial *poiesis*—is, then, necessarily done in the middle of things: poised between given circumstances and accumulated understanding, on the one hand, and necessary accountability, refinement, and anticipated actualization, on the other.

Such ecclesial *poiesis* cannot be a solo affair. It is necessarily a collegial process and this even whilst recognizing the decisive contribution that individuals are capable of making. The scientific community—albeit typically within somewhat narrowly focussed and distinct research teams—is much more *au fait* with this

---

[5] See Murray, *Reason, Truth and Theology in Pragmatist Perspective* (Leuven: Peeters, 2004), 3–4, 7–8, 75–7, 117–20.

[6] Healy, *Church, World and the Christian Life: Practical–Prophetic Ecclesiology* (Cambridge: Cambridge University Press, 2000).

mode of working than tends to be the case in the humanities. The conviction behind this volume, as also behind the project from which it derives, is that it should come just as naturally—indeed, more naturally—to ecclesial theologians both to recognize the ultimately collegial context in which their work is situated and to seek to develop projects that reflect this. The principle is that good ecclesial thinking, discerning, and learning require to be done together, with as many of the significant voices and perspectives as possible gathered in conversation. It is upon just such an exercise in collaborative ecclesial learning that we are engaged in this volume.

As to how all of this is reflected in the structure of the volume: there are basically five key movements at work.

Part I, 'Vision and Principles', starts out with the editor's chapter laying out the fundamental thinking behind the book and drawing out the agenda it poses. Following this is a series of chapters by Margaret O'Gara, Ladislas Örsy, Philip Sheldrake, Nicholas Lash, Walter Kasper, and Riccardo Larini, each also oriented in varying ways on the pertinent theological, methodological, and hermeneutical principles at play here.

In Part II, 'Receptive Ecumenical Learning Through Catholic Dialogue', chapters by Keith Pecklers, Michael Putney, David Chapman, William Rusch, and Paul McPartlan pursue, in turn, the possibilities that lie open for receptive ecumenical learning grounded in the respective dialogues between Catholicism and Anglicanism, Methodism, Lutheranism, and Orthodoxy. These are intended as indicative exploratory studies of what Receptive Ecumenism might mean and, to some extent, has already meant for Roman Catholicism when viewed through the lens of the specific gifts of other particular Christian traditions. None of these chapters claims to say the last word on potential Catholic Learning from the particular other traditions in view. Equally, it is clearly the case that the list of appropriate stimuli to such learning, at the level of entire traditions, requires to be far more extensive than is here modelled. Acknowledging this, these indicative exploratory forays into receptive Catholic Learning are not simply about taking stock of where we have got to; of what the story *has* been. Much more significantly, they are about exploring what lies open. They are, we might say, exercises in thinking the limits of the possible in the conviction that such limits may themselves expand as we move towards them. Or, expressed more theologically, they are guided by the conviction that grace not only opens and fills the available space, it expands current capacity in the very action of filling it.

Continuing in a related vein, James Puglisi, Denis Edwards, Joseph Famerée, Paul Lakeland, and Patrick Connolly turn in Part III, 'Receptive Ecumenism and Catholic Church Order', to probe how specific live issues in Roman Catholic thought and practice relating to apostolicity, primacy, collegiality, lay participation in ecclesial governance, and episcopacy might be constructively tended through appropriate receptive Catholic Learning from across the other Christian traditions.

So far, so good, as the invigorating air of ecclesial *poiesis*, of constructive theological exploration, is taken. But, even allowing for what is distinctive about the Receptive Ecumenism agenda,[7] there may, nevertheless, be a nagging question in the back of the reader's mind as to whether any of this potential Catholic Learning is, in itself, startlingly fresh? Are there not already shelves groaning under huge volumes of theological writings examining how particular traditions might understand each other better and even learn something from each other? Posing this question leads to a pivotal moment, for it, in turn, prompts the further question: given this considerable body of extant work, why has it generally led to such slight change in practice? Or, putting this more pointedly in relation to the host tradition: what factors hinder real receptive ecumenical learning within Catholicism? What is it that militates against Catholicism being a mature learning community? And how might this situation best be tended to, or ministered to, therapeutically in such a fashion as might help free the ecclesial body of Catholicism for greater flourishing?

These are the concerns that are to the fore in Part IV, 'The Pragmatics of Receptive Ecumenical Learning', where the focus turns from examining constructive possibilities and scrutinizing their viability (Parts II–III) to seeking to diagnose the various non-explicitly theological factors that contribute, for good or ill, and in varying degrees at various levels, to the health of Catholicism. This part of the process opens with two further case-study explorations by Mary Tanner and Donald Bolen, this time case-studies in good practice and poor experience in ecumenical receptivity. These explorations are then complemented by a sideways look at (with Brendan Tuohy) and theological reflection upon (with Eamonn Conway), related issues that have arisen in the process of seeking to manage organizational change in the Irish civil service—the principle being that it is generally easier to deal with difficult issues in relation to another than it is in relation to oneself. This, in turn, leads into a series of four chapters by Geraldine Smyth, Peter McGrail, James Sweeney, and Thomas Reese, drawing upon some of the various other diagnostic tools in addition to the explicitly theological—here, the psychological, the sociological, and the organizational— that are required if we are to make headway in understanding and ministering to the psyche, the culture, and the body politic of Catholicism.

The image has occurred a number of times here of the task of theology as one of therapeutic ministry. Given the explicitly collaborative nature of this exercise and the concern it evinces to draw together a variety of ecclesial voices and responsibilities, that image might be sharpened into the notion of ecclesial theology as being, in some respects, a process of family therapy, with all the combination of commitment, difficulty, and desire that that connotes. Furthermore, such a process of critical thinking about difficult issues is not to be confused with

---

[7] See 'Chapter 1: Murray, Receptive Ecumenism and Catholic Learning—Establishing the Agenda'.

an attitude of aggression or hostility. On the contrary, the motive is one of love, and here not the detached condescension conveyed by the English word charity but the full-blooded commitment of heartfelt passion, with all that suggests about gratitude, delight, desire, the determination to struggle for something worth struggling for, and the patience to bear with it, even, if necessary, to suffer for it.

In Part V, 'Retrospect and Prospect', the three-stranded conversation at work in the volume—*the poetic, the analytic, the pragmatic; the dreaming of dreams, the testing of such dreams,* and *the discerning of what hinders and promotes their realization*—is brought full-circle with a series of chapters reflecting back on aspects of earlier chapters and probing how the Receptive Ecumenism and Catholic Learning agenda might be taken forwards in divers ways. Here, the chapters by Andrew Louth and Nicholas Sagovsky are most explicitly in conversation with earlier chapters in the volume, whilst the chapters by Hervé Legrand, Gabriel Flynn, Gerard Mannion, and Dan Hardy explore the implications for ecumenical dialogues and for the very practice and task of ecumenism and ecumenical ecclesiology. In turn, the chapters by Jeffrey Gros and Peter Phillips are focused respectively on the key practical, pastoral issues of catechesis and eucharistic sharing.

The dreaming of dreams ... the having of dreams evoked in us ... the chapters in this volume are written in the conviction that some dreams are not simply subjective fantasy, idle diversion, or bulwarks against the terror of reality, but given to us by an Other whose dreams they are, and given to us precisely in order to be born into being. It is the hope of the contributors that something of this transformative potential will be mediated by this volume.

Feast of Saint Peter and Saint Paul, 2007

Acknowledgements

Given the collaborative nature of the endeavour, it is necessarily the case that thanks are due to a great many individuals and organizations without whose support the Receptive Ecumenism and Catholic Learning research project would have remained simply an interesting idea rather than a realized possibility.

At key points invaluable advice and encouragement were offered by Mrs Andrea Murray, Professor David F. Ford, Professor Daniel W. Hardy,[1] Dr David Barker, Mr David Carter, Dr Gerard Mannion, Ms Jane Leek, Mr John Wilkins, Dr Karen Kilby, Professor Margaret O'Gara, Revd Mark Woodruff, Professor Nicholas M. Healy, Professor Nicholas Lash, Revd Professor Paul McPartlan, Rt Revd Professor Stephen W. Sykes, Mrs Thérèse Pratt, and, most significantly, Mgr Donald Bolen of the Pontifical Council for Promoting Christian Unity. Without Don's interest, guidance, and care, the project, in this form, would have been stillborn and would certainly have lacked a considerable amount of its sparkle.

Sincere thanks are also owing both to those who prepared discussion papers for the January 2006 colloquium at Ushaw College, Durham and to all who subsequently prepared chapters for this volume. The enthusiasm each demonstrated was heartening and affirming of the timeliness of the project. Particular thanks are due here to: Margaret O'Gara, who generously agreed to co-facilitate the colloquium, bringing a calm clarity and gentle wisdom to the distracted passion and frayed energy of its convenor; Philip Endean, who committed to the demanding task of offering daily reflection 'in a different voice' on the unfolding work of the colloquium; and, pre-eminently, Cardinal Walter Kasper who, amidst a punishing schedule, committed to being the focus for the colloquium and this volume, as part of the celebrations surrounding his having conferred on him the honorary degree of Doctor of Divinity by the Chancellor of Durham University in Durham Cathedral on 12 January 2006.

In addition to advisers, contributors, and figureheads, projects of this kind also require both an appropriate institutional (and in this case also, ecclesial) home and significant financial sponsorship. As regards the former, it is less that the Receptive Ecumenism and Catholic Learning project found a home in Durham and more that it was conceived, nurtured, and born into life in the fertile space between Cuthbert, the pastor-saint, and Bede, the scholar-saint, that Durham Cathedral represents; itself a fitting witness to the distinctive partnership between

---

[1] As is similarly acknowledged in so many other works, conversation and engagement with Dan over many years have been vital ingredients in the shaping of the thinking behind this work. It is a gross understatement to say that his death, since first writing these acknowledgements, has left the academic theological community significantly poorer. *Requiescat in pacem.*

Church and academy that lay behind the project. Specifically, the two serving Heads of the Department of Theology and Religion at Durham University during the project's gestation and maturation, Professor Douglas J. Davies and Professor John W. Barclay, each gave their strong support, as did the newly arrived Dean of Arts and Humanities, Professor Seth Kunin, and the then Vice-Chancellor of the University, Sir Ken Calman, along with many other colleagues, most notably: Revd Professor Andrew Louth, Dr Mathew Guest, and Professor Philip Sheldrake. Similarly, Rt Revd Terry Drainey, then Rector of Ushaw College, along with the excellent staff of that venerable institution, immediately agreed to co-host the colloquium phase of the project. Indeed, it was in being thrown, whilst formerly on the staff of Ushaw College, into teaching on the module 'Church and Ministry in an Ecumenical Context'—in partnership with the local Anglican Theological College, Cranmer Hall, and the Wesley Study Centre, Durham as part of a collaborative degree programme in Theology and Ministry—that *Receptive Ecumenism and the Call to Catholic Learning* first began to take root.

Beyond this fruitful partnership between the now secular academy (Durham University) and the local theological colleges, of key importance to the project has been the desire that it should serve to model something of what is possible—and this for mutual benefit—in relation to creative collaboration more broadly between religious communities and departments of Theology and Religion situated within the public academy. In this regard, it was heartening that in addition to a considerable number of highly experienced ecumenists and ecclesial bureaucrats and, of course, the presence of Cardinal Kasper, the research colloquium at the heart of the project also attracted the active participation of five Roman Catholic bishops (Bishop Kevin Dunn of Hexham and Newcastle, Bishop Michael Evans of East Anglia, Bishop Michael Putney of Townsville, Australia, Bishop Tom Williams of Liverpool (Auxiliary), and Archbishop Mario Conti of Glasgow), three Anglican bishops (Bishop Stephen Sykes, formerly of Ely, Bishop John Flack of the Anglican Centre, Rome, and Bishop Tom Wright of Durham), one Orthodox Archimandrite (Ephraim Lash), and the General Secretary of the British Methodist Church (David Deeks). Here particular mention must be made of my own local ordinary, the late Bishop Kevin Dunn, who so warmly gave very significant personal and institutional support to the project throughout as the President of the colloquium. Along with the aforementioned death of Dan Hardy, it is a cause of immense sadness that the untimely death of Bishop Dunn on 1 March 2008 has prevented him from seeing the project come to published fruition. *Requiescat in pacem.*

As regards financial sponsorship, grateful thanks, for varying levels of support and mediation, are due, in alphabetical order, to: the British Academy, the Department of Theology and Religion (Durham University), the Diocese of Hexham and Newcastle, the Diocese of Salford, the Halley Stewart Trust, the Jerusalem Trust, Mr P. N. and Mrs A. L. Lanigan, St John's College (Durham), the *Tablet* and the *Pastoral Review*, and Ushaw College. It is hoped that sat-isfaction will be gained from knowing that the vital irrigation given to the original Receptive Ecumenism and Catholic Learning project is already bearing significant fruit beyond the immediate aims of that project in the dual form of: (1) having injected decisive momentum into the formal establishment of the Durham Centre for Catholic Studies and (2) having, in turn, stimulated the development of a further unique, fully ecumenical, collaborative research project in the form of a three-year regional study in Receptive Ecumenism and the Local Church involving all the major Christian traditions in the north-east of England.

At the sharp end of practical organization and assistance, invaluable help has generously been provided by: the secretarial team within the Department of Theology and Religion, particularly Mrs Anne Parker, Senior Secretary; the administrative, catering, and domestic staff at Ushaw College Conference Centre; those who prepared, led, and contributed to the immensely powerful liturgies that were a key part of the January 2006 experience (Revd Philip Gillespie, Revd David Chapman, Durham Palatinate, and Keith Wright and, most significantly of all here, Tim Harrison, Director of Music at Ushaw College); and those who generously gave all manner of other forms of practical assistance (Revd Anthony Currer, Luca Badini-Confalonieri, Revd Michael Fitzsimons, Revd Morrough O'Brien, Revd Philip Caldwell, and Theodora Hawksley). As all involved would recognize, in a class of his own here is Luca Badini-Confalonieri who, with irrepressible enthusiasm acted as the administrative assistant for the colloquium itself and subsequent assistant in the production of this volume.

Relevant also here, of course, is the excellent professional care of Oxford University Press and associates, particularly Lucy Qureshi, Tom Perridge, Alice Jacobs, Paul Smith and Mick Belson.

All Scripture citations are taken from the New Revised Standard Version, unless embedded within citations of other sources. All English language citations of the documents of the Second Vatican Council are taken from: *Vatican Council II: The Conciliar and Post Conciliar Documents*, ed. Austin Flannery (Leominster: Fowler Wright, 1980). Cardinal Walter Kasper's chapter and the Editor's opening chapter, along with some additional material from the Preface, were each first published ahead of this volume in the *International Journal for the Study of the Christian Church*, 7 (2007), 250–60 and 279–301. Gabriel Flynn's chapter draws on elements of an earlier essay published in *Lourain Studies* 31(2006), 196–213.

Finally, it remains for me to express my most heartfelt gratitude to and appreciation for my friends and family—the 'community of my heart', in David Ford's evocative phrase—who keep things in right perspective and put things in context; most particularly here is my immeasurable appreciation for Andrea, Anna, and Bede: for the privileged daily context they provide for my own continued schooling in the ways of receptive Catholic Learning and for the patient love they show on an equally regular basis to an inveterately slow learner.

Contents

PART III. RECEPTIVE ECUMENISM AND CATHOLIC CHURCH ORDER

PART IV. THE PRAGMATICS OF RECEPTIVE ECUMENICAL LEARNING

List of Contributors

Monsignor Donald Bolen is a priest of the Archdiocese of Regina (Saskatchewan, Canada), and, since 2001, has been assigned to the Pontifical Council for Promoting Christian Unity in Rome as the Vatican's officer for relations with the Anglican Communion and the World Methodist Council. In this capacity he is the co-secretary of the Anglican–Roman Catholic International Commission, the Anglican–Roman Catholic Commission for Unity and Mission, and the Joint International Commission for Dialogue between the World Methodist Council and the Roman Catholic Church. He also serves on the international commission responsible for preparing texts for the Week of Prayer for Christian Unity. He is the co-editor (with Gregory Cameron) of *Mary: Grace and Hope in Christ* (London: Continuum, 2006), text with commentaries and study guide.

David M. Chapman is an ordained minister of the Methodist Church of Great Britain. He is the Methodist co-secretary of the British Methodist–Roman Catholic Committee and a member of the Joint International Commission for Dialogue between the World Methodist Council and the Roman Catholic Church. His publications include *In Search of the Catholic Spirit: Methodists and Roman Catholics in Dialogue* (London: Epworth, 2004).

Patrick Connolly, a priest of the Diocese of Clogher, is a Senior Lecturer in the Department of Theology and Religious Studies at Mary Immaculate College, University of Limerick, where he is also coordinator of the department's taught postgraduate programmes. He was previously an assistant professor at Saint Paul University in Ottawa, Canada, and has also served in parish and church tribunal work. His area of expertise is canon law. Selected publications include 'Priest and Bishop: Implications of the Abuse Crisis', *The Furrow*, 57 (2006), 129–43 and 'Contrasts in the Western and Eastern Approaches to Marriage', *Studia Canonica*, 35 (2001), 357–402.

Eamonn Conway, a Catholic priest, is Professor and Head of Theology and Religious Studies at Mary Immaculate College, University of Limerick and co-director of the Centre for Culture, Technology, and Values. He is author of *The Anonymous Christian: A Relativised Christianity? An Evaluation of Hans Urs von Balthasar's Criticisms of Karl Rahner's Theory of the Anonymous Christian* (Frankfurt: Peter Lang, 1993) and has edited five other books, most recently *The Courage to Risk Everything. Essays Marking the Centenary of Karl Rahner's Birth* (Leuven: Peeters, 2004). He currently co-leads a pan-European research project on 'Culture, Technology, and Religion' funded by the Metanexus Institute. Until recently he served on the Irish Government's *Information Society Commission*. He is a former member of the Editorial Board of *Concilium: International Review for Theology*.

Denis Edwards is a Senior Lecturer in Systematic Theology in the School of Theology of Flinders University and at the Adelaide College of Divinity. He is a priest of the Roman Catholic Archdiocese of Adelaide. Currently he is the chair of the Ecumenical Commission of the Archdiocese of Adelaide, a member of the Australian Anglican–Roman Catholic Commission and co-chair of the national Lutheran–Roman Catholic Dialogue. He is a member of the Catholic Earthcare Australia Advisory Council. He has been involved with some of the international series of conferences on science and theology that have been co-sponsored by the Center for Theology and the Natural Sciences (Berkeley) and the Vatican Observatory. He has edited two books and written eight monographs, the most recent of which is *Breath of Life: A Theology of the Creator Spirit* (Maryknoll, NY: Orbis, 2004).

Philip Endean, SJ teaches theology in the University of Oxford and was formerly at Heythrop College, University of London. He has been editor of *The Way*, a journal of spirituality published by the British Jesuits, and has numerous articles to his name. His first monograph, *Karl Rahner and Ignatian Spirituality* (Oxford: Clarendon Press, 2001) has met with considerable critical acclaim.

Joseph Famerée SCJ is a member of the Congregation of the Priests of the Sacred Heart (Dehonians). He was educated at the Université Catholique de Louvain where, since 1995, he has been Professor of Ecclesiology, Ecumenism, the Theology of the Eastern Churches, and the History of Dogma. He has held Visiting Fellowships at the Istituto per le Scienze Religiose, Bologna, the Aristotle University of Thessaloniki, and St Vladimir's Orthodox Theological Faculty, New York. He is a member of the Académie internationale des sciences religieuses, the Praesidium of the European Society for Catholic Theology, and the Groupe des Dombes. He has numerous publications to his name.

Gabriel Flynn is currently Lecturer in Systematic Theology and Head of the School of Theology at Mater Dei Institute, Dublin City University. His main research interests are in the areas of ecclesiology and ecumenism, historical and political theology, and the great Catholic thinkers of the twentieth century. His publications include: *Yves Congar's Vision of the Church in a World of Unbelief* (Aldershot: Ashgate, 2004); *This Church That I Love: Essays Celebrating the Centenary of the Birth of Yves Cardinal Congar* (Leuven: Peeters, 2004); *Yves Congar: Theologian of the Church* (Leuven: Peeters, 2005); *Yves Congar: théologien de l'Église*, (Paris: Éditions du Cerf, 2007). He is currently editing, with Paul D. Murray, *Ressourcement: A Movement for Renewal in Twentieth Century Catholic Theology*, for Oxford University Press.

Jeffrey Gros, FSC was educated at St Mary's University, Winona, Marquette University, and Fordham University. He has taught secondary school, university, and seminary theology. He served for ten years as the Director of Faith and Order for the National Council of Churches, USA and for fourteen years as the Associate Director of the Secretariat for Ecumenical and Interreligious Affairs of the US Conference of Catholic Bishops. In addition to having edited numerous significant volumes in ecumenical theology, single and joint-authored books include: *Introduction to Ecumenism* (Mahwah,

NY: Paulist Press, 1998); *That All May Be One: Ecumenism* (Chicago, Iu.: Loyola University Press, 2000); *Handing on the Faith in an Ecumenical World* (Washington, DC: National Catholic Educational Association, 2005).

Daniel W. Hardy, American by birth, Dan Hardy was educated there and at Oxford before being ordained an Anglican priest. He held a variety of university posts: at the University of Birmingham; Van Mildert Professor at Durham University; Director (President) of the Center of Theological Inquiry, Princeton; and the University of Cambridge. His work was focused on the intelligibility of theology in modern times, fundamental theology, and ecclesiology. His published writings include: *Jubilate: Theology in Praise* (with David F. Ford) (London: Darton, Longman & Todd, 1984); *God's Ways with the World: Thinking and Practising Christian Faith* (Edinburgh: T. & T. Clark, 1996); and *Finding the Church* (London: SCM, 2001). Sadly, Dan died on 15th November 2007 before seeing this work in print.

His Eminence Cardinal Walter Kasper was appointed in 1964 to the Chair in Dogmatic Theology at the Catholic Faculty of Theology in Münster. From 1970 to 1989 he held the Chair in Dogmatic Theology at the Catholic Faculty of Theology in Tübingen. In 1989 he was appointed Bishop of Rottenburg-Stuttgart. In 1999 he was appointed by Pope John Paul II as Secretary to the Pontifical Council for Promoting Christian Unity and became President of the Pontifical Council after he was named a cardinal in 2001. His many published works include: *Jesus the Christ* (London and New York: Burns & Oates/Paulist Press, 1976), *The God of Jesus Christ* (London: SCM, 1984), *Theology and Church* (London: SCM, 1989), *Leadership in the Church* (New York: Crossroad, 2003); and *That They May All Be One: The Call to Unity Today* (London and New York: Burns & Oates, 2004).

Paul Lakeland holds the Aloysius P. Kelley Chair of Catholic Studies at Fairfield University, Connecticut. He is the author of six books, including *The Liberation of the Laity: In Search of an Accountable Church* (New York: Continuum, 2003) which won the Catholic Press Association 2004 Award for the Best Book in Theology, and of many articles on ecclesiology, religion, and politics, and the intersections of theology with cultural and critical theory. He recently completed a six-year term as Chair of the Theology and Religious Reflection Section of the American Academy of Religion, and is co-convener of the Workgroup for Constructive Theology, an independent ecumenical association of systematic and constructive theologians.

Riccardo Larini, subsequent to training in Physics at the University of Pavia, was a member of the ecumenical monastery of Bose from 1993 to 2004. Since 2004 he has been pursuing doctoral research at Cambridge University in biblical hermeneutics on the ecumenical implications of the dialogue between Hans Frei and Paul Ricœur. In 2007 he was appointed Director of Studies at Sarum College, Salisbury. He has published articles and encyclopaedia entries in Italian on ecumenism and the history of spirituality, and has edited several books on Orthodox and Anglican theology and on the history of Christian worship. In addition, he has collated, edited, translated, and introduced three major volumes: *Segno di unità. Le più antiche eucaristie delle chiese* (1996); *La sapienza del cuore: I padri monastici del XII secolo sulla coscienza e la vita spirituale* (1997); and *Il libro dei testimoni: Martirologio ecumenico* (2002).

Nicholas Lash is the Norris-Hulse Professor Emeritus of Divinity at the University of Cambridge. He is author of over 350 articles and numerous books, including: *Newman on Development* (London: Sheed and Ward, 1975), *The Beginning and the End of 'Religion'* (Cambridge: Cambridge University Press, 1996), *Holiness, Speech and Silence* (Aldershot: Ashgate, 2004); and *Theology for Pilgrims* (London: Darton, Longman, and Todd, 2008).

Hervé Legrand, OP studied at le Saulchoir (Paris), Bonn, Strasbourg, University of Saint Thomas (Rome), and Athens. He has been an Ordinary Professor at the Institut Catholique, Paris, during which time he was Director of the Department of Doctoral Studies, Director of the Advanced Institute for Ecumenical Studies, and an Associate Professor at the Faculty of Canon Law (Paris). He is a former member of the International Theological Commission between the Catholic Church and the World Lutheran Federation and he serves as an expert advisor to both the French Catholic–Orthodox Dialogue Commission and the Catholic Dialogue with the Lutheran and Reformed Churches in France. He is co-founder of the International Theological Working Group, Saint Irénée, between Catholics and Orthodox, and is currently an expert advisor to the Council of Bishops' Conferences in Europe.

Andrew Louth is a graduate of Cambridge and Edinburgh Universities. After academic posts at Oxford and Goldsmiths College, University of London, he is now Professor of Patristic and Byzantine Studies in Durham. He is author of several books and many articles, mostly on the Greek/Byzantine tradition, including works on Dionysios the Areopagite, Maximos the Confessor, and John Damascene. His most recent work is a history of the Church from 681 to 1071, the period during which Greek East and Latin West came to form their separate identities. He was ordained priest in the Russian Orthodox Diocese of Sourozh (Patriarchate of Moscow) in 2003 to serve the Orthodox community in Durham.

Gerard Mannion has held posts at Liverpool Hope University, Trinity and All Saints, University of Leeds, and Westminster College, Oxford. He was educated at King's College, Cambridge and New College, Oxford. Publications include: *Schopenhauer, Religion and Morality* (London: Ashgate, 2003) and *Ecclesiology and Postmodernity: Questions for the Church in Our Times* (Collegeville, Minn.: Liturgical Press, 2007). He has also co-edited a number of significant volumes, including *The Routledge Companion to the Christian Church* (with Lewis Mudge) (London: Routledge, 2007). He is presently co-chair of the Ecclesiological Investigations Program Unit of the American Academy of Religion.

Peter McGrail, a priest of the Archdiocese of Liverpool, holds a Licentiate in Sacred Liturgy (S. Anselmo, Rome) and a PhD (Birmingham University, 2003), published as *First Communion: Ritual, Church and Popular Religious Identity* (Aldershot: Ashgate,

2007). He spent four years as the Catholic incumbent in a shared Anglican–Roman Catholic church. From 1997 to 2006 he was Director of Pastoral Formation for the Archdiocese of Liverpool. Since 2003 he has been Senior Lecturer in Catholic Studies at Liverpool Hope University where he is Award Director for the MA (Theology and Religious Studies) and MMin programmes. He is Chair of the Liturgical Formation subcommittee of the Catholic Bishops' Conference of England and Wales. Publications include 'Display and Division: Congregational Conflict among Roman Catholics', in Mathew Guest and Karin Tusting (eds.), *Congregational Studies in the UK: Christianity in a Post-Christian Context* (London: Ashgate, 2004).

Paul McPartlan is a priest of the Archdiocese of Westminster and Carl J. Peter Professor of Systematic Theology and Ecumenism at the Catholic University of America in Washington, DC. He is a member of the International Theological Commission and also of two ecumenical commissions: the Joint International Commission for Dialogue between the World Methodist Council and the Roman Catholic Church and the Joint International Commission for Theological Dialogue between the Roman Catholic Church and the Orthodox Church. Prior to taking up his present position, he taught systematic theology for ten years at Heythrop College in the University of London. He is the author of *The Eucharist Makes the Church: Henri de Lubac and John Zizioulas in Dialogue*, 2nd edn. (Fairfax VA: Eastern Christian Publications, 2006[1993]); *Sacrament of Salvation: An Introduction to Eucharistic Ecclesiology* (London: Continuum, 1995); and many articles on ecclesiology and ecumenism. He is the editor of a recent volume of papers by John Zizioulas, *Communion and Otherness* (Edinburgh: T. & T. Clark, 2006).

Paul D. Murray, a married lay Roman Catholic, is currently Senior Lecturer in Systematic Theology at Durham University where he is also Director of the Centre for Catholic Studies. He has previously held posts at St Cuthbert's Seminary, Ushaw College, Durham; Newman College of Higher Education, Birmingham; and within the Department of Pastoral Formation of the Archdiocese of Liverpool. He serves on the British Methodist–Roman Catholic Committee and, formerly, on the Theology, Faith, and Culture Committee of the Catholic Bishops' Conference of England and Wales. His first monograph was *Reason, Truth and Theology in Pragmatist Perspective* (Leuven: Peeters, 2004). He has also contributed a number of well-received essays to various leading journals and scholarly collections. In June 2006 he was elected to the Editorial Board of *Concilium: International Review for Theology*.

Margaret O'Gara is Professor of Theology at the Faculty of Theology, University of St Michael's College, Toronto. She is a Roman Catholic who has been active in ecumenical dialogue for thirty years. She was a member of the Anglican–Roman Catholic Dialogue of Canada for eighteen years. She is presently appointed as a member of the US Lutheran–Roman Catholic Dialogue, the Disciples of Christ–Roman Catholic International Commission for Dialogue, the Lutheran–Roman Catholic International Commission on Unity, and the board of directors of the Collegeville Institute for Ecumenical and Cultural Research. She has published numerous essays and two books:

Triumph in Defeat: Infallibility, Vatican I, and the French Minority Bishops (Washington, DC: Catholic University of America Press, 1988) and *The Ecumenical Gift Exchange* (Collegeville, Minn.: Liturgical Press, 1998).

Ladislas Örsy, SJ, Educated in canon law at the Gregorian University, Rome, in law at the University of Oxford, and in Theology at Louvain, Ladislas Örsy has taught at the Gregorian University, Fordham University, New York, and the Catholic University of America, Washington, DC. He is currently Professor of Law at Georgetown University Law Center, offering courses on Philosophy of Law, Roman Law, and Canon Law. His main interest is in critically grounding the interpretation of Church structures and laws in theological values. He is the author of numerous essays and nine books, including: *Theology and Canon Law* (Collegeville, Minn.: Liturgical Press, 1992) and *The Church, Learning and Teaching: Magisterium, Assent, Dissent, Academic Freedom* (Wilmington, Del.: Michael Glazier, 1987).

Keith F. Pecklers, SJ has been Lecturer in Liturgical History at the Pontifical Liturgical Institute since 1996 and Professor of Liturgy at the Pontifical Gregorian University since 2002. He has six published books and numerous articles and reviews and is the co-editor of the recently published volume by Archbishop Piero Marini, *A Challenging Reform: Realizing the Vision of the Liturgical Renewal* (Collegeville, Minn.: The Liturgical Press, 2007). His book, *Worship* (London and Collegeville, Minn.: Continuum/Liturgical Press, 2003), won the Catholic Press Association first place book award in Liturgy. He is Founding President of the International Jungmann Society. He serves on the Board of the American Friends of the Anglican Centre Rome and is currently the Roman Catholic representative to the 'Cloud of Witnesses' Project co-sponsored by the World Council of Churches and the Ecumencial Monastery at Bose. He also serves as Vatican consultant and commentator for the American television network ABC News.

Peter Phillips is a parish priest in the Diocese of Shrewsbury. He is a member of the diocesan Ecumenical Commission and of the British Methodist–Roman Catholic Committee. He has been involved in tertiary theological education for a number of years, lecturing in Systematic Theology at Trinity and All Saints College, University of Leeds, and Ushaw College, Durham. While teaching in Durham he was involved with Catholic, Methodist, and Anglican colleagues in the setting up of a course in ecumenical theology which drew together students training for ministry at Ushaw, Cranmer Hall, and the Wesley Study Centre. He has had a number of essays published in leading journals and scholarly collections.

James F. Puglisi, SA entered the Franciscan Friars of the Atonement in 1964. Having completed studies in sociology, philosophy, and liturgical science at The Catholic University of America and in ecumenical studies at Boston University, he completed advanced degrees at the University of Paris–Sorbonne and at the Institut Catholique de Paris. Since 1991, he has been Director of the Centro pro Unione in Rome and Professor of Ecclesiology, Sacraments, and Ecumenism at the Pontifical Athenaeum S. Anselmo and other universities in Rome. He has participated in international bilateral dialogues with Mennonites and Seventh Day Adventists as well as in consultations organized by the Faith and Order Commission of the World Council of Churches. In 2004, he was elected Minister General of the Franciscan Friars of the Atonement. He has had numerous essays published in scholarly volumes and journals and is the author of the major three-volume study, *The Process of Admission to Ordained Ministry: A Comparative Study* (Collegeville, Minn.: Liturgical Press, 1996, 1998, and 2001). In addition he was editor of *Petrine Ministry and the Unity of the Church* (Collegeville, Minn.: 1999) and *Liturgical Renewal as a Way to Christian Unity* (Collegeville, Minn.: 2005).

Bishop Michael E. Putney, formerly a Lecturer in Theology at Pius XII Provincial Seminary in Brisbane, became an Auxiliary Bishop in Brisbane in 1995. He is a member of the National Uniting Church–Roman Catholic Dialogue in Australia and Roman Catholic co-chair of the Joint Commission for Dialogue between the World Methodist Council and the Roman Catholic Church. He is Chairman of the Australian Catholic Bishops' Committee for Ecumenical and Interfaith Relations. In 2001, he became Catholic Bishop of Townsville and in February 2004 was appointed by Pope John Paul II to the Pontifical Council for Promoting Christian Unity. He has had a number of essays published, including: 'The Holy Trinity and Ecumenism', in *God Down Under: Theology in the Antipodes* (Adelaide: Australian Theological Forum, 2003) and 'A Roman Catholic Understanding of Ecumenical Dialogue', *Ecclesiology 2* (2005), 179–94.

Thomas J. Reese, SJ is a Senior Fellow at the Woodstock Theological Center at Georgetown University. He was Editor in Chief of *America* from 1998 to 2005. He is a widely recognized expert on the American Catholic Church and is frequently cited by journalists. Prior to his appointment to *America*, he was a senior fellow at the Woodstock Theological Center where he wrote a trilogy examining Church organization and politics: *Archbishop: Inside the Power Structure of the American Catholic Church*; *A Flock of Shepherds: The National Conference of Catholic Bishops*; and *Inside the Vatican: The Politics and Organization of the Catholic Church* (Cambridge, Mass.: Harvard University Press, 1996).

William G. Rusch has been on the faculties of Augsburg College, Fordham University, the General Theological Seminary, the Lutheran Theological Seminary at Philadelphia, and the Ecumenical Institute at Tantur, Jerusalem. He is currently on the faculty of Yale Divinity School. He has served on the executive staff of the Lutheran Council in the USA, the Lutheran Church in America, and the Evangelical Lutheran Church in America. He has also been a member of several national and international ecumenical dialogues and a member of the Central Committee of the World Council of Churches. He has written over 100 articles on ecumenical and patristic themes and has authored or edited twenty books, including *Ecumenism: A Movement Toward Church Unity* (Philadelphia, Pa.: Fortress Press, 1985), *Reception: An Ecumenical Opportunity* (Philadelphia, Pa.: Fortress Press, 1988), and *Ecumenical Reception: Its Challenge and Opportunity* (Grand Rapids, MI: Eerdmans, 2007).

Nicholas Sagovsky is currently Canon Theologian at Westminster Abbey. He served a curacy at St Gabriel's Church, Heaton, Newcastle from 1974 to 1977 and a temporary curacy at Great St Mary with St Michael, Cambridge during 1981. From 1982 to 1986 he was Vice-Principal and Director of Studies at Edinburgh Theological College and from 1986 to 1997 Fellow, Dean, and Director of Studies in Theology, Clare College, Cambridge. From 1997 to 2002 he was William Leech Professorial Research Fellow in Applied Christian Theology, Newcastle University and from 2002 to 2003 Professor of Theology and Public Life at Liverpool Hope. He is the author of a number of books and articles on a wide range of subjects, including *Ecumenism, Christian Origins and the Practice of Communion* (Cambridge: Cambridge University Press, 2000) and, with Jeremy Morris, *The Unity We Have and the Unity We Seek: Ecumenical Prospects for the Third Millennium* (London: Continuum, 2003).

Philip Sheldrake, from January 2003 to December 2007 Philip Sheldrake held the William Leech Professorial Fellowship in Applied Theology at Durham University. He is also Honorary Professor of Theology at the University of Wales Lampeter and a regular visiting professor at the University of Notre Dame and at Boston College. Educated at Heythrop Pontifical Athenaeum and the universities of Oxford and London in history, philosophy, and theology, he has published extensively in the fields of Christian history and the history and theology of spirituality and has been a leading international figure in the development of Christian spirituality as an interdisciplinary academic field.

Geraldine Smyth, OP has a background in theology, ecumenics, and psychotherapy. She studied at Maynooth, the Irish School of Ecumenics (ISE), Trinity College Dublin. Between 1995 and 1999 she served as the Director of ISE and from 1998 to 2004 as the Prioress General of her Dominican congregation. She is currently a Senior Lecturer within ISE, Trinity College Dublin, teaching on ecumenical social ethics, and on conflict, religion and peace in Ireland, and is Coordinator of the Research Degrees Programme. Publications include *A Way of Transformation* (Berne: Peter Lang, 1995); *Distance Becomes Communion: Dominican Journeys in Mission and Hope* (Dublin, Dominican Publications, 2004); and *The Critical Spirit: Theology at the Crossroads of Faith and Culture* (Dublin: Columba Press, 2003)—co-edited with Andrew Pierce. She is a member of the Editorial Board of *One in Christ*, and has acted as a consultant to the World Council of Churches.

James Sweeney, CP, a Scottish Passionist priest, took his doctorate in the sociology of religion and teaches pastoral theology at Heythrop College, London, where he is Head of Department of Pastoral Studies. He was previously co-director of the Von Hügel Institute for the Study of Faith in Society at St Edmund's College, Cambridge. His publications include *The New Religious Order: The Passionists and the Option for the Poor* (London: Bellew, 1994).

Mary Tanner, OBE, taught Old Testament and Hebrew at Hull and Bristol Universities and at Westcott House, Cambridge before becoming the General Secretary of the Council for Christian Unity of the Church of England (1991–8). She served on the Meissen, Porvoo, and Reuilly Commissions. From 1991 to 1998 she was Moderator of the Faith and Order Commission of the World Council of Churches. She currently serves on the International Anglican–Roman Catholic Commission for Unity and Mission and the Special Commission on Orthodox Participation in the World Council of Churches. Recent publications include 'A Theology for Europe: The *Raison d'être* of the Church', in J. Barnett (ed.), *A Theology for Europe: The Churches and the Institutions* (New York: Peter Lang, 2005); 'Pneumatology in Multilateral Settings', in D. Donnelly, A. Denaux, and J. Famerée (eds.), *The Holy Spirit, The Church, and Christian Unity* (Leuven: Leuven University Press, 2005); 'Ministry in the Documents of Faith and Order: One Woman's Ecumenical Memory', in Tamara Grdzelidze (ed.), *One, Holy, Catholic and Apostolic* (Geneva: WCC, 2005).

Brendan Tuohy was Secretary General of the Department of Communications, Marine and Natural Resources, Eire from 2002–2007, and now works as an independent consultant. The Department is responsible for a number of sectors of the Irish economy including telecommunications, broadcasting, postal, e-commerce, fisheries, aquaculture, exploration, mining, energy, and renewable resources. He holds a degree in civil engineering from University College Cork and postgraduate qualifications in environmental engineering and management from Trinity College Dublin.

Abbreviations

AAS	*Acta Apostolicæ Sedis*
ARCIC	Anglican–Roman Catholic International Commission
BEM	The Faith and Order Commission, *Baptism, Eucharist and Ministry* (Faith and Order Paper, No. 111) (Geneva: World Council of Churches, 1982)
CCC	*Catechism of the Catholic Church* (1992) (London: Geoffrey Chapman, 1994)
CD	Vatican II, '*Christus Dominus*: Decree on the Pastoral Office of Bishops in the Church' (28 Oct. 1965), in Austin Flannery (ed.), *Vatican Council II: The Conciliar and Post Conciliar Documents* (Leominster: Fowler Wright, 1980 [1975]), 564–90
CDF	Congregation for the Doctrine of the Faith, Vatican City
CTS	Catholic Truth Society
Directory	Pontifical Council for Promoting Christian Unity, *Directory for the Application of Principles and Norms on Ecumenism* (London: Catholic Truth Society, 1993)
DS	*Enchiridion Symbolorum Definitionum et Declarationum de Rebus Fidei et Morum*, ed. Henricus Denzinger, rev. Adolfus Schönmetzer, 34th edn. (Freiburg and Rome: Herder, 1967).
DV	Vatican II, '*Dei Verbum*: Dogmatic Constitution on Divine Revelation' (18 Nov. 1965), in Austin Flannery (ed.), *Vatican Council II: The Conciliar and Post Conciliar Documents* (Leominster: Fowler Wright, 1980 [1975]), 750–65
EE	John Paul II, '*Ecclesia de Eucharistia*: Encyclical Letter on the Eucharist and the Church' (17 Apr. 2003) (London: Catholic Truth Society, 2003)
ELCA	Evangelical Lutheran Church in America
Formation	Pontifical Council for Promoting Christian Unity, *The Ecumenical Dimension in the Formation of Those Engaged in Pastoral Work* (1995)
GIA	Harding Meyer and Lukas Vischer (eds.), *Growth in Agreement: Reports and Agreed Statements of Ecumenical Conversations on a World Level* (Mahwah, NY and Geneva: Paulist Press/World Council of Churches, 1984)
GIA II	Jeffrey Gros, Harding Meyer, and William G. Rusch (eds.), *Growth in Agreement II: Reports and Agreed Statements of Ecumenical Conversations on a World Level, 1982–1998* (Geneva and Grand Rapids, Mich.: World Council of Churches/Eerdmans, 2000)

GS   Vatican II, '*Gaudium et Spes*: Pastoral Constitution on the Church in the Modern World' (7 Dec. 1965), in Austin Flannery (ed.), *Vatican Council II: The Conciliar and Post Conciliar Documents* (Leominster: Fowler Wright, 1980 [1975]), 903–1001

IARCCUM   International Anglican–Roman Catholic Commission for Unity and Mission

JDDJ   The Lutheran World Federation and the Roman Catholic Church, *Joint Declaration on the Doctrine of Justification* (Grand Rapids, Mich. and London: Eerdmans/Catholic Truth Society, 2000–1)

LG   Vatican II, '*Lumen Gentium*: Dogmatic Constitution on the Church' (21 Nov. 1964), in Austin Flannery (ed.), *Vatican Council II: The Conciliar and Post Conciliar Documents* (Leominster: Fowler Wright, 1980 [1975]), 350–423

LIC   Walter Kasper, *Leadership in the Church: How Traditional Roles Can Serve the Christian Community Today*, trans. Brian McNeil (New York: Crossroad, 2003)

LWF   Lutheran World Federation

PCPCU   Pontifical Council for Promoting Christian Unity, Vatican City

PL   J-P. Migne (ed.), *Patrologiæ Cursus Completus*, Series Latina, 221 vols. (Paris, 1844–64)

SC   Vatican II, '*Sacrosanctum Concilium*: The Constitution on the Sacred Liturgy' (4 Dec. 1963), in Austin Flannery (ed.), *Vatican Council II: The Conciliar and Post Conciliar Documents* (Leominster: Fowler Wright, 1980 [1975]), 1–36

SCM   Student Christian Movement Press

SOU   Walter Kasper, *Sacrament of Unity: The Eucharist and the Church*, trans. Brian McNeil (New York: Crossroad, 2004).

SPCK   Society for Promoting Christian Knowledge

TC   Walter Kasper, *Theology and Church*, trans. Margaret Kohl (London: SCM Press, 1989 [1987])

TEV   Faith and Order Commission, *A Treasure in Earthen Vessels: An Instrument for an Ecumenical Reflection on Hermeneutics* (Faith and Order Paper, No. 182) (Geneva: World Council of Churches, 1998)

TGJC   Walter Kasper, *The God of Jesus Christ*, trans. Matthew J. O'Connell (London: SCM Press, 1984 [1982]), 200–22

TTMABO   Walter Kasper, *That They May All Be One: The Call To Unity Today* (London and New York: Burns & Oates, 2004)

UR   Vatican II, '*Unitatis Redintegratio*: The Decree on Ecumenism' (21 Nov. 1964), in Austin Flannery (ed.), *Vatican Council II: The Conciliar and Post Conciliar Documents* (Leominster: Fowler Wright, 1980 [1975]), 452–70

USCCB	United States Conference of Catholic Bishops
UUS	John Paul II, '*Ut Unum Sint*: Encyclical Letter on Commitment to Ecumenism' (25 May 1995) (London: Catholic Truth Society, 1995)
WCC	World Council of Churches, Geneva
WJW	*The Works of John Wesley*, vols. i- (var. ed.) (Nashville, Tenn: Abingdon Press, 1984–)
WMC	World Methodist Council

PART I

VISION AND PRINCIPLES

Prologue to Part I
Acts 2: 1–13

Philip Endean, SJ

When the day of Pentecost had come, they were all together in one place. And suddenly from heaven there came a sound like the rush of a violent wind, and it filled the entire house where they were sitting. Divided tongues, as of fire, appeared among them, and a tongue rested on each of them. All of them were filled with the Holy Spirit and began to speak in other languages, as the Spirit gave them ability.

Now there were devout Jews from every nation under heaven living in Jerusalem. And at this sound the crowd gathered and was bewildered, because each one heard them speaking in the native language of each. Amazed and astonished, they asked, 'Are not all these who are speaking Galileans? And how is it that we hear, each of us, in our own native language? Parthians, Medes, Elamites, and residents of Mesopotamia, Judea and Cappadocia, Pontus and Asia, Phrygia and Pamphylia, Egypt and the parts of Libya belonging to Cyrene, and visitors from Rome, both Jews and proselytes, Cretans and Arabs—in our own languages we hear them speaking about God's deeds of power.' All were amazed and perplexed, saying to one another, 'What does this mean?' But others sneered and said, 'They are filled with new wine.'

Receptive Catholic Learning begins here. The church's liturgy encourages us to think that the story of Pentecost is a relatively short one. The disciples are filled with the Spirit and speak in tongues. But Luke's story in fact extends through the whole day (vv. 1–42). After a brief sneer from the onlookers about Catholic drunkenness, Peter connects the descent of the Spirit with the gospel of Resurrection (vv. 14–36). The fate of Christ is the fulfilment of ancient and cherished prophecy. The promises of Israel's psalms have been fulfilled, and humanity is challenged to repent (vv. 37–42).

The *communio* of the church, its unity in diversity, is not something complete, not an object of complacent veneration. Rather God's subversive touch is always opening that communion more widely. God's subversive touch is constantly leading us from darkness to light, from slavery to freedom, from death to resurrection. Ancient texts come to make startling new sense, and provoke us too into asking, 'sisters and brothers, what should we do?' Together we are being drawn to deepen the baptismal commitment we share, and to repent, to draw closer to God. And if we are coming closer to God, it must also be that we are coming closer to all God's children: those near, those far off, all those whom God is calling to Himself. May these essays draw all who read them, and indeed all who have written them, one step further along that paschal path.

1

Receptive Ecumenism and Catholic Learning—Establishing the Agenda[1]

Paul D. Murray

INTRODUCTION

This essay is concerned to introduce the Receptive Ecumenism and Catholic Learning project, the key thinking that drives it, and its core theological, ecclesiological, and practical implications. The essay unfolds in five steps. The first section briefly identifies the fundamental ecclesial–theological context and presuppositions within which the project is situated. Complementing this, the second and third sections deal, respectively, with the broader intellectual and ecclesial–historical contexts that have also helped shape the thinking and vision at work in the project. In turn, sections four and five give full articulation apiece to the twin key concepts of Receptive Ecumenism and Catholic Learning.

ON BECOMING WHAT WE ARE—THE PEDAGOGY OF THE CHURCH: ECCLESIAL–THEOLOGICAL PRESUPPOSITIONS

Somewhere in the vicinity of the main entrance of the many fine cathedral churches of England, towards the west end of the nave, is typically to be found a wooden scale model and architectural plan to aid the visually impaired in their interpretation of their magnificent surroundings. As any who have visited such places with young children will know, however, it is possible to become more fascinated by these models, these pedagogical aids, than by the cathedrals themselves. When compared with the prospect of play and exploration in miniature, nothing it seems to the small child is the beauty and quiet grandeur of the building, the view down the nave towards the east window, the combined sense of reassuring stability and prayerful possibility that a fine cathedral properly evokes.

Of course, focusing more on the models than on the cathedrals themselves is not the only way in which it is possible to mistake representation for reality when it comes to appreciating these magnificent buildings. Understood theologically, cathedral churches, for all their wonderful complexity and vibrancy of communication, are themselves but a representation of the more fundamental reality of the church as the communion of saints in God into which, in Christian understanding, all are called, both personally and collectively, to grow, ever more deeply, for all eternity. In this perspective, a key part of the purpose of a building such as Durham Cathedral is to be an enduring symbol of and witness to the life of the church as the deep story of creation's longing and destiny; a deep story reverberating back way further than the mere centuries of faith, failure, forgiveness, and creative endeavour that its stones have witnessed; a story stretching back to the originating purpose of God in bringing something other than God into being; similarly, a story reaching forth way beyond both our immediate preoccupations and the very limits of our imagining to the bringing of all things to consummation in dynamic configured communion in the Trinitarian being of God.[2]

In short, fully appreciating the reality of a cathedral church properly requires us to understand it as being situated within, as serving, and as showing forth the deep story of all things having their origin, existence, and end in the communion of the Trinity, and as inviting us to enter ever more deeply, ever more freely, more fully, more imaginatively, and more transparently into that reality. The pedagogy—the process of learning—that starts with the wooden representation is a pedagogy not simply in historical sensitivity, or aesthetic appreciation, or clan loyalty, or bourgeois respectability, but of lifelong (and beyond) initiation and growth into this fundamental reality of communion with each other in the life of God. In a beautiful passage, St Augustine gave eloquent expression to all of this early in the fifth century in the context of exploring with the newly baptized what it means to receive communion:

So if it's you that are the body of Christ and its members, it's the mystery meaning you that has been placed on the Lord's table; what you receive is the mystery that means you. It is to what you are that you reply *Amen*, and by so replying you express your assent. What you hear, you see, is *The body of Christ*, and you answer, *Amen*. So be a member of the body of Christ, in order to make that *Amen* true . . . Be what you can see, and receive what you are.[3]

Similarly, fundamental to the Receptive Ecumenism and Catholic Learning project is the conviction that the life of faith, personally and communally—or, better, ecclesially—is always in essence a matter of becoming more fully, more richly, what we already are; what we have been called to be and are destined to be and in which we already share, albeit in part. It is a process of growth and change—a process of conversion—that is at root not a loss, nor a diminishment but a finding, a freeing, an intensification, and an enrichment. As John Henry Newman, that great gift of Anglicanism to modern Catholicism, said: 'In a higher world it is otherwise; but here below to live is to change, and to be perfect is to have changed often.'[4] As a process of personal, interpersonal, and institutional growth, the proper dynamism of Christian tradition holds continuity and change together. As with personal development more generally, there is recognizable identity across time and diverse location but also real change, innovation, and development that goes beyond merely doing the same things in different ways and different locations to doing, when occasion demands, genuinely fresh things yet in familiar or recognizably coherent ways.[5]

In this perspective, the core concern of the Receptive Ecumenism and Catholic Learning project is to explore how ecumenical encounter, ecumenical engagement, ecumenical responsibility and calling can be privileged contexts for promoting this process of personal and ecclesial growth into more intensely configured communion in Christ and the Spirit. The conviction, as Thomas Reese, SJ has noted, is that whereas we might once have regarded ecclesial transformation within denominational traditions as being a necessary prerequisite for effective ecumenical progress, it is now more appropriate to view the capacity for receptive ecumenical learning *across* traditions as the necessary key for unlocking the potential for transformation *within* traditions.[6]

A PRAGMATIC–IDEALIST UNDERSTANDING OF ECCLESIAL EXISTENCE: BROADER CULTURAL–INTELLECTUAL PRESUPPOSITIONS

The intra-Christian ecumenical context—at least in the manner in which it is being engaged here—poses in a very proximate manner a far more pervasive contemporary cultural question: how are we to take traditioned particularity seriously, and the inevitable plurality of diverse traditioned particularities this suggests, without collapsing into the kind of closed, relativistic tribalism into which, for example, Richard Rorty's thought—against his better intentions—leads us?[7] Alternatively stated, what does it mean to seek to proceed reasonably beyond the demise of foundationalist objectivism; beyond the demise of an assumed neutral common ground on the basis of which differing particular perspectives and contrary claims can be independently assessed?

Such questions could be fruitfully pursued through close dialogue with a considerable range of contemporary thinkers—Jürgen Habermas,[8] Emmanuel Levinas,[9] Alasdair MacIntyre,[10] Paul Ricœur,[11] to name but a few. Equally, given that these questions come to one of their most influential expressions in Rorty's neopragmatism, it is both fitting and fruitful to pursue them also by seeking to retrieve a richer reading of the American pragmatist tradition than Rorty himself represents. In this regard, it is notable that the key thinking at work in the Receptive Ecumenism and Catholic Learning project has been shaped, in no small part, through just such close engagement with the broader, classical, pragmatist tradition; particularly so as this is mediated and creatively refashioned in the work of the Pittsburgh philosopher, Nicholas Rescher, and what he has come to refer to as his characteristic stance of pragmatic idealism.[12]

Variously contributing to a sophisticated combination of subtle realism, expansive coherentism, and recursive fallibilism in Rescher's thought are elements drawn from: an expansive Leibnizian concern for systematic coherence; a Kantian idealist recognition that our ways of understanding the world really are *our* ways (ways that would be different were we different); a Wittgensteinian conviction that there is no possibility of our attaining to a preconceptual, prelinguistic understanding of reality; an evolutionary presumption in favour of the basic adaptation of human reason to reality; and both a specifically Peircean regard for truth as an absolutely necessary, albeit elusive, aspiration and a more general pragmatist view of truth as extending beyond the cognitive alone to encompass also the practical.

Taken together, these emphases shape an understanding of human reason as always starting in the middle of things, already shaped by inherited stances, assumptions, values, and received knowledge, all with varying levels of associated significance and embeddedness. In this context, for Rescher the rational thing to do is to take one's situatedness seriously whilst continually opening it out to testing against what else there is and what else comes to light. Truth is something that we can legitimately assume ourselves to be articulating in part but which inevitably eludes us in *toto* and towards which, therefore, we need to understand ourselves as being oriented in the mode of aspiration rather than possession, or arrival. *Pace* Rorty, for Rescher it is continuing to take the question of truth seriously—rather than, à la Rorty, abandoning all such concern as inevitably confining and distorting—that serves to keep the conversation going. Here it is reasonable to hold to what one has as long as it continues to stand up and to show itself still to be cogent in the light of a recursive, expansive, self-critical engagement with the challenge of fresh understanding. Further, even more than simply being a matter of its critical testing, this process of recursive, expansive, self-critical challenge is envisaged by Rescher as being about the integral refreshment and renewal of what one/one's community already has in the light of what can be appropriately received.

Rescher's thinking is helpfully suggestive here of what might be referred to as a *committed pluralist* position and this in a dual sense: first, in the sense that it evinces a commitment to acknowledging the pluralist reality of the world of difference in which we exist and the need to negotiate this appropriately; secondly, in the sense that it makes a claim precisely for the legitimacy and rationality of particular rooted commitment in this context and for the way in which this might be appropriately lived. In each of these regards, I suggest that Rescher's instincts are uniquely well-suited to the contemporary Christian ecumenical context and to indicating a constructive way forwards in a difficult phase of the ecumenical journey.

DISCERNING THE ECUMENICAL
MOMENT—ANTICIPATING SPRING IN A WINTRY
SEASON: ECCLESIAL–HISTORICAL CONTEXT

As has been told many times, the modern ecumenical movement, already highly influential in the Protestant and, later, Orthodox traditions throughout the earlier part of the twentieth century, was given significant fresh impulse by the remarkable events of the Second Vatican Council (1962–5) when official Roman Catholic thinking made a historic development beyond its near recent previous stance of isolationist self-sufficiency and towards far greater ecumenical engagement.[13] In the years following the Second Vatican Council, this move released an enormous amount of ecumenical energy, goodwill, and optimism,[14] excessively and prematurely so, perhaps, in the latter regard. In contrast, we are now in a position where it is widely recognized that, on most fronts, the aspiration for programmed structural unity in the short–medium term is simply unrealistic.[15]

There are, of course, exceptions. Here, for example, the Church of England–Methodist Covenant is full of interesting possibilities, whilst also posing a number of potentially problematic issues requiring careful navigation.[16] Again, there have been other significant recent developments heralded as moving us incrementally closer to the goal of organic structural unity. Most notable here is the historic signing of the *Joint Declaration on the Doctrine of Justification* by the World Lutheran Federation (*WLF*) and the Roman Catholic Church in 1999, and its subsequent countersigning by the World Methodist Council in July 2006, declaring respective understandings of this doctrine no longer to be a cause of continuing division.[17]

More generally, however, the urgent hope for foreseeable structural unity—the mainstay of so much committed ecumenical activity from the late 1960s, throughout the 1970s and even into the 1980s—appears to have run out of steam. In contrast, there is now frequent talk of our being in a long ecumenical winter,[18] with the warming sun and abundant blooms of one summer but a nostalgic memory and the prospect of the next all too distant and uncertain to inspire much real enthusiasm.

Amongst the various factors contributing to this decisive change of climate we would have to acknowledge the immense disappointment occasioned by the failure of previous high-profile initiatives. Significant in the UK context, for example, was the failure of the 1969 and 1972 Church of England–Methodist unity schemes. Again, many felt disappointment at the tardy and largely negative authoritative judgement of the Catholic Church on the first phase of the Anglican–Roman Catholic International Commission's work, the response being jointly prepared by the Congregation for the Doctrine of the Faith and the Pontifical Council for Promoting Christian Unity (PCPCU), with the former having the final say.[19] This situation contrasted starkly with the very public way in which the relevant texts had already been discussed, and largely enthusiastically welcomed, by mixed groups of Anglicans and Roman Catholics in parishes throughout the UK and far more widely.

For the detractors, the Congregation's criticisms betrayed a misplaced concern simply to bring participants to a point of understanding and considered agreement with traditional Roman Catholic formulae rather than seeking together, on the basis of increased mutual understanding of each other's respective emphases and modes of expression, to find appropriate ways of giving fresh joint expression to a faith essentially held in common.[20] Equally, read more charitably, the concern of the Congregation was to avoid any ambiguity that simply served to cover over and to confuse continuing substantial differences.[21] Allied with this has been a further concern on the Congregation's behalf, as also the PCPCU, for consistency across the various bilateral agreements that a particular tradition might enter into, and with this also—more recently at least—a concern that dialogue partners should not take unilateral action in relation to significant fresh developments (e.g. women's ordination) that cannot be approved by all.

This contrast between the relatively slow and disappointing character of developments at the official level and the eagerness for more rapid progress amongst ecumenical enthusiasts on the ground has frequently bred a sense of impatience amongst the latter, leading some to regard the official processes as an irrelevance and to opt for anticipating in the immediacy closer degrees of communion than Roman Catholic teaching at least can currently sanction. More pervasive has been the sense that ecumenical engagement is made easier when it focuses on collaborating in practical activities of service and mission rather than on unravelling arcane matters of faith and order regarded as blocking the way to structural unity.

Such attitudes of impatience with the slowness of ecumenical progress and of the irrelevance of continuing structural divisions relative to the urgent need to proclaim the gospel find, perhaps, their clearest informal expression in the phenomenon of post-denominational Christianity, whether in the form of people committing themselves to Christ without understanding this as being tied, long-term, to any specific ecclesial context or, in the form of those who find themselves, over a period of years, moving fluidly between a variety of differing ecclesial traditions without ever viewing this as a process of ecclesial conversion.[22] More formally, it found expression in the shift within the World Council of Churches, under the leadership of Konrad Raiser, from a model prioritizing issues of doctrine and church order ('Faith and Order') to one effectively prioritizing matters of mission and evangelization ('Life and Works') and explicitly offering the structurally distinct yet fraternally associational character of the World Council of Churches as an adequate representation of the unity in diversity and universal catholicity of the church of Christ.[23]

In turn, however, pulling in the opposite direction of reinforcing differences rather than relativizing them have been factors such as the intensification of secularization and the consequent reduction in numbers of clergy and active laity across practically all of the traditions. This significant energy-drain can easily serve to promote a more inward-looking, preservationist mentality within congregations in contrast to the more outward-looking, mission-focused mentality that the ecumenical endeavour presupposes.[24] With this, in keeping with the characteristic late-modern or postmodern heightening of the particularity of identity over assumed commonality, a further significant contemporary factor in each of the Christian traditions is an increased appreciation for—and, in its most extreme forms, rigid defensiveness of—the particularity and distinctiveness of traditions.[25] Indeed, when allied with an impatience with any perceived coercion into the terms of another's debate, this postmodern turn to the particular can not only be invoked as a due celebration of difference but as justification even for its conscious deepening in the short–medium terms.[26]

Amidst all of this disillusioning of earlier hopes, frustration with formal ecumenical endeavours, and reassertion of the value of difference, what are we to make of the call to organic structural unity, to structurally configured communion in Christ and the Spirit, that lies at the heart of the Catholic instinct?[27] Does it, as Konrad Raiser formally maintains and as post-denominational Christianity informally expresses, necessarily recede out of proximate view and significant concern into the grand eschatological vista we started by considering earlier? Is reconciled diversity without structural unity simply the most that can be hoped for and worked towards in this context? Is just getting on with the business of living, working, and worshipping together in as creative ways as possible across traditional structural divisions all that really matters?

From the Catholic perspective the answer is both 'Yes' and 'No'. Clearly there *is* an unarguable sense in which the bringing of all things into fully actualized, differentiated communion in God is an eschatological reality—indeed, *the* eschatological reality. But it would be poor eschatology that led us to conclude that it is, therefore, a reality that is of no relevance to the contingencies of present existence.[28] On the contrary, when understood as a destiny breathed out in the originating fiat of creation, Christian existence is properly viewed as a living from and towards this promised end. As such, the point is not to relegate it to the irrelevant future but to live in the light of it, anticipating it and being drawn into it as fully as possible amidst present conditions. Authentic Christian hope, as Nicholas Lash recognizes, discounts *both* any ungrounded, misplaced optimism regarding our ability to construct the Kingdom according to our own time-scale *and* any unqualified pessimism regarding the in-principle impossibility of its realization.[29] In this perspective, the Christian task is not so much to assert and to construct the Kingdom as to lean into its coming; to be shaped and formed in accordance with it so as to become channels for its anticipatory realization and showing in the world. Further, as embodied, interpersonal, socio-structural beings, this anticipatory living into and out of the Kingdom itself properly requires embodied, interpersonal, institutional expression. In other words, it requires church and all this implies concerning the inevitability of order, structure, institution, and tradition.

Viewed in this way, 'reconciled diversity without structural unity' can simply never be a sufficient equivalent to the intended unity and catholicity of the church.[30] Sure, the ecumenical aspiration for forms of theological, practical, and structural unity that appropriately reflect this calling and creation's destiny will necessarily be a long haul. But to give up on it for that reason would be like giving up on the aspiration for economic justice which will likewise always be elusive in this order. The point is to ask what it means to live *now* oriented upon such goals? What does it mean to anticipate in present conditions the call to configured communion? What is the appropriate ethic for life between the times in relation to this calling? It is to such questions that the proposed strategy of *Receptive Ecumenism* seeks to respond.

RECEPTIVE ECUMENISM—A STRATEGY WHOSE TIME HAS COME?

In the subtitle of his hugely influential 1907 book of published lectures, William James, with some self-deprecation but perhaps also astute strategic sense, referred to pragmatism as but 'A New Name for Some Old Ways of Thinking'.[31] The same could, perhaps, be said of the twin notions of Receptive Ecumenism and Catholic Learning. What they each respectively seek to articulate and promote have been features of ecumenical thought and practice and of Catholicism throughout. But, of course, formally naming a way of thinking or proceeding and so drawing it to explicit attention can release its strategic potential and shaping influence in ways previously unforeseen. In an important sense Receptive Ecumenism and Catholic Learning each express the same core values of responsible hospitality to the other and dynamic integrity, and can be seen to express these values in relation to narrower and wider fields of play respectively.

For its part, as briefly noted, Receptive Ecumenism is concerned to place at the forefront of the Christian ecumenical agenda the self-critical question, 'What, in any given situation, can one's own tradition appropriately learn with integrity from other traditions?' and, moreover, to ask this question without insisting, although certainly hoping, that these other traditions are also asking themselves the same question. With this, the conviction is that if all were asking and pursuing this question, then all would be moving, albeit somewhat unpredictably, but moving nevertheless, to places where more may, in turn, become possible than appears to be the case at present. It is, as that suggests and as befits the character of Christian life, the way of hope-filled conversion.[32]

Within modern Roman Catholicism, the key relevant developments took place at the Second Vatican Council with the move beyond a straightforward identification, without remainder, of the church of Christ with the Roman Catholic Church to speaking of the former as *subsisting* in the latter[33] and, with this, maintaining that whilst the Catholic Church lacks none of the essential marks of the church of Christ, these marks cannot, therefore, be regarded as being present either exclusively (perhaps with the exception of Roman Catholic understanding of the unity of the church) or perfectly within Roman Catholicism.[34] On the contrary, the Catholic Church, itself always in need of purification, *semper purificanda*, can properly appreciate and receive from the aspects of catholicity present in other traditions which, as Cardinal Kasper has recognized, may be being lived there more adequately, in part, than within Roman Catholicism itself.[35] This, taken along with the recognition that Catholicism was itself complicit in the tragic events of the sixteenth century (*UR*, § 3), marked a significant development beyond the theology of one-way return that had previously explicitly characterized official Roman Catholic ecumenical thinking.[36]

This significant development in Catholic understanding was, in turn, fundamentally reaffirmed and further developed in Pope John Paul II's historic, 1995 encyclical letter, '*Ut Unum Sint*. On Commitment to Ecumenism'; particularly so in the remarkable invitation he issued to theologians and leaders in other Christian traditions to help reimagine the performance of Petrine ministry so that it might once again become a focus for unity rather than the continuing cause of division it currently is—an invitation which itself exemplifies the strategy and virtues of Receptive Ecumenism as here called for.[37]

Similarly, it would have to be acknowledged that the various developments achieved in bilateral dialogues over the last forty years in terms of increased mutual understanding and doctrinal clarification—together constituting some of the best examples of constructive Christian theology in a generation—have only been possible because the long-term participants have been prepared to commit to the challenge of attending closely to another tradition, seeking to gain clearer understanding of it and being open thereby to receiving of the other's particular gifts.[38] Again, whilst the dominant focus in bilateral processes has been upon painstakingly seeking to unpick knots of historic disagreement and attempting to reconcile differing doctrinal frameworks and formulations,[39] some—most notably the recent Methodist–Roman Catholic dialogue on the church, as also aspects of the ARCIC dialogues—have moved explicitly beyond the attempt simply to bring differing languages traditionally regarded as incompatible into reconciled conversation, to exploring the more open and more explicitly receptive question as to what each tradition might in practice fruitfully have to learn from the other, and this in a way that enriches rather than compromises their respective integrities.[40]

As such, the currently proposed strategy of Receptive Ecumenism by no means represents a rejection or criticism, in itself, of the patient search for bilingual agreement that has lain at the heart of most bilateral dialogues. Equally, nor does Receptive Ecumenism simply reduce to a concern to promote the approval, appropriation, and dissemination at the local level of the formulated results of higher-level bilateral processes, as—given the connotations of unidirectional passivity frequently, if inappropriately, associated with the concept of reception—the better-known phrase 'Ecumenical Reception' can potentially suggest.[41] Rather, Receptive Ecumenism represents the concern to bring to the fore the prior necessary disposition to receptive transformational learning that the bilateral processes presuppose.

The conviction here is that unless this commitment to transformational receptivity be made the explicit driving-motor of ecumenical engagement then no amount of refined conceptual clarification and reconciliation of differing theological languages alone will lead to real practical growth and change in the respective lives of the participating churches. Indeed, the conviction is that the strategy of conceptual and grammatical clarification, if pursued in isolation, is in danger of simply reinforcing each sponsoring church within its own current logic, even whilst clarifying that it need not be seen as being in necessary conflict with the differently expressed logic of other traditions. In this manner, a problem-driven strategy of conceptual and grammatical clarification would, on its own, basically leave the respective churches continuing on their separate ways, relatively unchanged apart from enjoying better terms and greater mutual understanding than before.[42] For all it has to offer, the problem-driven strategy of conceptual and grammatical clarification is, in itself, more a strategy of translation and interpretation than of actual conversion and real receptive learning.

As necessary complement, then, to the important work of conceptual and grammatical clarification, the strategy espoused here of a somewhat ad hoc yet nevertheless systematically tested and responsible receptive learning process has, it is assumed, the potential to take each tradition with integrity to a different place than at present; one resulting—in terms of the key Rescherian values summarized earlier—from the creative expansion of current logic rather than its mere clarification, extrapolation, and repetition. The further assumption is that the new places in which the various traditions might with integrity so find themselves could, in turn, give rise to contexts in which issues of apparently irreconcilable difference—viewed from within the respective current logic of things—become genuinely navigable as all grow with creative integrity but non-linearly beyond the present *impasse*.

Seen in this light, whilst the immediate aims of Receptive Ecumenism might appear relatively modest when compared with more structured concerns to explore and, hopefully, resolve differences in a programmed and systematic way, it should not, therefore, simply be viewed as a lesser option; merely the best that can be done in the circumstances, with the disappointment of past dialogues behind and the prospect of more recent and more significant difficulties ahead.

Rather, the fundamental principle of Receptive Ecumenism can be viewed as going to the very core of what is required for any real effective progress to occur at all. That is, Receptive Ecumenism is here being understood not simply as a compensatory second-best suited to the present interim situation, but as the essential way forwards towards the anticipated goal of organic structural unity. In turn, when viewed in this way, the situation in which we now find ourselves can begin to appear less as a problematic interim before the urgent striving for attainable structural unity can get back on track and more as a long-term learning opportunity in which the churches might progress towards their calling and destiny in the only way possible—by slow and difficult growth in maturity.

The realization of this opportunity requires the churches to make an analogous move to that advocated more generally by the philosopher Emmanuel Levinas in calling for a fundamental shift from each assertively defending their own perceived rights in competition with each other, to each instead prioritizing the need to attend to and to act upon their specific responsibilities revealed in the face of the other.[43] Only in this way can the closed logic of competitive assertion and defence be transcended by an imaginative dynamic capable of opening up fresh possibilities. For this to happen, for this process of overcoming stasis to begin, it requires some to take responsibility, to take the initiative, and this regardless of whether others are ready to reciprocate. As the therapeutic adage goes, 'We cannot change others. We can only change ourselves and, thereby, the way we relate to others.' But doing this will itself alter things and open up new possibilities. Similarly, the ethic at work in Receptive Ecumenism is one wherein each tradition takes responsibility for its own potential learning from others and is, in turn, willing to facilitate the learning of others as requested but without either requiring how this should be done, or even making others' learning a precondition to attending to one's own. In the jargon currently in use in education, learning here takes appropriate precedence over teaching.

Further, lest all this talk of ethic and responsibility should suggest otherwise, it is important to recall that the gospel is about promise before it is about obligation and that its challenge lies not in a call to stoic endurance but precisely in a call to greater life and flourishing. In this purview, receptive ecumenical awakening is properly a matter of the heart before it is a matter of the head; a matter of falling in love with the experienced presence and action of God in the people, practices, even structures of another tradition and being impelled thereby to search for ways in which all impediments to closer relationship might be overcome. As such, Receptive Ecumenism both resonates with Cardinal Kasper's and Archbishop Rowan Williams's joint advocacy of the need for 'spiritual ecumenism' and expands upon this by explicitly drawing out the interpersonal and structural–institutional dimensions alongside the more obviously personal that is the focus of spiritual ecumenism.[44] At all of these levels, Receptive Ecumenism is about having evoked in us the desire to become more fully, more freely, and more richly what we already are through the expansion of possibilities that relationship brings. From the Roman Catholic perspective, for example, this much-needed process of ecclesial growth, conversion, and maturing through receptive ecumenical learning is not a matter of becoming *less* Catholic but of becoming *more* Catholic precisely by becoming more appropriately Anglican, more appropriately Lutheran, more appropriately Methodist, more appropriately Orthodox, etc.[45]

In this manner, the assumption at issue in Receptive Ecumenism is that whilst the work of bilateral dialogues and formal ecumenical initiatives always needs to be driven by the kind of receptive passion and desire expressed here, such work alone cannot automatically reproduce or transmit this necessary prior desire. Its movement in our hearts is a work of the Spirit which stirs both in grace-filled delight in another's beauties and in a longing awareness of a fitting match between our own particular lacks and needs and the other's particular gifts. With this, the hope at issue in Receptive Ecumenism is that the current disappointing of earlier ecumenical aspirations may yet lead to a period in which, within each of our traditions, we become more sharply aware of our own respective lacks, needs, and sticking points and our inability to tend to them of our own resources without recourse to the particular gifts of other traditions. This is the kind of real ecumenical learning we now so urgently need and which will move us closer to finding ourselves in the other, the other in ourselves, and each in Christ.

Further, it remains to note that understood in this way, Receptive Ecumenism bespeaks a task, a responsibility—a Spirit-driven movement of the heart, mind, and will—that is of immediate potential relevance for *all* in the churches and not simply those with specific formal responsibilities, for it has implications, in analogous ways, at every possible level of ecclesial life, whether the personal, the local, the explicitly theological, or the structural. In short, it is a total ethic that is as simple yet all pervasive as the gospel it represents. With this, the conviction behind the Receptive Ecumenism and Catholic Learning project is that, like the gospel, it holds the promise of life within it and is worth our making the greatest of efforts to walk in its way.

CATHOLIC LEARNING—COMMUNION AND DIVERSITY

Where the phrase Receptive Ecumenism expresses the implications of the core values of responsible hospitality and dynamic integrity that shape the project, the paired concept of Catholic Learning complements and expands upon this at a number of levels.

Most obviously, Catholic Learning serves to identify the particular tradition in relation to which the generic strategy of Receptive Ecumenism is here being modelled and tested. This represents neither an imperialistic, nor a narrowly parochial disregard for other traditions but simply the authentic application[46] of the principle that lies at the heart of Receptive Ecumenism: that the primary call is to take responsibility for one's own and one's own community's learning in the face of the other, without first demanding that the other does likewise. Whilst one can always quite properly hope that the other will also heed and respond to the call to receptive ecumenical learning and whilst one can always be appropriately prepared to contribute to such a process if asked so to do, this can never be made a prior condition, either implicitly or explicitly, for taking responsibility for one's own and one's own community's learning. In this regard, one of the specific hopes behind the Receptive Ecumenism and Catholic Learning project is indeed that the examples of good practice it pursues in relation to Catholicism will serve, in turn, to encourage members of other traditions to embark upon and to embrace similar initiatives for themselves.

Beyond this first and most basic level of reference, Catholic Learning more substantively identifies the specific activity—*learning*—that Catholicism is here engaged upon. Here we are dealing with Catholicism in explicitly receptive, learning mode rather than its, perhaps more familiar, teaching, repeating, judging, and defending modes—which is not to claim any particular originality for according a strategic priority to Catholicism's learning mode,[47] nor to claim that these other modes do not also have their place. Indeed, in the latter regard, being a model learner would itself be a form of teaching; teaching in the mode of witness—arguably the most authentic form of Christian teaching.

With this, Catholic Learning at once also makes a claim for the authentically *Catholic* character of this learning. As noted earlier, the envisaged process of receptive ecumenical learning is not about becoming less Catholic (or less Methodist, less Anglican, or whatever)—as lowest common denominator versions of ecumenism and ecumenical ecclesiology imply—but about becoming more deeply, more richly, more fully Catholic (more fully Methodist, more fully Anglican, etc.), precisely through a process of imaginatively explored and critically discerned receptive learning from other's particular gifts. It is about the intensification, complexification, and further realization of Catholic identity, not its diminishment and loss.

In turn, Catholic Learning is intended to be suggestive of the universal, all-extensive range of the receptive dynamic that is properly at issue here. Where Receptive Ecumenism expresses this *ad intra* in relation to Christian ecumenism, Catholic Learning voices the claim *ad extra* that it is an authentically Catholic instinct always to ask—with due discernment, criticism, and appropriate concern for integrity intact—after the truth potentially to be learned from the other, whomsoever the other might be. In its inception, the Octave of Prayer for Christian Unity was well placed between the feasts of the Chair of St Peter on 18 January (now celebrated on 22 February in the reformed Roman Calendar) and the Conversion of St Paul on 25 January. More generally, there is a real sense in which Catholicism properly exists between the Petrine and the Pauline instincts: between the centripetal and the centrifugal forces of the Spirit's activity in the world; between constant gathering in communion and continual evangelical dispersal and engagement throughout the world; between the embracing arms of Bernini's colonnades in St Peter's square and the outward-facing stance of the basilica of St Paul Outside the Walls. Each of these instincts, each of these forces, each of these movements represents a vital aspect of what it means to think and live *kath' holon*, according to the whole truth in Christ. It is for this reason that Catholic Learning—duly discerned—from the multifarious others encountered is about becoming more not less Catholic: more fully, more richly Catholic and, hence, more fully, more richly the church of Christ; more clearly the 'sacrament of intimate union with God, and of the unity of all mankind', as Nicholas Lash has never tired of quoting from *Lumen Gentium*.[48]

Finally, as that last sentence suggests, Catholic Learning is intended to be evocative of a universal call and identifying mark pertaining to the entire church of Christ Catholic and to every confessing Christian, and not simply to the Roman Catholic Church uniquely. *Receptive Ecumenism and the Call to Catholic Learning: Exploring a Way for Contemporary Ecumenism* might first properly indicate that the strategy here advocated—of expansive, receptive ecumenical learning, with dynamic integrity—is being modelled in specific relation to Roman Catholicism. Beyond this, it is intended to indicate that what is here pursued in relation to Roman Catholicism is of much wider and direct relevance to the entire church of Christ Catholic and the church's calling to be witness to and sacrament of God's ways with the world.[49]

Here it is recognized that intra-ecclesial matters of structural, spiritual, and practical renewal and extra-ecclesial matters of witness, sacramentality, and mission are inextricably related. The ecclesial–structural and the ecclesial–practical are of intrinsic theological and evangelical significance. Here the medium *is*, in an important if qualified sense, the message. Or, more properly, here it is recognized that the lived reality of ecclesial existence either shows forth or contradicts, either discloses or disguises, the message to which the church is called to witness and the reality in which the church believes itself to exist.

Further, when viewed in relation to the all-pervasive situation of irreducible pluralism—even blood-soaked conflictual difference—that we late-moderns find ourselves in, it is here recognized that the call to the separated Christian traditions to embrace the way of Receptive Ecumenism and Catholic Learning represents not simply a piece of arcane ecclesial housekeeping; nor even simply a means of potentially enhancing the quality of ecclesial existence within each of these traditions when freshly orientated upon their eschatological goal. Rather, the call to embrace the way of Receptive Ecumenism and Catholic Learning comes to appear as the primary means by which, and the primary locus in which, the separated Christian traditions can witness to what it might mean to live difference as grace and blessing and for mutual flourishing.

CONCLUSION

This essay started out by attending, in turn, to the ecclesial–theological (I), cultural–intellectual (II), and ecclesial–historical (III) contexts in which *Receptive Ecumenism and the Call to Catholic Learning* is situated and by which it has been shaped. Following this, the twin key concepts of Receptive Ecumenism (IV) and, somewhat more briefly, Catholic Learning (V) have been explored. The essay then drew to a close by situating the call to Receptive Ecumenism and Catholic Learning within the mission and sacramentality of the church, suggesting that the appropriate performance of receptive ecumenical learning within and between the separated Christian traditions goes to the very heart of the evangelical call to witness to the possibility of living reconciled difference for mutual flourishing in a world of blood-soaked conflict.

This is the key issue of our living and dying together—the key question of our age—and is clearly of relevance way beyond the realms of ecumenically inclined theologians. Religious communities have the capacity for nurturing and transmitting unparalleled resources both for good and for harm in this regard. Given the socially and politically crucial nature of the issue that is in play, the potent implication of religious traditions in its unfolding, and the difficulties religious traditions frequently experience in opening and sustaining the crucial spaces for rigorous, critical–constructive exploration that are required for the navigation of fruitful ways forward, it is right and proper that the publicly funded, secular academy should provide such spaces for the good of all. Throughout the Receptive Ecumenism and Catholic Learning project, a key aim has been to model and to promote the significant possibilities that are, somewhat ironically but entirely appropriately, now open within the contemporary UK secular academy for pursuing imaginative (poetic), critical–constructive (analytic) and practically focused (pragmatic) ecclesial theology of the highest order.[50] The hope here is that the well-being and common good of society will be served precisely through—not in spite of—attending seriously to the intrinsic flourishing of the church.[51]

NOTES

1. This chapter, with additional material from the Preface, was first published in the *International Journal for the Study of the Christian Church*, 7 (2007), 279–301.
2. For a fascinating work arguing that there is theo-cosmological significance even in the maths employed—through the use of Platonic geometry—in the construction of many of the great cathedrals, see Nigel Hiscock, *The Wise Master Builder: Platonic Geometry in Plans of Medieval Abbeys and Cathedrals* (Aldershot: Ashgate, 1999); for specific discussion of Durham Cathedral, see ibid. 236–9; and for the more general

findings and conclusions, see ibid. 273–8. I am grateful to my former colleague David Brown for drawing my attention to this work.

3. St Augustine of Hippo, 'Sermon 272. On the Day of Pentecost to the *Infantes*, on the Sacrament', in *The Works of Saint Augustine: A Translation for the 21st Century, Part III, Sermons*, vol. vii. *Sermons (230–272B), On the Liturgical Seasons*, trans. Edmund Hill, ed. John E. Rotelle (New York: New City Press, 1993), 300–1.

4. Newman, *An Essay on the Development of Christian Doctrine* (1845), ed. J. M. Cameron (Harmondsworth: Penguin, 1974), chap. 1 § 1, 'On the Process of Development in Ideas', 100; also rev. edn. (London: Pickering, 1878), 40.

5. For further, see Murray, 'A Liberal Helping of Postliberalism Please', in Mark D. Chapman (ed.), *The Future of Liberal Theology* (Aldershot: Ashgate, 2002), 208–18 and id., *Reason, Truth and Theology in Pragmatist Perspective* (Leuven: Peeters, 2004), 131–61; also Terrence W. Tilley, *Inventing Catholic Tradition* (Maryknoll, NY: Orbis, 2000).

6. See Chapter 24: Thomas Reese, 'Organizational Factors Inhibiting Receptive Catholic Learning'.

7. See Murray, *Reason, Truth and Theology in Pragmatist Perspective*, 23–90, particularly 79–87.

8. See Nicholas Adams, *Habermas and Theology* (Cambridge: Cambridge University Press, 2006).

9. See Michael Purcell, *Levinas and Theology* (Cambridge: Cambridge University Press, 2006); also David F. Ford, *Self and Salvation: Being Transformed* (Cambridge: Cambridge University Press, 1999), particularly 30–44.

10. See MacIntyre, *Three Rival Versions of Moral Enquiry* (London: Duckworth, 1990); and for appreciative theological engagement, Gavin D'Costa, *Theology in the Public Square: Church, Academy and Nation* (Oxford: Blackwell, 2005), 25–37.

11. See, e.g., Ricœur, *Oneself as Another*, trans. Kathleen Blamey (Chicago, Ill.: University of Chicago Press, 1992); and for explicit theological appropriation, Ford, *Self and Salvation* particularly 82–104.

12. Rescher, *A System of Pragmatic Idealism*, vol. i., *Human Knowledge in Idealistic Perspective* (Princeton, NJ: Princeton University Press, 1992); vol. ii., *The Validity of Values* (Princeton, NJ: Princeton University Press, 1993); vol. iii., *Metaphilosophical Inquiries* (Princeton, NJ: Princeton University Press, 1994); also id., 'Précis of *A System of Pragmatic Idealism*', *Philosophy and Phenomenological Research*, 54 (1994), 377–90. For appreciative critical exposition, constructive development, and theological appropriation, see Murray, *Reason, Truth and Theology*, 91–130 and 131–61.

13. See Murray, 'Catholicism and Ecumenism', in Anne Hession and Patricia Kieran (eds.), *Exploring Theology: Making Sense of the Catholic Tradition* (Dublin: Veritas, 2007), 305–16.

14. Carl E. Braaten and Robert W. Jenson (eds.), Preface, in *The Ecumenical Future. Background Papers for 'In One Body Through the Cross: The Princeton Proposal for Christian Unity'* (Grand Rapids, Mich. and Cambridge: Eerdmans, 2004), p. vii.

15. For a significant counterblast to any complacent accommodation to this widespread shift in perception, see Braaten and Jenson (eds.) *In One Body Through the Cross:*

The Princeton Proposal for Christian Unity. A Call to the Churches from an Ecumenical Study Group (Grand Rapids, Mich. and Cambridge: Eerdmans, 2003), particularly 11, 15, 18, and 26; also *The Ecumenical Future*.

16. See Church of England and Methodist Church of Great Britain, *An Anglican–Methodist Covenant: Common Statement of the Formal Conversations Between the Methodist Church of Great Britain and the Church of England* (London: Methodist Publishing House and Church House Publishing, 2001).

17. The Lutheran World Federation and the Roman Catholic Church, *Joint Declaration on the Doctrine of Justification* (Grand Rapids, Mich.: and London: Eerdmans/CTS, 2000/2001). See also Chapter 11: William G. Rusch, 'The International Lutheran–Roman Catholic Dialogue—An Example of Ecclesial Learning and Ecumenical Reception'.

18. See, e.g., Walter Kasper, 'The Current Situation in Ecumenical Theology', *TTMABO*, 14; and Jeremy Morris and Nicholas Sagovsky, 'Introduction', in *The Unity We Have and the Unity We Seek: Ecumenical Prospects for the Third Millennium* (London and New York: T. & T. Clark, 2003), p. xvi. It is, perhaps, reassuring to note that this metaphor is actually of somewhat longer usage than these references might suggest, apparently recurring whenever the intrinsically counterfactual character of ecumenical hope and calling encounters significant difficulties. Donald Bolen, the Vatican's officer for relations with the Anglican Communion and the World Methodist Council at PCPCU, recounts that his colleague, John Radano, even recalls hearing the term used as far back as the late 1960s in amidst the burgeoning promise of the post-Second Vatican Council ecumenical spring!

19. See ARCIC, *The Final Report* (London: CTS/SPCK, 1982), also available at <http://www.prounione.urbe.it/dia-int/arcic/doc/e_arcic_final.html>; and CDF, *Observations on The Final Report of the Anglican–Roman Catholic International Commission* (London: CTS, 1982), § A. 2. iii (also *AAS*, 74).

20. See Chapter 18: Mary Tanner, 'From Vatican II to Mississauga—Lessons in Receptive Ecumenical Learning from the Anglican–Roman Catholic Bilateral Dialogue Process'.

21. See nn. 30 and 42 below for related concerns expressed, respectively, about the notions of 'reconciled diversity' and 'differentiated consensus'.

22. See Philip Richter, 'Denominational Cultures: The Cinderella of Congregational Studies?', in Mathew Guest, Karin Tusting, and Linda Woodhead (eds.), *Congregational Studies in the UK: Christianity in a Post-Christian Context* (Aldershot: Ashgate, 2004), 169–71; also Guest, 'Reconceiving the Congregation as a Source of Authenticity', in Jane Garnett, et al. (eds.), *Redefining Christian Britain: Post 1945 Perspectives* (London: SCM, 2007), 63–4; and Braaten and Jenson, *In One Body Through the Cross*, 38.

23. See Raiser, *Ecumenism in Transition: A Paradigm Shift in the Ecumenical Movement?*, trans. Tony Coates (Geneva: WCC, 1991), particularly 54–78; cf. Braaten and Jenson, *In One Body Through the Cross*, 6, 23–5, and 52.

24. See Chapter 22: Peter McGrail, 'The Fortress Church under Reconstruction? Sociological Factors Inhibiting Receptive Catholic Learning in the Church in England and Wales'.

25. Within the Roman Catholic context, see, e.g., George Weigel, *The Truth of Catholicism: Inside the Essential Teachings and Controversies of the Church Today* (New York: HarperCollins, 2001).

26. See Richard Harries, 'The Female Mitre', *Tablet* (15 July, 2006), available at <http://www.thetablet.co.uk/articles/8235/>.

27. See, e.g., here Benedict XVI's unqualified affirmation in his first statement as pontiff on 20 Apr. 2005, and many times since, that Roman Catholicism is irrevocably committed to the strong ecumenical aspiration for a structurally and sacramentally united church, 'First Message of His Holiness Benedict XVI at the End of the Eucharistic Concelebration with the Members of the College of Cardinals in the Sistine Chapel' (20 Apr. 2005), available at <http://www.vatican.va/holy_father/benedict_xvi/messages/pont-messages/2005/documents/hf_ben-xvi_mes_20050420_missa-pro-ecclesia_en.html>. See also 'Address of His Holiness Benedict XVI to the Delegates of Other Churches and Ecclesial Communities and of Other Religious Traditions' (25 Apr. 2005) available at <http://www.vatican.va/holy_father/benedict_xvi/speeches/2005/april/documents/hf_ben-xvi_spe_20050425_rappresentanti-religiosi_en.html>.

28. This has, of course, been a recurrent theme in near-recent eschatology, starting with Jürgen Moltmann, *A Theology of Hope: On the Ground and the Implications of a Christian Eschatology*, trans. James W. Leitch (London: SCM, 1967); also Karl Rahner, 'The Hermeneutics of Eschatological Assertions' (1960), *Theological Investigations*, vol. iv., trans. Kevin Smyth (London: Darton, Longman and Todd, 1966), 323–46.

29. See Lash, *A Matter of Hope: A Theologian's Reflections on the Thought of Karl Marx* (London: Darton, Longman and Todd, 1981), 250–80; id., 'All Shall Be Well: Christian and Marxist Hope', in *Theology on the Way to Emmaus* (London: SCM, 1986), 202–15; id., 'Hoping Against Hope, or Abraham's Dilemma', in *The Beginning and the End of 'Religion'* (Cambridge: Cambridge University Press, 1996), 199–218.

30. See Kasper, Introduction, *TTMABO*, 3; also Ola Tjørhom, *Visible Church—Visible Unity: Ecumenical Ecclesiology and 'The Great Tradition of the Church'* (Collegeville, Minn.: Liturgical Press, 2004), 73–83; and Geoffrey Wainwright, 'The Global Structures of Ecumenism', in Braaten & Jenson, *The Ecumenical Future*, 25.

31. See James, *The Works of William James*, vol. i., *Pragmatism*, ed. Frederick H. Burkhardt, Fredson Bowers, and Ignas K. Skrupskelis (Cambridge, Mass.: Harvard University Press, 1975).

32. See Kasper, 'Spiritual Ecumenism', *TTMABO*, 170.

33. See Vatican II, *LG*, § 8 (p. 357); and for commentary, see Kasper, '*Communio*. The Guiding Concept of Catholic Ecumenical Theology', *TTMABO*, 65–8.

34. See *LG*, §§ 8, 15, and 16; also *UR*, § 3 and 4 (pp. 455–9). Balancing this, for the most recent formal statement (reiterating the formulae adopted in the controversial year 2000 CDF document, *Dominus Iesus*) concerned to maintain that the *subsistit* clause of *LG*, § 8 is, nevertheless, to be correctly understood as making a claim in relation to Catholicism (i.e. that all the identifying marks of the church of Christ are to be found, even if only imperfectly, within the Roman Catholic Church) that does not apply in the same way to any other church or 'ecclesial communion', see CDF, 'Responses to Some Questions

Regarding Certain Aspects of the Doctrine of the Church' (29 June 2007), available at <http://www.vatican.va/roman_curia/congregations/cfaith/documents/rc_con_cfaith_doc_20070629_responsa-quaestiones_en.html>. For an earlier, magisterial discussion of the essential issues at stake, see Francis A. Sullivan, 'The Impact of *Dominus Iesus* on Ecumenism', *America*, 183 (28 Oct. 2000), 8–11, available at <http://www.americamagazine.org/content/article.cfm?article_id=2266>. For an incisive critique—on the grounds that it collapses an authentic Catholic appreciation for the properly analogical and, hence, wide-ranging and subtly differentiated application of theological concepts into a bald and improper univocity—of the judgement passed in *Dominus Iesus* and reiterated in the recent 'Responses' that the 'ecclesial ("churchly"!) communions' of the Protestant reformations cannot properly be called churches, see Nicholas Lash, 'Churches, Proper and Otherwise', *The Tablet* (21 July 2007), 13–14.

35. See *LG*, § 8; *UR*, §§ 6–7, and *UR*, § 4; also Kasper, 'The Current Situation in Ecumenical Theology', 17; id., '*Communio*: The Guiding Concept of Catholic Ecumenical Theology', 67.

36. e.g. '[F]or the union of Christians can only be promoted by promoting the return to the one true Church of Christ of those who are separated from it, for in the past they have unhappily left it'. Pope Pius XI, '*Mortalium Animos*: On Religious Unity' (6 Jan. 1928), § 10, available at <http://www.vatican.va/holy_father/pius_xi/encyclicals/documents/hf_p-xi_enc_19280106_mortalium-animos_en.html>.

37. *UUS*, §§ 95–6; also available at <http://www.vatican.va/holy_father/john_paul_ii/encyclicals/documents/hf_jp-ii_enc_25051995_ut-unum-sint_en.html>. For a summary of the various responses to this remarkable invitation, see 'Reports to the PCPCU Plenary: Petrine Ministry', *Information Service*, 109 (2002), 29–42.

38. See Chapter 2: Margaret O'Gara, 'Receiving Gifts in Ecumenical Dialogue' and Chapter 19: Donald Bolen, 'Receptive Ecumenism and Recent Initiatives in the Catholic Church's Dialogues with the Anglican Communion and the World Methodist Council'.

39. This is, perhaps, at its clearest in the dialogues relating to differing articulations of the doctrine of justification, see ARCIC II, *Salvation and the Church* (London: Church House Publishing/CTS, 1987), also available at <http://www.prounione.urbe.it/dia-int/arcic/doc/e_arcicII_salvation.html>; and, more recently, the *Joint Declaration on the Doctrine of Justification* between the Lutheran World Federation (LWF) and the Roman Catholic Church. Lying behind such dialogue processes is not only the groundbreaking substantive theological work of Hans Küng in *Justification: The Doctrine of Karl Barth and a Catholic Reflection*, trans. Thomas Collins, Edmund E. Tolk, and David Granskou (London: Burns & Oates, 1964), but also George Lindbeck's highly influential fundamental theological articulation of a grammatical, or cultural-linguistic, understanding of doctrine in *The Nature of Doctrine: Religion and Theology in a Postliberal Age* (London: SPCK, 1984), an understanding of doctrine that is itself derived from a professional lifetime of ecumenical commitment.

40. See the Joint International Commission for Dialogue Between the Roman Catholic Church and the World Methodist Council, *The Grace Given You in Christ:*

Catholics and Methodists Reflect Further on the Church (Lake Junaluska, NC: World Methodist Council, 2006); also, e.g., ARCIC II, *The Gift of Authority: Authority in the Church III* (London: Church House Publishing/CTS, 1999), available at <http://www.vatican.va/roman_curia/pontifical_councils/chrstuni/documents/rc_pc_chrstuni_doc_12051999_gift-of-autority_en.html>.

41. In contrast to this reduced understanding of reception, see Yves Congar's articulation of a rich and full understanding: 'By "reception", I understand... the process by means of which a church (body) truly takes over as its own a resolution that it did not originate in regard to itself, and acknowledges the measure it promulgates as a rule applicable to its own life.' Congar, 'Reception as an Ecclesiological Reality', trans., John Griffiths in Giuseppe Alberigo and Anton Weiler (eds.), *Church History: Election—Consensus—Reception, Concilium*, 77 (1972), 45; also Thomas P. Rausch, 'Reception Past and Present', *Theological Studies*, 47 (1986), 497–508. Similarly, for a full, constructive articulation of the concept of 'ecumenical reception' that also moves considerably beyond the mere notion of lower-level approval of higher-level formulation, to think rather in terms of the entire process by which one Christian tradition comes to the point of being able formally to affirm and appropriate an aspect of another Christian tradition's practice and belief, see Rusch, *Reception: An Ecumenical Opportunity* (Philadelphia, Penn.: Fortress Press, 1988), particularly 57, 58, 64, 65–6, 68, but cf. 31, 56, 70; and id., *Ecumenical Reception: Its Challenge and Opportunity* (Grand Rapids, Mich. and Cambridge: Eerdmans, 2007).

42. For a related claim to the effect that without a clear and consistent orientation towards the goal of structural unity, the powerful concept of 'differentiated consensus'—presupposed in practice, for example, in the *Joint Declaration on the Doctrine of Justification*—can all too easily serve to legitimate the permanent structural continuation of existing denominational differences as an acceptable feature of ecclesial life, see Annemarie C. Mayer, 'Language Serving Unity? Linguistic–Hermeneutical Considerations of a Basic Ecumenical Problem', *Pro Ecclesia*, 15 (2006), 206–8 and Wainwright, 'The Global Structures of Ecumenism', 26; see also n. 30 above for related comments in relation to the forerunner notion of 'reconciled diversity'.

43. See, e.g., Levinas, 'Philosophy and the Idea of Infinity' (1957), in *Collected Philosophical Papers*, trans. Alphonso Lingis (Dordrecht and Boston and London: Kluwer, 1987), 57–9 and 'Freedom and Command' (1953), ibid. 15–23, particularly 19 and 23; also see n. 9 above.

44. See Kasper, 'Spiritual Ecumenism', *TTMABO*, 155–72; 'The Current Situation in Ecumenical Theology', ibid. 16–17; and Rowan Williams, 'Keynote Address', in *May They All Be One ... But How?, Proceedings of the Conference Held in St Albans Cathedral on 17 May 2003* (St Albans: St Albans Centre for Christian Studies, 2003), 6–8.

45. Whilst there might, as the Groupe des Dombes claim, be the need for a dispossessive movement on behalf of the churches (see Groupe des Dombes, *For the Conversion of the Churches*, trans. James Greig (Geneva: WCC, 1993)) in the perspective taken here, and in accordance with a rounded Christian theology of conversion, this must be understood as but a moment in a greater flourishing. It is less a losing of identity and more a finding and freeing of a richer, fuller identity. As such, the strategy of

Receptive Ecumenism perceives as fundamentally mistaken—no matter how widely held and no matter how descriptively accurate of the common logic of things—the dichotomy sharply posed by Rusty Reno: 'The ecumenical process is stalled because the churches cannot square the circle. They cannot articulate their identities as churches, while at the same time admitting that they suffer an ecumenical need for unity with others.' Rusty R. Reno, 'The Debilitation of the Churches', in Braaten and Jenson, *The Ecumenical Future*, 47. See also Chapter 3: Örsy, 'Authentic *Learning* and *Receiving*—A Search for Criteria'.

46. Bearing in mind that the project was co-hosted by the then emerging *Centre for Catholic Studies* at Durham University, Ushaw, College, and the Roman Catholic Diocese of Hexham and Newcastle in honour of Cardinal Walter Kasper, President of the Pontifical Council for Promoting Christian Unity.

47. See, e.g., Pope Paul VI, '*Ecclesiam Suam*: Encyclical Letter on the Church in the Modern World' (6 Aug. 1964) (London: CTS, 1979), available at <http://www.vatican.va/holy_father/paul_vi/encyclicals/documents/hf_p-vi_enc_06081964_ecclesiam_en.html>, particularly §§ 78–87; also *GS*, § 1–3 and 44 (903–4, 946–7); Pope John Paul II, *UUS*, §§ 95–6.

48. *LG*, § 1; cf. Lash, *A Matter of Hope*, 75, 237, 252; id., Introduction, in *Theology on the Way to Emmaus*, p. xi; id., 'Theologies at the Service of a Common Tradition', ibid. 23–6; id., *Holiness, Speech and Silence: Reflections on the Question of God* (Aldershot: Ashgate, 2004), 41.

49. For the phrase 'God's ways with the world', see Daniel W. Hardy, *God's Ways with the World: Thinking and Practising Christian Faith* (Edinburgh: T. & T. Clark, 1996).

50. For a somewhat contrasting assessment—at least at the level of conclusions drawn, if not at the level of basic vision of the task of theology—see D'Costa, *Theology in the Public Square*.

51. Contra Raiser's dissociation of the structural–ecclesial from the missiological and his prioritizing of the latter to the detriment of the former.

2

Receiving Gifts in Ecumenical Dialogue

Margaret O'Gara

INTRODUCTION

Ecumenical dialogue allows the churches to receive gifts they need, but it also demands a readiness for such reception. I will consider receiving gifts in ecumenical dialogue in four steps: (1) ecumenical gift exchange as reception; (2) different ways of exchanging gifts; (3) gifts offered but not received; and (4) ecumenical partners and reception.

ECUMENICAL GIFT EXCHANGE AS RECEPTION

It was at Christmas that I first learned about the gift exchange. I married into a large family, and at Christmas each member of my husband's family would bring one gift to the family exchange and receive one in return. After the Advent season of repentance and hope, the gift exchange among members of this large family gave us renewed appreciation for each other and deepened the ties of mutual love.

Ecumenism is a gift exchange as well. In ecumenical dialogue, each Christian communion brings one or many gifts to the dialogue table, and receives riches from their dialogue partners as well. But in the ecumenical gift exchange, the gift-giving enriches all, since we do not lose our gifts by sharing them with others. The gift exchange of ecumenical dialogue means a mutual reception of gifts for which we have been prepared by repentance and hope. In fact, it is the gifts received from God, given for the good of the whole church, that in effect are now offered to be shared by all in ecumenical dialogue.[1]

Such a gift exchange is a constitutive part of ecumenical dialogue. We want to meet each other and receive the gifts that each has to offer. Like a good gift exchange in a big family, we want to open each gift slowly and take time to appreciate it, to savour it, before going on to the next gift. We know that some gifts are predictable, while others will be surprising. But each will be valuable. The gift exchange of ecumenical dialogue is a means of reception.

In *Lumen Gentium*, the Second Vatican Council taught that the catholicity of the church results in a gift exchange: 'In virtue of this catholicity each part contributes its own gifts to other parts and to the whole Church' (*LG*, § 13). It continues, '[S]o that the whole and each of the parts are strengthened by the common sharing of all things and by the common effort to attain to fullness in unity'. In turn, Pope John Paul II referred to this insight in his encyclical on commitment to ecumenism, *Ut Unum Sint*: 'Dialogue is not simply an exchange of ideas...In some way it is always an 'exchange of gifts'.[2]

Some people mistakenly think of ecumenical dialogue as a kind of melting pot which seeks the elimination of the distinctive gifts of the many churches. This would lead to a weakening of the distinctive traditions and emphases that each communion brings to the table of dialogue. It would be a loss of identity, not enrichment. But in fact I have found that the gifts exchanged in ecumenical dialogue are more like a mosaic, where every piece is valuable and every piece is needed for the full picture of the one church of Christ. The mosaic picture is damaged if any of the pieces is missing. Because of the divisions among Christians, explains the Second Vatican Council's *Unitatis Redintegratio*, 'the Church herself finds it more difficult to express in actual life her full catholicity in all its aspects' (*UR*, § 4).

At the same time, emphases within traditions that are exaggerated or distorted due to isolation are corrected and complemented in the emerging mosaic that results from ecumenical gift exchange. The Second Vatican Council teaches, 'There can be no ecumenism worthy of the name without interior conversion' (*UR*, § 7), and Pope John Paul II called for 'repentance' as the churches recognize their failings toward one another (*UUS*, § 15). Every one of our communions is wounded by our divisions. One of the gifts that Christian churches bring each other in dialogue is serious criticism, criticism that allows their weaknesses and sins to be acknowledged and overcome (*UR*, § 7). In this way, I believe the Holy Spirit is using the ecumenical dialogue today to bring about the renewal of the church in our time so that it will be strengthened for its mission in the coming years. By receiving gifts from each other, we are also prepared to offer gifts to the whole world through the proclamation of the Gospel together.

DIFFERENT WAYS OF EXCHANGING GIFTS

Ecumenical partners exchange gifts in different ways. Even when the exchange is mutual, such mutuality can take different forms depending on the topic and the partners in dialogue.

In the *Joint Declaration on the Doctrine of Justification* (*JDDJ*), the Lutheran World Federation and the Roman Catholic Church were able 'to formulate a consensus on basic truths concerning the doctrine of justification', in light of which 'the corresponding doctrinal condemnations of the sixteenth century do not apply to today's partner'.[3] But it is a differentiated consensus which is asserted, a consensus in which each tradition's language and forms of expression continue to be used and recognized as a valid, alternative way of confessing the commonly held faith.[4]

Even the form of the declaration reveals this style of agreement, beginning the discussion of each of the seven controverted topics with a paragraph of common confession, followed by separate paragraphs explaining the distinctive approach and concerns of Lutherans and Roman Catholics (§§ 19–39). But the distinctive emphases are maintained, though explained. For example, Catholics understand cooperation in accepting justification as 'itself an effect of grace' (§ 20), and Lutherans, in opposing the idea of cooperating in salvation, 'mean thereby to exclude any possibility of contributing to one's own justification' (§ 21). But both confess together 'that all persons depend completely on the saving grace of God for their salvation' (§ 19). Here, agreement permits varied emphases.

Discussions on the Eucharist often show a second kind of exchange as ecumenical partners have often combined several complementary insights in their agreement, each insight representing a focus by one partner that needs balance with another. So in the 1971 agreement of the Anglican–Roman Catholic International Commission on 'Eucharistic Doctrine', the members recognized the once-for-all character of Christ's death on the cross, sufficient for removing the sins of the world. 'There can be no repetition of or addition to what was then accomplished once for all by Christ.'[5] But this classically Anglican focus is immediately balanced by a Catholic understanding of the Eucharist as 'no mere calling to mind of a past event or of its significance, but the Church's effectual proclamation of God's mighty acts', such that the church even 'enters into the movement' of Christ's self-offering. By holding these two foci together, the statement corrects distortions in the approach to the sacrificial aspect of the Eucharist that could result from considering either of the partner's positions in isolation.

In discussing the presence of Christ in the Eucharist, a similar approach is used in which the characteristic foci of each communion are held together. Hence, members agree that 'communion with Christ in the Eucharist presupposes his true presence, effectually signified by the bread and wine which, in this mystery, become his body and blood' (§ 6). Yet they add to this classically Roman Catholic point the Anglican insight that Christ is present 'as an offering to the believer awaiting his welcome' (§ 8). The subsequent 'Elucidation' (1979) clarified that the becoming of the bread and wine 'does not imply a material change', does not imply that Christ's presence 'is limited to the consecrated elements', and does not imply that 'this *becoming* follows the physical laws of this world'[6]—all important clarifications for Anglicans to hear.

Hence the exchange of gifts represented by the ARCIC discussion of the Eucharist is different from the differentiated consensus of the *JDDJ*. Rather than affirming alternative formulations of the commonly confessed faith, the ARCIC statement binds together two complementary points that were once considered contradictory, showing the need each has for the other.

A third kind of gift exchange can be found in the dialogue between Mennonites and Roman Catholics. In the Mennonite–Roman Catholic movement called 'Bridgefolk', each tradition wants to receive a different gift from the other. Mennonites express their desire to recover a richer liturgical and sacramental heritage, one they feel they have lost, and Roman Catholics seek a deeper set of practices and insights to sustain long-term peacemaking. While Mennonites explore more frequent and liturgically richer eucharistic celebrations, Roman Catholics inch closer to a pacifist position in their strict reinterpretation of the just war theory in the contemporary situation of nuclear arms and increased global interdependence.[7]

This third kind of gift exchange is reflected in the official agreed statement of the international dialogue between the Roman Catholic Church and the Mennonite World Conference, 'Called Together to Be Peacemakers'.[8] Dialogue members found that they were able to reread the history of the church together and hence contribute to the 'development of a common interpretation of the past' (§ 27). This allowed them then to make breakthroughs in the areas of both sacraments and of peace and war. Mennonite members reported their experience of baptism as, 'not only a sign that points beyond the baptismal ritual to its historical and spiritual significance, but . . . in and through baptism, the individual and the community of faith undergo effectual change' (§ 123). Mennonite confessional documents reveal 'the expectation of transformation' through the practice of baptism (ibid.); and openness to 'effectual power . . . to bring change' carries over as well to the celebration of the Eucharist (§ 126). Roman Catholics can feel quite at home with this talk about the 'effects' of baptism and the Eucharist.

Meanwhile, in their discussion of peacemaking, Roman Catholic members note that Catholic teaching 'has increasingly endorsed the superiority of non-violent means and is suspect of the use of force in a culture of death' (§ 126). Even in Catholic teaching about just war, it explains, 'the criteria have grown more stringent in recent years, insisting that the function of the Just War Tradition is to prevent and limit war, not just legitimate it' (§ 158).

Of course this development has occurred in a discussion among Roman Catholics on peacemaking in the contemporary world, not primarily through their dialogue with Mennonites. Nevertheless, Mennonites hear in this development the recovery of an aspect of Gospel teaching that has been at the core of Mennonite identity. In a sense, this third form of gift exchange has meant that Mennonites and Roman Catholics can again listen to the Word of God together, rather than separated in hostility from each other. Listening together to the Word then also allows them to listen to each other.

Mutuality in the exchange of gifts can take many forms, and I have used three examples to illustrate this. But what happens when one partner offers a gift that its ecumenical dialogue partner does not want?

GIFTS OFFERED BUT NOT RECEIVED

I remember when I was choosing the title for my book *The Ecumenical Gift Exchange* and one of my ecumenical colleagues laughed and said that maybe he did not want some of the gifts my church communion was offering—for example, the papacy as it is currently exercised. His comment reminded me that one gift offered in the ecumenical gift exchange is serious criticism.

But it also raises the issue of the discernment of gifts: how do we distinguish the offer of bread from a stone? Churches engaged in serious ecumenical dialogue experience not only the mutuality of gift exchange, but also the refusal of the gift they enthusiastically offer to others. And they experience as well the fear within themselves of receiving a reading of the Gospel which their partner engagingly holds out to them.

In the Princeton Proposal for Christian unity, *In One Body through the Cross*, a group of ecumenical scholars criticizes the ecumenical movement for sometimes giving in to a kind of 'liberal indifference', leading others to react with 'divisive sectarianism'.[9] Wanting to avoid an indifferent relativism, some churches focus on older formulations to define their identity over against other churches. But, in fact, the Princeton Proposal argues, both liberal indifference and divisive sectarianism are often marked by a shift away from the question of truth and towards the question of identity: 'The question "Is it true?", that is, faithful to the divine revelation, was implicitly equated with "Is it authentically Catholic?", "Is it Evangelical?", "Does it express the mind of Orthodoxy?", "Is it congruent with the dynamics of the Reformation?"' (§ 41). The Proposal continues, 'This shift from truth to identity reflects a kind of tribalization of Christian communities' which can play into the hands of secular nationalism, ethnic conflict, or consumerist dynamics (§ 42).

Such reflections raise the need for repentance before any exchange of gifts is possible. It was a spirit of repentance which animated the US Lutheran–Roman Catholic Dialogue statement on *The Church as Koinonia of Salvation* when it used the language of 'woundedness' to describe the situation of each church. Rather than only mutual affirmations or exchange of gifts, the agreement asks Lutherans and Roman Catholics for a mutual recognition that the ordained ministries and communities of each are wounded because of the lack of full communion.[10]

The Princeton Proposal also speaks of the 'wound of disunity' affecting all Christians, and calls for disciplines of unity 'which are penitential' and ascetical.[11]

Christians need a spirit of repentance to help them learn whether it is divisive sectarianism or love for Gospel truth which leads them to reject a position offered to them as a gift by a partner church. Such discernment is not easy, and it leaves ecumenical dialogue with unfinished business.

This is a complicated issue. What seems in one communion like a gift of God for the church's up-building may strike another communion as a deeply unfaithful betrayal of the Gospel. A few examples reveal the complexity here.

In its statement on *Mary: Grace and Hope in Christ*, ARCIC[12] notes that teachings about Mary are being re-received in both the Roman Catholic and the Anglican communions. In fact, the Commission links these acts of re-reception. Because the Second Vatican Council sought 'consciously to resist exaggerations' in Marian teaching and practice 'by returning to patristic emphases and placing Marian doctrine and devotion in its proper Christological and ecclesial context' (§ 47), now the Anglican communion is able to consider the tradition about Mary in a fresh way. The Reformers had rejected 'real and perceived abuses surrounding devotion to Mary' (§ 47), with the result that 'to be a Roman Catholic came to be identified by an emphasis on devotion to Mary' (§ 47), while to be an Anglican came to be identified with the rejection of this emphasis.

But by reading the Scriptures together, members of ARCIC are able to present a fresh perspective on Mary based on Rom. 3: 30. For them, Mary embodies 'the "elect of Israel", of whom Paul speaks—glorified, justified, called, predestined' (§ 54). In this light, the statement presents a rereading of the teachings on the Immaculate Conception—seen as the 'prior preparation' of Mary for her unique role as Godbearer (§ 55)—and the Assumption—seen as part of the pattern of 'anticipated eschatology' in which Mary is 'a sign of hope for all humanity' (§ 56).

Could Anglicans receive the gift of these two teachings as they are offered here? The statement considers that perhaps 'explicit acceptance' of the two Marian dogmas 'might not be required of believers who were not in communion with Rome when they were defined', but that 'Anglicans would have to accept that the definitions are a legitimate expression of Catholic faith, and are to be respected as such, even if these formulations were not employed by them' (§ 63, n. 13). The statement points to the *JDDJ* as one example of 'an ecumenical agreement in which what one partner has defined as *de fide* can be expressed by another partner in a different way' (ibid.). This suggestion makes clear that a complex mutual reception of different gifts is being proposed for consideration by each communion.

In ARCIC's *The Gift of Authority*, the universal primacy of the Bishop of Rome is presented as a gift that the Anglican communion should now be ready to receive, 'a gift to be shared' that 'could be offered and received even before our churches are in full communion'.[13] Getting to such a recommendation involved ARCIC's earlier recognition of the complementarity of conciliarity and primacy within the exercise of authority in the church,[14] as well as a careful reinterpretation of the biblical and conciliar teachings about the papacy and infallibility. In particular, ARCIC emphasized that the primacy of the Pope must be exercised 'in collegial association with his brother bishops',[15] and that only the reception of a papal (or conciliar) teaching by the whole church is the 'final indication' that the teaching has been an exercise of infallibility.[16] In *The Gift of Authority*, ARCIC asks Anglicans to 'desire' the recovery and re-reception of the gift of the universal primacy and, in a poignant passage, it asks Roman Catholics to 'desire,' not only the re-reception of the primacy's exercise, but also 'the offering of such a ministry to the whole Church of God'.[17] This text suggests that receiving gifts is not the only difficult part of the dialogue. Even offering them suitably can be a challenge: we have to desire to offer them.

In the discussion on the ordination of women, we have a topic where the churches actually disagree about which teaching and practice really is a gift. Observing that some churches ordain men and women, while others ordain only men, the 'Ministry' statement in *Baptism, Eucharist and Ministry* of the World Council of Churches urged churches to face this question, adding, 'Openness to each other holds the possibility that the Spirit may well speak to one church through the insight of another'.[18]

What the Spirit is saying to the churches about this question, however, remains an area of disagreement. In 1976, the Congregation for the Doctrine of the Faith argued that 'the Church does not consider herself authorized to admit women to priestly ordination' because of the practice of Jesus and the apostolic community that did not include women among the twelve apostles or invest them with 'the apostolic charge'.[19] In 1994, Pope John Paul II argued from the will and practice of Christ 'that the Church has no authority whatsoever to confer priestly ordination on women' and that this judgment is to be held 'definitively'.[20] But in explaining the decision of some provinces within the Anglican Communion to ordain women, Robert Runcie, then Archbishop of Canterbury, also appealed to a Christological basis. Archbishop Runcie noted that some Anglicans believe that since in Jesus Christ the eternal Word of God assumed a human nature inclusive of both men and women, ordaining women as well as men would 'more perfectly ... represent Christ's inclusive high priesthood'.[21] Hence, he explained, for some Anglican provinces this doctrinal reason 'is seen not only to justify the ordination of women ... but actually to require it'.

Since the area of women's ordination remains in dispute among the churches, it is especially heartening to read a joint declaration by Archbishop Runcie and

Pope John Paul II that included comments directly on the question of women's ordination. Explaining that the ordination of women prevents Anglican–Roman Catholic reconciliation even where other progress has been made, they then added, 'No pilgrim knows in advance all the steps along the path'. And they continued, 'While we ourselves do not see a solution to this obstacle, we are confident that through our engagement with this matter our conversations will in fact help to deepen and enlarge our understanding' because of the Holy Spirit promised to the church.[22] 'We here solemnly recommit ourselves', they said, 'and those we represent to the restoration of visible unity and full ecclesial communion in the confidence that to seek anything less would be to betray our Lord's intention for the unity of his people'.[23]

ECUMENICAL DIALOGUE PARTNERS AND RECEPTION

By now it is clear that receiving gifts is not always easy. The work of the ecumenical gift exchange is nurtured by long-term dialogue among ecumenical partners who learn to give and receive from each other. Such long-term ecumenical dialogue has more than a sentimental or anecdotal significance: it provides a means and foretaste of reception among the churches.

First, long-term collaboration between dialogue partners forms the context for ecumenical research. Unlike some research, ecumenical discussion demands willingness and ability to listen to and cooperate with other scholars who hold very different viewpoints and to continue this collaboration for many years. It demands engagement in a common intellectual search for theological advance where none has seemed possible. Real ecumenical collaboration calls for willingness to enter into relationships, to risk vulnerability for the sake of the common effort, and to refuse competition as an acceptable mode for serious inquiry. Unlike some academic discourse in which competition is nurtured and even rewarded, ecumenical work only proceeds when competition is eschewed. By refusing to equate scholarship with its competitive forms, ecumenical research actually serves as a countercultural model within academic circles, recalling scholars to an earlier ideal of being truly a college together. In such a context reception becomes possible.

Secondly, long-term dialogue among ecumenical colleagues often enables improved understanding of their positions. Because dialogue partners can listen to each other sympathetically, without the presupposition of hostility or competition, they can often learn something new from each other's viewpoint. They can discover aspects of the other's position that previously they have distorted or neglected.

The *JDDJ* speaks of the 'new insights' that the Lutheran Church and the Roman Catholic Church have achieved, and adds, 'Developments have taken place that not only make possible but also require the churches to examine the divisive questions and condemnations and see them in a new light' (§ 7). This new light enables the two communions to 'articulate a common understanding' of justification, in which the emphases of each are recognized as legitimate alternatives (§ 5). When church communions see each other in this new light, then, they can be led to mutual recognition of the other's Christian faith, the basis for reception of ecumenical agreement.

Relationships between colleagues in the ecumenical movement parallel the relationships that have developed between communions once ignorant or hostile toward each other. In the past, churches addressed each other polemically, and emphasized each other's mistakes in interpreting the Gospel. But after a 'purification of memories', says Pope John Paul II, the churches are able to change their 'way of looking at things', yielding 'a calm, clear-sighted and truthful vision of things, a vision enlivened by divine mercy and capable of freeing people's minds and of inspiring in everyone a renewed willingness, precisely with a view to proclaiming the Gospel to the men and women of every people and nation'.[24] In ecumenical dialogue, this re-evaluation of each other's position is a necessary step on the way to reception of each other's insights.

Jean-Marie Tillard notes that reception is preceded by two aspects of mutual recognition. First, Christians recognize in each other the same faith given to the apostolic community and faithfully preserved over time in every generation. They must distinguish between what should be received from former generations and what is merely a contingent characteristic of a certain time in the church's history. 'Tradition cannot be confused with the museum of everything concerning faith', Tillard states.[25] Secondly, Christians recognize in each other the same faith given to the church at Pentecost and faithfully preserved throughout the world in every culture. Often the formulations and liturgical celebrations of the churches differ from culture to culture. But the churches do not receive merely a copy of the Spirit's gift given to the apostolic church, Tillard emphasizes. They receive in fact the same gift. He continues, 'Because they *recognize* it in each other, they are one church in the indivisible grace of Pentecost'.[26] If the soils in which the Gospel has grown are different, Tillard underlines, 'the seed is the very same, fully identical'.[27]

Reception then involves recognition of the identical faith in another person or another community. This identical faith, as Tillard notes, may be expressed through liturgical, theological, and cultural characteristics different from those that mark one's own faith expression. But it is the same gift given to all Christians, and, as Tillard says, 'because they *recognize* it in each other, they are one church'.[28] ARCIC explains reception in a similar way: 'By "reception" we mean the fact that the people of God acknowledge such a decision or statement because they recognize in it the apostolic faith.'[29] It is such a recognition that ecumenical partners sometimes experience with each other.

Here I can testify to the correctness of the phrase, 'the shock of recognition'. Arrogantly, I was convinced when I started teaching theology that I had little to learn about Christianity from evangelicals. But then I encountered evangelical dialogue partners who showed me they confess the same apostolic faith that I confess and that they also sought reforms within their own church communion parallel to those I was seeking in mine. Long-term ecumenists report many such experiences, when dialogue partners have opened our eyes in recognition of the common faith we share. Such a recognition is a kind of foretaste of the recognition our churches experience in dialogue together, a sudden gift of the new light in which to see each other more clearly.

I mentioned that one gift long-term ecumenical partners offer each other is serious criticism. Such criticism can be heard because of the basic mutual recognition that is present between dialogue partners. Henry Chadwick explains, 'Reception arises when it is recognized that the partner in dialogue loves God and his church and seeks to be obedient to the Gospel; moreover, that this obedience transcends allegiance to anything sectarian.'[30]

I have said that long-term collaboration between ecumenical colleagues in dialogue, first, sets the context of collaboration and, second, enhances understanding among dialogue partners, giving a foretaste of the reception between church communions that our dialogue seeks. I would add, third, that it supports the perseverance among scholars that is absolutely necessary for the success of ecumenical work.

The titles of two discussions of ecumenism tell us something important about dialogue today. Robert Bilheimer's study on spirituality for ecumenism is called *A Spirituality for the Long Haul*.[31] Thomas Ryan's guideline for ecumenical work is called *A Survival Guide for Ecumenically Minded Christians*.[32] These titles reveal something significant: ecumenical work today is a task for the long haul and it demands survival tactics. Put another way, ecumenical dialogue is a form of asceticism. It invites Christian scholars to enter into a process which may achieve no tangible success or rewards during their lifetime. During their involvement, ecumenists must follow various ascetical practices: they repeatedly fast from celebrations of the Eucharist when not in full communion with the presider; they spend their time and talents on lengthy study of positions they only gradually understand; they endure the embarrassment and frustration that flow from the sins of both their own and their dialogue partner's communion; and frequently their efforts are feared or suspected by members of their own church.

I do not think I could have survived in this ascetical way of life without the friendships of Roman Catholic colleagues and colleagues from other church traditions involved in ecumenical dialogue. Colleagues involved in ecumenism share the same poignant experience of love for their own traditions and restlessness within them—a kind of cognitive and emotional dissonance peculiar to the ecumenical task. Ecumenical friends and colleagues from other church communions offer each other intellectual and emotional hospitality on the journey towards full communion. They are oases of reception on the path. Ryan writes directly of the importance of such ecumenical hospitality, noting that ecumenists often have a 'primary home' in their own church communion but a 'secondary home' in their partner's communion where 'they have spent enough time to feel "at-home"'.[33] But, to be guests, he continues, 'we must be ready to go where the other lives, to see and understand the way things are done in the other's household, to develop an affection for that space and the things we find there'.[34] Visiting takes time, and friendship with colleagues from other church communions enables the time that hospitality demands. In experiencing the hospitality of our dialogue partners, we often experience the deeper hospitality of mutual reception that is the goal of our dialogue.

CONCLUSION

Yves Congar writes that 'those involved in the ecumenical movement have by virtue of that a *votum unitatis, votum catholicitatis* [desire for unity, desire for catholicity], which gives to their present belief a dynamic dimension in which their intention of plenitude is fulfilled'.[35]

Dialogue among long-term ecumenical partners provides a particularly intense experience of both the desire for unity and the foretaste of unity achieved. Perhaps this is the reason such relationships are so effective in nurturing ecumenical perseverance. Like the disciples on the road to Emmaus, we ecumenical colleagues walk along the road together with Christ as he opens the meaning of the Scriptures to us. Together we are amazed at what he is saying; but we do not recognize him yet for who he is. Sometimes, though, at the breaking of the bread in the other's home—even when we cannot partake—our eyes are opened and we recognize again: we indeed have a common Lord, and he is in our midst. Because we recognize a common Lord, ecumenical colleagues at such moments also recognize each other as his disciples and are again sustained for the long journey ahead.

NOTES

1. See George Tavard, 'Hospitality as an Ecumenical Paradigm', *Bulletin of the Centro Pro Unione*, 69 (2006), 11.
2. *UUS*, § 28.
3. *JDDJ*, § 13, also at <http://www.vatican.va/roman_curia/pontifical_councils/ chrstuni/documents/rc_pc_chrstuni_doc_31101999_cath-luth-joint-declaration_ en.html>.

4. See Chapter 11: William G. Rusch, 'The International Lutheran–Roman Catholic Dialogue—An Example of Ecclesial Learning and Ecumenical Reception'.

5. ARCIC, 'Eucharistic Doctrine' (1971), *The Final Report* (London: CTS/SPCK, 1982), 11–16, § 5.

6. Ibid. 17–25, § 6b.

7. See <http://www.bridgefolk.net>.

8. Available at <http://www.bridgefolk.net/calledtogether.htm>.

9. Carl E. Braaten and Robert W. Jenson (eds.), *In One Body through the Cross: The Princeton Proposal for Christian Unity* (Grand Rapids, Mich.: Eerdmans, 2003), § 24.

10. US Lutheran–Roman Catholic Dialogue, in Randall Lee and Jeffrey Gros (eds.), *The Church as Koinonia of Salvation: Its Structures and Ministries. Lutherans and Catholics in Dialogue*, vol. x., *Agreed Statement of the Tenth Round of the US Lutheran–Roman Catholic Dialogue with Background Papers* (Washington, DC: USCCB, 2005), 48 (§ 103), also available at: <http://www.usccb.org/seia/koinonia.shtml>.

11. *In One Body Through the Cross*, § 71.

12. ARCIC II: *Mary: Grace and Hope in Christ* (London: Continuum, 2005), available at <http://www.vatican.va/roman-curia/pomtifical_councils/chrstuni/angl-comm-docs/rc_pc_chrstuni_doc_20050516_mary-grace-hope-christ_en.html>.

13. *The Gift of Authority: Authority in the Church III* (London: Church House Publishing/CTS, 1999), § 60, available at <http://www.vatican.va/roman_curia/pontifical_councils/chrstuni/documents/rc_pc_chrstuni_doc_12051999_gift-of-autority_en.html>.

14. 'Authority in the Church I' (1976), *The Final Report*, 49–67 (§ 22).

15. 'Authority in the Church II' (1981), *The Final Report*, 81–100 (§ 19).

16. 'Authority in the Church: Elucidation' (1981), *The Final Report*, 68–78 (§ 3).

17. *The Gift of Authority*, § 62.

18. *BEM*, 20–32 (§ 54).

19. CDF, '*Inter Insigniores*: Declaration on the Question of the Admission of Women to the Ministerial Priesthood' (15 Oct. 1976), *Origins*, 6 (1977–8), 519–20, available at < www.womenpriests.org/church/interlet.asp>.

20. Pope John Paul II, '*Ordinatio Sacerdotalis*: Apostolic Letter on Reserving Priestly Ordination to Men Alone' (22 May 1994) (London: CTS, 1994), § 4, available at <http://www.vatican.va/holy_father/john_paul_ii/apost_letters/documents/hf_jp-ii_apl_22051994_ordinatio-sacerdotalis_en.html>.

21. 'Archbishop Robert Runcie to Cardinal Jan Willebrands' (18 Dec. 1985), *Origins*, 16 (1986–7), 157.

22. Pope John Paul II and Archbishop Robert Runcie, 'Common Declaration' (2 Oct. 1989), *Origins*, 19 (1989–90), 317.

23. Ibid., 316. Cf. Cardinal Walter Kasper's recent words to the Church of England's House of Bishops when he spoke of the then imminent likely decision to ordain women to episcopal office as representing 'a decision against the common goal we have until now pursued in our dialogue: full ecclesial communion' which would fundamentally alter 'the quality of the dialogue . . . Instead of moving towards one another we would co-exist alongside one another'. 'The Mission of Bishops in the Mystery of the Church: Reflections on the Question of Ordaining Women to Episcopal Office in the Church of England' (5 June 2006), § 3,

available at <http://www.vatican.va/roman_curia/pontifical_councils/chrstuni/card-kasper-docs/rc_pc_chrstuni_doc_20060605_kasper-bishops_en.html>.

24. *UUS*, §§ 2, 15.
25. 'Tradition, Reception', in Kenneth Hagen (ed.), *The Quadrilog: Tradition and the Future of Ecumenism. Essays in Honor of George H. Tavard* (Collegeville, Minn.: Liturgical Press, 1994), 334.
26. Ibid. 341.
27. Ibid. 342.
28. Ibid. 341.
29. 'Authority in the Church: Elucidation', § 3.
30. 'Reception', in G. R. Evans and Michel Gourgues (eds.), *Communion et Réunion: Mélanges Jean-Marie Roger Tillard* (Leuven: Peeters, 1995), 107.
31. Bilheimer, *A Spirituality for the Long Haul: Biblical Risk and Moral Stand* (Philadelphia, Pa.: Fortress Press, 1984).
32. Ryan, *A Survival Guide for Ecumenically Minded Christians* (Collegeville, Minn.: Liturgical Press, 1989).
33. Ibid. 126.
34. Ibid. 126–7.
35. Congar, *Diversity and Communion*, trans. John Bowden (London: SCM, 1984), 133.

3

Authentic *Learning* and *Receiving*—A Search for Criteria

Ladislas Örsy, SJ

INTRODUCTION

Receptive learning among Christian churches is a delicate operation: it is authentic when it is marked by truth and transfused by prudence. A community that is intent on it must first learn about valuable insights and praiseworthy practices in another church and then can receive them into its existing tradition: two distinct stages in a wholesome process.[1]

To bring such a process to a good resolution, there ought to be norms for authenticity. The persons learning and receiving must have the right dispositions, the doctrine received must be rooted in truth, and the practice accepted must be an expression of Christian love. The question emerges spontaneously: What are the criteria for identifying such subtle requirements?

The question is fair and just but there is not a standard response. Each Christian communion must find its own measures conditioned by their ancient traditions and present circumstances. My inquiry, therefore, must be restricted to the Roman Catholic Church. I hope, however, that searchers from other communities will undertake similar reflections in their own churches and eventually the singular quests will converge toward ecumenical conclusions.

THE SECOND VATICAN COUNCIL AND RECEPTIVE LEARNING

The documents of the Second Vatican Council contain probably as many conclusive statements as seminal propositions. Yes, on several points the bishops confirm a well-advanced doctrinal development, but on other issues they advance fresh insights and leave it to future generations to develop them further.[2]

Admittedly, the council said no word about receptive learning among the churches. But when the Fathers professed and articulated their faith in the

Roman Catholic communion, when they proclaimed their convictions about other Christian communities, and when they described the church of Christ that is and is to come they opened the way and set the scene precisely for receptive learning. What the bishops did not say emerges from the very state of the churches. Following here are some of the Council's relevant determinations.

First, the council asserts that

This Church [of Christ], constituted and organized as a society in the present world, subsists in the Catholic Church [*subsistit in ecclesia catholica*] ... (*LG*, § 8)

And

the Catholic Church has been endowed with all divinely revealed truth and with all means of grace ... (*UR*, § 4)

Thus, the council recognizes a particular fullness in the Roman Catholic communion but it does not say that the church of Christ does not in any sense exist in any other church, or that another church cannot reach a fuller understanding of a point of doctrine, or achieve a more intense practice than happens in the Roman Catholic communion.[3] The council leaves room for enrichment.

Then, the council affirms that

Catholics must gladly acknowledge and esteem the truly Christian endowments from our common heritage which are to be found among our separated brethren. It is right and salutary to recognize the riches of Christ and virtuous works in the lives of others who are bearing witness to Christ, sometimes even to the shedding of their blood. For God is always wonderful in his works and worthy of all praise. (*UR*, § 4)

In simple terms it follows that we Catholics—if we are willing to look and learn—may well find authentic 'riches of Christ' in other communions; riches that we not only *could* appropriate legitimately but which we *should* appropriate since they belong to Christ.

Finally, the council declares that

Whatever is truly Christian is never contrary to what genuinely belongs to the faith; indeed, it can always bring a more perfect realization of the very mystery of Christ and the Church. (*UR*, § 4)

And

Further, this Council declares that it realizes that this holy objective—the reconciliation of all Christians in the unity of the one and only Church of Christ—transcends human powers and gifts. (*UR*, § 24)

In other terms, the movement for unity has an objective goal, it is the 'one and only Church of Christ'. The Spirit of God, who is ultimately in charge, is leading the separated communions towards finding their unity in it. All are duty bound to follow the Spirit and perfect themselves. This process towards a fullness in the intelligence of faith and in discrete charity includes the honest will to learn and receive from each other 'whatever is true, whatever is honorable . . . whatever is pure, whatever is pleasing' (Phil. 4: 8)—so that God's peace be with them all (cf. Phil. 4: 9).

THE ALLEGORY OF THE WOUNDED BODY
IN NEED OF HEALING

For a good understanding of the state of the Christian communions, their unity, and their divisions, the allegory of the wounded human body may do good service: it speaks of an organic unity and it allows for internal dysfunctions. Further, it conveys the idea that when the one body is torn internally, every single part is the weaker for it; this is exactly the case in a living body. If this allegory is not *the* perfect symbol, it comes close to it.

Let the allegory unfold.

When a human body is healthy, it is transfused with energy and working in an orderly fashion. Each particular organ fulfills its own specific part in an operation that supports the well-being of the whole. Should, however, a serious disorder arise internally—as when an organ is harmed, or a vital balance is disturbed—the body ceases to function normally. Its unity is broken; its integrity is imperiled. Indispositions and breakdowns follow; the whole cannot operate well for the failing of the parts.

Our allegory recognizes an existing unity created by God's Spirit through the Word and the sacraments. It speaks of the hurts as being within the one body. It helps to see that healing must come from internal resources. Finally, it tells us that we all are affected by the tragedy since we *are* the body.

The allegory of the body suffering from internal wounds and in need of healing is more comprehensive than the one that sees progress in 'ecumenical exchange'. While to speak of 'exchange of gifts' as a means to unity is certainly legitimate, the expression puts more emphasis on the separate existence of the communities than on their existing unity.

Once we have a good understanding of the nature of the ailment, we are in better position to search for the remedy.

The starting point in this search must be the recognition that the healing is a gift of the Spirit. We cannot produce the needed medicine and—as it were—just administer it. All we can do is to dispose ourselves and to bring about the right environment for the reception of a gratuitous donation.

The very nature of ecumenical work consists, therefore, in doing all we can to create a climate of freedom where the Spirit of God can enlighten us and can overcome by divine impulses our stubborn prejudices and emotional resistances. For this, we need the virtues of humility and magnanimity, nurtured through individual and communal prayer and fasting.[4]

CRITERIA OF AUTHENTICITY 1: PRESERVING IDENTITY

Learning and receiving are authentic only if they support the identity of the receivers and bring them life in abundance. Thus, two questions: What is that identity? What is life giving?[5]

In relation to the first of these questions, the *Groupe des Dombes* is of good counsel about the problem of 'preserving identity'.[6] In an essay entitled *For the Conversion of the Churches* they offer an insightful analysis of the meaning and role of 'identity' in the various Christian assemblies.[7] They see three 'layers' that together make up the concrete historical character of each community. First, at the deepest level, the community has a Christian identity; it is permanent, it is the very core of their being—not subject to any negotiation. On that level all believers in Christ—justified and sanctified as they are—may have more in common then they realize. Then, each community has an ecclesial identity, which gives them their specific 'personality' within the larger Christian family. An example from history could be the distinct characteristics of the eastern and western churches as they developed in the first millennium. They did not differ in their substantial profession and practice of Christianity yet each had its own distinct theologies, organizational structures, and modes of operation. Such 'ecclesial identity' represents a wealth for all—it represents diversity in the church of Christ—never to be destroyed. Finally, over these two layers each communion has generated and built up a 'confessional character' that to this day marks them out among the others and gives them the specific 'historical personality' which we know today.[8]

The *Groupe* proposes that the time has come for each Christian denomination to look inwards—as it were—and ask how much each could shed or sacrifice of its own confessional identity in order to move closer to other churches and ultimately facilitate the progress towards the one church of Christ. The *Groupe* calls this a process of 'emptying', *kenosis*. It is a way (perhaps *the* way) for the churches to move towards the fullness of the church of Christ.

Learning and receiving could be considered as complementary to the *Groupe*'s proposal. Their emphasis is on the churches 'emptying themselves' from unnecessary historical accretions and obstacles to unity. Without denying this need, we go one step further: we focus on how the churches could enrich themselves by learning and receiving doctrinal insights and sound practices from each other. In addition (an important factor), learning and receiving are possible on any level of identity: new insights into the Tradition can enhance Christian identity; fresh initiatives in charity can enrich ecclesial personality; humility and magnanimity can make a denomination a better agent for unity.

CRITERIA OF AUTHENTICITY 2: TRUE AND FALSE RECEPTION

Learning and receiving are ultimately the acceptance of a gift—but how do we know a gift is genuine? How do we know that a new intelligence, or practice, of faith inspired by a sister communion is an authentic development of doctrine and not an abandonment of our Tradition? How do we know that an attractive proposition is true or false?

A never-proclaimed 'Doctor of the Church' who was an inspiration for the Second Vatican Council, John Henry Newman, should be our counsellor now.

In his *An Essay on the Development of Christian Doctrine*, published in its definitive form in 1878, Newman gathered the criteria for sound development under seven headings, contrasting each with the signs of destructive forces and providing ample evidence from history to support his conclusions.[9] While his book should be in the hands of every person who intends to play an active role in a process of learning and receiving, I try to indicate the wealth of his theory in a summary form under three headings.[10]

The signs of a true development are:

1. The new doctrinal insight confirms the identity and foundational components of the institution and leaves the leading principles of its operation intact.

2. The new development blends into the old tradition harmoniously; there is historical continuity between the two; the new can be rightly judged as the unfolding of a hidden potential in the old.

3. The development brings a new vigour of life; it fills the institution with new energy; its impact on the surroundings speaks of an abundance of life.

Such positive signs appear with greater clarity when each is contrasted with its negative counterpart. The signs of destructive trends are:

1. The new proposal could undermine the very identity of the community (Christian and ecclesial identity—in the terms of the *Groupe des Dombes*) and harm the core of its being; it could interfere with its vital operations.

2. The change would introduce an extraneous element that is not, and cannot be, an unfolding of the old tradition, a change that threatens with rupture.

3. The new project (a belief or an operational principle) would bring stag-
   nation and cause strife inside the community and would deprive it of the
   energy necessary to fulfil its mission to proclaim the Good News to the
   World.

The criteria, as they are enumerated here, are a summary of Newman's far
more nuanced expositions. The reader may want to go to the source!

CRITERIA OF AUTHENTICITY 3: PRUDENT AND IMPRUDENT RECEPTION

The criteria for truth operate in a realm of the abstract, universal, and impersonal;
in other terms, they work somewhat independently from the vicissitudes of
history.

Judgements, however, about the wisdom of introducing new ideas or inno-
vating practices into the life of a community move in a different world. They
must deal with the concrete, particular, even personal situations. They must
decide about the capacity of the would-be receiving community to move into
a new horizon, to find itself comfortable there, and then be able to operate in
an unfamiliar environment. Such practical judgements can be made only on the
basis of lived experience, or carefully gathered empirical evidence.

This leads us to say that in the process of learning and receiving, there comes
a stage when persons who are alert observers of events and well experienced in
community affairs are likely to be more reliable guides than subtle principles.
Persons who lived for long in the would-be receiving community can have a
better feel for what is suitable and attainable then dreamers who are roaming
the world of ideals. Such down-to-earth feeling persons—they could be prophets
or bishops—gather their knowledge from an affinity with the community. They
have the 'supernatural sense of faith', affirmed by the Second Vatican Council;
faith 'sustained by the Spirit of truth' that leads to 'right judgement' when applied
'more fully in daily life' (cf. *LG*, § 12).

THE RECEIVING COMMUNITY

The receiving community is the principal agent in the process of learning and
receiving. But what is a learning and receiving community? How could a local
church become one?

As a starting point, the community intent on learning and receiving must
be of one mind and of one heart. The enterprise cannot be successful if it
is undertaken merely (or mainly!) through authorities and representatives. A
significant majority—at least—must be behind it.

The Council of Florence should serve as a warning. Both Romans and Byzantines had the misconception that the reunion of the two churches could be accomplished by an agreement between the leaders of the two churches. They failed to realize that the existential reunion of two such complex social bodies with their sensitivities could never be accomplished by a theoretical agreement through their representatives; not even if the representatives are in the highest positions in the respective hierarchies. When the whole body is hurt, it is hurt throughout, and every organ must contribute to the process of healing. In other terms: the faithful at large must be involved. The violent rejection of the deed of reunion composed (that is, painfully hammered out under the threat of the advancing Turks) at Florence is an admonishment for today. Dialogues among experts (or among delegated officials) are not enough to lead to reunion—not even if they produce an agreement. This warning should not be construed as an argument against dialogues; they should continue. But their limits must be recognized. Only a unified community can create an authentic process of learning and receiving.

The following proposals—with some added comments—are an attempt to identify in greater details the attitudes, dispositions, and conditions needed for a successful process.

- The receiving community must look inwards and be well established in a position of humility; it must believe—with faith divine—in its own limitations and incompleteness; otherwise it cannot conceive a desire for enrichment.

The Catholic community may feel that such a humble attitude is contrary to their fundamental belief since 'the Church of Christ…subsists in the Catholic Church' (cf. *LG*, § 8; *UR*, § 4). What more can they learn and receive? They can learn and receive a lot: God is rich enough to give them more. The faithful can always progress in their intelligence of faith and their deeds of love. The church of Christ within the Catholic Church (and for that matter wherever it is present) is a dynamic theological reality always prompting the community to progress toward its eschatological perfection.

- The receiving community must look outwards; it must be alert to and observe the other communities with the eyes of faith; it must believe—with faith divine—that they too are sustained by the gifts of the Spirit; it must consider the others' insights and practices with sympathy.

In this exercise, love and wisdom must go hand in hand. Love commands respect for, and the acceptance of, the other community because a bond of communion (to a degree that may be hard for us to determine) already exists. Wisdom demands discernment: the integrity of the Christian and ecclesial character of the potentially receiving community must not be harmed. It is a process where the learning of the experts and the 'supernatural sense of faith' of experienced persons are equally indispensable.

- The community intending to receive must discover in the life of another communion an advanced insight into the evangelical message or a Christ-like practice that could enrich the receivers.

In such discovery critical doctrinal judgements and intuitive sense of faith must play their parts. Whatever is selected must correspond to the demands of orthodoxy and orthopraxis—I use these expressions in their classical senses, as they were current in the early centuries. In evaluating an attractive idea or custom the biblical criterion of judging the tree by its fruit offers reliable help.

- The receiving community must become a creative agent: it must develop the inspiration it received all over again, out of its own resources. It must progress in the intelligence of faith; it must achieve a more dedicated service in love.

Reception is not the bare copying of a belief or the mere imitating of a practice. Any act of reception is a move into a broader horizon: it transcends ordinary reasoning and goes beyond customary caution.[11] It is a move from the known into the unknown: it is not without risk. The ultimate criterion of authentic reception is in the crucible of life. The community ought to reach its final judgement through experience; after a certain period of time the capacity (or the lack of it) of the new initiative to produce good fruit should be manifest.

To sum it up: the dynamic of reception begins with critical self-knowledge, continues with the intelligence of the life of others, and concludes with the testing of new values in the crucible of the life and work of the receiving community. In this process an awareness of the Tradition, a capacity for discerning judgements, a good sense for practicalities are needed. They all together create the right dispositions and environment for receiving a gift of the Spirit.

IN THE CRUCIBLE OF LIFE: A TEST CASE

My reflections about learning and receiving have moved mostly on an abstract and theoretical level—'in the order of the essences', as the scholastics would define. Authentic reception, however, can happen only in the existential world, in the concrete and practical order. What happens there makes the difference between success and failure, reality and dream.

To come as close as possible to this existential crucible, let us try a thought-experiment, an exercise in theological and canonical imagination. Such a mental adventure involves a complex interplay of intuition and discovery, a series of value judgements followed by prudential recommendations, and finally an imaginary evaluation of a projected practice in the receiving community. We are attempting to construe a historical process, before it happens, so that we might handle it wisely when it does happen.

Let the theme of this exercise be the doctrine and practice of episcopal collegiality. It is a major issue in theology and canon law. The Second Vatican Council affirmed it, scholars are disputing it, bishops are asking for it, ecclesiastical documents are regulating it. It is an issue that touches the internal balances of the life of the Catholic Church intimately and has far reaching ecumenical consequences.

To start the exercise, we need a working definition. Let us assume that episcopal collegiality is the external, visible, and legal expression of an internal, invisible, and theological unity, which is often called—especially in the Orthodox church—'synodality'. In the Latin church the expression 'internal spiritual communion' comes closest to it. It exists among those who have the episcopal order: they have a common gift from the Spirit.[12] Like any other institutional charism, synodality or internal communion needs structures and norms to operate externally—this is an aspect of the law of incarnation.

The doctrine has never been denied in history, although hardly ever has it been defined with precision. But, as happened many times, practice preceded theory, and collegiality was operational at different degrees over 2,000 years before theologians theorized about it.

The Second Vatican Council reaffirmed the doctrine but not without having to overcome fierce minority resistance:

[I]n accordance with the Lord's decree, Saint Peter and the rest of the apostles constitute a unique apostolic college, so in like fashion the Roman Pontiff, Peter's successor, and the bishops, the successors of the apostles, are related with and united to one another. Indeed, the very ancient discipline whereby the bishops installed throughout the whole world lived in communion with one another and with the Roman Pontiff in a bond of unity, charity and peace . . . points clearly to the collegiate character and structure of the episcopal order (*LG*, § 22).

Again: 'Together with their head, the Supreme Pontiff, and never apart from him, they have supreme and full authority [*potestas,* power] over the universal Church' (*LG*, § 22).[13]

In this declaration, the term *potestas* must not be taken in a purely external and legal sense. It means also an internal and spiritual charism with restless energy, given for the sake of God's people. If God gives such a *collegial* gift, it is given to be used *collegially*; otherwise the divine project remains unfulfilled. A source of energy intended for action remains an abstraction.

The first step in our thought-experiment is to become aware that in the first millennium, and somewhat after it, the bishops of our western church practised effective collegiality with significant intensity. That is, collegiality *does* belong to our tradition. We must admit, however, that in recent centuries the idea nearly faded and collegial operations ceased significantly. In fact they were reduced to its exercise within an ecumenical council. We have reached a situation where canon law leaves no room for the practice of effective episcopal collegiality.

First step: we acknowledge our impoverishment; an act of humility.

Then, in our imagination, we discover that the practice of collegiality is a vital element in the life of, say, the Orthodox Church: their belief in synodality and their bishops' way of operating collegially is life giving.

Second step: we recognize a valuable Christian practice in a separated community; an act of magnanimity.

It would be unrealistic, of course, to think that such complex initial movements—humility and magnanimity—can take place all at once in the entire receiving community. There ought to be leaders, humble and magnanimous, to initiate and to sustain the process.

We are reaching a turning point in our thought-experiment. We must imagine what the practical steps should be in recreating an old Christian practice in the contemporary Catholic environment. Mere copying would not do. Nothing can be taken 'ready made' from the house of a community and implanted magically into a new home. The receiving community must generate new insights and operations. Such a conversion to a new way of thinking and to an unfamiliar manner of acting is bound to be slow.

Further questions emerge in our imagined exercise, questions not easy to answer a priori. In reality, would the bishops be ready and willing to function collegially? Could they leave behind the habit of continuously looking for directions from the Holy See and hardly using their own judgement and discretion?[14] Are they practised in building collegial decisions step by step, making their own contribution and accepting the suggestions of others? What about the communities at large: are the faithful willing to accept and respect the teaching and direction of their bishops?

If such questions cannot be answered in a positive way, the day for intense, responsible, and effective collegial government—desirable as it may be—has not come. Prudence may well dictate to work first on an educational programme that can guide the community—bishops and laity—towards a collegial mentality. But how can such mentality be created in the Catholic Church today? Who can do it? How can anyone do it?

At this point we must leave behind our imagination and face reality. Our mental exercise brought us to the threshold of the papal office. Without the help of Peter's successor, progress toward effective episcopal collegiality is virtually impossible. We have, perhaps more by human design than by divine intent, structures and norms that leave little space (virtually no space) for any significant decision by a gathering of the bishops—except for implementing decrees and directions emanating from the See of Rome. Immense energies latent in the episcopal college lie unused—perhaps waiting for the next ecumenical council!

Since all power to change the laws is reserved to the Pope, he alone can open the door to effective collegiality. Such a move, should it ever happen, would not mean that Peter's successor would lose his authority—quite the opposite! He would increase his authority by taking his brother bishops into decision-making processes where he alone would have the presidency with the final right of approval.

John Paul II in his 1995 encyclical *Ut Unum Sint*, asked the pastors and theologians of all the Christian churches to help him to find new ways of exercising his ministry; new ways in which all could recognize it as a service of love (cf. §§ 95–6).

Hardly anything could come closer to the late pope's wish and have a greater impact on the ecumenical movement than the exercise of the Petrine ministry in a collegial manner.

Once, in those blessed times when Christ walked with the apostles, he told Peter: 'I have prayed for you that your own faith may not fail; and you, when once you have turned back, strengthen your brothers' (Luke 22: 32). John Paul II comments that as Peter was in need of conversion, so is the Roman Catholic Church in need of perpetual conversion. In no way did the Pope exempt himself from this obligation; rather he declared that papal ministry was open to a new situation (cf. §§ 15, 91, and 95). Now, he spoke with apostolic authority. Does it mean, therefore, that the papacy is open to receptive learning—in matters such as episcopal collegiality?

CONCLUSION

The Son of God has come a long way to bring the Good News of salvation to the human family. His intent was 'to give light to those who sit in darkness and in the shadow of death, to guide our feet into the way of peace' (Luke 1: 79). The nations, however, are still sitting in the shadow of death—far from finding the way of peace.

For this sad state of the world, we Christians, to whom the message of peace has been entrusted, bear some responsibility. Due to our discords, the Word that gives light and life has become muted and obscured because we cannot speak with one voice, and because much of our energy that should be used for the proclamation of joyful tidings is needed for settling our differences.

We need to heal ourselves, if we want to heal the world. The medicine is at hand; the Word is among us; no Christian community is without it. The Spirit of God is willing to guide us and to lead us to finding and tasting the Word in its wholesome goodness.

To learn and receive from each other is part of this healing process.

NOTES

1. See Chapter 1: Paul D. Murray, 'Receptive Ecumenism and Catholic Learning—Establishing the Agenda'.
2. There is an interesting topic for historians and theologians: How far was the Second Vatican Council a 'seminal' council? The answer undoubtedly is that seminal ideas abound in the conciliar documents but—to my knowledge—no major work has been undertaken to identify them systematically and show how much the Council was and remains a 'beginning'.
3. For further on this, see Chapter 6: Walter Kasper, ' "Credo Unam Sanctam Ecclesiam"—The Relationship Between the Catholic and the Protestant Principles in Fundamental Ecclesiology', n. 10; also Chapter 1: Murray, 'Receptive Ecumenism and Catholic Learning—Establishing the Agenda', nn. 33 and 34.
4. What about a 'holy month' of prayer and fasting (yes!) observed by all Christian communities—as long as Christians remain divided—to sharpen our hearing for the word of God, and to dispose our will to follow it? This is not to exclude the dialogues but to create the proper environment for them.
5. For reflections prompted by the second question, see Part IV.
6. The ecumenical *Groupe des Dombes* was founded by Abbé Paul Couturier, priest of the Roman Catholic Diocese of Lyons, France, in 1937. It brought together Catholic and Protestant friends from France and Switzerland. They gradually construed and followed a method of 'ecumenical healing' that has produced extraordinary results and can serve as a model for all groups working for unity. See Bernard Sesboüé, 'Groupe des Dombes', in Nicholas Lossky, et al. (eds.), *Dictionary of the Ecumenical Movement*, 2nd edn. (Geneva: WCC, 2002), 503–5, and Catherine E. Clifford, *The Groupe des Dombes. A Dialogue of Conversion* (New York and Oxford: Peter Lang, 2005).
7. *For the Conversion of the Churches*, trans. James Greig (Geneva: WCC, 1993).
8. The dividing lines among these 'identities' may not be always clear but overall the observations of the *Groupe* are sound and historically demonstrable.
9. *An Essay on the Development of Christian Doctrine*, rev. edn. (London: Pickering, 1878).
10. For a more elaborate presentation of Newman's theory, see Örsy, 'Stability and Development in Canon Law and the Case of Definitive Teaching', *Notre Dame Law Review*, 76 (2001), 863–79.
11. See Chapter 7: Riccardo Larini, 'Texts and Contexts—Hermeneutical Reflections on Receptive Ecumenism'.
12. This is not the place to give a detailed theological explanation of episcopal communion and collegiality but it is fair to provide some doctrinal information. Episcopal ordination grants recipients the *uncreated* gift of the assistance of the Spirit and the *created* gift of a permanent charism. As in the church there is one Person (the Spirit) in many persons (the faithful), so it is in the episcopal college: the Spirit is holding many bishops together. The source of unity among them is ontological. This is *synodos*. This is *communio*. This is a theological reality in its deepest spiritual sense. In the visible body of the church, it demands an external, structural, operational expression; which in the Latin church is mostly referred to as collegiality.

13. The Council used the same three words—'supreme, full, and universal'—to describe the power of the episcopal college and the power of the Pope, and left it to the theologians to find a concordance in an apparent discordance. See the Commentaries on *Lumen Gentium* and in particular on the *Nota praevia,* which contains precious information but not without a hermeneutical problem: it was appended to the Constitution by 'higher authority'. It was meant to be the guide for the interpretation of the Constitution although it is not 'an act of the council'. The final solemn approval of the Constitution, however, was given after the publication of the *Nota.*

14. The force of this habit—in Rome and in the provinces—must not be underestimated. It is too deeply ingrained to change rapidly. In the Bull of Confirmation of the Council of Trent, Pius IV forbade theologians and canonists to publish their own comments on, or interpretations of, the council; see *DS,* § 1849. The merry times of the high Middle Ages, with their 'sic et non' method and ceaseless questionings, were over: all had to turn to Rome for help.

4

Becoming Catholic Persons and Learning to Be a Catholic People

Philip Sheldrake

[T]here is not much point in talking about being Catholic unless we try to make that pertinent to what our own wholeness might involve and that is immediately to start talking about holiness...The title 'Catholic persons' [is] a way of...trying to talk about the kind of human being that...Catholic Christianity...exists to foster.[1]

INTRODUCTION

This brief essay is a kind of manifesto—intended to set a particular tone and make a plea for a way of understanding our common enterprise. Fundamentally, I want to suggest that Catholic Learning and Receptive Ecumenism are more than purely ecclesiological concepts. Catholicity does not concern merely a certain *style*, distinct from other competing Christian forms. Catholic Learning does not simply refer to what (Roman) Catholicism might learn with integrity from other traditions. It also suggests that 'being Catholic' is something learned progressively and that we are to resist the siren voices both of premature certainty and of purification by processes of exclusion. It also suggests that there is a distinctively Catholic *way* of learning that is, by definition, integrated and that counteracts the separation of the intellectual from the practical and theology from spirituality— the conduct of a Christian life.

CATHOLICITY AND GOD

My first point is that 'catholicity' is a fundamental religious perspective that relates to the nature of God.[2] That is, while catholicity refers to a key feature of the church, how we describe and promote the life of the Christian community is rooted in a particular understanding of God. Only God is truly 'catholic' in the sense that God alone embraces the 'mystery of the whole'. What do we learn about becoming Catholic people if we begin with God? This is a complex question that I can only touch upon briefly.

God-as-Trinity speaks of a *koinonia* of co-inherent relationships in which the unique personhood of each is mutually substantiated. The implication of a Trinitarian doctrine of God for human existence is that God's presence-as-action is the source and goal of the inner dynamism of every person. God may be said to ground every person in their particularity. However, the 'catholicity' of God-as-Trinity not only grounds but also expands the inner dynamism of each person. If the Trinity expresses an understanding of God in which the particularity of the divine persons is shaped by mutual communion, the Trinitarian presence within every person underpins the uniqueness of particular identity whilst subverting self-enclosure by orienting us to what is other. We might say that a Trinitarian anthropology suggests an inherently social, rather than individualized and interiorized understanding of identity.[3]

In summary, I am suggesting that the 'Catholic' ideal of personhood is to be free enough, wise enough, and generous enough to give space to everyone and everything to whom and to which God gives space.

CATHOLIC PEOPLE

As the opening quotation from Rowan Williams suggests, to talk about being Catholic is to talk about holiness. Catholicity in this sense concerns how we 'perform' Christianity. So, in general terms, what vision of human holiness does Catholic Christianity espouse and exist to foster? Catholicity implies 'telling the whole truth', or 'telling the whole story'. A vital part of that telling, beyond mere exposition or proclamation, consists in living what might be called Catholic lives—that is, the way in which the fullness of God revealed in Jesus Christ's story is brought to realization in us. The catholicity of God-as-Trinity is expressed in time and space through the Incarnation. Thus, the heart of 'becoming Catholic', without which the concept remains insubstantial, is the person of Jesus Christ. In Christ, 'the whole fullness of deity dwells bodily, and you have come to fullness of life in him, who is the head of all rule and authority' (Col. 2: 9–10); 'And from his fullness have we all received, grace upon grace' (John 1: 16). So, the first element of Catholic holiness is a participation in God's catholicity in and through following Jesus Christ.

We struggle with how 'the whole story of Jesus Christ' is to be embodied in the particularities of our lives. I suggest that there are five key elements.

First, becoming Catholic people is not at the most fundamental level a matter of affirming certain beliefs in an objective, intellectual sense, although belief is certainly part of the equation. It is a matter of living Christ—in other words, a matter of how Jesus Christ's story of God-become-flesh, of the proclamation of God's kingdom, of the triumph of God-given life over suffering and death, is made present here and now in the lives of those who belong to the community of people bearing Christ's name.

So a second fundamental element of Catholic holiness is being part of a people, a universality of particularities, expressing unity in diversity by journeying with a family of faith that has integrity and yet is open to a God who cannot be confined within its boundaries.

Third, this also implies living in the stream of a tradition in the sense of practising a way of life shaped by the history of this people, this community. The two foundational sacraments of Baptism and Eucharist concern, among other things, incorporation into this people and this tradition. Becoming Catholic people, becoming holy, concerns the process by which we enter into an Easter narrative of human existence.

Living within the whole of Jesus Christ's story also implies getting to grips with the full story of our human existence—body *and* spirit, personal *and* social, sacred *and* secular. So a fourth element of Catholic holiness is that it is all-embracing. However, to 'tell the whole story' is also to speak of human incompleteness, failure, false aspirations—the ambiguity of lives that are both graced and sinful. The sacraments of Baptism and Eucharist speak of this as well, and of the process of reordering the disordered, healing what is broken, reconciling what is alienated—in other words, the gradual transformation of lives. Becoming Catholic people implies the ability to acknowledge a whole life in which our imperfections can paradoxically become the vehicles for receptive learning. Consequently, holiness is a process whereby the whole story of Jesus Christ and the whole story of each of us are effectively brought together.

This notion of 'becoming' is a crucial fifth element of Catholic holiness. 'Becoming Catholic people' is a process of hope, the hope of transformation that never ends within time and space. The whole truth of Jesus Christ is always in process of being realized in us. So, a fundamental quality of this vision of holiness, of becoming, is expectancy. Expectancy implies knowing there is more and becoming ever more receptive to 'the more' that we need. This receptivity is perhaps most sharply expressed in and through our engagement with people and communities that are unlike, other, strange, unnerving, even distasteful. By acknowledging that God, and the space God enables, is the fundamental reference point, Catholicity is, in this sense, self-subverting in that it undermines its own tendency to become fixed and to proclaim its own full self-sufficiency. This is perhaps counter-intuitive.

The process of transformation that we name as holiness is precisely a movement of being drawn ever more deeply into the depths of God. Inevitably, this is simultaneously a process of stepping into a way of unknowing or dispossession. To borrow a phrase from St Ignatius Loyola, 'becoming Catholic' is an engagement with the *semper maior*, the 'always more'. By 'the more' St Ignatius fundamentally implied what is more conducive to the glory of God or the service of God. However, a legitimate gloss on this would be that the 'more' is where the wholeness, the fullness, the catholicity of God is more effectively expressed. Only by an engagement with the depths of God (who alone expresses 'the mystery of the whole') may we ourselves be drawn into the mystery of catholicity. As St John of the Cross expressed it in *The Ascent of Mount Carmel*, to arrive at the mystery of the whole or to possess 'all' is not a matter of the accumulation, or possession, of more and more particular things. On the contrary, he emphasized a paradoxical theology of dispossession whereby the desire for more and more 'things' (that by definition are less than 'everything'—*todo*—in John of the Cross's language) is stripped away in favour of union with the 'all' that is God.

> To reach satisfaction in all
> desire its possession in nothing.
> To come to possess all
> desire the possession of nothing.
> To arrive at being all
> desire to be nothing.
> To come to the knowledge of all
> desire the knowledge of nothing.
> To come to the pleasure you have not
> you must go by a way in which you enjoy not.
> To come to the knowledge you have not
> you must go by a way in which you know not.
> To come to the possession you have not
> you must go by a way in which you possess not.
> To come to be what you are not
> you must go by a way in which you are not.[4]

BECOMING CATHOLIC—THE DEMANDS OF HOSPITALITY

The quest for the mystery of the whole necessarily involves a sense that we need continually to receive. Receptive Ecumenism is not simply a matter of structural adjustments or doctrinal refinement but is an encounter of people— a 'conversation' between two horizons that inevitably changes both. The very process of engagement and conversation is revelatory in that we come to realize that God speaks not simply in *my* tradition but in the very conversation and interaction that we share.

An important concept is 'hospitality'. Interestingly, the emphasis in both Hebrew and Christian scriptures is most strongly on hospitality to the stranger.

In the gospels, Jesus is frequently portrayed as the wanderer without a home (e.g. Matt. 8: 20) or dependent on the hospitality of others (e.g. Luke 9: 58) or, in the Gospel of John, as the stranger in our midst (John 8: 14 and 25 ff.). Hospitality to the stranger is presented as the vision of the Kingdom of God— and, in Matthew 25, as having a bearing on our eternal destiny. What is critical is that hospitality is not the same as assimilation of what is 'other' into me. It is not a question of finding the last piece of the jigsaw that completes my lack or our need—that ultimately gives me only what in a sense already belongs to me. Hospitality concerns the reception of what is strange and what remains strange, or at least 'other'.

There is a close relationship between the notions of 'hospitality' and of 'reconciliation'. As the South African theologian John de Gruchy suggested in his recent Hulsean Lectures, the doctrine of reconciliation is 'the inspiration and focus of all the doctrines of the Christian faith'.[5] There are specifically Christian characteristics to reconciliation—it is not simply a socio-political word with some incidental theological–spiritual gloss. Protestantism has tended to emphasize reconciliation between God and humanity as a result of the Cross (Rom. 5: 6– 11) and Catholicism has tended to emphasize how the love of God poured out upon us as a result of the divine–human reconciliation creates a new humanity in which the walls of division between people are broken down (cf. 2 Cor. 5: 17– 20; 6: 1). In practice, both dimensions need to be held in tension. Inter-human reconciliation is not simply a matter of giving each person their due but is really to give God *God's* due, by building a world and a church that God's all-embracing forgiveness demands.

The Christian narrative of redemption describes the nature and destiny, alienation and glory, of humanity. It speaks both of alienation (from God, from each other, and from creation) and of how God overcomes alienation, redeeming humanity from the bondage of sin. The Cross offers a new concept of reconciling love that risks everything, accepts death and rejection, and so enables the transformation of the unjust. The paradox is that it is out of weakness, rejection, and death that new life comes. However, reconciliation is not yet experienced in its completeness—for the evil of human division remains a reality. For now we merely have an assurance, a confident hope that God will finally establish justice and peace. The church, as prolongation of the mission of God, embodies proleptically the 'story' of reconciliation.

In addition, 'reconciliation' in Paul speaks of the one who is offended (God) as the one who takes the initiative in seeking an end to hostility. This contrasts with human assumptions that reconciliation should be initiated by 'the offender' and that an acknowledgment of guilt is an absolute precondition of reconciliation. Christian reconciliation also challenges the notion that difference should be viewed purely as part of the human predicament. Trinitarian theology speaks powerfully of a God in whom difference is the very foundation of existence.

Ephesians also relates reconciliation to participation in the church. A new covenant community becomes the carrier of the vision of a new humanity in which Jew and Gentile are reconciled as members of one body. Precisely by struggling to live this life we share in God's work of reconciliation. Linking together Eph. 2: 11–22 with Gal. 3: 23–9, Paul witnesses to a radical transformation of human status—the walls of enmity are broken down, those far off, even the enemy, are made near.

What is it to 'be in common'? Communion—existing in common—is more than sentiment. It is, at its heart, an expression of the life of the Trinity. Its roots lie in the Greek word *koinonia*. In 1 Cor. 1: 9 Paul expresses gratitude for the Corinthians having been called by God into *koinonia* with Christ—often translated as 'fellowship' but better expressed as participation in the life of Christ. *Koinonia* (2 Cor. 13: 13) is a gift from the Spirit so that our 'life in common' derives fully from our *koinonia* with Christ in the Spirit. Early Christian writers later developed the theme that the *koinonia* between believers, brought about by *koinonia* with Christ in the Spirit, is a sharing in the very life of God-as-Trinity, a *koinonia* of mutually co-inherent relationships. In the divine life we understand that to be the perfection of relationships. However, for us, living in contingent time and space, it is the measure of the promise into which we are called. But, existentially, it expresses patterns of relationship that are inherently ambiguous.

It will be helpful to consider three related illustrations of what a spirituality of 'becoming Catholic people' might imply. The first is the Rule of St Benedict. The second is the conversion of St Francis of Assisi as described in *The Testament*. The final element is a brief reflection on the Eucharist as a sacrament of human reconciliation.

HOSPITALITY IN THE RULE OF ST BENEDICT

The Rule of St Benedict deals directly with hospitality in Chapter 53. However, there is another related concept—listening.[6] The opening word of the Rule is actually the imperative 'Listen!'—*Obsculta!* This sets the tone for the whole Rule and its approach to Christian–human existence. At the heart of hospitality lies a commitment to listening. For this we need to learn silence, to cultivate attentiveness, so that we become capable of receiving what we are not. Silence counteracts a rush to judgement or destructive words. Listening and attentiveness are associated with true wisdom and this, in turn, is connected not only with our relationship to God but with the notion of obedience—obedience to the Rule but, by implication, to the community and its life together: listen contemplatively to the brethren for here God speaks; here is the 'school of the Lord's service', a school of discernment and wisdom. Listening implies giving oneself wholeheartedly rather than conditionally to a life in common. And, finally, listening implies being silent in order to learn or be taught. Chapter 6, On Silence, *De Taciturnitate*, reinforces this. The word used is *taciturnitas* not *silentium*. That is, not merely being quiet but sparing in what one asserts; being the opposite of domineering; keeping one's mouth firmly closed so that the evil thoughts or the lies in our hearts may not issue forth. In this discipline, we may slowly be converted to a gracious heart.

In Chapter 53 of the Rule of St Benedict, on hospitality, it says: *Omnes supervenientes hospites tamquam Christus suscipiantur*: 'All are to be received as Christ.' But note, the Rule continues by referring to Matthew 25: 35: 'I was a stranger and you welcomed me.' This is a deeper theology of hospitality than merely giving food and board to a passing visitor. Commentators have always noted the word *omnes* (all)—an inclusiveness linked particularly to strangers, or we might say to those who are 'other'. *Supervenientes*, 'those who arrive', underlines the point even more strongly. It literally means those who 'turn up out of the blue'. However, this is not a question merely of those people who did not warn us they were coming but those who are a surprise to us in broader terms. Close to the surface of the text is an understanding that Christians are not to be choosy about what company they keep. *Hospites* is a nicely ambiguous word that can be translated as 'stranger' as well as 'guest'. The former sense is reinforced by the reference to Matthew 25. Finally, *suscipiantur* literally means 'to be received' but its deeper sense is to be cherished—the stranger turns into someone who, while different, we learn to cherish as if they were one of our own.

THE *TESTAMENT* OF SAINT FRANCIS: EMBRACING THE LEPER

Closely related to the radical nature of the Rule of St Benedict's teaching on hospitality is the famous story of St Francis of Assisi's encounter with the leper. The first three verses of the *Testament* that Francis dictated shortly before his death identify the first moment of his spiritual life in his encounter with lepers.

The Lord granted me, Brother Francis, to begin to do penance in this way: While I was in sin, it seemed very bitter to me to see lepers. And the Lord Himself led me among them and I had mercy upon them. And when I left them that which seemed bitter to me was changed into sweetness of soul and body; and afterwards I lingered a little and left the world.[7]

The famous story of St Francis meeting and then embracing a leper on the road is a critical hermeneutical key to understanding Francis' life and teaching—not least his powerful vision of cosmic solidarity most famously expressed in his *Canticle of Creation*. The point is that meeting and kissing the leper was not a simple tale of courageous charity in the face of human suffering. Set in its medieval context, the story of the leper implies far more than this. Francis was here led to embrace what might be called the excluded 'other' of the society of his day. Lepers were not merely infected with a terrible disfiguring disease. In medieval society they symbolized the dark side of human existence on to which people projected a variety of fears and suspicions. Lepers were outcasts banished from society along with criminals, the mad, the excommunicated, sexual deviants, and Jews. In many respects, lepers were not only perceived as wretched and dangerous but also, because visibly symbolic of the overall corrupt nature of flesh, as scandalous. There was more than a hint that the sickness was a divine punishment for corrupted sexuality or for heresy (often associated with each other in the medieval mind).[8] So, as we reflect about Catholic Learning and receptivity, Francis' encounter with the leper reminds us that the process of becoming genuinely Catholic may be profoundly uncomfortable. Francis came to see that the catholicity of God revealed in Jesus Christ demanded that Christians should embrace precisely the categories of people that those who believed themselves to be spiritually pure preferred to exclude and reject.

THE EUCHARIST AS A SPACE OF RECONCILIATION

The catholicity of God is sacramentally expressed explicitly in the *koinonia* of believers filled with the Spirit of the risen Jesus and shaped by the Eucharist. The Eucharist is not simply a practice of piety but the enactment of the special identity of Christian community. As such it is an ethical practice although not simply in the superficial sense that it provides an opportunity for a didactic form of moral formation.[9] The link between ethics and the Eucharist is intrinsic rather than extrinsic.[10] Ethics embodies a way of being in the world that is appropriated and sustained fundamentally in worship, especially the Eucharist. Conversely, the eucharistic enactment of Catholic identity necessarily opens the community to appropriate ways of living in the world.

A sacramental perspective on reality demands a reordering of the existential situation in which we exist. To live sacramentally involves setting aside a damaged condition in favour of something that is offered to us by grace for 'where we habitually are is not, after all, a neutral place but a place of loss and need' which needs to be transformed.[11] Part of this damaged reality consists of our flawed identities—whether these suggest that we are people of power, or diminish us as people of no worth. The transforming dynamic of the Eucharist demands that the presumed identity of everyone be radically reconstructed. This necessitates honest recognition, painful dispossession and fearless surrender as a precondition of reconciliation.

To enter the 'space' of the Eucharist implies a radical transformation of human 'location' such that it is no longer centred on the individual ego, or on safe gatherings of the like-minded, but discovered in being (to borrow a phrase from Ignatian spirituality) a-person-for-others. Every time the Eucharist is celebrated, all those who participate commit themselves to cross the boundaries of fear, prejudice, and injustice in a prophetic embrace of other people, without exception, in whom we are challenged to discover the 'real presence' of an incarnate God:

Reconciled in the Eucharist, the members of the body of Christ are called to be servants of reconciliation among men and women and witnesses of the joy of resurrection. As Jesus went out to publicans and sinners and had table-fellowship with them during his earthly ministry, so Christians are called in the Eucharist to be in solidarity with the outcast and to become signs of the love of Christ who lived and sacrificed himself for all and now gives himself in the Eucharist.[12]

The Eucharist is very much a 'landscape of memory'—including ambiguous or conflicting memories. Beyond the immediate participants, there are wider and deeper narrative currents in all eucharistic celebrations. The central narrative, that is, the revelation of God's salvation in Jesus Christ, enables all human stories to have an equal place and yet at the same time reconfigures them. The eucharistic narrative makes space for a new history that tells a different human story beyond the selectivity of tribalism or sectarianism. It invites us to undertake the radical business of creating human solidarity and changing the status quo. The Eucharist, despite our various human attempts to regulate and control it, engages a power beyond the ritual enactments themselves to offer an entry point for the oppressed, the marginalized, and the excluded. The eucharistic action, according to its own inner logic, is the most Catholic 'space' there can be in the world of space and time.

There is, therefore, a perpetual and uncomfortable tension between the sacramental practice of God's reconciliation and the many efforts of Christians to resist the logic of reconciliation. At the heart of the Eucharist is the continual reaffirmation and consolidation of personal and collective human identities initially brought about in Baptism. Christian disciples are bound into solidarity with those they have not chosen or whose presence they have not negotiated and indeed would not choose of their own free will. Consequently, the new community, the new world, spoken of in Baptism and the Eucharist, is deeply subversive of humanly constructed social order.

The Eucharist does not simply bind individuals to God in a vertical relationship or bind people to each other in another kind of purely social construction. We are bound to one another *en Christo*. And Christ, the head of the body, is to be found persistently on the margins among those who are the least in the kingdom of the world. The margins include those who are other, foreign, strange, dangerous, subversive—even socially, morally, or religiously distasteful in our eyes. Yet, the Eucharist insists that humans find solidarity where they least expect it, and, indeed, least want to find it. We recall the story of Francis of

Assisi and the leper by means of which he passed from a romantic understanding of God's presence in the natural world to embrace the incarnate God in the excluded 'other'.

The most challenging dimension of the Eucharist is the question of recognition. Who do we recognize as our co-heirs with Christ, and who are we able to respond to in the real presence of Jesus Christ? The core of the eucharistic notion of real presence, however one understands this, is God's critical recognition of us; God's affirming and life-giving gaze. All are incorporated solely because of God's recognition. The demands on those who practise the Eucharist are consequently more powerful than any notion of solidarity based solely on a social theory, however inclusive or just it seeks to be.[13]

An affirmation of 'real presence' also stands in judgement on all our exclusions and negative judgements. A most challenging question is who and what we receive with Jesus? In receiving Jesus Christ the disciple receives at the same time all that makes up his Body. We find ourselves in communion not merely in some romantic way with the whole court of heaven, a communion of saints that safely visits us from elsewhere and represents merely the past and the future. We also find ourselves, if we dare to name it, in communion with the truly Catholic 'mystery of the whole' in present time and space as well. We know from the gospel narratives of the Last Supper that the catholicity of Jesus' act of incorporation included not only disciples like Peter who denied him but Judas who betrayed him. Those we prefer to exclude from communion with us in the public world are already uncomfortable ghosts at our eucharistic feast.

CONCLUSION

Becoming Catholic people is thus not a retreat into some kind of alternative, spiritual world. However, conversely, to draw our human identity simply from being born into this time, place, and community is not sufficient. To 'become Catholic people' involves some sense of vocation that demands discernment and then choice. To become Catholic people implies an identity that is first seen, then reflected upon, and finally intentionally embraced. Our contemporary culture too often suggests that choice (and ideally the multiplication of choices) is a right. However, to choose is more accurately a responsibility—even an obligation— because only choice makes moral responsibility possible. In this case, to become Catholic people—to commit oneself to the mystery of the whole—means dealing with the dilemma of engaging with the actual and contextual while doing justice to the eternal. It also involves a critical correlation of what makes sense in our existential situation with what is also appropriate to the tradition. In a sentence, becoming Catholic people is both an interpreted way of living in relation to a tradition and at the same time an authentic and challenging interpretation of our own existential situation.

NOTES

1. Rowan Williams and Philip Sheldrake, 'Catholic Persons: Images of Holiness. A Dialogue', in Jeffrey John (ed.), *Living the Mystery: Affirming Catholicism and the Future of Anglicanism* (London: Darton, Longman & Todd, 1994), 76.

2. See Sheldrake, 'Practising Catholic "Place"—The Eucharist', *Horizons: The Journal of the College Theology Society*, 28 (2001), 163–82.

3. See Colin Gunton, *The Promise of Trinitarian Theology* (Edinburgh: T. & T. Clark, 1997), 112 ff.; also id., *The One, The Three and The Many* (Cambridge: Cambridge University Press, 1995), 164.

4. *The Ascent of Mount Carmel*, Bk 1, Ch. 13: 11, in Kevin Kavanaugh (ed.), *John of the Cross: Selected Writings* (Mahwah, NY: Paulist Press, 1987), 78–9.

5. John de Gruchy, *Reconciliation: Restoring Justice* (London: SCM, 2002), 44.

6. For a modern scholarly edition of the Rule, see *Benedict's Rule: A Translation and Commentary*, ed. Terrence Kardong, (Collegeville, Minn.: Liturgical Press, 1996).

7. *Francis and Clare: The Complete Works*, eds. Regis Armstrong and Ignatius Brady (Mahwah, NY: Paulist Press, 1982), 154.

8. See Bronislaw Geremek, 'The Marginal Man', in Jacques Le Goff (ed.), *The Medieval World*, trans. Lydia G. Cochrane (London: Collins & Brown, 1991), 367–9, Robert Ian Moore, *The Formation of a Persecuting Society: Power and Deviance in Western Europe, 950–1250* (Oxford: Blackwell, 1994), 45–63.

9. See William Spohn, *Go and Do Likewise: Jesus and Ethics* (New York: Continuum, 1999), 175–84.

10. See Donald E. Saliers, 'Liturgy and Ethics: Some New Beginnings', in Ronald Hamel and Kenneth Himes (eds.), *Introduction to Christian Ethics: A Reader* (Mahwah, NY: Paulist Press, 1989), 175–86.

11. Rowan Williams, 'Sacraments of the New Society' (1996), *On Christian Theology* (Oxford: Blackwell, 2000), 209–10.

12. Faith and Order Commission of the World Council of Churches, *Baptism, Eucharist and Ministry* (Faith and Order Paper, No. 111) (Geneva: WCC, 1982), § 24.

13. Williams, 'Sacraments of the New Society', 212–14.

5

The Church—A School of Wisdom?[1]

Nicholas Lash

INTRODUCTION

The dons in one of the Cambridge colleges were recently conducting interviews with young people applying for admission. Seven people had applied to read theology, all of them bright creatures with strings of As at A-level either in prospect or achieved. On being asked how they had reached the decision that theology was the subject they most wanted to study, six of them mentioned reading the *Da Vinci Code* as being an influential factor.

At one point in the interview, the chaplain (himself a theologian) showed the candidates a passage from Mark's Gospel from which, in a minority of the ancient manuscripts, one sentence is missing. He asked them: 'Why?' Five of the seven came up with conspiracy theories of one sort or another: the ecclesiastical authorities were trying to hide something. Only one suggested that the omission might have originated from an error in transcription—and was promptly offered a place!

I take this bizarre little incident as a parable of two fundamental and related challenges faced by the church in this country. First, it is, I think, almost impossible to exaggerate the rapidity with which Christianity has become comprehensively illegible in British culture. Secondly, fuelling the fashionable and highly questionable dissociation of 'spirituality' from 'religion' is, I believe, the suspicion that 'They're up to no good'—this being the same suspicion that makes life difficult for politicians! Those inclined to look on the bright side might say that this shows how grown-up people have become: that they are no longer going to be bossed around and told how to live their lives. It is, I believe, more properly attributable to an individualism eating away at the very fabric of human existence. If 'pure religion' is a matter of caring for 'orphans and widows in their distress' (Jas. 1: 27), then one can see why it might prove unattractive to the egotism of the prosperous who find 'spirituality' so uplifting!

In 1992, I took part in a conference in Cambridge on *Consciousness and Human Identity*,[2] most of the participants in which were cognitive scientists, computer people, biologists, and psychologists. I rather dropped them in the deep end by saying something, in my paper, about the notion—central to Christian Trinitarian theology—of 'subsistent relations'. My reason for doing so went something like this. Émile Durkheim once defined 'religion' as 'the system of symbols by which society becomes conscious of itself'.[3] In classical Christian doctrine, God is not spoken of as three individuals variously related to each other. Much more strangely, and interestingly, God is simply said to be the relations that God is. We say God speaks, but God is, without remainder, God's act of uttering, just as God is, without remainder, the Word God utters. We say God breathes delight, the fecundity of joy that is the Holy Spirit. But, once again, God is, without remainder, the delighting and the outbreathed joy.

Now, the point that I made to my largely baffled scientific colleagues was this. If 'religion is the system of symbols by which society becomes conscious of itself', then a society—such as medieval Christianity—which described what we might call the character of God, in terms of absolute giving and receiving, pure mutuality, pure relation, must surely have been a society which understood human identity in similarly relational terms. It is not my intention to romanticize medieval Christianity—while mutual dependence may, indeed, be the freedom that is friendship, it may also, as Hegel brilliantly demonstrated, be enslavement. I merely want to indicate the herculean labour that will be required if, in a culture as radically and destructively individualistic as our own, we are to succeed, as a church, as a community, in imagining, in understanding, in realizing, in displaying, that primacy of relationship which is at the heart of Christian discipleship as it is at the heart of our understanding of the mystery of God.

I have entitled this chapter *The Church—A School of Wisdom?* To conclude these introductory remarks, I now want to say a word or two about the sense of 'wisdom' I have in mind. First, here is a lovely remark of St Augustine's, commenting on the Fourth Gospel: 'It is impossible to love what is entirely unknown, but when what is known, if even so little, is loved, this very capacity for love makes it better and more fully known.'[4] The argument, roughly, is that nobody will love what they have no prospect of making their own through understanding: faith without the hope of understanding would be no more than compliance with authority. And yet nobody will understand what they are not prepared to love.

Second, 'wisdom' according to Aquinas, is the virtue, or art, of sound judgement. But we make our judgements—and thereby display our wisdom or our foolishness—in different ways. On the one hand, there is the instinctive, almost intuitive sureness of touch of the person who has their head screwed on, their feet on the ground, and their heart in the right place! This is the wisdom of the virtuous, the gift of God's enlivening Spirit. It has nothing to do with erudition or the lack of it: it is calibrated on a different axis. On the other hand, there are judgements that are the fruit of reasoning and reflection. There is, therefore, a wisdom that is the fruit of study. Moreover, where the following of Christ, faith's quest for understanding, is concerned, wisdom in the second sense is dependent upon wisdom in the first, inasmuch as all our strenuous labours in libraries and laboratories simply serve to catch some glimmer of that eternal wisdom whose self-gift, in Word and Spirit, gives us the possibility of wise or 'faithful' thinking in the first place.

THE PROJECT

In the first of the two main parts of this essay, I want to try to indicate something of what is and is not entailed in pleading for that fundamental transformation of understanding and imagination which would enable us to recover and to sustain a sense of Catholic Christianity as a lifelong educational project.

Then, in a second part, I shall briefly consider some of the more intractable obstacles which, at present, work against the achievement of such a programme. These obstacles are partly external and partly internal; or, if you prefer, partly cultural and partly ecclesial.

Finally, by way of conclusion, I shall—with a stunning lack of originality—suggest that it is the quality of our liturgy which will decide whether such a project succeeds or fails.

In 1994, the central argument of my Teape Lectures was to the effect that

the modern dissociation of memory from argument, of narrative from reason, [has] made us forget...the extent to which the ancient traditions of devotion and reflection, of worship and enquiry [such as Christianity and Vedantic Hinduism, Judaism, Buddhism, and Islam], have seen themselves as schools...whose pedagogy has the twofold purpose...of weaning us from our idolatry and purifying our desire.[5]

In the year 2000, I wrote a little article in the *Tablet*, in which I said that

The move from an almost exclusive emphasis on Catholic schools to the recovery of an older vision, according to which the following of Christ is best understood as a lifelong process of adult education, will require such a revolution of imagination, such a fundamental redistribution of personal and financial resources, such a comprehensive rethinking of the ways in which we learn, teach and preach, that no single generation could accomplish it.[6]

In essence, the proposal is hardly revolutionary. To be a Christian is to be a pupil. That is what the word 'disciple' means, as does the Greek word, $\mu\alpha\theta\eta\tau\dot{\eta}\varsigma$, which it translates. And, if we are pupils, presumably we are members of some kind of school. As the excellent Heythrop report, 'On the Way to Life', put it in 2005: 'Education, catechesis and formation are . . . not just of internal benefit, they are part of what the Church has to offer humanity.'[7]

'Wisdom', said Newman in 1841, 'is the clear, calm, accurate vision, and comprehension of the whole course, the whole work of God', towards the luminosity of which faith, in contrast, feels its way, 'as if guessing and reaching forward to the truth, amid darkness or confusion'.[8] If Christianity is, indeed, a school of wisdom, this is because wisdom is its given goal, its promised end, not its achievement or possession. Hence the necessary note of pilgrimage, of interrogation, and enquiry. *Fides quaerens intellectum*: faith seeking understanding, not owning it or holding it nervously in its protective grasp.

If, then, we are members of a school, it is, we might say, a school with no fixed abode. But, at once, a word of warning is necessary because, in some contemporary sociology of religion, the notion of 'pilgrimage' is associated with self-construction and deracination,[9] neither of which is, or could ever be, a characteristic of members of the pilgrim church, because it is not we who set ourselves upon the journey which we undertake. As Stanley Hauerwas put it recently: 'Christianity is ongoing training to help us accept our lives as gifts.'[10]

The exercise of any virtue is, on an Aristotelian account of these things, the art of learning to keep one's balance between opposing vices. Where learning to accept our lives as gift is concerned, the contrasting vices are fatalism—resignation before the belief that we are simply products and victims of the system of the world—and the illusion that we are, or can be, whatever we decide to be: masters of the fantasy universe constructed by our egotism.

But in what kind of school might virtues such as this be learnt? I said earlier that the wisdom of the virtuous, the wisdom that is God's Spirit's gift, is calibrated on a different axis from that of the wisdom of the erudite. The point is worth emphasizing because, when an elderly Cambridge academic starts banging on about the importance of so re-imagining and restructuring Christian life as to render it more effectively a lifelong process of adult education, some will doubtless nurture the suspicion that I believe nobody without a PhD can really be a Christian.

If the church is, indeed, a school of wisdom, then it is a place in which we endlessly learn to know God better, and growth in the knowledge of God is not a matter of accumulating information or sharpening the quality of argument.

Nevertheless, important as it is not to confuse the two aspects of Christian wisdom which Aquinas so carefully distinguished, it is no less important not to dissociate them. One of the deformations of Catholicism in the UK used to be a kind of cult of people known as the 'simple faithful', celebrated for their devotion and obedience, and for stoutly resisting all temptation to be well informed or even—heaven forfend!—to think.

About forty years ago, when my uncle, Sebastian Moore, was—as prior of the Downside community in Liverpool—parish priest of St Mary's, Highfield Street, he wrote an article dismissing the idea of the 'simple faithful' as patronizing nonsense. He received a letter from Vincent Rochford, the outstanding and outspoken parish priest of one of the toughest areas in London's dockland. 'Dear Sebastian,' he wrote, 'for years I have searched, in the East End of London, for those "simple faithful" whom the bishops are so insistent that we must not in any way startle or disturb, and I have not found them. Now that you tell me that they are not to be found in the docks of Liverpool either, I am forced to conclude that they are but an exhalation of the hierarchy's subconscious.'

Ours is a society (and a church) of near 100 per cent literacy, nearly half of whose members continue their education, beyond school age, into institutions of higher and further education. But ours is also a society which, far from feeding and fostering what we might call a 'Christian imagination', is increasingly ignorant of and, to a disturbing extent, hostile to, the character and constituents of mainstream Christianity. Its ignorance is not that of acknowledged nescience—the nescience of those who say: 'I am afraid I know nothing about' this, that, or the other. What is much more difficult to deal with, much more malign, is the ignorance of those who are quite confident that they know exactly what Christianity is about—what Christians believe, and how they think—but whose confidence is, shall we say, misplaced.

A few years ago, in the Preface to a remarkable study entitled *Lost Icons*, Archbishop Rowan Williams spoke of 'our awkwardness in confronting the fact that certain styles of human self-understanding, styles that might conduce to a sense of irony or humility or trustfulness or solidarity, are fast becoming unavailable.'[11] And yet, if the church is, in these circumstances, to be a 'school of wisdom', an academy of discipleship, then it is a requirement, not only of 'mission', but even of 'maintenance'—not only in order that, in this culture, the Gospel be faithfully proclaimed, but even in order that the people called to be the Gospel's witnesses sustain their very identity as Christian—that the 'styles of human self-understanding' of which the Archbishop spoke are rendered once again available. Yet this will not happen, this cannot happen, I believe, unless, as I put it earlier, we recover and sustain a sense of Catholic Christianity as a lifelong educational project.

Here are four questions, which I put to the 2005 conference of the Catholic Theological Association of Great Britain:

1. How well, and in what manner, are adult Catholics in this country taught to pray?

2. How well, and in what manner, are adult Catholics in this country taught to read the Scriptures?

3. How well, and in what manner, are adult Catholics in this country equipped with a grasp of church history and doctrine commensurate with their general knowledge and grasp of public affairs?

4. To what extent, and in what manner, do we succeed in communicating the conviction that Catholic faith, is for every Catholic and in every context, '*fides quaerens intellectum*'?[12]

Perhaps paradoxically, I believe that one way of thinking about the kind of comprehensive transformation of structure and imagination I have in mind might be to consider some aspects of the religious life as distillations or parables of Christian discipleship in general.

Some years ago, the central directorate of the theological journal *Concilium* met in Einsiedeln, in Switzerland. At one point, the abbot of that vast and ancient Benedictine monastery indicated that he wished to address us. Listening to him, I had the sense that here was a man who thought of the great medieval universities—Paris, Bologna, Oxford—as innovations, representing, as he did, an educational tradition stretching back many centuries before their foundation. A tradition which had no truck whatsoever with the dissociation of heart from head, of prayer from understanding.

At one point in the *Summa*, Thomas Aquinas, considering what we would nowadays call Christ's 'lifestyle', asks whether, instead of dealing with other people, it would not have been better for him to have led a solitary life because, surely—as was generally agreed at the time and as he himself had argued earlier in the *Summa*—the contemplative life is the most perfect form of Christian living. That is true enough, in the abstract, he replies, but, in practice, even more perfect is the active life of those who, through preaching and teaching, hand on to others the fruits of contemplation: '*vita activa, secundum quam aliquis praedicando et docendo contemplata aliis tradit.*'[13] There you have the origin of the Dominican motto: '*contemplata aliis tradere*'. Or, as Aquinas himself put it in his commentary on the Psalms: 'We can bear witness only to what we have experienced.'[14]

A third and final snapshot. In February 2006, my wife and I were in Marrakesh. We visited the Medersa Ben Youssef, a sixteenth-century *medersa*, or Koranic school. A place of exceptional architectural beauty, of concentrated stillness and simplicity, with one of the student rooms furnished with bed, and desk, and prayer mat. To my surprise, the ethos of the school immediately reminded me of places such as Le Corbusier's great Dominican priory of La Tourette, or some of the Cistercian monasteries of southern France.

I am not suggesting, by the way, that, in order for the church to be, again, a school of wisdom, we should all dash off and become monks or Muslims! But I am suggesting that that integration of worship and enquiry, of thought and contemplation, which characterizes the traditions I have indicated, needs to become, in one way or another, characteristic of all forms of Christian discipleship.

OBSTACLES

I now turn to some of the cultural obstacles which stand in the way of our transforming the church into a lifelong process of adult education in the erosion of idolatry and the purification of desire.

Amongst these, I have already mentioned the endemic individualism which makes it so difficult to recover, in fact and in imagination, the primacy of relations—between each other, and between creatures and the mystery of God, through whose outbreathed Spirit and enfleshed Word all things exist. Two other fundamental obstacles might be named as 'the forgetfulness of memory' and 'the strangeness of virtue'.

Forgetfulness of Memory

'Whatever form it takes', say the authors of *On the Way to Life*, 'it is clear that the Catholic "memory" needs to be retrieved.'[15] In our dramatically globalizing world, in which we are becoming increasingly aware of the extent to which famine, poverty, disease, warfare, oppression, and the rape of natural resources—wherever they occur—impact, directly or indirectly, on everywhere and on everybody else, the illusions of optimism are (thank goodness) no longer available to us. Someone would have to be either wicked or insane seriously to maintain that everything is getting better! Nevertheless, we have, as a culture, inherited from the utopianisms of modernity the belief that such solutions as may be available are to be sought in the future rather than in the past. The past, it seems, is simply what we have left behind.

It has become commonplace for commentators on the Second Vatican Council to distinguish two tendencies in Catholic thought since the Council: a '*ressourcement*' tendency, concerned to ensure the church's maintained fidelity to its past, and an '*aggiornamento*' tendency, dedicated to ensuring that the church come up to date. This use of the terms is most misleading because, as the Council Fathers knew, it is only through the church's renewed remembrance of the richness of its history (*ressourcement*), that it can be brought into fresh, constructive, but by no means uncritical relationship with the forces shaping the world in which it lives (*aggiornamento*).[16]

All things are born and die in time, but only in the case of human beings is an awareness of temporality constitutive of their identity. Without remembrance, we know not who we are, can make no plans, and have no hope. Christians, Jews, and Muslims know these things, and know them to be true, not only of themselves, but of every society and of each individual. The retrieval of memory may be our urgent Catholic duty, but it is a duty we perform on behalf of everyone, not just ourselves. 'Tradition', says the Heythrop report, 'is the way in which we know and experience that the Truth is not our truth',[17] but the truth of God, the truth, or troth, or promise, that God is said to be.

The Strangeness of Virtue

Are there things which human beings can do such that, whatever their foreseen consequences, it is always wrong to do them? According to the moral climate of our culture, the answer is 'No', because it is always on the basis of the expected consequences of our actions that we should decide what is and is not to be done. Hence the term which Elizabeth Anscombe coined to describe the dominant moral philosophy of the English-speaking world: 'consequentialism'.[18] From the slaughter of the unborn to the bombing of Baghdad, from the erosion of human rights in this country to the unprincipled degeneracy of Guantanamo Bay, the evidence for the damage done to human flourishing by this style of thinking surrounds us on every side.

In marked contrast, 'it has', said Professor Anscombe, 'been characteristic of [the Hebrew–Christian] ethic that there are certain things forbidden whatever consequences threaten'.[19] But, if there are such things, how do we discover what they are, and how do we decide whether or not this particular action, carried out in these particular circumstances, fits the description of the forbidden deed?

Where the first of these questions is concerned, it is tempting to assume that the answer is in the book of rules. For some people, the rule book in question is the law of the land (which is why it is so widely assumed that it is quite all right to do anything that is not illegal), for others, perhaps, it is 'the law of God' or 'the church's teaching', or whatever.

Rules and regulations have their place, but what they cannot do is educate people into becoming mature and responsible moral agents, people equipped with the practical wisdom enabling them, often in appallingly difficult circumstances, to act appropriately, justly, kindly.

Indeed, if having the rule book to hand, and knowing that one ought to keep the rules, constituted an adequate moral education, then my whole argument in this essay would collapse. There would be no need for the church to be a school of lifelong adult education in holiness and wisdom— we could just teach children the rules in school, and the job would have been done!

I have been suggesting that the moral climate of our culture is a disastrous amalgam of consequentialism seasoned with the relics of an ethics of law. In this situation, the concept of 'virtue' seems very strange indeed. Yet Catholic Christianity has traditionally understood itself to be a school of virtue.

In order to lead the good life, where should we begin? Virtues are good habits, and the only possible place in which to begin is where we are, having acquired, from the particular society and tradition in which we were brought up, some 'set of habits of judgement, perception and desire'.[20]

The next stage is to recognize the various ways in which these habits are defective, as not equipping us very well to understand what friendship is, or happiness, what justice requires of us, and so on. It seems, paradoxically, that only by becoming good persons can we come to understand things in the way good people do. (We do not, I think, sufficiently advert to the fact that '*fides quaerens intellectum*' describes the character of Christian ethics.) As Alasdair MacIntyre writes, commenting on Herbert McCabe:

To be good is to be good at being human. It is to know how to play out one's part in social life. It is to have the kind of formed and developed character that enables one to enter into a life of friendship, and by so doing become better than one was: 'Virtues are dispositions to make choices which will make you better able to make choices.' And because our choices express our relationship to the community and to its flourishing, they have an ineliminable political dimension.[21]

We seem to need a school of lifelong adult education in the virtues. This is, of course, exactly what Catholic Christianity has traditionally supposed itself to be. I have simply tried to indicate the daunting difficulty of living, or even imagining, such a life in a culture to which the notion that being human means being educated in the virtues is so profoundly alien.

How Does the Church 'Teach'?

When people speak about 'the teaching of the church', to what are they referring? Education is what goes on in schools. And education is a process by means of which a group of people helps others to grow in expertise and understanding. We usually distinguish two aspects of this process: teaching and learning, although it is a mistake to draw the distinction too rigidly, because all good teachers know how much they learn from those they teach. Moreover, where Christianity is concerned, all of us, throughout our lives, are first and foremost pupils of one teacher, who is Christ. If, then, Catholic Christianity is a kind of school, the phrase 'the church's teaching' should presumably refer to that process, that lifelong pedagogy in the knowledge and the love of God, that is the church's *raison d'être*.

Except, of course, that this is not the way in which, at present, most Catholics see the matter. I have little doubt that the gravest internal obstacle preventing us from rediscovering the educational character of Christianity consists in the extent to which we have come to misconceive 'teaching' as a form of governance.[22]

In any educational process there is, of course, a place for the issuing of instructions and commands. But what a competent teacher looks for is not primarily obedience but illumination, 'something understood'. And yet, in recent decades, a language has grown up, in certain circles, according to which, on the one hand, the sense of 'the church's teaching' has virtually contracted to the issuing of instructions and commands from Rome while, on the other, only two reactions to these instructions are deemed possible: 'fidelity' (i.e. obedience) and 'dissent' or *dis*obedience. A good example of this would be an editorial, vigorously denouncing *The Tablet* ('Editorial after editorial has pursued a systematic dissent from . . . the church's teaching') which appeared in May 2005 in the magazine *Faith*.

This is the kind of thing that happens when 'teaching' is misconstrued as 'governance'. We are, as Christians, undoubtedly invited to obedience. But the model of Christian obedience is not the blind conformity of well-drilled cannon fodder but the courage, and the love, the generosity, of the garden of Gethsemane.

The Old Testament scholar Walter Brueggemann has remarked that

in situations where Christian life and thought is securely part of culture, the community's theological argument tends to be dogmatic . . . But where Christianity's legitimacy is contested . . . and is one voice competing with other voices . . . it must be marked by testimony, dispute and advocacy, where it recognises the claims made elsewhere in the world and counters them with its own different claims.[23]

'Testimony', 'dispute', 'advocacy'. Not only, however, with those outside the Christian family, but also those within it. One of the most remarkable parish priests I have ever known once said, commenting on a neighbouring parish: 'They have so little charity in that place that they can't even disagree with each other.' In the course of a long friendship with the late, great Dominican, Herbert McCabe, I only once succeeded in silencing him. He was waxing eloquent in defence of the proposition that deep and ongoing disagreement was at the heart of serious theological investigation, and I said: 'Herbert, you're so right!'

The faith we confess today is that confessed fifty, a hundred, a thousand years ago. Scripture has not changed, nor has the Creed. But the context in which we seek to bear faithful witness to love poured out on Calvary has changed dramatically, and is changing all the time. We are a people charged unceasingly to seek some understanding of how obedience to the Gospel is to be expressed and realized in the cultural, scientific, economic, and political circumstances of our time. What we need, at present, is not less debate, but more; more well-informed and serious argument, conducted with respect and courtesy, shaped by our commitment to the tradition of the Gospel. If the 'character' of Christian charity is, as the tradition has insisted, that of friendship, then to be a Christian school of holiness and wisdom is to be a 'society of friends'. And it is no sign of friendship that people never disagree.

In thus emphasizing the importance, for our school of wisdom, of conversation, argument, enquiry, I am not suggesting that, within the contours of the Creed, all questions are, as it were, equally open for debate. The disappearance of the Neo-Scholasticism which dominated Catholic thought between the Councils of Trent and the Second Vatican Council is, undoubtedly, cause for gratitude. Nevertheless, one of Neo-Scholasticism's strengths was 'the recognition', as Cardinal Avery Dulles has put it, 'that not all conclusions were equally certain'.[24] Each thesis in the textbooks had a 'note' attached, indicating whether the proposition in question was widely held, heretical, dogmatically defined, unsound, and so on. And the warrants for each note—indicating whether it was based on 'the definitions of popes and councils, the clear teaching of Scripture, theological reasoning, the general consent of the fathers or of the theologians',[25] and so on—were also indicated. The scheme became complex to the point of absurdity, but we badly need some agreed method of indicating what one might call the 'weight', in Catholic teaching, of whatever claim or counterclaim is under discussion.

Every member of the school of wisdom that is the Catholic Church is a pupil, and, in one way or another, all of us are teachers—for we have a duty to bear witness to the Gospel. The function of 'teachership', or *magisterium*, is therefore exercised by all of us. There is a *magisterium* of parents, exercised by each mother teaching her child to pray. There is a *magisterium* of scholarship, exercised by those engaged in teaching and research. Finally, there is a *magisterium* of pastoral 'oversight' or episcopacy, exercised by those who bear the grave responsibility of 'authentically interpreting' the Word of God (see *DV*, § 10). It is, to my mind, an impoverishment that, since the nineteenth century, we have got into the habit of using the term '*magisterium*' no longer to denote the function of teaching, but rather to name one group of 'functionaries', the bishops. It takes nothing from episcopal authority to keep in mind that there are other teachers in the church, including those from whom the bishops learnt their catechism and their theology.

After nearly a century of dangerously centralizing drift of power and structure in the Catholic Church, the Second Vatican Council sought to restore the balance of episcopal authority through its teaching on 'collegiality'. Thus far, the Council's intentions have been largely thwarted, making it more difficult for the church at large, and for the bishops in particular, to understand episcopacy in educational terms. (My impression is that one of the reasons why most bishops take so little interest in scholarship is because they do not consider the fostering of '*fides quaerens intellectum*' to be central to the episcopal vocation.)

A SCHOOL OF PRAYER

One hundred and fifty years ago, Newman preached a sermon, in Dublin, the title of which (at least in the published version) was: 'Intellect, the instrument of religious training.'[26] Towards the end of the sermon, he said this:

It will not satisfy me, if religion is here, and science there, and young men converse with science all day, and lodge with religion in the evening...I want the same roof to contain both the intellectual and moral disciplines. Devotion is not a sort of finish given to the sciences; nor is science a sort of feather in the cap...an ornament and set-off to devotion. I want the intellectual layman to be religious, and the devout ecclesiastic to be intellectual.[27]

The context determined the detail of his argument. He was preaching in the university church (solemnly opened just three days previously) of the infant Catholic university, now nearing the end of its second year, of which he was Rector. Nevertheless, it has been my argument in this essay that the broader drift of his remarks has application far beyond our schools and universities, to every aspect of the church's life.

Whether or not the church in England and Wales will have the imagination, the courage, and the dedication necessary to enable the lifelong adult education in faith's quest for understanding of every Catholic to be at least as high a priority in pastoral planning as the provision of primary and secondary schools, I do not know. One thing, at least, is certain: the school of wisdom that is Christianity is, at its heart, a school of prayer, and the 'engine room' of the transformation which we need must be the celebration of the liturgy. By way of conclusion, therefore, I would like to make one or two remarks about liturgical reform—with what one might call an ordinary parish Mass in mind.

Silence, speech, and song. Ours is a culture of relentless, restless noise. And yet, without some sense of stillness, of sustained attentiveness, we are rendered deaf to ourselves, to each other, and to the mystery of God.

James Crichton, parish priest of Pershore some decades ago, and perhaps the best pastoral liturgist in England, used to insist on the indispensability of 'pools of silence' during the celebration of the liturgy. Stillness is not a virtue easily acquired, but there is no better school of stillness than the liturgy—for good liturgy has not only shape, and structure, but also its distinctive rhythms.

Even tiny things can help, such as having the courage to sustain several seconds of silence between each 'bidding', in the Prayer of the Faithful, and the invocation: 'Lord, hear us.'

After silence, speech. Listening to the readings at Mass, one seldom gets the impression that the reader believes that Jesus Christ is as truly present in the proclamation of the word as he is in the consecrated bread and wine. As

Sacrosanctum Concilium puts it: 'He is present in His word, since it is He Himself who speaks when the holy Scriptures are read in the Church' (*SC*, § 7), and it is clear from the Latin that 'the Church' refers not to the building, but the congregation, God's gathered people.

After the reading, the homily. This is a topic on which only brevity can save me from ill manners. If, as *Lumen Gentium* has it, the preaching of the Gospel occupies the chief place amongst the duties of a bishop (§ 25), it surely follows that the quality of preaching in his diocese should occupy a very high place in every bishop's concerns. And yet if, as Saint Jerome said in his commentary on Isaiah, 'ignorance of Scripture is ignorance of Christ', it would seem that there are an awful lot of priests in this country who are unfamiliar with their Redeemer.

Silence, speech, and music. A good friend, a priest now in his mid-eighties, once remarked, 'I never regard myself as being on oath when singing hymns'—a wise precaution. Notwithstanding the excellent work done by people such as Mgr Kevin Nicholls,[28] too many of the hymns we sing are doctrinally illiterate, poor poetry, and set to third-rate tunes.

We are fortunate, in Great Britain, to have a composer of the quality of James MacMillan passionately interested in writing music for the liturgy. I recently tried to interest him in a hobby horse of mine, inspired by a marvellous lecture given by Geoffrey Turner to the 2005 conference of the Catholic Theological Association on Bach's cantatas. They are bit long for the average parish Mass, but Bach's liturgical purpose, in composing his cantatas, got me thinking. After the Word of God has been proclaimed, in the readings, and interpreted, in the homily, why could we not have three or four minutes of attentiveness, while one or two people sang some very simple setting of a phrase or two from the Gospel? Then, having 'digested' the bread of the Word in silence sustained by music, we would profess our faith.

To return to the four questions which, as I mentioned earlier, I put to that same conference, I do not know how well adult Catholics in this country are taught to pray, to read the Scriptures, and to acquire a grasp of church history and doctrine commensurate with their general knowledge and grasp of public affairs. I am, however, convinced that only by taking these questions with the utmost seriousness can we hope to become a church capable of bearing faithful and effective witness to the Gospel in these uncongenial times.

NOTES

1. First presented as 'The Gradwell Lecture', Liverpool Hope University, 4 May 2006.
2. See Lash, 'Recovering Contingency', *Consciousness and Human Identity*, ed. John Cornwell (Oxford: Oxford University Press, 1998), 197–211.

3. Durkheim, *Suicide: A Study in Sociology*, trans. John A. Spaulding and George Simpson (London: Routledge & Kegan Paul, 1952), 312.

4. St. Augustine, *Tract in Joh.* 96, 4, quoted by Peter Brown, *Augustine of Hippo* (London: Faber & Faber, 1967), 279.

5. Lash, *The Beginning and the End of 'Religion'* (Cambridge: Cambridge University Press, 1996), 21.

6. Lash, 'The Laboratory We Need', *The Tablet* (15 Apr. 2000), 514.

7. The Heythrop Institute for Religion, Ethics and Public Life, *On the Way to Life: Contemporary Culture and Theological Development as a Framework for Catholic Education, Catechesis and Formation* (London: Catholic Education Service, 2005), 55.

8. Newman, 'XIV. Wisdom, as Contrasted with Faith and Bigotry', *Newman's University Sermons: Fifteen Sermons Preached Before the University of Oxford, 1826–43*, 3rd edn., introds by D. M. MacKinnon and J. D. Holmes (London: SPCK, 1970), 292–3. Also Lash, ' "A Seat of Wisdom, a Light of the World": Considering the University', in Terrence Merrigan (ed.), *John Henry Cardinal Newman, 1801–1890: A Special Issue of Louvain Studies* (Louvain: Peeters, 1990), 200.

9. See *On the Way to Life*, 27.

10. See Rupert Shortt, *God's Advocates. Christian Thinkers in Conversation* (London: Darton, Longman & Todd, 2005), 182.

11. Williams, *Lost Icons: Reflections on Cultural Bereavement* (Edinburgh: T. & T. Clark, 2000), p. ix.

12. See Lash, Introduction, *New Blackfriars*, 87 (2006), 109.

13. Aquinos, *Summa Theologiae*, 3a.40.1, ad 2.

14. 'Nullus autem testimonium potest ferre nisi qui experitur.' Commenting on Ps. 18: 7.

15. *On the Way to Life*, 47.

16. See Lash, 'What Happened at Vatican II?', in Lash, *Theology for Pilgrims* (London: Darton, Longman, Todd, 2008), 240–8.

17. *On the Way to Life*, 37.

18. See Anscombe, 'Modern Moral Philosophy' (1958), *The Collected Philosophical Papers of G. E. M. Anscombe*, vol. iii. *Ethics, Religion and Politics* (Oxford: Basil Blackwell, 1981), 36.

19. Ibid. 34.

20. Alasdair MacIntyre, 'Review of Herbert McCabe, *The Good Life: Ethics and the Pursuit of Happiness* (London: Continuum, 2005)', *Tablet* (10 Sept. 2005), 22.

21. Ibid.

22. See Lash, 'Authors, Authority and Authorization', in Bernard Hoose (ed.), *Authority in the Roman Catholic Church. Theory and Practice* (Aldershot: Ashgate, 2002), 59–71.

23. Brueggemann, *Theology of the Old Testament: Testimony, Dispute, Advocacy* (Minneapolis, Minn.: Fortress Press, 1997), paraphrased by Nicholas Adams, 'Argument', in David F. Ford, Ben Quash & Janet Martin Soskice (eds.), *Fields of Faith. Theology and Religious Studies for the Twenty-first Century* (Cambridge: Cambridge University Press, 2005), 139–40.

24. Dulles, *The Craft of Theology: From Symbol to System* (New York: Crossroad, 1995), 43 (cited from Harold E. Ernst, 'The Theological Notes and the Interpretation of Doctrine', *Theological Studies*, 63 (2002), 814).

25. Ibid.

26. Newman, *Sermons Preached on Various Occasions* (London: Longmans, Green, & Co., 1900), 1–14.

27. Ibid. 13.

28. Who once taught in one of the constituent colleges that became Liverpool Hope University, and who died in Apr. 2006.

6

'Credo Unam Sanctam Ecclesiam'—The Relationship Between the Catholic and the Protestant Principles in Fundamental Ecclesiology[1]

Walter Kasper

INTRODUCTION

We find ourselves ecumenically in an interim period. Forty years of dialogue have produced many fine ecumenical texts, and efforts on many ecclesial levels have been made to bridge the differences between us. At the same time, new obstacles have emerged, and we do not see a clear path to full communion. As maintained in the opening essay here, the Catholic response in this situation is neither to become resigned to the current divisions, nor to rest content with a 'reconciled diversity' which stops well short of the unity Christ desires for his disciples. The theme of Receptive Ecumenism which binds together the chapters in this volume has as part of its premise the conviction that meaningful and fruitful ecumenical work remains possible in this interim period.

With the notion of Receptive Ecumenism in mind, but adopting an approach more akin to fundamental theology, this chapter reflects upon the relationship between Catholicism and Protestantism, understood as two principles, and offers a few reflections on Anglicanism within this context.

If I understand it correctly, what lies behind the Anglican principle of comprehensiveness is this: the endeavour somehow—and 'somehow' is the operative word—to achieve a harmonious balance between the positions of Catholicism and Protestantism; between Catholic and Protestant principles. *Summa summarum*, this chapter will basically reiterate the statement of my predecessor in this office, Cardinal Edward I. Cassidy, when as a guest speaker at the Lambeth Conference in 1998 he expressed the opinion that the principle of comprehensiveness was doubtless helpful and good, but should not be overdone.[2]

THE FLOWERING AND CURRENT CRISIS OF ECUMENISM

The subject of Catholicism and Protestantism leads us back to the beginnings of the ecumenical movement. It began with the insight, at the Mission Conference in Edinburgh in 1910, that the divisions within the church were the most profound impediment to world mission. It was precisely this link between ecumenism and mission which the Second Vatican Council later took up and adopted as its own (*UR*, § 1).

This insight was premissed on the rediscovery of the eschatological and historical dimension of the church. The church has of course been established once and for all, its apostolic foundation stands firm for all time; but the church is nevertheless not something finished, but rather a dynamic entity. As the old master of Catholic and ecumenical theology, Yves Congar, has shown, the church grows and matures internally in its striving for its own unity, and externally in its striving for the unity of the world. Through ecumenism and mission the church becomes that which it always has been and will always remain.[3] The church father of the as yet undivided church, Irenaeus of Lyons, said already in the second century that the Holy Spirit keeps the old church constantly youthful and as fresh as the dew.[4] It was of course a long process before this inner unity of the intrinsic being and the constant renewal of the church, of the church as an institution and as an ever new spiritual event, or of the Catholic sacramental and the Protestant prophetic understanding of the church, was able to assert itself.

Initially the two concepts diverged widely, not only at the time of the Reformation and Counter-Reformation but also at the beginning of the ecumenical movement. The First General Assembly of the World Council of Churches in 1948 in Amsterdam saw this variance as our most profound difference, describing it as the distinction between 'Catholic' and 'Protestant' fundamental attitudes and claiming that the two could not be harmonized. What is customarily designated as 'Catholic' was said to be characterized by a strong emphasis on the visible continuity of the church in the apostolic succession of the episcopacy; what is customarily designated as 'Protestant' was defined as accentuating the initiative of the word of God and the response of faith.[5]

Against this background, the initial reluctance of the Catholic Church to align itself with the ecumenical movement is all too easily understood. When the Catholic Church embraced the ecumenical movement at the Second Vatican Council, it was only possible because it had been preceded by a radical reconsideration of the essential nature of catholicity, carried out by theologians like Henri de Lubac, in his 1938 work *Catholicisme*,[6] Yves Congar, Hans Urs von Balthasar, and many others. Thus the Council was able to designate catholicity as a gift from the Lord, which as a gift at the same time represents a constantly renewed responsibility. Catholicity is to be understood as the involvement of all individuals, the various ministries and offices, all church bodies and peoples, collectively contributing their gifts under the one head, Christ. Accordingly, catholicity is understood as a dynamic unity in diversity (cf. *LG*, §§ 13 and 32).

These definitions allowed the Fourth General Assembly of the WCC in Uppsala in 1968 to venture a step which went far beyond Amsterdam. Under the title *The Holy Spirit and the Catholicity of the Church*, the statement is made that: 'The purpose of Christ is to bring people of all times, of all races, of all places, of all conditions into an organic and living unity in Christ by the Holy Spirit under the universal fatherhood of God.'[7]

On the basis of this rapprochement, the ecumenical movement was able to become a real success story in the years following the Second Vatican Council. This progress can be discerned not least in the documents of the Anglican–Roman Catholic International Commission, which began its work in 1970. At a meeting which brought together thirteen primates of the Anglican Communion, or their representatives, alongside thirteen Catholic bishops from the same countries, held in Mississauga near Toronto in the Jubilee Year 2000, the process of unification seemed to have progressed so far that many participants felt that significant steps towards unity were within our grasp.

Since then, of course, it has become clear that both the ecumenical mood and the ecumenical situation worldwide have changed so radically as virtually to run counter to the ecumenical movement towards unity. This change in the ecumenical climate is apparent in the southern hemisphere in the rapid expansion of Pentecostal and other charismatic movements and groupings premised on an immediate personal experience of the Spirit; in the northern hemisphere, and especially among us in the West, the changed situation is evident in a new polarization and fragmentation exemplified by divergent and even conflicting verdicts on ethical problems. The situation in the Anglican Communion is only one example of a development which can be observed also in other ecclesial communities of the Reformation tradition.

In what follows, I would like to elucidate the theological background of this development by discussing it in terms of the continental, and more precisely the German, context, with which I am understandably more familiar. It is striking that, whereas in the beginning of the ecumenical movement, in the wake of the renaissance in interest in Luther and the 'Word of God' theology propounded by Karl Barth and his disciples, questions of the individualistic profile of Protestantism (not Lutheranism) and issues regarding cultural Protestantism were treated almost contemptuously, at present these issues are once more forcing their way to the forefront. One can speak of a Schleiermacher renaissance. Nineteenth-century theologians like Ritschl, Harnack and Troeltsch are once more 'in'.

Individuality, interiority, freedom of the Christian individual, personal conscience—all subjects central to Harnack's 1900 lecture on 'The Nature of

Christianity'[8]—are surfacing once again. Regardless of all other contradictions, this reveals an individualistic approach similar to that of the Pentecostal and charismatic groupings, while on the other hand fitting easily into the context of postmodern pluralism. The visible unity of the church, then, is no longer a matter of urgency; the pressing issue is the involvement of contemporary culture in theological discourse.

The current President of the Council of the Evangelical Church in Germany, Bishop Wolfgang Huber (Berlin), has quite rightly drawn attention to the inherent risk of the self-secularization of the church.[9] There is a danger of arbitrary individualism leading to the loss of identity of the church. A church without identity can then no longer claim relevance. Inherent, then, in the liberally understood Protestant principle, isolated from Catholic substance, is a dialectic which—as Bishop Huber tells us—has the potential for self-destruction.

On the Catholic side we encounter a contrary movement in the direction of a rediscovery of the specifically Catholic. At the Second Vatican Council the Catholic Church expressed an openness towards the modern world; at the same time, however, the church affirmed the ecumenical witness of the martyrs of the twentieth century who gave testimony for Christ in their utmost resistance against the world and, in so doing, made the church a present reality (*UUS*, §§ 1 and 83). This contrary tendency is totally explicit in *Dominus Iesus*, the declaration of the Congregation for the Doctrine of the Faith (CDF) of 2000, which insists on the '*subsistit in*'; that is, on the realization of the fullness of ecclesiality in the Catholic Church alone.[10] As a consequence, from a Catholic perspective, the churches of the Reformation tradition cannot be called churches in the full sense of the word. Catholic doctrine therewith converged more closely with the Orthodox understanding, which upholds the Catholic principle even more strongly.[11]

Thus at the beginning of the twenty-first century we are confronted once more by the problematic constellation of the nineteenth and early twentieth centuries: Catholicism versus Protestantism. The problems raised by Schleiermacher, Tillich, and others have returned in a new guise. We have been thrown back to the beginnings of the ecumenical movement. It is understandable that the Anglican Communion, which hopes somehow to hold the two together, suffers particularly under this polarization. To me the only possible solution seems to be to turn back once more to the fundamentals of ecumenical theology. We must go back to the source, not so much in a temporal but more in the material sense of a reflection on the fundamentals.

THE UNITY AND SANCTITY OF THE CHURCH

If we go back to the biblical foundations—as is the norm in both our traditions—then the concept of *ekklesia* could initially suggest Schleiermacher's understanding of the church as proceeding from the individual Christian. *Ekklesia* originally means 'assembly', that is, the act of coming together. But in the Apostles' Creed, which we likewise both share, we immediately find a more precise definition: '*Credo unam sanctam ecclesiam.*' The church is more precisely defined by the two biblically based attributes of 'unity' and 'sanctity'.

Unity is a fundamental philosophical and theological concept. Philosophically, unity is the measure of multiplicity: it does not derive from multiplicity, but in the finite realm unity is self-evident only in multiplicity. In theology too unity is fundamental. The Bible speaks of one God, of one Lord and Saviour Jesus Christ, of one Spirit, of the one baptism and therefore also of the one church (Eph. 4: 4–5). The breakdown of unity and unanimity is sharply condemned already by Paul: 'Is Christ divided?'(1 Cor. 1: 13). Church division is thus antithetical to the essential nature of the church; it is a sin before God and a scandal to the world. That has nothing to do with the spectre of a uniform church. Unity in the New Testament is unity in the diversity of charisms, offices, local churches and cultures; unity is symphonic.

The attribute of holiness tells us more precisely where and how this unity is established: not through the amalgamation of its members or its local churches or the various denominations; ecumenical unity is not to be thought of along the lines of the fusion of worldwide mega-corporations in the course of globalization. Unity is *communio sanctorum*, that is, shared participation in the holy, in the life of God, in the Holy Spirit, in the Gospel, in the one baptism and in the one eucharistic body of the Lord. It is not we who construct and organize unity; it is a gift of the Holy Spirit.

Johann Adam Möhler, to whose ecclesiology and ecumenical theology I am indebted, therefore drew attention, in his debate with Schleiermacher, to the fact that this sharing has nothing to do with a community spirit engendered by the collaborative efforts of the members of the church, but involves instead shared participation in the Holy Spirit.[12] The church does not contain the ground of its existence and its unity within itself, it 'ex-ists'. In contrast to the tradition of enthusiasm, in the Catholic tradition this *extra nos* finds its expression in the external mediation of the Spirit through word and sacrament. This *extra nos* is also expressed in the fact that ecclesial office receives its commission not through the congregation but by virtue of sacramental ordination.

All of this tells us that the church does not draw its life from within itself, it does not produce itself or celebrate itself, nor does it contain its measure within itself. It is *communio sanctorum* in which communion with one another is established solely through shared participation in the holy. The church draws its life from word and sacrament and must again and again endeavour anew to measure up to this standard.

This precise point, the culmination of the Catholic sacramental principle, is at the same time the point where it becomes open to the more profound concern of the Protestant prophetic principle. The fact that the unity of the church is grounded in its participation in the holy does indeed have real consequences for the concrete form of the church. In the biblical sense holiness means distance from all that is worldly: it means not conforming to the spirit of 'this' world (Rom. 12: 2). The church is to be a holy people (Exod. 19: 6; 1 Pet. 2: 9). Only as a holy church can it be a prophetic sign to the world. The dividing lines which have unfortunately become evident on ethical issues since the latter half of last century are therefore not secondary or irrelevant for an understanding of the nature of the church; in touching on holiness, they touch on the essential nature of the church itself.

This holiness does not mean that the church is without spot, wrinkle, or blemish already during its time here on earth (Eph. 5: 27); indeed it harbours sinners within its bosom, and it can even include structures which are marked by sin (*UUS*, § 34). But caution is needed here. This does not mean that the church should no longer identify sin as sin. Justification of the sinner does not mean justification of the sin.[13] On the contrary, the church must again and again renew the struggle against sin in its own ranks; it must constantly follow the path of purification and sanctification, of repentance and renewal (*LG*, § 8; *UR*, §§ 4 and 6).

With the principle of the *ecclesia semper purificanda* the Catholic tradition takes up the legitimate concern of the Reformation principle of the *ecclesia semper reformanda*; but it does so not by reforming itself ultimately from within its own being as the holy church, but rather by becoming more and more the one holy church of Jesus Christ. The problem highlighted by reform and the reformers' protest against the secularization of the church is thereby taken equally as seriously as the danger of the self-secularization of the church inherent in cultural Protestantism.

Understood correctly, the sacramental Catholic view of the church is not necessarily antithetical to the self-critical Protestant prophetic principle. The Catholic sacramental principle can grasp the legitimate concern of the Protestant prophetic principle and make it its own. The two need not necessarily be contradictory, but can, if correctly understood, complement one another and achieve a state of balance. Avery Dulles has shown that leading Catholic theologians of the twentieth century have made this view their own.[14] This is of course—as John Henry Newman has shown[15]—not possible in the sense of a middle way but only through an internal mediation of both aspects. In this sense Newman arrived at the conviction that the Catholic Church is the apostolic and, therefore, the evangelical church.

In this sense we can speak of an evangelical Catholicity. This was Martin Luther's original intention, and it was taken up again by the Una-Sancta

Movement in the first half of the twentieth century (Friedrich Heiler, Hugo Asmussen, Max Lackmann, et al., and in another way by Hans Küng). But today the two principles are threatening once more—as so often throughout history— to diverge into ominous variance, to the detriment of the unity of the church and of its ministry for the unity and peace of the world.

At this point we have arrived at a critical moment in the current ecumenical discussion, at its '*hic Rhodos, hic salta*' as it were. It is not a matter of juxtaposition, or of merely external mediation, but of an internal mediation, a fusion of the Catholic sacramental and the Protestant prophetic principles. In the following I would like to concretize this argument by looking at three specific aspects of faith, each of which has ecumenical implications.

THREE SPECIFIC INSTANCES

The first specific example involves the unity and simultaneous existence of the universal church and local churches. In the second millennium Catholic ecclesiology developed from a communio ecclesiology to a unity ecclesiology.[16] The Second Vatican Council rediscovered the significance of the local church once more and determined that the universal church exists 'in and of' local churches (*LG*, § 23); by the same token one can also say that the local church exists 'in and of' the universal church. In their historical reality the local church and the universal church always exist simultaneously and mutually permeate one another.[17]

On the Anglican side, the *Windsor Report* (2004) highlighted this inter-connectedness and accordingly rejected the self-sufficiency, unilateralism, and absolute autonomy of an individual local church and demanded a reinforce-ment of the institutions of unity. From an ecumenically oriented Catholic perspective, that is a good starting-point and a good basis for dialogue, clearly demonstrating both the critical problem of division and the task of unification. If one adopts this view, two questions come into play: on the one hand the issue of Rome's ministry of unity, and on the other the question for Rome of how the relationship between primacy and collegiality or synodality can be better realized. This issue seems to me foundational for the reconcilia-tion of the Catholic and the Protestant principles and for future ecumenical rapprochement.

In addition to synchronic unity there is also a diachronic unity of the church, which leads us to the second specific point I would like to address in this context. The church is one and the same throughout all centuries. The individual local church must therefore not only strive for consensus with the other local churches as well as the universal church, it must also be in consensus with the apostolic church and the church of preceding centuries. We should not imagine that we possess more of the Holy Spirit today than the church of the early church fathers and the great theologians of the early Middle Ages. *Anamnesis/memoria* is therefore a fundamental category. It does not in any way exclude vital development and actualization, but must also be understood as 'dangerous memory',[18] disclosing for us the unresolved alternatives within the tradition and thus liberating us from the spell and the blindness created by prevailing fashions and plausibilities. In so far as tradition, understood as a living thing, is taken seriously as such, it validates the self-critical prophetic principle.

I cannot conceal the fact that for me as a Catholic theologian a fundamental problem of the Anglican Communion arises at this point, namely: how it is possible to designate Scripture and the Apostles' and Niceno-Constantinopolitan Creeds as normative in the Chicago–Lambeth Quadrilateral, but to disregard the binding force of the subsequent living tradition? While many Anglicans would accept only the first ecumenical councils, others would accept the first seven. In evaluating the resolutions of the later Councils, Henry Chadwick would go so far as to say that 'many of these Council's decrees could be received on the principle of accord with the apostolic tradition'.[19] Yet is this not an a-historical classicistic restriction of normativity to one specific epoch, justified in turn by establishing that it is in 'accord with Scripture'? Even here we find a chronological ranking which fails to discern in the many traditions the one tradition, borne by the Holy Spirit and spanning all ages.

A third and final point: both the synchronic and the diachronic aspects move on a horizontal plane. Ultimately, however—as Thomas Aquinas has shown—God himself is the actual *terminus* of faith.[20] So both the synchronic and the diachronic mode of reflection must transcend into the vertical plane. Ultimately all theology must be rooted in doxology and return to doxology again. The *lex orandi* determines the *lex credendi*. The fundamental significance which the Book of Common Prayer holds for the Anglican Communion underlines and affirms this concern. In the twentieth century, Anglican theologians (Michael Ramsey and Rowan Williams), Methodist theologians (Geoffrey Wainwright), and Lutheran theologians (Edmund Schlink and Wolfhart Pannenberg), together with Catholic and, not least, Orthodox theologians have been in agreement in stressing this liturgical and doxological dimension.

The ecumenical significance and value of this cannot be overstated. Ultimately it is not we, but the Spirit of God alone, who can create unity. Therefore, in the tradition of Paul Couturier, we can say that spiritual ecumenism is the soul of the ecumenical movement (*UR*, § 8). That encompasses prayer, conversion, and self-sanctification. Spiritual ecumenism also makes it clear that we should not be satisfied with such intermediate goals as better mutual awareness, cooperation, and peaceful coexistence. The goal of ecumenism is the shared celebration of the one Eucharist, partaking in the one bread and the one chalice (1 Cor. 10: 17).

CONCLUSION

In drawing us towards a conclusion, these three instances confront us with the fundamental question of ecumenical theology, which is none other than the task of all theology: the task of reflecting the living tradition. In ecumenical theology, however, this task is extended beyond the boundaries of each individual ecclesial tradition to encompass the other ecclesial traditions. The various ecclesial traditions need to be drawn into conversation with one another. Such an ecumenical dialogue is not just an exchange of ideas but an exchange of the gifts which are in the possession of each individual church (*UUS*, § 28). It is not a matter of finding the lowest common denominator but of reciprocal enrichment and growth towards the full stature of Christ (Eph. 4: 13).

Möhler has shown how this dialogue can liberate the specific gifts and concerns of the individual church from the self-inhibiting cocoon of egotistic isolation and contraposition, by reintegrating them into the whole and reconciling them with one another. In isolation they become heretical, one-sided, and sterile; through their reintegration a 'reconciled diversity' is achieved, or, as Möhler puts it: instead of contradictions they are to become reconciled—today we would say complementary—antitheses.[21] Whether, when, and how this can in the future become possible, not just in theory but also as an ecclesial reality with regard to the principles of Catholicity and Protestantism, is the great ecumenical question. The ecumenical movement and its theology are something like the building-site of the future structure of the church, where the one undivided church of the first millennium and the divided church of the second millennium are to become the one reconciled unity of the third millennium. Such a search for unity is not meant as going back to an 'ecumenism of return', but as a future-oriented movement towards a new reconciled form of unity.

This is not to speak of a 'new' church but certainly a spiritually renewed church, in which the church in its concrete form becomes to the fullest degree that which in its undeveloped nature it always has been and always remains: the one holy church which we confess together in the Apostles' Creed. When, how, and where that occurs we can confidently leave to another. I am convinced that He will bring to fruition that which He has initiated.

NOTES

1. This chapter was first published in the *International Journal for the Study of the Christian Church*, 7 (2007), 250–60.
2. Cardinal Cassidy noted: 'The commitment to unity is relativised if diversity and differences that cannot be reconciled with the Gospel are at the same time being embraced and exalted. It is put in question when pluralism in

the church comes to be regarded as a kind of 'postmodern' beatitude...The Virginia Report is surely right to argue that...the universal church sometimes has "to say with firmness that a particular local practice or theory is incompatible with Christian faith"'. 'Homily at Lambeth Ecumenical Vespers Service' (20 July 1998), *Information Service*, 98 (1998), 155–7; also available at <http://www.lambethconference.org/1998/news/lc034.cfm>.

3. Congar, *Vraie et fausse réforme dans l'Église*, 2nd edn. (Paris: Cerf, 1969); also id., *Diversity and Communion*, trans. John Bowden (London: SCM, 1984).

4. See Irenaeus, 'Against Heresies', III. xxiv. 1, in *The Ante-Nicene Fathers*, ed. and trans. Alexander Roberts and James Donaldson, rev. A. Cleveland Coxe (Grand Rapids, MI: Eerdmans, 1996), 458.

5. 'Report of Section I: The Universal Church in God's Design', in W. A. Visser't Hooft (ed.), *The First Assembly of the World Council of Churches Held at Amsterdam, August 22 to September 4, 1948* (London: SCM, 1949), 52.

6. For a translation of the 4th French edition of 1947, see *Catholicism: Christ and the Common Destiny of Man*, trans. Lancelot C. Sheppard (San Francisco, Calif.: Ignatius Press, 1988).

7. 'The Holy Spirit and the Catholicity of the Church: The Report as Adopted by the Assembly', § 6, in Norman Goodall (ed.), *The Uppsala Report 1968: Official Report of the Fourth Assembly of the World Council of Churches, Uppsala, July 4–20, 1968* (Geneva: WCC, 1968), 13.

8. Adolf von Harnack, *Das Wesen des Christentums* (Leipzig: J. C. Hinrichs, 1900); id., *What is Christianity?*, trans. T. B. Saunders (London: Williams & Norgate, 1904).

9. Huber, *Kirche in der Zeitenwende* (Gütersloh: Gütersloher Verlagshaus, 1999).

10. On the interpretation of this principle, see Kasper, 'The Nature and Purpose of Ecumenical Dialogue', *TTMABO*, 41–3; and id., '*Communio*: The Guiding Concept of Catholic Ecumenical Theology', ibid. 65–6; also Chapter 1: Paul D. Murray, 'Receptive Ecumenism and Catholic Learning—Establishing the Agenda', nn. 33 and 34.

11. John Meyendorff, *Orthodoxy and Catholicity* (New York: Sheed & Ward, 1966).

12. Möhler, *Unity in the Church, or, The Principle of Catholicism: Presented in the Spirit of the Church Fathers of the First Three Centuries*, trans. Peter C. Erb (Washington, DC: Catholic University of America Press, 1996), 209–13 (§ 49); also 428 n. 26.

13. See Dietrich Bonhoeffer, *The Cost of Discipleship*, ed. R. H. Fuller (London: SCM, 1948), 40–5.

14. See Dulles, *The Catholicity of the Church* (Oxford: Clarendon Press, 1985), 147–66.

15. See Newman, 'Preface to the Third Edition' (1877), in *The Via Media of the Anglican Church*, ed. H. D. Widner (Oxford: Clarendon Press, 1990), 10–57.

16. See Congar, *L'Ecclésiologie du haut moyen-age* (Paris: Cerf, 1968); also Kasper, 'Church as *Communio*', *Communio*, 13 (1986), 100–17.

17. See de Lubac, *Les Églises particulières dans l'eglise universelle* (Paris: Aubier-Montaigne, 1971).

18. See Johann-Baptist Metz, *Faith in History and Society: Toward a Practical Fundamental Theology*, trans. David Smith (London: Burns & Oates, 1980), 88–99, 200–4.

19. Chadwick, 'The Status of Ecumenical Councils in Anglican Thought' (1974), preparatory document for the Anglican–Orthodox Dialogue Commission and, subsequently, for ARCIC, held within the ARCIC archives, Centro Pro Unione, Rome.
20. *Summa Theologiæ*, vol. xxxi. (2a. 2æ. 1–7): Faith, ed. T. C. O'Brien (London: Eyre & Spottiswoode, 1974), 2a. 2æ. 1.1.
21. *Unity in the Church*, § 46 (pp. 194–8).

7

Text and Contexts—Hermeneutical Reflections on Receptive Ecumenism

Riccardo Larini

INTRODUCTION

A volume centred around the theme of Receptive Ecumenism undoubtedly represents a novelty in the world of ecumenical and, even more particularly, Roman Catholic theology. In fact, although the theme of reception has become central in ecumenical dialogue since at least the early 1970s,[1] its treatment in scholarly work is still uncommon.

A recurrent danger in ecumenical theological work—and this despite the numerous developments flowing from the dialogues—is to reduce the task to one of comparing the 'answers' provided by different confessional theologies to what are assumed to be similar issues or questions. The obvious risk here is that of undermining the potential enrichment which arises from truly listening to the 'other', even up to the point of reducing the demands of dialogue to refined monologue.

This essay focuses on the hermeneutical implications of Receptive Ecumenism, through the study of what leads to the rise of theological differences and of what happens when different theological traditions meet. What emerges provides some hints about how to understand and live true reception, from both theoretical and practical points of view, and indicates why academic theology *tout court* has a lot to benefit from the development of ecumenical hermeneutics.

THE IDEA OF RECEPTION AND THE RISE OF THE HERMENEUTICAL PROBLEM

In his often-cited original formulation, Yves Congar stated: 'By "reception" I understand...the process by which an ecclesial body truly makes its own a resolution which it had not given itself, recognising in the measure so promulgated a rule which is applicable to its own life.'[2] This definition reveals the origin of the reflection about reception in problems posed in the early church, particularly when decrees and canons promulgated by a group of churches demanded some form of adoption by other communities which had not been part of the originating discussions. If we compare Congar's definition with the one provided more than twenty years later at the Sixth Forum on Bilateral Dialogues, something interesting arises:

Ecumenical reception is the *comprehensive process* by which the churches make their own *the whole range of results of their encounters with each other*. It is thus far more than the official response to the results of dialogues, although such responses are essential. Reception is an integral part of the movement towards ... full communion.[3]

What has happened in between is both the development of a relevant number of bilateral and multilateral dialogues, and above all the deepening of the theological reflection on reception and on its link with the other key concept of contemporary ecumenism, *koinonia*.[4] The enrichment which emerges by comparing the two definitions of reception provided above is striking. It is now clear: (1) that reception is founded on the sense of already belonging to one church, although our different communities are still in an imperfect state of communion—what Ladislas Örsy refers to here as the one church that is internally divided;[5] (2) that reception relates not just to the solemn decisions of some ecclesial body but to any sort of comprehension of the Christian mystery/revelation which has arisen outside the boundaries of 'our' communities; (3) that encounters are necessarily bound to change the perception of our own traditions; (4) that reception is a comprehensive process.

In a few years' time the attention has therefore shifted from the legal to the ecclesiological implications of reception, and then to its hermeneutical basis. It is not by chance, then, that the 'Faith and Order Commission' of the World Council of Churches has been prompted, after examining the reception process of its highest achievement, the 1982 Lima document on *Baptism, Eucharist and Ministry*, to begin a study on ecumenical hermeneutics. The provisional outcome is a paper whose title reveals the fragility of present-day research on this theme: *A Treasure in Earthen Vessels: An Instrument for an Ecumenical Reflection on Hermeneutics* (*TEV*).[6] Suffice here to outline a few issues raised in it which are relevant to the argument of this essay.

First of all, *TEV* acknowledges that at the origin of all our theological interpretations lies the one and unique 'unsearchable mystery of God's love' (§ 1), 'which surpasses any human expression' (§ 10). It then reckons that the transmission of this mystery none the less 'relies upon human forms of expression and interpretation, dialogue and communication, all of which are fragile and all too often fragmented embodiments, none of which is completely adequate' (§ 2). The text then outlines the three main aims of ecumenical hermeneutics: (1) a greater coherence in the interpretation of the faith; (2) a mutually recognizable (re)appropriation of the sources of the Christian faith; (3) preparing ways of common confession and prayer (§ 6).

In a subsequent section, *TEV* makes its own the analysis of another Faith and Order document, the 1963 Montreal statement on *Scripture, Tradition and 'traditions'*,[7] which helped the churches to understand, in the light of contemporary biblical studies, the correct relationship between Tradition (the Gospel, the revelation of God's mystery of love), Scripture as its written deposit and normative reference, and 'traditions' as the different ways in which Tradition is lived and embedded and in which Scripture is interpreted throughout history.

At the end of this section, drawing upon the discussions of the Fifth World Conference of Faith and Order (Santiago de Compostela, 1993), it is stated that the present tasks of ecumenical hermeneutics should be: (a) to overcome and reconcile the criteriological differences with regard to faithful interpretation of the one Gospel; (b) to express and communicate the one Gospel in and across various contexts, cultures, and locations; (c) to work towards mutual account-ability, discernment, and authoritative teaching before the world (§ 12). In so doing, *TEV* takes up the greatest challenges identified in the last two decades, and points in helpful directions. None the less, despite noting the relevance of the contributions of the human sciences to contemporary hermeneutics, it makes very little use of them, limiting itself to the general principles that could be better defined with the aid of such tools.

The situation does not improve much even after analysing some major studies on reception and ecumenical hermeneutics published in recent years.[8] There are, as yet, practically no works which try to relate the present focus of the ecumenical dialogue on reception and *koinonia* to sociologi-cal theories about identity generation, literary theories about reception itself, and more deeply philosophical and hermeneutical theories on language and history.[9]

For this reason, what follows here is first of all an attempt to examine the birth and evolution of the diversified Christian identity. This will allow us to discern the implications of such identity generation processes for the encounter between the churches. More importantly, it will become clear why ecumenical hermeneutics—and ecumenism more generally—is vital for the future of acad-emic theology, and does not constitute just a secondary expendable branch of a wider theological curriculum.

FROM ONE TRADITION TO MANY THEOLOGIES

The 1963 Montreal Faith and Order statement on *Scripture, Tradition and 'traditions'* defines capital 'T' Tradition as 'the Gospel itself, transmitted from generation to generation in and by the Church, Christ himself present in the life of the Church', and 'traditions' as 'both the diversity of forms of expression and also what we call confessional traditions'.[10] While acknowledging that 'Montreal did not fully explain what it means that the one Tradition is embodied in concrete traditions and cultures' (§ 17), *TEV* fails both to define the content of Tradition better and to describe the hermeneutical process binding Tradition to 'traditions' and its implications for our own time.

However, if we follow the most important works on this theme in nineteenth- and twentieth-century scholarship, some legitimate questions arise: Does Christianity have a unique common origin? Is it therefore possible to define its 'pure essence'? Or rather does the plurality of the New Testament writings point towards a diversified beginning of Christian identity?

In an earlier piece of research, I have analysed the various relevant theories brought forward from F. C. Baur to Judith Lieu.[11] Using the tools provided by some contemporary sociological theories of identity construction, and examining all the extant Christian writings until AD 120, I came to the conclusion that the two shaping poles which emerge throughout all these works are: (1) the newness of life brought about by the unique mediation of Jesus Christ, and (2) the *koinonia* as participation in Christ's revelation and mutual accountability in the Spirit.

As is generally the case in relation to emergent religious identity definition, this 'logic' of Christian identity is attainable only through documents which belong to what Rowan Williams has referred to as a secondary, 'non-locative' phase of identity definition. Here Williams draws on Jonathan Z. Smith's distinction between a first 'locative' phase in the birth of a specific religious identity—normally 'located' within a very restricted community of people who have shared the crucial elements of the founder's message—and the transition to a new phase which occurs when the message is spread and meets the new challenges of reception in new places and of diachronic changes within the same context.[12]

Does this mean that the 'essence' of the gospel is no longer attainable? This is what some scholars would seem to suggest by saying that in the end every identity is 'made not born'.[13] In contrast, I would argue that a common given identity (more precisely, an identity that is both given and made, common and diversified) is now to be viewed as being embedded in different hermeneutical traditions, and capable of being reached, although not strictly defined, only through their living hermeneutical encounter.

I say reached but not strictly defined, both for theological and for literary–linguistic reasons: theological, because the mystery of God's love exceeds our possibility to circumscribe it, but is none the less open to our understanding and reception; literary–linguistic, because the creation of texts within the different contexts in which the original experience expands generates 'horizons of expectation', i.e. opens up the endless game of interpretation which arises when a potentially infinite range of questions meets texts which by their very nature generate a dialogue with their readers.

If my reading of the birth of Christian identity is correct, even before the fixation of a biblical canon, the appearance of written sources constitutes a decisive move towards both diversity of interpretations and common reference to the same origin. In fact, the shaping of relatively stable rites, ethics, and scriptures is vital for the establishment of what contemporary scholarship calls 'sign-systems'.[14] A sign-system makes religion a semeiotic phenomenon. Because of its stability, a sign-system constitutes the 'generative grammar' of a 'cultural–linguistic world'—to employ the Montreal language it is the instrument which gives voice to 'Tradition' as 'traditions' in a permanently creative way.[15]

However, it must be pointed out that, from the beginning, the plurality of 'traditions' is not generated just by the different contexts in which a supposedly unique original sign-system operates. There is no single and unilateral sign-system which imposes itself in early Christianity. There is more than one narrative of Jesus' life, death, and resurrection, probably not a unique way to celebrate the Eucharist, different meanings attached to baptismal rites, varying ethical emphases.

Nonetheless, within this partial variety (which retains always some form of inner kinship), scripture is the most stable element due to its very nature, and this makes biblical hermeneutics a crucial focus in the search for the *koinonia* which is a constitutive element of the Christian gospel. This is why if, as I believe, Averil Cameron is right in affirming that the real power which led to the expansion of Christianity is not its political success under Constantine, but its ability to generate a rhetoric, a 'discourse' capable of meeting the human quest and questions about meaning, I find even more appropriate the analysis provided by Frances Young of the role of biblical interpretation within the creation of Christian discourse.[16]

Moving one step further, we can say that the generative grammar of the Christian sign-system is expressed in particular linguistic forms, which privilege evocative, narrative, and poetic language. Nonetheless, it belongs to human nature to recur to further levels of rationalization once a certain cultural linguistic world is established.[17] Here is where 'speculative' theologies arise.

Theo-*logy* intended as language about God is certainly present in symbols and metaphors which are the first order product of human reason. The theological depth of symbolic and metaphoric speech is not necessarily less than what can be expressed in second-order rationalizations and speculations generated by the basic grammar of theological discourse. Nonetheless, the typical mark of speculative reason is its power to 'define' human knowledge, to raise human thinking to a fully conscious state, and to tend towards some form of universalism.

Defining means sharpening but also drawing boundaries; raising universalistic expectations means tending towards completeness and towards the fusion of all horizons of expectations generated by the experience reflected upon. By doing so, speculative theologies, like every form of reflective thinking (philosophy), hint at truth claims which make them both powerful tools but also systems which tend to resist dialogue and any sort of rival claim.[18]

We have considered so far the birth of Christian identity through the generation of sign-systems and the development of speculative theologies. We have therefore reached a point where we can seriously take into account what happens when the diversified Christian communities and their theologies meet.

THE ENCOUNTER BETWEEN DIFFERENT WORLDS
THAT SHARE THE SAME ORIGIN

Whenever two different Christian communities meet, what actually occurs is the encounter between different cultural–linguistic worlds. This is true even in the case of communities belonging to the same church, but differentiated in terms of geo-cultural location.

The psychological reaction prompted by such encounter is always of a double kind, and is due to the movement from common origin to a plurality of contexts: on the one hand, there is the impression of belonging together, of sharing something; on the other hand, there is the surprise, disturbance even, caused by the diversity of languages and theologies adopted to express supposedly analogous elements of the faith.

Every community encountering differences loses some control over the boundaries of its own identity. Listening to the other, we are brought not just to compare his or her answers to ours, but much more deeply to discern his or her questions and the whole process which brought an individual or a community from a common origin to a different theological construct.[19] If any judgement becomes possible at this point, it is only a judgement of consistency: there are in principle no illegitimate questions we may address to revelation, but only inconsistent answers. This presupposes a belief in the existence of forms of correct reasoning, and should be sustained by a new and agreed reformulation of the laws of rhetoric, where the latter, as used to happen in Aristotelian thought, is not reduced to the art of persuasion, but is inseparable from the philosophical enterprise of searching for the truth.[20]

Together with this understanding, and partly prompted by it, reception brings us to listen to our own tradition in order to unveil its crucial questions and developments, applying the same critical hermeneutical tools to ourselves as to our neighbours. In Ricœur's words, this *détour* through the other leads us to question ourselves and deepen our self-understanding.[21] More than this, it takes us back to our own quest enriched with further questions to address to the mystery of God's love. It is to this that ecumenical documents should refer when they speak of 're-reception'.

From a hermeneutical point of view, it is a fallacy to think of re-reception just in terms of rediscovering what we already had but have somehow lost or obscured: every new interpretation shares some continuity but also some elements of novelty, due to the very nature of language and human experience.[22] If we want to talk about 'receiving with integrity', as has been proposed in the opening chapter to this volume, we have to understand 'integrity' in terms of the rules of language and, above all, of the normative role of revelation, to which the church has to remain submitted.

What is achieved in our cultural–linguistic worlds through mutual reception is a kind of osmosis or, better, of corrective mirroring in each other up to the point of recognizing at the end of the process that the same logic of revelation is at work in our hermeneutics which will none the less always retain some legitimate differences. Such ideas are expanded in the following section in mere strictly hermeneutical terms.

THE PRIMACY OF THE TEXT AND THE HERMENEUTICAL CIRCLE

Our theologies, whatever the language through which they are conveyed (narrative, poetic, mythical, speculative), are all rationalizations of our encounter with the Christian revelation. Given that they are all generated by sign-systems, we can apply to them what some contemporary scholars have been saying about texts— that they generate horizons of expectation. For Hans Robert Jauss, the 'horizon of expectation' of a text is 'an intersubjective system or structure of expectations', which enters, and may substantially modify, the different 'horizon of expectation of the reader'.[23] Going beyond Hans-Georg Gadamer, who had simply affirmed that there is understanding when a fusion occurs between the text's and the reader's horizons,[24] Jauss not only reckons that interpretations of texts are events as important as the text itself, but also, paradoxically, ascribes a truly 'original' status to what lies at the beginning of the chain of interpretations. In this way, the whole history of successive interpretations generated by a 'sign' becomes relevant (both the whole history in itself and all 'traditions'), but above all a fundamental primacy is assigned to the original sign, where the germinal structures capable of generating further hermeneutics reside. As David Maybury-Lewis put it:

If I read a myth, select certain elements from it, and arrange them in a pattern, that 'structure' is bound to be in the material unless I have misread the text or demonstrably misrendered it. The fact of its being there does not, however, indicate that my arrangement is anything more than my personal whim ... A myth is therefore bound to have a number of possible 'structures' that are both in the material and in the eye of the beholder. The problem is to decide between them and to determine the significance of any of them.[25]

Such developments of literary criticism match quite properly the theological need to confer a primacy to revelation, to the Word of God, against human words prior or outside it. Although none of us meets texts without questions or biases, serious problems arise when we abandon the basic dialogic of a *fides ex auditu* (Rom. 10: 17), the fact that the initiative pertains to God who, speaking first, generates our world; in other words, the fact that it is God's appeal which continuously reshapes our horizons of meaning.

It is to this that Hans Frei refers when he stresses the primacy of the text over context, of the 'literal reading' of scriptures over post-critical ways of interpreting the Bible.[26] Although several critical remarks could be made regarding Frei's analysis of some modern authors, his plea for the 'primacy of the text' is pertinent to the theme of this chapter. In fact, even though texts are only one component of the sign-system which conveys the word of God and generates our world of discourse, they are certainly its most stable element and the most widely shared by all those who call themselves Christians. Furthermore, notwithstanding the role of Tradition and 'traditions' (using Montreal's language), scripture is and remains the *norma normans*, the mirror into which all our traditions have to be literally 'verified', and the most reliable deposit where Tradition—the Gospel and mystery of God's love—can be retrieved. Scripture, moreover, being the witness of an epoch already characterized by non-locative identity in different and diversified communities— therefore of different 'structures of expectation'—is also the instrument which allows churches of all time to build up a true *koinonia*, a reconciled diversity.

By stressing the primacy of the text, both in linguistic and in theological terms, we are able to correct all those hermeneutical theories which would somehow render the text superfluous. This applies first of all to those readings founded on 'correlation' between the biblical textual world and other worlds of meaning (the worlds of the readers).[27] But it also applies to structural hermeneutics, which, while concentrating apparently on the structures present in the text, easily ends up retrieving in the text general anthropological structures which could be reached independently of the text itself.[28]

Once the principle of the primacy of the text is established, there remains the problem of always maintaining the 'hermeneutical circle' between text and contexts, scripture and its readers. If, when different hermeneutics of the same sign-system meet, this circle is interrupted, the possibility that a text had to generate a reconciled diversity is definitely compromised. The theological systems generated by different interpretations of the same origin are identified with the origin itself, the end product of theological reflection becomes the new sign-system, and communication and reciprocal influence between cultural–linguistic worlds is more and more hindered.

If we bear in mind the hermeneutical considerations I have just outlined, true reception is a process in which all the steps of every tradition are valued, studied, and taken into account. This allows for movement back from the end product—confessional theologies—to the basic structures of the sign-systems which generated them, and allows the dialogue partners to start considering different aspects of revelation which had not been developed in their own traditions. Furthermore, this paves the way to some new shared hermeneutics which enrich and broaden every confessional tradition and act as a critical challenge to our previous partial readings.

Some recent ecumenical dialogues—particularly the bilateral ones—provide good examples of the benefits true reception can offer.

The report of the second phase of the Reformed–Roman Catholic dialogue has run through the different hermeneutical emphases on the church as *sacramentum gratiae* (Catholic) and *creatura Verbi* (Reformed), leading to new, shared, and deeper understandings on both sides.[29] In the first phase of the same dialogue, the debate on the eucharistic presence of Christ has led to increased understanding as to what lies behind two seemingly distant ways of depicting the real encounter between Christ and the congregation gathered in his name to worship the triune God. As a consequence, the term 'presence' has been enriched with new and further meanings.[30]

In contrast, in ARCIC II's *The Gift of Authority*, the strategy has been to begin with a new hermeneutic on some scriptural texts regarding authority (namely: 2 Cor. 1: 18–20) and then to seek to compare and readjust the different traditional confessional interpretations of authority with the aid of this new shared achievement.[31]

An interesting case for a thorough understanding of ecumenical reception and the hermeneutical process leading to it, has been provided by the 1999 Lutheran–Roman Catholic *Joint Declaration on the Doctrine of Justification* (*JDDJ*).[32] By choosing to adopt a differentiated agreement,[33] the two dialogue partners have shown how reception can enrich each confessional theology, but also how every human search for a single universal language in which to express communion is bound to remain incomplete. This means that, through dialogue and reception, discernment is made between what can be achieved in terms of a common language (hinting towards a certain universality of our statements) and what remains inextricably entangled with our own historical specificity.

If other dialogues have not always achieved the same level of theological depth, it is probably because they did not take into account the overall complexity of reception that I have tried to describe here through the analysis of its hermeneutical foundations.

CONCLUSION

By way of conclusion, I wish to draw out some implications relating above all to the way in which theology is now generally taught, particularly in Catholic institutions.

Different denominational approaches to theology are often confined either to the study of individual authors (the 'great' theologians) or to some minor courses on ecumenism. The problem of reception itself is presented mainly as the process of popularizing the results of official dialogues. Would not, however, theological studies be much deeper and more interesting if we introduced an explicitly comparative perspective and hermeneutical method in our courses? By this I mean a way of teaching theology which takes properly into account all the steps that generate different hermeneutics, and which does not limit itself to comparing the final linguistic formulation of different theological systems regardless of the history lying behind them.

If the previous remark applies more to denominational schools, whose aim is to form future pastors and leaders, a second remark applies to all theological institutions. That is, that at a more fundamental level, what is required is more attention in general to the role of hermeneutics in theological understanding. Hermeneutics is not just an optional tool, a sort of neutral discipline or an area destined to some specialists. It is deeply related with the philosophy of language and history. If Christians believe that 'the Word was made flesh', that the Word entered history to become part of it and transform it from within, it is vital to deepen our understanding of the realities of language and history which lie at the very heart of Christian theology.

In short, Receptive Ecumenism should not just be the limited passion of some people of good will in the different churches. Rather, it constitutes a great chance for the future development of academic theology more generally by modelling a particular approach to theological exploration that takes location and difference, commitment and criticism, and the possibility of constructive learning, all equally seriously. For Receptive Ecumenism to realize this potential, it will be necessary for its proponents to take radically into account its hermeneutical foundations and to be prepared to commit to the long but fascinating path towards the new and unpredictable horizons of understanding that such an enterprise entails. This chapter seeks to be but an initial foray in this direction.

NOTES

1. The key works were Aloys Grillmeier, 'Konzil und Rezeption: Methodische Bemerkungen zu einem Thema der ökumenischen Diskussion der Gegenwart', *Theologie und Philosophie*, 45 (1970), 321–52 (cf. 'The Reception of Church Councils', in Philip McShane (ed.), *Foundations of Theology: Papers from the*

International Lonergan Congress, 1970 (Dublin: Gill & Macmillan, 1971), 102–14) and Yves Congar, 'La "Réception" comme réalité ecclésiologique', *Revue des sciences philosophiques et théologiques*, 56 (1972), 369–403 (cf. 'Reception as an Ecclesiological Reality', *Concilium*, 77 (1972), 43–68). Earlier, prompted by the first Catholic–Orthodox meetings of the 1960s, the theme of reception was confined to legal philosophy or canon law. See W. Küppers, 'Reception, Prolegomena to a Systematic Study', in Lukas Vischer (ed.), *Councils and the Ecumenical Movement* (Geneva: WCC, 1968), 76–98.

2. 'La "Réception" comme réalité ecclésiologique', 370.

3. *Report: International Bilateral Dialogues, 1992–1994*, ed. Günther Gassmann (Faith and Order Paper, No. 168) (Geneva: WCC, 1995), 5 (italics mine).

4. See id., 'Rezeption im ökumenischen Kontext', *Ökumenische Rundschau*, 26 (1977), 314–27; E. J. Kilmartin, 'Reception in History: An Ecclesiological Phenomenon and its Significance', *Journal of Ecumenical Studies*, 21 (1984), 34–54; John D. Zizioulas, 'The Theological Problem of Reception', *One in Christ*, 21 (1985), 187–93; Thomas P. Rausch, 'Reception Past and Present', *Theological Studies*, 47 (1986), 497–508; William G. Rusch, *Reception: An Ecumenical Opportunity* (Philadelphia, Penn.: Fortress, 1988); W. Beinert (ed.), *Glaube als Zustimmung: Zur Interpretation kirchlicher Rezeptionsvorgange* (Freiburg: Herder, 1991); Jean-Marie R. Tillard, 'La Réception comme exigence œcuménique', in G. R. Evans and M. Gourgues (eds.) *Communion et réunion. mélanges J-M. R. Tillard* (Leuven: Leuven University Press, 1995), 75–94; Ángel Anton, 'La "recepción" en la Iglesia y eclesiología, I.' and 'La "recepción" en la Iglesia y eclesiología, II.', *Gregorianum*, 77 (1996), 57±96 and 437–69; G. R. Evans, *The Reception of the Faith: Reinterpreting the Gospel for Today* (London: SPCK, 1997); Gassmann, 'From Reception to Unity: The Historical and Ecumenical Significance of the Concept of Reception', in Colin Podmore (ed.), *Community—Unity—Communion: Essays in Honour of Mary Tanner* (London: Church House Publishing, 1998), 117–29; Tillard, 'Authentic *Koinonia*, Confessional Diversity', ibid. 262–73.

5. See Chapter 3: 'Authentic *Learning* and *Receiving*—A Search for Criteria'.

6. Faith and Order Paper, No. 182 (Geneva: WCC, 1998), available at <http://wcc-coe.org/wcc/what/faith/treasure.html>. For a first group of studies, see Peter Bouteneff and Dagmar Heller (eds.), *Interpreting Together: Essays in Hermeneutics* (Geneva: WCC, 2001).

7. P. C. Rodger and L. Vischer (eds.), *Scripture, Tradition and Traditions: The Fourth World Conference on Faith and Order, Montreal 1963* (Faith and Order Paper, No. 42), (London: SCM Press, 1994), 50–61; cf. Congar, *Tradition and Traditions: An Historical and a Theological Essay*, trans. Michael Naseby and Thomas Rainborough (London: Burns & Oates, 1966).

8. See Bouteneff and Heller, *Interpreting Together*.

9. For some hints, but without concrete examples, see Hermann Pottmeyer, 'The Reception Process: The Challenge at the Threshold of a New Phase of the Ecumenical Movement', in Lawrence S. Cunningham (ed.), *Ecumenism: Present Realities and Future Prospects, Papers Read at the Tantur Ecumenical Center, Jerusalem, 1997* (Notre Dame, Ind.: University of Notre Dame Press, 1998), 149–68; also relevant are Rush, *The Reception of Doctrine: An Appropriation of Hans Robert Jauss' Reception Aesthetics and Literary Hermeneutics* (Rome: Pontificia Università Gregoriana, 1997) and id.,

Still Interpreting Vatican II. Some Hermeneutical Principles (New York: Paulist Press, 2004).

10. *Scripture, Tradition and Traditions*, 53.

11. Larini, 'The Birth of Christian Identity: Criteria for Unity and Room for Diversity in the New Testament and Apostolic Fathers' Time', unpub. MPhil diss., Univ. of Cambridge, 2005.

12. See Williams, 'Does it Make Sense to Speak of Pre-Nicene Orthodoxy?', in Williams (ed.), *The Making of Orthodoxy: Essays in Honour of Henry Chadwick* (Cambridge: Cambridge University Press, 1989), 1–23; cf. Jonathan Z. Smith, *Map is Not Territory: Studies in the History of Religions* (Leiden: Brill, 1978).

13. See Judith Lieu, *Christian Identity in the Graeco-Roman World* (Oxford: Oxford University Press, 2004), 310–16.

14. See Gerd Theissen, *A Theory of Primitive Christian Religion* (London: SCM, 1999), 2 ff.; also Clifford J. Geertz, 'Religion as a Cultural System', *The Interpretation of Cultures* (New York: Basic Books, 1973), 87–125; Fritz Stolz, *Grundzüge der Religionswissenschaft* (Göttingen: Vandenhoeck & Ruprecht, 1988), 79 ff.

15. For 'generative grammar', see Noam Chomsky, *Current Issues in Linguistic Theory* (The Hague: Mouton, 1964), 7 ff.; also id., *Cartesian Linguistics: A Chapter in the History of Rationalist Thought*, ed. James McGilvray, 2nd edn. (Christchurch, New Zealand: Cybereditions, 2002). For the relationship between generative grammars, cultural–linguistic worlds, and ecumenism, see George A. Lindbeck, *The Nature of Doctrine: Religion and Theology in a Postliberal Age* (London: SPCK, 1984).

16. See Cameron, *Christianity and the Rhetoric of Empire: The Development of Christian Discourse* (Berkeley, Calif.: University of California Press, 1991); also Young, *Biblical Exegesis and the Formation of Christian Culture* (Cambridge: Cambridge University Press, 1997).

17. See Paul Ricœur, 'The Hermeneutics of Symbols and Philosophical Reflection', *The Conflict of Interpretations: Essays in Hermeneutics* (Evanston, Ill.: Northwestern University Press, 1974), 287–334.

18. See id., *History and Truth* (Evanston, Ill.: Northwestern University Press, 1965), particularly 'The History of Philosophy and the Unity of Truth,' 41–56.

19. I am adapting here some ideas of Rowan Williams from 'Christian Theology and Other Faiths', in Michael Ipgrave (ed.), *Scriptures in Dialogue: Christians and Muslims Studying the Bible and Qur'an Together* (London: Church House Publishing, 2004), 131–43.

20. See Ricœur, *The Rule of Metaphor: Multi-Disciplinary Studies of the Creation of Meaning in Language* (London: Routledge & Kegan Paul, 1978), 9–13.

21. This theme runs through all Ricœur's works, originating in his reflection on the philosophy of history (see *History and Truth*, 31 ff.), and being deepened through his hermeneutical reflections on myth and symbolic language (see *The Conflict of Interpretations*, 211–22).

22. See id., 'Structure, Word, Event', *The Conflict of Interpretations*, 79–96.

23. See Jauss, *Toward an Aesthetic of Reception* (Minneapolis, Minn.: University of Minnesota Press, 1995), 139–85.

24. See Gadamer, *Truth and Method*, trans. Joel Weinsheimer and Donald G. Marshall, 2nd edn. (New York: Crossroad, 1989), 245 ff.

25. Cited in Smith, *Map is Not Territory*, 19.

26. See Frei, *The Eclipse of Biblical Narrative: A Study in Eighteenth and Nineteenth Century Hermeneutics* (New Haven, Conn. and London: Yale University Press, 1974); id., *Theology and Narrative: Selected Essays*, eds. George Hunsinger and William C. Placher (New York and Oxford: Oxford University Press, 1993), in particular 'The "Literal Reading" of Biblical Narrative in Christian Tradition: Does it Stretch or Will it Break?', 117–52.

27. See Paul Tillich, *Systematic Theology*, vol. i. (Chicago, Ill.: Chicago University Press, 1951), 60 ff. For a critique concerned to maintain the primacy of the text, see Frei, *Types of Christian Theology*, ed. Hunsinger and Placher (New Haven, Conn. and London: Yale University Press, 1992). Whilst correlation in some form is important, this cannot be at the expense of the generative power of the text.

28. See Ricœur's critique of Levy Strauss, 'Structure and Hermeneutics', *The Conflict of Interpretations*, 27–61.

29. 'Toward a Common Understanding of the Church,' *GIA II*, 780–818.

30. See 'The Presence of Christ in Church and World', *GIA*, 434–63.

31. *The Gift of Authority: Authority in the Church III* (London: Church House Publishing/CTS, 1999), also at <http://www.vatican.va/roman_curia/pontifical_councils/chrstuni/documents/rc_pc_chrstuni_doc_12051999_gift-of-autority_en.html>.

32. See Chapter 11: William G. Rusch, 'The International Lutheran–Roman Catholic Dialogue—An Example of Ecclesial Learning and Ecumenical Reception'.

33. By which is meant that on crucial issues something can be said together, whilst other non-divisive things have to be formulated in different ways according to each cultural–confessional world, without envisaging the possibility of full linguistic reconciliation; see esp. *JDDJ*, § 5.

PART II

RECEPTIVE ECUMENICAL LEARNING THROUGH CATHOLIC DIALOGUE

Prologue to Part II
Philippians 1: 3–7

Philip Endean, SJ

> I thank my God every time I remember you, constantly praying with joy in every one of my prayers for all of you, because of your sharing in the gospel from the first day until now. I am confident of this, that the one who began a good work among you will bring it to completion by the day of Jesus Christ. It is right for me to think this way about all of you, because you hold me in your heart.

The chapters which follow contain many erudite words about how Catholic Learning can be enriched as it draws on Anglicanism, Methodism, Lutheranism, and Orthodoxy. But none of us would be reading them were it not for one simple truth. Each of us, when we think of at least some Christians from other traditions, can make our own those words of Paul about the Christians at Philippi: 'I thank my God every time I remember you ... because of your sharing in the Gospel. ... It is right for me to think this way; you hold me in your heart ...'

These reflections at the beginning of each section are not yet more essays veiled in pious disguise. They represent, rather, an acknowledgement that theological reflection is always part of a more comprehensive process. The journey to God involves our bodies and our emotions as well as our minds.

Some twenty years ago, as part of my preparation for being ordained, I spent some time exploring with some of my contemporaries my own faith history. One startling moment came when I reconnected with how I had first learnt the word 'Catholic'. I was four or five years old, at my first school. Since I had no sisters, school meant, for the first time in my life, girls. I took a fancy to one Hester. After a couple of weeks, I finally summoned up the courage to approach Hester in the playground before school began, and managed to get talking with her. The bell then went, and we were shepherded into assembly. In my innocence, I thought it might be nice to continue the beautiful relationship with Hester by standing next to her during morning prayers. But it was not to be. A large nun, clothed in a formidable black habit, separated us, and sent me to one side of the partition and Hester to the other. Confronted by my furious protest and demand to know why, Sister's response was unequivocal: 'Because you're a Catholic and she's a non-Catholic.' So it was that I learnt what the word 'Catholic' meant. And at the same time I learnt the word 'partition'.

Of course time has moved on. I have been given, thank God, more positive images of Catholic identity; I have become reasonably skilled and sophisticated in my handling of theological words; I have learnt how to mind my p's and q's in distinguished ecclesiastical circles, and to make sage noises about not being too simplistic when it comes to questions of intercommunion. Nevertheless, the child is father of the man. Whenever I am dealing with issues involving women and religion (especially nuns), whenever I am thinking about issues of Church authority, whenever I wonder about where and how Christians of different traditions can pray together, I still feel within me an energy coming from the sense of childhood outrage that arose at that moment so many years ago. How dare they keep us apart!

No doubt this history is idiosyncratic, and I have no wish to project its details on to the readers of this volume. But there is, nevertheless, an important point to be made about method. As each of us reads this book, we are bringing to it a set of passions and commitments, nourished by a history of relationships with Christians of other traditions. Perhaps these relationships have been difficult; perhaps, for both good and bad reasons, they have been frustrated in their development. But we would not care about ecumenism enough to be reading this book if such relationships were not fundamentally nourishing, godly, or—to use a term from Ignatian spirituality—consoling. Of course, we need to be critical and discerning about that history—but we cannot be reflective and discriminating about our history unless we are in touch with it in the first place.

The following pages contain many words. Before you read them, I suggest you take a few minutes of silence. During that time, call to mind before God one or two significant relationships you have had with Christians from other traditions, and simply pray in whatever way seems appropriate as you ponder those memories. Perhaps you can make your own Paul's tone of affection and gratitude; perhaps the reality of those relationships will lead you in another direction. The important thing is that we be as honest as possible before God about our personal engagement in the movement of Christian unity. For it is only when we are honest with ourselves about our emotional commitments that God will be able to take the good work begun among us, and bring it to completion.

8

What Roman Catholics Have to Learn from Anglicans

Keith F. Pecklers, SJ

INTRODUCTION

Prior to the Second Vatican Council the title given to this chapter would have appeared odd at best—Catholics, apparently, had nothing to learn from Anglicans, or from any other non-Roman Catholics for that matter! As Paul Murray details in the opening chapter here, the Council changed all that by setting us on an ecumenical path from which we cannot and will not turn back. Indeed, one of the greatest gifts of the Second Vatican Council was the recognition that the church is always on pilgrimage toward the reign of God (*LG*, § 7, 21, 48, 50), something reaffirmed in an ecumenical context by Pope John Paul II in his 1995 ecumenical encyclical (*UUS*, § 25).

This image offers much as we consider the particular relationship between Anglicans and Roman Catholics within the one, divided Body of Christ. The way of pilgrimage is fundamentally a way of slow and patient conversion rather than convergence. Those on pilgrimage travel the road together and a certain interdependence is implied. Food and lodging are shared, strangers become friends, and even those with expertise become students and disciples together along the way.[1]

Lumen Gentium also notes the unique gifts present within this pilgrim church—gifts that contribute to the 'bond of close communion whereby spiritual riches, apostolic workers and temporal resources are shared' (§ 13). Again, 'All . . . are called to this catholic unity which prefigures and promotes universal peace. And in different ways to it belong, or are related: the Catholic faithful, others who believe in Christ, and finally all [hu]mankind, called by God's grace to salvation' (§ 13).

The Council's Decree on Ecumenism, *Unitatis Redintegratio*, takes this further when it speaks of the many 'significant elements and endowments' of the 'one Church of Christ' that exist 'outside the visible boundaries of the Catholic Church' (*UR*, § 3). It specifies 'the written Word of God; the life of grace;

faith, hope and charity...the other interior gifts of the Holy Spirit', and 'many liturgical actions' which 'truly engender a life of grace, and...can aptly give access to the communion of salvation'. Consequently, whilst still considered defective in various ways, the separated churches are viewed as having their own 'significance and importance in the mystery of salvation' (*UR*, § 3). The following section is even more direct:

It is right and salutary to recognize the riches of Christ and virtuous works in the lives of others who are bearing witness to Christ, sometimes even to the shedding of their blood...Nor should we forget that anything wrought by the grace of the Holy Spirit in the hearts of our separated brethren can contribute to our own edification. Whatever is truly Christian is never contrary to what genuinely belongs to the faith; indeed, it can always bring a more perfect realization of the very mystery of Christ and the Church (*UR*, § 4).

As Anglicans and Roman Catholics, we share a communion that is imperfect, yet we are nonetheless woven together, in John Paul II's words, 'by a true union in the Holy Spirit' (*UUS*, § 11). We have increasingly come to recognize the presence of fundamental elements of sanctification and truth present in each other, through which the 'one Church of Christ is effectively present'.[2] Indeed, without denying the real issues that continue to divide our churches, we must honestly admit and celebrate the dual truth that (1) we hold much more in common, and (2) there is much we have to learn from one another, and this, as Pope John Paul II eloquently expressed, at a level far deeper than a mere 'exchange of ideas'.[3] As Bishop Michael Putney explores here, Pope John Paul's image of ecumenical dialogue as properly an 'exchange of gifts' itself suggests that some essential ecclesial elements found in the Roman Catholic Church have been more developed in other traditions. More generally, each of our churches possesses Christian characteristics and ideals that are not as pronounced in our respective others. In this regard, this essay explores the gifts that Roman Catholics have to receive from Anglicans under four headings: Church, Authority, Worship, and Spirituality.

CHURCH

The Second Vatican Council drew deeply on eastern and western patristic sources in the renewal of the church's self-understanding and identity. The church came to be presented as a 'universal sacrament of salvation', as the 'people of God', as 'a communion of life, love, and truth'. In turn, the Anglican–Roman Catholic International Commission took as foundational what might be called a '*koinonia* ecclesiology':

The *koinonia* is grounded in the word of God preached, believed and obeyed...The Church is the community of those reconciled with God and with each other because it is the community of those who believe in Jesus Christ and are justified through God's grace. It is also the reconciling community, because it has been called to bring to all mankind, through the preaching of the Gospel, God's gracious offer of redemption.[4]

This theme was further developed in a 1991 agreed statement specifically focusing on *Church as Communion* which Nicholas Sagovsky regards as 'the best short presentation of an ecumenical ecclesiology of communion'.[5] Here it is explicitly noted that speaking of the Church 'in terms of communion confronts Christians with the scandal of our divisions' that 'obscures God's invitation to communion for all humankind and makes the Gospel we proclaim harder to hear'.[6] Again, ARCIC II reminds us that taking the communion of the Church seriously means embodying the vocation and mission of the Gospel together, as a prophetic sign of what God is accomplishing in the world:

The communion of the Church demonstrates that Christ has broken down the dividing wall of hostility, so as to create a single new humanity reconciled to God in one body by the cross (Eph. 2: 14–16). Confessing that their communion signifies God's purpose for the whole human race the members of the Church are called to give themselves in loving witness and service to their fellow human beings...In this way the Church not only signifies the new humanity willed by God and inaugurated by Christ. It is itself an instrument of the Holy Spirit in the extension of salvation to all human beings in all their needs and circumstances to the end of time.[7]

That paragraph makes abundantly clear how much Anglicans and Roman Catholics share an understanding of the essential ecclesial elements of the church of Christ: reconciliation to God through Christ's passion, death, and resurrection; proclaiming the saving Gospel of Christ in the power of the Holy Spirit, and witnessing to that message through humble service of others. With this, the document explores the sacramentality of the church both as foretaste of the eschatological communion for which we long and the place where God's salvific plan for the world is realized. More specifically, *koinonia* ecclesiology is necessarily expressed in its concern for the world and the living out of the Gospel within the context and fabric of human society. In this it echoes the emphasis placed upon the church's social role and prophetic voice in the Second Vatican Council's 'Pastoral Constitution on the Church in the Modern World' (e.g. *GS*, § 41).

Similarly, recent popes have spoken out strongly against injustice, as evidenced by Pope John Paul II's criticism of the Iraq War, much to the disappointment of the Bush Administration. The Anglican Communion has also been a credible voice within the modern world. Indeed, Roman Catholics have much to learn from the Anglican capacity to engage in dialogue with contemporary culture on complex and controversial issues rather than, as tends to be the case within Roman Catholicism, closing the door to any such discussion.

Happily, our churches are finding a common voice in speaking out against social problems and taking action together. In most places where Anglicans are found in significant numbers—the Western World and Africa—they live in the same cultural worlds as their Roman Catholic counterparts, in contrast to Orthodoxy where there is a real cultural gap needing to be bridged. Consequently, even where real differences keep us apart, Anglicans and Roman Catholics generally find it easy to work together, to cooperate on social questions, and to pray together, as was notably evident in the joint statement from the Archbishop of Canterbury, Dr Rowan Williams, and the Archbishop of Westminster, Cardinal Cormac Murphy-O'Connor in February 2003 counselling against the then imminent move towards war in Iraq.[8]

Of special significance has been the work of the International Anglican–Roman Catholic Commission for Unity and Mission established in 2001 after the meeting of Anglican and Roman Catholic bishops held at Mississauga, Canada in May 2000. At the conclusion of that historic meeting, the bishops decided that a body should be formed to promote their relationship and to find new ways of putting into practice the Christian faith that we share in terms of common life and mission. IARCCUM was designed to have a different function from the existing theological dialogue of ARCIC. While using ARCIC documents as the basis for their activity, its members were to discern together ways in which those texts might lead them towards new means of joint witness and mission within the world. The very existence of this new ecumenical body offers encouragement and a framework in which to work together on common projects of mission and outreach in service of broadened and deepened communion. In the context of the broader ecumenism of religious pluralism and of the need to find new ways of engaging in dialogue with followers of other religious traditions, it is essential that we find our common voice as Christians. IARCCUM's existence reminds us that there is an urgency to our ecumenical collaboration as we consider our common witness within the world.

AUTHORITY

In the context of his extraordinary 1995 encyclical on ecumenism, John Paul II explored the issue of papal primacy in the following terms:

Whatever relates to the unity of all Christian communities clearly forms part of the concerns of the primacy . . . I am convinced that I have a particular responsibility in this regard, above all . . . in heeding the request made of me to find a way of exercising the primacy which, while in no way renouncing what is essential to its mission, is nonetheless open to a new situation. (*UUS*, § 95)

He continued, 'I insistently pray the Holy Spirit to shine his light upon us, enlightening all the Pastors and theologians of our Churches, that we may seek—together, of course—the forms in which this ministry may accomplish a service of love recognized by all concerned.' But the most astounding statement is found in the following paragraph:

This is an immense task, which we cannot refuse and which I cannot carry out by myself. Could not the real but imperfect communion existing between us persuade Church leaders and their theologians to engage with me in a patient and fraternal dialogue on this subject, a dialogue in which, leaving useless controversies behind, we could listen to one another, keeping before us only the will of Christ for his Church and allowing ourselves to be deeply moved by his plea 'that they may all be one ... so that the world may believe that you have sent me' (John 17: 21)? (*UUS*, § 96)

Here, on that most controversial subject of teaching authority, is a formal Catholic invitation to explore the matter ecumenically. In a sense, it authorizes a discussion which has been going on for decades. For example, ARCIC has directly addressed the subject of authority in three agreed statements and one follow-up text.[9] These statements arguably constitute the most significant work done by any ecumenical bilateral commission on the subject of authority. They indicate a wide range of agreement on the purpose and nature of ecclesial authority, and take significant steps towards resolving issues that were at the origins of the Reformation separation between the Church of England and the Catholic Church. Equally, they are candid about addressing remaining areas of difference requiring ongoing dialogue.

The co-chair's preface to Authority I is especially pertinent in that it notes the need for both the Roman Catholic Church and the Anglican Communion to be ready to learn and then identifies something of what each has to learn from the other:

On both sides the readiness to learn, necessary to the achievement of such a wider *koinonia*, would demand humility and charity ... Communion with the see of Rome would bring to the churches of the Anglican Communion not only a wider *koinonia* but also a strengthening of the power to realize its traditional ideal of diversity in unity. Roman Catholics, on their side, would be enriched by the presence of a particular tradition of spirituality and scholarship ... [and would have] much to learn from the Anglican synodical tradition of involving the laity in the life and mission of the Church.[10]

Twenty-five years later, drawing *The Gift of Authority* to a close, is a series of questions probing where each communion needs to learn from the other. The issues facing Anglicans were described as follows:

We have seen that instruments for oversight and decision making are necessary at all levels to support communion. With this in view the Anglican Communion is exploring the development of structures of authority among its provinces. Is the Communion also open to the acceptance of instruments of oversight which would allow decisions to be reached that, in certain circumstances, would bind the whole Church?... To what extent does unilateral action by provinces or dioceses in matters concerning the whole Church, even after consultation has taken place, weaken *koinonia*? Anglicans have shown themselves to be willing to tolerate anomalies for the sake of maintaining communion. Yet this has led to the impairment of communion manifesting itself at the Eucharist, in the exercise of *episcope* and in the interchangeability of ministry. What consequences flow from this? Above all, how will Anglicans address the question of universal primacy as it is emerging from their life together and from ecumenical dialogue?[11]

The text then presented issues facing Roman Catholics:

The Second Vatican Council has reminded Roman Catholics of how the gifts of God are present in all the people of God. It has also taught the collegiality of the episcopate in its communion with the Bishop of Rome, head of the college. However, is there at all levels effective participation of clergy as well as lay people in emerging synodal bodies? Has the teaching of the Second Vatican Council regarding the collegiality of bishops been implemented sufficiently? Do the actions of bishops reflect sufficient awareness of the extent of the authority they receive through ordination for governing the local church? Has enough provision been made to ensure consultation between the Bishop of Rome and the local churches prior to the making of important decisions affecting either a local church or the whole Church? How is the variety of theological opinion taken into account when such decisions are made? In supporting the Bishop of Rome in his work of promoting communion among the churches, do the structures and procedures of the Roman Curia adequately respect the exercise of *episcope* at other levels?[12]

In the first millennium, the church functioned with collegial structures of synodality and consultation not unlike what one finds today throughout the Anglican Communion. Laity were active participants with clergy in the choice of bishops.[13] While some Roman Catholic bishops and theologians have called for a recovery of synodal structures of governance,[14] they remain more the exception than the norm within the Catholic Church, at least in the West.

At the end of the day, Anglicans and Roman Catholics have much to learn from one another on the exercise of authority in the church. Both begin with the same principles and sources of authority but different structures are established for emphasis. As we have seen, within Roman Catholicism there is a strong, unified teaching authority combined with some room for theological discussion. Within Anglicanism, there is a strong commitment to synodal structures at all levels of church life.

In this regard, one of the specific gifts Anglicans can give Roman Catholics is manifest in the earlier extracts from *The Gift of Authority*: the gift of asking questions which need to be asked. Of course, this is a reciprocal matter, and Roman Catholics also do well to ask Anglicans pointed questions. Anglicans exhibit a willingness to engage in difficult questions, to set forth all of the arguments—from Scripture, from Tradition, from reason (drawing on contemporary scholarship in diverse fields), and from experience (including those who find themselves marginalized)—in order to discern a way forward.

Such discernment is a complex and often messy process, but because of the theological diversity within Anglicanism, it does tend to get all sides of an issue out into the open where rigorous discussion can take place. Anglicans may not always be happy with the outcome, but they do not often have the sense that significant issues have been avoided and discussion suppressed. On various questions—most recently the role of women in the church and the question of human sexuality—Anglicanism has ventured into rigorous theological discussion, both in the academy and at the levels of provincial and diocesan synodal structures.

Some within Anglicanism might wish that their Communion had a more centralized structure to deal with such delicate matters. Indeed, the possibility of an authoritative voice that would speak out and ultimately make the final decision would solve divisive problems—at least on one level. But within apparent weakness can also be found strength from which Roman Catholics can learn a great deal. To quote one Anglican: 'Anglicans insist on washing their dirty laundry in public. But at least we wash it!' Within Roman Catholicism, it would be terribly naive to think we do not have to deal with some of the same problems, but there can be a tendency to avoid the questions, hoping they will go away.

Anglicans, then, teach Roman Catholics a great deal by their ability to live with the questions in an open, honest, and transparent way. While Roman Catholicism has at times sought to safeguard unity by cutting off discussion on certain issues, the Anglican Communion has been reluctant to close down discussion on controversial issues. At times this can appear as a gift; at times, as something approaching internal chaos. While there are many positive aspects to Anglican willingness to engage difficult questions, there is also a problematic aspect, and the Anglican Communion has had a difficult time maintaining internal unity as a result. As *The Windsor Report* of 2004 noted: 'One matter that has struck us forcefully is the way in which the views of the Instruments of Unity have been ignored or sidelined by sections of the Communion.' Again, referring to *The Virginia Report*'s description of Anglicanism's core structures as 'a complex and still evolving network of authority', the *Windsor Report* noted that whilst 'in many ways such dispersed authority is a great strength ... in relation to the issues that have recently confronted the Communion, its inherent weakness has been illustrated only too clearly'.[15]

It has been most impressive to observe the ecumenical consultation which has taken place as the Anglican Communion discerns a way forward amidst current difficulties. Given the challenges discussed in *The Windsor Report*, the Archbishop of Canterbury invited Cardinal Kasper to join him in setting up a sub-commission of IARCCUM to address the ecumenical implications of the current situation. In an address to the Anglican Consultative Council in June 2005, reflecting back on the decision taken in December 2003 to put the work of IARCCUM on hold in the light of developments in the Episcopal Church, USA and in the Anglican Church of Canada, the Cardinal said:

During the period which followed, we were encouraged by the attentiveness to ecumenical concerns which has characterized the Anglican Communion's discernment of a way forward...at the initiative of the Archbishop of Canterbury, we jointly established a sub-commission of IARCCUM which prepared a document...reflecting on the current ecclesiological situation in the Anglican Communion in the light of the work of ARCIC over the past 35 years. When the *Windsor Report* was published, again the Archbishop of Canterbury invited written reflections on possible ecumenical implications, and asked that I lead a delegation of the PCPCU to meet him and Anglican Communion staff at Lambeth Palace to carry forward the discussion.[16]

This willingness to consult long-standing ecumenical partners in the midst of important theological discussion is once again something from which the Catholic Church could learn.

WORSHIP

Anglicans and Roman Catholics hold a great deal in common in the area of Christian worship and sacramental practice, and the subject of liturgy offers much fertile ground for mutual learning and ecumenical exchange.[17] Indeed, our common liturgical heritage is something to be celebrated and even promoted in the wider ecumenical context. Unlike other liturgical books of the Reformation, the origins of the Book of Common Prayer are fundamentally Catholic. The Anglican Baptismal Rite, for example, was strongly influenced by the Mozarabic Rite, and the Daily Offices of Morning and Evening Prayer are drawn from the Benedictine tradition.[18]

In the twentieth century, Anglican liturgical pioneer Arthur G. Hebert, SSM (+ 1963) attributed his own liturgical formation and inspiration to the Benedictine monks at Maria Laach in the Rhineland where the German liturgical movement had been launched.[19] Conversely, in the United States during the 1940s members of the Vernacular Society proposed adopting the Book of Common Prayer as a base text (typical edition) for Roman Catholic worship in English because of its beautifully crafted and theologically rich prayer texts. In our own day, Roman Catholics have much to receive from Anglicans in terms of both prayer texts and liturgical style. The Collect for the Feast of the Nativity of Mary found in the Church of England's *Common Worship* offers but one example:

Almighty and Everlasting God, who stooped to raise fallen humanity through the child-bearing of the blessed Mary: grant that we, who have seen your glory revealed in human nature and your love made perfect in our weakness, may daily be renewed in your image and conformed to the pattern of your Son, Jesus Christ our Lord, who is alive and reigns with you and the Holy Spirit, ever one God, world without end. Amen.[20]

The Anglican Communion and the Roman Catholic Church agree that the Eucharist is the fulfilment of the process of Christian Initiation and that in its anamnetic, epicletic, and sacrificial dimensions, the Eucharist celebrates the paschal mystery of Christ and is the self-realization of the church in all its fullness. Bread and wine are transformed into Christ's sacramental body and blood in order that communicants themselves might become that body and blood of Christ within the world. But Anglicans and Roman Catholics have different disciplines regarding eucharistic sharing. Anglican churches regularly welcome other Christians to Holy Communion while the Roman Catholic Church regards eucharistic sharing by those who are not yet in full communion as something exceptional—only in rare and specific cases.

Nonetheless, even as our communion remains imperfect at the level of eucharistic sharing, there is an enormous amount of common liturgical ground that Anglicans and Roman Catholics do share, and we need to commit our-selves ever more intentionally to gather together for common prayer so that the 'exchange of gifts' we desire will more and more become a reality. In the words of Pope John Paul II,

If Christians, despite their divisions, can grow ever more united in common prayer around Christ, they will grow in the awareness of how little divides them in comparison to what unites them. If they meet more often and more regularly before Christ in prayer, they will be able to gain the courage to face all the painful human reality of their divisions, and they will find themselves together once more in that community of the Church which Christ constantly builds up in the Holy Spirit, in spite of all weaknesses and human limitations. (*UUS*, § 22)

When we do gather together for common worship, Roman Catholics have much to receive from Anglicans on the level of pastoral practice. For example, many Anglicans have maintained and fostered a sense of the holy and the transcendent within worship—a sense of reverence and mystery—that Roman Catholics would do well to recover. Anglican worship demonstrates well that it is possible to celebrate a participative, reformed liturgy without losing worship's transcendental dimension. Similarly, Anglicans have been more successful at sustaining and promoting ancient non-eucharistic forms of liturgy—Morning and Evening Prayer—and this despite various attempts at the Council of Trent (1545–63) and the Second Vatican Council to encourage laity to join their clergy in praying Sunday Vespers together.

Another liturgical gift that Anglicans can offer Roman Catholics, and from which they have already been receiving, is the rich musical tradition of Even-song with its numerous beautiful settings of the Psalms, the *Magnificat*, the *Nunc Dimittis*, and the glorious anthems sung by choirs in Anglican churches throughout the world. Similarly, Anglican hymnody is a gift from which Roman Catholics have been receiving since the Second Vatican Council's decision to worship in the vernacular.

More generally, for more than forty years now, Anglican and Roman Catholic liturgical scholars have met regularly to consult on the liturgical reforms of their respective churches and collaborate on research projects of common interest. In 1997, Anglican liturgist Canon Donald Gray visited Rome to deliver a lecture at the Pontifical Liturgical Institute on the topic of 'Ecumenical Liturgical Cooperation'. Gray argued that although we remain divided at the altar of the Eucharist, we need not be divided around the Altar of God's Word, and then he spoke candidly about a certain frustration with the Holy See's reluctance to accept the proposed *Common Lectionary*:

Some of us find it hard to understand that there is hesitation on the part of the Roman Catholic Church when it is substantially the *Ordo Lectionum Missae* which is being proposed for ecumenical use. It is an unnecessary offence to the Spirit to decline this opportunity. The recently published *Ecumenical Directory* (1993) envisages such cooperation when it says 'agreement for common scriptural readings for liturgical use should (also) be explored'.[21]

Such honesty within ecumenical discussions is itself a gift because it ultimately enables dialogue partners to get beyond formalities to the heart of the matter where real progress can be made.

In the area of worship, progress is evident in several examples. A newly composed eucharistic Prayer by the International Commission on English in the Liturgy (ICEL) intended for the new English edition of the Revised Roman Missal was eventually included in a redacted form in *Common Worship*.[22] Again, in recent years as the Church of England's Liturgical Commission has been revising its Ordination Rites, several of us Roman Catholics were involved in the process of evaluating and reworking those proposed texts, an invitation that has particular importance, given that Anglican ordination rites were judged to be deficient in the 1896 papal bull *Apostolicae Curae*. Similarly, when the International Anglican Liturgical Consultation (IALC) meets every two years—a subsidiary body of the Anglican Consultative Council (ACC)—there is always an ecumenical observer invited to attend who, in recent years, has been a Roman Catholic. Most recently, the Archbishop of Canterbury concluded his November 2006 visit to Rome by presiding at a solemn Anglican Eucharist in the Basilica of Santa Sabina on the Aventine Hill. He did so at the very altar where the Pope has traditionally celebrated on Ash Wednesday since the fifth century and in the presence of several Vatican representatives. Forty years ago the mere concept of an Anglican Eucharist in an ancient Roman basilica would have been unthinkable but is indicative of just how far we have come.

SPIRITUALITY

Deeply steeped in Benedictine foundations, Anglican spirituality has much
to offer Roman Catholics. In the eleventh and twelfth centuries Benedictine
monasteries rapidly increased in England, and towns and villages formed around
them. The daily order was structured around the hinges of morning and
evening prayer and reinforced with the minor liturgical hours, culminating in
the eucharistic celebration.[23] From the thirteenth century, however, the parish
church began to replace the monastery as spiritual centre of the English people,
even as the monastic tradition continued to flourish. When the monasteries were
destroyed at the Reformation, Archbishop Thomas Cranmer carried forth their
rich tradition of daily common prayer by including the Morning and Evening
Offices in The Book of Common Prayer, along with a service of the Sunday
Eucharist.[24]

The evangelical revival of the eighteenth century helped Anglicans to link their
own personal spirituality and search for holiness with special care for the poor
and destitute.[25] In turn, in the nineteenth century, the Oxford Movement gave
impetus to the mystical and spiritual dimensions of Christianity within a strongly
Anglo-Catholic framework. Led by John Henry Newman, Edward Pusey, John
Keble, and others, the movement emphasized the sacramental life of the church,
especially the centrality of the Eucharist.[26]

The excellent volume on Anglican spirituality, *Love's Redeeming Work: The
Anglican Quest for Holiness*, compiled by three bishops—Geoffrey Rowell, Kenneth Stevenson, and Rowan Williams,[27] captures in its subtitle what lies at
the heart of Anglican spirituality. That was what drew believers to English
monasteries in the Middle Ages and then to cathedrals and parish churches. It
is also what inflamed the evangelical revival of the eighteenth century and the
Oxford Movement of the nineteenth. This Anglican quest for holiness is a gift
from which Roman Catholics could greatly benefit. It would be enough to think
of the Anglican contribution to the integration between poetry and spirituality
thanks to the work of John Donne and George Herbert, to name but two.

Within contemporary Anglicanism, a particularly rich contribution to spirituality has been made through the person and writings of the current Archbishop of
Canterbury, Dr Rowan Williams. In a conference entitled 'Shaping Holy Lives',
given at Holy Trinity, Wall Street, New York in April 2003, he spoke about
transparency, honesty, and peacemaking as hallmarks of Benedictine spirituality
which offer a deeper invitation to the whole church:

The community that freely promises to live together before God is one in which both
truthfulness and respect are enshrined. I promise that I will not hide from you—and that
I will also at times help you not to hide from me or from yourself. I promise that your
growth towards what the good God wants for you will be a wholly natural and obvious
priority for me; and I trust that you have made the same promise...But how often do

we understand the promises of baptism as bringing us into this sort of group? How often do we think that the Church is a natural sort of place for honesty, where we need not be afraid?[28]

More recently, in an address to the 'Third Annual Global South to South Encounter' in Ain al Sukhna, Egypt, the Archbishop spoke eloquently of holiness as the church lives out its worship in daily life:

Our holiness takes us where Jesus goes; our holiness takes us to those Jesus died for; it takes us into the neighbourhood of those who are forgotten, who have no voice; those who need healing and forgiveness. It takes us into very strange places indeed, and the holy person, as we all know, is often found in very odd company.

Similarly:

A holy church is one that...stands alongside those who live with the scourge of HIV/AIDS; a holy church is a church that labours...alongside those who have been made homeless or bereaved by natural disaster...A holy church...is a church which will go into the heart of the city and sit with the homeless and the addicts and the destitute.[29]

Those comments of the Archbishop of Canterbury remind us that the holiness of the church is deeply bound up with its mission within the world—washing the feet of others and doing as Christ would have us do. Today, there are many areas of social outreach and mission where the Anglican Communion is seriously engaged around the world, and, thanks to the impetus of IARCCUM, much of this work is increasingly done through bilateral ecumenical commissions or jointly encouraged there. During the last week of June 2005, Anglican and Roman Catholic Bishops in Sudan organized an ecumenical meeting in Mukono, Uganda that gathered together Sudanese church leaders on the topic 'Building Peace in Sudan Through United Church Leadership'. At the end of that week they issued a joint pastoral letter entitled 'May They All Be One' making a plea for the overcoming of ethnic divisions and discrimination in Sudanese society.

Such an ecumenical initiative in Africa could not have happened were it not for the bonds of affection and the close working relationship that have grown over the years between Anglican and Roman Catholic bishops there in Sudan. But it is precisely that sort of ecumenical collaboration on a daily basis that enables our common quest for holiness to be pursued in efforts of common mission, in which our churches speak out prophetically with one voice as the Body of Christ within the world.

A further aspect of the church's mission within the world involves its capacity for dialogue with other religious traditions, and, once again, the Anglican Communion offers us a great example here, especially in the initiative of the former Archbishop of Canterbury, Dr George Carey, to open an ongoing dialogue with

Muslims. Appropriately called 'Building Bridges', this initiative has been carried forth by the current Archbishop of Canterbury and, each Spring, Christian and Muslim scholars gather together at the Jesuit University of Georgetown in Washington, DC for their deliberations. The depth of commitment among those who are involved in that dialogue is already beginning to bear fruit in terms of increased Muslim and Christian scholarly collaboration. It is instinctual for Anglicans to think to include scholars who are not Anglican, so that Christians of different churches can work together on the dialogue and can also be seen by the dialogue partners as working together.

CONCLUSION

Walking the pilgrim path towards the reign of God involves genuine faith that is lived out in action along the road. Together, we participate in the life of the one God whose mission within the world is to draw all people into a graced communion of love. And together we are compelled to give common witness to the Gospel not through our division but through the unity that we already share in Christ thanks to the grace of baptism. Thus, what we can do together we must do together, as Christ would have us do. This is not one option among the many choices we are offered within our respective ecclesial traditions. Rather, it is a Gospel imperative, 'that they may all be one'.[30] The pilgrim path always begins in humility and trust, believing that the God who has led us to this point is faithful and will lead us forth toward the unity for which we long. As we seek a way forward, there is much that we can learn from one another's churches and there is much that we can do in the concrete visibly to express our common faith in Jesus Christ.

Whatever we can accomplish together always begins in prayer, and we need to be gathering together for common prayer much more frequently than we are doing at present. Common blessing of palms to inaugurate Holy Week ecumenically, common Evening Prayer, joint processions, pilgrimages, and retreats all offer viable options for a greater ecumenical exchange of gifts between Anglicans and Roman Catholics.

During the Sunday Eucharist, it would be a further powerful symbol of our desire for unity if Anglican and Roman Catholic communities were to pray for the diocesan bishop of the other church in the Prayers of the People, and even for the Archbishop of Canterbury in Roman Catholic parishes and for the Pope in Anglican churches. As in Sudan, Anglican and Roman Catholic bishops in other parts of the world are beginning to issue pastoral letters in common so that the same message is being communicated ecumenically to those who live in the same geographical area.

In the area of theological, liturgical, spiritual formation, Anglicans and Roman Catholics could benefit greatly from joint lectures, study days, seminars, and conferences, whether as inter-parish initiatives or on the diocesan level.

Finally, there is tremendous room for collaboration on projects of social outreach and mission: care for immigrants and the homeless, the sick and the elderly; finding a common voice in speaking out against world hunger and other injustices within human society; combining efforts in the struggle against HIV/AIDS and in offering assistance to those living with that disease. Greater fidelity and commitment to common prayer and works of justice between Anglicans and Roman Catholics might actually begin to transform the way we think and act—the way we view our respective churches in relation to the world. And that more intentional commitment to such an ecumenical pilgrimage might even lead us to believe deep within our hearts that what unites us is, in fact, infinitely greater than what divides us.

NOTES

1. See Keith Pecklers, 'Il pellegrinaggio cristiano: ritorno alle sorgenti della grazia', *Ecclesia Orans*, 16 (1999), 101–7.
2. *UUS*, § 11; also §§ 12–13.
3. *UUS*, § 28; cf. Chapter 2: Margaret O'Gara, 'Receiving Gifts in Ecumenical Dialogue'.
4. ARCIC, *The Final Report* (London: SPCK/CTS, 1982), 8.
5. ARCIC II, *The Church as Communion: An Agreed Statement by the Second Anglican–Roman Catholic International Commission* (London: Church House Publishing/CTS, 1991), available at <http://www.prounione.urbe.it/dia-int/arcic/doc/e_arcicII_communion.html>; cf. Sagovsky, *Ecumenism, Christian Origins and the Practice of Communion* (Cambridge: Cambridge University Press, 2000), 21.
6. *Church as Communion*, § 4.
7. Ibid., § 22.
8. Anglican Communion News Service (ACNS), 3314, 'Statement from the Archbishop of Canterbury and the Cardinal Archbishop of Westminster' (20 Feb. 2003), available at <http://www.anglicancommunion.org/acns/news.cfm/2003/2/20/ACNS3314>.
9. 'Authority in the Church I' (1976); 'Authority in the Church: Elucidation' (1981); and 'Authority in the Church II' (1981), all in ARCIC, *The Final Report*, 49–67, 68–78, 81–98; also ARCIC II, *The Gift of Authority: Authority in the Church III* (London: Church House Publishing/CTS, 1999), available at <http://www.vatican.va/roman_curia/pontifical_councils/chrstuni/documents/rc_pc_chrstuni_doc_12051999_gift-of-autority_en.html>.
10. *The Final Report*, 50.
11. *The Gift of Authority*, § 56.
12. Ibid., § 57.

13. See Chapter 16: Paul Lakeland, 'Potential Catholic Learning Around Lay Participation in Decision-making'.

14. See Michael J. Buckley, *Papal Primacy and the Episcopate: Towards a Relational Understanding* (New York: Crossroad/Herder, 1998); John R. Quinn, *The Reform of the Papacy: The Costly Call to Christian Unity* (New York: Crossroad/Herder, 1999).

15. The Lambeth Commission on Communion, *The Windsor Report, 2004* (London: Anglican Communion Office, 2004), available at <http://www.aco.org/windsor2004/downloads/windsor2004full.pdf>, § 97, citing The Inter-Anglican Theological and Doctrinal Commission, *The Virginia Report* (Harrisburg, Pa: Morehouse, 1999), 42, available at <http://www.lambethconference.org/1998/documents/report-1.pdf>.

16. See 'Cardinal Walter Kasper's Message to the 13th Anglican Consultative Council Meeting' (18 June 2005), *Information Service*, 119 (2005), 101.

17. See Pecklers, *Dynamic Equivalence: The Living Language of Christian Worship* (Collegeville, Minn.: Liturgical Press, 2003), 127–69.

18. H. Boone Porter, 'Hispanic Influences on Worship in the English Tongue', in J. Neil Alexander (ed.), *Time and Community: in Honor of Thomas J. Talley* (Washington, DC: Pastoral Press, 1990), 171–84.

19. Hebert, *Liturgy and Society: The Function of the Church in the Modern World* (London: Faber & Faber, 1935).

20. *Common Worship: Services and Prayers for the Church of England* (London: Church House Publishing, 2000).

21. Donald Gray, 'Ecumenical Liturgical Cooperation—Past, Present and Future', *Studia Liturgica*, 28 (1998), 241.

22. Eucharistic Prayer G, *Common Worship*, 201–3.

23. Mark Pellew (ed.), *Anglicanism and the Western Christian Tradition: Continuity and Change* (Guide to the Anglican Exhibition at the Vatican Museums in 2002) (Norwich: Jarrold Publishing, 2002), 6–7.

24. Ibid. 5, 7.

25. Ibid. 15.

26. See Christopher Dawson, *The Spirit of the Oxford Movement* (London: Saint Austin Press, 2001).

27. Rowell, Stevenson, Williams (eds.), *Love's Redeeming Work: The Anglican Quest for Holiness* (Oxford: Oxford University Press, 2001).

28. Williams, Rowan, 'Shaping Holy Lives: A Conference on Benedictine Spirituality' (29 Apr. 2003), n.p.; see also his lecture 'Saint Benedict and the Future of Europe' (S.' Anselmo, Rome, 21 Nov. 2006), *Tablet* (25 Nov. 2006), 8–11, also available at <http://www.archbishopofcanterbury.org/657>.

29. 'One Holy Catholic and Apostolic Church' (28 Oct. 2005), available at <http://www.archbishopofcanterbury.org/965>.

30. John 17: 21.

9

Receptive Catholic Learning Through Methodist–Catholic Dialogue

Michael E. Putney

INTRODUCTION

For his year 2000 Père Marquette Lecture in Theology, Geoffrey Wainwright took as his topic 'Is the Reformation Over?'.[1] He identified five different ways in which one could press this claim, evocatively captured in the following questions: (1) Has the Catholic Church turned Protestant? (2) Has Protestantism poped? (3) Were they mere misunderstandings? (4) Does doctrine (still) matter? (5) Are matters now settled? Or, less provocatively expressed:

The idea might be that the Roman Catholic Church has now, for good or ill, accepted the proposals by which Luther launched the Reformation. Alternatively, it could be...that Protestant truth has sold out to Rome, or...that Protestantism is on the point of being welcomed back into the Catholic fold. A third, and more irenical possibility, would be that the unfortunate mutual 'misunderstandings' of the sixteenth century have at last been cleared up. Or again, the sixteenth-century controversies may be thought...to have since become irrelevant or at least no longer church-dividing. Fifth and finally, it might be considered that genuine and substantial differences, which were insoluble when they first arose, can now be reconciled and overcome through the discovery of new insights...or...the recovery of more original perceptions that anti-date the Reformation.[2]

None of these proposals would justify the claim that the Reformation is completely over but each of them affords a way of reviewing developments in the state of ecumenical relationships since the Catholic Church officially embraced the ecumenical movement at the Second Vatican Council. As to why none of them could claim a complete resolution of Reformation divisions, Wainwright concluded that the most basic and comprehensive issue still needing to be dealt with was 'the nature, identity and location of the church, the question of fundamental ecclesiology'.[3]

Related to this, I would suggest that for as long as our starting-point is our historical relationship with each other as brought about by the Reformation, then we will never be able to answer definitively questions such as 'Is the Reformation over?' or 'Are our divided churches finally able to accept each other in the embrace of full communion?' The desired reconciliation will never be achieved simply by looking back or looking at each other as divided. In contrast, I believe that Pope John Paul II's description of dialogue as 'not simply an exchange of ideas', but as in some ways 'always an "exchange of gifts"' (*UUS*, § 28) gives us a new starting-point for describing our present relationships and thereby indicates a possible way to future reconciliation.

Further, this exchange of gifts should not be viewed thinly in terms of some potentially enriching ecclesial practices or elements which might simply be added on to the fundamental gift of deepened understanding that should always occur through dialogue. Obviously, such a practical exchange does already occur. We receive from each other not just new insights into the Gospel but even new ways of perceiving ourselves or the way in which we and others stand within the apostolic tradition. One startling example of this occurred through the dialogue between the Catholic Church and the Assyrian Church of the East which led to the recognition of the latter's Eucharist despite its lacking an explicit proclamation of the words of institution.[4] Again, other very practical changes occur because of our ecumenical engagement. One need only think, for example, of the biblical and liturgical renewals that have been shared between Christian communions. However, the exchange of gifts to which Pope John Paul II referred, developing the teaching of Pope Paul VI in his 1964 encyclical *Ecclesiam Suam*, describes a more profound exchange and deeper relationship than the practical alone. It is the nature of this more profound exchange that I would like to explore.[5]

DIALOGUE, EXCHANGE, AND DEEPENED COMMUNION IN CHRIST

In a 1970 document of the then Secretariat for Promoting Christian Unity, it was presumed that 'those who take part [in ecumenical dialogue] recognise one another as existing in Christ' and so are able 'through the Holy Spirit to hear their brethren tell them of the marvellous works of God' and to recognize 'a certain communion' existing between them.[6] The document could then speak of dialogue leading not just to the discovery of truths held in common, or truths which have been obscured because of separation, but also the discovery of new insights indicative of the unique, divinely grounded fruitfulness of the relationship of dialogue.[7]

In a more recent document produced by the Joint Working Group between the Roman Catholic Church and the World Council of Churches, one reads:

Dialogue entails walking with the other; pilgrimage is an apt metaphor...Dialogue represents a word—neither the first nor the last—on a common journey, marking a moment between the 'already' of our past histories and the 'not yet' of our future. It images the disciples' conversation on the road to Emmaus, recounting the wonders the Lord has worked during a journey culminating in the recognition of the Lord in the breaking of bread at a common table.[8]

Dialogue, then, looks not only to the past but also to the future. It is always a process of discovery of the divine presence and activity in the other and so always opens each partner to receiving a new gift from the Lord.

I draw attention to these texts because they point to a way of viewing dialogue which starts from the common participation of the dialogue partners in Christ, their common sharing in the leading of the Holy Spirit, and their communion in the very life of the Triune God. If one perceives this deeper relationship as occurring not only for individuals but also for ecclesial communities, and if one believes that anyone or any communion living in Christ will be drawn by Christ toward the full realization of his will for their ecclesial identity, then one can look at Christian communions that may have been divided over many centuries of acrimony with the eyes of a faith that makes one expectant of discovering in them some version of all of those elements which one believes Christ wills for his church and which one believes are found in one's own ecclesial communion. Indeed, one can look at them in the faith-filled expectation that some aspects of the full richness of the church of Christ may be more evident in other communions than in one's own.

This positive and hope-filled perception of inter-ecclesial relationships has only become possible because of the new context created by the ecumenical movement, which can itself be seen as a movement of conversion. In this perspective, ecclesial communities grow towards each other as they grow closer to Christ. Already having some level of relationship with each other through their common immersion into Christ and so into the life of the Triune God, they are drawn to reclaim their relationship with each other in him and to discover the developments within each other which have occurred both because of him and because of the Spirit who was sent by the Father to remind all his followers of what he has said. This 'living memory' of the church, which is the Holy Spirit, is a living memory that has existed in different communions. Because it is the memory of the same Christ, and it is the same Spirit who is keeping it alive, what each communion which strives to be faithful will grow to understand and endeavour to put into practice will be the same gospel, the same apostolic tradition, and the same requirements for the full realization of the church of Christ.

In other words, contemporary dialogue between Christian communions involves a process of discovering in the other what the Holy Spirit has done to conform them to Christ and his wishes for the church. The exchange of gifts then becomes an exchange not just of other insights, other ways of living the Gospel, and other ways of remaining faithful to those which have developed in one's own communion. Beyond all of this, it can also involve an exchange of those gifts which are yet to develop as fully in one's own communion or which may be present only very embryonically but yet belong to Christ's vision for his church.

METHODIST–CATHOLIC DIALOGUE—A CASE IN POINT

To look specifically at the Methodist–Catholic dialogue over the past forty years is to discover a very good illustration of this way of seeing the relationship between divided Christians and the potential for a new way of reconciling them. In the opening chapter of *The Grace Given You in Christ*, the latest report of the Methodist–Catholic dialogue, an attempt is made to explore the new context which exists for a mutual reassessment by Methodists and Catholics.[9] Such a reassessment needs to include a new understanding of the past which would not only be guided by contemporary historical research but would also be the result of the openness created through decades of dialogue, collaboration, and prayer. The report contains the following key insights:

Neither Methodists nor Catholics should regard their separation as acceptable. Some may believe that certain separations were necessary in the past for the sake of the Gospel. Others may view all separations as failures...which have obscured the unity of Christ's church. In 2003 the Archbishop of Canterbury said of the divided histories of the Church of England and the Methodist Church of Great Britain, 'Wesley came to the point where he believed that he and his followers could only be fully obedient to Jesus Christ if they took the risk of separation. No-one can easily pass judgement on this costly decision, and no-one is seeking to do so; what we can be sure of is that by God's direction it bore fruit in witness and transforming service to the Kingdom of God in this nation and far beyond.' Similarly, the separate histories of Methodism and the Roman Catholic Church can show how God has worked in both of them for the fulfilment of the divine purpose...(§ 13)

Later, taking up a reflection of Pope John Paul II, it continues:

The separations of the last five hundred years cannot simply be condoned even if they cannot simply be condemned and blame apportioned. Reflecting on why the Holy Spirit had permitted all the divisions between Christians, Pope John Paul II noted: 'Could it not be that these divisions have been a path continually leading the Church to discover the untold wealth contained in Christ's Gospel and in the redemption accomplished by Christ? Perhaps all this wealth would not have come to light otherwise...'[10]

In the light of this, *The Grace Given You in Christ* continues:

A review of past history suggests that God has led each of our churches in new ways that came through the separations. Catholics can recognise that God has used Methodism, both in its beginning and throughout its history, to develop gifts which eventually ought to bless all Christians everywhere. Similarly, Methodists can recognise that God has been at work in the Catholic Church's preservation of important traditions and in its pursuit of fresh presentations of the Gospel for the benefit of all Christian believers.

The most recent phase of the dialogue has in fact endeavoured to harvest the work of previous phases and, in the light of what has been achieved, to deepen and extend the recognition that each communion is able to offer the other. A deliberate attempt has been made to describe the elements of each communion which represent to the others' eyes, genuine elements of the church of Christ. This recognition cannot at this point in history be complete. It is, nevertheless, of an extraordinary depth and breadth which none would have imagined even a few decades ago. We are each able to acknowledge that the relationship is radically different from that which existed when the dialogue began and can now speak easily of the gifts we have received and hope still to receive.

Of course, one properly faces here the obvious fact that all members of the communion do not share this new level of mutual recognition. This is a practical problem which confronts all dialogues and which always needs to be dealt with by both partners: how the different levels of the church, its leaders, theologians, ordinary women and men can all move together through increasing levels of relationship and mutual recognition.

In this regard, in *The Grace Given You in Christ* it is acknowledged that there are some core elements of each communion that are equally precious to both, such as the quest for holiness, the commitment to mission and the recognition that life in Christ is one lived in communion or 'connexion'. In addition, of course, both communions share a fundamental Trinitarian faith and a fundamental centring on the person of Jesus Christ, the Word Incarnate. We recognize too that in regard to the Reformation controversy concerning cooperation with God's grace, Catholics and Methodists are largely of one mind. This became obvious in Seoul in 2006 when Lutherans and Catholics were able to sign a new agreement concerning Justification with the World Methodist Council. On these points at least, if full communion were to be restored between Methodists and Catholics, far from this diminishing or even challenging respective identities, it would serve only to enhance these fundamental characteristics of ecclesial life which are already so central to each communion.

Equally, beyond these points already held in common, it is acknowledged that there are also gifts to be exchanged which can only be received through this new relationship. On the one hand, Catholics should be able to see that there are elements that the Holy Spirit has led Methodists to grasp in ways that are exemplary for all communions. Examples explored in *The Grace Given You in*

Christ and also treated very fully in the 2001 Brighton Report are the Methodist understanding of lay ministry based on baptism and of the priesthood of all believers.[11] This leads Methodists in practice to give laypeople a very significant place in ecclesial governance. On the other hand, there is the Catholic understanding of ordination as a sacrament and its sacramental understanding of the ministry, authority, and ecclesial significance of those who are ordained. What could cause a certain polarization between Methodists and Catholics, with the priesthood and authority of the ordained being defended over against the priesthood and authority of the faithful can, it is hoped, become in a mutual exchange of gifts an enrichment to both. In one sense, this could be an example of a 'clash' of gifts, or an exchange of gifts which requires that one gift be adjusted in order to make room for the other to be received.

Again, in dialogue over the decades both parties have come to describe the particular attributes and dimensions of the church to which they have steadfastly adhered in language increasingly acceptable to the other party because there is no longer any need to define them over against the other. In this redefinition, which takes place continually in ecumenical dialogue, the true gift which was perhaps hidden by polemical language over the centuries begins to emerge and can be welcomed, although not uncritically, by the other as indeed a gift of the Spirit. This takes time, a long time, and when there is an apparent 'clash' in the gifts themselves dialogue over time is the only way forward. As the true character of the other's gift emerges, it should threaten less and less the gift being offered in turn. It may well be that it is only through such dialogue that the Holy Spirit can lead each of us to recognize the limitations in our current interpretations of our respective gifts and so to corresponding possible adaptations in our ecclesial lives which may have appeared unthinkable some decades ago or only as a capitulation to the different or opposed other. In contrast, at this point such an adaptation may rather be seen as the proper adjustment necessary for the reception of a gift from God through the other.

Lest the contrary should be assumed, however, it should be noted that this process does not require that an element which Catholics recognize to be more developed in Methodism than in their own communion ought, therefore, simply to be adopted on the automatic assumption that it is necessarily a work of the Spirit. Likewise, there are many gifts which the Catholic Church would like to offer Methodism which Methodism may, despite forty years of dialogue, still find hard to recognize as unalloyed gifts. For its own part, the particular gift of lay participation in ecclesial governance and, hence, in authoritative decision-making, is a gift which the Catholic Church would discern very carefully given its own understanding of the unique role of the ordained ministry. But, precisely because of this dialogue, it is called before God to do this discerning. Fellow Christians have, in Christ, asked us to do so. I do not wish to discuss this question in detail here but there are many elements which could be brought into the discussion, such as various examples in the history of the undivided church and the consultative bodies called for by Second Vatican Council, the significance of which is undermined when they are described as 'only' or 'just' consultative.

This remains a question for further dialogue: a dialogue based on the positive premiss of seeking to find the gift hidden within the Christian experience of another communion which may at first sight appear as unacceptable but which can emerge through the unveiling that takes place in dialogue as a gift which comes from Christ and is meant for all. When this happens, the receiving party will normally have already found within itself some traces of the gift in question precisely because it is integral to Christ's wishes for the church; or, at least, a 'space' or lack within their own ecclesial experience which requires such a gift to fill it and complete it.

Reflecting such a spirit, in *The Grace Given You in Christ*, the Methodist participants were able to say the following concerning gifts they were increasingly open to receiving from the Catholic Church: 'At a basic level, the diversity in unity of the Roman Catholic Church is one such element; another is its concrete expression of the universality of the Church.' And, specifically, 'Whilst treasuring the Wesleyan emphasis on the sacrament of the Lord's Supper, Methodists would benefit from a more developed theology of the Eucharist, such as can be found in Roman Catholic teaching.' (§ 111) They also identified some Catholic devotions which they might be willing to adopt in the future and even addressed the question of 'veneration of Mary . . . subject to continuing dialogue about the later Marian dogmas' (§ 111). More generally, they added: 'Greater awareness of the communion of the saints and the Church's continuity in time, the sacramental use of material things and sacramental ministry to the sick and dying are also ecclesial elements and endowments that Methodists might profitably receive from Roman Catholics.' Again, after acknowledging a renewed appreciation of the whole of Church history rather than only those extraordinary moments when they perceived the Holy Spirit as acting, they were able to make the following comments about episcopacy:

Accordingly, Methodists acknowledge the episcopal college and the historic succession of bishops within the Roman Catholic Church to be a sign (though not necessarily a guarantee) of the unity of the Church in space and time . . . Historically, *episcopé* in Methodism has mostly been exercised corporately, even in those parts of the world where Methodism is endowed with bishops. However, Methodists increasingly recognise the value of *episcopé* properly exercised by individuals within the context of a collegial ministry of oversight. Thus Methodists are open to receiving from Roman Catholics fresh insights into the exercise of individual forms of *episcopé* for the building up of the Body of Christ. (§ 112)

Finally, they were able to express openness to the gift of the ministry of the Bishop of Rome:

Methodists around the world responded positively to Pope John Paul II's invitation to engage in dialogue about the exercise of the Petrine ministry of the Bishop of Rome (*UUS*, 96). In the light of the present crisis of authority in the Christian Church, Methodists may come to value a Petrine ministry at the service of unity. In particular, with proper safeguards, Methodists may be prepared to receive a Petrine ministry exercised collegially within the college of bishops as a final decision-making authority in the Church, at least insofar as essential matters of faith are concerned. (§ 113)

In turn, Methodists hoped that Catholics might be able to welcome some of their ecclesial elements and endowments as gifts to be received with thanksgiving. They began by inviting Roman Catholics to consider 'how their own appreciation of the spiritual gifts bestowed upon lay people may be informed by Methodism's fruitful experience of the spiritual empowerment of lay people for ministry and mission' (§ 115). They then focused specifically on the ministry of women who in the movement's early years and again more recently, 'have made a full contribution to the mission and ministry of Methodism' (§ 116). So it is that Methodists 'do not restrict any ministry or office in the Church to either men or women, believing that to do so would be contrary to God's will as they discern it in obedience to the Scriptures'. With this, they invited Roman Catholics to consider 'how the Methodist experience and practice of ordained ministry might contribute to their own understanding of the Church's ministry' (§ 116). In the light of their own flexible and pragmatic approach towards ecclesial structures borne out of their commitment to mission, they also invited Roman Catholics to consider 'how greater flexibility and pragmatism might enhance their own missionary activity' (§ 117). Again, alongside these more ecclesiological elements, the Methodists also focused on the characteristic spiritual gifts of their tradition:

[A] significant feature of the historic mission of Methodism has been an emphasis on the crucial importance of personal experience of Jesus Christ and his redeeming love. However else it may be described, the Church is a community of Christians whose personal experience of Jesus Christ compels them to join with other Christians in worship, fellowship, mission and service in the world. Methodists invite Roman Catholics to consider how this same emphasis, and the forms that it takes, might contribute to their own pastoral ministry and mission. (§ 118)

In turn, after reflecting on the consequences of their own commitment to Christian unity, they asked of Catholics whether their commitment to ecumenism might influence 'their own understanding of their particular identity, and their willingness to distinguish between what is essential and what is changeable' (§ 119). From this they went on to discuss their own 'characteristic ethos in worship and spirituality' and concluded by inviting Roman Catholics to consider how these same ecclesial elements and endowments might enhance their own worship and spirituality. Given that these gifts and, likewise, those being offered by Catholics to Methodists would not all be recognized easily or by all as truly gifts of Christ, it is fair to say that the agenda for future dialogue has come to clear definition in *The Grace Given You in Christ*.

THE WESLEYS, HOLINESS, AND CONNEXIONALISM

One gift of Methodism which stands out for me from my ten years' experience in this dialogue is the gift of John and Charles Wesley themselves. They were extraordinary Christian men. In speaking of them and of the Methodist movement in his homily at Ponte Sant'Angelo Methodist Church in Rome on 22 June 2003, in a celebration to mark the 300th anniversary of the birth of John Wesley, Cardinal Kasper spoke of their being 'characterised by a desire to make known the love of Christ, to reform the inner life of the church, to encourage participation in the celebration of the Eucharist, to foster Christian education, to serve the poor, to impassion professed Christians into articulate witness for Christ's sake'.[12] In that same homily he compared the imprint that John Wesley left on Methodism to that of St Ignatius on the Jesuits and went on to say: 'In like manner, just as you continue to turn to the ministry of John Wesley for inspiration and guidance, we can look to see and find in him the evangelical zeal, the pursuit of holiness, the concern for the poor; the virtues and goodness which we have come to know and respect in you.'[13] Later that year, a letter from Cardinal Kasper was read during the liturgy marking the 225th anniversary of Wesley's Chapel, City Road, London. In that letter he explained that by means of his homily at Ponte Sant'Angelo he had hoped to contribute to a Catholic 'reassessment' of Wesley. He saw this reassessment as rich with possibilities given the new context created by the Methodist–Catholic dialogue.[14]

Were John and Charles Wesley members of the Catholic Church, they would certainly be on the list of those whose causes would be put forward for canonization. I look forward to a day when in the Litany of the Saints in the ordination ceremony of a bishop we would sing together 'Saints John and Charles Wesley, pray for us'. One can rejoice also in the hymns that flowed from their pens, especially that of Charles, which have already enriched the Catholic communion and certainly challenged it to accept the gift not just of these hymns, but of hymn singing itself as a form of prayer and spiritual enrichment which has clearly proved its worth in the Methodist tradition. Of these hymns, Cardinal Kasper said in the message referred to, that they have been the means for members of the Catholic Church to discover some of the insights of John and Charles Wesley into the call to holiness.[15]

Linked to this, Methodists believe that holiness is the basis for the church's unity and communion. Methodism emerged because of the desire in the hearts of

John and Charles Wesley and others to preach scriptural holiness to the people of England and Ireland and in a special way to poor working men and women. Indeed, Methodism was primarily a renewal movement within the Church of England which sought to foster social and personal holiness in response to the proclamation of the Gospel. It grew apart from the Church of England without major conflict over the Gospel or the faith but, positively speaking, because of this commitment to evangelism and holiness.

Just as the Church of England in that day, so the Catholic Church today, needs to ask itself how true it is to claim that holiness is a major pastoral goal for the preaching of its clergy and the pastoral life of its parishes? There have been and still are many like John and Charles Wesley within the Catholic Church who endeavour to make these the church's priorities. The Methodist communion bears this gift in abundance, and the Catholic Church would be blessed enormously were it to receive it.

In this regard, one of my major learnings from ten years of dialogue with the Methodist Church is the discovery of the fundamental difference between Catholic and Methodist understandings of the holiness of the church. What is true of Methodists would also be true of many other Christians. Catholics are determined to protect the holiness of the church from those who would say the church itself is sinful. They distinguish between the church as the Body and Sacrament of Christ which cannot but be holy and the holiness or sinfulness of its members.[16]

Other Christians do not always make this distinction because of the evidence of sinfulness and distortion or corruption which they perceive at all levels and in all aspects of the church, including its teaching. Their fundamental commitment to reform or renewal seeks to change this and to bring genuine holiness to every aspect of the church's life. There is also a reluctance to canonize any structure, aspect, or teaching of the church because of the frailty, fallibility, and sinfulness of the human members of the church who are responsible for what it does or says. The Catholic principle—which relies on the certainty of the divine presence and activity in sacraments, teaching, and ministerial activity on account of the church being the Sacrament of Christ's presence and activity in the world—can too easily lead to a neglect of the human contribution which can distort as well as enhance the communication of the divine presence and activity.

The emphasis in *Lumen Gentium* on the universal call to holiness (*LG*, § 8) and the recognition that the church is holy but always in need of purification and renewal (*LG*, § 39–42) are very important insights for the church which are, as yet, insufficiently explored for their potential to bring about a change in priorities for the Catholic Church. The emphasis in the ministry of Pope John Paul II upon the witness of saints and martyrs and their authority is also a sign of a Catholic reaffirmation of the fundamental call to holiness. The gift of Methodism and other Christian churches may be both a rediscovery of holiness as an essential mark of the church and an admission that no matter how holy the teaching, sacraments, and ministerial structures of the church, they are inadequate without a constant renewal by the Holy Spirit bringing genuine scriptural holiness into all aspects of the church's life.

Finally, a gift of enormous importance for the Catholic Church as it grows in an ecclesial spirituality of communion is the Methodist experience of always 'living in connexion', and hence of ensuring that structures of communion are such that pastors and people, congregations and larger regions, all people on every level of ecclesial life take each other into consideration and actually care about each other, seek each other's wisdom and serve each other's needs. Methodists obviously do this imperfectly but they have structures which ensure that communion is lived and not just loved. Catholics have a beautiful rhetoric about communion, collegiality, participation, and collaboration which is variously realized in the daily life of the church. For their own part, Methodists have a practice of connexion or communion which challenges Catholics the more fully to live what they confess. It would be a worthy gift indeed if Methodists were to help Catholics to establish other structures of collaboration and mutual accountability which ensured that communion was much more than an ideal on every level of the church's life and in every place.

CONCLUSION

It is easier to recognize the validity and the value of an exchange of gifts when one is talking about such gifts of renewal or new theological insights, as are the regular fruit of dialogue. It becomes harder, however, when one speaks of the way a church structures its ministry and the way in which authority is exercised in a communion, or the doctrinal weight that a church gives to some of its teachings which may not be part of the teaching of another Christian communion. There can be no rushing this particular process of learning, receiving, and giving. Nor should there be any delay. It cannot be carried out by theologians and church leaders alone but must draw upon the experience of ordinary men and women of each communion who live the life of Christ daily in ordinary human situations and therefore test the authenticity of the claims of theologians and church leaders about what Christ wills for his church. At the same time, this is always undertaken in the hope that Christ who dwells in each communion is drawing each to grow more like his vision for his one church and that our task is to seek him in the other and so to discover the gifts that he has in store for us, if only we can finally see.

NOTES

1. See Wainwright, *Is the Reformation Over? Catholics and Protestants at the Turn of the Millennia* (Milwaukee, Wis.: Marquette University Press, 2000).
2. Ibid. 9–10.
3. Ibid. 61.
4. See Robert F. Taft, 'Mass Without the Consecration? The Historic Agreement on the Eucharist Between the Catholic Church and the Assyrian Church of the East, Promulgated 26 October 2001', in James F. Puglisi (ed.), *Liturgical Renewal as a Way to Christian Unity* (Collegeville, Minn.: Liturgical Press, 2005), 199–226.
5. See Paul VI, '*Ecclesiam Suam*: Encyclical Letter on the Church in the Modern World' (6 Aug. 1964) (London: CTS, 1979), particularly §§ 78–85.
6. Secretariat for Promoting Christian Unity, 'Reflections and Suggestions Concerning Dialogue' (15 Aug. 1970), in Austin Flannery (ed.), *Vatican Council II: The Conciliar and Post Conciliar Documents* (Leominster: Fowler Wright, 1980), 543.
7. Ibid. 547–8.
8. 'The Nature and Purpose of Ecumenical Dialogue: A JWG Study', in *Eighth Report, 1999–2005* (Geneva and Rome: WCC, 2005), 76, available at <http://www.oikoumene.org/fileadmin/files/wcc-main/documents/p1/8thjointworkinggroup.pdf>.
9. The Joint International Commission for Dialogue Between the World Methodist Council and the Roman Catholic Church, *The Grace Given You in Christ: Catholics and Methodists Reflect Further on the Church* (Lake Junaluska, NC: World Methodist Council, 2006).
10. Ibid., § 14, citing Pope John Paul II, *Crossing the Threshold of Hope*, ed. Vittorio Messori, trans. Jenny McPhee and Martha McPhee (London: Jonathan Cape, 1994), 153.
11. *Speaking the Truth in Love: Teaching Authority Among Catholics and Methodists* (Lake Junaluska: World Methodist Council, 2001).
12. 'The 300th Anniversary of the Birth of John Wesley: Cardinal Kasper's Statements', *Information Service*, 114 (2003), 184.
13. Ibid.
14. Ibid. 185.
15. Ibid.
16. See Karl Rahner, 'The Church of Sinners' (1947), *Theological Investigations*, vol. vi., trans. Karl-H. Kruger and Boniface Kruger (London: Darton, Longman & Todd, 1969), 253–69; id., 'The Sinful Church in the Decrees of Vatican II' (1965), ibid. 270–94.

10

A Methodist Perspective on Catholic Learning

David M. Chapman

INTRODUCTION

Central to Margaret O'Gara's contribution to this volume is reflection on and development of the motif affirmed by Pope John Paul II when he declared: 'Dialogue is not simply an exchange of ideas. In some way it is always an "exchange of gifts".'[1] This chapter, accordingly, explores the subject of Catholic Learning from a Methodist perspective, identifying a number of characteristic Methodist ecclesial endowments from which Catholics might fruitfully receive. Whilst, of course, Catholics likewise possess distinct gifts which Methodists might fruitfully receive, limitations of space and the specific focus of this volume prevent extensive treatment of these here.[2]

That said, the assumed principle throughout is that just such a mutual exchange of gifts between Catholics and Methodists is an essential step in achieving the goal of our full communion in faith, mission, and sacramental life; an exchange, moreover, that needs to preserve all the specific endowments that Catholics and Methodists respectively possess since 'we dare not lose any of the gifts with which the Holy Spirit has endowed our communities in their separation'.[3] Further, precisely because their source is believed to be the Holy Spirit, no one has proprietorial rights over these gifts, which are held in trust for the sake of the one, holy, catholic and apostolic church and its mission to the world.

In fact, Methodism claims no special gifts beyond those ordinarily bestowed upon the church for the sake of its mission. Methodism's distinctive endowments are not, therefore, necessarily absent from the Catholic Church, although in some cases they may have been obscured by Reformation disputes or, for some other reason, be currently more visible within Methodism. Understanding itself as a movement raised up by God to spread scriptural holiness, Methodism's gifts have sustained a historic mission resulting in a worldwide community currently numbering about 70 million people. Given this fruitfulness, what ecclesial elements and endowments might Catholics appropriately receive from Methodists? I will explore this question under six headings: Corporate Christianity; Watching Over One Another in Love; Connexionalism and Christian Conference; The Contribution of Laypeople; The Call to Holiness; and The Means of Grace.

CORPORATE CHRISTIANITY

The *General Rules* of the original Methodist societies are important for under-standing what distinguishes Methodism from other renewal movements in the history of the church. According to John Wesley, a Methodist society was no other than 'a company of men "having the form and seeking the power of godliness", united in order to pray together, to receive the word of exhortation, and to watch over one another in love, that they may help each other to work out their salvation'.[4] As Wesley tirelessly insisted, 'working out' one's salvation was not Pelagian since justification was attained only by God's grace through faith. Rather, it meant pressing on towards the goal of entire sanctification or Christian perfection.

This concise definition tells us a great deal about Methodism in its classical Wesleyan form. For Methodists, Christian life is essentially corporate. When still a young man at Oxford, John Wesley was given advice that he evidently took to heart: 'Sir, you are to serve God and go to heaven. Remember you cannot serve him alone; you must, therefore, find companions or make them; the Bible knows nothing of solitary religion.'[5] Many years later, Wesley advised a correspondent: 'It is a blessed thing to have fellow travellers to the New Jerusalem. If you cannot find any, you must make them; for none can travel that road alone. Then labour to help each other on that you may be altogether Christians.'[6]

The idea of Methodists 'helping each other on' is a recurring theme in the Wesleys' writings. The following verse from one of Charles Wesley's 'Hymns for Christian Friends' gives such assistance an eschatological orientation:

> Then let us ever bear
> The blessed end in view,
> And join with mutual care,
> To fight our passage through;
> And kindly help each other on
> Till all receive the starry crown.[7]

Indeed, one of the factors in the growth of Methodism was undoubtedly its corporate ethos.

Despite changing social patterns, 'helping each other on' towards salvation is still characteristic of Methodism. The local church is a community of fellow travellers in the caravan to the New Jerusalem, concerned not to leave anyone behind through neglect. Admittedly, a strong sense of community has potential defects: Methodism may, unintentionally, appear unnecessarily inquisitive into private spirituality, and close-knit groups can become 'holy huddles' withdrawn from the world. Fortunately, a traditional concern for social justice has led Methodists to be fully engaged in wider society.

Methodists recognize the sense of community within Roman Catholicism. Catholics are one body because they all share in one bread. Catholics also express their belonging in other ways, just as they support one another in the Christian life. But there is frequently a qualitative difference, since the demise of the traditional Catholic sodalities at least, in the way 'community' functions in our two communions. For Methodists, the idea of community may include eucharistic communion but normally also denotes an affective sense of 'fellowship' and corresponding formation of ecclesial relations that bind Christians together in small groups for Bible study, prayer, youth fellowship, or similar activities. In the New Testament, *koinonia* denotes fellowship in the Holy Spirit (2 Cor. 13: 14) as well as eucharistic communion (1 Cor. 10: 16), suggesting that both aspects are required to give Christian community its full shape. What might Catholics learn from Methodism about the nature of Christian communion as affective and effective fellowship in the Spirit?

WATCHING OVER ONE ANOTHER IN LOVE

The concept of 'watching over one another in love' is another classical feature of Methodism. In his *Advice to the People called Methodists* (1745), Wesley observed: 'if, lastly, you unite together to encourage and help each other in thus working out your salvation, and for that end watch over one another in love—you are they whom I mean by Methodists.'[8] As Wesley saw it, since the followers of Christ are susceptible to temptation, watching over one another is necessary to avoid temptation and facilitate growth in holiness. Accordingly, the early Methodists met weekly in small groups, or classes, for self-examination and mutual encouragement. Supported by other members, it was the task of the class leader 'To advise, reprove, comfort, or exhort, as occasion may require'.[9] Failure to maintain the rules of the Methodist societies was a serious matter: 'If there be any among us who observe them not, who habitually break any one of them, let it be made known unto them who watch over that soul...'[10] In *A Plain Account of the People called Methodists* (1749) Wesley urged his followers: 'Strengthen you one another. Talk together as often as you can. And pray earnestly with and for one another, that you may "endure to the end and be saved".'[11] Note the allusion to Peter's 'strengthening' of the other apostles (Luke 22: 32).

Nowadays, Methodist discipline is more enlightened than in the eighteenth century, though the principle of 'watching over one another' continues to be expressed in various ways. While the class meeting may have shed some of its original features, small groups that meet for fellowship, prayer, and mutual encouragement are still relatively common in Methodism. Likewise, in most churches there is some system whereby pastoral visitors maintain contact with a group of members, reporting any pastoral concerns (such as illness) to the minister. The pastoral committee and church council are courts exercising discipline. A collegial outlook means that ministers are never alone in exercising their ministry. Although the Superintendent is entrusted with particular responsibilities, there is a strong sense of mutual accountability among ministers, as demonstrated in the ministerial synod where ordination vows are renewed annually.

At every level in Methodism authority and discipline are exercised corporately. None is exempt from 'watching over one another' by virtue of their position. The Conference, to which all ministers and laypeople are accountable, is the ultimate forum for this. Nevertheless, whilst all ecclesial relations in Methodism are mutual and reciprocal, they are not necessarily symmetrical. The essential equality among the baptized notwithstanding, there is a clear duty of obedience to instruments of authority in the church.

Methodists recognize that mutuality is expressed in various ways within Roman Catholicism, the collegiality of the bishops being a prime example. *Koinonia* ecclesiology tends to emphasize the reciprocity of ecclesial relations within and throughout the church.[12] Equally, there is an unresolved tension between ecclesiologies of communion and versions of Catholic ecclesiology that tend to construe the church in exclusively hierarchical terms. Whilst the principle of 'watching over one another' might extend sideways and downwards in a hierarchical institution, it does not obviously apply in an upward direction. There may, however, be scope for developing the notion of *consensus fidelium* in the direction of appropriate modes of mutual accountability.

The particular ministry of the Pope raises some interesting questions in relation to 'watching over one another in love'. Jean-Marie Tillard used the metaphor of 'watchman' to describe the special ministry of the Bishop of Rome: the Pope is alert to prevent the church from sinking into a sleep in which the apostolic faith and the *koinonia* of the churches might be threatened.[13] Where the apostolic faith and *koinonia* are endangered, it is his responsibility to sound the alarm and intervene by lending assistance to the bishop of the local church.

More generally, the universal primate states authoritatively the fundamental conditions required for the visible expression of communion. As end point of ecclesial discernment, the authority of such formal papal teaching—in its

extraordinary/infallible mode rather than its ordinary/non-infallible mode—
stands in its own right (*ex sese*) rather than on the basis of subsequent ecclesial
consent (*ex consensu ecclesiae*). But far from negating the need for prior consent,
it rightly presupposes such prior consent.[14] The point is that in sound Roman
Catholic understanding, teaching does not become infallible simply because the
Pope declares it. Rather, the Pope is regarded as speaking infallibly when he gives
formal, final articulation to the discerned mind of the church on matters pertaining to the identity of the church. As Tillard recalled, it was frequently stated
at the First Vatican Council that 'the Pope's function and ... power ... exist *ad
aedificationem Ecclesiae non ad destructionem*, for the building-up of the Church,
not its destruction.'[15]

Describing the Pope's ministry in terms of 'watching over' the universal
church resonates with Methodists. John Wesley exercised just such a ministry
in relation to Methodism in the eighteenth century. To the Methodist way of
thinking, however, describing the Pope as 'watchman' prompts the question:
who watches over the watchman? Or, what are the structures and mechanisms
by which papal ministry is appropriately held in bonds of mutual accountability?
For Methodists, this question arises most acutely in connection with the Pope's
ordinary *magisterium*, which some sections of the Catholic Church invest with a
quasi-infallibility that makes it difficult to engage in a critical debate about the
actual exercise of papal ministry.[16]

Without abandoning their ecclesiology, Catholics may then have something
to learn, both in the local church setting and in the college of bishops, from the
way in which Methodists have interpreted Luke 22: 32 in terms of 'watching over
one another in love'. What might Catholics learn from Methodists about the
corporate exercise of oversight? How might Catholics benefit from Methodist
experience of developing small groups that meet for fellowship, prayer, and
mutual encouragement?

CONNEXIONALISM AND CHRISTIAN CONFERENCE

The connexional principle in Methodism holds that each part of the church
is inseparably bound to every other. 'It witnesses to a mutuality and interdependence which derive from the participation of all Christians through
Christ in the very life of God himself.'[17] This interdependence is expressed
in ecclesial structures, including those of oversight and authority. 'Insofar
as such interdependence involves submission to higher authorities (at any
level), that submission is to an authority representative of the churches over
which it is set.'[18] This connexional principle 'has been intrinsic to Methodism
since its origins'.[19] In the eighteenth century, the term 'connexion' denoted
a circle of people related to a particular individual. Thus, John Wesley

regarded his itinerant preachers as being in connexion with himself. Over time, 'the connexion' came to be used as an umbrella term for the network of Methodist societies, equivalent to 'denomination' or 'church'. Even today Methodists often speak of 'the connexion' when referring to Methodism in general.

Although it is not a Scriptural term, connexionalism is closely related to *koinonia*. If we imagine *koinonia* as having three dimensions—sacramental, juridical, and spiritual—connexionalism most closely corresponds to the juridical. It denotes those ecclesial structures that give visible form to the sacramental and spiritual dimensions of *koinonia*. Catholics and Methodists agree that the nature of the church is fundamentally connexional.[20] Whereas bishops are the nodal points of connexionalism in the Catholic Church, the connexional nature of Methodism is expressed in the Conference.

John Wesley held the first Methodist Conference in 1744 with a few hand-picked lieutenants. After prayer, the company decided upon a simple agenda for their five days of deliberation: '(1) what to teach; (2) How to teach; and (3) What to do; i.e. how to regulate our doctrine, discipline, and practice.'[21] Thereafter the Conference was held annually, steadily growing in size as the number of itinerant preachers permitted to attend increased. Wesley presided, and at first the power of the Conference was limited to giving 'advice concerning the best method of carrying on the work of God'.[22] Conference business proceeded by way of question and answer, Wesley or another attendee raising an issue for discussion before Wesley gave his answer, which was definitive. After his death, the Conference became the supreme doctrinal, legislative, and disciplinary court in Methodism. One Methodist theologian describes it as 'Methodism's corporate *magisterium*'.[23]

Disputes over whether laypeople should be allowed to participate in the Conference were among the primary causes of schism in Methodism in the century following the death of Wesley. Eventually, in 1878, laypeople were admitted to membership of the Wesleyan Conference in equal numbers with ordained ministers. Secular movements for greater democracy in British society played a part, though retrospectively Methodists interpreted the development as providential. Whilst a ministerial session of the Conference continues to deal with a few matters relating to ministers, the representative session, comprising lay members and ministers, exercises jurisdiction. The vast majority of Conference members, lay and ordained, are elected by District Synods as representatives rather than mandated delegates.

Something of the original intention and method of the Conference is preserved in the system of 'memorials' whereby circuits and districts may present written questions for Conference to address. A committee drafts replies on behalf of the Conference. If, however, members of Conference are dissatisfied with the proposed reply, there is a procedure for allowing memorials to be debated. The annual Conference agenda containing the memorials from circuits and districts together with the proposed replies provides a snapshot of current concerns within Methodism.

The Methodist Church Act (1976) empowered the Conference to amend the Deed of Union, including the doctrinal clause, by means of special resolutions requiring a 75 per cent majority. If approved, these resolutions become provisional legislation, which the District synods are required to ratify by a similar majority. Given sufficient support, the ensuing Conference is able finally to adopt the legislation. In the case of changes to the doctrinal clause, a two-year consultation is required. Occasionally, the Conference directs districts and circuits to register their mind before taking a decision on major issues—for example, when the Conference voted in favour of the Anglican–Methodist Covenant in 2003.

This whole process of Christian conference, including its subsidiary consultations, provides a means of discerning the mind of the Methodist Church. As an agent of discernment, the Conference is not intended merely to be a forum for debate. Members participate in worship and devotions and are expected to engage with issues within the framework of Scripture informed by tradition, reason, and experience. The possibility of Conference acting as an instrument of authority is based on the conviction that the Holy Spirit will guide the church with sufficient certainty for it to continue on its pilgrim journey, as expressed in the words of Charles Wesley, based on the Exodus story, sung annually at the Conference:

> By thy unerring Spirit led,
> We shall not in the desert stray;
> We shall not full direction need,
> Or miss our providential way.[24]

Along with being an agent of discernment and instrument of authority, the Conference is also a means of reception, acting as a necessary brake over disputed matters until a consensus emerges. If Conference pronounces authoritatively, its decisions are binding but not inviolable. The Conference can and does change its mind over a period of time. Whether the provisional nature of its decisions is an indication of the strength or weakness of Conference as an instrument of authority is debatable, though Methodists believe that the exercise of authority is always subject to future revision since the Holy Spirit continues to lead Christians into all truth.

None of this is to suggest that the Conference is free from limitations. Some complain that by controlling the way in which business is presented, connexional leaders curtail the opportunity for true conferring. There are perennial complaints, particularly from those whose view has not prevailed, that the Conference is insufficiently representative. There is also a critique of the Conference from a Catholic perspective, which Methodists need to hear.[25] Still, the idea of Christian conference is one that merits attention from Methodism's ecumenical partners. It is not simply a variant of Church of England synodical government. Nor is it merely an assembly constituted on democratic principles. Christian conference is compatible with episcopal forms of governance, though it allows the voice of the laity to be heard independently of the bishops. Christian conference expresses the synergy and co-responsibility of Christians within the body of Christ, lay and ordained together, to discern the will of God for the church.

THE CONTRIBUTION OF LAYPEOPLE

One consequence of the societal origins of Methodism is the immense contribution of laypeople to ecclesial life and leadership. From its origins, Methodism has been heavily dependent upon laypeople to sustain its life and mission, even if Wesley was initially hesitant about their assuming a prominent role. In the end, a combination of necessity and undeniable signs of fruitfulness overcame his scruples.

Methodist churches and circuits continue to be sustained by a cadre of lay officers who exercise 'stewardship' in conjunction with ordained ministers. Church councils, circuit meetings, and district synods are authorized to determine policy within the constitutional limits imposed by Conference. Since there have never been enough ministers to meet the needs of the circuits, 'local' preachers are trained and authorized to lead worship and preach under the direction of the Superintendent. Moreover, there are various forms of lay ministry. In these and other ways lay leadership alongside ministers is a hallmark of Methodism at every level.

While the history of Methodism illustrates how difficult it is to maintain a theology that does justice to both ordained and lay ministry, nevertheless Methodists discern that laypeople are not merely adjuncts to the ordained but the People of God empowered by the Holy Spirit to exercise their royal priesthood. As such, they have a proper contribution to the development of the church's doctrine, discipline, and ethics. Indeed, Methodists regard laypeople as being empowered by their baptism and experience of the Holy Spirit to contribute in virtually every area of ecclesial life, including the instruments of authority. Furthermore, a commitment to the ministry of the whole people of God means that Methodists are expected to live out their faith through personal evangelism. What might Catholics learn from the vast experience Methodism has of lay participation in the ministry and mission of the church? How might Catholics make more visible the royal priesthood of the People of God?

THE CALL TO HOLINESS

In Methodism Christian life is understood as one of scriptural holiness. John Wesley's writings contain frequent references to 'holiness of heart and life', 'holiness of true religion', and 'inward and outward holiness'. For Wesley, the goal of Christian life was nothing less than entire sanctification or perfect love.

Whilst Catholics and Methodists place similar emphasis on the call to holy living, holiness in Methodist understanding has certain distinguishing characteristics. Reflecting Puritan influence, Methodism has adopted a pattern of holy living which makes significant claims upon every aspect of life. According to the *General Rules* of the original Methodist societies, those who wished to continue in membership were expected to evidence their desire for salvation: 'By doing good, by being in every kind merciful after their power, as they have opportunity of doing good of every possible sort and as far as possible to all men.'[26] The examples cited by Wesley are all practical: 'by giving food to the hungry, by clothing the naked, by visiting or helping them that are sick, or in prison.'

This practical slant on holiness has given Methodism a reputation for commitment to radical social action. Membership entails personal commitment to Christian service and a willingness to render material support for the church's mission. Without a culture of sacrificial giving, Methodism could never have financed its burgeoning global mission. Even today, Methodist circuits must finance their mission and ministry through local giving. Methodists are acutely aware of the direct correlation between the Sunday offering and the ability to sustain their ministry and mission.

While Catholics will recognize themselves to some degree in this description of holy living, the societal origins of Methodism have bequeathed an ethos that positively urges individuals to fulfil their commitment to holiness. This is underpinned by the annual Covenant service in which Methodists renew their baptismal covenant corporately and individually. Even if the content has been toned down over the years, the Covenant service still makes heavy demands. In the words of the Covenant prayer:

Christ has many services to be done: some are easy, others are difficult; some bring honour, others bring reproach; some are suitable to our natural inclinations and material interests, others are contrary to both; in some we may please Christ and please ourselves; in others we cannot please Christ except by denying ourselves. Yet the power to do all these things is given to us in Christ, who strengthens us.[27]

The congregation respond:

I am no longer my own but yours. Your will, not mine, be done in all things, wherever you may place me, in all that I do and in all that I may endure; when there is work for me and when there is none; when I am troubled and when I am at peace. Your will be done when I am valued and when I am disregarded; when I find fulfillment and when it is lacking; when I have all things, and when I have nothing. I willingly offer all I have and am to serve you, as and where you choose. Glorious and blessèd God, Father, Son and Holy Spirit, you are mine and I am yours. May it be so for ever. Let this covenant now made on earth be fulfilled in heaven. Amen.[28]

How might Methodism's pattern of holy living influence Catholic understanding of holiness? What might the Methodist Covenant service contribute to Catholic worship and spirituality?

THE MEANS OF GRACE

John Wesley placed considerable emphasis on the experience of conversion and assurance whilst maintaining the necessity of the means of grace as administered in the Church of England.

By 'means of grace' I understand outward signs, words, or actions ordained of God, and appointed for this end—to be the *ordinary* channels whereby he might convey to men preventing, justifying or sanctifying grace ... The chief of these means are prayer, whether in secret or with the great congregation; searching the Scriptures (which implies reading, hearing and meditating thereon) and receiving the Lord's Supper ... and these we believe to be ordained of God as the ordinary channels of conveying his grace to the souls of men.[29]

For Wesley, baptism and the Lord's Supper were chief among the 'covenanted' means of grace; there were also other 'prudential' means of grace. We will attend here to four such prudential means.

Searching the Scriptures

What Wesley called 'searching the Scriptures' is central to Methodism. Methodists read the Scriptures with a very real sense that Christ is present and operative in them as a means of grace. *Sacrosanctum Concilium* likewise affirms that: 'He is present in his word since it is he himself who speaks when the holy scriptures are read in the Church' (§ 7). As *Dei Verbum* explains: 'The Church has always venerated the divine scriptures as she venerated the Body of the Lord, in so far as she never ceases, particularly in the sacred liturgy, to partake of the bread of life and to offer it to the faithful from the one table at the Word of God and the Body of Christ' (§ 21). Since the Second Vatican Council, Roman Catholicism has experienced a remarkable return to the Bible. But, whereas the Catholic emphasis here is primarily upon the liturgical context, Methodists have a strong sense—akin to the traditional monastic emphasis on *lectio divina*—that even outside worship God encounters his people through the pages of Scripture. Without abandoning the need for an ecclesial interpretation of Scripture, Methodists consider that the Bible speaks to individual Christians in their private devotions. Thus, Bible reading and study belong to the life of the individual and the community. For Methodists, 'the task of interpreting Scripture is not merely for theologians but for every Christian person.'[30] As participants in the process of searching the Scriptures, laypeople are qualified to be part of the church's instruments of authority.

Conscious of their own shortcomings, Methodists invite Catholics to consider how they might encourage a stronger ethos of Bible reading and study. Here, it is good to acknowledge the lead taken by the Catholic bishops of England and Wales, and of Scotland, in *The Gift of Scripture*.[31] The bishops admit that until comparatively recently the Catholic Church rejected the use of historical–critical methods in biblical studies (§ 82). Given the sea change that occurred within Catholicism during the twentieth century, might not further developments in the use of the Bible be possible? Methodists ask why, having been encouraged to read and study the Bible, laypeople should not be allowed to participate in its authoritative interpretation?

Prayer

For Methodists prayer also ranks among the means of grace. Puritan influence taught Wesley to value extempore prayer in Christian worship and fellowship, and its persistence as a normative feature of Methodist worship testifies to an enduring need for prayer that is directly inspired by the Holy Spirit. In Methodist experience, extempore prayer enables Christians to pray with confidence in their own words, expressing not just personal feelings but articulating the contemporary needs of the community.

In contrast, from a Methodist perspective, Catholics seem not to value extempore prayer in a liturgical setting, perhaps fearing that it would lead to excessive individualism. While such fears are understandable, the Methodist sense is that the Holy Spirit cannot be domesticated within prescribed liturgical forms. That said, Methodists have learned to appreciate prescribed forms of prayer in their worship alongside extempore prayers and, likewise, invite Catholics—beyond the realms of those involved in Catholic charismatic renewal—to discover the benefits of such a combination.

Hymns and Singing

John Wesley regarded edifying hymns as an essential element of Christian worship and devotion, and the continual flow of hymns from the pen of Charles Wesley confirms their importance in the early Methodist societies. The *Collection of Hymns for the Use of the People called Methodists* (1780) is commended to the pious reader 'as a means of raising or quickening the spirit of devotion, of confirming his faith, of enlivening his hope, and of kindling or increasing his love to God and man' (Preface). Consequently, Methodists take seriously the liturgical role of corporate hymn singing, believing that hymns reinforce the ministry of the Word. As the Preface to *Hymns and Psalms* (1983) explains:

[Hymns] unite the intellect, the emotions, the will, and the voice, in the human response to God's grace; and they also point beyond our human faculties and abilities, for God addresses us in them, and through them applies the good news of Jesus Christ to our lives. Their combination of music and poetry provides a medium for God's Word, and a way in which our hearts and minds may become open to that Word.

Roman Catholic worship does not rely on the use of hymns in the same way. Of course, the Mass often includes hymns, and some fine compositions by Catholic writers have found their way into the hymn books of Methodists and others. Still, the use of hymns is essentially auxiliary to the order of the Mass. Methodists invite Catholics to consider whether a stronger emphasis on the liturgical use of hymns could enrich their experience of worship.

Preaching

Even if the sermon no longer dominates the shape of Methodist worship, evangelical preaching remains at its heart. As part of 'searching the Scriptures', such preaching is experienced as a means of grace, though not by necessarily and directly producing an experience of conversion or assurance. Instead, it involves presenting the truths of the Gospel in a way that makes a personal claim upon all who hear, addressing them in their particular pastoral situation. Evangelical preaching may take a broad theme or else it may focus on one particular aspect of the Gospel. Either way, it is closely related to the Scriptures, which it seeks to relate to contemporary discipleship. That candidates for presbyteral ministry must be local preachers reflects the importance that Methodists attach to preaching as part of the ministry of word and sacrament.

Reforms within Roman Catholicism since the Second Vatican Council have gone a long way towards restoring preaching as an integral component of the Mass. However, from a Methodist perspective the comparatively low priority generally attached to homiletics in priestly formation reflects the muted culture of preaching in Catholicism. Methodists accordingly invite Catholics to consider whether evangelical preaching could not have a higher priority in their ecclesial life.

CONCLUSION

There are other topics that could fruitfully be explored in relation to the potential contribution of Methodism to receptive Catholic Learning, the Methodist experience of women's ministry being an obvious example, though one of fairly recent provenance. Aware of the sensitivities involved, Methodists urge Roman Catholics to learn from the Methodist experience of women's ministry as part of the process of Receptive Ecumenism.

The history of Methodism bears testimony to the fact that God raises up diverse forms of ministry for particular purposes. As a result, Methodism is characterized by a flexible and pragmatic approach towards ecclesial structures for the sake of the church's mission to the world. Methodists invite Catholics to consider whether and how the pressing needs of mission in today's world might inform their own understanding of ecclesial structures.

In the past, the Methodist doctrine of assurance was a source of controversy with Catholics. However, Catholics and Methodists now agree that Christian assurance 'should not be seen as a form of certainty which removes the need for hope. Assurance, itself a gift of the Holy Spirit, [is] no guarantee of perseverance, nor even a necessary accompaniment of saving faith'.[32] Furthermore, 'Christian religious experience includes the assurance of God's unmerited mercy in Christ, the inner witness of the Spirit that we are indeed children of God, pardoned and reconciled to the Father (Rom. 8: 12–17)'.[33] Far from providing a form of guarantee that quietens the continual need to grow in holiness, appropriate Christian assurance should serve rather only to quieten distorted anxiety concerning believers' standing before God and so free them precisely *for* due growth in holiness. Methodists invite Roman Catholics to consider whether and how this experience of assurance might find greater expression in their spirituality.

Finally, in offering gifts to an ecumenical partner it is as well to consider how these might appear from the other side. The Lutheran theologian Michael Root warns about 'dead mouse' gifts in ecumenism. Whereas the cat fondly imagines it is offering a treasured possession, its owner instinctively recoils at being presented with a dead mouse. Analogously, the treasured ecclesial elements and endowments of one community may generate bewilderment or distaste when offered to another. While that is always a risk, Catholics and Methodists have journeyed sufficiently far in dialogue over the past forty years to establish a robust relationship capable of frank and honest discussion of the obstacles impeding progress towards full communion.[34]

Receptive Ecumenism is never a one-way process. Methodists, in turn, should expect to receive gifts and be open to learning from Catholicism. Examples here would include: fresh insights into the exercise of individual forms of *episkopé* within a collegial ministry of oversight; a more developed theology of the sacraments, especially of the Eucharist; alternative ways of expressing the diversity in unity of the church and its continuity or connexion in space and in time; and a stronger sense of the possibility of authoritative teaching in the church.

It is evident, then, from our past and present dialogues, both nationally and internationally, that Catholics and Methodists have a great deal to offer each other, and our willingness to commence an exchange of gifts—and, more importantly, a mutual process of receptive ecumenical learning—along the lines envisaged above, will ultimately serve the unity of the one, holy, catholic and apostolic church.

NOTES

1. *UUS*, § 28, in turn echoing *LG*, § 13.
2. See the Joint International Commission for Dialogue Between the Roman Catholic Church and the World Methodist Council, *The Grace Given You in Christ: Catholics and Methodists Reflect Further on the Church* (Lake Junaluska, NC: World Methodist Council, 2006), particularly ch. 4, 'Principles and Proposals for Developing Relations Between Catholics and Methodists', 60–70.
3. United Methodist–Roman Catholic Dialogue, *Through Divine Love: The Church in Each Place and All Places* (Washington, DC: USCCB, 2005), § 178, available at <http://www.usccb.org/seia/finalUMC-RC5–13masterintro.pdf>.
4. 'The Nature, Design and General Rules of the United Societies in London, Bristol, Kingswood, and Newcastle upon Tyne' (1743), *WJW*, ix. 69; cf. 2 Tim. 3: 5; Phil. 2: 12.
5. Cited in John Telford, *The Life of John Wesley*, 4th edn. (London: Epworth, 1924), 147.
6. 'To Frances Godfrey' (2 Aug. 1789), in Telford (ed.), *The Letters of The Rev. John Wesley*, vol. viii., *July 24, 1787 to February 24, 1791* (London: Epworth, 1931), 158.
7. *WJW*, vii. 685.
8. *WJW*, ix. 125.
9. 'The Nature, Design, and General Rules', ibid., 70.
10. Ibid. 73.
11. Ibid. 256; cf. Matt. 24: 3.
12. See *LIC*, 158–75.
13. See *The Bishop of Rome*, trans. John de Satgé (London: SPCK, 1983), 90–2.
14. See Paul D. Murray, 'On Valuing Truth in Practice: Rome's Postmodern Challenge', *International Journal of Systematic Theology*, 8 (2006), 163–83 (168–70); also in Laurence Paul Heming and Susan Frank Parsons (eds.), *Redeeming Truth: Considering Faith and Reason* (London: SCM, 2007), 184–206 (189–91).
15. *Bishop of Rome*, 28.
16. See Murray, 'On Valuing Truth in Practice', 170–1, 175.

17. British Methodist Conference, *Called to Love and Praise: The Nature of the Christian Church in Methodist Experience and Practice* (Peterborough: Methodist Publishing House, 1999), § 4.6.1.
18. Ibid., § 4.6.5.
19. Ibid., § 4.6.1.
20. See Joint International Commission, *The Grace Given You in Christ*, § 60.
21. Wesleyan Methodist Church, *Minutes of the Methodist Conferences*, i. *(1744–98)* (London: John Mason, 1862), 1.
22. Ibid. 61.
23. Stephen Dawes, 'Revelation in Methodist Practice and Belief', in Clive Marsh, et al. (ed.), *Unmasking Methodist Theology* (London: Continuum, 2004), 115.
24. British Methodist Conference, *Hymns and Psalms* (London: Methodist Publishing House, 1983), No. 62.
25. See, e.g., Clifford Longley, 'Methodism: Distinctive, or just Catholic?', in *Unmasking Methodist Theology*, 198–203.
26. *WJW*, ix. 72.
27. British Methodist Conference, *Methodist Worship Book* (Peterborough: Methodist Publishing House, 1999), 288.
28. Ibid.
29. 'The Means of Grace' (Sermon 16), *WJW*, i. 381.
30. British Methodist Conference, *A Lamp to My Feet and a Light to My Path: The Nature of Authority and the Place of the Bible in the Methodist Church* (Peterborough: Methodist Publishing House, 1998), § 8.4.
31. Catholic Bishops of England and Wales, and of Scotland, *The Gift of Scripture* (London: CTS, 2005).
32. The Joint International Commission for Dialogue Between the Roman Catholic Church and the World Methodist Council, *Growth in Understanding* (Dublin: World Methodist Council, 1976), § 12, n. 6.
33. Id., *Towards an Agreed Statement on the Holy Spirit* (Lake Junaluska, NC: World Methodist Council, 1981), § 24.
34. See David M. Chapman, *In Search of the Catholic Spirit: Methodists and Roman Catholics in Dialogue* (Peterborough: Epworth, 2004).

11

The International Lutheran–Roman Catholic Dialogue—An Example of Ecclesial Learning and Ecumenical Reception

William G. Rusch

INTRODUCTION

The purpose of this chapter is twofold: (1) to give a short history and review of the international Lutheran–Roman Catholic dialogue, including its results, development, and methodology, and (2) to demonstrate how this dialogue may be viewed as an example of ecclesial learning and ecumenical reception by the sponsoring churches.

'Ecumenical reception' is here understood to mean

all phases and aspects of an ongoing process by which a church under the guidance of God's Spirit makes the results of a bilateral or multilateral conversation a part of its faith and life because the results are seen to be in conformity with the teachings of Christ and of the apostolic community, that is, the gospel as witnessed to in Scripture.[1]

In view of this definition, it needs to be stressed that this reception is not a mere exchange of ideas. Rather, churches receive, in a most profound sense of that word, insights of the Christian faith and life from other churches. This process of reception is ongoing and may take years. These insights of Christian faith and life then become a part of the identity of the other church. For example, Lutherans will gain a new richness about sanctification and works; Roman Catholics will acquire new awareness of the unmerited nature of God's grace in Christ.

THE INTERNATIONAL LUTHERAN–ROMAN CATHOLIC DIALOGUE

The origin of this world-level bilateral dialogue was in the summer of 1965. Even before the conclusion of the Second Vatican Council, a Roman

Catholic–Lutheran working group was authorized by the Vatican and the Lutheran World Federation (LWF). This working group decided that a theological dialogue should be initiated between the Roman Catholic Church and the LWF on an international level.

This decision was of critical importance. Three characteristics were clear: (1) there was to be a dialogue, (2) it was to be theological in nature, and (3) it was to be international, although not to the exclusion of appropriate regional and national dialogues. In fact, almost simultaneously efforts were undertaken to establish an American Lutheran–Roman Catholic dialogue, which in many ways contributed to the ongoing work of the international effort. In the following years a number of other regional dialogues between Catholics and Lutherans were put in place. All these dialogues contributed to a redefining of Lutheran–Roman Catholic relations in the twentieth century.

The dialogue participants for the international dialogue were soon appointed by the then Secretariat for Promoting Christian Unity of the Vatican (later the Pontifical Council for Promoting Christian Unity, PCPCU) and the Executive Committee of the LWF. There were seven Roman Catholic and six Lutheran members of the first dialogue team. The dialogue mandate was not completely clear, but it was accepted that the dialogue was not to study the theological controversies of the sixteenth century as such, but to explore the confessional differences in the light of contemporary biblical theology and church history as well as from the perspectives expressed by the Second Vatican Council. Thus, the task was to be more than a merely historical review, but one of addressing the issues that were keeping the present Lutheran and Roman Catholic churches divided.

In 1972, the dialogue issued its first report under the title, 'Report of the Joint Lutheran–Roman Catholic Study Commission on The Gospel and the Church', often referred to as the 'Malta Report'.[2] The tentative nature of this early work can be observed in the Preface, signed by André Appel, the General Secretary of the LWF, and Jan Willebrands, the President of the Secretariat for Promoting Christian Unity, when it states, 'This report has no binding character for the churches.'[3]

Nevertheless the 'Malta Report' affirms the authority of the Word of God in and over the church. Respective misunderstandings about the doctrine of justification and sanctification are corrected. Agreements are noted on the sacrificial character of the Eucharist and the real presence of Christ. Partial agreements are expressed on ministry and order in the church. These agreements led the 'Malta Report' to recommend the possibility of a mutual recognition of ministries and even intercommunion, although four of the Catholic members had reservations on this last point. The report indicated theological subjects to be taken up in later dialogues.

It was clear already in 1972 that the dialogue between these two churches must be an ongoing process. For an initial dialogue report, this text has much to commend itself in the quality of its work. Yet it also discloses how it is possible for one text to attempt to accomplish too much. A new dialogue group was appointed. This group decided that three topics were not sufficiently covered in the first report and required further treatment. These included: Eucharist, the episcopal office, and ways to a structured community.

As a result of this decision, in 1978, the dialogue issued a report, 'The Eucharist', in German, followed two years later with an English text.[4] The report contains two appendices: one offers examples of liturgies used by both churches in different countries; the other contains six essays by the participants. The members of the dialogue concluded that agreement was possible on a number of key topics and unanimously presented the report to the churches for study.

Two years later the dialogue published in German a text dealing with issues involving the nature of community, published in English in 1981 under the title, 'Ways to Community'.[5] The report describes the goal of unity and concrete steps towards that goal. It is a summary of agreement rather than an examination of previously undiscussed or unresolved subjects. The dialogue approved the text unanimously and expressed the hope that it might hasten the unity of the churches. This text did not provide a specific model for Catholic–Lutheran unity: only later in the dialogue would this prove possible.

The year 1980 marked the 450th anniversary of the Augsburg Confession, the defining document of Lutheran identity and the most irenic of the Lutheran Confessions. The dialogue noted this occasion with the publication of a document, entitled 'All Under One Christ'.[6] This document, drawing on recent Catholic and Lutheran scholarship, sought to place the Confession in its historical context, to show how the Augsburg Confession reflects a common faith between Catholics and Lutherans, and to identify a broad but incomplete accord between Catholics and Lutherans. It represented a new type of text from the dialogue, but one that would be repeated later.

The next publication was 'The Ministry in the Church', published first in German in 1981 and in English in 1982.[7] Special attention is unsurprisingly paid to the topic of the episcopate. The report wished to demonstrate what Lutherans and Roman Catholics share in regard to ministry, while not ignoring significant remaining differences. The dialogue members acknowledged that they had not solved all these differences. They nevertheless believed that their conclusions were of extreme importance for the churches and could draw them closer together, even on this controversial subject. Accordingly, the report requested the churches to consider seriously the dialogue's work and its implications. Behind this request is the growing recognition that dialogue work, in some way, must be judged by the sponsoring churches. This is something that had not occurred by 1981, although there was an obvious willingness for the dialogue to be continued.

In 1983, the 500th anniversary of the birth of Martin Luther, the dialogue published 'Martin Luther—Witness to Jesus Christ'.[8] Like 'All Under One Christ', this text was brief and drew upon recent scholarship, especially theological and historical work done by Roman Catholics on Luther. Specifically, it moved beyond the unhistorical idealism of Lutherans about Luther and the highly charged and frequently inaccurate polemics of Catholics. By so doing, the text disclosed how much common ground in the late twentieth century Lutherans and Roman Catholics could share about the sixteenth-century figure.

The next dialogue report must be regarded as one of its most impressive achievements. Bearing the title in English 'Facing Unity', this text explored, as few other dialogue statements do, the concept of unity and models of union, and proceeded to describe a process which included forms and phases of Catholic–Lutheran fellowship.[9] In this respect it moved beyond the earlier 'Ways to Community'. While not yet adopted in a Catholic–Lutheran context, 'Facing Unity', was an influential dialogical text that bore fruit in assisting Anglicans (Episcopalians) and Lutherans to move toward full communion. This is evident both in the Episcopal–Lutheran texts from the United States, *Concordat of Agreement* and *Called to Common Mission*, and in documents from dialogue in the Nordic countries.[10]

Clearly an ongoing issue of discussion between Catholics and Lutherans has been the topic of ecclesiology. This is because of the church-dividing character of disagreements in this area. Thus, a new dialogue team took up this subject and published in 1993, 'Church and Justification'.[11] This dialogue report is lengthy and seeks to show the many things that Catholics and Lutherans can state together about the church. The dialogue members obviously recognize the importance of this topic for further advance. A long section is devoted to the significance of the doctrine of justification for the understanding of the church. Often the text follows the pattern of describing what Lutherans and Catholics can say together on a particular aspect of ecclesiology, and then moves on to indicate the specific emphasis of each tradition. Although a text of some seventy pages with 396 footnotes, 'Church and Justification', does not resolve or move very far towards resolution the church-dividing issues in ecclesiology. Yet, it was patently necessary that the dialogue at that stage provide some indication of what could be mutual Catholic and Lutheran thought and affirmation about the church.

When the thirty-year history of this dialogue is examined it must be accorded high praise. It has shown itself to be a persistent enterprise to address the historic and theological reasons for Lutheran–Roman Catholic disunity. It has done this with the official support and encouragement of its sponsoring bodies—a fact of considerable importance. It has offered a way forwards to overcome many theological differences between the two traditions. In a remarkably short period of time, it has done much to offer the opportunity to move

Catholics and Lutherans closer to some form of visible unity. Moreover, as the dialogue accomplished its work, it both developed a methodology and raised the urgent matter of ecumenical reception. Attention must now be turned to these topics.

THE METHODOLOGY OF THE LUTHERAN–ROMAN CATHOLIC DIALOGUE

With the hindsight of several decades, it is possible to observe how the dialogue achieved its work. This has been demonstrated with particular clarity by Harding Meyer who has shown that the dialogue did not begin with a preconceived method, but actually worked out a means of identifying a specific kind of agreement in the course of its activity.[12] This type of agreement has come to be described more and more by the term 'differentiated consensus'. Although the actual use of this term is rare or practically non-existent in the dialogue texts, the reports show a remarkable consistency in claiming an agreement with certain characteristics.

In this regard, the dialogue rejected two possible ways forward: first, that one side would capitulate to the other and accept their formulations, something virtually impossible for any dialogue partner to do; and second, that the dialogue would have to develop new teaching on a topic, an equally difficult assignment for anyone in dialogue. Instinctively, members of the dialogue recognized the impracticality of both approaches.

Thus, they claimed an agreement, a consensus that was 'differentiated' without actually employing the word in dialogue texts. Such a consensus is not a mere compromise. This is to misunderstand it. Nor is it partial or preliminary in the sense a fuller agreement on a specific point is possible or needed. On any particular topic, unity requires no consensus beyond differentiated consensus. This point is often overlooked in critiques of the concept.

This differentiated consensus is distinguished by two characteristics. First, on a particular doctrine there is the declaration of a basic agreement. Secondly, differences are recognized. These differences continue, and there is no attempt to reconcile them. They remain. But these differences have a certain characteristic, viz., they do not challenge or place into question the declared basic agreement. They can even be positive and enriching. Therefore the consensus is 'differentiated'.

Meyer refers in this regard to two examples from the Lutheran–Roman Catholic dialogue: the 'sacramentality' of ordination and the 'sacrificial character' of the Eucharist.[13] He shows how in both examples Catholics and Lutherans can claim a consensus and live with a difference. This understanding of consensus is something new. It is a result of the ecumenical movement, and especially the bilateral dialogues.

Still it should not be overlooked that *within* churches this type of consensus has existed for centuries, whether or not it has been described as 'differentiated'. Members of a particular tradition are rarely in total agreement with all the other members of that tradition. What is new here is recognizing this kind of consensus across church lines, declaring that it is sufficient to resolve any issues of a church-dividing character on a certain doctrine, and employing the expression 'differentiated consensus'.

Therefore, in the course of its history the international Lutheran–Roman Catholic dialogue evolved a new theological methodology, addressed a significant number of historically church-dividing topics, and in a number of instances showed how the church-dividing nature of those differences could be overcome.

THE LUTHERAN–CATHOLIC DIALOGUE, ECCLESIAL LEARNING, AND ECUMENICAL RECEPTION

As any careful examination would disclose, this dialogue work had its influence on the churches. In many ways, often difficult to discern, the relationship between the Lutheran churches and the Roman Catholic Church on the international level and in many local settings changed for the better. There was ecclesial learning from the bilateral dialogue taking place. Polemics and inaccurate and unfortunate caricatures were replaced by friendships, new levels of trust, and cooperative work in areas of justice and peace. Catechetical materials and educational literature all began to reflect new understandings that Catholics and Lutherans had of each other, although this has been an uneven and slow process.[14] Members of each tradition found themselves on theological faculties of the other church. Leaders of both churches on the world scene visited each other. These events were more than publicity occasions. They revealed a growing sense of communion between the churches, as imperfect as that communion may have been.

All of this meant that an informal process of ecclesial learning was taking place within both churches. But it must be emphasized that this developing process, as positive as it was, was an informal process. By the late 1990s, a perception was growing in both Catholic and Lutheran circles that if the progress in the dialogue and other relationships was to be preserved and expanded some official action was required. Hints of this concern can be documented already in the mid-1980s. The question was: What could that action be that underscored progress to date, showed the challenges still to be confronted, and could find a common affirmation in both Catholic and Lutheran circles?

The successful response to that critical question led to a new type of ecumenical document and the placement of the international Lutheran–Roman Catholic dialogue in an unusual, if not unique, spot among the bilaterals: unlike other dialogues between the Roman Catholic Church and churches of the Reformation experience, a highly important part of this dialogue's work has received official acceptance by the sponsoring churches.

The description of this development has been told in a number of places and need not be repeated here in detail.[15] What is critical for present purposes is to stress this development is an example of the results of a dialogue being learned (accepted) by the churches so that it led to a clear instance of formal ecumenical reception.

'Reception' has always been a feature of the life of the church. What is new about 'ecumenical reception' is that divided churches are challenged to receive a text which comes from outside them, from a bilateral or multilateral dialogue in which they have taken part. With this, until the Second Vatican Council raised the question of reception in first a Roman Catholic context and then an ecumenical setting reception had largely dropped from active theological consideration.[16]

In 1993, the Evangelical Lutheran Church in America signalled, on the basis of the international and American Lutheran–Roman Catholic dialogues and the joint study of the sixteenth-century condemnations between Lutherans and Roman Catholics, conducted in Germany, that it was prepared to declare the condemnations on justification no longer applicable to the contemporary Roman Catholic Church.[17] Such a contemplated action would have been a clear case of ecumenical reception.

In this regard the ELCA sought the advice of the LWF. This action, as intended, set off a process that led the LWF to work with the PCPCU of the Vatican to produce a common declaration on justification. The sign from the ELCA had been clear: it was prepared as one church to take such action unilaterally if necessary. Yet, the desire of the ELCA was also equally clear. It wished to take such action in concert with its fellow-member churches of the LWF, and it was hoped with the Roman Catholic Church at an appropriate level.

This process was not easy. The first target date of 1997, the anniversary year of the Decree on Justification of the Council of Trent, had to be abandoned. Serious objections were raised, especially in Germany, by the Lutheran side, including a number of theological professors. Issues of methodology and Lutheran identity became part of a heated debated. A lingering question was: How is it possible that Lutherans and Roman Catholics could find agreement on this doctrine which more than any other caused the sixteenth-century splits in the western church? For some the answer was apparent: it could not be possible! More than once the project almost failed because of missteps on both sides. It was evident in this undertaking both traditions were entering into new unexplored territory. This will be continually true as other churches encounter ecumenical reception. But, finally, success was obtained.[18] In the process three documents were produced: *Joint Declaration on the Doctrine of Justification* (*JDDJ*), *The Official Common Statement*, and *Annex to the Official Common Statement*.[19]

On 31 October 1999, in the city of Augsburg, Germany, Bishop Christian Krause, President of the LWF, with other officers of the Federation and Cardinal Edward Cassidy, then President of the PCPCU, signed the *Official Common Statement* as the means by which the *JDDJ* was confirmed jointly. Shortly after the signing Pope John Paul II announced that a milestone had been reached on the difficult path to re-establishing full unity among Christians.

It is important to understand what the *JDDJ* is and what it is not. It is a brief text of some ten pages in English. Its purpose is to show and to declare that an understanding has been reached on an extremely critical doctrine of Christian faith, especially between Catholics and Lutherans. The *JDDJ*'s purpose is to allow the formal reception of a dialogue conclusion by the sponsoring churches. As such, it is an example of ecumenical reception.

Therefore, the *JDDJ* is not merely another dialogue report. It moves beyond other dialogue reports by the virtue of its official acceptance by the churches of the LWF and the Roman Catholic Church. It declares that these churches are no longer in a church-dividing dispute about the doctrine of justification and so the respective condemnations of the sixteenth century do not apply to the teaching of either the Roman Catholic Church or the Lutheran churches as presented in the *JDDJ*. Its distinctiveness is its official character. It is not the dialogue team speaking, but the churches are speaking in the *JDDJ*.[20]

This breakthrough took place because the *JDDJ* adopted as its methodology the concept of differentiated consensus without ever using this expression explicitly. Throughout the *JDDJ* there is the double goal: (1) an agreement in basic truths, and (2) an acknowledgement of remaining differences that do not call into question the agreement in basic truths with the result that mutual condemnations on justification do not apply to the present ecumenical partner.

For example, the *JDDJ* addresses the basic consensus on justification in § 15. This is then developed at several points (§§ 19, 22, 25, 28, 31, 34, and 37). In these sections the *JDDJ* is describing the commonality on the basic truths point by point.

Then the *JDDJ* turns to the remaining differences: cooperation on the Catholic side, passivity on the Lutheran (§§ 20–1); different views of grace (§§ 23–4); 'simuls' and concupiscence (§§ 29–30); and issues of merit (§§ 38–9). As indicated above, what is critical is that these differences are open to each other, and they do not rescind the basic truths of the doctrine of justification. It is upon the basis of this differentiated consensus that the non-applicability of the condemnations on justification can be asserted.

The *JDDJ* has occasioned ample study and reflection.[21] It has been fittingly seen as an example of ecumenical reception at the highest level of authority.[22] Both Lutheran and Catholic churches have officially acknowledged through the *JDDJ* and its attendant documents that this conclusion of their dialogue is now received. It is a rare example of what I mean by 'ecumenical reception'.

CONCLUSION

The *JDDJ*, then, is both a vehicle for an ongoing process of reception and a witness to the acceptance of that specific dialogue conclusion by the member churches of the LWF and the Roman Catholic Church. But, as the *JDDJ* itself notes, Catholics and Lutherans together need further dialogue about aspects of the doctrine of justification and other topics that prevent their full communion. The *JDDJ* is thus an instance of both ecclesial learning and ecumenical reception. In this regard it is a notable achievement. Yet it should not and cannot be seen as closure. Both ecclesial learning and ecumenical reception must be viewed as dynamic ongoing processes that continue to challenge divided churches.

Finally, the further potential of the *JDDJ* should be mentioned. Even prior to the signing of the *Official Common Statement*, the question was raised whether the *JDDJ*, or an appropriate version of it, could be utilized in Roman Catholic–Methodist, Roman Catholic–Orthodox, Roman Catholic–Pentecostal, and Roman Catholic–Reformed relations.[23] Such hopes were given their first definitive confirmation when on 23 July in Seoul the World Methodist Conference also formally committed to the *JDDJ*, further establishing it as a unique example of ecclesial learning and ecumenical reception. As Pope John Paul II declared in Rome on 31 October 1999, within minutes of the signing of the *JDDJ* in Augsburg, 'a milestone' has been reached on the journey to reunite Christians. For such progress within the last century, only thanks can be offered.

NOTES

1. Rusch, *Reception: An Ecumenical Opportunity* (Philadelphia, Penn.: Fortress Press, 1988), 31. This definition builds on the earlier work of Aloys Grillmeier and Yves Congar. See Grillmeier, 'Konzil und Rezeption: Methodische Bemerkungen Zu einem Thema der ökumenischen Diskussion der Gegenwart' *Theologie und Philosophie*, 45 (1970), 321–52; Congar, 'La "Réception" comme réalité ecclésiologique', *Revue des sciences philosophiques et théologiques*, 56 (1972), 369–403.
2. See *GIA*, 168–89.

3. *GIA*, 168.
4. *GIA*, 190–214.
5. *GIA*, 215–40.
6. *GIA*, 241–7.
7. *GIA*, 248–75.
8. *GIA II*, 438–42.
9. Ibid. 443–84.
10. See William A. Norgren and Rusch (eds.), *Towards Full Communion and Concordat of Agreement*: *Lutheran-Episcopal Dialogue USA, 3rd series, 1983–1991* (Cincinnati, Ind. and Minneapolis, Minn.: Augsburg & Forward Movement Publications, 1991); also eid., *Called to Common Mission: A Lutheran Proposal for a Revision of the 'Concordat of Agreement'* (Chicago, Ill.: Evangelical Lutheran Church in America, 1999). For the Nordic dialogue, see C. Podmore (ed.), *Together in Mission and Ministry: The Porvoo Common Statement with Essays on Church and Ministry in Northern Europe* (London: Church House Publishing, 1993).
11. *GIA II*, 485–565.
12. Meyer, 'Die Prägung einer Formel: Ursprung und Intention', in Harald Wagner (ed.), *Einheit aber Wie? Zur Tragfähigkeit der ökumenischen Formels 'differenzierten Konsens'* (Freiburg: Herder, 2000), 36–58. Whilst the entire volume merits attention, the Meyer article is particularly helpful to understand the development and nature of differentiated consensus.
13. Ibid. 44–6.
14. See Darlis J. Swan, 'The Impact of the Bilateral Dialogues on Selected Religious Education Materials Published by the Lutheran Church in America', PhD thesis, Univ. of Michigan, 1988.
15. See Rusch, 'The History and Methodology of the *Joint Declaration on Justification: A Case Study in Ecumenical Reception*', in Jean-Marie Tillard (ed.), *Agapè: études en l'honneur de Mgr Pierre Duprey M. Afr.* (Chambésy and Geneva: Centre Orthodoxe du Patriarcat Œcuménique, 2000), 169–84.
16. See Rusch, *Reception: An Ecumenical Opportunity*; also Frederick M. Bliss, *Understanding Reception: A Backdrop to its Ecumenical Use* (Milwaukee, Wis: Marquette University Press, 1993).
17. See Karl Lehmann and Wolfhart Pannenberg (eds.), *The Condemnations of the Reformation Era: Do They Still Divide?*, trans. Margaret Kohl (Minneapolis, Minn.: Fortress Press, 1999).
18. See 'III. Final Report of the Joint Ecumenical Commission of the Examination of the Sixteenth-century Condemnations', ibid., esp. 178–81.
19. The Lutheran World Federation and the Roman Catholic Church, *Joint Declaration on the Doctrine of Justification* (Grand Rapids, Mich. and London: Eerdmans/CTS, 2000/2001); also at <http://www.vatican.va/roman_curia/pontifical_councils/chrstuni/documents/rc_pc_chrstuni_doc_31101999_cath-luth-joint-declaration_en.html>. Both the English and German texts are official.
20. Note, e.g., the footnote placed in the most recent German edition of the Lutheran Confessions in regard to article 4 of the Augsburg Confession, which acknowledges the *JDDJ*, and how this article must be read in the light of the *JDDJ*; see Horst Georg Pöhlmann, (ed.), *Unser Glaube: Die Bekenntnisschriften der evangelisch-lutherischen*

Kirche (Gütersloh: Güthersloher Verlagshau, 2000), 62–3. Unfortunately, the most recent English edition of the Lutheran Confessions, *The Book of Concord: The Confessions of the Evangelical Lutheran Church*, ed. Robert Kolb and Timothy J. Wingert (Minneapolis, Minn.: Fortress Press, 2000), 38–40, does not contain any reference to the *JDDJ*.

21. e.g. Pawel Holc, *Un ampio consenso sulla dottrina della giustificazione: Studio sul dialogo teologico cattolico-luterano* (Rome: Editrice Pontificia Università Gregoriana, 1999); Rusch (ed.), *Justification and the Future of the Ecumenical Movement: The Joint Declaration on the Doctrine of Justification* (Collegeville, Minn.: Liturgical Press, 2003); Wayne C. Stumme, (ed.), *The Gospel of Justification in Christ: Where Does the Church Stand Today?* (Grand Rapids, Mich.: Eerdmans, 2006).

22. Although for critical views from Catholics and Lutherans respectively, see, e.g., Steven D. Paulson, 'The Augustinian Imperfection: Faith, Christ, and Imputation and its Role in the Ecumenical Discussion of Justification', *The Gospel of Justification in Christ*, 104–24 and Avery Dulles, 'Justification and the Unity of the Church', ibid. 125–40; also, from the Catholic perspective and reflecting an apparent misunderstanding of the nature and intention of differentiated consensus, Christopher J. Malloy, *Engrafted into Christ: A Critique of the Joint Declaration* (New York: Peter Lang, 2005).

23. Papers on this question were given at the meeting of the North American Academy of Ecumenists in 2000. See also Rusch, *Justification and the Future of the Ecumenical Movement*, esp. Valerie A. Karras, 'Beyond Justification: An Orthodox Perspective' (pp. 99–131) and Frank D. Macchia, 'Justification and the Spirit of Life: A Pentecostal Response to the *Joint Declaration* (pp. 133–49).

12

Catholic Learning and Orthodoxy— The Promise and Challenge of Eucharistic Ecclesiology

Paul McPartlan

EUCHARISTIC ECCLESIOLOGY AND THE SECOND VATICAN COUNCIL

In October 2005, the Synod of Bishops met to consider the topic of 'The Eucharist: Source and Summit of the Life and Mission of the Church'. On 11 October, Metropolitan John (Zizioulas) of Pergamon addressed the Synod as a Fraternal Delegate, representing the Ecumenical Patriarchate. He spoke warmly of the theme of the Synod as highlighting vital common ground between Catholics and Orthodox and providing the way forward for Catholic–Orthodox dialogue. His words have added moment because he is the Orthodox Co-Chairman of the newly reconstituted Joint International Commission for Theological Dialogue between the Roman Catholic Church and the Orthodox Church, Cardinal Walter Kasper being the Catholic Co-Chairman. Here is part of what he said:

> We Orthodox are deeply gratified by the fact that your Synod, too, regards the Eucharist as the source and summit of the life and mission of the Church... There may still be things that separate our two Churches, but we both believe that the Eucharist is the heart of the Church. It is on this basis that we can continue the official theological dialogue of our two Churches, which is now entering a new phase. Eucharistic ecclesiology can guide us in our efforts to overcome 1000 years of separation. For it is a pity to hold the same conviction on the importance of the Eucharist but not be able to share it at the same Table... The Eucharist belongs not simply to the well-being but to the being of the Church. The whole life, word and structure of the Church is eucharistic in its very essence.[1]

These are significant words, identifying eucharistic ecclesiology as the common theological matrix within which issues that continue to divide Catholics and Orthodox can be constructively addressed. Metropolitan John's final reference to the 'structure of the Church' being eucharistic is particularly significant, because there is, in fact, only one truly outstanding theological issue that needs to be resolved between Catholics and Orthodox and it is the structural issue of primacy. Metropolitan John clearly urges a eucharistic approach to this issue and we shall see that Catholic theology has indeed been moving towards a eucharistic understanding of primacy in recent decades.

Two statements from the 1992 *Catechism of the Catholic Church* serve to summarize what eucharistic ecclesiology is. The *Catechism* states with emphasis the key principle, 'the Eucharist makes the Church', and makes it plain that this principle has structural consequences for the shape of the church.[2] 'The Church', it says, 'is the People that God gathers in the whole world. She exists in local communities and is made real as a liturgical, above all a Eucharistic, assembly' (§ 752). Further indication of Catholicism's formal espousal of eucharistic ecclesiology is to be found in Pope John Paul II's final encyclical, *Ecclesia de Eucharistia*,[3] and by the title of the 2005 synod itself, in turn repeating a phrase used in both the Second Vatican Council's Dogmatic Constitution on the Church (*LG*, § 11), and its Constitution on the Sacred Liturgy (*SC*, § 10). Together with this is the Second Vatican Council's description of the eucharistic assemblies of local churches, presided over by their bishops, as 'the principal manifestation of the Church' (*SC*, § 41) in which and 'formed out of them ... the one and unique Catholic Church exists' (*LG*, § 23).[4]

Of the latter formula, Walter Kasper has noted that it significantly reinstates perspectives lost around the start of the second millennium when the eucharistic ecclesiology of the early church fell 'into general oblivion' in the wake of eucharistic controversy, leading to the church subsequently being understood mainly as a 'social, hierarchical structure'. In his judgment:

The recourse to the first millennium and its *communio*-ecclesiology means, namely, parting with the one-sided unity-ecclesiology of the second millennium, which was and has been until today one of the essential reasons for the separation of the Eastern churches. The understanding of the unity of the Church as a *communio*-unity leaves space again for a legitimate multiplicity of local churches within the greater unity in the one faith, the same sacraments and offices. With that, the road is smoothed for the Church's way into the third millennium.[5]

At this point we may note that eucharistic ecclesiology and *communio* ecclesiology are essentially the same thing—in the *Eucharist* we receive holy *communion*. As Yves Congar concluded, between the eleventh and thirteenth centuries, the West developed 'an ecclesiology of the universal Church' as 'a single society under the apostolic monarchy of Peter', which was foreign to the East.[6] He tellingly described this as a change 'from an ecclesiology of the *ecclesia* to an ecclesiology of powers, from an ecclesiology of communion and holiness to an ecclesiology of the institution and of the means of salvation founded by Christ'.[7] The East

retained much more of a *communio* vision and, in due course, it was a Russian
Orthodox, Nicolas Afanasíev, who coined the term 'eucharistic ecclesiology' and
advocated the principle that 'where there is a eucharistic assembly, there Christ
abides, and there is the Church of God in Christ.'[8]

Afanasíev was one of a very influential group of theologians who left Russia
after the 1917 Revolution. Many, including Afanasíev, settled in Paris and taught
at Saint-Serge, while others moved on to the USA. Gonzáles de Cardedal notes
the impact they had on Catholic theology:

> They...were provoked...to accentuate the discordant elements between modern West-
> ern culture and Christian faith, between the Westernized Roman Church and the Ortho-
> dox Church, showing the latter to be in greater fidelity to the apostolic and patristic
> periods...This Eastern presence...made Catholic theology feel the distance...between
> the historical look of the Roman Church and that of the Orthodox Church.[9]

Afanasíev was an ecumenical observer in the final period of the Second Vatican
Council. As well as the broad influence that he and his colleagues exerted on
Catholic theology in the pre-conciliar period, there was a very specific instance
of 'Catholic Learning' from Afanasíev early in the activity of the council itself.
One of the most notable sections of *Lumen Gentium* from the point of view of
eucharistic ecclesiology is § 26 in the final 1964 text. There, with reference to
Ignatius of Antioch, the council teaches that the bishop is the prime celebrant
of the Eucharist in the local church and refers to the Eucharist as being that
'from which the Church ever derives its life and on which it thrives'. This
text was introduced into the second draft of the schema, *De Ecclesia*, in 1963,
with an explanatory footnote stating: 'If only the Church makes the Eucharist,
it is also true that the Eucharist makes the Church.' This statement bears
the hallmark of Henri de Lubac, though he is not acknowledged.[10] Instead,
Augustine, Jerome, Leo the Great, Aquinas, and Cardinal Franzelin, who took
a leading role at the First Vatican Council, were cited, with the note remarkably
concluding: 'Regarding the link between ecclesiology and the Eucharist, cf. also
N. Afanassieff.'[11] Catholic bishops receiving the draft and wanting to deepen
their knowledge of this topic were thus referred to Augustine, Aquinas, and
Afanasíev!

Afanasíev's significant, even catalytic, influence on the council's teaching on
the church is again clear from a lengthy footnote attached to chapter nine of
the original 1962 draft of the schema *De Ecclesia*. There it was noted that the
Eucharist was central to Orthodox life and that many Orthodox theologians were
following Afanasíev in setting up an opposition between a Catholic 'universalistic
ecclesiology' of one universal Church hierarchically organized and an Orthodox
'eucharistic ecclesiology' of particular churches, not authoritatively subordinated
iure divino. 'Therefore', said the note strategically, 'it seems very useful to show in
what way the Catholic Church itself starts from a eucharistic ecclesiology which
at the same time is universalistic'.[12]

The conviction being expressed there is that the very Eucharist which local churches celebrate itself requires that they be bound together in an overall unity. The Eucharist itself generates bonds of communion not just within but also between the communities which celebrate it. No local church which wants to be truly eucharistic can cut itself off from the others and declare independence. It can fairly be said that the one crucial theological issue confronting Catholic–Orthodox dialogue today is that of identifying the structure of unity that properly corresponds to the mystery of the one Eucharist celebrated by local churches spread over the face of this world—and I stress *this* world, not an ideal world in which perfect charity reigns. It is within that context that the question of primacy needs to be resolved.

Afanasíev believed that any juridical structure of unity was alien to eucharistic ecclesiology, and that a local church could celebrate the Eucharist with full integrity in isolation from the others. This position was unsatisfactory to the drafters of *Lumen Gentium*. Interestingly, it also proved unsatisfactory to some Orthodox theologians in the generation following Afanasíev. Outstanding among these is John Zizioulas who describes a eucharistic community that would close itself to others as betraying 'the catholic character of the eucharist'.[13]

On the other hand, any overall structure of unity must respect the full catholicity of each local church and not effectively reduce them to 'parts' of a whole, as pre-Second Vatican Council Catholic ecclesiology tended to. In other words, structure cannot exist for itself and be imposed simply for reasons of good order; that is 'universalism'. On the contrary, structure must arise from the Eucharist and correspond to the Eucharist, and it must respect and release the catholicity that the Eucharist gives to each local church. Afanasíev's emphasis upon the Eucharist, but extreme reaction against ecclesial structures, precipitated a searching critique of those structures that really do not have a eucharistic justification but arise from other, more worldly considerations. It has ultimately led to the concerted effort nowadays in Catholic ecclesiology, in Orthodox ecclesiology, and perhaps most promisingly in Catholic–Orthodox dialogue, to identify those structures that the Eucharist itself generates and requires. The international dialogue has been committed to this path since its first agreed statement, in 1982, which contained the following bold and programmatic declaration:

[T]he Church finds its model, its origin and its purpose in the mystery of God, one in three persons . . . [T]he eucharist thus understood in the light of the Trinitarian mystery is the criterion for the functioning of the life of the Church as a whole. The institutional elements should be nothing but a visible reflection of the mystery.[14]

Around the same time, Zizioulas himself said 'there is a need for special attention and creative theological work to keep an adequate balance between the "local Church" and the "universal Church" ', and 'it is the eucharist itself which will guide us in this, for, by its nature, it expresses simultaneously both the "localization" and "universalization" of the mystery of the Church'.[15] The complex debate several years ago between Cardinal Kasper and the then Cardinal Ratzinger about the relationship between the local church and the universal church gives an indication of the delicacy of the task in hand.[16]

EUCHARIST AND PRIMACY

At first sight, eucharistic ecclesiology may seem necessarily to foster the 'localism' that Afanasíev so displayed and Zizioulas so rejects. Suspicions to this effect were voiced in the 1992 letter from the Congregation for the Doctrine of the Faith to Catholic bishops on 'Some Aspects of the Church Understood as Communion' which, nevertheless, showed a remarkable desire to adopt a eucharistic ecclesiology and to identify the need that such an ecclesiology truly has for a universal primacy. Referring to the danger of seeing local churches as independent entities, it said: 'it is precisely the Eucharist that renders all self-sufficiency . . . impossible.' The papacy has its place within the necessary openness to one another of truly eucharistic local churches: 'the existence of the Petrine ministry . . . bears a profound correspondence to the Eucharistic character of the Church'.[17] Likewise, the *Catechism*: 'The whole Church is united with the offering and intercession of Christ. Since he has the ministry of Peter in the Church, the Pope is associated with every celebration of the Eucharist, wherein he is named as the sign and servant of the unity of the universal Church' (*CCC*, § 1396).

The fact that, in major official Catholic texts, the papacy is being set within the mutual eucharistic openness of local churches that Zizioulas espouses, is profoundly promising for progress between Catholics and Orthodox on this most thorny of topics. Also deeply encouraging are Zizioulas's own recent contributions to reflection upon the proper place of a universal primacy within eucharistic ecclesiology.[18] Here he has articulated a consistent approach to primacy from within the Orthodox tradition itself, based on the necessary complementarity between primacy and synodality: 'In Orthodox tradition there has never been and there can never be a synod or a council without a *protos*, or *primus*. If, therefore, synodality exists *iure divino*, primacy also must exist by the same right.'[19] His point is that many Orthodox draw a mistaken contrast between an Orthodox adherence to synodical government and a Catholic advocacy of papal primacy. He proposes that the 34th Apostolic canon, dating from the fourth century, can provide 'the golden rule of the theology of primacy',[20] and stresses the primordial nature of this canon for an ecclesiology of communion, because it arises directly from Trinitarian theology.

This canon provides that all the bishops of a region (ἔθνος) must recognise their 'first one' (πρῶτος) as their 'head' (κεφαλὴ) and do nothing without him, while he should equally do nothing without them. The canon, significantly enough, ends with reference to the Holy Trinity, thereby indicating indirectly that canonical provisions of this kind are not a matter of mere organisation but have a theological, indeed a triadological, basis.[21]

In short, the one and the many go together in an ecclesiology truly rooted in the communion of the Holy Trinity, and this applies at all levels of church organization, including the universal. Orthodox have emphasized the many and need to rediscover the one, particularly in the form of a universal primate; Catholics have emphasized the one and need to recover the many. The Second Vatican Council's teaching on the status of the bishop in the local church and on episcopal collegiality in the universal church are therefore big steps in the right direction,[22] but more are needed. Zizioulas' proposal makes demands both of his fellow Orthodox and of Catholics. With regard to the latter, perhaps his biggest outstanding request is that Catholics recognize that a proper universal primacy, which is by no means just a 'primacy of honour',[23] need not necessarily involve universal jurisdiction, that is, the right to intervene in local churches over the heads of the local bishops; for that, in his view, violates the 'full catholicity of the local Church'.[24] There can be and should be, he stresses, a true primacy at the universal level of the church that respects and complements the full catholicity of all the local churches.

This proposal is serious, generous, and urgent. It merits a serious, generous, and urgent response. Suffice to note here that the medieval West did indeed allow jurisdiction to detach itself from the sacramental life of the church and particularly from the Eucharist so as to form an independent mechanism of church unity. Joseph Ratzinger refers to 'the separation of the doctrine of the Eucharist and ecclesiology, which can be noted from the eleventh and twelfth centuries onwards', as 'one of the most unfortunate pages of medieval theology.'[25] He highlights 'the increasing distinction between sacrament and jurisdiction, between liturgy and administration':

The essential unity of Church and eucharistic assembly, of Church as *communio*, was no longer evident. Like any other society, the Church was now, in a certain sense, a juridical instrument, a complex of laws, ordinances, claims. In addition, of course, she had also what was peculiarly her own: the fact that she was the *situs* of cultic acts—of the sacraments. But the Eucharist was just one of these—one liturgical act among others, no longer the encompassing orbit and dynamic centre of ecclesial existence per se.[26]

Clearly, one important step towards responding to Zizioulas' proposal would be to reforge the link between liturgy and administration, between Eucharist and jurisdiction. Happily, as noted, there are clear indications that Catholic theology is already embracing that task.[27] Jurisdiction needs to be brought back within the ambit of the church's eucharistic life, instead of floating above it, and this task is obviously linked to the endeavour to bring the hierarchy itself back within the ambit of the People of God as a whole, in order to have what Congar called a 'total ecclesiology', instead of an ecclesiology that is just a 'hierarchology'.[28] The Second Vatican Council made large strides towards a total ecclesiology, particularly by finally putting the chapter on the hierarchy after the chapter on the People of God in *Lumen Gentium*.[29] However, Orthodoxy still has much to teach Catholicism about the development of a truly total ecclesiology.[30]

MUTUALITY

It is very important in a chapter such as this to remain even-handed. I have already mentioned de Lubac, who made a massive contribution to the development of eucharistic ecclesiology in the Catholic Church,[31] and we should note the explicit tribute that Zizioulas paid to de Lubac and other twentieth-century western pioneers of *ressourcement* in 1980 when he wrote: 'the return to the ancient patristic sources, which has characterised Western theology in our century, is largely responsible for the Orthodox theological renaissance.'[32] A book which greatly influenced Zizioulas as he began his own research on Eucharist and church in the early 1950s was de Lubac's magisterial study, *Corpus Mysticum*.[33]

It was in 1952 that Congar coined what was to become a familiar metaphor in Catholic–Orthodox relations: 'It is not in vain that the Christian world has always contained an East and a West from the beginning; this is an indispensable feature of its providential character. Theology is only fully "catholic" when, like a healthy organism, it breathes deeply and uses both its lungs.'[34] This image of breathing with both lungs was much used by Pope John Paul II—for example, in his 1995 encyclical letter on commitment to ecumenism (*UUS*, § 54). The broad invitation he momentously extended there to church leaders and theologians to engage with him in 'a patient and fraternal dialogue' regarding the exercise of the primacy (*UUS*, § 96) arose from the desire he specifically expressed to the Ecumenical Patriarch eight years earlier that the Holy Spirit enlighten the pastors and theologians of the Catholic and Orthodox Churches 'that we may seek—together of course—the forms in which this ministry may accomplish a service of love recognised by all concerned' (*UUS*, § 95).

The 'dialogue of charity' between Catholics and Orthodox and the theological dialogue (the 'dialogue of truth') that built upon it have led Catholics to love and respect the Orthodox Church, marvelling at its otherness while being convinced that Catholicism and Orthodoxy at root are one. Congar pondered the mysterious providential relationship between the 'two lungs': 'Between East and

Catholic West, everything is similar and yet all is different, even what is essentially the same thing!'[35] With particular regard to Catholic and Orthodox doctrine on the Trinity, he recognized 'two constructions of the mystery...which cannot be superimposed'. 'It is a case for applying [Niels] Bohr's saying, "The opposite of a true statement is a false statement, but the opposite of a profound truth can be another profound truth".'[36] Orthodoxy has challenged and continues to challenge Catholicism to acknowledge a complementary 'Other', to realize, therefore, that it has no monopoly on understanding and explaining the fundamental truths of the Christian faith, and thereby to grow in wisdom and holiness.

Identifying specific Orthodox influences upon Catholic Learning is a delicate task as there are many kinds of learning in such a complex relationship. What is certain is that, in receptive contact with Orthodox, Catholics have grown in their appreciation and articulation of the Christian mystery. It is much to be hoped that that process has been mutual.

A FRUITFUL DECADE: THE *CATECHISM* AND CATHOLIC–ORTHODOX DIALOGUE

We may reflect on those gains by focusing on a very fruitful decade for international dialogue between Catholics and Orthodox, namely, the 1980s, which saw the production of three major agreed statements: 'The Mystery of the Church and of the Eucharist in the Light of the Mystery of the Holy Trinity' (1982); 'Faith, Sacraments and the Unity of the Church' (1987); and 'The Sacrament of Order in the Sacramental Structure of the Church' (1988).[37] In particular, I would like to highlight the ten years from the first agreed statement of 1982 to the production of the *Catechism*, and the many resonances that exist between the latter's teaching and the statements of the dialogue.

As we have seen, the Eucharist has been at the heart of the international Catholic–Orthodox dialogue from the outset. It is instructive to note several dimensions of the Eucharist and of the Christian mystery more widely that, after lengthy intervals of neglect, have been strongly recovered by Catholic theology in recent times. As earlier noted, thanks to the work of de Lubac and other Catholic theologians and liturgists, and with a significant influence from Afanasíev, Zizioulas, and other Orthodox theologians, eucharistic ecclesiology has been re-established in Catholic thought in the course of the twentieth and twenty-first centuries. In his first book, *Catholicism*, de Lubac lamented 'the swamping of the spiritual life by the detestable "I"', and set out the essentially corporate, social nature of the Eucharist and of the whole Christian mystery.[38] He battled against individualism in order to restore an ecclesial perspective.

In Orthodox theology, the ecclesial dimension of the Eucharist is intrinsically linked to its pneumatological and eschatological dimensions. Zizioulas stresses that the Bible shows Christ himself to be constituted by the Holy Spirit, who is the gift of the final days and the giver of communion. Christ himself is therefore an eschatological corporate personality (Servant of God, Son of Man).

> The Person of Christ is automatically linked with the Holy Spirit, which means with a *community*. This community is the eschatological company of the 'Saints' which surrounds Christ in the kingdom. The Church is part of the definition of Christ. The body of Christ is not first the body of an individual Christ and *then* a community of 'many', but simultaneously both together.[39]

Zizioulas implicitly acknowledges that this understanding is difficult for western theology when he says: 'This de-individualisation of Christ is in my view the stumbling-block of all ecclesiological discussions in the ecumenical movement.'[40] Nevertheless, his broader statement that the church is 'an eschatological community existing in history, taking upon itself Christ's Cross, suffering in this world, celebrating its true identity in the Eucharist'[41] would now find many western echoes.

It would not be too much of a caricature to say that Catholics and western Christians in general have often thought of the Eucharist as the occasion when I as an individual encounter Christ in a re-enactment of the past event of the Last Supper, a solemn memorial of his passion and death. This true but rather limited perception has recently been expanded by three complementary considerations: the Eucharist is the occasion when the church in the power of the Spirit anticipates the coming of the future kingdom. As such, a full understanding of the Eucharist involves not just 'I' but also the church; not just Christ, but also the Holy Spirit; not just the past but also the future.

Those three complementary dimensions of the Christian mystery—ecclesial, pneumatological, and eschatological—are amply represented in the three Catholic–Orthodox agreed statements of the 1980s and also in the *Catechism*, with multiple and strong resonances between these texts. I have shown those resonances elsewhere,[42] and I suggest that the previous decade of Catholic–Orthodox dialogue can be seen to have contributed to the remarkably rich presentation of Catholic faith to be found in the *Catechism*.

I offer briefly here just three examples of such resonance. With regard to the *ecclesial* dimension, the first agreed statement simply but profoundly said: 'each eucharistic assembly is truly the holy Church of God' (III, 1), 'because the one and only God is the communion of three Persons, the one and only Church is a communion of many communities and the local church a communion of persons' (III, 2). As we have already seen, the *Catechism* stated that the church 'exists in local communities and is made real as a liturgical, above all a Eucharistic, assembly' (*CCC*, § 752). With regard to the pneumatological dimension, the first agreed statement said of the Eucharist that 'the entire celebration is an *epiclesis*, which becomes more explicit at certain moments'. 'The Church is continually in a state of *epiclesis*' (I, 5c). In turn, whilst the *Catechism* taught that there is an *anamnesis* as well as an *epiclesis* at the heart of every Eucharist, it effectively extended the latter to cover the former by referring to the Spirit as 'the Church's living memory' (*CCC*, § 1099) and then extended the *epiclesis* to cover the entire life of the Church (*CCC*, § 1109). Finally, regarding the eschatological dimension, where the first agreed statement said: 'The Church comes into being by a free gift, that of the new creation' (II, 1), and the Eucharist is 'the sign of the Kingdom to come' (I, 2), the *Catechism* strikingly spoke of the earthly Church as the 'sign and instrument' of 'the full realisation of the unity yet to come' (*CCC*, § 775).

Such statements concerning the ecclesial, pneumatological, and eschatological dimensions of the Eucharist still serve to stretch the minds and hearts of Catholics into a fuller understanding of the mysteries we celebrate. If, as I have suggested, the *Catechism* did indeed benefit from the dialogue, it follows that further consolidation of these important dimensions in Catholic awareness depends to a significant degree upon the continuance of a vigorous dialogue between Catholics and Orthodox.

Before returning to the theme of the 'new creation', let us recall that the production of the *Catechism* was an initiative that sprang from the 1985 Extraordinary Synod of Bishops held to commemorate the twentieth anniversary of the closing of the Second Vatican Council. Placing the spotlight on the notion of communion that was present but not prominent in the documents of the council, the synod said: 'The ecclesiology of communion is the central and fundamental idea of the Council's documents.'[43] Moreover, it related the Council's teaching that the church itself is 'the universal sacrament of salvation' (*LG*, 48) directly to the church's communion life. 'The Church as communion is a sacrament for the salvation of the world.'[44]

Soon afterwards, the fact that these two ideas—of the church as communion and sacrament—are rather new to Catholics, still needing to be learnt and assimilated, was pointed out by Walter Kasper[45] and Joseph Ratzinger, respectively. Ratzinger said: 'it becomes clear how far the Council is still ahead of us: the idea of the Church as sacrament has hardly entered people's awareness.'[46]

With a particular accent on mission, the *Catechism* very clearly taught both the communion nature and the sacramentality of the church: 'The Spirit, who is the Spirit of communion, abides indefectibly in the Church. For this reason the Church is the great sacrament of divine communion which gathers God's scattered children together' (*CCC*, § 1108). Again, '[I]n her whole being and in all her members, the Church is sent to announce, bear witness, make present and spread the mystery of the communion of the Holy Trinity' (*CCC*, § 738).

When they hear the word 'sacrament' Catholics still tend instinctively to think of the seven sacraments, rather than of the church, or more primordially of Christ himself. Orthodox can help with the learning necessary here. Alexander Schmemann points out that, until its own theology fell under western influence in recent centuries, Orthodoxy never isolated and defined the sacraments:

The word *sacrament* was never restricted by its identification with our current seven sacraments. This word embraced the entire mystery of the salvation of the world and mankind by Christ and in essence the entire content of the Christian faith. The fathers of the Church perceived the Eucharist both as the revelation and the fulfilment of this universal mystery—'hidden from the angels', but to us, the new people of God, manifested in all its abundant fullness.[47]

Rejecting the western influence and reasserting what he considers a more authentic Orthodox understanding, he continues:

The Church is not an organisation but the new people of God. The Church is not a religious cult but a *liturgy*, embracing the entire creation of God. The Church is not a doctrine about the world to come but the joyous encounter of the kingdom of God. It is the sacrament of peace, the sacrament of salvation and the sacrament of the reign of Christ.[48]

CURRENT CONCERNS: CREATION AND THE ENVIRONMENT

Owing to controversy over the issue of 'uniatism', the international Catholic–Orthodox dialogue fell into difficulties in the early 1990s. A notable feature of the period since has been a growing worldwide environmental concern and an increasing sense of ecological crisis. Has the church a specific contribution to make on this issue? The answer from the Christian West has been uncertain, whereas the Christian East has responded with a resounding, Yes. We can identify here another important area for Catholic Learning.

As well as being linked to the Holy Spirit, the church and the future, the Eucharist in Orthodox theology is also intrinsically linked to the salvation of creation, as the quotation from Schmemann indicates. Though the *Catechism* teaches that in the Eucharist 'the whole of creation loved by God is presented to the Father through the death and Resurrection of Christ' (*CCC*, § 1359), this can hardly be said to be an aspect of the Eucharist that is vivid for Catholics.

Schmemann, however, expressly links the very meaning of the Eucharist to creation. It is the restoration of humanity to its proper relationship both with God and with creation, and the restoration of the whole of the cosmos to its proper activity of praise: 'The only real fall of man is his non-eucharistic life in a non-eucharistic world. The fall is not that he preferred [the] world to God . . . but that he made the world *material*, whereas he was to have transformed it into "life in God", filled with meaning and spirit.'[49] In Orthodox understanding, man is 'priest of creation' at every moment but primarily in the Eucharist, and 'Man has to become a liturgical being before he can hope to overcome his ecological crisis'.[50] Zizioulas is critical of western scholasticism because it reinforced the idea that the sacraments are largely 'irrelevant to the material world'. Instead of being 'a blessing over the material world . . . a reference of it with gratitude and dedication to the Creator', the Eucharist had become in the West 'primarily a memorial service of the sacrifice of Christ and a means of grace for the nourishment of the soul'.[51]

The schism between East and West occurred at the time of the rise of scholasticism. Zizioulas invites us to recognize the West's neglect of the cosmic aspect of the Eucharist as a significant factor in the distancing of East and West. It follows that a recovery of this aspect of the Eucharist and of the Gospel is vital for Catholic–Orthodox rapprochement. Moreover, if the requirement of an effective mission to humanity inspired ecumenical efforts through much of the twentieth century (John 17: 21), it may well be that now, at the start of the twenty-first century, it is the urgency of an effective mission to creation that can revive our ecumenical inspirations and energies.

Few Catholics know that in recent years Ecumenical Patriarch Bartholomew has organized a series of environmental symposia, bringing together scientists and theologians, politicians and church leaders, ecologists and journalists, to reflect upon the perilous state of our world in human hands. The fourth symposium was held from 5 to 10 June 2002 on board a ship in the Adriatic Sea. On 9 June 2002, for the first time in twelve centuries, the Patriarch celebrated the Orthodox liturgy in the Basilica of Sant' Apollinare in Classe in Ravenna, and the next day, via a televised link between Pope John Paul in Rome and the Ecumenical Patriarch in Venice, the two church leaders signed a 'Common Declaration on Environmental Ethics'. In it they said: 'The problem is not simply economic and technological; it is moral and spiritual'. More specifically:

A solution at the economic and technological level can be found only if we undergo, in the most radical way, an inner change of heart, which can lead to a change in lifestyle and of unsustainable patterns of consumption and production . . . A new approach and a new culture are needed, based on the centrality of the human person within creation and inspired by environmentally ethical behaviour stemming from our triple relationship to God, to self and to creation. Such an ethics fosters interdependence and stresses the principles of universal solidarity, social justice and responsibility, in order to promote a true culture of life.[52]

CONCLUSION

What has been mentioned here may serve to indicate what a unique forum of Catholic Learning—and, one hopes, of mutual learning—is provided by Catholic–Orthodox dialogue. Happily, the official international theological dialogue between these two churches restarted in December 2005. May the Holy Spirit warm the hearts of all involved in that dialogue, and of Catholics and Orthodox across the world, that they may be open and receptive to one another, truly longing to overcome past hurts and to grow together in love and praise of the living God, in the fullness of faith.

NOTES

1. See *L'Osservatore Romano* (English edn.) (2 Nov. 2005), 13.
2. *Catechism of the Catholic Church* (1992) (London: Geoffrey Chapman, 1994), § 1396 (p. 315). For a detailed study of this principle, see McPartlan, *The Eucharist Makes the Church. Henri de Lubac and John Zizioulas in Dialogue* 2nd edn. (Fairfax VA: Eastern Christian Publications, 2006 [1993]); also, id., *Sacrament of Salvation. An Introduction to Eucharistic Ecclesiology* (London: Continuum, 2005).
3. John Paul II, '*Ecclesia de Eucharistia*: Encyclical Letter on the Eucharist in its Relationship to the Church' (17 Apr. 2003) (London: CTS 2003).
4. For a valuable study, see Olegario González de Cardedal, 'Development of a Theology of the Local Church from the First to the Second Vatican Council', *The Jurist*, 52 (1992), 11–43.
5. 'Church as *Communio*', *Communio*, 13 (1986) 107, 109–10.
6. *L'Ecclésiologie du haut moyen-âge* (Paris: Cerf, 1968), 388–90.
7. 'L'Ecclesia ou communauté chrétienne, sujet intégral de l'action liturgique', in J-P. Jossua and Congar (eds.), *La liturgie après Vatican II* (Paris: Cerf, 1967), 261.
8. Afanasíev, 'Una Sancta', *Irenikon*, 36 (1963), 459.
9. González de Cardedal, 'Development of a Theology of the Local Church', 18. It is important to note that these Orthodox theologians also benefited from the patristic revival that was then underway in the West. See below.
10. For an almost identical expression, see de Lubac, *The Splendour of the Church*, trans. Michael Mason (San Francisco, Calif.: Ignatius, 1986), 134, also 152.
11. See Francisco Gil Hellín, *Concilii Vaticani II Synopsis. Constitutio Dogmatica de Ecclesia: Lumen Gentium* (Vatican City: Libreria Editrice Vaticana, 1995), 270. The particular work of Afanasíev cited was 'L'Église qui préside dans l'amour', English translation in N. Afanasíev, et al. (eds.) *The Primacy of Peter in the Orthodox Church*, trans. Katherine Farrer (London: Faith Press, 1963), 57–110, repr. John Meyendorff

(ed.), *The Primacy of Peter: Essays in Ecclesiology and the Early Church* (St Vladimir's Seminary Press, 1992), 91–143.

12. See Gil Hellín, *Concilii Vaticani II Synopsis. Constitutio Dogmatica de Ecclesia*, 650.

13. Zizioulas, *Being as Communion: Studies in Personhood and the Church* (London: Darton, Longman & Todd, 1985), 157, also 24–5.

14. Joint International Commission for Theological Dialogue Between the Roman Catholic Church and the Orthodox Church, 'The Mystery of the Church and of the Eucharist in the Light of the Mystery of the Holy Trinity' (1982), repr. in *GIA II*, 652–9, also available at <http://www.prounione.urbe.it/dia-int/o-rc/e_o-rc-info.html>.

15. *Being as Communion*, 25; also id., *L'Être ecclésial* (Geneva: Labor et Fides, 1981), 20.

16. See McPartlan, 'The Local Church and the Universal Church: Zizioulas and the Ratzinger–Kasper Debate', *International Journal for the Study of the Christian Church*, 4 (2004), 21–33, where I argue that this debate was not really resolved owing to shared presuppositions regarding eschatology which look weak from an Orthodox point of view.

17. CDF, '*Communionis Notio*: A Letter to the Bishops of the Catholic Church on Some Aspects of the Church Understood as Communion' (28 May 1992) (London and New York: CTS/St. Paul Books & Media, 1992), § 11, available at <http://www.vatican.va/roman_curia/congregations/cfaith/documents/rc_con_cfaith_doc_28051992_communionis-notio_en.html>; cf. McPartlan, *Sacrament of Salvation*, 68–71.

18. See Zizioulas, 'Primacy in the Church: An Orthodox Approach', in James F. Puglisi (ed.), *Petrine Ministry and the Unity of the Church* (Collegeville, Minn.: Liturgical Press, 1999), 115–25; id., 'Recent Discussions on Primacy in Orthodox Theology', in Walter Kasper (ed.), *The Petrine Ministry: Catholics and Orthodox in Dialogue* (Mahwah, NY: Newman Press, 2006), 231–46; also the interview Zizioulas gave to Gianni Valente, 'Where the Eucharist is, There is the Catholic Church', *30 days*, 8 (2005), 8–12; cf. McPartlan, *The Eucharist Makes the Church*, 203–11.

19. 'Where the Eucharist is, There is the Catholic Church', 10.

20. Ibid. 11, 12.

21. 'Primacy in the Church', 121–2.

22. Ibid. 124–5.

23. 'Where the Eucharist is, There is the Catholic Church', 9–10.

24. Ibid. 12; also 'Primacy in the Church', 124.

25. 'The Pastoral Implications of Episcopal Collegiality', *Concilium*, 1 (1965), 28.

26. Ratzinger, *Principles of Catholic Theology. Building Stones for a Fundamental Theology*, trans. Mary Frances McCarthy (San Francisco, Calif.: Ignatius, 1987), 254–5.

27. See also McPartlan, 'Eucharistic Ecclesiology', *One in Christ*, 22 (1986), 314–31.

28. See Congar, *Lay People in the Church: A Study for a Theology of the Laity*, trans. Donald Attwater, rev. edn. (Westminster, Md.: Newman, 1965), pp. xvi, 51, and 214.

29. See id., 'The Church: The People of God', *Concilium*, 1 (1965), 9; cf. also ref. to the 'whole Church' in *DV*, § 10 and *GS*, §§ 11 and 44.

30. See id., 'L'≪Ecclesia≫ ou communauté chrétienne', 282. From an Orthodox point of view (frankly acknowledging Orthodoxy's failings to live up to its own principles), see Nikos A. Nissiotis, 'The Main Ecclesiological Problem of the Second Vatican Council', *Journal of Ecumenical Studies*, 2 (1965), 60–1; also id., 'Pneumatological Christology as a Presupposition of Ecclesiology', *Oecumenica*, 2 (1967), 235–51.

31. See also McPartlan, 'Liturgy, Church and Society', *Studia Liturgica*, 34 (2004), 147–64.

32. Zizioulas, 'Ortodossia', in *Enciclopedia del Novecento*, vol. v. (Rome: Istituto della Enciclopedia Italiana, 1980), 6.

33. *Corpus Mysticum. The Eucharist and the Church in the Middle Ages*, trans. Gemma Simmonds with Richard Price (London: SCM, 2006); cf. McPartlan, *The Eucharist Makes the Church*, pp. xiii–xiv.

34. Congar, 'The Human Person and Human Liberty' (1952), in *Dialogue Between Christians: Catholic Contributions to Ecumenism*, trans. Philip Loretz (Westminster, Md.: Newman, 1966), 244; also Elias Zoghby, 'Eastern and Western Tradition in the One Church', in Hans Küng, Yves Congar, and Daniel O'Hanlon (eds.), *Council Speeches of Vatican II* (Glen Rock, NJ: Paulist, 1964), 32–5; Edmund Schlink, 'The Significance of the Eastern and Western Traditions for the Christian Church', *The Coming Christ and the Coming Church* (Edinburgh and London: Oliver & Boyd, 1967), 285–95.

35. Congar, *Diversity and Communion*, trans. John Bowden (London: SCM, 1984), 90.

36. Ibid. 76.

37. See *GIA II*, 652–9, 660–8, 671–9; also at <http://www.prounione.urbe.it/dia-int/o-rc/doc/e_o-rc_05_valamo.html>.

38. De Lubac, *Catholicism: Christ and the Common Destiny of Man*, trans. Lancelot C. Sheppard. (San Francisco, Calif.: Ignatius, 1988), 16, 109–11.

39. Zizioulas, 'The Ecclesial Presuppositions of the Holy Eucharist', *Nicolaus*, 10 (1982), 342; also, id., *Being as Communion*, 145–7, 182–3.

40. Id.,'The Mystery of the Church in Orthodox Tradition', *One in Christ*, 24 (1988), 299.

41. Ibid. 301.

42. McPartlan, 'The *Catechism* and Catholic–Orthodox Dialogue', *One in Christ*, 30 (1994), 229–44.

43. Extraordinary Synod, 'Final Report', *L'Osservatore Romano* (English edn.), (16 Dec. 1985), 6–9; II. C. 1.

44. Ibid., II. D. 1 (cf. also *LG*, § 1).

45. 'The Church as Communio', *New Blackfriars*, 74 (1993), 239.

46. *Church, Ecumenism & Politics*, trans. Robert Nowell (Slough: St Paul, 1988), 19.

47. Schmemann, *The Eucharist* (Crestwood, NY: St Vladimir's, 1988), 216–17.

48. Ibid. 242; likewise, 'The Church of Christ is not an institution; It is a new life with Christ and in Christ, guided by the Holy Spirit,' Sergius Bulgakov, *The Orthodox Church*, trans. Lydia Kesich (Crestwood, NY: St Vladimir's, 1988), 1; also Zizioulas, *Being as Communion*, 15.

49. Schmemann, *For the Life of the World* (Crestwood, NY: St Vladimir's, 1973), 18.

50. Zizioulas, 'Preserving God's Creation: Lecture One', *King's Theological Review*, 12 (1989), 2–3; also Paul Evdokimov, 'Nature', *Scottish Journal of Theology*, 18 (1965),

12; Bishop Kallistos (Ware) of Diokleia, 'Through the Creation to the Creator', *Ecotheology*, 2 (1997), 18–26.

51. Zizioulas, 'Preserving God's Creation', 3.
52. The 'Common Declaration on Environmental Ethics' (10 June 2002) is available at < http://www.vatican.va/holy_father/john_paul_ii/speeches/2002/june/documents/ hf_jp-ii_spe_20020610_venice-declaration_en.html>.

PART III

RECEPTIVE ECUMENISM AND CATHOLIC CHURCH ORDER

Prologue 3 to Part III
Ephesians 4: 7, 11–16

Philip Endean, SJ

> But each of us was given grace according to the measure of Christ's gift.... The gifts he gave were that some would be apostles, some prophets, some evangelists, some pastors and teachers, to equip the saints for the work of ministry, for building up the body of Christ, until all of us come to the unity of the faith and of the knowledge of the Son of God, to maturity, to the measure of the full stature of Christ. We must no longer be children, tossed to and fro and blown about by every wind of doctrine, by people's trickery, by their craftiness in deceitful scheming. But speaking the truth in love, we must grow up in every way into him who is the head, into Christ, from whom the whole body, joined and knitted together by every ligament with which it is equipped, as each part is working properly, promotes the body's growth in building itself up in love.

The chapters in this part of our volume are about receptive Catholic Learning: about what Roman Catholics, without losing their integrity, can take on board from other traditions in order to realize more fully the vision of the church which the author of Ephesians sets out before us. We hear in this scripture of a body with differing gifts, and of how each of us must be built up until all of us come to the unity of faith. In the chapters which follow, we will be looking at collegiality in both narrow and broad senses; we will be reminded that the biblical witness about apostolicity is patient of many different readings; and we will be considering how all the baptized might be drawn into the decision-making of the church.

These essays are intended as an exercise in first-rate ecclesial theology within the academic context. So, it is of course the case that the insights they contain are based on cutting-edge, recent experience and research. But, true though this is, the basic themes they are rehearsing are hardly new to students of Catholic ecclesiology. We have had rich, creative theologies of collegiality since the 1960s. The problems are not intellectual, but moral. Catholic ecclesiology has stagnated because we will not allow ourselves to imagine change.

It is only nice people who are going to read this book. Many contemporary influential Catholics see the opening up of questions about authority and the nature of the church during the conciliar period as a big mistake, a typically sixties aberration. I would love to think that I am sensitive to these voices only because I live in Oxford, the home of lost causes; but I fear that such an assessment of the matter is merely wishful thinking. Many Christians from other churches would welcome a Petrine ministry that was collegially exercised, with appropriate safeguards against abuse. But they cannot accept the Roman Catholic exercise of authority in its current forms. However you evaluate that impasse, it is clear that theology has said as much as it can, and that the remaining problems are about what people want. The emotions here are quite difficult to handle. Cynicism and bitterness can take us over. It is of faith that there have to be constructive ways of coping with this situation, but it is not easy always to see them or to live by them.

'The gifts he gave were that some would be apostles, some prophets, some evangelists, some pastors and teachers . . . for building up the body of Christ.' We would not be reading this book if the vision enshrined in Ephesians had not at some point in our lives gripped us, if we were not hungering and thirsting for ways in which that vision could be more a reality than it currently is. But the realization of the vision is not in our hands; it lies within the providence of God and the freedom of the church. And 'the freedom of the church' includes the freedom of many who will not bother to read this sort of book, and indeed of some who would never be seen dead reading it.

Nevertheless, the vision of Ephesians is a godly vision. The fact that the vision is not yet reality is no reason to question its authenticity, any more than an alcoholic's relapse indicates that the desire to kick the habit is somehow misguided. Ephesians should awaken our longing: God, through the inspired scripture, is placing a desire within us. We must nurture that desire, and cherish it—even when the climate feels wintry.

13

Catholic Learning Concerning Apostolicity and Ecclesiality

James F. Puglisi, SA

INTRODUCTION

The issues of apostolicity and ecclesiality are complex and complicated themes to treat of and this for several reasons. First, we are in the presence of theological realities with underlying philosophical presuppositions. Furthermore, there is more than one philosophical system which could be driving differing opinions on how to deal with the topic. This problematic may be illustrated by an analogy from the world of computers. To make a computer function one needs an 'operating system' such as Windows or Linux or VMS, which is always running in the background and on top of which programs are placed. More specifically, the operating system enables the computer to interpret data that the programs input. Not all programs can run on all operating systems. Applying this to our subject, we see that the concept of apostolicity is understood in its historical context that includes its own development down through the centuries. We know that in the context of theological development a philosophical shift occurred from a Platonic/Neoplatonic to an Aristotelian system at a certain point in time. This change may correspond to certain shifts in attributing meaning to the concept. An example from eucharistic theology is the debate over the presence of Christ based on the understanding of 'true/*veritas*' or 'real/*realiter*'. Hence we need to be aware of the serious methodological issues involved.

Another issue rendering the topic complicated comes from the human sciences—the question of 'true discourse'. From the field of the sociology of knowledge the question is posed: Who determines what a true discourse is? Cultural issues of dominance within the structure of society and the 'authority' they exercise in the determination of the components of true or false discourse are important. The issue here is who may or may not produce 'verbal capital' in the construction of true discourse?[1]

Thirdly, the very nature of apostolicity touches upon symbolic as well as discursive elements. The use of ritual elements in liturgical services as well as faith statements expressed in canons, creeds, and other discursive forms are all constitutive of the understanding of apostolicity. This interweaving of levels of understanding makes it more difficult for interpretation.

With these issues in mind, let us summarize some of the learnings we have been able to glean from the various ecumenical discussions that have taken place on the theme of apostolicity.

WHAT DO WE MEAN BY APOSTOLICITY?

Taken as a starting-point, the *Dictionary of the Ecumenical Movement* offers a helpful definition deriving from the Faith and Order study project 'Towards the Common Expression of the Apostolic Faith Today':

The church is *apostolic* (1) in that it recognizes its fundamental identity with the church of Christ's apostles, as presented in the NT; (2) in its faithfulness to the word of God lived out and understood in the apostolic tradition, guided by the Holy Spirit throughout the centuries and expressed in the creeds; (3) by its celebration of the sacraments instituted by Christ and practised by the apostles; (4) by the continuity of its ministry... initially taken up by the apostles, in the service of Christ; (5) by being a missionary church which, following the example of the apostles, will not cease to proclaim the gospel to the whole of humankind until Christ comes again in glory.[2]

The concept is here placed in a new context that takes into account the historical and eschatological dimensions. This statement clearly manifests the impact and influence of the 1982 multilateral statement on *Baptism, Eucharist, and Ministry* that articulates two realities together: the apostolic continuity of the church and the apostolic succession of the ministry. Here 'the apostolic tradition of the church as a whole' is regarded as the 'primary manifestation of apostolic succession' (§ M35). This is an important learning for the churches because it identifies elements which are constitutive of the apostolic character of the church (such as the Word of God, the lived witness of faith, hope, charity, ministry, etc.) and does not reduce apostolicity to one specific element, e.g., the transmission of the ministry. Instead, the succession in the ministry is seen as being a service to the whole. § M23 states:

The Church as the Body of Christ and the eschatological people of God is constituted by the Holy Spirit through a diversity of gifts or ministries. Among these gifts a ministry of *episkopé* is necessary to express and safeguard the unity of the body. Every church needs this ministry of unity in some form in order to be the Church of God, the one Body of Christ; a sign of the unity of all in the kingdom.

The same understanding may be found in the statement of the International Theological Commission's 1972 text 'The Apostolic Continuity of the Church and Apostolic Succession'.[3] Likewise, a similar methodology is employed in *Lumen Gentium*, first treating of the ministerial dimension of the whole church before speaking of a special ministry at the service of the general. This pattern is seen in Ephesians 4 where the general ministry of the whole body (i.e. the Gospel project) is built up by charisms given by God for the sake of others. The category of 'testimony' or witness expresses an essential part of the apostolic mission entrusted to the whole church with the ministry oriented towards maintaining the whole project oriented towards Christ.

PROBLEMS IN THE INTERPRETATION

In this context the question of pluralism versus unity is posed—the legitimate and necessary tension between the many and the one. There is a plurality of members in Christ who form the one people of God and, as Ephesians recognizes, a pluralism of vocations and ministers. Similarly, the New Testament is a plurality of traditions receiving and transmitting the essential Gospel message that forms the one book of Scriptures. These traditions require that nothing can be forfeited that is part of one's fidelity to Christ since these elements are considered necessary for salvation. Accordingly, from the very beginning there was and still remains 'an expression of diversity and pluralism in a single communion of faith and Church life'.[4]

This is seen in the history of the early church which had a great variety of cultural diversity in expressing the same faith. Hence, different liturgical forms and customs could be used to express the same apostolic faith. The example of the date for the celebration of Easter bears this out: where priority was accorded to the meaning of what was being celebrated.

Similarly, we may affirm that there was no one single pattern of ministerial leadership within the New Testament. Forms eventually evolved according to cultural spheres of influence, as is seen in the evolution of the form of the episcopate. In most places it evolved from a plural, collegial form to a mono-episcopal form to a monarchical form of exercise. Several of the important early churches, however, maintained the plural form of the episcopate up into the second century. Indeed, scholars are in agreement that the Church of Rome is itself an example of this.[5]

Another lesson from history has been presented by Metropolitan John of Pergamon. In studying the Syriac patristic sources and comparing them to the Greek and Latin traditions, he discovered another way of articulating the question of apostolicity and apostolic succession. Whereas in the later traditions the apostles are seen as individuals, in the Syriac and Oriental traditions they are seen as a college. The church is seen as an eschatological community in which the apostolic ministry is exercised by the apostles headed by Christ in the presence of the community gathered together. This means that apostolic continuity and succession take place in and through the entire structure of the community. With this, in the Syriac tradition, James, brother of Jesus, occupies a central and important place in the structure of the church and in apostolic succession, being referred to as 'lord and bishop of the church' (*Epistle of Peter to James*, Preface) or 'lord and bishop of bishops' (*Epistle of Clement to James*, Preface). In each local church there exists continuity with the original community of Jerusalem whose structure is transferred and copied with James at its head.

The Syrian tradition, then, understands succession as a transmission not of certain authority from individual to individual but of the original Jerusalem community in its entire structure, having Christ as its head replaced, in the first instance, by his brother James and finally by the bishop of every local church. It is a continuity of communities. Theologically this means each local church in its eucharistic structure is the image of the New Jerusalem coming down from heaven. Here we find an eschatological rather than historic outlook. Each succession has continuity with Jerusalem as the image of the eschatological community in which Christ occupies the throne of God imaged on earth by the bishop. The bishop is seen not as an individual but as the head of his community which in turn is the image of the community of the New Jerusalem of the last days.[6]

These two historical observations remind us that there is still much to be learnt from a (re)examination of history, especially of the entirety of the Patristic traditions. Hence, there was great diversity but yet still communion in the faith. There was diversity in the way continuity was understood: either through the transmission from person to person or through a continuity of communities all linked to the mother community of Jerusalem (both geographic and eschatological) through the eucharistic structure of the community. Problems arise when a rigid way of reading this material excludes those 'messy' historical cases which do not neatly fit into our ready made moulds and when one church pretends dominance over another. Eventually what happens is the sense of the continuity of communities (their faith, life witness, canonical traditions, sacramental rites, etc.) gives way to the emphasis placed on the transmission of authority and power to an individual through ordination or apostolic succession in ministry. The central focus shifts: the person of the minister becomes the centrepiece and not the ministry or diaconia.

WHAT HAVE WE LEARNED FROM THE DIALOGUES?

First of all the concept of 'apostolicity' is used in many of the dialogues when speaking of or describing the church. It is most frequently used when talking about issues of ministry especially a ministry of *episkopé* where the content of apostolicity usually refers to teaching that is true and in some way connected to the apostolic tradition.

Let us begin then by talking about the apostolicity of the church. There is an overwhelming consensus that affirms the church to be apostolic to the degree that she stands firm in fidelity to the witness of the Apostles and lives from the gifts of the Spirit. *BEM* puts it clearly when it says:

The Spirit keeps the Church in the apostolic tradition until the fulfilment of history in the Kingdom of God. Apostolic tradition in the Church means continuity in the permanent characteristics of the Church of the apostles: witness to the apostolic faith, proclamation and fresh interpretation of the Gospel, celebration of baptism and the Eucharist, the transmission of ministerial responsibilities, communion in prayer, love, joy and suffering, service to the sick and the needy, unity among the local churches and sharing the gifts which the Lord has given to each. (§ M34)

The text tries to answer the question of the relationship between the apostolic continuity of the whole church and episcopal succession by underlining the Christological foundation (the sending of the apostles by the Lord and his continued presence in the Church) and the pneumatological and eschatological foundations of apostolicity (the assistance of the Spirit given to the church until the completion of the kingdom is accomplished). Bilateral dialogues have developed also along this same line.[7]

In §§ 27–31 of the 1990 ARCIC II statement 'The Church as Communion' there is a description of how the tradition is a living tradition by the introduction of the concept of memory: 'This dynamic process constitutes what is called the living tradition, the living memory of the Church.'[8] The text states that the apostolic tradition of the church is formed by 'this memory, realized and freshly expressed in every age and culture' and 'if the Church is to remain faithfully rooted and grounded in the living truth and to confess it with relevance, then it will need to develop new expressions of the faith' (§ 31).

Another example can be found in the 1996 Rio de Janeiro Report of the Joint International Commission for Dialogue Between the World Methodist Council and the Roman Catholic Church: 'The Church is like a living cell with Christ as its centre; the community, as it grows and multiplies, retains its original pattern. Apostolic communities need people to do for their own time what the apostles did in theirs: to pastor, teach and minister under the authority of the Good Shepherd and Teacher, the Servant Lord.'[9] This affirmation clearly links the role of the ordained to the mission of the church and to apostolicity. The basis for this identification is found in the pattern of the relation of the Apostles to the early church. The work of the 1991 Singapore Report on *The Apostolic Tradition* laid the foundation for the above-cited statement where the Trinitarian foundation of the patterns of Christian Community (sect. V) provided the basis for understanding how the church in its structures (especially its ministerial dimension) has developed and continues in the present time.[10]

Even though we have only cited a few of the dialogues, an agreement on the apostolic nature of the whole church may be seen. In 1980, the International Lutheran–Roman Catholic Dialogue remarked that: 'The goal of unity is *given* to us *beforehand*. It is not constructed or manipulated, but is received. It is not a totally new reality reserved for a distant future, but is in its fundamental elements already present and active among us.'[11] Moreover, whilst this apostolicity is an abstract reality, it is related to the concrete mission of the church. *The Apostolic Tradition*, cited above, puts it this way:

Jesus Christ was sent among us by God the Father to make known and to bring to completion the divine purpose of salvation . . . In the power of the Holy Spirit, this mission continues in and through the Church, the family Christ gathers together in common obedience to the Father's will. As Christ's servant, the Church proclaims to the world the message of his victory over sin and death, provides a living sign of that victory, and summons everyone to repent and believe the gospel and so receive the promised Spirit. (§ 1)

Apostolicity is seen in terms of its continuity in history as a succession of faithful teaching from generation to generation. Hence, in the 1972 Lutheran–Roman Catholic 'Malta Report':

The basic intention of the doctrine of apostolic succession is to indicate that, throughout all historical changes in its proclamation and structures, the Church is at all times referred back to its apostolic origin. The details of this doctrine seem to us today to be more complicated than before. In the New Testament and the early fathers, the emphasis was obviously placed more on the substance of apostolicity, i.e., on succession in apostolic teaching. In this sense the entire Church as the *ecclesia apostolica* stands in the apostolic succession.[12]

We may glean from this that the apostolicity of the church is historically founded, rooted in the original witness of the apostles which ultimately points to the ministry of Jesus Christ, the original one sent by God. This witness was not intended to remain fallow or static but, rather, was destined to expand, looking beyond history to God's purpose in the fulfilment of the Kingdom, ushering in the end times. This double dimension of apostolicity is very important and needs to be articulated by means of diverse elements, symbols, and activities of the church.

Two examples of these elements are found in the earlier-cited *BEM* § M34 and in the 1972 Anglican–Lutheran 'Pullach Report'. In the latter case:

The succession of apostolicity through time is guarded and given contemporary expression in and through a wide variety of means, activities and institutions: the canon of Scriptures, creeds, confessional writings, liturgies, the activities of preaching, teaching, celebrating the sacraments and ordaining and using a ministry of Word and Sacrament, the exercising of pastoral care and oversight, the common life of the Church, and the engagement in mission to and for the world.[13]

These examples show that there is a general convergence as to what are considered the marks of apostolicity of the church and its constitutive elements.

This fundamental apostolicity of the church is the regulating force of the apostolicity of a local church and of a particular bishop and even of the episcopal ministry. This observation not only arises out of the results of the dialogues but also from a careful study of the process of access to the ordained ministry.[14] This will lead us to consider our last point, namely: the relationship of succession to continuity.

APOSTOLICITY AND SUCCESSION

Once again in almost all of the dialogue statements there is a reference to the ministry of oversight or *episkopé* and the apostolicity of the church. While there is not universal consensus on what is the essential nature of this relationship, there is some convergence at the heart of the matter.

The Joint Working Group between the World Council of Churches and the Secretariat (now Pontifical Council) for the Promotion of Christian Unity made a preliminary study on the subject in 1968. It affirmed the necessity of the apostolic ministry as one of the necessary elements for the apostolicity of the church: 'In the life of the church, the apostolic preaching transmitted by Scripture and Tradition, the apostolic ministry, and life in accordance with the Gospel are inseparable. All three are essential to its apostolicity.'[15]

From a Catholic perspective, the question of the extent to which other churches possess 'true sacraments' is related to the question of ministerial succession. We may cite two interesting positions, one by Walter Kasper and the other by the International Theological Commission. Building on the Second Vatican Council's recognition of elements of sanctification outside of the Catholic Church (*LG*, § 15 and *UR*, § 3) and in particular relation to the sacraments celebrated in other churches and ecclesial bodies, Kasper reasons thus:

In the same way that we find *vestigia ecclesiae* beyond the visible limits of the Church, we also find *vestigia successionis et ministerii* beyond succession in its visible and verifiable form. With reference to the churches of the Reform, Vatican II merely talks about a *defectus* with regard to the full form of ministry, a lack, but not a complete absence. Thus a certain degree of recognition has been conceded.[16]

A few years earlier, the International Theological Commission's 'The Apostolicity of the Church and Apostolic Succession' took more or less the same stance:

[Protestant] ministers have edified and nourished their communities. By baptism, by the study and the preaching of the word, by their prayers together and celebration of the Last Supper, and by their zeal they have guided men toward faith in the Lord and thus helped them to find the way of salvation. There are thus in such communities elements that certainly belong to the apostolicity of the unique Church of Christ.[17]

One could say that within the Roman Catholic theological community there is the opinion, in relation to the Protestant churches, that while there is not an immediate recognition of a ministerial succession such as is known to the Catholic Church, there is, nevertheless, not a complete lack thereof. But what do some of the dialogues say to the issues of oversight in their understanding of apostolic succession?

The 1981 Lutheran–Roman Catholic text 'The Ministry in the Church' states what is held in common:

As regards the succession of the ministers, the joint starting point for both Catholics and Lutherans is that there is an integral relation between the witness of the gospel and witnesses to the gospel (cf. Malta Report, § 48). The witness to the gospel has been entrusted to the church as a whole. Therefore, the whole church as the *ecclesia apostolica* stands in the apostolic succession. Succession in the sense of the succession of ministers must be seen within the succession of the whole church in the apostolic faith (cf. Malta Report, § 57).[18]

Continuing to reflect on this understanding, the dialogue stated some years later that:

The vigilance with regard to the apostolicity of the faith that belongs to the bishop's duty is bound up with the responsibility for the faith borne by the whole Christian people. Members of the church participate in the election of their bishop and receive the person who is to exercise the apostolic ministry. In addition, when the candidate answers the ordination questions and confesses his faith in the presence of the congregation, the congregation is witness that the bishop represents the authentic apostolic faith. All this shows that the apostolic succession is not really to be understood as a succession of one individual to another, but rather as a succession in the church, to an episcopal see and to membership of the episcopal college, as shown by the lists of bishops.[19]

The final sentence of this statement in particular underlines a vital learning for the future progress of the question of succession which, in turn, allows me to make a digression concerning the diverse understandings of succession found in history.

First, it is not without significance that all ordinations take place in the context of the Eucharist, i.e. in the presence and participation of the entire community. This means that succession has to come to us not only from the past but also from the future, from the eschatological community with which the Eucharist relates each local church at a given time in history.

Second, no ordination to the episcopate is possible without mention of the place to which the ordained bishop is attached. Therefore, succession means in fact continuity of communities, not individuals. If the bishop is crucial in this kind of succession it is because he is head of a community imaging the eschatological gathering of all around Christ and not because he has received apostolic authority as an individual. This role is clearly seen both in the role of the neighbouring bishops at the ordination of a bishop and the action of the community concerned in the election of their bishop. In both cases their involvement signifies theologically the activity of the Holy Spirit. This pneumatological dimension of ordination is rooted in the concept of witnessing, thereby demonstrating the confessional dimension of the process of access to the ordained ministry of bishop.[20]

Thirdly, ordination as a sign and visible means of apostolic succession must be an insertion into the life of the community. When this happens, the ordained bishop both gives and receives apostolicity from the community into which he is inserted. Therefore, we cannot consider apostolic succession outside of the apostolic continuity of the specific church in question. Apostolic continuity cannot be created *ex nihilo* through episcopal ordination unless it is somehow already there. And it cannot be taken for granted unless it is somehow affirmed, sealed, and proclaimed through episcopal ordination. Every bishop participates in the episcopal college via his community, not directly. Apostolic succession is a succession of apostolic communities via their heads.[21]

Lastly, Zizioulas affirms that apostolic continuity is not something that concerns a particular local church taken by itself. It is a matter concerning all the local churches at a regional or even universal level. The church is an entity that receives and re-receives what her history transmits to her (*paradosis*), but this transmission is never a purely historical affair. It takes place *sacramentally* or, better, *eucharistically*. That is, it is experienced as a gift coming from the last days; from what God has promised and prepared for us in His Kingdom—the work of the Holy Spirit (Acts 2: 17).[22]

If Lutherans and Roman Catholics can agree upon this way of understanding the relationship between ministerial succession and the continuity of the church, then we need to consider the Lutheran caution in 'Church and Justification' (1993) concerning human error by bishops who are separated from the faith of the community. We understand that the bishop does not possess apostolicity as an individual but only as the head of an apostolic church. It is the apostolic faith of his church that is reconfirmed in the ordination service because no local church is assured of being in the apostolic faith unless she has been attested to by other churches. This is represented by the obligatory presence of the neighbouring bishops in an ordination service. The apostolic faith is kept by all the faithful of that local church which is the meaning of the witness that they give to the elect. In her comment upon 'Church and Justification', Margaret O'Gara notes that 'while Catholic tradition holds "that the episcopate as a whole is ... kept firm in the truth of the gospel" (§ 217), the teaching office exercised by the episcopate "remains anchored in the life of faith of the whole people of God" who are involved in a "many-sided exchange" with the bishops as all sharers in Christ's prophetic office (§ 216)'.[23]

Other churches that have discussed these issues have been able to come to a similar understanding of the relationship of episcopal succession to the apostolic continuity of the church. For example, the discussions held between the Nordic churches and the Anglican churches of Great Britain and Ireland, issuing in the 1993 'Porvoo Common Statement', recognized an episcopal succession that is signified by the ordination of a bishop as 'a visible and personal way of focusing the apostolicity of the whole Church'.[24] The Lutheran and Anglican churches in question make a strong statement together affirming the value of the historic episcopate while at the same time realizing that it is not a guarantee:

To ordain a bishop in historic succession (that is, in intended continuity from the apostles themselves) is also a sign. In so doing the Church communicates its care for continuity in the whole of its life and mission, and reinforces its determination to manifest the permanent characteristics of the Church of the apostles. . . . The use of the sign of the historic episcopal succession does not by itself guarantee the fidelity of a church to every aspect of the apostolic faith, life and mission. . . . Nor does the sign guarantee the personal faithfulness of the bishop. Nonetheless, the retention of the sign remains a permanent challenge to fidelity and to unity, a summons to witness to, and a commission to realize more fully, the permanent characteristics of the Church of the apostles. (§ 50)

Let us look at one more example from the discussions between Methodists and Roman Catholics. This is an interesting dialogue because the Methodist World Council has member churches that are both episcopal and non-episcopal. Early on in this dialogue, Methodists understand succession in the ministry as 'a valuable *symbol* of the Church's continuity with the church of the New Testament, though they would not use it as a *criterion*'.[25] While the dialogue has progressed and while each side has clarified the meaning given to a ministry of oversight, there still resides a difference in light of the necessity for a personal office of bishop. In the 1986 Nairobi statement we read:

Both Roman Catholics and Methodists believe that *episkopé* of the churches is a divinely given function. The Roman Catholic Church and many Methodist Churches express *episkopé* through bishops. It is the belief of the Roman Catholic Church and these Methodist Churches that for the exercise of their ministry the bishops receive special gifts from the Holy Spirit through prayer and the laying-on of hands. Methodist Churches which have an ordained ministry but do not have bishops, believing them not to be essential to a church, have considered adopting them as an enrichment of their own life and to promote the unity of Christians; such bishops would be a focus of unity and a sign of the historic continuity of the church.[26]

HOW TO USE WHAT WE HAVE LEARNED

The learnings from these forty years or more of dialogue and experience together need somehow to be assimilated into the way we think and act as church. The difficult question of what a united church might look like needs at some time to be considered. My first response when I am asked this question is to say quite frankly that I do not know. However, it is necessary immediately to add that it will not look like any of our current churches! Whatever else, we have learned that the ecumenical movement is not a movement of conversion from one flock to another but rather a conversion to the one Shepherd himself. At the heart of the teaching of the Second Vatican Council is that call to conversion to Christ which is the central movement of the reconciliation that God asks of all those who are baptized.

Moreover, polite refusal to consider this question as to the possible shape of a united church should not satisfy any Christian because we need to deal concretely with such shifts as have already occurred—for example, in the thinking on the relationship between apostolicity, ecclesiality, and episcopacy.

Implications for Catholic thinking and practice could involve a greater effective collegiality. This would mean concretely that heads of local churches assume their responsibility for the inculturation of the faith and its practice according to a model that is collegial (among those who are ordained for service of the local church [bishop, presbyters, deacons]) as well as synodical (with the responsibility of all the baptized for the Gospel). This approach would require a continual catechesis of the faithful and an ongoing education of the clergy (from bishop to deacons). Only in this way will a local church remain apostolic because it continually breaks open afresh the Word of God and seeks to conform its life and witness to that Word. Only then will all be able to assume their proper responsibility and role in the spread of the Gospel at service to the world.

The advantages would be the slowing down of the process of secularization because the church would, in its entirety, constantly be hearing the Word as the new living Word which continually challenges the hearer to a renewed conversion to God. With the Second Vatican Council there was much optimism and enthusiasm engendered by the Council's teaching on collegiality, the theology of the local church, and the participation of the laity in the life and mission of the church.

However, one of the *periti* at the Council, Yves Congar, who hoped that the Second Vatican Council's teaching would counterbalance the First, noted more soberly before the Council even concluded that its real ecumenical impact would only be felt if the theology of the local church really became *the* way of being church. Of course, he was not against the necessary role that the petrine office was to exercise but he was sure that without the application of the theology of the local church, the hoped-for ecclesiological equilibrium never be achieved.[27]

In this regard, it must be recognized that lessons that Roman Catholicism might learn as to the ways in which collegial and synodical systems work in other churches have yet to be learned. As here noted, relevant dialogues with the Anglican Communion and the Lutheran Church have made good progress along the theoretical lines of the Council but have not, unfortunately, found much of an echo in practice.

What would have to be done in order to cull the most from these dialogues? Clearly all parties need first to consider relevant potential structural changes in their own churches. From the Roman Catholic side, there needs to be far more responsible involvement of the laity in the life of the church—from the possibility of voicing their needs in the choice of their bishops, to the daily functioning of the local church. A more collaborative style of governance is needed which, without ceasing to govern, would enable bishops to develop practices of and structures for decision-making with Christians. With this, a synodical lifestyle would complete the Second Vatican Council's teaching on collegiality and subsidiarity. It needs to be determined when it is necessary to decide together, to teach together, and to celebrate together. This means learning how 'to travel the road together'.[28]

On the other hand, it will likewise be necessary for the Protestant and Anglican churches to learn what are the instances when they cannot act alone, in isolation from other churches, since every decision made impacts others. The days of believing that decisions made in one church do not have an impact on another church are over. Because of the ecumenical movement the churches have become more interconnected. A synodical form of government and dialogue are therefore absolutely essential for the being of the church and the health of its mission.

One of the most serious issues remaining is the recognition of the ordained ministries of other churches. As noted earlier, Cardinal Kasper helpfully clarifies that the Council did not speak in terms of a complete absence of ordained ministry in churches other than the Roman Catholic, but of a lack (*defectus*). In the past, the implications for this lack was that these churches were deficient in regards to their apostolicity. This was due to the fact that there was a confusion between apostolic succession (in ministry) and the apostolic continuity of the church.

We have seen that these two realities are to be articulated together, with the former serving the latter. Therefore, the wider reality is the apostolic continuity of the church which has many components, one of which is the ministry. The ministry is seen to be at the service of this continuity and, as we have seen, needs to be inserted into a community. One does not possess apostolicity but is inserted into a church which is recognized by other churches to be apostolic. This is the importance of the ecclesial, confessing, and juridical process that we call ordination (particularly that of the head of a local church).

We may even say that there is already a type of recognition of heads of other Christian churches that may be seen in the way these heads are received by the Bishop of Rome himself. Lutheran and Anglican bishops who have been received by the Pope often receive a symbolic gift (a stole, a pectoral cross, a chalice). Would the Pope offer such gifts to a 'simple layperson'? Obviously not! This means that these individuals are recognized as spiritual leaders of their people and, therefore, as the Council would say, as providing the means for the action of the Holy Spirit. Could this not then mean that they are effective ministers of the Holy Spirit and to be recognized as being in communion with the corpus of ministers who have the duty to build up the body of Christ?[29] We need to draw even more from this realization concerning the status of the office of *episkopē* in other traditions and their recognition as authentic ministers of the Gospel and sacraments.

One last observation is in order before drawing some conclusions. In the minds of many people in the church today, there is still a basic confusion between unity and uniformity. The church of Christ is one, but Christians are divided. This unity requires diversity, a legitimate pluralism, otherwise there could not be unity. With uniformity, one presupposes that everything will be the same. In the early church this mentality did not exist. For example, some churches had an individual leader responsible for the oversight of the *ecclesia*. This fact did not impede them from recognizing other churches who had a plural form of ministry as being authentic apostolic churches. The question to ask today is: if this situation could be in the past why not so today? It is obvious that the form of the ministry was not the determining factor but rather the recognition that it was the same apostolic faith being proclaimed, celebrated, and lived that counted not its diverse form. Hence the unity of the church will likewise demand a diversity of forms and expressions of the same faith.

CONCLUSIONS

What may we conclude that we have learned from all of this? I believe there are several points that can be confirmed.

First, there is now a general agreement about apostolicity, namely: that first and foremost apostolicity is applied to the whole church and not just to some elements of the church.

Second, in general, all recognize the place of the apostolic ministry within the apostolicity of the whole church.

Third, there is recognized to be an intimate relationship between the apostolic continuity of the whole church and the apostolic succession of the ministry.

Fourth, there is agreement on the role of a ministry of oversight/*episkopē* in maintaining the church oriented towards its source, Christ.

Fifth, even though the historical dimension of apostolicity is important there is also the eschatological dimension of the purpose of the ministry which must be taken into account. When we speak of the 'living memory' of the apostles and their teaching we are also speaking of their eschatological role as judges of the nations and as ones who prefigure the reality of the kingdom which is coming into our midst.

Sixth, there is a symbolic/ritual dimension to the issue of continuity and succession that cannot be neglected. This gives us access to the sacramental or mysteric dimension of ordination so that it does not simply become a historic, material transmission of power and authority to an individual but 'orders' the constellation of diverse actors in the body with a new and lasting relationship to the other Christians in the body. In this way the ministerial succession is seen as a service to the whole.

Seventh, from a consideration of the patristic understanding one can see that there were two approaches to the question of succession: one which was linear and traces back to a particular apostle and the other which is eschatological and traces its source back to a continuity of communities. While this was not explored that much by the dialogues themselves but rather by theologians it merits further exploration. By considering the whole of the ancient church, we may arrive at a more balanced and flexible paradigm for the questions that still are raised by the churches in terms of mutual recognition of ministries and reception of the apostolic constitution of churches which do not have the same structure (i.e. concerning the relationship between non-episcopal and episcopally structured churches).

NOTES

1. See Peter L. Berger and Thomas Luckmann, *The Social Construction of Reality. A Treatise in the Sociology of Knowledge* (New York: Doubleday, 1967). For a related discussion, see Paul D. Murray, 'On Valuing Truth in Practice: Rome's Postmodern Challenge', *International Journal of Systematic Theology*, 8 (2006), 163–83; also in Laurence Paul Hemming and Susan Frank Parsons (eds.), *Redeeming Truth: Considering Faith and Reason* (London: SCM, 2007), 184–206.
2. Peter Staples, 'Apostolicity', in Nicholas Lossky, et al. (eds.), *Dictionary of the Ecumenical Movement*, 2nd edn. (Geneva: WCC, 2002), 50; also John J. Burkhard, *Apostolicity Then and Now: An Ecumenical Church in a Postmodern World* (Collegeville, Minn.: Liturgical Press, 2004).
3. Michael Sharkey (ed.), *International Theological Commission: Texts and Documents, 1969–1985* (San Francisco, Calif.: Ignatius Press, 1989), 93–104.
4. E. Lanne, 'Pluralism and Unity. The Possibility of a Variety of Typologies Within the Same Ecclesial Allegiance', *One in Christ*, 6 (1970), 431.
5. See J. Füllenbach, *Ecclesiastical Office and the Primacy of Rome: An Evaluation of Recent Theological Discussion of First Clement* (Washington, DC: Catholic University

of America Press, 1980); also Francis A. Sullivan, *From Apostles to Bishops: The Development of the Episcopacy in the Early Church* (Mahwah, NY: Newman Press, 2001), esp. 218–30.

6. See John D. Zizioulas, *Eucharist, Bishop, Church: The Unity of the Church in the Divine Eucharist and the Bishop During the First Three Centuries*, trans. Elizabeth Theokritoff (Brookline, Mass.: Holy Cross Orthodox Press, 2001), 128–62; id., 'Apostolic Continuity of the Church and Apostolic Succession in the First Five Centuries', *Louvain Studies*, 21 (1996), 153–68.

7. For some examples from the International Lutheran–Roman Catholic Dialogue, see 'Report of the Joint Lutheran–Roman Catholic Study Commission on *The Gospel and the Church*, 1972 ("Malta Report")', § 57, *GIA*, 181–2; 'The Ministry in the Church' (1981), § 16, *GIA*, 252; 'The Church and Justification' (1994), § 47, *GIA II*, 498–9 .

8. ARCIC II, *The Church as Communion: An Agreed Statement by the Second Anglican–Roman Catholic International Commission* (London: Church House Publishing/CTS, 1991), § 27, available at <http://www.prounione.urbe.it/dia-int/arcic/doc/e_arcicII_communion.html>.

9. *The Word of Life* (Rio de Janeiro) (World Methodist Council, 1996), § 86, repr. *GIA II*, 637.

10. *The Apostolic Tradition* (Singapore) (World Methodist Council, 1991), §§ 83–5, repr. *GIA II*, 614.

11. 'Ways to Community' (1980), § 4, *GIA*, 215.

12. § 57, *GIA*, 181.

13. 'The Pullach Report', § 74, repr. *GIA*, 24.

14. See Puglisi, 'Ecumenical Developments in Ordination Rites', in Tamara Grdzelidze (ed.), *One, Holy, Catholic and Apostolic. Ecumenical Reflections on the Church* (Geneva: WCC, 2005), 226–41 and, more extensively, id., *The Process of Admission to the Ordained Ministry: A Comparative Study*, vols. i–iii (Collegeville, Minn.: Liturgical Press, 1996–2001).

15. 'Study Document on Catholicity and Apostolicity' (1968), *One in Christ*, 4 (1970), 460.

16. Kasper, *Apostolic Succession in Episcopacy in an Ecumenical Context* (Baltimore, Md.: St Mary's Seminary and University, 1992), 12.

17. In Sharkey, *International Theological Commission: Texts and Documents, 1969–1985*, 104.

18. 'The Ministry in the Church', § 60, *GIA*, 267.

19. International Lutheran–Roman Catholic Dialogue, 'Facing Unity' (1984), § 110, repr. *GIA II*, 468.

20. See Puglisi, *The Process of Admission to Ordained Ministry*, i. 27 ff.

21. See B-D. Dupuy, 'La Succession apostolique dans la discussion œcuménique', *Istina*, 12 (1967), 398.

22. Zizioulas, *Being as Communion: Studies in Personhood and the Church* (London: Darton, Longman & Todd, 1985), 201 ff. and 236–7.

23. O'Gara, 'Apostolicity in Ecumenical Dialogue', *Mid-Stream*, 37 (1998), 189.

24. *The Porvoo Common Statement*, Occasional Paper, 3 (London: Council of Christian Unity of the General Synod of the Church of England, 1993), § 46, repr. C. Podmore (ed.), *Together in Mission and Ministry: The Porvoo Common Statement with Essays*

on Chruch, and Ministry in Northern Europe (London: Church House Publishing, 1993).

25. Joint International Commission for Dialogue Between the World Methodist Council and the Roman Catholic Church, *Growth in Understanding* (Dublin) (World Methodist Council, 1976), § 87, repr. in *GIA*, 358.

26. Id., *Towards a Statement on the Church* (Nairobi) (World Methodist Council, 1986), §§ 34–5, repr. *GIA II*, 589–90.

27. Congar, *Le Concile au jour le jour: quatrième session* (Paris: Cerf, 1966), 134.

28. See the insightful and lucid observations of H. Legrand concerning the functioning of the teaching of the Vatican Council on collegiality and what does and does not work for ecumenism: 'The Bishop is in the Church and the Church is in the Bishop', *The Jurist*, 66 (2006), 70–92, esp. 76–7.

29. Cf. Eph. 4: 12–13.

14

The Holy Spirit as the Gift—Pneumatology and Catholic Re-reception of Petrine Ministry in the Theology of Walter Kasper

Denis Edwards

INTRODUCTION

Two issues have particular priority in the discussion of Catholic ecumenical receptivity: first, and arguably most fundamentally, is the general need for western receptivity to the East with regard to a proper balance between pneumatology and Christology; second is the particular, strategically important issue, which many would view as constituting a logjam in present ecumenical relations, of Petrine ministry. My proposal is that the pneumatological theology of Walter Kasper illuminates both issues.

Noting the oft-repeated assumption that the issue of ministry cannot be the only reason we live in separate churches and do not participate together at the Lord's Table, Cardinal Kasper insists 'Yet it is!'[1] Differences over ministry, above all episcopal and Petrine ministry, constitute the central challenges for ecumenism in the twenty-first century. Even where there is agreement about the ministries of bishop and priest, the ministry of the Bishop of Rome, above all the claims made at the First Vatican Council, block the movement towards full communion.

Further, Kasper points out that Orthodox and Protestant ecumenical partners see a deeper issue below the surface in all discussions about ministry—pneumatology. Orthodox theologians find a neglect of the Spirit in the western tradition, speaking specifically of a tendency to a one-sided Christomonism in Roman Catholicism, which results in an ecclesiology that gives priority to authority, to the juridical institution, and to the papacy. While Kasper rejects the reproach of Christomonism with regard to the Roman Catholic tradition taken as a whole, he finds a significant kernel of truth when it is applied to post-Reformation ecclesiology, 'which was indeed often more a hierarchology'.[2] In turn, Protestant ecumenical partners give priority to the Word of God in and over the church and emphasize the freedom of the Spirit over against a juridical–institutional view of church and the priestly–sacramental system. From a very different perspective they too challenge the Roman Catholic Church to a renewed pneumatology.

Kasper proposes that the way forward involves a deeper pneumatology that opens out into a theology of church as communion, where the church is understood as both institution and ever-new charismatic event.[3] He argues that such a theology, already initiated by the Second Vatican Council, will be able to hold to what is essential in the Roman Catholic position whilst also being able to respond creatively to the criticisms and gifts of ecumenical partners. I believe this line of thought is fundamental to Roman Catholic receptivity in ecumenical relations. The most important gift Roman Catholicism can receive from the East is a deeper pneumatology. More precisely, I think this is an invitation to retrieve from the whole Christian tradition a living theology of Word and Spirit who, in Congar's phrase, always 'do God's work together'.[4] By restoring the balance and the interrelationship between Christology and pneumatology it will be possible to find the balance and right interrelationship between freedom and institution, the priesthood of all believers and the ordained, the local church and the universal church, the episcopacy and the Bishop of Rome.[5] It is important to recognize that if the gift offered is an invitation to a more balanced and dynamic pneumatology, the Spirit is also that in us by which we are enabled to receive the gift. The Spirit is both the gift, and the very principle of ecumenical receptivity.

The great example here is Yves Congar. Kasper speaks of him as 'the theological pioneer of ecumenism'[6] and the 'master of ecumenical theology'.[7] What is being suggested is that Kasper is a second radical example of Catholic ecumenical receptivity in the area of pneumatology and it is this that bears fruit in his ecumenical theology and practice. I use the word radical because Kasper grounds his pneumatology where it must be grounded, in Christology. I will trace his Spirit theology from his Christology to his Trinitarian theology and his view of the church, and then to one example of this pneumatology at work in ecumenical theology, the critical issue of the Petrine ministry.

CHRISTOLOGY IN THE PERSPECTIVE OF PNEUMATOLOGY

Kasper's major systematic work on Christology appeared in 1974.[8] Writing at an early stage in the western renewal of pneumatology, Kasper led the way, particularly among Roman Catholic scholars, in locating his Christology within a rich theology of the Spirit, arguing that the mediation between the divine and the human in Jesus can only be understood as an event in the Spirit. What is required is a 'pneumatologically oriented Christology'.[9]

Kasper identified dangers in both western and eastern theologies. With Joseph Ratzinger, he saw the West as in danger of an exclusively Christ-centred theology.[10] In the East, the danger is of a spirituality that becomes indifferent to the institutions of church and world. Kasper takes from the East a theology that begins from the Father, with the Spirit understood as the excess, the overflow of divine love manifest in the Son: 'In the Spirit, the love manifested in the Son again impels onwards and outwards to a further revelation of God. The Spirit is as it were God's outermost and uttermost.'[11] Through the Spirit, understood in this way, God acts in creation, history, and in the incarnation itself.

A pneumatological Christology needs to go beyond scholastic theology, which had so emphasized the one divine essence and the unity of divine action *ad extra* that it could hold that any one of the divine persons might have become incarnate. The result is a complete disjunction between biblical history and theological metaphysics. Kasper insists, by contrast, on approaching the issue from the concrete perspective of biblical history and argues for a theology in which the divine persons are involved together in the incarnation but according to the distinctive character of each.

Scholastic theology spoke of the *gratia unionis* to express the effect of the incarnation on Jesus' humanity which, as a consequence of its union with the eternal *Logos*, is filled with the grace of the Spirit. This outpouring of the Spirit on the humanity of Jesus is ascribed to its union with the eternal *Logos*. The action of the Spirit is understood as the result of the union. Patristic theology had used the language of 'unction' or 'anointing' and had seen this as divinizing the humanity of Jesus. Kasper insists on two corrections to these positions. First, the patristic thesis of the divinization of Jesus' humanity is correct, but only when it is understood according to the principle that the closer we are to God the more fully human we are. Second, the action of the Spirit on Jesus is not simply a consequence of the presence of the *Logos*, but its *presupposition*. The Holy Spirit is the creative principle who sanctifies the humanity of Jesus, enabling him to respond to God's self-communication in radical freedom and love, and thus enabling him to be this self-communication made incarnate for the world.[12]

Because Jesus' humanity is transformed by the Spirit, he can be the Word of God. Because Jesus is anointed by the Spirit, he is the Christ. As created in the Spirit, and transformed by the Spirit, Jesus is the Son of God. The incarnation is understood as beginning with the freedom of God's loving self-communication in the Spirit, rather than in a more Hegelian way with the necessary self-communication of the *Logos*. It is an utterly gracious event flowing from the excess of divine love that is the Spirit.

A Spirit Christology best communicates the meaning of salvation in Christ: through the Spirit, divine love finds expression outside the Trinity in Jesus; in the Spirit-filled humanity of Jesus, the Son gives himself in love unto death to the Father; in the death and resurrection of Jesus, the Spirit, as it were, breaks free and is poured out for us. Salvation is 'participation in the life of God in the Holy Spirit through the mediation of Jesus Christ'.[13] Jesus, anointed with the Spirit and installed by the Spirit as the messianic one, is the bearer and dispenser of the Spirit. The Spirit, as the *gratia unionis*, is not a private endowment of Jesus but is also the *gratia capitis*, the grace that flows from Christ the head to his body the church, and is transmitted by the church to the world. Jesus is the salvation of the world because 'he is filled with the Holy Spirit and we share in this plenitude'.[14] The distinction between Christology and soteriology is overcome.

A Spirit Christology can integrate God's universal action with salvation in Christ. The Spirit and salvation are at work wherever human beings take upon themselves the risk of their existence, seek for truth, and take up responsibility, above all when they commit themselves in love of God and neighbour. While universal history is the place of the Spirit, it is also the place of sinful refusal. The Spirit's influence in history is disfigured by sin and easily misunderstood. Jesus is the only instance where the Spirit finds acceptance in a complete and undistorted way. He is wholly a receptacle for God's self-communication through the Spirit in the Word: 'The universal historical activity of the Spirit therefore reached its goal in him in a way that is ultimate. Light falls from Jesus Christ on the rest of history.'[15] Only in Christ does the work of the Spirit find its fulfilment and meaning. In him, the needs and hopes of humanity are met by God's explicit self-communication.

Kasper's Christology shows how incarnation and salvation are to be seen as events of the Spirit. Congar has added another dimension, insisting strongly on the ever-fresh historical, event-character of the Spirit in the conception, life, ministry, death, and resurrection of Jesus.[16] Kasper's Christology can also be developed in the direction of a real history of the Spirit with Jesus, thereby grounding more fully a view of the church also as always needing to invoke the Spirit and be open to the new gift offered by the Spirit in new historical moments.

A TRINITARIAN THEOLOGY OF THE SPIRIT AS GIFT

In his Trinitarian theology, Kasper again insists that the starting-point for a pneumatology must be the experience of the Holy Spirit in history. He lays the foundations for his approach by tracing the biblical account of the Spirit in creation and the history of salvation, and by then offering an account of the emergence of the doctrine of the Spirit and of the different theologies of East and West.[17] In the process he discusses the *filioque*, arguing for respect for both traditions, calling both to a deeper theology of salvation in the Spirit, and suggesting that further dialogue may open a way forward.[18]

In building his own pneumatology, Kasper turns to what he considers to be the historically most influential image—the Holy Spirit as gift and as love. In the New Testament, the Spirit is the gift without qualification (Acts 2: 38; 8: 20; 10: 45; 11: 17; Heb. 6: 4; cf. John 4: 10). The Spirit is God's eschatological gift, the one who completes the works of God, the first instalment of eschatological fulfilment of human beings and the whole creation (Rom. 8: 18–23; 2 Cor. 1: 22; Eph. 1: 14). The theology of the Spirit as gift was taken up by theologians of East and West, and was developed by Augustine and Aquinas. Kasper points out that for Christian theology, understanding God is only possible as the gift of the Spirit of God (1 Cor. 2: 11). With theologians like Karl Barth, Kasper sees the Spirit as the subjective possibility of revelation.[19]

If the Spirit as gift really does reveal God to us, the Spirit cannot be gift only for us, but must be gift in the life of God. The Spirit must be not only God's gift and love in our history, but the giver of the gift and God's love in person. But how can the Spirit be called God's love and gift in person when love and giftedness are the very nature of God and common to the divine persons? Kasper follows Augustine in distinguishing between love in the sense of substance and love in the sense of person: in the substantial sense, love is the very being of God and common to the divine persons; in the personal sense, it is special to the Holy Spirit. The Spirit expresses in a personal way the love and giftness of the Father and the Son and is in person the reciprocal love of Father and Son.

Unlike the Son, the Spirit proceeds from the Father as given (*quomodo datus*) rather than as born (*quomodo natus*). The Spirit, then, does not become gift only in the economy, but is God from all eternity as the gift of God and as givable (*donabile*):

The Spirit . . . expresses the innermost nature of God—God as self-communicating love—in such a way that this innermost reality proves at the same time to be the outermost, that is, the possibility and reality of God's being outside of himself. The Spirit is at it were the ecstasy of God; he is God as pure abundance, God as the overflow of love and grace.[20]

The love of the Father and the Son reaches its goal in the Spirit. Thus the Spirit becomes the possibility of love reaching out to embrace creation, not in a necessary way, but as a free streaming out in gracious self-communication. As completion in God, the Spirit is also the eschatological completion of creation. Kasper sees the divine indwelling of the Spirit in us as not simply appropriated to the Spirit, but as personal and proper to the Spirit. The Holy Spirit is the giver and the gift, the condition for the possibility of salvation in Christ and the realization of the work of God in the whole economy. Kasper traces this work of the Spirit in the three areas of creation, grace, and the life of the church.

First, as divine love in person, the Spirit is the source of creation because creation is the overflow of divine love and participation in God's being:

But the Spirit is also the source of movement and life in the created world. Whenever something new arises, whenever life is awakened and reality reaches ecstatically beyond itself, in all seeking and striving, in every ferment and birth, and even more in the beauty of creation, something of the activity and being of God's Spirit is manifested.[21]

Kasper agrees with Rahner that because of the presence and action of the Spirit, creation is always more than 'pure nature'. It is always graced. It has a supernatural finality and character.

Second, the Spirit is the source of grace. The Spirit is 'at work everywhere that human beings seek and find friendship with God'.[22] In the Spirit, we become friends of God, and daughters and sons of God. It is only in the Spirit that we are in God and God is in us. Through faith in Jesus Christ we participate in the law of the new covenant, which, as Aquinas has shown, is the law that moves us from within, the law of freedom, the grace of the Spirit which manifests itself in its many charisms (1 Cor. 12: 4–11) and fruits (Gal. 5: 22).

Third, all of this has consequences for an understanding of church. Wherever there is love, the Spirit is at work and the reign of Christ becomes a reality, even without the church's institutional forms and formulas. The offices of the church exist for the sake of the gift of the Spirit. The Spirit is 'the internal life-principle or soul' of the visible church.[23] The church always lives and renews itself by the Spirit. The Spirit makes Jesus Christ present 'ever anew in his newness'.[24] The Spirit preserves the church in its fidelity to tradition by leading it in a prophetic way into the entire truth and making known what is coming (John 16: 13). The Spirit is not an 'ideological guarantee of the Church's *status quo*, but rather the Spirit of continual renewal'.[25] The Spirit leads the church anew into mission and teaches it to heed and interpret the Spirit's own action in the 'signs of the times.'

The Trinity, for Kasper, is a communion that is a unity in love. It is a dynamic movement of giving and receiving love. The Father, the unoriginate origin, is giver and the sender. The Son receives from the Father in order to pass love on. The Spirit is a 'pure receiving, pure donation and gift'. As gift within God, the Spirit is God's eschatological gift to creation, its definitive sanctification and completion. With the help of insights of Richard of St Victor, Kasper sees the distinctions in the Trinity as distinctions in the way love is given and received: 'In the Father, love exists as pure source that pours itself out; in the Son it exists as a pure passing-on, as pure mediation; in the Spirit it exists as the mode of pure receiving.'[26]

At this point, I find Kasper's formulation somewhat unhelpful. If the Spirit exists as pure receptivity, this can seem to limit the Spirit to a passive role. This would not, I think, be Kasper's intention, since he is using this language to describe the Trinitarian relations of origin. I think it is extremely important to insist that the Spirit is dynamically active in the perichoretic relations of the Trinity and, as Kasper makes abundantly clear, is the active, life-giving power of God at work in creation, grace, incarnation, and the church. In Kasper's theology, it is because God is pure gift, that God is able to give God's self to creatures in the Spirit.[27]

ECCLESIOLOGY AS A FUNCTION OF PNEUMATOLOGY

In his *Introduction to Christian Faith*, Kasper points out that in the first millennium ecclesiology was seen as a function of pneumatology.[28] In the second millennium, by contrast, western pneumatology has tended to become a function of ecclesiology, with the Spirit simply the guarantor of the church and pneumatology an ideological superstructure of ecclesiology. This shift has had a visible effect on the theology of church, which comes to be seen more or less as a political and juridical power structure. The Gospel and the Spirit tend to become possessions of the church, administered by the church. This leaves the church without an external standard and in danger of becoming a self-contained system, inoculated against questions and challenges.

Kasper sees the alternative as 'an ecclesiology built on pneumatology', in which the church is seen 'more as an event in which the truth, freedom and justice which entered the world with Christ remain alive in history and are constantly given new life'.[29] The church exists when the 'cause of Jesus' is made present by the Spirit, taken up in faith, and lived in love. Kasper makes it clear that the idea that church is primarily an event in the Spirit does not exclude but includes institutional forms of church. Because the church is grounded in the person of Jesus Christ it includes doctrine. It is always both institution and event. A pneumatological view of the church includes authority and is the basis for authority, but it takes the church beyond the limits of the institutional. The Spirit always calls the church to break out of rigidity to be open to the new. The institutional elements are not safeguards and guarantees of the Spirit, but sacramental signs of the Spirit. Even the apostolic succession of ministries is not itself the continuity of the church with its apostolic origins, but a sign of the continuity that the church possesses in the Spirit.

Central to an ecclesiology that is a function of pneumatology is the scriptural teaching that the Spirit has been given to all the baptized. While this was forgotten for a long time in the life of the church, it was recovered in the teaching of the Second Vatican Council and has found expression in the idea that the *sensus fidei* characterizes the whole People of God. According to Kasper, this means that where there is a difference between magisterial teaching and the laity's everyday faith experience, the truth of the Gospel will come not from tightening up traditional doctrinal formulations, but by a consensus that emerges from listening to, and learning from one another.[30] Kasper finds in the Council's work three criteria for discernment: the first is to listen to the Spirit, seeking to discover the consensus of the faith at work in the whole church; the second is to relate this sense of the faith to the whole tradition that goes back to Christ; the third is to be in union with the authority of the church.

It is no accident that authority is set in the third place. It is fundamentally a service, a service to the Word and to the community. It represents and gives effect to the priority and otherness of the Gospel. The authority of the magisterium is not a power to force one's will on another. It is a Gospel authority that seeks to serve the faith and the freedom of the children of God. In Kasper's view, authority has a mediating function. It seeks to articulate the faith in such a way that people of good will can see themselves as represented in it: 'Unfortunately', he comments, 'authority has largely lost this mediating function because it has become a faction within the Church.' He notes the traditional Catholic teaching that authority can also take decisions alone and give final rulings. Kasper suggests that in contemporary law this extraordinary form of the magisterium might be called an emergency power. Its use, he argues, should be limited to extreme situations, with the goal always being to return to proper forms of collective and synodal discovery of truth.[31]

Kasper sees orthodoxy in faith as orthodoxy through dialogue:

A person is orthodox and a member of the Church as long as he or she is prepared to preserve the connection of dialogue with the ecclesial community, as long as he or she allows its statements a binding claim, accepts them as a challenge to which he or she gives full weight in relation to his or her own subjective religious convictions.[32]

This does not mean that the church cannot draw clear boundaries. It needs to be able to speak with one voice on fundamental issues such as those to do with salvation in Christ.

Kasper's pneumatology governs all aspects of his ecclesiology, particularly his fundamental understanding of church as communion,[33] but also his view of the relationship between the local and the universal church,[34] his theology of the Eucharist,[35] and his understanding of the ministries of the deacon, priest, and bishop.[36] It is at work in his ecumenical theology of the doctrine of justification,[37] apostolic succession,[38] sister churches,[39] participation in the Eucharist,[40] the nature of ecumenical dialogue,[41] and his strong commitment to spiritual ecumenism.[42] I will take up his treatment of one issue, the Petrine ministry, because I see this as fundamental if the Roman Catholic Church is to be receptive of what its partner churches have to offer in terms of synodality and collegiality.

RE-RECEPTION OF THE FIRST VATICAN COUNCIL ON THE PETRINE MINISTRY

In a globalized world, there is an increased openness to the idea of a ministry of unity in a reconciled church. At the same time, many Christians find it difficult or impossible to accept the Petrine ministry as it is defined in the First and Second Vatican Councils, and particularly as it is interpreted and lived in the life of the Catholic Church. On the Roman Catholic side, there is not only an abiding commitment to the Petrine ministry, but also recognition that a spiritual and institutional renewal is fundamental for the future of ecumenism.

In this context, Pope John Paul II opened up a new ecumenical discussion with his 1995 encyclical letter, *Ut Unum Sint*. He recognized that the Petrine ministry constitutes a difficulty for most other Christians, and committed to finding a new way of exercising the primacy, without renouncing what is essential to its mission. He asked 'the Holy Spirit to shine his light on us, enlightening all the pastors and theologians of our churches, that we may seek—together, of course—the forms in which this ministry might accomplish a service of love recognized by all concerned' (*UUS*, § 95). He invited church leaders and theologians to a 'patient and fraternal dialogue' on this subject (*UUS*, § 96). This invitation has been taken up in official replies from some churches and in theological responses in journals, books, and conferences.[43]

Cardinal Kasper seeks to take this discussion into a second phase. With the Catholic Church bound to the First and Second Vatican Councils, and its ecumenical partners committed to their confessional writings and historical positions, how can honest progress be made? Kasper suggests the beginning of an answer from the Roman Catholic side. According to Catholic theology there can be an evolution in the understanding of faith. It recognizes the need for interpretation of doctrine and offers criteria for its interpretation. For this reason, Joseph Ratzinger could long ago call for a rereading, and Congar for a re-reception, of the First Vatican Council.[44] The reception of doctrine does not happen once and for all. It is not an automatic passive acceptance, but a 'lively and creative evolution of appropriation and integration'.[45] Kasper proposes that the teaching of the First Vatican Council on the primacy and infallibility of the Pope needs to be re-received in a new ecumenical context. This means reinterpreting the teaching of the Council according to the principles of dogmatic hermeneutics. Kasper offers four hermeneutical principles as guides for such a re-reception.[46]

The first principle is to interpret the primacy within the whole context of ecclesiology. The introduction to the First Vatican Council Constitution, *Pastor Aeternus*, states that the Petrine ministry exists for the sake of the unity of the church. Kasper sees this as *the* theological principle that must guide interpretations of the Council. The First Vatican Council did not intend to cancel but to confirm, strengthen, and defend the direct power of the bishops. But because of the outbreak of the Franco-Prussian war, it was never able to finish its work, and its teaching on primacy was never integrated into a broader view of the church. Historically this led to one-sided interpretations of the Petrine Ministry. The Second Vatican Council situated this ministry within a fuller ecclesiology, involving a sacramental theology of episcopacy, the dignity of lay ministry, the importance of the local church, and, above all, the ecclesiology of communion. But it was not able to achieve a full integration, and in this sense the work of both councils remains incomplete. Kasper points to a number of open questions: 'the integration of the Petrine ministry within the whole of ecclesiology, the relation between primacy and collegiality, the relation between the universal and the local church, the interpretation of the direct jurisdiction of the pope in all local churches, the question of the principle of subsidiarity . . .'[47] There is need for further interpretation and reception of both councils. Such a re-reception could lead to the replacing of a one-sided pyramidal concept of church with a communal one in which the different ministries have their own irreplaceable and interrelated roles.[48]

The second principle is to interpret the First Vatican Council in the light of the whole tradition and its integration into it. Because the Holy Spirit guides the church in every age, the ancient tradition is not to be understood as only the first phase of a later development. Later developments need to be interpreted in the light of the older tradition. So, Kasper argues, the communion ecclesiology of the first millennium—reaffirmed by the Second Vatican Council—is the hermeneutical framework for reinterpreting the First Vatican Council. This is why Joseph Ratzinger could say, in his famous conference at Graz in 1976, that Rome need not require of the East today a higher doctrine of the primacy than that which was formulated and lived in the first millennium.[49] What was right and of the Spirit for centuries cannot be wrong today. This would apply, for example, to the relative autonomy of the eastern churches and their patriarchates. While Kasper notes that the Second Vatican Council has already begun to interpret the First Vatican Council within an ecclesiology of communion, he sees a corresponding reception on behalf of the churches of the East as only at its beginning. What is needed is not mechanical acceptance or submission, but a lively and creative process of appropriation, which would enrich both East and West, so that the church as a whole might begin to breathe with both lungs. This would lead to different forms and expressions of the Petrine ministry, as exemplified in the first millennium and also in the Oriental churches in full communion with Rome today.

Kasper's third principle is to interpret the teaching of the First Vatican Council by taking into account its historical context and the historical meaning of the concepts used. The majority of the participants in the First Vatican Council saw the church besieged on all sides: 'They were traumatized by the Enlightenment, the French Revolution, the absolutism of modern states, by Gallicanism and Episcopalism, and wanted to make sure the church would remain capable of action in an extreme situation.'[50] Because of this, they turned to the modern idea of sovereignty. They defined the papacy in terms of absolute sovereignty, enabling the Pope to act even if he were unable to communicate with the church. The Council's statements on primacy 'were conceived for extreme and exceptional conditions'.[51] Of course, in the Catholic tradition, the Pope's power is always limited by revelation, the tradition, the sacramental and episcopal structure of the church, and by God-given human rights. But these limits were forgotten in maximizing interpretations of the power of the papacy on all sides. This maximizing interpretation has turned an exceptional situation into a normal one. Uniformity of law and liturgy, and Roman appointment of bishops do not belong to the primacy as such. Kasper says that if we separate the declarations on primacy from their historical forms, we find their essential and binding meaning: 'that the pope is free to act according to the specific and changing necessity of the Church'.[52] As Pope John Paul II has made clear, the ecumenical situation now requires the church to find new ways in which the Petrine ministry may be faithfully exercised for the good of the whole church.

The fourth principle is to interpret the Petrine ministry according to the Gospel. Kasper points out that Roman Catholics believe that the Petrine ministry has its foundation in the biblical witness, and ultimately in Jesus himself. He refers not only to the well-known Petrine texts, whose exegesis he recognizes as controversial ecumenically, but to the whole Petrine tradition in the New Testament, and of the first millennium. However, he also goes deeper to a New Testament theology of primacy and power: 'whoever wishes to be first among you must be your slave' (Matt. 20: 27). He points to Ignatius of Antioch's description of the primacy of Rome as the 'primacy of love' and to Pope John Paul II's interpretation of the primacy as 'not one of jurisdiction based on the idea of sovereignty, but a spiritual one based on the idea of service—as service to unity, service and sign of mercy and love'.[53] The Petrine ministry is an *episkopē*, a pastoral love based on Jesus the Good Shepherd who gives his life for his sheep (John 10: 11). Kasper does not want to oppose jurisdiction and service, but to understand jurisdiction in the biblical sense of an authority that is in the service of *episkopē* and of the *oikodomē* of unity within the church.

With the aid of these principles Kasper seeks to uphold what he sees as the binding essence of the Petrine ministry and also to open up a spiritual re-reception of it within his own church, in dialogue with his church's ecumenical partners. He offers this in the hope that it can also facilitate a broader ecumenical reception of the Petrine ministry. He does not offer concrete answers to the question of the future of the Petrine ministry, but hopes to pave the way for such answers.

CONCLUSION

I have been proposing that two issues have a certain priority in thinking about Catholic ecumenical receptivity. The most foundational is pneumatology. Particularly in receptive dialogue with the East, Catholic theology needs a renewed theology of the Spirit, and a new balance between pneumatology and Christology in the life of the church. At another level, the Petrine ministry is a pressing and strategically important issue for ecumenical progress. Only when this is addressed in an ecumenical context will the Roman Catholic Church be able to be fully receptive to what its partners have to offer in terms of synodal theology and participatory structures. And only in this context will the ecumenical partners of the Roman Catholic Church be able to address the issue of the Petrine ministry creatively from their own tradition.

Walter Kasper's theology is one which is pneumatological from the ground up. His early Christology is already a Spirit Christology, his Trinitarian theology involves a rich theology of the Spirit as the *ekstasis* of the divine love in creation, grace, and the life of the church, and he sees ecclesiology as a function of pneumatology rather than the other way around. All of this means that he is well placed to think about the pressing issues that confront us in ecumenical theology. On the issue of the Petrine ministry, he offers us a way of re-receiving the teaching of the First Vatican Council, in dialogue with ecumenical partners, which in my judgement loosens the logjam and offers hope for new movement forward under the impetus of the Holy Spirit.

NOTES

1. 'The Current Situation in Ecumenical Theology', *TTMABO*, 24.
2. Ibid. 25; also 'The Renewal of Pneumatology in Contemporary Catholic Life and Theology: Towards a Rapprochement between East and West', *TTMABO*, 96–121.
3. 'The Current Situation', 27.
4. Congar, *The Word and the Spirit*, trans. David Smith (London: Geoffrey Chapman, 1986), 21–41.

5. See Edwards, *Breath of Life: A Theology of the Creator Spirit* (Maryknoll, NY: Orbis, 2004), 87–101.

6. Kasper, 'Ecumenical Perspectives on the Future: *One Lord, One Faith, One Baptism*', *LIC*, 180.

7. 'Ecumenism of Life and Eucharistic Fellowship: *Future Perspectives*', in *SOU*, 65.

8. *Jesus the Christ*, trans. V. Green (London and New York: Burns & Oates/Paulist Press, 1976).

9. Ibid., 249.

10. Ibid., 257–8; Ratzinger, *Introduction to Christianity*, trans. J. R. Foster (London: Burns & Oates, 1969), 256–7.

11. *Jesus the Christ*, 258.

12. Ibid., 250–1.

13. Ibid., 253.

14. Ibid.

15. Ibid., 267

16. Congar, *The Word and the Spirit*, 87.

17. See Kasper, *TGJC*, 200–22.

18. He notes that only the future will reveal whether a new common formula is possible, such as the procession of the Spirit from the Father *through* the Son (*TGJC*, 222). See also 'The Renewal of Pneumatology', *TTMABO*, 96–121, where he argues for the hermeneutical priority of the common creed of 381, suggesting that 'the easiest solution at the moment would probably be to insert into the Latin Missal for ecumenical use the Latin version of the creed as proclaimed at the Council of Chalcedon (451), i.e. the creed without the *filioque*, beside the Latin creed of the second millennium with the *filioque*'. (p. 111).

19. *TGJC*, 225.

20. Ibid., 226.

21. Ibid., 227.

22. Ibid., 228.

23. Ibid., 229.

24. Ibid.

25. Ibid.

26. Ibid., 308–9.

27. Ibid., 311.

28. *An Introduction to Christian Faith*, trans. V. Green (London: Burns & Oates, 1980), 138.

29. Ibid., 139.

30. Ibid., 142–3.

31. Ibid., 149.

32. Ibid., 150.

33. See 'The Church as Communion: Reflections on the Guiding Ecclesiological Idea of the Second Vatican Council', *Theology and Church*, trans. Margaret Kohl (London: SCM, 1989), 148–65; id., 'Communio: The Guiding Concept of Catholic Ecumenical Theology', *TTMABO*, 50–74.

34. See 'The Universal and the Local Church A Friendly Rejoinder', *LIC*, 158–75.

35. See 'Sacrament of Unity—Plurality of Aspects: Fundamental Theological Reflections on the Eucharist', *SOU*, 84–116.

36. See chs. 1–3, *LIC*, 15–113.
37. See 'The Joint Declaration on the Doctrine of Justification', *TTMABO*, 122–35.
38. See 'The Apostolic Succession: An Ecumenical Problem', *LIC*, 114–43.
39. See 'Open Questions in the Ecclesiology of Sister Churches', *TTMABO*, 75–95.
40. See 'Ecumenism of Life and Eucharistic Fellowship. Future Perspectives', *SOU*, 57–83.
41. See 'The Nature and Purpose of Ecumenical Dialogue', *TTMABO*, 33–49.
42. See 'Ecumenism of Life and Eucharistic Fellowship', particularly 73–83; also 'Spiritual Ecumenism', *TTMABO*, 155–72.
43. See *Information Service*, 109 (2002), 29–42.
44. See *TTMABO*, 140.
45. Ibid.
46. On this, see also Chapter 27: Hervé Legrand, 'Receptive Ecumenism and the Future of Ecumenical Dialogues—Privileging Differentiated Consensus and Drawing its Institutional Consequences'.
47. Kasper, *TTMABO*, 142.
48. Ibid., 143.
49. Ratzinger, *Principles of Catholic Theology: Building Stones for a Fundamental Theology*, trans. Mary Frances McCarthy (San Francisco, Calif.: Ignatius Press, 1987), 199; cf. Kasper (*LIC*, 236, n. 21), 'this lecture was reprinted without any changes after its author had become a cardinal...He has never retracted these words, but has later sought to defend them against misunderstandings by emphasizing that they do not mean that we should return to the first millennium, practicing an ecumenism of a "return to the past"...'
50. 'A Discussion on the Petrine Ministry', *TTMABO*, 145.
51. Ibid.
52. Ibid., 146.
53. Ibid., 148.

15

What Might Catholicism Learn from Orthodoxy in Relation to Collegiality?

Joseph Famerée, SCJ

INTRODUCTION

To grasp the Orthodox notion of collegiality or, more exactly, synodality, it is necessary to understand the vision of ecclesial communion that flows from Orthodoxy's apophatic and Trinitarian anthropology.[1] The first part of this chapter interprets the diverse institutional forms of conciliarity in the East from this perspective. In turn, the second part asks what Catholicism, especially at the universal level, might learn from Orthodox ecclesiology and institutional functioning in these regards.

ORTHODOX ECCLESIOLOGY

Trinitarian Theology and Anthropology

Within orthodox theology and anthropology, and similarly ecclesiology, the human being is seen, not as a 'closed', 'self-sufficient' entity, but as a dynamic reality determined in its very existence by its relation to God. This dynamic reality is understood as an ascending process and a communion: created in the image of God, the human being is called to achieve a 'divine likeness' in a free effort of love. To express this, the Byzantine theologians used the Greek notion of 'theosis' or 'divinization'. The human being is called to 'know' God, to 'take part' in God's life by 'becoming divine': it is a new expression of the life 'in Christ' or of the 'communion of the Holy Spirit' evoked by the New Testament.

At the same time, an antinomy is at the heart of the eastern theology: God has revealed himself truly in Jesus Christ, and the knowledge of this truth is essential for salvation, but God, in God's essence, is beyond human comprehension and cannot be expressed by words fully or completely. So, it is by indicating what God is not that the theologian most truly teaches. God is above any human word or thought. Eastern theology is, as such, negative or apophatic. However, by the communication of the Holy Spirit to the human being, which is the experience of 'deification', a 'contemplation greater than knowledge' (Gregory Palamas) is made possible.[2]

More precisely, Orthodox understanding of the Trinity stresses the singularity and the uniqueness of each hypostasis: the Father (principle without principle) does not have the same relationship to the Son (generation) as to the Holy Spirit (procession). The three divine hypostases are united by their mutual distinction and distinguished by their union. This ineffable mystery suggests a difference which asserts itself by asserting the others: absolute diversity in absolute identity, difference in communion. The divine person appears as a coincidence of unity and uniqueness.

This Trinitarian revelation constitutes the foundation of any Christian anthropology, because the human being is 'in the image of God'. The life of humankind has 'to imitate the divine nature'. Just as there is a unique God in three persons, there is a 'unique human being' in a multitude of persons: this 'unique human being' has been divided by the Fall, but restored in its unity as the Body of Christ. So Orthodoxy holds the radical uniqueness of the person together with the ontological unity of humankind. In this perspective, the human person, being in the image of God, is as 'ineffable' as its archetype. Just as one speaks of the *Deus absconditus*, one can also speak of the *homo absconditus*. The created person is also a mystery and cannot be reduced to a simple 'object' of knowledge. Thus, one can speak of a negative or apophatic anthropology.

Through holiness, human beings stop appropriating, and therefore breaking up, the human nature: they discover its unity in Christ. The personal conscience is not self-consciousness, but consciousness of communion, of 'consubstantiality' with all people. Russian thought has greatly emphasized this 'transcendent', communal aspect of the conscience, especially through the theme of *sobornost*, which expresses the conciliarity or spiritual catholicity of the church. So, Orthodox anthropology finds fulfilment in its ecclesiology. The fulfilment of salvation will consist in the universal communion of all human beings and of all things; the eschatological 'pleroma' of deified humankind and a transfigured universe; a cosmos of which the human being is already centre, steward and 'microcosm'.[3]

It is from this mystical perspective of a transcendent God, incarnate for the salvation of the world, that Orthodox Christianity considers the church as the community in which the liturgy, through the Holy Spirit, anticipates already the final transfiguration of all things. This is the key to the eastern conception of the church: the church is both hierarchical and collegial; she is universal, but finds fulfilment only in the local eucharistic assembly, where a group of sinners becomes fully the People of God. One can already note that the synodal life of the church (relationships between faithful and bishops, between bishops and primate) is a matter of sacramental (eucharistic) communion in the faith, before being a matter of authority and canonical rules.

Local Church

The church, as we have mentioned it, has her origin and her source in the mystery of the Trinitarian communion.[4] She finds concrete fulfilment in the local churches, each of which manifests the presence in a specific place of the one catholic and apostolic church.

The Holy Spirit unites the baptized in one and the same body, that of Christ: the baptized are both equal by baptism yet different in terms of the varied charisms received and the resultant functions exercised with a view to the edification of the one body. The Holy Spirit builds up the church through the proclamation and the reception of the Gospel, and through the celebration of the sacraments, especially the Eucharist. The eucharistic body of Christ is indeed the source of his ecclesial body, and so the eucharistic celebration is the fullest manifestation of the church. This celebration, in which the mystery is every time present in its fullness, is always that of a local church. Consequently this church is truly the presence in its place of the unique church of Christ.

The local church is 'presided over' by a 'pastor' whose task is to guide her and to take care of her unity and of her living faithfulness to the Gospel received from the Apostles. This pastoral 'presidency' has particularly strong expression in the 'presidency' of the Eucharist which the 'pastor' celebrates with the faithful of his church.[5]

Communion of Local Churches

Every local church, so gathered by the Eucharist, is in principle the full manifestation in a particular place of the unique catholic and apostolic church of Christ. However, it cannot be such a manifestation in an isolated or autarkic (self-sufficient) way, but only by keeping living and active links of communion with the other local churches, which are also, each of them, the one church of God. Since each of the churches is constituted by the Holy Spirit, the Gospel, the sacraments, and the pastoral ministry, they all need to be in communion with one another, in a dynamic process of mutual reception and exchange. So the one and universal church is concretely a communion of sister local churches. Consequently, in a correct Orthodox theology of the ecclesial mystery, there cannot be a priority, either historical or ontological, of the universal church over the local church(es) and vice versa, the local church and the communion of the local churches having the same foundations (Spirit, Gospel, sacraments, ministry).[6] However, one has to recognize that Orthodoxy, owing to historical circumstances, has tended to stress the local and national characteristics, even independence, of each church (manifesting the autocephalic temptation of phyletism),[7] whereas Roman tradition developed a universal, or even universalist ecclesiology.[8]

Institutional Expressions of the Communion of Churches

It is only on the basis of this Trinitarian, pneumatological, sacramental, and eucharistic theology of local church and *communio Ecclesiarum* that we are able to understand the diverse ways in which ecclesial communion is structured.

If the ministry of the bishop is to preside over the edification and communion of a local church through his witness to the apostolic faith, his ministry also involves maintaining the vital bonds of communion with the other 'apostolic' churches. It is because of the reciprocal nature of eucharistic and ecclesial communion that the 'president' of a church's Eucharist also has the ministry of preserving bonds of communion with the other churches. So the bishops each represent their own church and assure its integration into the *communio Ecclesiarum*, just as they represent the apostolic faith in which all the churches share. On this basis, one may speak of a 'synod' or a 'college' of bishops: their 'synodality' or 'collegiality' is rooted in episcopal ordination and is inseparable from the communion of the churches it must express and serve. Therefore, each bishop has a (co)responsibility with regard to the communion of all the churches in the same faith.[9] This (co)responsibility has been and can be exercised in different forms. The two main forms are synods or councils, and the existence of leading or primatial sees. These sees are considered as 'centres of mutual agreement and communion'.

Synods or councils, at different levels, are the particular loci where the communion of the churches is manifested and realized through the bishops which represent them. However, the bishops in the synods are never to be considered separately from the local churches over which they preside. Similarly, the 'college' or 'synod' does not constitute an authority located above the churches. It is a ministerial sign of the communion of the churches in the apostolic faith and tradition. It is only within this framework, and on the basis of the ministry of presidency, peculiar and common to all bishops, that it is possible to understand the primatial function exercised by the principal sees, amongst them Rome, recognized as the first during the first millennium and which it could be again, under certain conditions.[10]

To restate two key premises: (i) because of the mutual interiority (*perichoresis*) between universal church and local churches, the mission of every bishop includes solicitude for the universal communion of the churches; (ii) conversely, given that the local church is constitutively open to the other churches which, together, form the universal church, the existence of principal sees does not in itself infringe the full ecclesiality of local churches. From these, certain consequences follow.

(1) Any primatial function has the aim of serving the edification and the communion of the local churches. The primate is not located above the churches, but at the heart of the bonds of communion.

(2) The reasons why a primatial function has been attributed to a see may be theological/ecclesiological in character (e.g. apostolicity of a church, antiquity of its foundation, 'motherhood' toward daughter churches), but also political/cultural (importance of the city etc.). This *taxis* amongst churches has found canonical expression in the councils, particularly those received by both eastern and western churches. The difference between East and West concerning the universal primacy of the Church of Rome was not church-dividing during the first millennium.[11] In addition, as noted, the existence of primatial functions does not undermine the equality of all the bishops. Indeed, whatever be its concrete forms, the primatial function has no other theological foundation than that of the episcopate itself. It is the same for the more specific service of universal communion. This is only the particular implementation of a solicitude for the communion of churches which belongs to the episcopal function, and which each bishop must exercise. For the conditions of exercise of this particular primacy, the canons of the Council of Sardica (AD 343) offer a possible figure of reconciliation in spite their diverse reception in East and West.[12]

(3) The 'honour' attributed to a primate includes an effective responsibility and authority. If he is *inter pares*, he is also *primus*.[13] His power, which must be regulated in a canonical way, should never be unrelated to the communion amongst the churches and bishops: ecclesiastical legislation should never be separated from the sacramental nature of the church, upon which it is founded.

(4) True communion amongst the local churches, in each of which the one and holy church is truly present, presupposes interdependence between the *primus* and the other bishops. This is well expressed by the 34th Apostolic canon, always very dear to the Orthodox and to a large extent recognized also by the West during the first millennium:

The bishops of each nation must know the primate amongst them and consider him as (their) head, and do nothing without the consenting opinion (*gnomes*) of this one; but may everyone do only that which concerns his district and the country belonging to it! But may (the primate) also do nothing without the consenting opinion of all! As a result of this, there will be concord, and God will be glorified, through the Son, in the Holy Spirit.[14]

So a dialectical tension between the multiplicity of local centres (poles) and the regional centres of mutual agreement, of which one is the first, exists within the one episcopal ministry. However, these centres (poles) should never either absorb or result from each other. This interdependence between the 'one' and the 'many', which exists analogically at all levels of ecclesial life, is based on the

Trinitarian mystery: the Father makes the church exist through the joint mission of the Son who institutes her and the Spirit who constitutes her. So, whatever the need for canonically regulating relationships between the diverse functions or persons in the church, the last word is always for the Spirit. The *sensus Ecclesiae* of the baptized, assisted by the Spirit, always takes precedence over the diverse ministers, and manifests itself notably in their reception of these ministers. Only on the basis of this fundamental ecclesiology is it possible to interpret correctly the different forms of conciliarity in the East.

(1) The ecumenical council is the supreme authority in the universal church. But, for Orthodoxy, the division of Christendom since 1054 makes a new ecumenical council impossible for the time being.

(2) In the absence of ecumenical councils, a panorthodox council, with representatives of all autocephalous churches, could be the supreme authority for the whole Byzantine Orthodox Church. Unfortunately, there are divergences amongst the autocephalous churches over its status and its agenda.[15]

(3) At the regional level (patriarchates, autocephalous and autonomous churches, archdioceses), supreme authority belongs to the councils, because the primate (patriarch, archbishop, or metropolitan) is only *primus inter pares* within the episcopate of his church, and has a role of coordination in domains exceeding the competence of a diocesan bishop. However, he does not intervene in, nor has immediate jurisdiction over, the internal affairs of a diocese. For instance, in the Russian Orthodox Church dogmatic authority belongs to the 'local' or 'national' council, which gathers together bishops, clergy, monks, and laity, whilst the 'episcopal council' is the supreme organ of hierarchical administration. During the inter-conciliar period the patriarch of Moscow and all Russia governs the church together with the bishops of his permanent Holy-Synod. In the Church of Greece there is no council with the participation of laity; the supreme power belongs to the synod of all bishops, presided over by the Archbishop of Athens and all Greece.[16] Thus, the archbishop or metropolitan has the obligation to ensure unity amongst the bishops of his church and to settle conflicts, but only with the cooperation of the other bishops.

(4) In the diocesan church, the supreme authority belongs to the bishop who governs his church with the cooperation of the clergy and the people. Usually the bishop is elected by the episcopal synod of the 'regional' church, but, currently, particularly in the Orthodox churches of the Slavic Diaspora, the election of the bishop by the laity has been restored. The bishop is elected by an assembly of all the clergy of the diocese and an equivalent number of lay representatives elected by their parishes. Independently of the manner of election, the Christian people must ultimately approve of the candidate by proclaiming during the ordination 'axios' (he is worthy) or 'anaxios' (he is unworthy). In the latter case, which is very rare, the ordination stops. More globally, both parishes and dioceses gather in general assemblies, which have voting powers for all practical questions, and are

consultative for all spiritual and pastoral questions. In both cases, the assembly elects a council. In the parish council, laity are always in the majority, whereas the diocesan council is at parity (clergy and laity). Both councils are consultative, the final decision being always that of the president, priest, or bishop. Internal appeals to the hierarchy or to a joint diocesan commission are possible.[17]

On the basis of this ecclesiology and its institutional expressions, what might Catholicism learn from Orthodoxy in relation to collegiality?

CATHOLIC LEARNING FROM ORTHODOXY IN MATTERS OF COLLEGIALITY

The communion ecclesiology of Orthodoxy should challenge Catholicism at many points: in its ecclesiology, in its related anthropology, and in regard to institutional forms of ecclesial and sacramental communion.

Ecclesiology

Since the Second Vatican Council, Catholic theologians have also developed a communion ecclesiology very close to that of Orthodoxy.[18] This ecclesiology is based on a theology of the local or particular church as diocese, 'in which the one, holy, catholic and apostolic church of Christ is truly present and active',[19] and of the universal, but also regional communion of these local churches.[20] Nevertheless, there is here currently a dispute over the correct interpretation of the Second Vatican Council: did the Council truly endorse a *communio Ecclesiarum* theology, or did it teach a universalist ecclesiology, according to which the universal church (and thus the Pope) has priority over the local church(es), the monarchical principle over the collegial?

The Orthodox understanding of the church is an incentive for Catholics to reinterpret the Council properly from diachronic (historical) and synchronic (the whole *corpus*) perspectives, taking into account also Scripture and the ancient patristic and conciliar traditions. In doing so, it is impossible in my opinion not to identify the foundations and first developments of an authentic *communio Ecclesiarum* ecclesiology within the Second Vatican Council texts, whilst recognizing that the Council also took care to safeguard the particular role of the Roman see. That particular ministry could and should be rethought and reshaped in accordance with this theology of the communion of the local churches, in a way that would be more faithful to the functioning of the Roman primacy during the first millennium. This should, as we will see, have many consequences for the understanding and practice of collegiality in the Roman Catholic Church. Equally, it is necessary also to deepen the notion of communion, especially from an anthropological point of view. There is a close

correlation between anthropology and ecclesiology in as much as ecclesiology is
the social and collective form of Christian anthropology and its fulfilment. Here
too Roman Catholicism should receive some stimulus from Orthodoxy.

Anthropology

Roman Catholicism also has a rich Christian anthropology, whilst emphasizing
other aspects than Orthodoxy. First, Catholic theology is more cataphatic than
apophatic. It has great confidence in the capacity of human reason to know the
Truth. Admittedly, it knows that God is transcendent and God's very essence,
therefore, beyond the capacities of human knowledge, but it also asserts that
God's existence may, nevertheless, be known by the natural light of reason,
reflecting on the created order.[21] The human being is *capax Dei*. It is possible,
apart from revelation, to say and know something about God, even if only
analogically.

As God's creature, human being has value in itself. It is endowed with intelligence and freedom; in other words, real autonomy. Admittedly, this natural
freedom is wounded by sin, but it is not radically corrupted, and by the salvific
grace of Christ received in baptism the human being is justified and sanctified,
and made collaborator in his or her own salvation.[22] In this relatively optimistic
conception of humanity, salvation is Christocentric, anthropological (the rest of
Creation is not directly involved), and rather individualistic (focused on the level
of personal sin), whilst Orthodoxy is more pneumatological and displays a more
cosmological understanding of salvation (more a matter of receiving eternal life
than the remission of sins, and concerning the *whole* cosmos), and a more social
or communal conception of humankind.

Without abandoning its own characteristics, could not Roman Catholicism
integrate some aspects of Orthodox anthropology into its understanding by
giving more prominence to the Holy Spirit, by trying to conceive of a real
communion between humans and nature, and by looking for a better expression
of the link between the individual and communal aspects of the human being?
This has a direct influence on the conception of the church, and vice versa. If the
church, whether local or universal, is really a eucharistic communion of all the
faithful in the Holy Spirit, then the life of the church must be synodal or collegial
by essence: it is an existential, even an ontological necessity for the church in
order to be truly the church. Ultimately, nothing is good for the church if it is
not finally accepted and received by the whole People of God, assisted by the
Spirit and served by its pastors. In ecclesiastical life, the last word rests with
the *sensus fidei* (*fidelium*) or the *sensus Ecclesiae*.[23] Roman Catholicism still has
a lot to do to take on board effectively this basic synodality (collegiality) of all
the baptized, either within the local, the regional, or the universal church. For
instance, parish and diocesan councils should have more voting powers. Again,
the representatives of the whole People of God in a single diocese should have the

right of electing the (three) candidates to the episcopate—for instance, before the provincial bishops choose the future bishop from amongst the elected candidates. Many expressions of this fundamental synodality of the whole People of God are possible. Similarly, this basic conciliarity calls for an authentic collegiality amongst the pastors.

Institutional Forms of Ecclesial Communion

As earlier noted, Roman Catholicism also has a liturgical and sacramental, especially eucharistic, understanding of the church, in particular of the local diocesan church.[24] The unity of the local church, and thus of the whole church (or communion of the local churches), is realized 'in the Holy Spirit through the Gospel and the Eucharist'.[25] So this unity is pneumatological, Christological, and sacramental. From her own teaching, but also from that of Orthodoxy, it is very important for Roman Catholicism to remember that ecclesial unity or communion is essentially spiritual and sacramental before being a juridical matter, and to act accordingly. In contrast, since the Council of Trent the traditional temptation of Catholicism has been towards a certain juridical authoritarianism and centralization.

Therefore, it is first on a pneumatological, Christological, and sacramental basis that Roman Catholicism should look for institutional expressions of the communion of the local churches, and thus of the collegiality of their bishops. The universal level of this collegiality particularly interests me.

The whole College of bishops (pope and bishops) is the supreme authority within Roman Catholicism, even if the Pope alone also 'has full, supreme and universal power over the whole Church' (*LG*, § 22). *Lumen Gentium* continues: 'The supreme authority over the whole Church, which this college possesses, is exercised in a solemn way in an ecumenical council.' It would be more appropriate to keep the appellation 'ecumenical council' for a truly ecumenical council, which would gather together representatives of all Christian churches, and to use the term 'general council of the Roman Catholic Church' in this case. Anyway, general councils are not very frequent. The last one ended more than forty years ago. Therefore, the true question is: how to ensure permanently an authentic collegiality at the universal level within Roman Catholicism?

Within an ecclesiology of the communion of equal local churches, the local church of Rome (and thus her bishop), essentially as the church of Peter's and Paul's martyrdoms, has traditionally a particular role at the service of the communion of all local churches in love and apostolic faith. However, she is not a super-church (more church than the others) and her bishop is not a super-bishop (more bishop than the others). If episcopacy is a sacrament (ordination), papacy is not one. In the perspective of a true *communio Ecclesiarum*, the special (universal) primacy of the local church of Rome cannot be exercised except in a real relationship of reciprocity with all other local churches, based on the Trinitarian model, according to the 34th Apostolic Canon.

Here, I will not discuss the content and the extent of this universal primacy, but only its functioning. Nor will I discuss the possible difference of extent between the universal and the patriarchal primacy of the Pope in the West. As regards the mode of functioning of the universal primacy within the Roman Catholic Church, I think Catholicism could learn a lot from the relationships between a (regional) primate and the bishops of his ecclesiastical region, as regulated within Orthodoxy.

So, an effective interdependence between the *primus* and the other bishops is necessary in my opinion to express the *communio Ecclesiarum*: the bishops must know the primate amongst them and consider him as their head and do nothing without his consenting opinion; conversely, the primate must do nothing without the consenting opinion of all bishops.[26] This indispensable interdependence between pope and bishops could be expressed and exercised through a permanent Roman synod with voting powers.

Since 1965, a Roman synod of bishops has existed. It was instituted by Pope Paul VI, and is in fact completely subject to the power of the Pope. As a concrete assembly of bishops, it is not permanent (it meets triennially), it is consultative unless the Pope gives it voting powers and ratifies its decisions. Thus, the Roman synod is always dependent on the Pope as someone outside of itself, while the Pope is its president by right: the synod, Pope included, has no autonomy of decision and, even if it receives voting powers from the Pope, its decisions still require a papal ratification. Conversely, the Pope remains always totally independent (by right) and not bound by the advice and recommendations of the synod unless he wants to be. So the *motu proprio, Apostolica Sollicitudo*, of 15 September 1965, instituting the synod of the bishops, was in fact a primatial and monarchical act giving birth to an institution purely subject to the universal primate.[27] It is interesting to note that this synod was far more restricted that that advocated by Maximos IV on 6 November 1963, with the agreement of several Fathers. For the Antiochian Patriarch of the Melchites, the synod should have been a restricted group of bishops from around the world, representing their colleagues in the concrete charge of helping the Pope with the general government of the church. It should have been a 'true *Sacred College* of the universal Church', made up of the apostolic and residential patriarchs, of the cardinals who were residential archbishops or bishops, and of bishops chosen by the episcopal conferences of each country. Some members of this 'Sacred College' would succeed one another in turn to be beside the Pope, who has always the last word; it would be the supreme permanent council of the universal church, executive and decisive, to which the whole Roman Curia should be subjected; it would be a centre by definition open to the world and not closed in on itself to regiment everything.[28]

A true association of the Catholic episcopate with the universal government of the church should, in my opinion, develop along the lines of Maximos IV's *votum*, and conform even more fully with the Orthodox theology of synodality, even though the actual Orthodox practice of synodality does not, unfortunately, always correspond with its theology.[29] So the Pope could establish forthwith an authentic Roman Holy Synod, or a permanent supreme Council of the universal church, which would consist of several bishops (the number and the geographical proportions to be determined) elected by the whole Catholic episcopate for a fixed term. The bishops should be necessarily diocesan bishops, heads, and thus representatives, of real local churches. They could subsequently be re-elected or replaced. The Holy Synod (the Pope always included) would have voting powers and would assist the Pope in making necessary decisions for the entire Roman Catholic Church. The Pope would only make these sorts of decisions with the agreement of a large majority of the Holy Synod, perhaps even, when it is possible, only with the completely unanimous consensus of the bishops acting in the power of the Holy Spirit, according to the 34th Apostolic canon. The universal decisions of the Pope with his Holy Synod would be rare (they should be perhaps determined by a general council) and would concern ecclesiastical discipline or matters of doctrine when the faith as such is not at issue or in danger. Both in this last case, when faith is at stake (*fidei causa*), and for the most important, and even grave matters of discipline (*causae maiores*), a general Roman Catholic council should be convoked. All the other problems not requiring universal identity of view would be decided on by the particular (national or provincial) councils, or the bishops' conferences at the continental, regional, or national levels.[30] Without prior Roman recognition, their decisions would be communicated to the other local churches, and particularly to that of Rome, for reception or even fraternal correction if necessary.[31] Then one would be able to speak of true decentralization, better still of legitimate autonomy of the local and regional churches in communion with the other churches, especially that of Rome. This legitimate autonomy would respect the full ecclesiality of each local church according to the witness of the New Testament and of the ancient Tradition, to which Orthodoxy has remained faithful, whereas, within Roman Catholicism, the apostolic letter *Apostolos Suos* of 21 May 1998 did not promote this understanding.[32] These local and regional forms of collegiality could also be developed from the perspective of the Orthodox synodality, but this is not directly my point here.

The collegiality exercised by the Holy Synod would be real and effective, although partial. It is only in a general council, gathering together all bishops of the Roman Catholic Church, that full episcopal collegiality is solemnly exercised. Anyway, even before rereading with the Orthodox (and, one hopes, all other Christians) the First Vatican Council dogmas concerning the Pope's universal primacy and infallibility, the synergy between the Pope and a Holy Synod would alter the usual exercise of the universal primacy in a significant way, proving to the Orthodox (and other Christians) that synodality within Roman Catholicism was real, and thus opening up new lines of ecumenical dialogue.

CONCLUSION

In this chapter I have wanted to show what Catholicism might learn from Orthodoxy in terms of collegiality, especially for the usual exercise of the Pope's universal primacy. For this, synodal interdependence between the primate and bishops could, as we have seen, be a good model, as it could also for other levels of ecclesial life. In addition, the regional and local churches should enjoy a true autonomy of decision for their own affairs, whilst preserving communion with the rest of the church. With this synodal life at all levels, especially at the universal one, the *communio Ecclesiarum* would find a better institutional expression, as in Orthodoxy.

However, it is also always necessary to remember that the institutional forms in the church should be the best possible expression of a fundamental ecclesiology, a sacramental ecclesiology of communion amongst the faithful and amongst the churches. This ecclesiology is also intrinsically related to a fundamental anthropology. Both are based on Trinitarian presuppositions. This is the divine depth of ecclesial communion. Before being a matter of power or canon law, the relationships between a primate and his bishops are always a matter of ecclesial, sacramental, and anthropological communion in the Holy Spirit. In precise terms, the conciliarity or communion of the whole church in the Holy Spirit always takes precedence over the collegiality of the pastors. This conciliarity of all the faithful is particularly well 'shown in the supernatural appreciation of the faith (*sensus fidei*) of the whole people, when, "from the bishops to the last of the faithful" they manifest a universal consent in matters of faith and morals' (*LG*, § 12).

NOTES

1. By Orthodox or Orthodoxy, I mean primarily Byzantine (Chalcedonian) Orthodoxy, though my description would, in the main, apply also to the Oriental (pre-Ephesian and pre-Chalcedonian) churches.
2. See John Meyendorff, Introduction, *Byzantine Theology: Historical Trends and Doctrinal Themes* (New York: Fordham University Press, 1983), 1–15.
3. See Olivier Clément, *L'Église orthodoxe*, 4th edn. (Paris: Presses Universitaires de France, 1991), 57–60; also N. Berdiaev, *Freedom and the Spirit*, trans. D. Fielding (London: G. Bless/Century Press, 1935); Vladimir Lossky, *The Mystical Theology of the Eastern Church* (London: James Clarke, 1957); P. Evdokimov, *L'Orthodoxie* (Paris-Neuchâtel: Delachaux et Niestlé, 1959).

4. e.g. see Comité Mixte Catholique–Orthodoxe en France, *La Primauté romaine dans la communion des Églises* (Paris: Cerf, 1991), 113–25.

5. This conception of the local church was outlined in the first joint statement of the Roman Catholic–Orthodox International Theological Commission (Munich, 1982), 'The Mystery of the Church and the Eucharist in the Light of the Mystery of the Holy Trinity', I. 1–6 and II. 1–4, *GIA II*, 652–9.

6. See ibid., III. 1–4.

7. See J. H. Erickson, 'The "Autocephalous Church" ', *The Challenge of Our Past. Studies in Orthodox Canon Law and Church History* (Crestwood, NY: St Vladimir's Seminary Press, 1991), 91–113.

8. See Klaus Schatz, *Papal Primacy: From its Origins to the Present*, trans. John A. Otto and Linda M. Maloney (Collegeville, Minn.: Liturgical Press, 1996), 78–127.

9. See 'The Mystery of the Church and the Eucharist', III. 1–4.

10. See B. Pseftongas, 'L'unità nella Chiesa e le istituzioni che l'esprimono', in Antonio Acerbi (ed.), *Il ministero del Papa in prospettiva ecumenica* (Milan: Vita e Pensiero, 1999), 33–50.

11. This difference appeared at the Council of Chalcedon (451), of which the Roman legates refused to recognize the 28th canon, in turn a development of the 3rd canon of Constantinople (381). The 28th canon of Chalcedon attributed the same ecclesiastical prerogatives to the see of the new Rome (Constantinople) as to the see of the older Rome, because the former was then the city of the emperor as the latter had been in the past, Constantinople being second after Rome. See A. De Halleux, 'Les deux Rome dans la définition de Chalcédoine sur les prérogatives du siège de Constantinople', and id., 'Le Décret chalcédonien sur les prérogatives de la Nouvelle Rome', *Patrologie et œcuménisme: recueil d'études* (Louvain: Peeters, 1990), 504–19, 520–35.

12. According to these canons, the Bishop of Rome has the right to hear a unanimous sentence of a provincial synod when a condemned bishop appeals to him with the agreement of his own synod or the support of bishops of a neighbouring province. The Bishop of Rome has the right either to confirm the first decision or to order a new trial, which will take place in a province bordering that one where the point at issue has been settled the first time. Thus the Pope has the right to declare the first judgement valid, but he has not the right to judge the case again by himself. See Hervé Legrand, 'Brève note sur le synode de Sardique et sur sa réception: Rome, instance d'appel ou de cassation', and id., 'Conclusions du comité mixte', in *La Primauté romaine dans la communion des Églises*, Comité Mixte Catholique–Orthodoxe en France (Paris: Cerf, 1991), 47–60, 113–25.

13. See De Halleux, 'La Collégialité dans l'Église ancienne', *Revue théologique de Louvain*, 24 (1993), 433–54.

14. See Marcel Metzger (ed. and trans.), *Les Constitutions Apostoliques*, vol. iii., Sources chrétiennes, 336 (Paris: Cerf, 1987), 284–5. The 34th canon is quoted as normative by, for example, Pope John VIII, in his letter to Anspertus, Archbishop of Milan, in 879 (cf. *Epistola 223*, *PL*, 126, col. 837, A13–B15). For commentary on this canon, see the third joint statement of the Roman Catholic–Orthodox International Theological Commission, 'The Sacrament of Order in the Sacramental Structure of the Church' (Valamo, 1988), IV. 52–5, *GIA II*, 678–9.

15. See Hilarion Alfeyev, 'La Primauté et la conciliarité dans la tradition orthodoxe', *Irénikon*, 76 (2005), 24–36.
16. Ibid. 30.
17. See Jean Gueit, 'Démocratie dans les Églises: le cas de l'"orthodoxie"', in Jean Bauberot, Joseph Famerée, Roger T. Greenacre, and Jean Gueit (eds.), *Démocratie dans les Églises: Anglicanisme, Catholicisme, Orthodoxie, Protestantisme* (Brussels: Lumen Vitae, 1999), 77–9.
18. See Chapter 12: Paul McPartlan, 'Catholic Learning and Orthodoxy—The Promise and Challenge of Eucharistic Ecclesiology'.
19. See *CD*, § 11; also *SC*, § 41; *LG*, § 26.
20. See *LG*, §§ 13, 23.
21. See Vatican I, '*Dei Filius*: Dogmatic Constitution on the Catholic Faith' (24 Apr. 1870), in Norman P. Tanner (ed.), *Decrees of the Ecumenical Councils*, vol. ii., *Trent to Vatican II* (London: Sheed & Ward, 1990), 804–11.
22. See Council of Trent, 'Decree on Justification' (13 Jan. 1547), ibid., 671–81.
23. See *LG*, § 12.
24. See n. 19, above.
25. See *LG*, § 23 and *CD*, § 11, in particular.
26. Whilst Vatican II required that the faithful and the pastors must always be in communion with the Pope, reciprocity was not explicitly required. See, e.g., *LG*, §§ 13, 22, 23, 25.
27. See '*Apostolica Sollicitudo*: Apostolic Letter Issued Motu Proprio on Establishing the Synod of Bishops for the Universal Church' (15 Sept. 1965), *AAS*, 57 (1965), 775–80, also at <http://www.vatican.va/holy_father/paul_vi/motu_proprio/documents/hf_p-vi_motu-proprio_19650915_apostolica-sollicitudo_en.html>; also Famerée, '"Responsabilisation" des conférences épiscopales et concession de "facultés" aux évêques: signes de décentralisation?', in J. Doré and A. Melloni (eds.), *Volti di fine concilio: Studi di storia e teologia sulla conclusione del Vaticano II* (Bologna: il Mulino, 2000), 39–41; A. Borras, 'Considérations corrélatives sur l'exercice de la primauté romaine', in P. Tihon (ed.), *Changer la papauté?* (Paris: Cerf, 2000), 91–7.
28. See Maximos IV, 'Intervention', *Acta Synodalia Sacrosancti Concilii Oecumenici Vaticani II*, vol. ii/4 (Vatican City: Typis polyglottis Vaticanis, 1972), 516–19; also Famerée, 'Bishops and Dioceses and the Communications Media (5–25 Nov. 1963)', in G. Alberigo and J. Komonchak (eds.), *History of Vatican II*, vol. iii. (Louvain and Maryknoll, NY: Peeters/Orbis, 2000), 124–5; also id., ' "Responsabilisation" des conférences épiscopales', 42.
29. See Chapter 25: Andrew Louth, 'Receptive Ecumenism and Catholic Learning—An Orthodox Perspective'.
30. It could be argued that such a practice would correctly implement in the ecclesial sphere that central tenet of Catholic Social Teaching, subsidiarity. For its first official full formulation, see Pius XI, '*Quadragesimo Anno*: On Reconstruction of the Social Order' (15 May 1931), §§ 79–80, available at <http://www.vatican.va/holy_father/pius_xi/encyclicals/documents/hf_p-xi_enc_19310515_quadragesimo-anno_en.html>; also John Paul II, '*Centesimus Annus*: On the Hundredth Anniversary of *Rerum Novarum*' (1 May 1991) (London: CTS, 1991), § 48, available

at <http://www.vatican.va/holy_father/john_paul_ii/encyclicals/documents/hf_jp-ii_enc_01051991_centesimus-annus_en.html>.

31. See H. Legrand, J. Manzanares, and A. García y García (eds.), *The Nature and Future of Episcopal Conferences*, trans. Thomas J. Green, Joseph A. Komonchak, and James H. Provost (Washington, DC: Catholic University of America Press, 1988).

32. See Famerée, ' "Responsabilisation" des conférences épiscopales', 44–5; also id., 'La Fonction du pape: éléments d'une problématique', in Tihon, *Changer la papauté?* 82–3.

16

Potential Catholic Learning Around Lay Participation in Decision-making

Paul Lakeland

INTRODUCTION

It is probably no coincidence that the great Dominican ecclesiologist, Yves Congar, was an equally passionate ecumenist. Feeding into the more radical implications of his work on the laity, especially his late preference for the language of 'different ministries', was a profound historical familiarity with the plurality of Christian churches. The extreme defensiveness of early twentieth-century Roman Catholicism was in the end largely overcome by the force of historical precedent in the guise of the liturgical reform movement, the recovery of the historical Aquinas, and the theological explorations of *la nouvelle théologie*. A historian as learned as Congar knew quite well that church polity and the theology of orders continued to be works in progress.

In this regard, it might seem likely that Roman Catholicism would have much to learn about lay roles in governance from other churches. Maybe so, but it will have to be at a deeper level than simply focusing on the practical lessons to be gleaned, for example, from the Lutheran experience of synodal government or the Methodist concept of connexionalism. For most of Catholic history, 'lay' has been a remainder concept defined by negatives and at a level deeper than mere exclusion from the clerical caste.

More recently, Roman Catholic laity are commonly identified by their 'secularity'. Whilst helpful in some ways, this term can also support an unhealthy view of the church. On the one hand, it helps us understand that the church itself is secular, in the fundamental sense that it is located in the world and properly oriented towards it in service. On the other hand, the legitimate stress on the laity's mission to the world can occlude their real responsibility as baptized adults for the community of faith itself. This presents particular difficulties in relation to the important post-Second Vatican Council emergence of 'lay ecclesial ministers' who can be viewed either as temporary expedients in a time of shortage of ordained ministers or as no longer properly *lay*.

This question of the status of the laity becomes particularly acute when we turn to the issue of lay role in governance. The broad ecumenical witness is that there are a number of successful ways in which the laity play a part here, from synodal structures with elected representatives, to the selection of local ministers by a lay board or the elders of the community. While traditions vary considerably, almost all except Roman Catholicism have clearly defined expectations of lay participation in governance at some level. Why Catholicism should be the exception here is a complex matter.

A first lesson to reflect on is that there is no necessary connection between the theological understanding of the *lay* vocation and the part the laity play in governance. Some fundamentalist Christianity categorically rejects all notion of orders while insisting on a highly authoritarian structure. Equally, the Anglican, Methodist, Lutheran, and Orthodox churches maintain a serious commitment to orders while building a substantial role for the laity into the polity of their communities. Roman Catholicism is, therefore, on shaky ground if it rests its exclusion of the laity from governance solely on the basis of a strong theology of orders. It may, indeed, be time to reconsider the monopoly the ordained have of jurisdiction within Catholicism and to ask if there might be a dimension to governance and leadership that is separable from the eucharistic presidency that seems to be the one indisputable role of the ordained.

The time for such discussion is especially ripe since the turmoil in which much of the Roman Catholic Church currently finds itself—provoked by the ongoing scandal of clerical sex abuse of minors—is clearly a crisis of leadership more than one of faith or doctrine. This, in turn, has led to a crisis of authority, and laypeople and others have begun to turn a searchlight upon both the cultural phenomenon of clericalism and the politics of episcopal appointments over the last quarter of a century. In an age in which Roman Catholic laypeople frequently have considerable professional responsibilities and leadership experience, it is not surprising that they have begun to realize that ecclesial structures have infantilized them and that an adult and thoroughly accountable church requires a much greater voice for the laity.

The bright spot, then, in this crisis is that Catholic laity are increasingly becoming aware of it and asserting their own rights and responsibilities to speak out on such a crucial matter. In this, they are taking their cue from the Second Vatican Council's teaching on the church (*Lumen Gentium*) and the lay apostolate (*Apostolicam Actuositatem*) and are beginning to enact something of the same historical scenario to which John Henry Newman alluded when he identified the laity as having saved the church in the Arian crisis. Likewise, in their increasing interest in having a role in the selection of bishops and pastors, the laity are returning to ancient practices, even when they are accused of creeping congregationalism or an uncritical adoption of the querulous spirit of our age.

In what follows we will trace some of the issues along four paths: historical, theological, ecumenical, and political. On the historical path, we will look at where the question of lay governance had generally arrived with the Second Vatican Council's seminal work on the laity. On the theological path, we will examine recent developments in thinking on ordained and baptismal priesthood within Catholicism, partially inspired by ecumenical learning. We will pursue this ecumenical debt in a third moment, inquiring of the usefulness of various patterns of lay governance to Catholicism and, on the political path, we will turn to developments in the Roman Catholic Church in the United States in the last five years.

THE LAY ROLE IN THE SECOND VATICAN
COUNCIL'S ECCLESIOLOGY

The Second Vatican Council was a remarkable moment for serious theological reflection upon the place of the laity in the church, the first such time in official Roman Catholic teaching. While the early years of the church showed no sense of a theologically significant division between lay and ordained, as attention progressively focused upon the roles of ministers and leaders, laypeople came by degrees to be forgotten: a theology of the laity was not so much abandoned, as never really developed. The laity were defined by what they were not—not ordained and, later, not monks. The priestly and missionary significance of baptism faded into near oblivion, baptism coming to be understood solely as a sacrament of initiation. As recently as the early twentieth century, Pius X could say 'the one duty of the multitude is to allow themselves to be led and, like a docile flock, to follow the Pastors'.[1]

Only fifty years later the voice of the institutional church was utterly transformed, reflecting a remarkable theological ferment in the first half of the twentieth century. *Lumen Gentium*'s treatment of the laity revolves around four themes: the priority of baptism, the priesthood of the laity, the specific character of lay ministry, and the solidarity of laity and pastors. These ideas were taken from the pioneering work of theologians such as Congar, Marie-Dominique Chenu, Henri de Lubac, and Jean Daniélou, concerned to equip the church for mission in secular society. Pope Pius XII had effectively squelched this movement with the publication of *Humani Generis* in 1950. Ten years later, their ideas found a place at the Second Vatican Council under a very different pope, John XXIII.[2]

Among the more important aspects of the Second Vatican Council's teaching on the laity is the recovery of attention to the priestly character of the whole people of God anchored in a renewed understanding of baptism as not just about membership but as initiation into a missioned community. In *Lumen*

Gentium, the whole people of God are 'a kingdom of priests' in virtue of their baptism, who share equally the responsibility to proclaim Christ (*LG*, § 10). In the eucharistic sacrifice, all the baptized offer the divine victim to God and themselves along with it. Neither priesthood is derivative of the other, but rather they differ 'essentially and not only in degree'. Baptismal priesthood is said to be related to ordained priesthood because both are a sharing in the one priesthood of Christ, and it is characteristic of all the faithful, not a 'vocation' to which only some are called. Indeed, ordained ministers do not abandon their baptismal priesthood: ordination adds onto the first priesthood. In itself, therefore, baptismal priesthood has nothing to do with *lay* ministry. But it has a lot to do with ministry in general, an idea to which we will return.

Also important for the role of laity in decision-making is the prominence the Second Vatican Council gives to the *sensus fidelium* in helping to maintain the church in truth. Alongside a restatement of the First Vatican Council's treatment of papal infallibility and the promotion of the college of bishops, with the Bishop of Rome as their head, as being able to speak infallibly, the council fathers, in words reminiscent of John Henry Newman, asserted that when the whole body of the faithful is united in belief, they too express a form of infallibility (*LG*, § 12). The consequence is clear: the spirit of truth fills the laity just as it fills the ordained; though some may possess a charism of teaching with authority through the word, the whole community teaches with authority through its lived faith.

A third dimension of importance can be found in the prominence given in both *Lumen Gentium* and *Apostolicam Actuositatem* to the right and responsibility of the laity to speak out for the good of the church. *Apostolicam Actuositatem*, in particular, recognizes that the laity sometimes possess special competencies or technical knowledge in this regard, which empowers or obliges them to speak out.[3] While there is no suggestion that there ought to be structures through which these actions can be systematically directed, it is clearly implied that the wise pastor will defer to greater knowledge, recognizing the legitimate exercise of baptismal responsibilities and encouraging this kind of lay initiative.

Alongside these three key aspects of the Second Vatican Council's treatment of the laity, is the significance of the broader ecumenical spirit of the Council, representing a shift from an exclusively teaching stance to one also of potentially learning from the secular world and from those with other religious commitments. With specific reference to relations with other Christian churches, Ormond Rush points out that the first stage of post-conciliar ecumenical dialogue involved a comparative approach that highlighted differences and led to very little progress.[4] Progress began to be made when attention shifted to showing how each tradition was itself faithful to the witness of the apostolic church. In other words, rather than trying to negotiate the boundaries of present-day pluralism, dialogue revealed that today's differences were anchored in the pluralism of the early church. This turn to the pluralism of the early church is of great importance for the consideration of lay roles. While the earliest witness seemed to see little significance in the term *laos*, within a century or so there were different practices in different churches, from the narrower understandings of Catholicity in Irenaeus to the broader inclusiveness of Cyprian. The possibility that the early church has much to teach us leads into more theological considerations.

BAPTISM, MINISTRY, AND THE TWO PRIESTHOODS

Whilst taking great inspiration from the work of the Council, subsequent theology of the laity also moved beyond it in various ways. Specifically, it has probed much further: (1) the relationship between baptism and orders; (2) the supposedly 'secular character' of the lay vocation; and (3) the demerits of too exclusive a focus on ordination as effecting ontological change. This theology has been influenced throughout by three of Congar's insights that the Council did *not* incorporate: sustained attention to *ressourcement*, the 'principle of lay consent', and the shift from a lay–clergy polarity to the concept of 'different ministries'.

It is commonly said that the twin impulses of the Second Vatican Council were *aggiornamento* and *ressourcement*. The 'updating' that John XXIII called for was to be accomplished by a return to the sources. Both steps were necessary if the church was to emerge from the stultifying ahistoricality of neoscholasticism. Without *aggiornamento* there would be no ability to respond to the particular concerns of the day; without *ressourcement*, there would be no testing and informing against the tradition.

Congar's magisterial work, *Lay People in the Church*,[5] is a shining example of *ressourcement*. This work above all others drew attention to the rich patristic resources concerning the roles of the laity. While the early centuries evinced no sustained reflection on the status of the layperson, they provided innumerable examples of laypeople being incorporated in serious decision-making, implying the view that baptismal equality had practical consequences for governance. Many texts provide clear evidence that laypeople were consulted as a matter of course about the work of the church, and especially about the selection of leaders. Where they did not necessarily directly elect them, they were closely involved in the process, sometimes choosing by acclamation from a shortlist presented by the bishops of the province. So, for example, Cyprian of Carthage was quite clear that 'it is our custom when we make appointments to clerical office to consult you beforehand, and in council with you to weigh the character and qualities of each candidate'.[6] Indeed, he is adamant that he has always been committed 'right from the beginning of my episcopate, to do nothing on my own private judgment without your counsel and the consent of the people'.[7] Likewise, the third-century text the *Apostolic Tradition* maintained that the bishop should be chosen first by the people and subsequently approved by bishops and presbyters. Again, when in the fifth century Pope Leo the Great stated, 'Let the one who is going to rule over all be elected by all', he was only confirming his predecessor Celestine I's position that 'a bishop should not be given to those who are unwilling to receive him'.[8]

Congar enacts a particularly important instance of *ressourcement* in recalling the 'principle of lay consent' which he describes 'as a principle, not of structure but of life, as a concrete law of all the great acts of ecclesial life, beginning with that of designation to the highest offices'.[9] In Congar's view, while the hierarchical authority of the church can take decisions which are always in some abstract sense 'true', without the active consent of the laity they may never become effective. Subsequent to Congar, of course, these ideas have developed into the whole concept of 'reception theory'. If a teaching is not received then, while one may claim it is true in some abstract sense, it is not useful, it does not contribute to building up the body of Christ. At root, this depends upon the conviction that the Spirit cannot be at war with itself. If, over a sufficiently extended period, a magisterial teaching does not gain the active consent of the people one might conclude that the Spirit is speaking more clearly through them than through the hierarchy. A case in point is *Humanae Vitae*, Paul VI's 1968 encyclical letter on birth control.[10]

Whilst recognizing that the principle of consent should not be applied too liberally, nor equated with a simple majority vote, it may nevertheless be pertinent to the fact that polls taken in the United States over the past five years or so by the Zogby company, the *National Catholic Reporter*, and Andrew Greeley regularly show a clear majority of active Roman Catholics favouring an end to mandatory celibacy, a lay role in the selection of bishops, and the admittance of women to ordination. Furthermore, since for the last twenty-five years the hierarchy has been forbidden to discuss such matters in public, it is appropriate to ask whether the Spirit of God might be more likely to be heard where people can speak freely out of concern for the church, than where artificial constraints are imposed.

Some ten years after his great work on the laity, Congar began to have second thoughts about the way he had construed the problem. Influenced by his Jesuit friend, Jean Daniélou, he produced a second edition of *Lay People in the Church* in which he admitted he had remained overly wedded to a clerical model. At about the same time, he rethought his theology in the category of 'different ministries'.[11] Now he was able to say that while priesthood is a distinct ministry, it has its meaning only within the common ministries of the faithful. Consequently, the community must have a role in recognizing the gifts that confirm the claim to a vocation. He famously concluded, 'Since the Council it is no longer the layman who stands in need of definition, but the priest'.[12]

The most promising recent development in Roman Catholic ministry studies is indebted to Congar's ideas on different ministries and is to be found in renewed attention to baptism as the basis for all ministry. Whilst this does not eliminate the particular ministry of ordained priesthood, it does clarify its status as one ministry alongside others, which, whatever 'essential' distinction pertains, can only be understood in relation to the priesthood of the baptized. This fresh 'relational' understanding of ministry promotes the idea that the distinctiveness of ordained ministry lies in the particular character of the relation of the priest to the rest of the community, not in some interior change.[13]

In this perspective, in baptism we are all inserted into a missionary community and called to mission. Our mission grows naturally from our particular talents and the church can recognize this mission in a variety of ways. Ordination is one of these ways which, like other ministries less directly connected to leadership, places us in a new particular relationship to the community of faith. In ordination, the priest acquires a new 'ordo', a new set of relationships to the community. It is in this new ecclesial relationship that the 'real change' of ordination consists; the implication being that 'ontological change' is a misleading way of describing this.

The language of ontological change and character theology, like that of transubstantiation, is a time-conditioned effort to express the timeless truth of real change or real presence. Roman Catholics are obliged to hold to the doctrine of real eucharistic presence. We are not obliged to find the language of transubstantiation helpful. Similarly, we believe that ordination makes a real difference, but we are not obliged to find the language of ontological change helpful. Pope John Paul II frequently expressed his belief in the qualitative rather than merely quantitative difference between the priesthood of all and the 'hierarchical priesthood', intending thereby to indicate that the latter derives directly from Christ, rather than from the community of believers and is, thus, independent of the priesthood of the baptized. The problem is that the language of qualitative distinction obscures the fact that the biggest qualitative change occurs at baptism. It is there that we become a new creation. Again, to say that 'real change' occurs in ordination is not to say that 'real change' does not equally occur in the commissioning of those called to other ecclesial roles. In each case, commissioning/ordination places the individual in a new relation to the whole community.

At first sight it might seem that this relational understanding displaces the standard view of the hierarchical ministry being directly established by Christ, but this does not necessarily follow. An exclusive focus on the Christological origins of priesthood can serve to obscure the pneumatological basis for ministry as a whole. All genuine calling to ministry is the work of the Spirit, expressed in the will of the local church and the local community, and finding resonance in the generosity of the individual heart. If priesthood is structurally different in virtue of its historical origins in a direct act of Christ—which is too often misunderstood as Jesus' direct institution of the tripartite ministry of bishop, priest and deacon—there are no degrees of difference between the way the Spirit calls one to leadership and another to teaching. There may be difference between the two priesthoods, but the dynamics of calling are identical.

ECUMENICAL WITNESS AND THE POTENTIAL FOR LEARNING

There are many practices in a number of Christian churches which have direct relevance to the status of the Roman Catholic laity and their potential for involvement in governance. This is particularly true of those churches which retain an ordained ministry such as Episcopalianism and Methodism. Their attachment to different forms of synodal government and the attendant philosophy of common oversight of all members for one another and for the church as a whole can be enormously instructive.

The first thing that strikes the more ecumenically minded Roman Catholic is that the flavour of the relationship between minister and layperson within Protestantism is entirely different from that even within more enlightened Roman Catholic communities. Whilst most Roman Catholic communities in Europe and North America have long abandoned the patriarchal relationship of priest and people, they have not managed to accomplish a genuine sense of equality. Among many Protestants, as among many Jews, the minister/rabbi is a professional, respected for the special skills that he or she brings to the role. Within Roman Catholicism, even where that same professional respect exists, it continues to be coloured by the structural phenomenon of clericalism which is, in part, a product of Roman Catholic theology of orders and, in part, a consequence of lifestyle differences between priest and people.

If, then, the first lesson is that the eradication of lifestyle differences between ordained and lay should result in a better climate for lay leadership, this on its own may be simplistic. Clericalism is the culture of separation that has grown up around clerics. An end to mandatory celibacy would be quite possible, theologically speaking, and would surely deal a huge blow to clericalism, though not necessarily a fatal one. Without the admission of women to ministry, itself a wholly more difficult issue within Roman Catholicism, some aspects of clerical exclusivity would continue to be likely. Moreover, there is no guarantee that married men would value prestige and special status any less than their celibate counterparts.

A second possible lesson is that the flattening of the difference between lay and ordained within Protestant theology of orders might contribute to a healthier vision of ministry as a spectrum of gifts. As suggested earlier, there are good reasons to rethink ministry as involving 'relational' rather than 'substantial' ontological change. Such revisioning would curtail the unhealthy accentuation of difference between ordained and lay ministry. The bigger problem is how to assert this new way of thinking while maintaining the claim that ministry comes from the commission of Christ and the call of the Spirit, rather than the community's delegation. A way forward, in line with the attitudes of many Protestant traditions, might involve two moves. First, there must be consistent and serious theological attention to the two priesthoods, which in practice means a whole campaign of revalorization of the baptismal priesthood. Second, the Roman Catholic Church needs to restore the lay voice in the calling of ministers. If the call of Christ is one pillar of ordained ministry, the role of the Holy Spirit is the second. While the call of Christ may be confirmed by the judgement of the institutional church, the Spirit speaks through the whole people.

If it is true that attitudes of mind and theologies of orders impede a renewed role for the laity in governance and leadership, calls for a change of consciousness will not be enough. Patterns of synodal government and community account-ability within Episcopalian, Methodist, Lutheran, and other traditions strongly suggest themselves as structural ways to deal with what is a structural problem. Moreover, the Receptive Ecumenism possible here is less a matter of importing alien practices into Roman Catholicism than of re-energizing dormant processes and of activating structures already on the books, but, for one reason or another, not taken seriously.

There is nothing unCatholic, for example, about diocesan synods.[14] Synods were the standard way the church of the first few centuries governed itself and today diocesan synods are recognized as approved structures for assisting a bishop. Canon Law describes them as 'an assembly of selected priests and other members of Christ's faithful of a particular church which, for the good of the entire diocesan community, assists the diocesan bishop...'[15] They are to be summoned into existence by the bishop with representation from among the laity. The *Directory for the Pastoral Ministry of Bishops* lists among the ways they might help the adaptation of church law to local conditions, the resolution of administrative problems, encouraging diocesan projects, and correcting errors in doctrine and morals.[16]

While the Lutheran and Episcopal churches continue the practice of synodal government, the diocesan synod within Catholicism is somewhat different. It is typically a 'one-off' and can only be called at the bishop's pleasure. Its scope is only diocesan, while Lutherans and Episcopalians have regional and national synods. Its make-up is to a large degree dependent on the bishop (canon 463, § 1). Nevertheless, it could be an enormously important adjunct to the workings of the diocese. Any bishop who wished to institute regular synods would have much to learn from the synodal traditions within Protestantism.

What impedes the emergence of a viable synodal structure within Roman Catholicism is an inability to countenance the subordination of the hierarchy, in any fashion, to the legislative authority of laypeople. For example, canon law makes clear that: 'The diocesan Bishop is the sole legislator in the diocesan synod. Other members of the synod have only a consultative vote' (canon 466). Accordingly, the Vatican response to the American Bishops' 2002 *Charter for the Protection of Young People* ruled, contrary to the intentions of the American bishops, that the diocesan review boards, staffed overwhelmingly by well-qualified laypersons, were to have only advisory roles.[17]

In contrast, Protestant notions of what the United Reformed Church has called 'whole-body ecclesiology' offer a possible way forward here for the Roman Catholic Church. The term 'whole-body ecclesiology' suggests the communal dimension of oversight (*episcope*) through which all the members of the congregation and all the congregations unite in an active concern for the life of their communities. This form of conciliarity may have differing representative structures in the various churches, but they all provide for the active principle of 'whole-body' consent. Synods are part of this process but they in turn build upon an ethos of communal oversight at the grassroots level. One particularly interesting expression of this is the Methodist commitment to connexionalism which combines a sense of corporate ecclesial responsibility with a recognition of 'the need for ministries of unity and oversight'.[18]

'Whole-body ecclesiology' is close kin to the Second Vatican Council's notion of collegiality, especially as extended to the whole people of God in their shared 'co-responsibility' for the church. Where it differs is in the structured accountability enshrined through systems of election, representation, and participation in decision-making processes. Whilst allowing for the Roman Catholic commitment to a particular role for episcopacy and ordained ministry, it challenges Catholic practice in timely ways by suggesting that the 'power of orders' might cede a little jurisdictional responsibility to a theology of oversight appropriate to a church of adults.

LAY VOICE AND ECCLESIAL DECISION-MAKING IN AMERICA TODAY

Turning to the contemporary scene and future possibilities, the focus will be on the Roman Catholic Church in the United States which, for a number of reasons, presents a fitting case study. In the last decade at least, it is in North America that the issues have been most openly debated, above all because of the crisis in leadership precipitated by the sexual abuse scandal. Again, the Roman Catholic Church in the United States—a vital going concern—evinces

an extraordinary level of dependence upon 'lay ecclesial ministers', a phenomenon which may be remaking the church in a direction in which lay
decision-making becomes inevitable.[19] With this, the size and mostly progressive
complexion of the Catholic theological community in the United States is also
an important factor.[20] Finally, American Catholicism, unlike its European, Asian,
African, and Latin American counterparts, is indelibly marked by the Protestant
individualism of the culture in which it has achieved a measure of national
acceptability and by the continuing tensions between a previous attempt to
forge a truly American Catholicism and the ultramontanism of the immigrant
church that was superimposed upon it. Thus, the particular character of the
American Roman Catholic Church makes it almost inevitable that the question
of lay roles in governance and decision-making would sooner or later achieve
prominence.

'Sooner or later', of course, means the year 2002, a year which began with
an avalanche of lawsuits over abusive priests in the United States in general and
in the Archdiocese of Boston in particular, and which ended with the removal
of Cardinal Bernard Law as Archbishop of Boston. In *Call to Action* the church
had had a lively progressive group of mostly lay Roman Catholics for over thirty
years, but in 2002 there emerged a much more centrist organization, *Voice of the
Faithful*. This association, formed in Boston at the end of 2001, rapidly grew to
over 25,000 members on a three-point programme of support for the victims of
sexual abuse, support for honourable clergy, and structural change in the church.
Under the banner of 'Keep the Faith, Change the Church', and the outstanding
leadership of Jim Post, a professor of management at Boston University, they
have gone on to become a major force in American Catholicism, though not one
with which all bishops are happy.

The nervousness of the American hierarchy about *Voice of the Faithful* is a
product of suspicion of the ambiguous third point of the organization's platform,
'to promote structural change'. Does this mean that the usual liberal Pandora's
box will be opened and out will pop more pressure for women priests and an
end to mandatory celibacy? Certainly, such concerns have been expressed by
those more conservative bishops who have effectively banned *Voice of the Faithful*
from their dioceses. But there may also be wider concern about the challenge to
episcopal authority and clerical culture itself in the more modest call for a lay
voice in decision-making.

One of the healthiest signs being shown by movements for lay decision-
making is their awareness of the practices and patterns of the early church, briefly
reviewed earlier. It is theologically sound, tactically significant, and personally
satisfying to realize that lay decision-making was part of the ancient past of
the church. If so, no one can declare it to be somehow contrary to the nature
of the church now. Somehow, in large measure thanks to a concerted effort
by theologians and others, this historical awareness has reached the lay Roman

Catholic population at large.[21] Cyprian of Carthage is frequently quoted at *Voice of the Faithful* meetings in the Diocese of Bridgeport, Connecticut, surely a turn of events that is as surprising as it is hopeful! Sadly, at the insistence of the bishop, those meetings must take place somewhere other than on diocesan property.

While it is clearly the case that *Voice of the Faithful* represents a wholly healthy move towards a more adult and accountable church, it is also true that there are further steps that need to be taken, reflecting the theological developments outlined in the second section of this essay. Roman Catholic laity have already begun to take the first step, corresponding to the earlier work of Congar, in which *ressourcement* has empowered them to ask searching questions about their rights and responsibilities. The two further steps will be more challenging. The second, paralleling the work of the later Congar, is to shift attention away from a lay/clerical division to construing the church according to the concept of 'different ministries'. Whilst the ground is already well prepared for this by the growth of lay ecclesial ministries, the theological implications have yet to sink in. As they do, a third step will be reached, in which ministry itself will need to be revisioned in categories of 'baptismal priesthood', 'relational ontological change', and 'ecclesial repositioning'.

There is, of course, a distinct difference between rethinking the theology of ministry and investigating ways in which laypeople can participate in decision-making, but within Roman Catholicism the two cannot easily be separated. While the Second Vatican Council wrote movingly about the importance of a lay voice in the church, Roman Catholic polity continues to allow for absolutely no effective voice, and no formal roles, in ecclesiastical structures. This polity derives from that failure to anchor Christian life in the baptismal priesthood of all which led to the exclusion of the laity from anything other than passive roles. Though the Second Vatican Council began to recover baptismal priesthood, clericalism has continued to bar laypeople from formal voice. Asking the question about lay participation in decision-making thus necessarily entails attending to the understanding of ministry.

The dynamism of the movements for greater lay participation in decision-making is consequently towards more radical questioning of the nature of ministry, its relation to orders, and the 'essential' distinction between ordained and baptismal priesthood. In terms of the North American church, it means that *Voice of the Faithful* cannot stop at a call for participation but must press on to more fundamental questioning. Otherwise, any future lay involvement in decision-making will be conceived merely as the extension of a more generous form of patronage than has been accorded laypeople in the past.

In the end, therefore, we cannot simply say that the way forward is by means of some kind of synodal organization in which the lay estate will have its say. In the

Roman Catholic context, this is to perpetuate the dramatic division between the ordained and the laity. More substantially, moving forward will require recovering the idea of a priestly people in a faith community in which all are called to mission. It is because all the baptized are in some way intended to be missioned that they need to have a voice in the decision-making processes of the church. Certainly, among the baptized there are those who are called to a ministry of liturgical or jurisdictional leadership (must these always be the same people, since the two roles seem to require quite different competencies?) and those who are called to other ministries. But there is no way to argue responsibly that the Spirit speaks only through the ordained.

If there is to be responsible participation in decision-making on the part of all, it cannot occur without the creation of appropriate structures. The details of those cannot be suggested here, though they have been hinted at in the previous section's discussion of 'whole body ecclesiology'. Which brings us to the Americanist question: What is so terrible about democracy? Perhaps Rome only knows the marketplace democracy of classical Athens and fears that it leads inexorably to the Great Terror of revolutionary Paris? Perhaps Rome has not heard of the checks and balances of the American experiment in democracy, or of the lessons learned in the great democracies of Europe? Furthermore, what is it that has allowed Rome to embrace democratic solutions in civil society while rejecting them for the church? If democracy is based on the equal dignity of all before God, how is it that authoritarianism can be the appropriate political form for a church founded upon the equality of all in the baptismal priesthood?

NOTES

1. Pius X, '*Vehementer Nos*: Encyclical Letter on the French Law of Separation' (11 Feb. 1906), § 8, available at <http://www.vatican.va/holy_father/pius_x/encyclicals/documents/hf_p-x_enc_11021906_vehementer-nos_en.html>.
2. See Etienne Fouilloux, *Une église en quête de liberté: la pensée catholique française entre modernisme et Vatican II, 1914–1962* (Paris: Desclée de Brouwer, 1998) and Lakeland, *The Liberation of the Laity: In Search of an Accountable Church* (New York: Continuum, 2003), 23–48.
3. See *AA*, § 3; also § 7; § 25; *LG*, § 37.
4. See Rush, *Still Interpreting Vatican II: Some Hermeneutical Principles* (New York: Paulist Press, 2004), 67.
5. Congar, *Lay People in the Church: A Study for a Theology of the Laity*, trans. Donald Attwater rev. edn. (Westminster, Md.: Newman, 1965).
6. See 'Letter 38: 1–2', *The Letters of St Cyprian of Carthage*, trans. G. W. Clarke (New York: Newman, 1984), ii. 52–3 and Francis A. Sullivan, 'St Cyprian on the Role

of the Laity in Decision Making in the Early Church', in Stephen J. Pope (ed.), *Common Calling: The Laity and Governance of the Catholic Church* (Washington, DC: Georgetown, 2004), 39–49.

7. 'Letter 14: 4', *Letters*, i. 89.

8. For these and other examples, see Michael J. Buckley, 'Resources for Reform from the First Millennium', in *Common Calling*, 71–86, also, significantly, Antonio Rosmini, *The Five Wounds of the Church*, trans. Denis Cleary (Leominster: Fowler Wright, 1987), 67–132, 157–94.

9. *Lay People in the Church*, 247.

10. For a particularly important treatment of reception, see John E. Thiel, *Senses of Tradition: Continuity and Development in Catholic Faith* (Oxford: Oxford University Press, 2000), specifically 109–11 in relation to *Humanae Vitae*.

11. See Congar, 'Ministères et laicat dans les recherches actuelles de la théologie catholique romaine', *Verbum Caro*, 18 (1964), 127–48; id., 'Ministères et structuration de l'Église', *La Maison Dieu*, 102 (1970), 7–20; id., 'Quelques problèmes touchant les ministères', *Nouvelle revue théologique*, 93 (1971), 785–800, also id., 'My Pathfindings in the Theology of Laity and Ministries', *Jurist*, 2 (1972), 169–88.

12. 'My Pathfindings', 181–2.

13. See Susan Wood (ed.), *Ordering the Baptismal Priesthood* (Collegeville, Minn.: Liturgical Press, 2003), particularly Richard Gaillardetz, 'The Ecclesiological Foundations of Ministry Within an Ordered Communion' (pp. 26–51).

14. I am indebted here to an unpub. paper by Tom Reese.

15. The Canon Law Society of Great Britain and Ireland, *The Canon Law: Letter and Spirit. A Practical Guide to the Code of Canon Law* (London: Geoffrey Chapman, 1995), canon 460.

16. Congregation for Bishops, *Apostolorum Successores. Directory for the Pastoral Ministry of Bishops* (Vatican: Libreria Editrice Vaticana, 2004).

17. <http://www.usccb.org/ocyp/norms.shtml>. The best place to see the subtle but important changes that the Vatican-required 'mixed commission' made to the original Dallas document is at <http://www.bishop-accountability.org/resources/resource-files/churchdocs/MixedChanges.htm>. See esp. norms 4–5.

18. See *Conversations on the Way to Unity*, a document of the British United Reformed Church summarizing the history of their dialogue with the Methodist Church and the Church of England between 1995 and 2001, available at <http://www.urc.org.uk/conversations/conciliarity.htm>.

19. There are now over 30,000 lay ecclesial ministers in the American Roman Catholic Church, including chancellors, parish associates, youth ministers, religious educators, and chaplains. About 75 per cent work full time and some 80 per cent are women. They serve on the staff of 66 per cent of parishes and 41 per cent care for parishes without a resident pastor. One can then generalize that the typical lay ecclesial minister is a laywoman working full-time for the local church. See United States Conference of Catholic Bishops, *Co-workers in the Vineyard of the Lord: A Resource for Guiding the Development of Lay Ecclesial Ministry* (Washington, DC: USCCB, 2005), also at <http://www.usccb.org/laity/laymin/co-workers.pdf>.

20. The size and character of the American Catholic theological community is principally a product of the importance of Catholic higher education. Over 720,000 students attend 221 Roman Catholic colleges, all of which have programmes of theology or religious studies staffed by faculty with doctoral-level qualifications, the majority of whom are Roman Catholic. Most are laypeople, a large minority women, and as a group they mirror the generally liberal face of American academia at large.

21. See, e.g., Francis Oakley and Bruce Russett (eds.), *Governance, Accountability and the Future of the Catholic Church* (New York and London: Continuum, 2004); also *Common Calling*.

17

Receptive Ecumenical Learning and Episcopal Accountability Within Contemporary Roman Catholicism—Canonical Considerations

Patrick Connolly

INTRODUCTION

Roman Catholic theology has beautiful language about the church yet there is often a gap between the rhetoric and practical realities. In this regard, a number of the chapters in this volume touch on what Roman Catholicism might appropriately learn from other Christian traditions in relation to the increased transparency and accountability of its structures of governance.[1] This chapter, accordingly, probes the extent and limitations of the resources that exist within the 1983 Code of Canon Law of the Latin Catholic Church[2] for addressing one particular perceived area of weakness in the internal governance of the Roman Catholic Church, namely: episcopal accountability, as this has come under scrutiny in the light of the sexual abuse scandals in the English-speaking world. The ensuing crisis has given these matters a new and compelling relevance as it becomes obvious that such weaknesses have practical implications and significant consequences for the church's credible preaching of the Good News in a sceptical world. The concern here is to explore how in this specific regard the gap that can open up between the high rhetoric of Roman Catholic self-understanding and the actual reality of practice and structure might be narrowed. In this, the chapter follows in the spirit of the call expressed in ARCIC II's *The Gift of Authority* for a renewal of respective internal structures through a process of what is here being referred to as receptive ecumenical learning.[3]

A PARTICULAR WEAKNESS

At one level the Roman Catholic Church is a highly centralized institution (e.g. in terms of episcopal appointments within the Latin church). At another level, however, power is highly devolved to the local bishop, certainly in terms of administrative and day-to-day decision-making. The theologian may respond that this is how it should be. A local church is not a province or department of the world church, but the church in one particular place.[4] The bishop in his diocese is not the delegate of the Pope, but one commissioned by Christ with a proper responsibility of his own (*potestas propria, ordinaria et immediata*), rooted in the sacrament of orders (*LG*, § 27; also *CD*, § 8).

Canonically, there is a basic unity of episcopal governing power rooted in sacramental ordination.[5] Some aspects of that *potestas sacra* are completely personal (e.g. the power to ordain, canon 1012), while others can be exercised through vicars (canons 475–481). So within a unified governing power there is a differentiation of functions but no true separation of powers as in secular governments. The difficulty is that the exercise of episcopal administrative authority remains largely unstructured in the 1983 Code, with few effective mechanisms to ensure the bishop's ongoing accountability, especially in his executive function. There is indeed appeal possible for a bishop's allegedly arbitrary administrative act in a particular case, by means of hierarchical administrative recourse.[6] However, if a bishop is seriously failing in the way he runs the diocese—through mismanagement or ill-thought-out policies and decisions, rather than moral weakness necessarily—little usually happens unless it becomes public or is of such obvious significance as to receive Roman attention.

To take one example, the secretive mismanagement of abuse cases by many bishops over such a long period has focused attention on this lack of effective canonical means of ensuring episcopal accountability in diocesan governance. In following a policy of reassignment of priests known to have engaged in the sexual abuse of minors, there appears to have been a general lack of accountability, and indeed the wider church only became aware of the problem as a result of the courage of victims and the power of the media, leading to lawsuits and criminal investigations. Because dioceses did not share information about incidents of alleged abuse, many bishops failed to realize that the problem was widespread in scope. This is not to impute bad faith or arrogance to individual bishops. No doubt they made decisions in good faith as best they could in the circumstances, decisions which of course in hindsight can be seen to have been profoundly ill-judged and ill-thought-out. The difficulty is that the clear impression was given that many bishops were not used to explaining their decisions and there were few formal mechanisms to cause any questioning of the policy. Looking at it from another angle, there were no effective formal procedures to help bishops evaluate their policies and decisions. *De facto*, a policy of reassignment and cover-up could be pursued in the knowledge that bishops were in reality answerable to no one. This failure of bishops to hold themselves accountable for their decisions and to make use of the existing minimal governance structures was identified as a key factor exacerbating the problem by the National Review Board in the USA.[7]

As has been noted by John W. O'Malley, the first characteristic of this scandal is its extent; it was not limited regionally.[8] The consistent pattern in how these cases were handled indicates that this was not a one-off management problem, but a more systemic issue as to how dioceses are governed on a day-to-day level. Since the Second Vatican Council and the revision of canon law, the discussion of possible mechanisms of accountability has been rather academic, in the sense that it has been contended that certain ecclesiological ideas lack an effective canonical implementation, but the crisis has demonstrated in a very practical and compelling way just how damaging such a lack can be.

This lack of accountability, along with other aspects of the crisis, has raised widespread problems of credibility for the whole church, particularly in the English-speaking world. Aside from the effect on the perception of ecclesiastical authority within the church among Roman Catholics, the scandals have undermined the church's social mission. Since some clergy have committed grave injustices of abuse against young people and since many bishops failed to deal with the problem effectively or covered it up, it is not surprising many people now feel that official church teaching on justice rings hollow. Thus, the church's proclamation of Gospel values experiences a renewed reaction of scepticism and indeed cynicism in a western culture already dubious about institutional organized religion. No longer can questions of governance and accountability be discounted as a navel-gazing preoccupation with ecclesial reform. Such failures seriously damage the witness and mission of the church.

Leaving aside the particular issue of the scandals and how they were handled by bishops, this question has a wider relevance.[9] We mention the scandals because they have renewed and heightened interest in how ecclesiastical structures for accountability are currently underdeveloped or underutilized. It is to these structures that we now turn.

ACCOUNTABILITY: THEORY AND PRACTICE

The notion of accountability is very broad, because there are different dimensions to it, ranging from the accountability of church leadership due to the faith community to that due to the wider society beyond the church. To speak in general terms, accountability involves various forms of openness so that leadership decisions affecting the church's mission are, in principle, available to the relevant people for informed comment. Accountability is, of course, a concept which goes beyond the juridical and which is not limited to the intra-ecclesial, the focus of this chapter. And we need always to remember that even comprehensive legal processes of accountability can sometimes themselves be used to evade true accountability.

Accountability is a word with democratic connotations. Moreover, it is commonly a somewhat harsh term, suggesting—in the way it is habitually used in secular public discourse at least—the need to call leaders to judgement for their actions. The question may, therefore, arise as to how suitable it is for ecclesial discourse. The context of its use is that it is increasingly suggested that the church has much to learn about its own governance from secular bodies such as companies, hospitals, educational, and political institutions. Whilst that is indeed true, we need also to be careful that we do not uncritically import managerial ideas without significant theological reflection on them. The church is not a business corporation or a department of the public service. Nonetheless, this is not to say the church should not adopt useful elements from civil society, as she did in the past. As Cardinal Kasper has noted:

In the past, the Church adopted a number of feudal and monarchical elements in order to provide a concrete articulation for its own constitution. In the same way, it can and must take up some democratic structural elements and procedures today, in a manner both critical and creative, in order to express in the forms appropriate to human law its own constitution, which is prescribed antecedently to the Church's action, since it belongs to the sphere of divine law and hence is inviolable.[10]

There can, of course, be no simple and undifferentiated importation of structural theory or concepts from the secular world, and we need to avoid viewing the church simply through a socio-political rather than a properly theological lens.[11] Yet the church cannot remain completely detached from contemporary secular organizational forms and ideas when they are not in conflict with its unique nature and divine constitution. Indeed, this must be the case if the church's structures are to serve as effective signs and instruments in the world. Archbishop Martin of Dublin has insightfully observed that a church with participatory structures will be more effective than an authoritarian one.[12] So, while accountability remains primarily a word from the secular world rather than a theological term per se, and though a complete theological notion of it has yet to be developed—one which would take sinfulness and forgiveness into account—this does not discount its use in an ecclesial context.

In theory, both theologically and canonically, there is indeed a form of episcopal accountability. Theologically, as a matter of Roman Catholic doctrine, the authority of bishops finds its source in the Holy Spirit and as the successors of the apostles. Bishops exercise a divinely given authority. Yet this authority is not in any way diminished by holding that bishops are to be accountable—to the Pope, to other bishops, and to the faithful. The episcopacy is an honour only in so far as it is a form of service. Indeed authority exists in the church for the purpose of service and pastors are servants (*LG*, § 27). The bishop is a servant-leader, and accountability is certainly congruent with that concept of authority—which concept is not, of course, immune from its own danger of disguising the reality of power. Again, having to render an account of one's ecclesial stewardship and setting standards for ministry are in line with New Testament teaching.[13]

Fundamentally, the notion of accountability in the church is pastoral in nature and intent: the ecclesial office-holder is answerable for the pastoral work for which the office is responsible.

So in principle church leaders are accountable for their actions. First and foremost, as vicars of Christ in their dioceses, bishops are answerable to God for their ministry. This type of accountability ultimately lies in the forum of conscience, which is beyond canonical regulation. In a certain wide sense, bishops are also accountable to all the People of God. Whilst these dimensions of accountability are not the focus of this chapter, they are nonetheless of fundamental significance and should not be minimized. In practice, however, the means for ensuring episcopal accountability are structured canonically and exist in two senses, vertical and horizontal.

VERTICAL ACCOUNTABILITY

Vertically, each diocesan bishop answers directly to the Pope. This relationship is rooted in the Petrine office and the Roman primacy as taught by the First Vatican Council and confirmed by the Second; the Pope has the power of jurisdiction over all the pastors of the Roman Catholic Church. *De facto*, the exercise of this primacy is structured through the various dicasteries of the Roman Curia.

There are two canonical modes of this vertical accountability: exceptional and regular. The exceptional, or extra-ordinary, mechanism is that of an apostolic visitation of a diocese; these special investigations are quite naturally rare and tend to arise when some matter has come to the attention of the Roman Curia, and sometimes involves public controversy.[14] Also, canonical procedures exist for the correction and punishment of a diocesan bishop, but again this is meant to address rare crisis situations of wrongdoing rather than to be a regular review of diocesan operations.[15] On the other hand, the only regular ongoing mechanisms of vertical accountability are the bishop's personal *Ad limina apostolorum* visit to Rome and his quinquennial written reports (canon 399). Despite the impression you might get from some commentary, the Roman Curia is relatively small in organizational terms and staff numbers, considering the size of the church worldwide. There are approximately 2,700 diocesan bishops, each of whom is directly accountable to the Pope. So, unless there is some urgent matter demanding Rome's attention or to which the Curia has decided to give special attention, most bishops are left to get on with their work basically unsupervised in any real sense. That is fine as long as things are going well.

Among various ideas put forward to remedy the current weakness regarding structures for episcopal responsibility, some have argued for some type of regular diocesan visitation process, similar to that required for parishes. One suggested American version, drawing upon the re-accreditation processes used in higher education, would involve a comprehensive diocesan self-study, followed by a report to the diocesan bishop by a team made up of laypeople and a number of experienced pastors or other bishops.[16] This would be carried out in conjunction with the *Ad limina* visit every five years. Such a process would be entered into voluntarily, bringing an outside fresh perspective, and also indicating that the bishop believes in accountability. This is an interesting idea, though the implementation would need to go beyond the obvious and stated need for people with managerial training and experience, and integrate other experience and gifts, while especially not forgetting the necessity of theological formation for all those involved. One also wonders how this kind of process would ensure ongoing day-to-day accountability.

Returning to the current situation, there is another line of vertical account-ability, that of the metropolitan: an archbishop at the head of an ecclesiastical province (a geographic grouping of dioceses) charged with exercising a very limited degree of authority over the bishops within his province. Historically, the authority of the metropolitan was quite important, but has waned in recent centuries, so that he now has a very circumscribed oversight with respect to the other bishops. In current Roman Catholic canon law it is of such limited scope as to make its capacity for ensuring episcopal accountability negligible. Specifically, the Roman Catholic metropolitan's powers are considerably less than those of the Church of England archbishop. There the right to effect episcopal discipline lies, unlike in the Roman Catholic Church, with the archbishops. In the Church of England the archbishop has in his province authority 'to correct and supply the defects of other bishops', and he can hold metropolitan visita-tions during which time he possesses jurisdiction as Ordinary, except in places and over persons exempt by law or custom.[17] The institution of archiepiscopal visitation can be found in other churches of the Anglican Communion, and it is a general principle of Anglican canon law worldwide that metropolitans are in a legal position of superiority over the bishops of a province.[18] In the Church of England, the metropolitan is superintendent of all ecclesiastical matters. Every person to be made diocesan bishop must take an oath of 'due obedience' to the archbishop and his successors. As Norman Doe notes, this is 'the general basis' of the archbishop's 'disciplinary powers' over other bishops.[19] In the Roman Catholic Church the arrangement is at present very different indeed (see canon 436). The metropolitan does not correct defects in diocesan episcopal ministry, but is to report these to the Pope. Moreover, the archbishop may only visit a diocese in his province if the diocesan bishop fails to do so, and to do this must obtain the prior approval of the Holy See. Beyond the function of vigilance, the metropolitan archbishop has no power of jurisdiction within the suffragan dioceses.

In short, this ancient office has become largely honorary in the Roman Catholic Church. One cannot speak of it as a method of vertical accountability in any real legal sense, though a certain moral authority may be present. During the 1983 Code's redaction, efforts to upgrade the status of the metropolitan were unsuccessful, probably out of concern not unduly to restrict the diocesan bishop.[20] However, Pope John Paul II urged in his November 2003 post-synodal Apostolic Exhortation, *Pastores Gregis*, that the bishops restore vitality to this ancient institution.[21] Learning from Anglican structures, which in this case are probably more faithful to ancient traditions, the office of metropolitan could be reinvigorated, and its oversight functions expanded. So far there seems little sign of follow-up in canonical discussion or, more importantly, any move towards a practical implementation by the supreme church authority of such a restoration. In terms of practical signs of a possible reinvigoration of the office, the only one worth noting is that the United States Conference of Catholic Bishops has recommended each diocesan bishop confirm to his metropolitan every year that the diocesan finance council exists, meets regularly, and is carrying out oversight of diocesan finances.[22] This is a welcome if fairly minimalist measure.

HORIZONTAL ACCOUNTABILITY

To turn now to horizontal accountability: practically, this involves relationships at two levels—with fellow bishops and with diocesan bodies. First, in terms of accountability and episcopal relationships, there is the hallowed notion of fraternal correction, finding its origins in Paul's remonstrance to Peter in the New Testament (Gal. 2: 11). Although fraternal correction is a logical consequence of episcopal collegiality, one bishop taking another to task is, perhaps unsurprisingly, the exception rather than the rule. In any event, such correction is likely to be a very occasional event, and could not be a regular way of ensuring accountability, as it is not something easily amenable to canonical ordering.

Historically, provincial or plenary councils were the traditional organization for accountability between bishops, and served as instruments of reform in the church. In the early centuries of the church, provincial councils pronounced judgement on bishops for wrongdoing and more generally held them responsible for their ministry. However, such councils have fallen into disuse, and though there is still much about them in the revised canon law, practically speaking there is little sign of their widespread revival anytime soon. Another possible modern instrument of accountability is the episcopal conference. During the latter stages of the revision of the 1983 Code, the proposed decision-making powers of the conference were reduced, apparently out of concern for preserving the discretion of the diocesan bishop.[23] Consequently, the canonical authority of the episcopal conference is so limited as to deprive it of any legal role in ensuring accountability. So the role of the college of bishops, as expressed from time to time in the traditional structure of particular councils, is no longer effective, and in the newer instrument of episcopal conferences it lacks the necessary canonical authority to promote accountability. By way of contrast, in the Anglican communion, 'central episcopal assemblies have a determinative, decision-making power over a very wide range of subjects'.[24]

There seems to be no compelling theological reason why intermediary level authority structures like provincial councils or episcopal conferences (or indeed the metropolitan as mentioned above) could not be given a certain supervisory competency over diocesan bishops. Given the history of Gallicanism and Febronianism and understandable Roman wariness of 'national churches', it would probably be better to speak of 'regional' or 'provincial' or 'intermediary' ecclesial structures. In one sense, this would be a form of 'peer review'. Such review might be more effective in promoting authentic episcopal accountability than the current system whereby Rome is responsible for the oversight of so many bishops. Given the Roman Catholic understanding of Roman primacy, any such review mechanism would have to contain provision for appeal or recourse to the Pope.

We turn now to horizontal episcopal accountability as it relates to diocesan councils. In the structure of the Roman Catholic Church there is a requirement for bishops to seek the advice, and sometimes even the approval, of consultative bodies. Every diocese, in so far as pastoral circumstances suggest, is to have a pastoral council which investigates, considers, and proposes practical conclusions about those things which pertain to pastoral work in the diocese (canon 511), the members of which are designated in a manner determined by the diocesan bishop (canon 512, § 1). The role of this council is consultative only and it is required to meet only once a year. In addition, every diocese should have a presbyteral council (consisting of some priests elected by their fellow priests and others selected by the bishop) whereby priests can make their concerns known to the bishop and assist the bishop in promoting the pastoral welfare of the people of the diocese (canons 495, 497). The utility of these bodies will depend upon whether the bishop actually uses them, whether the members of the councils speak openly, and whether the bishop pays any attention to their advice. *De facto*, a bishop can treat these bodies as window-dressing and does not have to be accountable to them in any real sense.

Every diocese also is to have both a finance council, with members appointed by the bishop (canon 492), and a college of consultors (canon 502), a group of six to twelve priests chosen by the bishop from among the members of the priests' council. Canon law requires that the finance council and the college of consultors alike be consulted on the more important acts of ordinary administration, and that they approve all acts of 'extraordinary administration' as defined by the episcopal conference (canon 1277), any proposed alienation of property beyond an amount stipulated by the episcopal conference, and any other transaction which could worsen the financial condition of the diocese (canons 1292, § 1, 1295). Certainly when it comes to making larger financial transactions, canon law tries to impose some accountability on the bishop. While a diocesan bishop could choose from the priests' council as consultors only those priests whom he knows will tell him what he wants to hear, and likewise appoint acquiescent people to the finance council, that would be contrary to the spirit of the law. Canon 127, which establishes the legal elements for 'consent' and 'advice' when they are required by the law, speaks of the sincere opinion of those whose advice or consent are required. It is not meant to be a rubber-stamp process. One difficulty is that if a bishop ignores these canonical requirements, it may never come to light or it may take time to make hierarchical recourse to Rome, and meanwhile his actions often are valid in the civil law, making it impossible to rescind them.[25] None the less, and perhaps not too surprisingly, it seems to be in the area of finance that current canon law makes most effort to impose some form of horizontal accountability on the diocesan bishop.

Comparing Roman Catholic diocesan councils to those found within the Church of England, in a sense they have much in common—for instance, the Roman Catholic diocesan pastoral council not being dissimilar to the Anglican diocesan pastoral committee.[26] However, there is a fundamental difference overall: 'whilst formally in the Church of England diocesan bodies are broadly responsible to and under the direct control of the clerical and lay diocesan synod, in the Roman Catholic Church control is reserved to the bishop.'[27] All churches in the Anglican Communion share the practice of having a diocesan synod or assembly, the work of which is carried out by a representative standing committee and other bodies answerable to the assembly itself.[28] In the Church of England, the diocesan synod is the primary administrative body of the diocese, consisting of houses of bishops, clergy, and laity, and it is assisted in its work by various executive bodies. The synod has deliberative, advisory, and consultative functions. In the Roman Catholic situation, the diocesan synod typically has no ongoing administrative or executive functions, but rather functions, at least in theory, as the pre-eminent consultative body, composed of a group of priests and other Christian faithful summoned to offer assistance to the diocesan bishop (canon 460).[29] However, in practice many diocesan synods do not meet frequently and only at the discretion of the diocesan bishop (canons 461, § 1; 462, § 1), and in some places never at all; moreover, if a synod is convened, the bishop is the sole legislator in the assembly (canon 466).

While ecumenical reception cannot be a simple act of copying, this surely is an area where Roman Catholicism could learn something from the Anglican synodical practice. A revival and expansion of the diocesan synod, making it a regular feature of ecclesial life, to which the existing diocesan councils related and reported, could assist in ensuring episcopal accountability.

CONCLUSION

Curiously enough, a good deal of Roman Catholic discussion about renewing structures to ensure accountability revolves primarily around learning from the secular world, rather than from other Christian denominations. However, given that ecclesial communions have more in common than divides them, and given also that they struggle with the same problems, it would seem both appropriate and highly desirable that we turn to one another in our search for suitable models for structural renewal. As this preliminary reflection has indicated, Roman Catholics can learn much about oversight of leadership from other Christian traditions who also seek to ensure accountability.

In an ecumenical dialogue which speaks of 'an exchange of gifts', it is necessary to note that receiving gifts is not a pain-free exercise, because of the need for an acknowledgement of current Roman Catholic inadequacies, and of the consequent need for ecclesiastical adaptation. There is also a sometimes unspoken Roman Catholic reluctance to learn from other Christian traditions such as Anglicanism because of the awareness of difficulties in that other tradition's own structures, and a tendency to focus on these difficulties rather than on those structural aspects from which something could be fruitfully learned. In addition, we need to be aware that current Roman Catholic canonical structures have not been planned with a view to ecumenical reception.

Finally, promoting episcopal accountability through receptive ecumenical learning is not meant to make the task of the diocesan bishop within Roman Catholicism more difficult. Ultimately, mechanisms which ensure accountability are also a protection and indeed help for the bishop in his ministry of governance. Canon law and its application must correspond with the church's ecclesiological self-understanding. By way of conclusion, it is worth recalling that in September 2004, Pope John Paul II asserted that a 'commitment to creating better structures of participation, consultation and shared responsibility should not be misunderstood as a concession to a secular "democratic" model of governance, but as an intrinsic requirement of the exercise of episcopal authority and a necessary means of strengthening that authority.'[30]

NOTES

1. See, e.g., Chapter 10: David Chapman, 'A Methodist Perspective on Catholic Learning'; Chapter 16: Paul Lakeland, 'Potential Catholic Learning Around Lay Participation in Decision-making'; and Chapter 8: Keith F. Pecklers, 'What Roman Catholics Have to Learn from Anglicans'.
2. I will be dealing here only with the Latin church, not with the Eastern Catholic churches governed by the 1990 *Codex Canonum Ecclesiarum Orientalium*. The Latin

church may well have much to learn from these *sui iuris* Catholic churches, but that is a subject for another day.

3. See *The Gift of Authority: Authority in the Church III* (London: Church House Publishing/CTS, 1999).

4. See *LG*, § 26; *CD*, § 11; also Chapter 12: Paul McPartlan, 'Catholic Learning and Orthodoxy—The Promise and Challenge of Eucharistic Ecclesiology'.

5. See Roman Catholic Church, *Codex iuris canonici auctoritate Ioannis Pauli PP. II promulgatus* (Vatican City: Libreria Editrice Vaticana, 1983), canon 375, § 2. English translation of the canons found in *Code of Canon Law Annotated, Prepared Under the Responsibility of the Instituto Martín de Azpilcueta*, 2nd English edn. (rev. and updated) of the 6th Spanish edn., ed. E. Caparros and H. Aubé, with J. I. Arrieta, et al. (Montreal: Wilson & Lafleur, 2004).

6. This is the process of appealing against an administrative act and its consequences, to the superior of the responsible person or to an administrative tribunal. Because of the lack of any administrative tribunals at episcopal conference or infra-universal levels, the only recourse available against episcopal administrative acts is to the Roman Curia (see canons 1732–1739).

7. See National Review Board for the Protection of Children and Young People, *A Report on the Crisis in the Catholic Church in the United States* (Washington, DC: USCCB, 2004), 125, available at <http://www.nccbuscc.org/nrb/nrbstudy/nrbreport.pdf>.

8. See O'Malley, 'The Scandal: A Historian's Perspective', *America*, 186 (27 May 2002), 15.

9. See James H. Provost, 'Towards Some Operative Principles for Apostolic Visitations', *The Jurist*, 49 (1989), 543–67.

10. Kasper, 'Priestly Office', in *Leadership in the Church: How Traditional Roles Can Serve the Christian Community Today* trans. Brian McNeil (New York: Crossroad, 2003) 63.

11. See Donald W. Wuerl, 'Reflections on Governance and Accountability in the Church', in Francis Oakley and Bruce Russett (eds.), *Governance, Accountability, and the Future of the Catholic Church* (London and New York: Continuum, 2004), 13–24.

12. See Diarmuid Martin, 'Will Ireland be Christian in 2030?', Twenty-fifth Patrick MacGill Summer School (18 July 2005), Glenties, Co. Donegal, available at <http://www.dublindiocese.ie/index.php?option=com_content&task=view&id=89&Itemid=21>.

13. e.g. Matt. 24: 45–51; Luke 12: 42–6; 2 Tim. 4: 1–5.

14. See John P. Beal, 'The Apostolic Visitation of a Diocese: A Canonico-Historical Investigation', *The Jurist*, 49 (1989), 347–98.

15. See John Huels, 'The Correction and Punishment of a Diocesan Bishop', ibid. 507–42.

16. See Thomas J. Healey, 'A Blueprint for Change', *America*, 193 (26 Sept. 2005), 15–16.

17. See Norman Doe, *The Legal Framework of the Church of England* (Oxford: Clarendon Press, 1996), 122; also Mark Hill, 'Authority in the Church of England', in James Conn, Norman Doe, and Joseph Fox (eds.), *Initiation, Membership and Authority in Anglican and Roman Catholic Canon Law* (Rome and Cardiff: Pontifical Gregorian

University and Pontifical University of St Thomas Aquinas/University of Wales, Cardiff, 2005).

18. See Doe, *Canon Law in the Anglican Communion: A Worldwide Perspective* (Oxford: Oxford University Press, 1998), 75–6, 107, 126–7; also id., 'Canonical Dimensions of ARCIC on Authority: An Anglican Perspective', *Initiation, Membership and Authority*, 222–3.

19. See Doe, *The Legal Framework of the Church of England*, 122.

20. See Thomas J. Green, 'Subsidiarity During the Code Revision Process', *The Jurist*, 48 (1988), 780, n. 32.

21. See Pope John Paul II, '*Pastores Gregis*: Apostolic Exhortation on the Bishop, Servant of the Gospel of Jesus Christ for the Hope of the World' (16 Oct. 2003) (Vatican City: Libreria Editrice Vaticana, 2003), § 62.

22. See Wuerl, 'Reflections on Governance and Accountability in the Church', 21.

23. See Green, 'The Normative Role of Episcopal Conferences in the 1983 Code', in Thomas J. Reese (ed.), *Episcopal Conferences: Historical, Canonical and Theological Studies* (Washington, DC: Georgetown University Press, 1989), 150–3; also Pope John Paul II, '*Apostolos Suos*: Apostolic Constitution Issued *Motu Proprio* on Episcopal Conferences' (21 May 1998), available at <http://www.vatican.ca/holy_father/John_paul-ii/motu_proprio/documents/nf_Jp-ii_motu_proprio_22071998_apostolos-suos_en.html>.

24. Doe, *Canon Law in the Anglican Communion*, 125.

25. See Sharon Euart, 'Clergy Sexual Abuse Crisis: Reflections on Restoring the Credibility of Church Leadership', *The Jurist*, 63 (2003), 136.

26. For a discussion of diocesan administrative bodies (e.g. the pastoral committee, the board of finance, etc.) in the Church of England, see Doe, *The Legal Framework of the Church of England*, 97–100.

27. Ibid. 100.

28. See id., *Canon Law in the Anglican Communion*, 61–5, 70.

29. See Congregation for Bishops and Congregation for the Evangelisation of Peoples, 'Instruction on Diocesan Synods' (8 July 1997), available at <http://www.vatican.va/roman_curia/congregations/cbishops/documents/rc_con_cbishops_doc_20041118_diocesan-synods-1997_en.html>.

30. John Paul II, 'Address to the Bishops of the Ecclesiastical Region of Pennsylvania and New Jersey (USA) on their "Ad Limina" Visit' (11 Sept. 2004), § 3, available at <http://www.vatican.va/holy_father/john_paul_ii/speeches/2004/september/documents/hf_jp-ii_spe_20040911_ad-limina-usa_en.html>.

PART IV

THE PRAGMATICS OF RECEPTIVE
ECUMENICAL LEARNING

Prologue to Part IV
John 11: 43–53

Philip Endean, SJ

Jesus cried with a loud voice, 'Lazarus, come out!' The dead man came out, his hands and feet bound with strips of cloth, and his face wrapped in a cloth. Jesus said to them, 'Unbind him, and let him go.' Many of the Jews therefore, who had come with Mary and had seen what Jesus did, believed in him. But some of them went to the Pharisees and told them what he had done. So the chief priests and the Pharisees called a meeting of the council, and said, 'What are we to do? This man is performing many signs. If we let him go on like this, everyone will believe in him, and the Romans will come and destroy both our holy place and our nation.' But one of them, Caiaphas, who was high priest that year, said to them, 'You know nothing at all! You do not understand that it is better for you to have one man die for the people than to have the whole nation destroyed.' He did not say this on his own, but being high priest that year he prophesied that Jesus was about to die for the nation, and not for the nation only, but to gather into one the dispersed children of God. So from that day on they planned to put him to death.

John's Jesus performs the last and greatest miracle of his public life: he raises Lazarus from the dead, and many come to believe in him. The forces of darkness—which for John are symbolized as 'the Jews'—panic, but Caiaphas indicates a way forward: 'it is better for one man to die for the people than to have the whole nation destroyed.'

The following chapters are exercises in diagnosis of the various factors that support or hinder the proposed practices of Receptive Ecumenism and Catholic Learning. Some evoke—with the courtesy, of course, that marks good dialogue—the disappointments that ecumenists have had to sustain over the last decades. The ecumenical project involves conflict, and the temptations to regression are frequent. The call to a richer form of discipleship brings darkness to the surface. The touch of God, the coming of Christ, evokes resistance. Indeed, John's Jesus suggests that his coming is itself a judgement, in that people's reactions to that event make it quite clear who is of the light and who is of the darkness. Disappointment is an inevitable part of the process.

Yet, of course, for John, the plottings of Caiaphas and his cronies fail utterly to impinge on the divine, glorifying sovereignty. Even here, Caiaphas is prophesying despite himself about how Jesus will die for the nation in another, far richer sense—and not for the nation only, but to gather into one the dispersed children of God. The judicial murder that ensues is, for those with eyes to see, an enthronement. When Jesus gives up the ghost, it is the Spirit which is handed over. The light shines in the darkness—a light which the darkness cannot master.

We need to hear the message here about assurance in times of discouragement. The prospects, if we are honest, are disappointing. There can be a sense of second best about putting organic reunion on hold and settling instead for Receptive Ecumenism. In such a situation, we can easily become discouraged, and find ourselves in what Ignatius Loyola called desolation: the very opposite of faith, hope, and love. We need to fortify ourselves in advance against such discouragement. We need to remember the words of Cardinal Kasper earlier in this volume to the effect that whatever our experience now may be, we can confidently leave to Another the when and the how and the where of the reconciled church confessed in the Creed. We can be convinced that God will bring to fruition what God has initiated.

But true and unexceptionable though that sentiment is, it needs to be appropriated carefully. When the devout invoke divine providence, there is a danger that we are simply legitimating laziness. By contrast, a Catholic trust in providence needs to be interpreted according to the authentic teaching of the Council of Trent, and not according to some quietist travesty of what the Reformers were saying about grace. Trent and the Reformers are one in the conviction that God's action of sheer grace occurs only in and through our empowered co-working. When it comes to ecumenism, there is much reason to be impatient with exhortations to patience. Patience alone is not enough; we need also generosity, open-mindedness, and—above all—imagination.

Here our model can be the evangelist John himself. His imagination is uncomfortably dualist, and his thought patterns, read in retrospect, can appear shameful and disastrous in what they imply about the Jews. But, nevertheless, his creative genius enabled his own community to interpret the stories of Jesus in ways that opened up new possibilities not only for themselves but for all the scattered people of God in whom their text has lived on as Scripture. Perhaps the method of dialogue and reinterpretation, so well pursued by the various dialogue commissions, has taken us as far as it can. What we need now, in a situation of impasse, may be something more like a poetic reframing of the terms in which we conceive the problems. One example of such thinking has been offered to us here by Ladislas Örsy, with his suggestion that we should stop thinking about divided churches, and begin instead to think about the one church that is already united, albeit with wounds needing to be healed. An imaginative shift of this kind, the introduction of new metaphors and images, has the potential to set our discussions on completely new footings, and to open up possibilities so far unenvisaged.

If we let the imagination run free, perhaps dead ends might suddenly become new awakenings. And situations that tempt us to put our heads down, give up the ghost, and settle for Receptive Ecumenism, may suddenly be revealed as epiphanies, in which the divine design is finally accomplished, and the Spirit in person given to us: that Spirit promised by Jesus, that Spirit who will lead us into the fullness of truth.

18

From Vatican II to Mississauga—Lessons in Receptive Ecumenical Learning from the Anglican–Roman Catholic Bilateral Dialogue Process

Mary Tanner

INTRODUCTION

The rationale behind this volume has been clearly set out. While commitment to hope and work for 'structural unification' continue to represent core Catholic instincts—as, indeed, for Anglicans also[1]—it nevertheless 'seems clear that the aspiration for programmed re-unification in the short term is unrealistic'. The answer in this situation is not, it is suggested, to move towards a lesser goal of 'reconciled diversity without structural unity', but rather to envision how 'Christian traditions might most effectively and genuinely learn or receive, from one another with integrity', now. This notion of Receptive Ecumenism encourages reflection which is both realistic in the face of current difficulties and, at the same time, imaginative and bold. How are we to live in the interim not giving up on the vision; not tempted to settle for less? How might we learn and receive from one another in this middle time with its challenges and problems?

In this regard it is instructive to examine the story of Anglican–Roman Catholic relations since the heady days following the Second Vatican Council to see what has proved effective and what counterproductive in receptive ecumenical learning. It is perhaps worth noting at the outset that what is here being referred to as Receptive Ecumenism is a new feature of the life of Christian churches that has emerged over these years. There are no generally accepted principles and no formulated rules. The years since the Second Vatican Council have been a voyage of discovery for all churches in the ecumenical movement. The January 2006 Durham Colloquium provided a useful opportunity to reflect on what has happened and to envisage what might stimulate Receptive Ecumenism in the future.

THE IMPORTANCE OF THE PERSONAL AND RELATIONAL

When Pope Paul VI and Archbishop Michael Ramsey issued their *Common Declaration* at the end of the momentous visit of the Archbishop to Rome in 1966, they talked of 'a new atmosphere of Christian fellowship between the Roman Catholic Church and the churches of the Anglican Communion ... a new stage in the development of fraternal relations, based on Christian charity, and of sincere efforts to remove the causes of conflict and to re-establish unity'.[2] The gesture of the Bishop of Rome, placing his own ring on the Archbishop's finger, spoke volumes for the respect and fraternal love about which they had written. On parting, Pope Paul VI remarked that he looked forward to the time when 'affective communion' would become 'effective communion'. It is worth recalling this for it is a reminder that friendship is the seedbed in which Receptive Ecumenism flourishes. The personal and relational are always prior to the structural and institutional. Journeying out of our isolations, meeting, learning to know and trust one another, establishing friendships form the climate in which separated communities become open to receiving gifts from each other. It is the climate out of which a passion for unity is born and sustained. Nevertheless, however important symbolic gestures are between those whose ministry focuses the unity of the church, that same relationship of trust and mutual affection has to be built up between all of the members of the two Communions if Receptive Ecumenism is to flourish and lead to visible unity.

THE MALTA VISION OF STEPS AND STAGES

In 1968, two years after the historic meeting, a Preliminary Anglican–Roman Catholic Commission set out a realistic and imaginative programme for the progression of Anglican–Roman Catholic relations, a plan for what was called 'phased *rapprochement*'.[3] Anglicans and Roman Catholics would move together by taking bold steps and entering new stages of officially sanctioned relationship on the basis of the degree of explicit agreement in faith reached in theological conversation. A first stage had already been reached by the Pope and the Archbishop in their *Common Declaration* recognizing all that Anglicans and Roman Catholics already shared in common. A second stage of closer relationship lay in the future. This second stage would begin with a statement of mutual recognition and acknowledgement based upon the degree of agreement in faith discovered to exist through theological conversation. The theological agreements would support binding commitments to intensify relationships and to act together wherever possible in life and mission. What was envisaged was a period in a new stage of closer fellowship in which the two communions would reform their own lives in light of the theological agreements, receive the insights and gifts of the other, including, in time, the gifts of ordained ministry, and live as closely together in mission and ministry as the advance in doctrinal convergence made possible. This second, officially recognized stage, would lead to a third and final stage in the quest for what the Preparatory Commission called 'full organic unity of our two Communions'.

Looking back at the 'Malta Report', what stands out is its firm commitment to 'organic unity' as the stated goal of Anglican–Roman Catholic relations and its intention to move towards that goal by taking clear steps into officially sanctioned, fresh stages of relatedness, thereby creating a new context in which each might confidently receive gifts from the other. The 'Malta Report' was clear that theological agreed statements and advances in lived relationship had to be kept together. Indispensable as the doctrinal statements are, they are not themselves capable of delivering a structurally united church. However, no thought seems to have been given to the relevant procedures for responding to theological documents. Nor was there any view on who would sanction any developments in relationship and by what means. This posed a particular challenge because each Communion had very different structures of consultation and decision-making as well as different polities concerning the relation of the regional to the international aspects of the church. The provincial structure of the Anglican Communion enables a certain degree of progress to take place in the regions on the way towards the unity of the worldwide Communions. The more centralized Roman Catholic structure makes regional development more difficult.

RECEPTIVE ECUMENISM IMPLEMENTED IN ANGLICAN-LUTHERAN/REFORMED/MORAVIAN AND METHODIST RELATIONS

The idea of the 'Malta Report', concerning entering into new and officially recognized stages of relatedness on the way to full visible unity, was one that proved hospitable to Anglicans. The same pattern was some years later implemented in a series of new regional relationships with Moravian, Lutheran, and Reformed Churches in Europe and North America and, most recently, in England in the Covenant with the Methodists.[4] These agreements are in each case regional and not between world Communions. Nevertheless, it was the 1988 Lambeth Conference that, after assessing the results of existing international bilateral conversations with Lutheran and Reformed partners, encouraged the way of regional development where relations allowed. There was thus an international affirmation that this was an appropriate way for Anglican provinces to proceed. There was also care for consistency and coherence between the different relationships entered into in the different regions. The fact that each was based upon the doctrinal agreements which the bishops at the 1988 Lambeth Conference affirmed after widespread discussion in the regions themselves went a long way to safeguarding the coherence of the different regional agreements.

Each regional agreement sets out the goal of visible unity to which the partners are committed and harvests the agreements in faith reached in the international statements. They also take account of the fact that the regional churches had already been on a voyage of mutual discovery and had already expressed a genuine desire to move together. On the basis of all of this, commitments were then made to live a closer life in mission and ministry, each appropriate to the degree of theological agreement reached. In the case of the Meissen Agreement (with the Evangelical Church in Germany), the stage reached is a step on the way to visible unity, with no interchangeability of ministries because of the remaining outstanding disagreement on the historic episcopate. On the other hand, the Porvoo Agreement (with Nordic and Baltic Lutheran Churches) goes further, establishing, with its expressed agreement on apostolicity and succession, an interchangeable ministry. The fact that all the agreements are committed to the same goal of visible unity, and that they each harvest the same agreed statements, ensures coherence and consistency. The participating churches in each agreement have established a committee or commission to monitor the development of the new relationship, the implementation of the commitments made, and to oversee the continuation of the theological dialogue on remaining areas of difference.

Concerned for the coherence and consistency of these regional developments, the 1998 Lambeth Conference established an International Anglican Standing Committee on Ecumenical Relations charged with the task of overseeing in advance any future regional proposals. What had become clear by 1988 was that this new development in ecumenical *rapprochement* required new procedures to monitor coherence and consistency, both for the sake of the unity of the Anglican Communion and for the development of coherent ecumenical partnerships. In the interest of Receptive Ecumenism Anglicans have accepted that the ecumenical landscape will not be tidy and, as the 1988 Conference said: 'the process of moving towards full, visible unity may entail temporary anomalies...some anomalies may be bearable when there is an agreed goal of visible unity, but...there should always be an impetus towards their resolution and, thus towards the removal of the principal anomaly of disunity.'[5] It is worth noting that although the Roman Catholic Church finds it difficult to move at a regional level, a not dissimilar model has recently emerged in the Covenant between Anglicans and Roman Catholics in Papua New Guinea.

The intention of the 'Malta Report'—that convergence in faith, expressed in doctrinal statements, should be kept together with convergence in life—became a major concern of the Faith and Order Commission of the World Council of Churches (WCC). Many had come to understand ecumenical reception as merely the affirmation, articulated at the highest level of authority in a Communion, that the faith of the church through the ages could be recognized in the various agreed statements emanating from bilateral and multilateral dialogues. Beyond that, however, it came to be understood as the reception of such recognized common faith in the fabric of reformed lives and practices, and changed relationships with other communions. Ecumenical reception came, consequently, to be understood as a receptive converting process: conversion of churches to the truth of the Gospel in the depths of their own ecclesial life, and conversion to others in new and committed relationships, oriented to the establishment of visible unity. Reception came to be understood as a costly transformative process: both the exchange of gifts and reformation of life which was seen to be inconsistent with the understanding of the faith of the church through the ages.

THE ANGLICAN–ROMAN CATHOLIC INTERNATIONAL COMMISSION—A SUCCESS IN ECUMENICAL DIALOGUE, BUT A FAILURE IN RECEPTIVE ECUMENISM

After Malta, as from 1970, the Anglican–Roman Catholic International Commission (ARCIC) made extraordinary progress in its work on Eucharist, ministry, and authority. From the outset, the Commission worked in conversation with the two communions, encouraging reflection on early drafts and soliciting a response from national Anglican–Roman Catholic Committees which included a lay voice, Roman Catholic bishops' conferences, and Anglican diocesan and national synods. In some areas of the world there was considerable enthusiasm for studying the agreed statements—in clergy groups, seminaries, and local parishes, often in joint Roman Catholic and Anglican groups. The Commission continued its conversation with the wider constituency by, in turn, responding to the responses it received in a series of Elucidations.[6] The result of this dialogical process between the Commission and the two communions was twofold. First, Anglicans and Roman Catholics locally, not just theologians, increased their understanding of one another, breaking down false stereotypes, discovering how much faith they in fact had in common. In some places the discovery led to a greater sharing at the local level in common prayer and witness. But, at the same time, an expectation grew amongst the laity that a change in relationship could not be far off. Many saw this in terms of an opening up of some form of eucharistic sharing, perhaps on significant ecumenical occasions, and a move towards the recognition, if not yet reconciliation, of ministries. What happened in this energetic time of getting to know one another, through conversation around the work of ARCIC, was the preparation of a climate for Receptive

Ecumenism. However, in spite of these promising signs, things began to go wrong.

In 1982, ARCIC's *Final Report* was submitted to the two communions with two questions: first, they were asked whether the agreed statements were 'consonant in substance' with the respective faith of Anglicans and Romans Catholics, and, secondly, what 'concrete steps' ought to be taken on the basis of these agreements. By harnessing these questions together those who framed them were faithful to the vision of the 'Malta Report' in keeping theological advance together with the practical and relational, indicating the hope that theological agreement would lead to changed relationships, to a genuine Receptive Ecumenism.

However, the formulation of the first question—inviting each communion to ask whether the statements were consonant with their own faith rather than with 'the faith of the church through the ages'—seemed to encourage them to compare the agreed statements with their own internal position, thus reinforcing and entrenching, rather than challenging, denominational identity. To look for precise conformity with one's own confessional statements can be a way of sidestepping the challenges to costly renewal in the light of the faith of the church through the ages. Moreover, the fact that there was no question inviting the two communions to consider what reform and renewal was required in their own lives in response to faith of the church reflected in the agreed statements, meant that an opportunity was lost to challenge them to appropriate internal renewal in the light of the mirror of the ARCIC agreed statements. The response process became more an academic exercise than a move in Receptive Ecumenism.

If there was a problem in the way the questions were formulated there was also a failure on the part of both communions to understand the point of the questions being harnessed together. Attention was given by both communions to answering the first, doctrinal, question, but almost no attention was given to the second about reception in life, renewal in the light of the Gospel. Thus an opportunity for the intensification of Receptive Ecumenism was missed. At the end of the 1980s the *Malta* vision of Receptive Ecumenism in Anglican–Roman Catholic relations was lost.

There was another difficulty that became apparent. The two Communions had very different procedures for responding to ecumenical documents and little understanding of each other's processes, and often not much understanding of their own processes either. The process had revealed weakness in the structures of communion in both churches.

The Anglican Communion sought the responses of provinces, most of which were formulated on the basis of widespread study and synodical action involving lay people. These responses were published and collated as a resource to be used by the bishops at the 1988 Lambeth Conference in helping them discern and articulate the mind of the Communion. The fact that the Roman Catholic response was not finished in time to be reported to the Conference and that only two or three responses of national bishops' conferences were placed in the public domain led to Anglican disappointment, and a growing suspicion that there was a struggle going on within the Roman Catholic Church to reach a common mind. When the final response did arrive it echoed some of the difficulties already noted in the initial *Observations* of the Congregation for the Doctrine of the Faith and required ARCIC to show more consonance with the teachings of the Roman Catholic Church. This seemed to suggest a lack of understanding of the method of ecumenical dialogue which seeks to go back to Scripture and the early Tradition and to re-state afresh the faith of the church for today. In such restatement, neither party can expect to find its own internal language. It also became clear how difficult it was to respond in the same way, or within the same timescale, when the two communions had such different processes for taking decisions. This led to suspicion among the laity and a loss of interest in the process, not only of doctrinal discussion but of Receptive Ecumenism itself. Both communions suffer today from a loss of the enthusiasm of the first generation of ecumenically committed enthusiasts who felt genuinely let down.

There was another factor that militated against Receptive Ecumenism. By now some provinces of the Anglican Communion had moved to ordain women to the priesthood and by the late 1980s the matter of women and the episcopate was already being debated in America, while the Church of England, having ordained women as deacons, was intensifying its debate on the ordination of women to the priesthood. For the Roman Catholic Church this unilateral action on a matter that touches the unity of the church appeared to call into question the Anglican Communion's ecumenical commitment to visible unity, to the progress thus far made in the ARCIC conversation, and the existing 'degree' of communion. The unilateral action made any concrete step towards the recognition of ministries impossible, dashing with it hopes of any form of mutual eucharistic hospitality. So, what was most needed to encourage and support Receptive Ecumenism—a closer sharing of ministry and sacramental life—became even less likely to happen. With this, the closer relational context in which new issues in faith, order, or moral life arising in one communion might be creatively explored together failed to develop. In retrospect, it is not difficult to see that the absence of some agreed process for consultation and mutual account-ability affected the situation. Nor had there been any discussion of whether the close degree of communion between the two communions should actually have suggested the need for restraint, at least while serious consultation took place.

It was not only Roman Catholics who were puzzled and disappointed. There was also disappointment on the Anglican side. In taking their decisions relating to the ordination of women, Anglicans had recognized that this was a matter that touched the ministry of the universal church and, therefore, provincial decisions and actions on the matter were necessarily to be understood as being in 'an open process of reception', both in the Anglican Communion itself and in the fellowship of all churches.[7] The fact that the Roman Catholic Church declared the subject not one for open discussion and took the matter off the agenda of ARCIC II was a blow for Anglicans for it precluded that continuing discernment and ongoing open reception on which their resolutions and legislations were based.

While Roman Catholics might well press the question on Anglicans whether in a period of Receptive Ecumenism unilateral decisions on matters touching the unity of the church ought to be avoided and restraint exercised, Anglicans might ask their Roman Catholic partners whether Receptive Ecumenism does not require the acceptance that no matter of faith, order, or moral life ought to be excluded from the ecumenical agenda?

In the open correspondence between the Pope and Archbishop Runcie on the subject of the ordination of women following the 1988 Lambeth Conference, the Pope referred to the serious erosion of the degree of communion between the two churches because of what had happened but also affirmed the degree of communion that continued to exist. The exchange highlighted that there is no longer such a thing as a unilateral action that has no consequence for the other. At the same time the reference to the degree of communion that still exists was an important reminder that if Receptive Ecumenism is to flourish at all then it will require care for the degree of communion that already exists and an avoidance of those things that damage existing communion. What was becoming obvious was the urgent need, within the existing degree of communion, for some mechanisms for consultation, joint discernment, and perhaps even joint decision-making to avoid unilateral action.

THE WORK OF ARCIC II

The work of ARCIC II has gone largely unrecognized in both Communions. There never was the same official encouragement to study, nor a request for response which had accompanied the work of the first Commission, nor a dialogical process between theologians and the wider church. As a result the process of increasing knowledge of one another was slowed down and there was an apparent loss of interest (particularly among the laity) in theological conversations, which seemed only to produce more documents for library shelves. When no concrete changes were made in relationships at the level experienced by congregations there was an increasing feeling that pursuing the goal of visible unity was no longer realistic.

However, in its own discussions ARCIC II came to recognize the importance of the notion of reception and re-reception. This became a major theme treated in the agreed statements themselves. *The Gift of Authority* not only offers a statement on authority, it includes sharp challenges to both communions to reform their internal lives now, and boldly challenges both to re-receive the ministry of the Bishop of Rome even ahead of any move to visible unity.[8] The challenges ARCIC puts to Anglicans are on target and echo those the Inter-Anglican Theological and Doctrinal Commission independently put to Anglicans but which sadly received little attention from the bishops at the 1998 Lambeth Conference.[9] The agreed statement thus moves beyond doctrinal agreement and encourages what is here being referred to as 'Receptive Ecumenism' through renewal and reformation of internal structures and processes of each communion now. This would mean, if responded to by both, that they would move closer to one another and be more capable of receiving one another in visible unity.

In a similar way the most recent agreed statement, *Mary: Grace and Hope in Christ*, moves beyond doctrinal statement to urge re-reception of the tradition of Mary's place in God's redemption and so hasten a process already begun in recent Anglican liturgical renewal and in the Roman Catholic Church in *Lumen Gentium* and *Marialis Cultus*.[10]

Both of the recent ARCIC documents then insist that reception is not simply about acceptance of words on a page but about the readiness to change and to be changed—it is about 'Receptive Ecumenism' in its deepest sense. This raises acutely questions of whose responsibility it is in each communion to devise and guide a response process to the work of ARCIC, to see that the challenges to life and witness are taken seriously, and to implement and monitor renewal and change? What effective structures would encourage radical renewal and oversee their implementation? Both our communions seem happy to set up theological conversations but are less sure about how to follow through by promoting change which should flow from the theological convergences. It is surely time in two episcopally ordered churches for the bishops to take responsibility for pursuing the implications of the theological dialogue and for actively promoting Receptive Ecumenism.

A NEW INITIATIVE IN RECEPTIVE ECUMENISM: MISSISSAUGA, 2000

An unprecedented initiative in 'Receptive Ecumenism' was in fact taken in May 2000 when Archbishop George Carey and Cardinal Cassidy, with Pope John Paul II's blessing, gathered together Anglican and Roman Catholic bishops from thirteen countries in order to review where the two communions were and where they were going at the beginning of a new millennium. At last it seemed as if the ecumenical baton was passing from a few ecumenical enthusiasts to those whose ministry of oversight entails a care for the unity of the church. The intention was for the bishops to reflect on their own experiences of Anglican–Roman Catholic relations in their dioceses, listen to what was happening in other parts of the world, and then review this experiential ecumenism in the light of the convergence of the theological work of ARCIC. The intention was to pose the question 'What is the relation between theological agreement and lived relations?'[11]

At the end of their time together the bishops issued a Statement and an Action Plan. In their statement they affirmed that the communion that exists between Anglicans is 'no longer to be viewed in minimal terms...it is a rich and life giving multifaceted communion'. They claimed to have discerned that Anglicans and Roman Catholics have in fact moved much closer to the goal of visible unity than they had at first dared to believe. They even offer a picture in words of the sort of unity they believe God is calling the two communions to live together.[12] The bishops listed those things held in common which they claimed put outstanding differences (namely: the exercise of authority, the precise nature of universal primacy, Anglican Orders, the ordination of women, and moral and ethical issues) in context.

The most important suggestion made by the bishops was that they believed it was time, at the beginning of a new millennium, to enter into a new stage of relationship by signing a Joint Declaration of Agreement which would set out the shared goal of visible unity, would bank the theological agreements discovered through the work of ARCIC, and, on the basis of this, express definite commitments to live a closer life and shared mission. The bishops hinted at the sort of shared life they considered possible now and stressed the need for new forms of consultation, an acceptance that there is no longer such a thing as a purely internal statement. They emphasized the importance of episcopal sharing, shared collegiality, and the need for the bishops themselves to take responsibility for this new phase of Receptive Ecumenism.

The suggestion of the bishops at Mississauga was in line with the original *Malta* vision, with its intention that theological advance and advance in lived experience should be held together and that a new relationship should be inaugurated with explicit affirmation and recognition of one another from the highest level of authority appropriate to each Communion and be celebrated locally. The bishops left with high hopes for moving Anglican–Roman Catholic relations into a new period of closeness, in which there could be a real reception of one another and a heightened sharing in mission and service. Very quickly a new international commission (IARCCUM) was charged with the task of drawing up a Common Declaration to inaugurate this new stage of committed relationship, this new stage of openness to one another, this new stage of what is here called Receptive Ecumenism.

SOME TENTATIVE CONCLUSIONS

So, what can we learn from the story of the last forty-five years about Receptive Ecumenism?

First, if there is to be a real reception of one another in faith and life then the personal and relational is prior. There has to be a real getting to know one another at all levels of the life of the two communions, a real appreciation of the gifts the other has to offer, and an inclination to receive as well as to give.

Secondly, Receptive Ecumenism requires the involvement not just of leaders and theologians but of whole communities that desire to get to know one another, are open to learn from each other, and accept that renewal and change is required for the sake of fidelity to the Gospel and for more credible mission and service.

Thirdly, Receptive Ecumenism requires effective leadership. Those charged with a ministry of unity must be committed to the visible unity of the church and prepared, as part of their ministry, to take responsibility, personally and collegially, and increasingly in shared collegiality, for nurturing the communion that already exists and directing the processes of Receptive Ecumenism.

Fourthly, Receptive Ecumenism requires a better understanding of the structures and processes of reception both in one's own communion and in the partner.

Fifthly, Receptive Ecumenism requires the formation of new mechanisms to ensure ongoing close communication which would also implement effective practices of reception. The two communions need a greater sense of being mutually accountable.

Sixthly, Receptive Ecumenism requires some rigorous consideration of what mutual accountability means when a subject raised in one communion touches the basic bonds of communion of the church, and what we can expect of one another in coming to decisions. There is no such thing as a unilateral action, as Cardinal Kasper has said, when the matter touches the bonds of the church's unity, which does not now have consequences for both communions.[13]

Seventhly, the theological conversation has to continue but with a greater involvement of the members of both communities and with greater clarity about what questions should be put to an agreed statement and what procedures of response would include the community of the faithful. Theological dialogue needs to be complemented by a dialogue in the lives of the two communities. The gap between faith and its tangible expression in life has always to be addressed.

Finally, if Receptive Ecumenism is to deepen then there has to be a constant restatement of the goal of visible unity; restatement which speaks not of domineering structural unity but which offers to the faithful a convincing, motivating, vision of the sort of unity God calls Anglicans and Roman Catholics to live together. Any restatement should challenge us all to affirm the rich diversity that can blossom in unity as well as what structures and processes are most likely to sustain authentic diversity in communion, holding together the local and the universal. Restatement of the goal has to convince that unity is for God's sake and for the sake of credible witness to the Gospel of reconciliation. In their study here of the factors militating against organizational change in the Irish Civil Service, Brendan Tuohy and Eamonn Conway stress the importance of vision: 'The ability to envision and articulate a future and to look from the future back to today, to determine the gap that needs to be closed, is not easy and demands specific training.'[14] If this is true in the secular world, it is all the more so in the life of the churches. The motivating power of a communicable vision ought not to be underestimated.

Structural unification will not happen overnight and it may be 'unrealistic in the short-term'. But confident and authentic steps taken and new stages entered into in phased *rapprochement* now on the basis of agreements already reached might provide a new context in which we can gladly receive from one another in a new phase of receptive ecumenical living.

NOTES

1. This commitment was clearly expressed by Pope Benedict XVI in his first message at the end of the eucharistic concelebration with members of the College of Cardinals in the Sistine Chapel, 20 Apr. 2005; see <http://www.vatican.va/holy_father/benedict_xvi/messages/pont-messages/2005/documents/hf_ben-xvi_mes_20050420_missa-pro-ecclesia_en.html>. Similar sentiments can be found in the speeches of the Archbishop of Canterbury and the bishops of the Anglican Communion at the 1998 Lambeth Conference; see Mark J. Dyer, et al. (eds.), *The Official Report of the Lambeth Conference, 1998* (Harrisburg, Penn.: Morehouse Publishing, 1998), 10 and 404. Again, in Nov. 2005, Her Majesty the Queen urged the General Synod of the Church of England to have the commitment to visible unity at the centre of its work, see General Synod, *Report of Proceedings*, 36 (2005), 2.
2. See 'The Common Declaration', in Alan C. Clark and Colin Davey (eds.), *Anglican–Roman Catholic Dialogue: The Work of the Preparatory Commission* (Oxford: Oxford University Press, 1974), 1–2.
3. See 'The Malta Report', ibid. 107–16.
4. See Colin Podmore (ed.), *Anglican–Moravian Conversations: The Fetter Lane Common Statement with Essays in Moravian and Anglican History*, Council for Christian Unity, Occasional Paper 5 (London: Church House Publishing, 1996); Council for Christian Unity, *The Meissen Agreement*, Council for Christian Unity Occasional Paper, 2 (London: Church House Publishing, 1992); Podmore, *Together in Mission and Ministry: The Porvoo Common Statement with Essays on Church and Ministry in Northern Europe (Conversations Between the British and Irish Anglican Churches and the Nordic and Baltic Lutheran Churches)* (London: Church House Publishing, 1993); id., *Called to Witness and Service: The Reuilly Common Statement with Essays* (London: Church House Publishing, 1999); *An Anglican–Methodist Covenant: Common Statement of the*

Formal Conversations Between the Methodist Church of Great Britain and the Church of England (London: Methodist Publishing House and Church House Publishing, 2001).

5. In Dyer, et al. (eds.), *Official Report of the Lambeth Conference, 1998*, 404.

6. See ARCIC, *The Final Report* (London: CTS/SPCK, 1982). It remains debatable whether the publication of original texts together with elucidations is the best model for ecumenical documents or whether a redrafted text taking into account the responses would have been more satisfactory.

7. See The Anglican Consultative Council, *Women in the Anglican Episcopate* (London: Church House Publishing, 1998).

8. ARCIC II, *The Gift of Authority: Authority in the Church III* (London: Church House Publishing/CTS, 1999).

9. Inter-Anglican Theological and Doctrinal Commission, *Virginia Report* (Harrisburg, Pa.: Morehouse, 1999), available at <http://www.lambethconference.org/1998/documents/report-1.pdf>.

10. See ARCIC II, *Mary: Grace and Hope in Christ* (London: Continuum, 2005), available at <http://www.vatican.va/roman_curia/pontifical_councils/chrstuni/angl-comm-docs/rc_ pc_chrstuni_doc_20050516_mary-grace-hope-christ_en.html>; also Pope Paul VI, '*Marialis Cultus*: Apostolic Exhortation for the Right Ordering and Development of Devotion to the Blessed Virgin Mary' (2 Feb. 1974), available at <http://www.vatican.va/holy_father/paul_vi/apost_exhortations/documents/hf_p-vi_exh_19740202_marialis-cultus_en.html>.

11. See Mary Tanner, 'A Unique Meeting in Mississauga', *One in Christ*, 39 (2004), 3–6.

12. 'A eucharistic communion of churches: confessing the one faith and demonstrating by their harmonious diversity the richness of faith; unanimous in the application of the principles governing moral life; served by ministries that the grace of ordination unites together in an episcopal body, grafted on the company of the Apostles, and which is at the service of the authority that Christ exercises over his Body. The ministry of oversight has both collegial and primatial dimensions and is always open to the community's participation in the discernment of God's will. This eucharistic communion on earth is a participation in the larger communion which includes the saints and martyrs, and all those who have fallen asleep in Christ through the ages.' 'Communion in Mission: The Report of the Meeting of Anglican–Roman Catholic Bishops, Mississauga, May 2000', *Information Service*, 104 (2000), 138 and 139 respectively.

13. See 'The Mission of Bishops in the Mystery of the Church: Reflections on the Question of Ordaining Women to Episcopal Office in the Church of England' (5 June 2006), available at <http://www.vatican.va/roman_curia/pontifical_councils/chrstuni/card-kasper-docs/rc_pc_chrstuni_doc_20060605_kasper-bishops_en.html>.

14. Chapter 21: Brendan Tuohy and Eamonn Conway, 'Managing Change in the Irish Civil Service and the Implications for Transformative Ecclesial Learning'.

19

Receptive Ecumenism and Recent Initiatives in the Catholic Church's Dialogues with the Anglican Communion and the World Methodist Council

Donald Bolen

INTRODUCTION

The ethic of Receptive Ecumenism—'wherein each tradition takes responsibility for its own potential learning from others and is, in turn, willing to facilitate the learning of others as requested but without either requiring how this should be done, or even making others' learning a precondition to attending to one's own'[1]—is not foreign to bilateral dialogues, but neither is it synonymous with them. This essay reflects on two international bilateral dialogues and their initiatives relating to the theme of receptive ecumenical learning.

The starting-point is the acknowledgement of sizeable gaps between: (1) the reports and agreed statements of bilateral dialogues on the one hand and their reception on the other, and (2) the degree of faith shared by our churches and its full expression in our ecclesial lives. These gaps are not so much something to lament, but the space of possibility where work of reception and ecumenical learning can and should move forward, while theological work continues to address remaining fundamental differences.

The first section of this chapter looks to the methodologies adopted and developed within the Roman Catholic Church's dialogues with the Anglican Communion and the World Methodist Council, reflecting on aspects attentive to ecumenical learning, and which to some degree could be adapted or replicated in other contexts. The second section looks to recent initiatives within Anglican–Roman Catholic relations, in particular, the work of the International Anglican–Roman Catholic Commission for Unity and Mission, as a means of bridging the gaps mentioned above. Here some of the external factors and developments which have facilitated or complicated relations between the Anglican Communion and the Catholic Church will be identified. The third section looks to recent developments in Methodist–Catholic relations and the focus on a mutual exchange of gifts in the most recent statement of the Joint International Commission for Dialogue Between the World Methodist Council and the Roman Catholic Church. Finally, the chapter offers concluding reflections on Receptive Ecumenism in the light of these dialogues.

METHODOLOGY OF BILATERALS

As is normative in bilateral dialogues, during the meetings of the Anglican–Roman Catholic Commission and the Joint International Commission for Dialogue Between the World Methodist Council and the Roman Catholic Church, members live, plan, discuss, and draft together. ARCIC's Authority I noted the importance of the Commission's methodology in stating: 'For a considerable period theologians in our two traditions, without compromising their respective allegiances, have worked on common problems with the same methods. In the process they have come to see old problems in new horizons and have experienced a theological convergence which has often taken them by surprise.'[2] The shared prayer which is a part of each commission's gatherings serves to deepen the spiritual communion among its members. Through this process, and in light of the fact that members generally serve for a number of years, a close working relationship tends to develop, even where theological approaches seemed most disparate.

Long-time ARCIC member Jean Tillard noted how his friendship with Anglican Evangelical Julian Charley during the first phase of ARCIC was referred to by fellow member Bishop Christopher Butler as 'the miracle of the conciliatio contradictorium'.[3] Similarly, Bishop Christopher Hill, Anglican co-secretary for most of ARCIC I, noted that there was a forging of communion among members, such that they increasingly became 'a stable and trusting group of Christian friends, dedicated to the restoration of communion'.[4] Tillard observed that 'as a Commission we found ourselves living and experiencing the tragic drama of our two churches'; the unity being sought was one which 'together we were already experiencing'.[5] Similar comments could be evoked from ARCIC II members or members of other bilateral dialogues, where the real but imperfect communion between churches is at times experienced with immediacy and forcefulness.

While it is vital that dialogue participants be able to articulate their church's teachings and beliefs with confidence, the context is also highly conducive to recognizing the faith of the other, and to seeing the integrity of the dialogue partner as one who desires to love God, to be a faithful disciple of Christ, to be obedient to the Holy Spirit. George Tavard, who served on ARCIC I and was a member of the Methodist–Catholic Commission from 1982 to 2006, notes that dialogues foster a desire to 'enter as deeply as possible into the mindset of the other side'.[6] In turn, this has enabled a constructive approach to past areas of conflict, allowing members to approach the separated history of their dialogue partners empathetically and with the fewest possible obstacles to reception. Each church has the opportunity to look to the history of the other during the period of separation 'to ask if it should not learn from the other...a memory that it has itself missed'.[7] In this way, commissions tend to be well situated not only for their primary task—articulating the degree of common faith discerned, and seeking to broaden that consensus—but also for receptive learning in the process.

In a lecture first presented at the 2003 Biennial Conference of Catholic Ecumenical and Interfaith Commissions, Melbourne, Cardinal Kasper noted that ecumenical dialogue is not a process of protracted negotiation, but of standing together before Christ, seeking to discern what he is asking of the Church, mindful that he desires that his disciples be one: 'In the ecumenical movement the question is the conversion...of all to Jesus Christ....As we move nearer to Jesus Christ, in him we move nearer to one another. Therefore, it is not a question of church political debates and compromises...but of...reciprocal spiritual exchange and a mutual enrichment.'[8]

Working within the framework of Catholic ecclesiology, Bishop Michael Putney, Co-Chair of the International Methodist–Catholic Dialogue, has expanded on this by offering the premise that if we believe our dialogue partners are bound to Christ, we can trust that they 'will be drawn by Christ toward the full realisation of his will for their ecclesial identity'. Therefore we can properly look to our dialogue partners 'expectant of discovering in them some version of all of those elements which one believes Christ wills for his Church'. Dialogue 'involves a process of discovering in the other what the Holy Spirit has done to conform them to Christ and his wishes for the Church'.[9] Approaching dialogue from this perspective allows for a receptivity consistent with Catholic participants bearing witness to their own faith and understanding of work of the Spirit in the Catholic Church.

FROM ARCIC TO IARCCUM

During the Vespers celebration commemorating the fortieth anniversary of the Second Vatican Council's Decree on Ecumenism, *Unitatis Redintegratio* (*UR*), Pope John Paul II noted that the ecumenical path ahead 'is still long and arduous', but then proceeded to say: 'Rather than complaining about what is not yet possible, we must be grateful for and cheered by what already exists and is possible. Doing what we can do now will cause us to grow in unity and will fire us with enthusiasm to overcome the difficulties.'[10] This perspective of an ecumenism of the possible is helpful in looking at recent developments within Anglican–Roman Catholic relations, developments which have grown out of difficulties that have emerged in those same relations.

Mary Tanner's essay in this volume sets forth how the 'Malta Report' of 1968 gave an initial thrust for Anglican–Roman Catholic relations to proceed with theological convergences and practical ecclesial steps being taken in tandem. In 1974, four years after ARCIC was initiated, Pierre Duprey, an ARCIC member and then Under-Secretary at the Secretariat for Promoting Christian Unity, set forth a scenario for the future of relations with the Anglican Communion which indicates a shift from this dual emphasis. The first step was for ARCIC to address the communion-dividing issues, then, through the publication of its texts, foster and invite discussion within the two communions, which could subsequently lead to a revising and improving of the texts. The Commission's work could then be submitted for an official pronouncement, and if 'judged to be positive and acceptable', could, in turn, clear the way for 'many questions of a more practical order' to be broached.[11] This approach was not, in itself, contrary to Malta's thrust. Duprey was more than likely suggesting that the Commission's treatment of Eucharist and ministry, if judged positively, could establish a new context for the reassessment of Anglican Orders. None the less, the priority at the time Duprey was writing was clearly to reach theological agreement, with practical consequences following as a second step.

Once again, Mary Tanner's essay details some of the difficulties which complicated the reception of ARCIC I's agreed statements, drawing out key factors in the unfolding relationship between the two communions through the 1980s and 1990s which help to explain why the significant initiatives which ARCIC documents called for were not undertaken.[12] From the Catholic perspective, developments within various provinces of the Anglican Communion leading to the ordination of women to the priesthood and the episcopate in effect blocked the ARCIC strategy to put in place all that was necessary for a reappraisal of Anglican Orders. Hence there was a genuine possibility of relations being interrupted or downgraded.

But, in 1996, during a visit of Archbishop George Carey to Pope John Paul II, the two church leaders signed a common declaration which noted that, given the new situation, 'it may be opportune at this stage in our journey to consult further about how the relationship between the Anglican Communion and the Catholic Church is to progress'.[13] This further consultation led to the Mississauga meeting of May 2000, and in 2001, the establishment of the International Anglican–Roman Catholic Commission for Unity and Mission (IARCCUM).

The choice of name for the new commission indicated the importance of bringing together the search for unity and a commitment to common mission.

Following the 'Malta Report' and the Mississauga meeting, IARCCUM's principal leitmotiv was to give expression in the lives of the churches to the degree to which Anglicans and Catholics hold a common faith. The Commission understood its mandate to be threefold, as set forth in the Mississauga text 'Communion in Mission': 'This Commission will oversee the preparation of (a) Joint Declaration of Agreement, and promote and monitor the reception of ARCIC agreements, as well as facilitate the development of strategies for translating the degree of spiritual communion that has been achieved into visible and practical outcomes.'[14]

Three subcommissions were accordingly established: the first was mandated to prepare a joint statement which would distil from ARCIC's agreed statements the principal receivable elements, and would thus identify in a moderately thorough way the extent of our shared faith; the second was asked to look to other means to foster the reception of ARCIC's work; the third was to explore and reflect upon possible practical initiatives which would give more tangible expression to the 'rich and life-giving' partial communion already shared.[15] IARCCUM's *raison d'être* resonates with the concerns of Receptive Ecumenism, and in relating something of its history we will be able to draw some concluding reflections in the final section regarding practices, decisions, and developments which have been either conducive or detrimental to receptive ecumenical learning.

The task which has most occupied IARCCUM has been the preparation of a common statement of faith. While it was established principally as a commission of bishops, a number of theologians who had experience drafting for bilateral commissions were brought on to IARCCUM, either as members or as consulters, in order to assist with this task. Events in the life of the Anglican Communion necessitated that the project be put on hold for just over a year between late 2003 and early 2005.

The Commission's intent has been to prepare a text which draws together theological agreement and practical steps which can consequently be taken.[16] A proposed opening section of the text is to offer an appraisal of what has been achieved through the two phases of ARCIC dialogue, identifying areas of shared faith as well as candidly pointing to areas where further theological work is needed. A second part of the text is to be shaped by the desire to give tangible expression to the incontrovertible elements of shared faith, and to offer practical suggestions on the way in which joint prayer and study, common witness and mission, could be responsibly fostered and carried forward within the existing boundaries of appropriate ecumenical engagement. A communiqué issued after IARCCUM's November 2005 meeting noted:

Despite a realistic estimation of the current state of relations between the Anglican Communion and the Catholic Church, the Commission believes that the mission given us by Christ in his prayer the night before he died (cf. John 17: 21) obliges and compels us to seek to engage more deeply and widely in a partnership in mission, coupled with common witness and joint prayer.[17]

The Commission's hope is that the text will be put forward for evaluation and reception by Anglican and Catholic churches; the Commission also hopes that the text's practical suggestions will call forth local discernment in order to identify initiatives and actions appropriate to each particular local context.

IARCCUM's brief existence has been lived against the backdrop of tensions, as the churches of the Anglican Communion have entered into a period of dispute over certain moral issues and a consequent reappraisal of the nature of the relationship between the churches of the Communion. Recent decisions in the Dioceses of New Westminster in the Anglican Church of Canada and New Hampshire in the Episcopal Church have been well documented elsewhere. Here it will suffice to speak about the implications of the current unrest on relations between the Anglican Communion and the Roman Catholic Church, and on the way in which the Anglican Communion has engaged its dialogue partners in its discernment process.

Dr Rowan Williams made his first visit to Rome as Archbishop of Canterbury at the beginning of October 2003, two months after the Episcopal Church's General Synod had confirmed the election of Canon Gene Robinson, and a month before his episcopal ordination. During the course of the Archbishop's visit, candid discussions were held at the PCPCU regarding the developments in the Episcopal Church and the Anglican Church of Canada, and Roman Catholic opposition to these decisions was clearly set forward, from both moral and ecclesiological perspectives. Cardinal Kasper noted that as an ecumenical partner the Catholic Church was not simply an observer; the decisions of one partner impinged upon relations with the other. He also added that it was precisely in the midst of problems that dialogue was most necessary.[18]

While the decision was taken in November 2003 to put IARCCUM on hold given that it was an unstable context in which to propose new initiatives in our relations, Archbishop Williams invited Cardinal Kasper to join him in setting up an ad hoc subcommission of IARCCUM to reflect jointly upon the ecclesiological issues raised by recent developments within the Anglican Communion in the light of the relevant Agreed Statements of ARCIC. A subcommission was formed, and, within seven months, prepared a substantial report, which was in turn submitted by the Archbishop of Canterbury to the Lambeth Commission.[19] As such, it was part of the process which led to the *Windsor Report*, allowing the agreed statements of ARCIC to be attended to amidst a vital discernment process regarding the future and shape of the Anglican Communion.[20]

While the content of IARCCUM's submission to the Lambeth Commission and Cardinal Kasper's letter are of interest in their own right, suffice it to say here that the long-standing constructive relations between the Anglican Communion and the Catholic Church, and the gracious requests from the Archbishop of Canterbury for contributions both from an instrument of Anglican–Roman Catholic relations and directly from the Holy See, have made it possible in the midst of the present situation to have frank discussion in the context of friendship and the pursuit of unity.

METHODIST–CATHOLIC RELATIONS AND AN EXCHANGE OF GIFTS

While Methodist–Catholic relations receive less publicity than many bilateral dialogues, relations between the WMC and the Catholic Church have grown steadily over the past forty years. The International Methodist–Catholic Dialogue began in 1967, and has published a report every five years. The most recent report, completed in the Spring of 2006, is entitled *The Grace Given You in Christ: Catholics and Methodists Reflect Further on the Church*.[21] The title is taken from 1 Cor. 1: 4, where Paul writes: 'I give thanks to my God always for you because of the grace of God that has been given you in Christ Jesus.' As the Pauline reference suggests, the text develops the conviction that God's grace has been operative in the dialogue partner and that at the present stage in Methodist–Catholic relations it is appropriate for the dialoguing churches to look to each other and to identify gifts of the Spirit which could fruitfully be received from the other.

As the report relates, it has taken a long time for Methodists and Catholics to come to appreciate that there could be anything to learn from each other. The first chapter of *The Grace Given You in Christ* looks to the way in which Methodists and Catholics have historically understood and assessed each other ecclesially. While early Methodism 'shared in the habitual anti-Catholic attitude of English and American Protestantism' (§ 20), early Catholic reactions to Methodism 'largely reflected the principle that the Reformation had been an unmitigated evil' and saw Methodism as a sectarian growth which further undermined the church's unity and apostolicity (§ 26; also §§ 27, 31). The text proceeds to identify theological and hermeneutical perspectives which have allowed us to come to assess each other much more positively in recent years: Methodists have come to see the Catholic Church as a true church and a means of grace for salvation; Catholics in turn have come to recognize Methodists as fellow Christians and Methodist churches as ecclesial communities in which the grace of salvation is present and effective. With that mutual recognition as a starting-point, the report proceeds in three steps, which provide a model for receptive ecumenical learning through bilateral dialogue.

First, *The Grace Given You in Christ* draws from the previous results of the dialogue in identifying 'very considerable agreement' regarding our respective understandings of the nature and mission of the church (§ 97; also chap. 2). In doing so, it also candidly points to five remaining areas of divergence: the sacramental nature of ordination; the episcopate in apostolic succession; the 'assurance' of certain authoritative acts of teaching (i.e. infallibility); the place and role of the Petrine Ministry; and the role of the laity in authoritative teaching (§ 92).

Secondly, the text asks what Catholics and Methodists can acknowledge to be truly of Christ and of the Gospel, and thereby of the church, in each other's lived faith, and proceeds to identify various ecclesial elements and endowments that might form part of a fruitful mutual exchange of gifts. Catholics can see in Methodists a vigorous Trinitarian faith, which gives great emphasis to the ministry of the Word, is strongly committed to mission and to social responsibility, has a great zeal for the salvation of all, and upholds the importance of lay ministry and the place of lay people in ecclesial governance. For their part, Methodists are increasingly recognizing that the fifteen centuries prior to the Reformation constitute a shared history with Catholics, and are gaining new appreciation for neglected aspects of the Catholic tradition. They can see value in a sacramental approach to the church, appreciate the benefits of a more developed ecclesiology and theology of the Eucharist, and see the richness of diverse forms of spirituality and ecclesial life within the Catholic Church which foster a growth in holiness. The report proceeds to reflect upon these and other aspects of Christian life, especially on gifts deriving from the Spirit which are more prominent in the other, and which could be fruitfully received in order to deepen and make more visible our real but imperfect communion.

Thirdly, the text's final chapter offers a number of specific proposals which could help Methodists and Catholics advance towards the full communion we seek. These proposals—reflecting the recognition of gifts of God present in the other—are attentive to both the constitutional practice and discipline of Methodist churches and the norms of the Catholic Ecumenical Directory. The text systematically grounds its specific proposals for common prayer, witness, and mission in a clear articulation of the existing degree of common understanding of the church, and the recognition of authentic elements of the church in the other. This gives the practical proposals a strength and solidity which is helpful. Coupled with the candid identification of doctrinal areas where further work is needed, this should facilitate the ecclesial reception of the report and the implementation of those proposals which are deemed appropriate in various local contexts.

In December 2005, representatives of the WMC paid an official visit to the Holy See to discuss the future of Methodist–Catholic relations. The delegation, which included the Chair and General Secretary of the WMC as well as Methodist members of the Methodist–Roman Catholic Joint International Commission, met with Pope Benedict XVI and held meetings with Cardinal Kasper and staff at the PCPCU. The principal purpose of the visit was to discuss how Methodists and Catholics might practically build on our theological dialogue. Various proposals were discussed. In his message to Pope Benedict, WMC Chair, Bishop Sunday Mbang noted that while 'there are still doctrinal matters to be settled between us, we wish now to consolidate these interim achievements.' Picking up on the thrust of the recent round of dialogue which has now come to fruition in *The Grace Given You in Christ*, Mbang proceeded to state: 'we know that we have much to learn and accept from the Catholic Church and we believe and hope that we also have a contribution to make towards the fullness of catholicity in the one church of Jesus Christ.'[22]

CONCLUSIONS

The focus of this chapter has been on international dialogues—their methodologies and, most particularly, recent developments within two of those dialogues which have deliberately sought to implement the results of nearly four decades of work: moving their churches to give more tangible expression to the degree of faith we share. These developments of IARCCUM and the Methodist–Catholic dialogue are kindred to the notion of receptive ecumenical learning. In this conclusion, we look to these international dialogues and their methodologies with an eye to the larger ecumenical enterprise, asking what can be learned here about both good practice for Receptive Ecumenism and obstacles or dynamics which are detrimental to such learning.

Methodology

Early on in the ARCIC process, Commission members recognized that the experience they lived somehow needed to be translated and shared by the participating churches. Addressing the Church of England's General Synod in 1974, Catholic Co-Chair Bishop Alan Clark noted: 'It is only when our communities accept that the faith portrayed in our consensus documents is indeed their faith that something dramatic has occurred. This can happen only if our communities—using perhaps the Statements as guidelines—themselves go through exactly the same process as the members of the Commission.'[23] While three decades of experience suggest that the exact dynamics of a dialogue commission are not easily replicated, many of the elements which have proved fruitful in international dialogue also assist in ecumenical learning at all levels of ecclesial life: long-term ecumenical friendships and working relationships, learning to know and understand the other, coming to challenge distorted understandings of the other inherited from the past, coming to recognize the integrity of the other's faith, reflecting on the Scriptures together, engaging in joint study, standing together before Christ in common prayer, and joining in common mission or witness, all foster a context where ecumenical learning can take place. Each of these activities, especially when combined, has potential to serve the cause of reconciliation and conflict resolution in areas other than Christian doctrine, bringing to light previously hidden new paths. Each offers a foretaste of the full communion we seek, giving density to the notion of real but imperfect communion. Perhaps that experience, more than any argumentation, can effectively challenge the sceptical claim that ecumenism is going nowhere at present.

In turn, the fostering of an understanding of ecumenical relations which trusts that the Holy Spirit is at work in the other, conforming them to Christ and to what Christ wills for the church, invites a receptivity to learn from the other on all levels of ecclesial life without compromising one's own ecclesial identity.

Resources and Virtues for the Long Haul

Edward Yarnold formulated the principle that 'if x is the number of years it takes to establish a schism, the number of years it takes to heal it seems to be in the order of 100x'.[24] It was not a formulation arising out of cynicism or even of profound discouragement, but from recognition of the complexity of recovering and maintaining visible Christian unity. Because reconciliation involves not only a resolution to the matters at the origins of our separation, but also necessitates a bridging of centuries of separate development and growth, there is no short path to full communion. It is a Spirit-led journey. But, after forty years in the wilderness, there is every indication that the Spirit continues to nourish in us the twin virtues of patience and perseverance required for the long haul.

The bilateral dialogues, notes Tavard, represent 'a new kind of theological literature' which challenge the churches to rethink their self-definition along ecumenical lines.[25] Such rethinking does not come easily, and our churches' structures and operational patterns are not oriented towards such a new self-understanding. Given that our bilateral dialogues are not going to bring us easily into the promised land of full communion, we need to ask what is possible in the present. It is both ironic and instructive that when full communion was in sight—even if only from a distance—in Anglican–Roman Catholic relations, very few practical steps were taken on an international level to bring our churches closer together, whereas in the current context where we no longer see a path to full communion, there is significant investment of time and energy to take what-ever steps are open to us in terms of common prayer, witness, and mission. In this interim context, a key task of the churches, at every level, is the discernment of what resources are most needed to take the steps open to us at present, then finding ways to allocate those resources.

Bridging the Gaps

Both Methodist and Anglican international dialogues with the Catholic Church are seeking to complement the theological work of the past forty years with other structures or means of reception. In both instances, there has been a sense that the gaps between the corpus of texts and their reception, between the level of agreement in faith which they register and the tangible expression of that faith in the ecclesial lives of the dialogue partners, need to be addressed. IARCCUM and recent initiatives in the Methodist–Catholic dialogue are both seeking to foster an exchange of gifts within our churches, and to encourage practical initiatives in the present context which are thoroughly grounded in clear statements articulating the extent to which we hold a common faith.

These initiatives from bilateral commissions are travelling into new territory as they do so. As they proceed, they will need to learn what international commissions can do to foster what to a large degree needs to happen at a local level, and what structures are appropriate and constructive in bridging the gaps mentioned above. These gaps are fertile places for receptive ecumenical learning at all levels of the church. Relations between churches at local and regional levels could certainly benefit from a thorough acquaintance with the international dialogue reports and the possibilities opened up therein. The challenge will be to engage the whole church in the process of reception, and there is no easy formula for doing so.

Communication, Consultation, and Internal Coherence

Ecumenical relations are necessarily affected by significant changes or developments in the ecclesial life or teachings of a dialogue partner. The current tensions and subsequent discernment process within the Anglican Communion have certainly had an impact on relations with the Catholic Church. While much has been said in this regard in the IARCCUM subcommission's report on the ecclesiological implications of the current situation, and in the correspondence between Cardinal Kasper and the Archbishop of Canterbury on the *Windsor Report*, I will restrict myself here to making two brief and somewhat general points.

The first and faraway most self-evident thing to be said is that ecumenical relations are built on the recognition of a degree of shared faith. When part of that shared faith is called into question, when a dialogue partner is in the midst of a serious discernment process, when the nature of the relationship between the churches of the communion is under discussion, then ecumenical relations do not proceed unaffected; for these are matters which are key determinative factors in shaping what is possible or not possible, what is appropriate or not appropriate in advancing relations. While certain actions or initiatives can be undertaken, there is also a sense in which the dialogue partner needs to wait, and possibly to find an appropriate way to accompany the communion which is in the midst of discernment.

Secondly, the current situation brings to light the importance of communication, consultation, and mutual accountability in ecclesial life and ecumenical relations. Indeed reflection on appropriate consultation and accountability between provinces is near the heart of internal discussions within the Anglican Communion at present. In terms of relations between the Anglican Communion and the Catholic Church, there are numerous structures and means of maintaining close communication, and these have been tremendously important in navigating relations through the current situation. The Anglican Communion's decision to engage the Catholic Church and other dialogue partners in their discernment process was an indication of the importance given to ecumenical relations, and has allowed dialogue partners to accompany the discernment process—through prayer, but also through dialogue about matters at the heart of present discussions. Consultation with ecumenical dialogue partners prior to making decisions which will significantly affect our relations remains something of a long-term goal for all churches in the ecumenical movement.

Reconciliation and the Past

Reconciliation between churches has to negotiate what Gillian Evans has referred to as 'a loss of common context in the past'. A vast amount of history needs to come into play, especially history which has taken the form of 'separated experiences, formulations, elaborations, understandings, and the altering of the common tradition into distinct traditions'.[26] Henry Chadwick makes the point concretely in terms of painful moments of the separated past in observing that 'one can still meet theologians for whom those disasters occurred as it were yesterday afternoon'.[27]

The treatment of past assessments of each other in the most recent Methodist–Catholic report is a constructive attempt to deal with our separate histories and the impact that difficulties of that period continue to hold for the present. While international commissions can constructively address difficult periods of the past, ultimately the purification or healing of memories which will allow us to proceed towards unity unencumbered by the weight of separate histories involves the whole church and all its members. There is no single way, no strategic approach, which can bring about this purification of memories. Rather, it will require study, pastoral attentiveness, creativity, and patience at all levels of the church's life.

Receptive ecumenical learning is in its own way a healing process. Hopefully the impetus at an international level to engage in this process will be of assistance and will encourage local and regional attempts creatively to do likewise.

NOTES

1. Chapter 1: Paul D. Murray, 'Receptive Ecumenism and Catholic Learning— Establishing the Agenda'.
2. ARCIC, 'Authority in the Church I' (1976), § 25, *The Final Report* (London: CTS/SPCK), 66.
3. Butler, 'J. M. R. Tillard', in G. R. Evans, Lorelei F. Fuchs, and Diane C. Kessler (eds.), *Encounters for Unity: Sharing Faith, Prayer and Life* (Norwich: Canterbury Press, 1995), 199.
4. Hill, 'ARCIC-I and II: An Anglican Perspective', in Albert Denaux (ed.), *From Malines to ARCIC: The Malines Conversations Commemorated* (Leuven: Leuven University Press, 1997), 137.
5. 'J. M. R. Tillard', 199–200.
6. Tavard, 'For a Theology of Dialogue', *One in Christ*, 15 (1979), 15.
7. Id., '*The Final Report*: Witness to Tradition', *One in Christ*, 32 (1996), 122.
8. See *TTMABO*, 17.
9. Chapter 9: Michael E. Putney, 'Receptive Catholic Learning Through Methodist– Catholic Dialogue'.
10. 'Homily, 13 Nov. 2004, St Peter's Basilica, Rome', *Information Service*, 118 (2005), 30; also available at <http://www.vatican.va/holy_father/john_paul_ii/homilies/2004/documents/hf_jp-ii_hom_20041113_unitatis-redintegratio_en.html>.
11. Duprey, 'Anglican/Roman Catholic Dialogue: Some Reflections', *One in Christ*, 10 (1974), 362.
12. See *The Final Report*, 98–9.
13. 'The Common Declaration of 5 Dec. 1996', *Information Service*, 94 (1997), 20–1, available at <http://www.vatican.va/roman_curia/pontifical_councils/chrstuni/angl-comm-docs/rc_pc_chrstuni_doc_19961205_jp-ii-carey_en.html>.
14. Anglican–Roman Catholic Bishops, 'Communion in Mission: The Report of the Meeting of Anglican–Roman Catholic Bishops, Mississauga, May 2000', § 12, *Information Service*, 104 (2000), 138–9, also available at <http://www.vatican.va/roman_curia/pontifical_councils/chrstuni/angl-comm-docs/rc_pc_chrstuni_doc_20000519_iarccum-mississauga_en.html>.
15. Ibid., § 5.
16. The IARCCUM agreed statement *Growing Together in Unity and Mission: Building on 40 Years of Anglican–Roman Catholic Dialogue* (London: SPCK, 2007) was published after this essay was prepared for publication.
17. 'IARCCUM's 2005 Meeting', *Information Service*, 120 (2005), 185.
18. See 'Visit to Rome of the Archbishop of Canterbury Dr Rowan Williams', *Information Service*, 114 (2003), 173–80.
19. International Anglican–Roman Catholic Commission for Unity and Mission, 'Ecclesiological Reflections on the Current Situation in the Anglican Communion in

the Light of ARCIC', *Information Service*, 119 (2005), 102–15; also available at <http://www.prounione.urbe.it/dia-int/iarccum/doc/e_iarccum_2004.html>.

20. Following the publication of the *Windsor Report*, Archbishop Williams once again invited the Anglican Communion's ecumenical partners to offer their reflections. For Cardinal Kasper's letter of 17 Dec. 2004 in response, see *Information Service*, 118 (2005), 38–9, also available at <http://www.vatican.va/roman_curia/pontifical_councils/chrstuni/card-kasper-docs/rc_pc_chrstuni_doc_20041217_kasper-arch-canterbury_en.html>.

21. The report was published by the World Methodist Council (Lake Junaluska, NC, 2006), also available at <http://www.vatican.va/roman_curia/pontifical_councils/chrstuni/meth-council-docs/rc_pc_chrstuni_doc_20060604_seoul-report_en.html>.

22. Pontifical Council for Promoting Christian Unity, 'Visit to Rome by Representatives of the World Methodist Council', *Information Service*, 120 (2005), 164.

23. Clark, 'Address to General Synod' (7 Nov. 1974), *One in Christ*, 11 (1975), 191.

24. Yarnold, 'Tradition in the Agreed Statements of the Anglican–Roman Catholic International Commission', in Kenneth Hagen (ed.), *The Quadrilog: Tradition and the Future of Ecumenism. Essays in Honor of George H. Tavard* (Collegeville, Minn.: Liturgical Press, 1994), 239.

25. Tavard, 'For a Theology of Dialogue', 11–12.

26. G. R. Evans, *Method in Ecumenical Theology: The Lessons So Far* (Cambridge: Cambridge University Press, 1996), 114–15.

27. Chadwick, 'Canterbury and Rome', *Month*, 5 (1983), 153.

20

Jerusalem, Athens, and Zurich—Psychoanalytic Perspectives on Factors Inhibiting Receptive Ecumenism

Geraldine Smyth, OP

INTRODUCTION

'What has Athens to do with Jerusalem?' And, similarly, what has Zurich or Tavistock to do with the ecumenical movement?[1] This is not a query that Walter Kasper would raise, since for him theology can fulfil its purpose only 'by facing up to the dialogues with other disciplines, and by rendering an account of Christian hope before the forum of reason (1 Pet. 3: 15).'[2] He specifically refers to 'the urgently required but badly neglected dialogue with the modern sciences' and to the need to hold together the perspectives of a creation theology and of a historically determined salvation theology through appeal to a 'wisdom Christology and theology'.[3] With reference to the proper relative autonomy pertaining to the created order, he notes that: '[I]n evaluating the particular personal, cultural, social or political situation, the church has no particular spiritual authority and competence. Here it is dependent on human experience, human judgment and the relevant human sciences.'[4]

Commenting on the continuing process of reception of the Second Vatican Council and the challenges this entails, Kasper acknowledges a crisis in contemporary Catholic identity according to which 'the contours of what is Catholic have largely speaking become blurred', manifesting in a 'general lack of drive, perspective and hope'.[5] In this regard, whilst mindful of his judgement that 'the council's interest was too much confined to the church' and that it 'paid less attention to the real foundation and content of faith, which is God, than it did to the church's mediation of faith',[6] the purpose of this chapter is to examine the relationship between the challenge of Receptive Ecumenism and psychoanalytic dynamics relating to the loss and reconfiguration of identity. Accordingly, following two brief opening sections respectively indicating the relevance of psychoanalytic factors to matters of faith and introducing some methodological considerations, the heart of the chapter focuses on issues relating to the loss of meaning and the loss of identity before considering the character of ecclesial identity. These last three sections are organized in relation to the cardinal virtues of faith, hope, and love respectively.

COUCHING THE PROBLEM: PSYCHOANALYTIC FACTORS IN MATTERS OF FAITH AND ECUMENICAL RECEPTIVITY

It is notable that whilst the various ecumenical dialogues have necessarily grappled with obstacles linked to divergent patterns of belief and worship, scarce attention has been devoted to the anatomy of institutionalized prejudice, particularly vis-à-vis other churches. This bespeaks a reluctance on the part of divided churches as they go deeper into dialogue to enter into the consequent reality of loss, through processes of ecumenical learning, rituals of repentance and lamentation (so needed in contexts like Northern Ireland), and through pastoral cooperation. Thus, with historical identities staked out in opposition, issues of competitiveness and institutional power are often the controlling hermeneutical key to understanding interchurch encounters, rather than the imperatives of unity and mission.[7]

Historical, cultural, and theological factors have disposed the churches, in the context of protracted conflict, trauma, and loss, and centuries of institutionalized division, to resist the means of other churches securing their own patterns of identity in doctrine, worship, and service.[8] In contrast, more recent philosophical psychology (Martin Buber, Emmanuel Levinas, John Macmurray) and developmental psychology (Erik Erikson, Robert Kegan, Carol Gilligan) have each demonstrated that identity-formation requires a delicately balanced dynamic of security and change; attachment and loss; distance and intimacy; independence and reciprocity.[9] There is no human flourishing outside of communicative relationship—although distance is an intrinsic aspect of this. Severe rupture injures the capacity to trust, and is restored only through the healing of relationship. I need the other to become myself.[10] It is regrettable, then, that churches, so often, fail to pay attention to these socio-psychological realities of interchurch relationship and ecumenical reception.

Consequently, in what follows I set out to explore some aspects of this engagement, through a discursive psychoanalytic-cum-theological reflection on the significance of loss as it relates to the need for meaning, belonging, and social exchange. Giving space in this way to recognize the psychodynamics of ecumenical relationships and ecclesiology evokes openess to the divine mystery, allowing it to radiate in every aspect of the church's confessional, liturgical, and institutional life and witness. A key focus will be the ecumenical significance of the paradox of loss in terms of transpersonal psychology, where—as is central to the understanding and practice of Receptive Ecumenism—the way of loss can become the way of blessing.[11] I shall propose psychological insights which correlate with religious experience, revelation, and theological tradition. One such example relates to the development in early learning of a secure base, which involves the recursive process of moving between the known and 'the strange situation', and which serves paradoxically to strengthen independent responsibility and trustful dependence. Gradually, one learns to let go of identification with the object of attachment, and, with it, the anxious craving for certainty, dependence, and self-sufficiency.[12] This psychodynamic understanding of the self resonates with Christ's teaching on losing and finding one's life (e.g. Luke 17: 33). It is, likewise, relevant to how churches understand the ecumenical tension and process of integrity *through* a decentring loss, as they endeavour to live in the ecclesial space between faithful assurance and provisionality.[13]

SUPPORTIVE AND NECESSARY TOOLS: A DIALOGUE OF METHODOLOGIES

Several conceptual and methodological objections remain to be addressed. Some may object, for example, to the importing of conceptions of personal agency into the socio-structural domain. While one must be careful not to make unregistered moves from one realm to the other, research and common observation demonstrate that the personal and the systemic are recursively connected, bearing on the exercise of freedom, including the freedom to resist change.[14]

Ecclesially speaking, the interplay of personal and institutional is clear. Thus, the church may be construed on a number of levels including, the transpersonal (Mystical Body, Communion of Saints), the personal/interpersonal (the People of God), and the institutional (the New Temple, sacred hierarchy). Such ecclesiological models as 'conciliar fellowship', *koinonia*, and 'differentiated consensus' exemplify the dialectic of personal and structural aspects.[15] Indeed, some theologians have not hesitated to attribute personal qualities and psychological stances to the church in the context of conflictive interchurch relationships.[16]

Additionally, one must briefly acknowledge the sophistication of analysis and method as developed in the fields of conflict transformation and process learning and their potential in refining ecumenical self-reflection, negotiating ways through deadlock, for distinguishing prejudice from preference, or matters of fundamental difference from matters of indifference (*adiaphora*).[17] In terms of organizational change, Thomas Kuhn's classic, *The Structure of Scientific Revolutions*, repays reflection, with its acute analysis of the typical defensiveness exemplified by the arbiters of knowledge and power in clinging to manifestly outmoded scientific paradigms. Such arbiters can be adamantine in upholding vested interests or the *ancien régime*, but intellectually flaccid in the face of new intellectual challenges.[18] Likewise, Michel Foucault's trenchant analysis of the dynamics of knowledge and power should not be disregarded.[19] Other pertinent psychological studies critically examine the dynamics of change in specifically religious organizations.[20] More generally, already located within the diction of organizational psychology are terms which find echoes in our ecclesial and ecumenical experience and observation: fight, flight, repression, fear, resistance, denial, chaos, apathy, vision, identity, community, leadership, limits, breakdown, loss, and, increasingly, even in secular contexts, spirituality and transformation.[21] There are valuable insights here to enhance Catholic Learning and Receptive Ecumenism.

Enlightening as such insights may be, however, it cannot simply be a question of 'add management theory and stir'. First-order ecclesial change does not follow *tout court* from imported change-management techniques. Faith and grace form our primary context. Indeed, organizational theory also is not above poaching the spiritual woods intent on their quarry of religious models ('mission statements', 'retreats', 'wilderness experiences', etc.). To be eschewed, then, is any reductionism of ecumenical ecclesiology and mission to cybernetics, in a frenzy of organizational Pelagianism. Neither, as intimated above, should churches resort to a discourse of docetist mystification, above human science. In seeking for ways in which psychology and theology can cooperate creatively, one must bear in mind the two orders given with creation (nature and grace), together with the different modes of knowing and of knowledge-inquiry adequate to them.[22] It is necessary to avoid confusion of levels, whether by way of reductionism, repression, or sublimation.[23] MacNamara puts it in a nutshell: 'If in the past, religion was divorced from human psychic experience, the fear now is that it will be confined to such.'[24]

Specifically addressing the nature of the church, Peter Scherle (drawing on insights of Max Weber and Ernst Troeltsch), illustrates the need for an inclusive church theory which views the church on three distinct but interrelated levels: the church as *Communio Sanctorum*, as worshipping community, and as social institution.[25] None of these separately constitutes the church in its integrity. Such a model holds together the necessary distinctions between creedal, liturgical-ethical, and sociological-juridical dimensions and their interrelationship in any theory of the church. It may serve as a helpful touchstone in what follows.

RECEPTIVE ECUMENISM: BY WAY OF LOSS?

The Second Vatican Council 'Decree on Ecumenism', *Unitatis Redintegratio*, spoke in both a spiritual and theological register of conversion as being at the heart of ecumenism. Likewise, in John Paul II's encyclical, *Ut Unum Sint*, conversion is crucial. Again, the long-constituted *Groupe des Dombes* has pressed the notion of conversion in relation to ecumenical ecclesiology, calling the churches to assume responsibility for their histories of mutual hostility, historical exclusions, *anathemata*, and divers moral and theological failures.[26] The *Groupe's* astringent realism in its allusion to institutional sin underscores the stark power of memory to hold others hostage, endlessly. Acknowledging, then, that grace builds on nature, it is now in order to explore what might be involved—diagnostically, therapeutically, and transformatively—from the perspective of psychology, and specifically, using the focus of attachment and loss, to consider Receptive Ecumenism as a journey of transformation.

Loss of Meaning: Invitation to Seek the Truth in Faith

Many today are speaking the language of loss, but not with hope for transformation. Within Northern Ireland, for example, one hears daily the peace process construed in terms of political and religious loss, particularly with reference to Protestant-Unionist alienation. More widely, western social theorists from Richard Sennett to Zygmunt Bauman expound upon the breakdown of shared belief systems in the postmodern context.[27] Uncertainty and ambiguity reign over the ruins of a consensus on meaning and morality. Cultural and religious narratives which once gave coherence are decentralized, casting erstwhile devotees adrift upon a sea of multiple consumer choices and lifestyle options. Archbishop Rowan Williams eloquently expands on this cultural bereavement through the metaphor of 'lost icons', intimating that in the prevailing ethos of confusion people are affected in the deepest sense of who they are in their orientation to mystery. This disorientation and loss of sacral symbolic competency in turn provokes a withdrawal into closed perceptions of others, heightening anxiety and causing a reduction of social presence.[28] Paradoxically, amidst this cultural bereavement, the dominant cultural voices deny limits and overplay the scope of will. Subliminal and overt messages insist that every difficulty can be mastered, every dream is achievable, and nothing is off-limits[29]—nothing except, of course, traditions that insist upon the necessary existence of appropriate limits. At this point the notion of narcissism comes into view, associated as it is with self-referring grandiosity and denial of limits.

Since Freud's classic study of narcissism,[30] there has been continuing interest in this topic, both as it relates to a particular phase and turning-point in infant–parent relations (linked with the new-found cognitive and emotional freedoms and insecurities which come with the ability to walk), and as it is analysed in later patterns of expressing independence and reciprocity. This understanding indicates consequences in respect of the person's internalized ways of dealing with difference—along a spectrum from narcissistic egoism to respect and empathy. The dramatic shift in perspective on self, parent, others, and the world that comes with being able to break free of former constrictions both shapes and distorts ego-identity.[31] Fixations associated with this phase include shows of omnipotence and narcissistic grandiosity.[32] An inherent task at this phase is to develop a repertoire of appropriate judgements in self–other relations (dependence, independence, and interdependence).

In respect of interchurch relations, self-fixation may flaw our philosophical interpretations of the one and the many, or our theological constructions of unity in diversity, amounting to 'a refusal to take a back-seat to anybody'.[33] It is necessary, therefore, to reflect as churches on our habitual paradigm of interchurch dialogue, so as to come to a critical view of where we 'place' ourselves–others–Christ. If we tend to place our church and its particular doctrinal formulations at the centre, rather than Christ and his reconciling mission, we will probably expect to be centre stage and the pivotal point of reference in interchurch exchange. Humility is behovely if grandiose idealization of our own church is to be modified in favour of openness to the other.[34] Thus did the Faith and Order Conference in Lund (1952) argue the need to move from a self-centred, comparative ecclesiology to a focus upon common witness to Christ as the core ideal and constant point of reference.[35] It is a principle with potentially fruitful relevance for receptive ecumenical learning.

In this respect, it is often asserted—not without truth—that those who would engage in ecumenical interaction must first be secure in their own beliefs and ready to forefend against compromise (cf. *UR*, § 11). Otherwise, justice will not be done to either tradition. Equally, it is important to submit one's own position to critique and to desist from pre-emptive claims to revealed truth which masks a politics of certainty or a will to control, rather than a dynamic of dialogue—as implied in Newman's dictum that truth is wrought by many minds working together freely.[36]

Furthermore, within the Roman Catholic Church, as with other churches and ecclesial communions, beliefs are neither univocally, nor unanimously held. The human context of faith calls for its inner character of search to be manifest, and for the courage to live in trust.[37] Relevant again here are Möhler's words concerning the need for the church to go beyond egoism in order to learn from different perspectives, to compromise sufficiently to listen and eschew self-sufficiency. Dialogue implies complementarity, as implied in the interdependent notions of 'Protestant Principle and Catholic Substance'.[38]

I have referred above to the psychological idea of the 'secure base' as a condition for a child's graduated confidence in 'object constancy'. Thus, as the capacity for interdependent relationship grows, there evolves also a facility in being less anxiety-ridden in the face of doubt, in learning from mistakes, negotiating ambiguity, and taking into account the needs of others.[39] There are other implications significant to our present concern, not least relating to the matter of identity. Included in a healthy sense of identity, as intimated already, is the ability to keep the other in view and to form relationships. There is also an expectation that one will develop a sense of meaning through the exercise of self-knowledge, critical reflection, fidelity, and openness towards one's tradition, and the ability to make prudent judgements when facing moral complexity and limit-situations.[40] In such ways humans mature into the realization that they live in relationship and according to narratives larger than themselves.

In some contrast, recent generations of Roman Catholics have grown up knowing a centralization of authority, with little place for debate or questioning of the prevailing norm.[41] In addition, in some contexts Catholic identity has been politically honed in resistance to a hostile state and psychologically conditioned in opposition to other churches, with the pattern tending towards dependence on being told what and how to think, according to a 'hierarchical displacement of uncertainty'.[42] More generally, it is hardly surprising that ecumenical receptivity has been impeded where coercive modes of teaching hold sway, where adult faith formation is a low priority and critical thinking disapproved.

In short, warnings about safeguarding the integrity of truth and resisting compromise should not be marked by defensiveness. Acknowledging that leaders, in situations of confusion, need to exercise a concern for stability and due guidance, it should equally be recognized that people in such circumstances also appreciate leaders who can stand alongside them in their struggle, who can encourage them to be faithful even as they seek for fresh articulations of paschal faith attuned to changing experience, and who will share their burden of uncertainty.[43] In the context of church, truth, compromise, and integrity cannot be comprehended simply in terms of abstract propositions or determinate self-understandings, but in terms of a living, unfolding history in which the Spirit is creative.[44] Where churches are divided, truth needs to leave room for imagination and permit history to be freed from the clamp of sectarian ideology. In sponsoring opportunities for people to meet and learn together, church leaders can open the way to more truthful evaluations of their own and other's traditions, to reconciling memories and healing histories.[45]

In my own country, people have died for want of compromise. Divided churches have cost lives. The prior condition of 'being secure in one's own identity before engaging in ecumenical dialogue' has too often failed to take context into account: a recipe for sectarianism. Asseverations to 'preserve' and 'be wary', echoing into situations of rampant division, risk strengthening the sinews of prejudice. Conversely, where opportunities for ecumenical study and sharing are provided, participants repeatedly testify that their understanding of their own tradition has been enhanced because of their study, conversation, and friendship with those of other traditions. Neither denying diversity, nor exaggerating existing division, students and teachers together build an atmosphere of trust in which study, mutual questioning, and explaining ensure that stereotypes are relinquished and Receptive Ecumenism increases.

Freud observed that, in situations of conflict, petty distinctions become infused with potency, to the extent that a group's very identity is thought to be at stake in upholding them.[46] Churches too need to recognize—given their own formation in contexts of conflict and trauma—that leaders are liable to pummel 'minor differences' by intensifying their emotional appeal and elevating them to the status of core doctrines. Interestingly, a century earlier than Freud, Möhler argued against fabricated oppositions between Catholic and Protestant, asserting it not a rare circumstance 'that an ignorance of the true points of difference leads to the invention of false ones. And this certainly keeps up a hostile, uncharitable spirit of opposition between parties, far more than a just and accurate knowledge of the distinctive doctrines could do; for nothing wounds and embitters more than unfounded charges.'[47]

In short, the negative effects of the re-inscribing of warnings about compromise begs a question as to the way in which such warnings serve to occlude the 'real but imperfect communion' (see *UUS*, §§ 80 and 96) already given and to obstruct the vital reception of what has been formally approved. Is there scope here for Christians and churches to reflect on whether their default position towards others is that of the ecumenical exchange of gifts, or that of rejuvenating the narcissism of minor differences? Here the question of identity casts its shadow over the Body of Christ.

Losing Hardened Identities: Invitation to Let Go in Hope

The recent resurgence of identity discourse has been spectacular, prompted by a complex intermixture of identity politics, rebellion against globalization, and the massaging by the self-help industry of the zeitgeist of existential self-preoccupation.[48] The questions 'Who am I?', 'Where do I belong?' prompt further self-concern about, 'Which identity fits my changing, unstable situation?' Bauman speaks of 'liquid modernity'[49] and 'liquid love'[50] to suggest the melting of boundaries and bonds and tension between the desire to relinquish commitments which may lack meaning tomorrow, and a yearning to belong. Thus, he views the irreducible need for freedom *and* security (flattened somewhat crudely by Freud to aggression and sex), as having mutated bizarrely:

Longing for identity comes from the desire for security, itself an ambiguous feeling. However exhilarating in the short run...floating without support in a poorly defined space...becomes in the long run an unnerving and anxiety prone condition. On the other hand, a fixed position amidst the infinity of possibilities is not an attractive prospect either. In our liquid modern times, when the free-floating, unencumbered individual is the popular hero, 'being fixed'...gets an increasingly bad press.[51]

Within identity discourse, two opposed frames of thought are detectable. Some early social identity theorists embraced a primordial construction, ascribing definitive importance to the fixed and inherited nature of identity. Identity was viewed as ab-original and driven by collective myths, enacted commemoration of founding events, which marshalled groups into 'patterns of ethnic, political or religious behaviour, and [consolidated]...collective identity and self-esteem'.[52] Others argued that identity is constructed, shaped by deliberate choices and reflecting 'greater plurality and complexity of influences'.[53] Drawing out Peter Berger's metaphor, Vamik Volkan views the allure of the 'canopy of identity' as an ethnic tent that provides a sense of protective belonging while highlighting difference from other groups.[54] Torn between this tension of seeking both security and freedom, some regard their 'canopy of identity' as a 'fortress' resistant to any change from outside and impose severe sanctions against inner dissent.[55] Bauman thus views identity as 'a hotly contested concept' that 'comes to life only in the tumult of battle'.[56] Church communities might take note.

CHURCH IDENTITY—INVITATION TO LOVE BETWEEN THE ALREADY AND THE NOT-YET[57]

Given that ecumenical relations come burdened with conflicted, indeed violent histories, it is little wonder that 'Identity', with its embattled semantic field, affects the ethos of encounter, rarely without anxiety. Suspicion of strangers seems perennial and ubiquitous. But often there is a counter-thread: in the Judaeo–Christian tradition, the stranger stands also as invitation and promise.[58] Ricœur, commenting on Emmanuel Levinas, agrees that 'ethics unfolds outside the field of ontology',[59] by which he means that inclusion of the other in one's own vision arises from a summons, and has ethical priority over claims of essentialist differences of identity. The *Groupe des Dombes* speaks of collective identity as 'always a paradoxical phenomenon',[60] liable to evoke sectarian separation, fixations on security, and a sacralizing of the past. Yet, they insist, identity is conclusively disclosed only in the future, in journeying with others. Churches might recall here Jesus' pointing to a transcendent horizon of identity, as when challenging those who would base their religious credentials on Abrahamic descent (Matt. 3: 9); or when asserting that kinship with him was constituted not by blood ties but in doing 'the will of my Father in heaven' (Matt. 12: 47–50).

Here the ineluctable tension between belonging and freedom cuts both ways.[61] It draws churches into the force-field of the already and the not-yet. It offers the grace of life transformed through the embracing of failure. In the context of ecumenical learning and the relinquishing it invites, it is wholesome to take account of emotional attachments, the pain of impasse, and the necessary 'work of mourning',[62] correlating this again with Jesus' paradoxical declaration that only those laying down their life would find it. This offers an illuminating hermeneutical key to understanding the account of Jesus' conversation with Mary of Magdala near the tomb (John 20: 11–18). It is as if in speaking her name Jesus confirms her identity in continuity with their past. It is necessary that nothing of the 'already said' be lost. But, in bidding her not to cling, Jesus appears to be urging Mary to detach from the former master–disciple relationship. In the power of the Resurrection, she is now graced to go and preach—to announce the vision not yet spoken. The implication is that followers of Christ will rediscover who they are at the empty tomb. One can similarly read the Philippians hymn (Phil. 2: 6–11) where Jesus is portrayed as not taking advantage of his identity with God. This opens up the paradox of authentic Christian identity consisting in a self-emptying obedience that surrenders to death and to being raised up by God.[63]

In the light of such readings, it is important that churches perceive the theological and moral challenge to transcend the role of guardians of cultural or confessionalist boundaries. Too easily, identities have 'crystallized in history as a result of the occurrence of divisions', traditions adrift from that larger Tradition in which those identities subsist.[64] Hence the *Groupe des Dombes* insist that where confessional identity has become an end in itself, aggressive rejection of other Christian groups has resulted. Legitimate '*confession-alité*' calcifies into '*confessionalisme*' and self-justification. Hardened identity 'withdraws into itself, and rejects real confrontation with other confessions or denominations'.[65]

The central thrust here is to challenge divided churches to recognize that divided identities will not be healed without openness to conversion and that authentic ecclesial identity is to be discovered in repentance and grace.[66] To this end, John Paul II, echoing *UR*, § 7, speaks of dialogue not simply as a means of resolving disagreements but as ongoing commitment to a 'dialogue of conversion' and an 'exchange of gifts' leading to 'fraternal *koinonia*' (*UUS*, §§ 35 and 82).

One of the most troubling aspects of interchurch controversies in Ireland in recent years on the issue of eucharistic hospitality is the spirit of animosity which crept into the discussions. Specific interpretations of eucharistic doctrine were instrumentalized as fence-posts of confessional identity. In the language of social identity theory, the boundary was kept 'hot',[67] as if the mere underscoring of divergence was more urgent than taking the opportunity to create spaces for ecumenical dialogue (where different doctrinal perspectives might be explained sensitively) without undermining the fragile relationships between churches, or denying the legitimate diversity of liturgical understanding and expression. Thus, in a spirit of ecumenical learning, reciprocal theological illumination might have resulted,[68] and attention called to Christ's eucharistic self-emptying as an ecumenical paradigm for reconciling broken relationships, offering an antidote to violence—'medicine for a world diseased'.[69]

It is, of course, no cause for surprise that churches rebound into psychological 'reaction formations', for this is typical of groups who have lived in mutual isolation, and then begin to move closer together. In the context of peace processes, Volkan describes this as the 'accordion phenomenon' whereby following upon the achievement of formal agreement, reflexes of fear or anxiety come into play, with a pull back to old positions and a reheating of the boundary. In the light of what has been indicated about the need for a secure base, it can be helpful for churches to construe this as a temporary reaction, more successfully negotiated through a show of ecumenical tact, a prayer for patience, or words that encourage, than through a reflex taking of offence.

Are there transferable lessons here about the painful and painstakingly slow nature of institutional reconciliation? In feeling the vicarious pain of Protestant-Unionist loss, in the context of the peace process in Ireland, it becomes clearer that change will not be brought about via new inclusive political structures. The latter is a managed legal process which takes no account of collective pain or insecurity. Without empathic imagination, whereby we see through the eyes of the other, sectarian stories forever reassert themselves and a shared future remains a vision postponed. Is there not a role here for churches?[70] More broadly, this accordion metaphor offers a better analogous insight on the slow, contested reception of the Second Vatican Council in the Catholic Church, and also of ecumenical reception.

With the peace processes or the ecumenical movement, I conclude, nevertheless, that something more than the human and historical is needed. We cannot free ourselves—whether through more personal effort or striving to overcome collective apathy or in the comfort zone of churchly narcissism. Reconciliation will be found not by denying that we find ourselves at a loss but in acknowledging that it is a grace within us and beyond us.

LOSS AS BLESSING: CONCLUDING REFLECTIONS

This chapter started out from Walter Kasper's recognition of the need for the church to learn from other disciplines, reflecting the concern of Schleiermacher before him to hearken to and bring together both 'ecclesial interests' and 'scientific spirit'. I have shown my own agreement with this assertion—specifically that the church, in fulfilling its ecumenical call, needs greater openness to the insights of social and developmental psychology. The underlying concern, we recall, is that '[U]ltimately what is at stake is the question of God.'[71]

In this regard, Constance Fitzgerald, a Carmelite nun, drawing from the Christian mystical tradition and the insights of Christian feminism, speaks of the Sophia-God whose wisdom turns life upside down.[72] This Sophia-God unmasks self-sufficiency and invites an authentic mutuality, dwelling among the little ones of this world whose beauty shines through their suffering. This Sophia-God comes to meet each one in the shadows of their sinfulness and loss. Then, avows Fitzgerald, 'hope, forfeiting the struggle to press meaning out of loss, becomes a free, trustful commitment to the impossible . . .'[73]

Likewise, Rowan Williams's image of 'lost icons' is again apropos, as is the sacred icon of the harrowing of hell where Christ is envisioned going into the depths, stretching out his wounded hand to lead the lost towards his cross, which acts as bridge. Here we contemplate the green of hope interfused with the blood-red of suffering. So it is for those who would follow the one in whose eye darkness is not dark any more (Ps. 138). From Christ's face shines the gold of transformation. This hope comes to us only when we accept that we have come to a dead end—incapable of tracing any secure sense of meaning, wholeness, or promise. Is this the hour in the ecumenical movement when churches must stand face-to-face in the impasse? Even at the terminus of human capacity can we make an act of faith in God's future, entrusting ourselves to the guiding power of the Spirit, and search out new paths? In conversion and journeying together our necessary losses will be transformed in hope.

Concluding on this spiritual note, my purpose is not to reduce everything upwards into a pseudo-harmony. Ecumenism is a task and challenge. Tough work remains, and now is not a time to sit back in complacency or give up in despair. But we betray Christ's vision if we fail to remember that this unity is ultimately the work of the Holy Spirit. Accordingly, in a world marked by conflict (in the words of a perhaps forgotten ecumenical text), '[T]he Church is called to work for unity, under the sign of the cross';[74] and, bearing the tension of conflicts within itself, 'to be a visible sign of the presence of Christ, who is both hidden and revealed to faith, reconciling and healing human alienation'.[75] Because we do not fully know how to embody that reconciliation and 'must refuse too easy forms of unity', we are urged to a different level of relationship, more patient and more receptive; a *Receptive Ecumenism*:

This means to be prepared to be a 'fellowship in darkness'—dependent on the guidance of the Holy Spirit for the form which our fellowship should seek and take for strength to reconcile within the one body of the Church all whom the forces of disunity would otherwise continue to drive apart. For there is no 'fellowship of darkness' without some sign of the reconciling judgement and love.[76]

NOTES

1. Zurich was Sigmund Freud's base for many years. Following the split in the young psychoanalytic movement, the Tavistock Clinic, London became home of the Psycho-Analytic Society where Freud's ideas were developed in more empirically grounded directions; see Jeremy Holmes, *John Bowlby and Attachment Theory* (Hove: Brunner-Routledge, 1993), 24–7.
2. Kasper, 'Introduction: Systematic Theology Today and the Tasks Before it', *TC*, 8.
3. *TC*, 10, 13.
4. 'The Continuing Challenge of the Second Vatican Council: The Hermeneutics of the Conciliar Statements', *TC*, 174.
5. *TC*, 176.
6. Ibid.
7. See Alan D. Falconer, 'The Reconciling Power of Forgiveness', in Alan D. Falconer and Joseph Liechty (eds.), *Reconciling Memories*, 2nd edn. (Blackrock, Co. Dublin: Columba Press, 1998), 179–86; also Faith and Order Commission of the World Council of Churches, *Christian Perspectives on Theological Anthropology* (Faith and Order Paper, No. 199) (Geneva: WCC, 2005), 14–18, 31–2.
8. See Cardinal Jan Willebrands, 'Anglican–Roman Catholic Dialogue', *One in Christ*, 15 (1979), 291.
9. See Kegan, *The Evolving Self: Problem and Process in Human Development* (Cambridge, Mass.: Harvard University Press, 1982), 82 ff., 184–91, and *passim*; also Bowlby, *Attachment* (New York: Basic Books, 1969); id., *Separation: Anxiety and Anger* (New York: Basic Books, 1973); id., *Loss: Sadness and Depression* (London: Pimlico Press, 1998), 38–43 and *passim*.
10. See Macmurray, *The Form of the Personal*, vol. ii., *Persons in Relation* (London: Faber & Faber, 1961), 27.
11. One recalls the French word, *blessé* with its double-meaning of hurt and healing. So, too, in the post-Resurrection appearance of Christ to Thomas, his revealed wounds are an emblem of blessing and an invitation to believe (John 20: 27–9).
12. Holmes, *The Search for the Secure Base: Attachment Theory and Psychotherapy* (Hove: Brunner-Routledge, 2001), 65–94; also M. D. Ainsworth, M. C. Blehar, E. Waters, and S. Wall, *Patterns of Attachment: Assessed in the Strange Situation and at Home* (Hillsdale, NJ: Lawrence Erlbaum, 1978); Ainsworth, 'Attachments Beyond Infancy', *American Psychologist*, 44 (1989), 709–16.
13. Cf. Christian Duquoc, *Provisional Churches: An Essay in Ecumenical Ecclesiology*, trans. John Bowden (London: SCM, 1986), 12, 32–3.
14. See Holmes, 'Attachment Theory: A Secure Base for Policy?', in Sebastian Kraemer and Jane Roberts (eds.), *The Politics of Attachment: Towards a Secure Society* (London: Free Association Books, 1996), 27–42; also Peter Dickens, *Society and Nature* (Cambridge: Polity Press, 2004), 38, 172–4. For insightful theological appropriation of related thinking, see Dietrich Ritschl, *The Logic of Theology: A Brief Account of the Relationship Between Basic Concepts in Theology*, trans. John Bowden (London: SCM, 1986), 50 ff.
15. e.g. the basic notion of 'differentiated consensus', anticipated in essence by Johann Adam Möhler, was pressed into helpful service in enabling the holding together of

fundamental agreement and persisting differentials without the denial of either in the Lutheran–Roman Catholic *JDDJ*; see Chapter 11: William G. Rusch, 'The International Lutheran–Roman Catholic Dialogue—An Example of Ecclesial Learning and Ecumenical Reception'; also Kasper, 'The Joint Declaration on the Doctrine of Justification', *TTMABO*, 129. The notion has been further explicated by Harding Meyer. See Rusch, 'Structures of Unity: The Next Ecumenical Challenge—A Possible Way Forward', *Ecumenical Trends*, 34 (2005), 1–8; Meyer, 'Differentiated Participation: The Possibility of Protestant Sharing in the Historic Office of Bishop', ibid. 10–14; also Chapter 27: Hervé Legrand, 'Receptive Ecumenism and the Future of Ecumenical Dialogues—Privileging Differentiated Consensus and Drawing its Institutional Consequences', n. 16.

16. Writing in 1825, Möhler commented on the two extreme stances of '*each as an individual* or *one individual* wishes to be all' as each being rooted in 'egoism': 'In the latter case the bond of unity is so narrow and love so warm that one cannot free oneself of its strangling hold. In the first case everything falls apart, and love grows so cold that one freezes.' He insists that 'Neither one nor another must wish to be all. Only all can be all and the unity of all can only be a whole. This is the idea of the Catholic Church': *Unity in the Church, or, The Principle of Catholicism: Presented in the Spirit of the Church Fathers of the First Three Centuries*, § 70, trans. Peter C. Erb (Washington, DC: Catholic University of America Press, 1996), 262.

17. See Jill Tabart, *Coming to Consensus: A Case Study for the Churches* (Geneva: WCC, 2003).

18. Kuhn, *The Structure of Scientific Revolutions* (Chicago, Ill.: University of Chicago Press, 1970); also Geraldine Smyth, *A Way of Transformation: A Theological Evaluation of the Conciliar Process of Mutual Commitment to Justice, Peace and the Integrity of Creation, World Council of Churches, 1983–1991* (Berne: Peter Lang, 1995), 10–11.

19. Foucault, *An Archaeology of Knowledge and the Discourse on Language* (New York: Harper Colophon, 1972).

20. e.g. G. R. Evans and Martyn Percy (eds.), *Managing the Church? Order and Organization in a Secular Age* (Sheffield: Sheffield University Press, 2000).

21. See Donna J. Markham, *Spiritlinking Leadership: Working Through Resistance to Organizational Change* (Mahwah, NY: Paulist Press, 1999); also Danah Zohar and Ian Marshall, *Spiritual Capital: Wealth We Can Live By* (London: Bloomsbury, 2004).

22. Ken Wilber, *A Sociable God: A Brief Introduction to a Transcendental Sociology* (New York: McGraw-Hill, 1983), 111–19; id., *The Eye of Spirit: An Integral Vision for a World Gone Slightly Mad* (Boston, Mass. and London: Shambhala Publications, 1997), 80–95.

23. See Vincent MacNamara, *New Life for Old: On Desire and Becoming Human* (Dublin: Columba Press, 2004), 40–3, 61–3, drawing on Roberto Assagioli's account of the self from the perspective of transpersonal psychology in *Psychosynthesis* (Harmondsworth and New York: Penguin, 1971).

24. MacNamara, *New Life for Old*, 62.

25. Scherle, 'Nachhaltige Kirchenentwicklung', in Wolfgang Nethowfel and Klau-Dieter Grunwald (eds.), *Kirchenreform Jetzt! Projekte—Analysen—Perspektiven* (Schenefeld: EB-Verlag, 2005), 39–60. Yves Congar articulated a similar ecclesiological model

(mystery, sacramental life, and institution) from a Roman Catholic perspective, see *The Mystery of the Church*, rev. trans. (London: Geoffrey Chapman, 1965), 125–32.

26. See Groupe des Dombes, *For the Conversion of the Churches*, trans. James Greig (Geneva: WCC, 1993).

27. See Sennett, *The Uses of Disorder: Personal Identity and City Life* (London: Faber & Faber, 1996); Bauman, *Liquid Modernity* (Cambridge: Polity Press, 2000); id., *The Individualized Society* (Cambridge: Polity Press, 2001); id., *Identity* (Cambridge: Polity Press, 2004).

28. Williams, *Lost Icons: Reflections on Cultural Bereavement* (Edinburgh: T. & T. Clark, 2000), 1–9, 77, 178–81.

29. Ibid. 49–52.

30. Freud, 'On Narcissism—An Introduction' (1914), in *The Standard Edition of the Complete Psychological Works of Sigmund Freud*, vol. xiv (1914–16), *The History of the Psycho-Analytic Movement: Papers on Metapsychology and Other Works*, ed. James Strachey (London: Hogarth Press, 1957), 73–102.

31. See S. Waldgogel, J. Coolidge, and P. Hahn, 'The Development, Meaning and Management of School Phobia', *American Journal of Ortho-Psychiatry*, 27 (1957), 757, cited in Kegan, *The Evolving Self*, 155.

32. Freud, 'On Narcissism', 91, 101.

33. Wilber, *The Eye of Spirit*, 129.

34. We recall Möhler's words that catholicity means that 'there is no need for one person or for each person to want to be everything' (n. 16 here). On, variously, the role of conscience in holding us open to 'the other as that which defines me', see Terence P. McCaughey, 'Conscience as Consciousness of the Other', in *Memory and Redemption: Church, Politics and Prophetic Theology in Ireland* (Dublin: Gill & Macmillan, 1993), 89, also 90–102; John Paul II, *UUS*, § 34; Freud, *The Ego, the Id and Other Works*, 94–5.

35. The now classic 'Lund principle' was couched as a series of related questions: 'Should not our Churches ask themselves whether they are showing sufficient eagerness to enter into conversations with other Churches, and whether they should not act together in all matters except those in which deep differences of conviction compel them to act separately? Should they not acknowledge the fact that they often allow themselves to be separated from each other by secular forces and influences instead of witnessing together to the sole Lordship of Christ who gathers His people out of all nations, races and tongues?' Michael Kinnamon and Brian E. Cope (eds.), *The Ecumenical Movement: An Anthology of Key Texts and Voices* (Geneva and Grand Rapids, Mich.: WCC/Eerdmans, 1997), 462–3.

36. 'Letter to Robert Ornsby' (26 Mar. 1863), in *The Letters and Diaries of John Henry Newman*, ed. Charles Stephen Dessain (London: Thomas Nelson, 1970), xx. 426.

37. See Paul D. Murray, 'Faith, Fallibilism and Theology', *Reason, Truth and Theology in Pragmatist Perspective* (Leuven: Peeters, 2004), 131–61.

38. See Paul Tillich, *The Protestant Era*, trans. and ed. James Luther Adams (London: Nisbet, 1951), 13; also Gabriel Daly, *One Church: Two Indispensable Values—Protestant Principle and Catholic Substance* (Dublin: ISE Publications, 1998).

39. See Kegan, *The Evolving Self*, 80–3, 103–4, 293–4.

40. Cf. David Tracy, *The Analogical Imagination: Christian Theology and the Culture of Pluralism* (London: SCM Press, 1981), 165 and 363.

41. Cf. Daly, 'Catholic Fundamentalism', in Angela Hanley and David Smith (eds.), *Quench Not the Spirit: Theology and Prophecy for the Church in the Modern World* (Dublin: Columba Press, 2005), 125–36; Wilfred Harrington, 'Scribalism in the Church', ibid. 44–55; also Franz König, *Open to God, Open to the World*, ed. Christa Pongratz-Lippitt (London and New York: Continuum, 2005), 17–35.

42. Peter Marris, *The Politics of Uncertainty: Attachment in Private and Public Life* (London and New York: Routledge, 1996), proposing that typical consequences of long-term acquiescence in the allure of defensive structures are: apathy and denial of interest, exploitation of power and meaning in debasing the authority of sacred texts and rituals, and retreat to autonomous worlds (pp. 114–15, 128).

43. Ibid. 67.

44. See Congar, *The Mystery of the Church*, 48–9, 103–4; also Murray, 'On Valuing Truth in Practice: Rome's Postmodern Challenge', *International Journal of Systematic Theology*, 8 (2006), 163–83, also in Laurence Paul Hemming and Susan Frank Parsons (eds.), *Redeeming Truth: Considering Faith and Reason* (London: SCM, 2007), 184–206.

45. See Irish Interchurch Meeting, *Sectarianism: A Discussion Document* (Belfast: Irish Interchurch Meeting, 1993), 28–30, 45 ff.; also Frank Wright, 'Reconciling the Histories of Protestant and Catholic in Northern Ireland', in Falconer and Liechty, *Reconciling Memories*, 128–48. This collection emerged from an interdisciplinary research project of the Irish School of Ecumenics. The work continues through the School's twenty and more community-based programmes, *Education for Reconciliation*.

46. See 'The Taboo of Virginity (Contributions to the Psychology of Love III)' (1918), *The Standard Edition of the Complete Psychological Works of Sigmund Freud*, vol. xi (1911), *Five Lectures on Psycho-analysis; Leonardo da Vinci; and Other Works*, ed. James Strachey (London: Hogarth Press, 1957), 199; 'Civilisation and its Discontents' (1930), ibid., vol. xxi (1927–1931), *The Future of an Illusion; Civilization and its Discontents, and Other Works*, ed. Strachey (London: Hogarth Press, 1961), 114; also Ritschl, *The Logic of Theology*, 85–91.

47. Möhler, *Symbolism: Exposition of the Doctrinal Differences Between Catholics and Protestants as Evidenced by their Symbolical Writings*, trans. James Burton Robertson (New York: Crossroad Herder, 1997), p. xxviii.

48. See Bauman, *The Individualized Society*, 140.

49. Id., *Liquid Modernity*, 2–4, 200–1.

50. Id., *Liquid Love: On the Frailty of Human Bonds* (Cambridge: Polity Press, 2003), 14–28, 113.

51. Id., *Identity*, 29.

52. See Smyth, 'Envisaging a New Identity and a Common Home: Seeking Peace on our Borders', *Milltown Studies*, 46 (2000), 64, referring to Harold R. Isaacs, 'Basic Group Identity: The Idols of the Tribe', in Nathan Glazer and Daniel P. Moynihan (eds.), *Ethnicity: Theory and Experience* (Harvard: Harvard University Press 1975), 29.

53. Smyth, 'Envisaging a New Identity', 64.

54. Volkan, *Bloodlines: From Ethnic Pride to Ethnic Terrorism* (Boulder, Colo.: Westview Press, 1997), 27–8, 114.

55. See Smyth, 'Envisaging a New Identity', 66; also Paul Ricœur, *Oneself as Another*, trans. Kathleen Blamey (Chicago, Ill.: Chicago University Press, 1992), 2–3, 116–19, where Ricœur explores closed and open views of the self. Self-identity understood as *idem* demonstrates unchanging continuity, with the assurance that one is the *same* person from birth to death. In contrast, *ipse* denotes identity as formed through the different interactions, exchanges, choices, and expressions of freedom.

56. Bauman, *Identity*, 77.

57. I draw here on Smyth, 'Churches in Ireland—Journeys in Identity and Communion', *Ecumenical Review*, 53 (2001), 155–66.

58. e.g. see Gen. 18; 1 Kings 17; Exod. 22–3; Lev. 17–23; Eph. 2: 19.

59. Ricœur, 'Emmanuel Levinas: Thinker of Testimony', *Figuring the Sacred: Religion, Narrative and Imagination*, ed. Mark I. Wallace, trans. David Pellauer (Minneapolis, Minn.: Fortress Press, 1995), 119; also *Totality and Infinity: An Essay on Exteriority*, trans. Alphonso Lingis (Pittsburgh, Penn.: Duquesne University Press, 1998), 46–7.

60. Groupe des Dombes, *For the Conversion of the Churches*, 18.

61. Bauman, *Identity*, 77; id., *The Individualized Society*, 41–56.

62. The designation is John Bowlby's, and the choice of the word 'work' here intimates the cathartic value of grieving rituals, which enable those in mourning to honour intensively what has gone before, thus integrating the loss and opening gradually towards the future. I would none the less wish to suggest that this move is more passive in quality, and its expression calls for a stance of receptivity to the transcendent. Nonetheless, it is 'the *work* of mourning' to lead those bereft, through its symbolic rituals of lamentation and protest, into acceptance of a different future.

63. For a reading that takes account of feminist misgivings about *kenotic* theologies, see Sarah Coakley, '*Kenōsis* and Subversion: On the Repression of "Vulnerability" in Christian Feminist Writing' (1996), in Coakley, *Powers and Submissions: Spirituality, Philosophy and Gender* (Oxford: Blackwell, 2002), 3–39. Most significant for our reflection on ecumenical *reception* is Coakley's identification of the motif of contemplative *receptiveness to the divine* as the feminist hermeneutical key to *kenosis*.

64. WCC, 'Scripture, Tradition and Traditions: Report of Section II', in P. C. Rodger and Lukas Vischer (eds.), *The Fourth World Conference on Faith and Order: The Report from Montreal 1963* (New York: Association Press, 1964), §§ 39–71.

65. Groupe des Dombes, *For the Conversion of the Churches*, 23.

66. Ibid. 26.

67. See Fredrik Barth (ed.), 'Introduction', in *Ethnic Groups and Boundaries: The Social Organisation of Culture Difference* (London and Bergen-Oslo: Allen and Unwin/University of Forlaget, 1969), 9–38; also Daniele Conversi, 'Nationalism, Boundaries and Violence', *Millennium Journal of International Relations: Territorialities, Identities and Movement in International Relations*, 28 (1999), 553–84.

68. Cf. PCPCU, *Directory for the Application of Principles and Norms on Ecumenism* (London: CTS, 1993), § 172; also Jeffrey Vanderwilt, *A Church Without Borders:*

The Eucharist and the Church in Ecumenical Perspective (Collegeville, Minn.: Michael Glazier, 1998), 104.

69. 'Hymn for Good Friday Morning Prayer', Roman Catholic Church, *The Divine Office: Liturgy of the Hours According to the Roman Rite, Approved for Use in Australia, England and Wales, Ireland, New Zealand, Scotland*, vol. ii. (London and Glasgow: Collins, 1974), 299.

70. See Smyth, 'A Habitable Grief: Forgiveness and Reconciliation for a People Divided', *Milltown Studies*, 53 (2004), 94–130.

71. *TC*, 176.

72. Fitzgerald, 'Desolation as Dark Night: The Transformative Influence of Wisdom in John of the Cross', *The Way Supplement*, 82 (1995), 106.

73. Ibid. 105.

74. WCC, 'Towards Unity in Tension', § 11, in Günther Gassmann (ed.), *Documentary History of Faith and Order, 1968–1993* (Geneva: WCC, 1993), 144–7.

75. Ibid., § 12.

76. Ibid.

21

Managing Change in the Irish Civil Service and the Implications for Transformative Ecclesial Learning

Brendan Tuohy and Eamonn Conway

INTRODUCTION[1]

The dual core aim of this volume, and of the broader project to which it relates, is 'to explore with rigor, integrity and imagination what, in the first instance, Catholicism might have to learn from the other Christian traditions . . . and, what the factors militating against such potential learning might be and how they might best be negotiated.'[2] In the latter regard, this is recognized as requiring analytic resources beyond the explicitly theological, such as anthropological, social-psychological, political-scientific, and systems/organizational.

Openness to receptive learning is a particular instance of openness to the process of change. This chapter will contribute to the diagnosis of factors militating against receptive learning by pursuing a case study of how factors relating to change in the Department of Communications, Marine, and Natural Resources of the Irish Civil Service were diagnosed and how a change process was embedded through a strategic management initiative that commenced in 1992 and which is still ongoing. This material will then be examined with regard to its implications for the strategic management of change in the church.

The purpose of strategic management is to enable an organization to make choices and decisions regarding its future and the process or processes by which the future can be realized. It involves:

- diagnosis of likely developments both internal and external to the organization;
- identification of strategic direction and policy objectives;
- appointment and resourcing of appropriately skilled staff;
- adaptation/replacement of organizational structures, systems, and procedures;

- development of plans designed to maximize effectiveness and efficiency in expected circumstances;
- implementation of these plans;
- continual evaluation and review, making adjustments as required.

Thus, strategic management involves: strategic thinking; strategic planning and strategy formulation; strategic implementation (including organizational structures, processes, systems, staff skills, organizational culture, style, and values); strategic control; systematic review of the process.

TWO INITIAL OBSERVATIONS

Two issues initially emerged as needing particular attention. The first relates to what, drawing upon the work of Selfridge and Sokolik, can be referred to as the 'covert', as distinct from the 'overt', culture of the organization.[3] Overt dimensions are publicly observable and generally appear quite reasonable and practical. Examples include job titles and descriptions, mission statements, committees, and other structures. However, covert dimensions, which, by definition are more elusive, can be effective in enabling but also influential in hindering strategic management. Examples of covert components include: perceptions of work group sentiments and norms; perceptions regarding how such qualities as trust, openness, and risk-taking are valued; memories with regard to attempts at change in the past; and affective relationships between office-holders and subordinates.

Learning from previous failed attempts to bring about change, it is clear that the task was more about encouraging a change of hearts and minds than a mere technical matter of producing sets of plans for implementation.

A second observation also proved to be critical. There was great concern at the outset that the strategy would be sustainable and enjoy 'durable capability'. It was noted that while previous analysis and prescription of changes needed, and of the obstacles that had to be overcome, was quite good, less effort had been put into setting up systems and processes for implementation and delivery. A good 'delivery system' was considered just as important as a good strategy.

THE PROCESS

The process put in place involved:

- regular off-site meetings of the Management Committee of the Department of Communications, Marine, and Natural Resources to deal with strategic management issues;

- weekly Management Committee meetings, with agenda available to all staff in advance;
- establishment of specialist committees and networks of staff;
- identification of mission and aims for the Department and objectives for each division;
- investment of resources in staff training, development, and mentoring;
- development of structures for greater participation of staff in management decisions;
- implementation of effective systems of accountability;
- publication of regular progress reports on the strategic management process and on the outputs and outcomes.

An integral part of the process was the willingness to put the process itself under regular review while at the same time providing the process with clear direction and leadership. This involved allowing issues to be surfaced at any stage, including debate and even dissent with regard to the process itself, and taking time to address such issues. Significant questions raised included:

- Why undertake strategic management? (supported by such comments as: 'after all, the Government will always be here'; 'the current problems are just part of a cycle and we will survive them'; 'we are not like businesses').
- Whose job is strategic planning? (supported by: 'it is the politicians' job to tell us what they want not for us to propose'; 'we do not have the permission or power to do it'; 'we do not have the resources to do it').
- What constraints are there, on the scope for strategic thinking? (supported by: 'must we stick solely to existing policy or can we think the unthinkable?'; 'which items are currently not for discussion and how can we make them open to discussion?').
- Is there any point in undertaking a planning process without the guarantee of resources being made available in advance? (supported by: 'why go to all this trouble without commitment to support the outcome?').
- Why bother with planning if other departments are not also doing it? (supported by: 'we will be wasting our resources and others will get the benefits'; 'this can only be effective if we all do it').
- Have we the necessary competencies and resources? (supported by: 'this is a new area and we do not have the resources or skills base').

For the purposes of this chapter, the responses do not need to be detailed. What is worth noting is the importance placed by the Management Committee upon creating a 'covert' culture which allowed such questions to surface, and an 'overt' process that meant such questions were dealt with in an open, transparent, and timely fashion. This approach promoted trust in the process and a sense of ownership by participants appropriate to their role in the organization.

Other supporting developments that took place more broadly included the introduction of legislation to encourage much greater openness, transparency, and accountability in the public sector. Real accountability in any organization is not possible without an openness and transparency in the processes and unless there is clear articulation of the objectives and outputs/outcomes. In an organization that traditionally valued secrecy and opacity and had little accountability as a result, it was a real challenge to switch to being open and transparent with corresponding personal and institutional accountability.

LESSONS LEARNED

Strategic Management as a Process

Strategic management is about changing an organization. It is a long-term process that demands a great deal of senior management time and energy. It is not just about producing a glossy plan or simply promising better customer service.

Civil servants are quite happy dealing with documents and their training has tended to put much emphasis on writing things down. But strategic management is not about documents, rather it is about change processes and it may take some time for staff to become comfortable with processes as opposed to documents.

There was a debate for a number of years in the academic journals about which should come first—structure or strategy. From our experience, the relationship is symbiotic in that the initial strategy is a function of the structure in place at the time. Once the initial strategy is being implemented, it is likely that the structure will itself change and this will lead to a new strategy being developed. Therefore, it would appear reasonable to develop a strategy within the existing structure but to include a facility to review both the strategy and the structure.

There is a need for periodic reviews or audits of the strategic management process to ensure that it is progressing as planned. An outside facilitator was used to undertake these reviews which helped to present a factual report on the state of the strategic management process. It also allowed for feedback comments concerning staff perceptions of the process.

Importance of Vision

An integral part of strategic management is scanning the environment and looking at changes to better position the organization in the future. The ability to envision and articulate a future and to look from the future back to today, to determine the gap that needs to be closed, is not easy and demands specific training. The aim is to instil a sense of empowerment and a culture of innovation in staff so that they proactively seek to influence outcomes rather than just responding to events.

The Management of Change

Staff attitudes to change are deeply engrained, based on previous experiences of attempts at change in the public sector and on perceptions concerning the forces (if any) currently driving change. In the main, such previous experiences have been quite negative and these memories still remain. With this, structural obstacles to change exist. These can be in the form of existing structures and processes more geared to dealing with, perhaps even protecting, the existing systems and practices than looking at how best the organization should be structured to carry out its mission.

It is important that a climate-setting process is established aimed at getting staff to recognize and accept the need for change and the scale of the change required. This can be very time-consuming and demands top management time. Staff need to buy into the need for and urgency of change and they must feel their views are taken seriously. Likewise, the approach adopted towards introducing change is very important. If it is accepted that the most desirable form of change is one in which staff and management see the need for change, are involved in determining the change strategies, and are committed to the changes, this will again take a long time. It will demand the sustained commitment of senior management and the establishment of appropriate structures and processes for staff participation.

Leadership and Management Style

Much of the literature about strategic management refers to the critical importance of leadership. Experience whole-heartedly supports this. The three most critical things that top management can give to support the process are time, time, and time. To say one is supportive of strategic management but not to follow this up with visible time commitment by listening to staff and managers and engaging in the various constitutive activities of the process will be quickly seen for what it is—token commitment—and will predictably provoke a cynical reaction.

Writing mission statements and aims may bring one into the lofty realms of pious statements and well-meaning sentiments. The reality for staff is often very different and it is their experience of what happens in the organization, not what the organization says in its published aims and values, which is important. Therefore, top management's style of doing business—what it actually rewards and values as important, what behaviour it encourages, and how it treats staff—is critical. This must be consistent with its stated aims and values or the potential for cynicism will be created.

The Role of Managers

The involvement of principal officers (i.e. divisional heads) and professional equivalents (e.g. engineers) in the process highlighted a number of issues:

- their previous experience of civil service planning had often resulted in much work being done by themselves but with no resulting changes. This tended to colour their initial view of this initiative and it required a sustained effort by both the Management Committee and principal officers to keep the process moving along;
- their pattern of work was such that operational matters tended to predominate. Whilst understandable, this needed to be changed;
- there was a need to bestow legitimacy on managers taking time out to think about strategic issues and to accept that this should be regarded as an activity proper to principal officers.

Three roles were defined for principal officers: (1) strategic role—responsible for developing and overseeing the implementation of a strategy for the sector for which they have responsibility, e.g. electricity sector, telecommunications sector; (2) architectural role—responsible for putting in place a suitable infrastructure for the delivery of the strategy for their sector, e.g. what skill base and competencies are required? what processes are required to develop and implement the strategy? (3) managerial role—responsible for the lead management of a departmental division and for the collegial management of the Department.

Inter-dependent Issues that Need to be Addressed

Raising expectations of managers and staff about a better way of running the Department will quickly turn to cynicism if they do not see actual changes on the ground. Many of the issues identified in our Department as requiring change were in the management support areas and, in particular, personnel. It became apparent that a number of issues were interdependent (e.g. devolving responsibility for financial and personnel matters requires the prior existence of information systems and the advance training of managers). Some of the issues were outside the control of departmental management, being the responsibility of the Department of Finance with its centre role in personnel matters (e.g. recruitment, promotion, and remuneration of staff).

The role of the management support units (e.g. personnel, finance, information technology, organizational development, planning information, and library) has tended to be played down in the past. If strategic management is to succeed, it will mean totally revamped roles for these units, with increased emphasis being placed on the expertise and advice they can offer to line managers.

Alongside such lessons, an important query arose about the appropriateness of the application to the public sector of principles initially developed for the world of business. This tended to highlight some of the particular obstacles to introducing change in the public sector.

POTENTIAL OBSTACLES TO CHANGE IN THE PUBLIC SECTOR

As in the private sector, there are many potential obstacles to change in the public sector. But there are quite distinct differences between them. The following are some of the potential obstacles.

No Catalyst for Urgent Change

Government departments and public sector agencies generally do not collapse, resulting in large-scale job losses if they fail to provide a service at a reasonable price to the public. There is no 'bottom line' of profit being essential for survival. Neither is there exposure to the reality of the marketplace; public agencies tend to be monopolies and consumers do not have a choice of suppliers. That sharp focus and awareness of market competitors, apparent in most private sector companies, is noticeably missing.

Attitudes of Manager, Staff, and Staff Associations

The key question that many managers and staff ask is 'Why change?' The experience of staff is generally such that they perceive that their success in not cooperating with previous major change initiatives has been validated, particularly when aligned with a similar attitude by many managers. With this, many see that the move towards a more business-like approach, based to some degree on new public management theory and similar new right philosophies, is fundamentally flawed and capable of seriously undermining the traditional public service values of independence, fairness, and probity, and similarly negatively affecting the democratic accountability of ministers to the electorate through the *Oireachtas* (Parliament). Likewise, staff associations, that have a very important role in the public service, are particularly concerned with the effects on their own members' working conditions and career prospects.

Unclear Direction or Vision

There tends to be uncertainty at national level, and even at Departmental level, about the future vision of the public service. This lack of clarity may act as an obstacle to change in the minds of staff, although clarity can only come through a process of consultation with staff.

Structural Obstacles

There is a need to assign specific resources to the change process and this at a time when resources are being cut back generally in the civil service. When changing from an old to a new system, it is essential to keep both in operation simultaneously. This requires resources and some specific skills that may not be currently available.

Conflicting Mandates

The public service is often expected to operate with conflicting mandates. For example, it may be asked to become more commercial yet provide uneconomic services; or it may be asked to provide new services but not be supplied with resources. It is often asked to prioritize, but may find when it endeavours to close down certain non-priority services that it is not allowed to do so.

Ambiguities Concerning the Role of the Public Service

Getting the civil service to change itself is only part of the solution. Elected representatives also have a major part to play in the public service. As the relationship between the civil servants and the elected representatives becomes more complex, there is a need to clarify this relationship and to develop new models for the relationship that can handle these growing complexities. For example, the range and complexity of issues handled by Government departments, together with the speed at which matters regularly require dealing with, often require decisions to be made without prior ministerial approval. This is an accepted modus operandi, yet many members of the public still believe and expect that the minister is involved in all decisions.

The move towards greater managerialism could be seen by some as deepening the democratic deficit. If the move in the public service is towards a greater focus on outputs with an expectation that ministers will extricate themselves from the minutiae and be accountable for the broader policy issues only, then the business of the Oireachtas will also have to be looked at. As the political process and the electoral system have a major effect on the behaviour of elected representatives, any effort at reforming the public service must be matched by congruent reforms of the political process.

IMPLICATIONS FOR THE MANAGEMENT OF CHANGE IN THE CHURCH AND RECEPTIVE ECCLESIAL LEARNING

The final section of this chapter will deal with the possible objection that the uniqueness of the church makes the application of any such secular case study to the church inappropriate or even invalid. It will then suggest a few areas where concrete lessons might be learned, with a view to contributing to a climate of receptive ecclesial learning.

The Unique Nature of the Church: An Obstacle to Learning from Secular Case Studies?

The Second Vatican Council's 'Dogmatic Constitution on the Church', *Lumen Gentium*, situates all discussion of the church's nature within the rubric of the church as the 'mystery of Christ' (Eph. 3: 4), the universal Spirit-endowed sacrament of salvation. Accordingly, a true understanding of the church is considered possible only through the eyes of faith because the church is a sign and instrument of 'intimate union with God and the whole human race' (*LG*, § 1).

Some thirty years ago, Walter Kasper warned against any naive appropriation of secular structural theories. Equally, he acknowledged that the church must become incarnate in the structures of its era, and that it is as legitimate for the church to be influenced in this regard by twentieth-century democratic forms as by those owing their origins to the Roman Empire or to the Byzantine court.[4]

The church exists in order to draw the world as a whole into the presence of the mystery of which it is sacrament. Of necessity, the church must be a visible, institutionally structured reality. As Karl Rahner pointed out, there is no 'ideal' church, only the 'concrete' church; only in the concrete is the church the church.[5] Consequently, the church's structures must serve as *effective* signs and instruments in the world, even if their meaning cannot be entirely grasped, illuminated, or exhausted by it. With this, God's grace must also be understood to be at work in and through 'the world', i.e. in and through secular structures.

The church simply cannot choose to remain historically and socially disembodied, aloof and apart from the forms of life operative in the societies it seeks to serve. The church's only choice is to choose wisely, in fidelity to its nature, the structures that best serve its mission in any particular time and place. In so far as the church is inevitably embodied in forms that show secular influence if not also origin, then it is entirely appropriate for the church to seek, as here, to learn from the ways in which secular structures undergo critique and change.

At the same time, care must be taken to avoid viewing the church through a sociological rather than theological lens. This is something that the then Joseph Ratzinger has consistently warned against, specifically concerning the concept of the church as 'people of God'. From the moment the Second Vatican Council began promoting this concept, Ratzinger expressed concern that it could become used in a non-biblical and profane way.[6] As he has repeatedly reiterated in recent years:

[F]or many, the Church is a human invention, an institution created by the Christian community, which could easily be reorganized according to the needs of the historical and cultural variables of the time. The message is precisely to recover the persuasion of faith that the Church is not ours, but the Lord's; to reconstitute a truly Catholic climate means to want to understand once again the meaning of the Church as Church of the Lord, as a place of the presence of the mystery of God and the Lord resurrected in the world.

And 'Sadly, the Council's view has not been kept in mind by a good part of post-Conciliar theology, and has been replaced by an idea of the "people of God" that, in not a few cases, is almost banal, reducing it to an a-theological and purely sociological view.'[7]

With these important cautionary words in mind, we will proceed to examine what can be learned from the above case study.

The Need for a Systematic Diagnosis

One of the key benefits of strategic management is that it requires a systematic diagnosis of factors both internal and external to an organization which help and hinder change, thus facilitating an integrated and coherent response. In Europe, an audit of internal factors affecting the church would have to take account of the decline in vocations, a diminishing and ageing priesthood, a similarly diminishing and ageing churchgoing population, demands for more participative models of leadership, the loss of credibility of office-holders, and the widespread impact of various abuse scandals on the church's mission—not least through the diversion of energies and resources into managing this crisis. External factors would include: emigration and immigration, globalization, the role of women in society and the decline of patriarchy, the impact of Information and Communications Technologies, the rise of Islam in Europe, consumerism, pluralism, secularism, post-modern cultural consciousness, and changing attitudes to sexuality.

Since the Second Vatican Council, various synods have meant to go some way towards meeting the need for 'strategic management' at both regional and universal levels within the church. However, bishops have complained about the 'controlled' way in which synods are conducted and subsequent documents produced. In recent times, bishops have complained that discussion, for example of the ordination of married men, has not been sufficiently encouraged, though there would seem to have been considerable progress at the 2005 Synod.[8] At the same time, the lack of adequate lay participation has also given cause for concern.

Difficulties with the synodal process notwithstanding, ecclesial authorities locally and universally have produced many excellent documents on the church and its responsibility in contemporary culture. However, as Eugene Duffy has noted, the production of finely written documents does not make for sound or effective teaching, and does not, in itself, bring about desirable change.[9]

Fundamentally, the problem with the Roman Catholic Church lies not at the level of diagnosis, but at the level of an operative culture that is resistant to change, and which is neither demanded by fidelity to the Gospel, nor in the best interest of the mission of the church. As Rahner has commented:

> It is strange that we Christians . . . have incurred the suspicion both in the minds of others and in our own that so far as we are concerned the will to guard and preserve is the basic virtue of life. In reality, however, the sole 'tradition' which Christianity precisely as the people of God *on pilgrimage* has acquired . . . is the command to hope in the absolute promise and . . . to set out ever anew from social structures which have become petrified, old and empty.[10]

Or, with George Tavard:

> The action of the Spirit and the believers' forward-looking anticipation of divine gifts to be received in the future have taken second place, being subordinated to the church's memory of Christ and to its preservation of the deposit of faith. The hierarchy has acted as the trusted keeper of the deposit, hence a more authoritative conception of hierarchy, a more systematic regulation of episcopal authority, a more centralising trend in organisation, a tendency to bring unity close to uniformity, a desire for clarity of formulation in defining and teaching the Christian faith and for uniformity of liturgical language and of canon law, a submission of theological speculation to the process of decision-making, a subordination of contemplation to action, a domination of ministerium by magisterium.[11]

Where does this resistance to warranted change come from?

Attentiveness to the 'Covert' Culture

From the present case study we can see that many of the obstacles to change, and likewise many of the opportunities, lie within the 'covert' culture of an organization. As detailed here, previous well-conceived proposals for change within the Irish Civil Service were frustrated by various covert factors. Attentiveness is similarly needed to the 'covert' culture of the church in a number of respects:

- the 'healing of memories' in relation to previous unsuccessful attempts at reform and the constraining influence such failed attempts exercise over subsequent processes for change;
- covert 'clerical' culture, including perceptions regarding power and influence, unwritten rules regarding promotion and the bestowal of symbolic rewards (e.g. ecclesiastical titles), operative sanctions against 'thinking outside the box', the prevalence of 'groupthink' (i.e. the tendency for like-minded people within a cohesive group to agree on issues without challenging each other's ideas or realizing that the seeming consensus may not represent the actual views of the group);
- the constraining nature of some operative theologies—for example, of revelation, understood as static rather than dynamic; or of priesthood, understood as *representatio Christi* rather than *representatio Ecclesiae*;[12]
- the lack of transparency with regard to the establishment and functioning of various committees and church bodies—for example, the blurring between 'being consulted' and actual participation in decision-making on parish councils;
- the laity–clergy division, despite church teaching on the common priesthood of all the faithful;
- the constraining nature of fear, covertly operative among office-holders at a number of levels, including: the fear of making changes that would be unfaithful to tradition;[13] the fear of incurring disfavour from superiors in a hierarchical structure that enforces a high level of dependency; the fear of enabling changes that would impact negatively on office-holders' own role identity (cf. the issue of lay empowerment and employment).

At the 'covert' level, much needs to done to create a climate of mutual respect, openness, and trust that would enable the diminishment of fears and a genuine sense of ownership of the process of change. Above all, the following reality has to be accepted. The choice for any organization, the church included, is not whether or not it changes, but whether or not such change is chosen on the basis of strategic thinking and wise discernment, or is merely an unavoidable reaction to circumstances that have overtaken the church.

Overt Constraints—Reformable and Irreformable Teaching

One of the questions that emerged early in the Strategic Management Initiative under review here was whether or not the scope of strategic thinking by civil servants would have to be circumscribed, given that ultimately their role is to implement Government policy. Initially, because of the presence of the various 'covert' factors just outlined, it was found that there was insufficient questioning of overt systems that had been long in place. The result was that the analyses of strengths, weaknesses, opportunities, and threats (SWOT) tended towards a past and, at best, current view, rather than the anticipation of future circumstances. It was therefore considered vital that strategic thinking would challenge the status quo and the 'conventional wisdom'.

Perhaps an important point needs to be noted here with regard to the differing services provided to the church by the magisterium and by theologians. Whereas it is characteristic of the magisterium to 'safeguard' the 'conventional wisdom', theologians should be encouraged and enabled to understand their ecclesial responsibility as that of interrogating the 'conventional wisdom' and not merely clarifying it or justifying it on behalf of the magisterium.

In the church context, overt constraints take the form of teachings that are in principle irreformable as well as other teachings that are in principle reformable, but have a long and unbroken tradition behind them. Without straying too much into the concerns of other chapters in this volume, it is none the less worth noting that from the very beginning Christianity found itself facing unanticipated futures and did not understand itself as having a 'fixed structural mould' that would have to be applied in all circumstances. Many of the questions that emerged, for example, in the very early encounter with Hellenism, were ones to which Jesus was understood as not having already given fixed or unambiguous answers. Creative processes had to be put in place in order to discern 'the will of God' under the guidance of the Holy Spirit.[14]

Fidelity to Tradition requires the development of structures and ministries which best serve the communication of the Good News in the context of the culture and the time, trusting that God is with the Christian community in its efforts to remain faithful. This is central to the tradition which is received and handed on. From its past the Christian community learns the art of searching out what is needed to achieve its task. It inherits a tradition of determination and persistence in realizing the Good News. It rejoices in the history of its efforts which proved successful. It bears the burden of its failures. But the church lives and breathes in history and has its own history. Each generation, to be faithful, must be prepared to take the risk of evolving new forms which serve its mission here and now, inspired and in keeping with, but not imprisoned by, what has happened in the past. Genuine fidelity means letting go of particular forms of ministry which stifle the church's mission and creatively establishing new forms which facilitate it. And in discerning the right thing to do the Christian community must, just as in New Testament times, be open to learning from the culture and context in which it serves.

The Need for Attentiveness to 'Durable Capability'

We noted at the outset that for Strategic Management a good 'delivery system' is just as important as a good strategy. This is an important lesson for the church to learn. Failure to 'follow through' has contributed to the resistance often met when new proposals for ecclesial renewal are made. Related to this, whether as a result of fear or neglect, rarely are adequate processes of evaluation built in to planning processes. Yet, ongoing evaluation builds confidence and contributes to the sense of shared ownership and responsibility for change.

The Need for Ownership of the Process, and for Accountability

One of the principal obstacles to change is the lack of a sense of ownership of the change management process by those who will be most affected. Experience shows that in the absence of a sense of ownership and shared responsibility, people often engage in passive resistance and this can be sufficient to ensure that changes simply do not take place. In church terms, conveying ownership requires:

- taking time, especially to bring people to acceptance of the inevitability of change;
- providing people with the means to make their views known, means which are both effective and appropriate to their role in the church;
- for priests, helping them to envision a viable and vibrant future for themselves within the revised structures;
- for all, quality education with regard to the desirability and inevitability of the changes proposed.

Without accountability, a sense of ownership is impossible. Significantly, it has been widely noted that systems of accountability now need to be put in place before confidence in the leadership of the Roman Catholic Church can be restored in the wake of the child sexual abuse crisis. Here again, operative theologies play their part in stoking resistance to such systems being put into place. For example, the then Archbishop of Pittsburgh, Donald Wuerl, now Archbishop of Washington, DC, would have accountability understood as primarily a vertical reality, from the people, through their priests and bishops to the Pope and ultimately to Christ.[15] At the same time, he sees the value of openness and acceptance of merited critique. Paul Lakeland, on the other hand, stresses the need for genuine visible horizontal accountability to the Christian community, and critiques how 'the hierarchical principle precedes the community'.[16]

The Need for Commitment of Resources

It was noted in the case study that, before all else, senior management needed to invest time in the process of managing change. It was also noted that serious investment was also required with regard to the continuing education of all those responsible for implementing change. Probably the single greatest catalyst for change in the Roman Catholic Church would be the development of a culture of continuing education for clergy and others responsible for the mission of the church.[17]

CONCLUDING COMMENTS

This chapter has argued that there is much for the church to learn from observation of the processes of strategic management within the Irish Civil Service. The central concern of this volume is to identify factors capable of promoting a climate of receptive ecumenical learning within Roman Catholicism. This, it has been argued, presupposes openness to the process of change. Specifically, this chapter has argued that where the church is concerned resistance to change needs to be tackled at the 'covert' level where the greatest problem is one of fear. Scripture tells us that 'There is no fear in love, but perfect love casts out fear . . . and whoever fears has not reached perfection in love' (1 John 4: 18). The prevalence of fear is evidence that the church is still the *ecclesia peregrinans*, still journeying from fear to faith and love, still needing to grow in confidence in the presence of the Risen Lord in its midst. As the Second Vatican Council noted, the church will only attain full perfection in the glory of heaven, until which time 'the pilgrim Church in her sacraments and institutions, which pertain to this present time, has the appearance of this world which is passing and she herself dwells among creatures who groan and travail in pain until now and await the revelation of the sons of God' (*LG*, § 48). The church is inevitably involved in change; the only choice relates to the processes put in place for discerning and managing such change.

While urging that there is much to learn from this case study, at the same time it should not be forgotten that the church is also uniquely resourced to fulfil its mission by the abiding presence of the Holy Spirit. Paradoxically, by showing its openness to learning from the world, it will become evident that the church also has much to offer the world.

NOTES

1. The first four sections of this chapter draw upon work first presented in a paper by Brendan Tuohy, 'Strategic Management Choices and Imperatives'; the remainder was written by Eamonn Conway.
2. See Paul D. Murray, Preface, above.
3. Richard J. Selfridge and Stanley L. Sokolik, 'A Comprehensive View of Organization Development', *MSU Business Topics*, 23 (1975), 46–61; also Edgar H. Schein, *The Corporate Culture Survival Guide* (San Francisco, Calf.: Jossey-Bass, 1999).
4. See Kasper, *Glaube und Geschichte* (Mainz: M. Grünewald, 1970), 371–87; id., 'Die Funktion des Priesters in der Kirche', *Geist und Leben*, 42 (1969), 103; cf. id., 'Priestly

Office', *Leadership in the Church: How Traditional Roles Can Serve the Christian Community Today*, trans. Brian McNeil (New York: Crossroad, 2003), 63.

5. See Rahner 'The Church of Sinners', *Theological Investigations*, vol. vi., trans. Karl-Heinz Kruger and Boniface Kruger (London: Darton, Longman & Todd, 1969), 261.

6. See Ratzinger, 'Pastoral Constitution on the Church in the Modern World', in Herbert Vorgrimler (ed.), *Commentary on the Documents of Vatican II*, vol. v., trans. W. J. O'Hara (London: Burns & Oates, 1969), 118–19.

7. From a 1999 interview with *Famiglia Cristiana*; Eng. trans. available at <http://www.zenit.org/english/visualizza.phtml?sid=49464>.

8. See Archbishop Keith O'Brien's comments in 1999, available at <http://ncronline.org/NCR_Online/archives/102999/102999h.htm; and http://ncronline.org/NCR_Online/documents/JA10–22.htm>.

9. See Duffy, 'On Proclaiming Sound Doctrine: Theology of Method', *The Furrow*, 50 (1999), 77–89.

10. 'On the Theology of Hope' (1968), *Theological Investigations*, vol. x., trans. David Bourke (London: Darton, Longman & Todd, 1973), 258–9.

11. George Tavard, *The Church, Community of Salvation: An Ecumenical Ecclesiology* (Collegeville, Minn.: Liturgical Press, 1992), 52.

12. See Conway, 'Operative Theologies of Priesthood: Have They Played a Part in Child Sexual Abuse?', *Concilium*, 3 (2004), 72–86.

13. Drawing upon empirical research, P. M. Zulehner and A. Hennersperger characterize the majority of church office-holders as 'anxious wardens' or 'sentinels'; see Zulehner and Hennersperger, *'Sie gehen und werden nicht matt' (Jes 40: 31), Priester in heutiger Kultur* (Ostfildern: Schwabenverlag, 2001), 35, 151–3.

14. Peter Schmidt, 'Ministries in the New Testament and the Early Church', in Jan Kerkhofs (ed.), *Europe Without Priests?* (London: SCM, 1995), 62.

15. See Wuerl, 'Reflections on Governance and Accountability in the Church', in Francis Oakley and Bruce Russett (eds.), *Governance, Accountability and the Future of the Catholic Church* (New York and London: Continuum, 2004), 17.

16. See Lakeland, *The Liberation of the Laity: In Search of an Accountable Church* (New York: Continuum, 2003), 211.

17. See Conway, 'A Long Way To Go', *The Furrow*, 57 (2006), 648.

22

The Fortress Church Under Reconstruction? Sociological Factors Inhibiting Receptive Catholic Learning in the Church in England and Wales

Peter McGrail

INTRODUCTION

Forty years on from *Unitatis Redintegratio*, the Second Vatican Council's ground-breaking document on ecumenism, the involvement of the Roman Catholic Church in England and Wales in the ecumenical project appears secure. The church participates in formal ecumenical bodies at national and regional levels, and ecumenical covenants involving Roman Catholics in their local neighbourhoods suggest a flourishing of ecumenical good will. Similarly, a willingness to collaborate with other Christian bodies at national level has proved extremely significant in responding, for example, to national crises. However, at this time it is apposite to ask whether this very visible ecumenical engagement actually constitutes receptive ecumenical learning on the part of the English and Welsh Roman Catholic community.

If by such receptivity we understand the 'potential to take each tradition with integrity to a different place than at present',[1] then learning implies transformation. Within Christianity, with its essentially corporate self-understanding, such transformative learning cannot remain on a purely conceptual plane, nor at the level of the individual. Instead, it ought to have a profoundly social dimension. The ultimate measure of a genuinely transformative ecumenical learning is not simply agreement on matters of faith and morals, but a renewal of interpersonal engagement at a structural or institutional level, within denominations and across them.

As such, true receptive learning would impact upon relational patterns within the Roman Catholic community itself, and at the same time inform and animate a commitment to social engagement and solidarity with many others beyond the confines of the Christian churches. For Roman Catholicism, wedded as it is to a rich sacramental economy, ecumenical learning ought to have an incarnational thrust as the community seeks to be true to the vision set forth in *Gaudium et Spes*, the Second Vatican Council's 'Pastoral Constitution on the Church in the Modern World'.[2] In the UK this takes place within a social realm shared by all Christians. Therefore, surely it is not overambitious to hope that all the churches have here a great deal to learn from each other as each denomination seeks to renew its sense of mission while it renegotiates its way within a rapidly changing society.

However, despite four decades of ecumenical dialogue, at the socio-institutional level Roman Catholicism remains largely untouched by the ecumenical experience. Many Catholics do indeed speak of the profound effect that engagement in prayer, shared action of various kinds, and dialogue with members of other denominations has had upon their lives. Yet when the focus is lifted from the individual to the institutional, very little transformation is visible. At parish, diocesan, and national levels, there appears to be institutional resistance to ecumenical learning in the profound sense outlined above. There are a number of reasons for this, one very obvious one being the international frame of reference within which the Catholic community operates. In terms of its theology, its canonical discipline, and the appointment of its bishops, the Roman Catholic Church in England and Wales is not autonomous, and its primary dialogue partner is the international bureaucratic organs of the Roman Catholic Church. A sense both of a broader identity and of responsibility to systems of power and authority beyond the national level exercise a powerful pull away from a sustained learning partnership at local and ecumenical levels.

That, however, is not the only reason and it would be inauthentic to use it as an excuse. Within the freedom of thought and action that the community enjoys there are ample possibilities for learning from other Christians that would be perfectly legitimate and acceptable to the Vatican. As other contributors to this volume also explore, Roman Catholics could, with complete integrity, and utter fidelity to the vision of church outlined by the Second Vatican Council, learn an immense amount from other Christians concerning, for example, how to balance a sense of outreach and service to the broader community with the need to support members' faith; or how the apostolate of lay members could better be drawn into collaborative consultative structures; or how the church at local level can be structured at a time of ministerial shortages. Yet, there appears to be an unwillingness to engage in depth with these issues. The Roman Catholic Church in England and Wales tends to seek solutions to its practical difficulties primarily framed in terms of its own tradition and experience. The principal reason, I suggest, is primarily sociological in nature. In saying this, I am aware of a profound irony: the fruits of receptive ecumenical learning could be the sociological renewal of the Catholic community—both internally and in its relationship with broader society—yet it is precisely tensions arising from its own social make-up that most impede its learning.

In this essay I wish to draw out those sociological factors that impede receptive ecumenical learning. This requires an exploration of the complex relationship between two sets of processes. The first traces broader changes in British society; the second refers to the Roman Catholic community itself, and outlines the social structures and expectations that have historically emerged within it. My thesis is that the interaction today between these sociological processes has forced the Roman Catholic community into a situation of profound structural crisis. Yet, determining a response to that crisis places the community on the horns of a dilemma. In a real sense this should be a golden opportunity for receptive ecumenical learning—as every Christian denomination in Britain has to face the challenges posed by broader societal trends. However, the weight of the Roman Catholic community's traditional social configuration retains a powerful emotive pull that risks drawing it back into seeking solutions entirely framed in terms of its own discourses. Therefore, Catholics in England and Wales face a choice of either embracing ecumenical learning or of rebuilding the 'fortress' model of church that was its default position across the twentieth century.

To illustrate the nature of this choice more concretely I shall examine two contrasting contemporary loci. These demonstrate how the processes of sociological change both interact with the Roman Catholic community's construct of its own social identity and impact upon the potential for ecumenical learning. The first examines the Roman Catholic community at its most local—the parish. The second arguably places the Roman Catholic community at its most aspirational, as it negotiates a terrain in which receptivity might be expected to be paramount—the university chaplaincy. In each case I shall draw on my own fieldwork to identify a number of factors that inhibit ecumenical learning. Lest the analysis of these two loci appear overly negative, I shall go on to consider how in the contemporary context receptive Catholic Learning might be enabled, drawing upon my own experience of ministering in a shared Anglican–Roman Catholic Church. Finally, I shall draw out a number of broad questions that the Roman Catholic community needs to ask if it is to move forward constructively.

SOCIOLOGICAL CHANGE IN BRITAIN

On 19 December 2005 our television screens were filled with the image of a group of Christian protesters confronting two lesbian women making their way into Belfast City Hall to become the first same-sex couple to register their civil partnership under new UK legislation. Forty years ago that event would have been unimaginable anywhere in these islands, perhaps above all in the North of Ireland. Today it offers a barometer not only for the rapid pace of change in our society, but also for the challenges such change presents to the churches. The legislative changes embodied in British society's accommodation of an increasingly broad range of civil partnerships and lifestyles drives home the fact that all the churches are seeking to be faithful to the call of the Gospel in a setting that is far from static and that impacts—often directly—upon their members. The Catholic community finds itself enmeshed in a complex web of structural instabilities. Society is in a state of flux, and so is every social institution with which it engages—including the family, the parish, the school, the diocese, and national institutions. Many are subject to greater or lesser degrees of breakdown. The civil partnership issue illustrates the difficulties inherent in such instability, and draws from the Christian community a wide range of responses. These embrace protest, be it from Protestant groups in Belfast,[3] or from the English and Welsh Roman Catholic hierarchy,[4] alongside the nuanced and disputed formal position of the Church of England,[5] and support from prominent Roman Catholic gay commentators.[6] The landscape that Christians are required to negotiate is changing rapidly.

As we have seen, the breadth of opinions on such issues renders a response all the more complex. It is impossible to discuss the impact upon the churches of such changes in society's attitudes and norms without at least acknowledging the concept of secularization. This is itself an intensely debated field. There is general agreement that active engagement in church life has significantly declined across the twentieth century. Similarly, there is a clear sense that the Judaeo–Christian tradition has a diminishing significance in developing norms for European societies—whether those norms relate to legislation or social policy. However, there is widespread disagreement among academics as to how the data should be interpreted.[7] In the broadest terms, British academic debate is polarized between those who argue that the data point to the progressive disappearance of religion from mainstream life[8] and a more nuanced position—referred to by Grace Davie as 'believing without belonging'—in which it is argued that the decline in religious practice does not necessarily imply a corresponding abandonment of religious belief.[9] Davie's approach has the advantage of attempting to locate the decline in church involvement against the background of broader social trends.[10] However, as I will show below, there are reasons for thinking that the axiom 'believing without belonging' does not accurately describe the situation within Roman Catholicism. What is important for our present purposes is to note that there is a significant repositioning of the role and status of religion and religious institutions in Britain that impacts upon the whole of society, Roman Catholicism included. That being so, there ought to be ample reasons for that community to engage in careful listening to other Christians. However, as we shall now consider, even in the midst of broader processes of secularization, the fundamental instinct of the Roman Catholic community is to look principally within itself to identify both the causes of and potential responses to its difficulties.

CHANGE IN THE ROMAN CATHOLIC COMMUNITY

The underlying reasons why the English and Welsh Roman Catholic community might be instinctively unreceptive to ecumenical learning lie in its history. Michael Hornsby-Smith's now classic description of the English Catholic parish as akin to a 'fortress' can be extended to the Roman Catholic community as a whole, and to its attitude towards ideas generated within other Christian denominations.[11] Even before the 1850 restoration of the hierarchy a socio-religious and educational system had begun to be set in place to parallel that of society at large, and to provide a bulwark against the incursion of external ideas into the Roman Catholic body. The rapid expansion of Roman Catholicism in the major towns at the time of the Irish famine extended its social role to that of providing a safe environment within which an ethnically distinct and economically underprivileged minority could flourish.[12] A remarkable synergy thus emerged between the social function of the Roman Catholic community and its religious self-identity. A great deal was posited upon the construct of the community as distinct, self-contained, and counterpoised against a broader society. Within this setting, the primary focus for mission (at least at home) was internal: energy was directed towards forming successive generations within the self-referential meaningful universe of Roman Catholicism.

Perhaps the clearest expression of this construct of an enclosed Catholic identity was the corresponding construct of the 'non-Catholic'. This expression, common among Catholics, defines other Christians in terms of what they are not, reducing them to the category of the 'other'. The reduction serves two related purposes. First, it clarifies the boundaries of the Roman Catholic community by establishing a clear conceptual distinction between its members and the rest of society. Secondly, the negating definition introduces a note of the deficient into its conceptualization of other Christians. Such a construct of fellow Christians as 'other' not only reduced openness to receptive ecumenical learning; it was entirely inimical to that possibility. In so far as other Christians remained within the category of 'other', such dialogue would have risked jeopardizing Roman Catholic identity itself. There are, undoubtedly, some who continue to fear that possibility.

This model of the enclosed Catholic community reached its apogee in the years leading up to the First World War, as the doctrinal, legislative, and liturgical reforms of Pope Pius X solidified the conceptual boundaries of Roman Catholicism. Yet, the very implementation of those reforms indicated that the walls of the 'fortress' were far from secure. For example, the archives of the Archdiocese of Liverpool suggest that the 1907 attempt to enforce endogamy had a very limited impact.[13] Here we can recognize the emergence of the dichotomy that still plays out today. A significant minority of Catholics always sat relatively loosely with the church's formal position on a range of issues; that minority is now probably a majority. As some of their predecessors did, so now most Roman Catholics on a personal level have renegotiated their identity by a degree of engagement with ideas drawn from outside the Catholic community.[14] This process of progressive renegotiation has both contributed to and been intensified by the Roman Catholic Church's dismantling of many features that had demarcated the external boundaries of the fortress. Examples would be the abolition of the requirement for Friday abstinence,[15] or of head-coverings for women. Some would even say that the post-Second Vatican Council openness to ecumenical engagement has itself contributed to the demolition of the fortress's defences. The dissolution of a distinctive Catholic subculture has served to highlight the extent to which Catholics, like most groups in society, are exposed to external social change, and its consequences. Despite this, there is a tendency for the institution to continue to construct its identity without any reference to the progressive repositioning of its members. Today the dissonance between formal discourses and identity-expectations and the reality of the lives of Roman Catholics is becoming ever louder.

The markers of such renegotiated Roman Catholicism are easy to identify and quantify—for example, by surveying the steady decrease in the numbers regularly attending Mass; or the reduction in the numbers of active priests and vocations to the priesthood, or the steadily increasing number of parish closures. Such data pose the question why such traumatic change should be under way. It is seductive to focus on explanations expressed solely in terms of discourses internal to the Catholic community—for example, perceived failings in the religious education of children, or the internal divisions within Catholicism over the interpretation and implementation of the Second Vatican Council. However, whilst these issues do undoubtedly play a part in the debate, the causes of such significant change are ultimately to be located beyond the narrow confines of the Roman Catholic community itself, as individuals renegotiate their personal identity in the face of the explosion of change that has taken place within society as a whole.

My own research into the celebration of First Communion[16] has suggested that many people persist in incorporating the category of 'Catholic' into their construct of their own identity. However, this does not normally carry implications either for religious practice or for observance of the Roman Catholic Church's moral teaching, particularly around marriage and family formation. Many Catholics appear to opt for the opposite of the paradigm 'believing without belonging': they do not necessarily believe, at least in terms of faith as expressed in formal ecclesial discourses, but they very much want to belong. Being Roman Catholic is their cultural heritage; access to the church's rituals such as baptism and first communion is their birthright. This is I think largely because it is through the celebration of rituals such as first communion that a sense of inter-generational continuity is both articulated and achieved. Catholicism interprets the ritual of first communion in terms of the individual embarking upon a lifelong pattern of weekly repetition of the Eucharist; many participants, however, understand it in terms of a very different pattern of repetition. This is not the week-by-week rhythm presumed by formal Roman Catholic teaching, but the much broader wavelength of the enactment of the ritual of first communion, once in the life of each individual in each generation. A phrase I encountered several times during my fieldwork summed up this inter-generational approach: 'My Nan did it for my Mam, my Mam did it for me, and I'm doing it for my children.' The church's rituals reinforce continuity between generations, and help to reinforce familial identity. They help to mark and reinforce a constituent element of that identity—'being Catholic'—but they carry few or no implications for belief as a consequence of that belonging. This is especially true when ecclesial expectations with regard to normative religious practice and lifestyle choices are brought into the frame.

THE PARISH

The social changes here outlined do not of themselves constitute a barrier to receptive ecumenical learning. Indeed, by breaking down the distinctiveness of the Roman Catholic community they expose the common ground that might become a fertile seedbed for ecumenical openness. Arguably, the issue is not with the processes of sociological change in themselves, but with the response of many within the Roman Catholic community. There are two dimensions worth noting here. The first is intolerance for those Catholics who manifest the renegotiated Catholicism that has resulted from their engagement with broader trends in society. The second is the attempt to create (or, rather, to recreate) the fortress model, in which a self-referencing Roman Catholicism seeks to stand foursquare against the onslaughts of society. Neither of these dimensions is hospitable to openness to learning from the experience of other Christians—even though that experience could prove highly illuminating.

The buttressing reflex is particularly strengthened by two related developments within the Roman Catholic community that directly impact on both diocesan planning and parish life. The first is the continued fall in the numbers attending Mass each Sunday. Censuses of Mass attendance in the Archdiocese of Liverpool, for example, show a drop from 150,000 in November 1986 to 70,000 in November 2004. If an age profile is included in the equation, it becomes very clear that the Mass-going population is not regenerating itself. The second feature maps onto the first—this is the reduction in the numbers of active clergy able to staff parishes. The result is the progressive dismantlement of the parish system across the country. The social structure that has held (contained, perhaps) and sustained the Catholic community in this country for over 150 years is rapidly breaking down.

At this stage, the impulse to preserve an appearance of 'business as usual' is uppermost: dioceses generally prefer to merge parishes or to draw them into clustering arrangements by which one priest assumes responsibility for more than one parish. Even these limited processes of change can prove extremely painful, as parishioners sense there are winners and losers, with a frequently expressed sense that the parish in which the priest lives enjoys an advantage over the others for which he is responsible. To engage with the possibility that a priest may not be resident within the parish boundaries jeopardizes a number of expected norms of Roman Catholic life. In pastoral work I carried out with a number of parishes as they prepared for clustering, the questions most frequently asked turned upon fears of a withdrawal of access to priestly ministry at points of crisis: 'Who is going to sign the Mass cards?' and 'What happens if someone is taken sick?' were recurring themes.

These expressions of dependence introduce a further paradox, and one that once again risks hardening the community against the possibilities of ecumenical learning. After a relatively brief post-conciliar period in which the mission and role of the laity were spotlighted, the person of the priest is once again becoming more dominant. As the number of active Roman Catholics declines and ages, so too do the ranks of those willing to assume positions of leadership and responsibility in their parishes. At the same time, the reduction in the number of priests raises the profile of the remaining clergy within the community and enhances the premium invested in their ministry. The risk is the reinforcement of what Desmond Ryan describes as 'paidomorphic Catholicism,' that is the preference of very many Catholics to avoid having to take mature responsibility for their own faith development and parish management.[17]

These structural shifts over the coming decade will radically change the local face of the Roman Catholic Church in England and Wales. They should also present great opportunities for ecumenical learning—the same processes of ministerial shortage, congregational diminution, and consequent restructuring have happened and continue to happen in other churches. This, however, does not appear to be the general case, and the reason, I suspect, is that the primary driving factor in the current reconfiguration of Roman Catholicism is not ultimately a concern with the church's mission. Rather, the focus for current energy and thought is on the deployment of clergy and the management of dwindling personnel and financial resources, generally regarded as entirely internal matters. The default point of reference all too easily becomes the church's own internal discourses—particularly given that diocesan authorities, priests and parishioners have a fundamental orientation towards the maintenance of the status quo. The result is twofold: the emergence of a new clerical culture, and a tendency, as the questions around providing Sunday Mass becomes paramount, to a further retreat into viewing the Roman Catholic community as constituted only by the liturgical assembly.

The danger of this approach is that the Roman Catholic community could slip into an unarticulated but effectively congregationalist position. Instead of the parish making present at local level the church in its universality, it could become merely the focus for the gatherings of like-minded individuals around a priest, who could represent just about any shade of Roman Catholic opinion—from liberal to neo-Tridentine. Whilst Catholicism seeks to maintain its presence across the country, albeit spread more thinly, the end result could be its fragmentation. Those Catholics who remain committed to regular participation in its worship could become liturgical consumers, shopping around for those celebrations that best match their own needs with a reduced sense of their identification with the church in their own immediate neighbourhood. Any sense of the parish as exercising a mission to the broader local community risks being subsumed into an internally directed concern for the needs (liturgical, emotional, theological) of those who gather, whilst a sense of context is lost.

Avoidance of this position calls for a willingness on the part of the Roman Catholic community to learn from other Christian denominations how they manage congregational involvement in the life and mission of their church. Catholics are, as a whole, probably too naive in their understanding of and engagement with consultative processes within their community. The Code of Canon Law requires every parish to have a Finance Committee,[18] though the extent to which that legislation is observed is debatable. However, the Code leaves the establishing of parish pastoral councils to the discretion of the local bishop.[19] Where such councils do exist, they frequently have few frames of reference, and can be created or dissolved by a parish priest at will. Yet they ought to be capable of providing checks and balances on any internalist tendencies by representing to the parish the broader issues at stake within the local community. Paradoxically, perhaps, it is exactly those denominations that would regard themselves as 'congregational', from whom the Catholic community might have the most to learn, not least because they have centuries of experience of the potential pitfalls of the model and have built safeguards into their procedures. Learning from Protestantism can furnish tools to protect the catholicity of the church!

CHAPLAINCY IN HIGHER EDUCATION

As we have seen, it is possible for the local life of Roman Catholics to be carried out and restructured without any sustained reference to the experience of other Christians. Internally directed discourses can and do dominate. What, however, happens when the Roman Catholic community has much of its freedom to operate taken away from it, or when collaboration is, at least in theory, a given requirement? This is the case with the community's ministry to secular institutions, such as prisons, hospitals, or the Higher Education sector. During the academic year 2004/5 I carried out a research project into chaplaincy provision in nine Higher Education institutions, whose findings cast light on the questions here addressed.

Across the Higher Education sector a range of attitudes emerged on the part of Higher Education institutions towards the provision of chaplaincy, and the presence on campus of denominational chaplains. Some institutions were highly supportive, but the more general tenor was that chaplaincy was at best tolerated, and sometimes viewed with considerable wariness. Frequently the institution was hoping, and sometimes actively trying, to integrate chaplains and chaplaincies into a departmental structure which veiled the distinctive features of each Christian denomination. This approach resonated strongly with some chaplains, and certainly could be mapped onto the broad expectations of the established church in some campuses. However, such an approach severely compromises the ability of the denominations to stand in their own integrity and from there to learn from each other. Because of this the openness to ecumenical learning that one might have expected to be paramount— not least for survival and mutual support among the chaplains—was far from what I actually found. At an individual level, chaplains generally got on well with each other, and active ecumenical engagement took place, involving both chaplains and students. However, receptive ecumenical learning, in the profound sense discussed above, was not in evidence at any institution I studied.

One major factor in this was the replication on campus of the strong link between priest, Roman Catholic community, and sacramental provision already noted. The expectation of both diocesan authorities and most students was that the Roman Catholic chaplaincy should mirror the sociological structures of the old parish model. These do not fit at all comfortably with the institutions' structural expectations, nor with the ecclesiological paradigm often informing the approach to chaplaincy of other Christian chaplains on campus. Most Roman Catholic chaplains (and almost all students) saw the chaplains' role as being primarily to minister to the body of Roman Catholic students and staff—and above all else to ensure the provision of a Sunday Mass. On the other hand, chaplains from other denominations—in line with the institutions' expectations, different ecclesiological paradigms, and in the interests of ecumenical cooperation—would see their role as crossing denominational boundaries and ministering to the institution as a whole. These ill-matching perceptions often found their focus over the celebration of the Eucharist. In several locations, the other chaplains aspired to an inter-denominational Sunday Eucharist to which all students and staff were welcomed. Whilst there was a general appreciation on the part of other denominational groups that this did not accord with the Catholic position on inter-communion, there was nonetheless a sense of strong disappointment that a greater degree of sharing was not possible, with consequent tensions. The particular circumstances of a Higher Education institution highlight the Roman Catholic tendency towards cultural isolation. This is intensified where, for the reasons discussed, the Catholic community senses the institution to be hostile, and other Christians to be at least unsympathetic. These tensions play out under a strong spotlight. Whereas in a parish setting it is relatively easy to ignore the needs and expectations of other Christian denominations, this cannot be the case here. Shared chapels and worship spaces manifest the extent to which separate lives are being led.

Thus, even when our focus moves from the traditional stronghold of the parish, and we find ourselves instead in what might be expected to be an environment strongly favourable to receptive ecumenical learning, a mutated set of sociological factors nonetheless lead to the same outcome. It may be that a similar outcome awaits Roman Catholicism whenever it needs to step outside its own traditional boundaries and engage in partnership with other Christians in a context where secular institutions and bodies hold the balance of power. This does not preclude the possibility of receptive ecumenical learning; indeed, it accentuates its importance and value. However, it does point to the need to achieve a true mutuality between the ecumenical parties, which secular departmental and managerial models do not favour. In the Higher Education institutional setting Roman Catholicism has much to learn from other Christians; not least with regard to their broader sense of mission. Conversely, the learning needs to be mutual, and founded in mutual respect for the other's integrity— in this case, the sacramental disciplines governing the Roman Catholic community.

ST BASIL'S AND ALL SAINTS, WIDNES: WHAT MIGHT BE POSSIBLE?

On a more positive note, let us finally look briefly at one setting in which much receptive ecumenical learning has taken place. From 1994 to 1998 I was the parish priest of a Roman Catholic parish which shared a church building with an Anglican congregation. The two parishes had been founded as the only Christian presence in a large housing estate built on a greenfield site towards the end of the twentieth century. The population faced considerable social problems, including high youth unemployment, low income households, and widespread drug abuse. The primary learning, for the Catholics especially, was twofold.

First, from the outset, the formal sharing agreement required that a joint church council be established, with members from both communities. Its function was to handle the day-to-day use and management of the shared property. This pragmatic need gave the Roman Catholic members of the joint council close experience of the well-established workings of an Anglican Parochial Church Council, whose lay members were accustomed to exercising real shared responsibility and decision-making with their pastor. This impacted on the Catholic participants' engagement with the joint council and also on the workings of their own parish council which mirrored the Anglican Parochial Church Council. This fostered a much more responsible and involved approach on the part of the Catholics, particularly to the whole area of collaborative ministry, and was a healthy antidote to the prevailing Catholic dependence on the clergy.

The second key area of learning flowed out from the first. As the two communities participated together in decision-making, they also began to develop a shared sense of mission to the locale. Sharing the same neighbourhood, they encountered the same social problems and increasingly sought to respond to problems of welfare and support of families as a body rather than along denominational lines. Again, for the Catholics the learning here was to look beyond the traditional walls of the fortress and to recognize the importance of outreach, not least social, to the community at large.

This was all possible because the learning was mutual. Although the two communities shared much worship in common, the particular exigencies of Roman Catholic sacramental teaching were not only respected, but increasingly understood. The pain that this could cause was always allowed to speak: genuine receptive ecumenical learning is not without its cost, and does not accommodate quick-fix, easy solutions.

CONCLUSION

If the overall demand placed on the churches today is to respond in a changing social landscape to Christ's call to evangelization, then each denomination must negotiate a way forward that permits it to hold with integrity what is essential to its authentic existence and yet be open to the real opportunities presented by learning from and with other denominations. Openness to receptive ecumenical learning is needed now more than at any time since the restoration of the hierarchy in the last century. Yet, faced with the choice between seeking to secure that which is known, and moving into a different terrain, especially one with a new ecumenical dimension, the instinct to maintain the known can prove overwhelmingly attractive. However, that instinct will not respond to the demands that the Gospel places upon us. Nor will it form a secure basis for re-imagining the Roman Catholic community within this country. That is a delicate task that requires that we resist simple responses and easy solutions, and calls instead for creative imagination, an openness to learn, and a willingness to revisit and re-engage with one's own tradition beyond the constraints of the socio-religious construct within which one was originally formed.

NOTES

1. See Chapter 1: Paul D. Murray, 'Receptive Ecumenism and Catholic Learning—Establishing the Agenda'.
2. Most iconically in the opening sentences: 'The joy and hope, the grief and anguish of the men [and women] of our time, especially of those who are poor or afflicted in any way, are the joy and hope, the grief and anguish of the followers of Christ as well. Nothing that is genuinely human fails to find an echo in their hearts'. *GS*, § 1.
3. See ' "Gay weddings" first for Belfast' (19 Dec. 2005), available at <http://newswww.bbc.net.uk/1/hi/uk/4540226.stm>.
4. See 'Cleric attacks "gay weddings" law' (4 Dec. 2005), available at <http://newswww.bbc.net.uk/1/hi/wales/south_west/4492024.stm>.
5. Bishops of the Church of England, 'Civil Partnerships—A Pastoral Statement from the House of Bishops of the Church of England' (25 July 2005), available at <http://www.cofe.anglican.org/news/pr5605.html>; also *Church Times* (16 Dec. 2005).
6. Martin Prendergast, 'Compatible Not Competing—Pastoral Practice and Civil Partnerships' (2003), available at <www.titipu.demon.co.uk/samesexunions/compatcompete.htm>.
7. For an overview of the secularization debate, see William H. Swatos Jr. and Daniel V. Olson (eds.), *The Secularization Debate* (Lanham Md., Boulder Colo., New York, and Oxford: Rowman & Littlefield, 2000); Grace Davie, Paul Heelas, and Linda Woodhead (eds.), *Predicting Religion: Christian, Secular and Alternative Futures* (Aldershot: Ashgate, 2003). For a more recent revisiting of the terrain, see David Martin, *On Secularization: Towards a Revised General Theory* (Aldershot: Ashgate, 2005).
8. See Steve Bruce, *Religion in Modern Britain* (Oxford: Oxford University Press, 1995); id., *God is Dead: Secularization in the West* (Oxford: Blackwell, 2002).
9. See Davie, *Religion in Britain Since 1945: Believing Without Belonging* (Oxford: Blackwell, 1994); id., *Europe the Exceptional Case: Parameters of Faith in the Modern World* (London: Darton, Longman & Todd, 2002).
10. See Bruce, 'Praying Alone? Church-going in Britain and the Putnam Thesis', *Journal of Contemporary Religion*, 17 (2002), 317–28; Davie, 'Praying Alone? Church-going in Britain and Social Capital: A Reply to Steve Bruce', ibid., 329–34.
11. Michael P. Hornsby-Smith, *Roman Catholics in England: Studies in Social Structure Since the Second World War* (Cambridge: Cambridge University Press, 1987); also David G. Barker, *Change, Communication and Relationships in the Catholic Church* (Chelmsford: Matthew James, 2002).
12. See John Bohstedt, 'More than One Working Class: Protestant–Catholic Riots in Edwardian Liverpool', in John Belchem (ed.), *Popular Politics, Riot and Labour: Essays in Liverpool History, 1790–1940* (Liverpool: Liverpool University Press, 1992), 173–216; Tom Gallagher, 'A Tale of Two Cities: Communal Strife in Glasgow and Liverpool before 1914', in Roger Swift and Sheridan Gilley (eds.), *The Irish in Victorian Britain: The Local Dimension* (Dublin: Four Courts Press, 1999), 106–29.
13. Liverpool Archdiocesan Archives, Chancellor's Returns, Box IX.

14. For an example from Liverpool in the 1950s, see Madeleine Kerr, *The People of Ship Street* (London: Routledge & Kegan Paul, 1958).

15. See Mary Douglas, *Natural Symbols: Explorations in Cosmology* (London: Routledge, 2003).

16. McGrail, *First Communion: Ritual, Church and Popular Religious Identity* (Aldershot: Ashgate, 2006).

17. Ryan, *The Catholic Parish: Institutional Discipline, Tribal Identity and Religious Development in the English Church* (London: Sheed and Ward, 1996), 199 ff.

18. The Canon Law Society of Great Britain and Ireland, *The Canon Law: Letter and Spirit. A Practical Guide to the Code of Canon Law* (London: Geoffrey Chapman, 1995), canon 537.

19. Ibid., canon 536.

23

Receptive Ecumenism, Ecclesial Learning, and the 'Tribe'

James Sweeney, CP

INTRODUCTION

In the heady days of Catholic ecumenism just after the Second Vatican Council, I attended a great public lecture in Dublin given by one of my philosophy teachers, in which he situated ecumenism in a grand historical perspective as the inner religious requirement of a unifying (or, as we would now say, globalizing) world. Ecumenism was 'just right', and especially right in the prospective the 1960s were unveiling. Looking back now from our postmodern perch it is easy to think this naive and scorn the implicit suggestion of historical inevitability. And yet, the link between religious impulse and social and political forces should not be underestimated.

What was underestimated, of course, were the countervailing forces to unity—how globalization mobilizes localism, Utopias re-engage traditions, levelling down provokes a re-marking of boundaries. Victor Turner alerted us to the liminal moments when structure is displaced by *communitas*, but of course the contrary movement is inevitable when structure re-emerges—apparently stronger than ever.[1] Driven not only by theological imperatives but by real-life impulses and repulses, sociological and anthropological dynamics are inevitably engaged in the ecumenical project. Consequently, the socio-logic of ecumenism has to be respected as well as its theo-logic.

Ecumenism has been described as an exchange of gifts, so it has to take account of a certain 'ritual' aspect. Gift-giving is rule-governed, an orderly process, and there are cramps and opportunity costs to be reckoned with. A gift is not always welcome; some would be inopportune; the wrong gift at the wrong time miscommunicates and may destroy a relationship. Ecumenical Greeks bearing gifts warrants wariness—and clearly ecumenism must beware of making any offers others 'cannot refuse'!

As this volume explores, it is precisely in the receiving rather than the giving that the real challenge lies. The present paradox is that all are agreed that ecumenism is the non-negotiable call of the Lord, but no one knows how to surmount the *new* obstacles that diverging ecclesial practices and moral positions are creating. The temptation is to turn away sadly. More challenging is to receive the gift.

However, we need not be naive. These are not the most generous of times. We struggle with sweeping transformations of society and church. We inhabit a remarkably fluid world; familiar landmarks are obscured, if not demolished, leaving us on the lookout for whatever comfort comes to hand. Religion is caught up in a clash of cultures, bursting anew upon the scene in a guise to confirm the worst secularist fears—fanatical, absolutist, intolerant. More 'reasonable' variants are still to be found, but the archetype to which it is feared even well behaved Anglicanism or Catholicism might regress is what Peter Berger has dubbed 'furious religion'.[2] In all the din of controversy—religious conservatives settling policy in the White House and Downing Street, more faith schools to peddle creationism and intelligent design, a law against religious hatred suppressing freedom of speech, the Muslim veil challenging school uniform policy—what hope is there of calm receptivity?

As Catholics, we might be tempted to regroup behind the barricades. The sociological take on Catholicism is that over the last forty years it has begun to transcend its self-imposed institutional impregnability. The code for that was 'the fortress church'—a Catholicism closed to external sources of learning and content in its ideological self-sufficiency.[3] The counterpart at the local level, especially in Britain, was the 'ghetto parish', the Catholic system of cultural defence over against a hostile society.[4] This, to use the anthropological term, is 'the Catholic tribe'.

Tribalism is usually thought of negatively. But for the anthropologist the tribe is a virtuous term: a social grouping at a certain stage of economic and cultural development with a clearly delineated identity; a distinct people with its own special characteristics and history; a coordinated system of mythical beliefs and practices; the repository of cultural values and artefacts. The tribe's delicate ecology is perennially under threat from the remorseless logic of globalization, and anthropologists quickly become tribal defenders. It is not surprising, then, that it was anthropologists such as Mary Douglas and Victor Turner who were quick to raise critical questions about the post-Second Vatican Council dissolution of 'tribal Catholicism'.

What capacity do religious 'tribes' have for ecumenical openness? Are they capable of the necessary self-transcendence? And what does that involve? Receptive Ecumenism may be ingenious theologically, but a cost–benefit analysis at the popular level shows the difficulties. Skilled ecumenists can negotiate the theological obstacles in the path of unity, deftly framing contradictory positions on, say, the Eucharist as deriving from different theological paradigms, so that, as a fuller vision loosens their grip, the way opens for a re-articulation of the common inheritance. At the grass-roots level, however, theology has other resonances:

as a marker of communal identities reinforced by the legacy of history—the Mass (Catholic) and the Bible (Protestant); devotion to Mary and the saints versus one unique Saviour; the authority of the Pope over against individual religious freedom. The Second Vatican Council itself stands as a warning. The Council threw open the gates of the fortress, which was in tune with the church's deep sense of its own universality and properly rebalancing its relationships with others, but it also put established Catholic identities under pressure. Tribal ecology came under threat.

How can the underlying processes of communal identity formation be accommodated? How to get beyond the simple tribalism of establishing identity over, against, and, even hostile to, the foreign 'other'? Can we envisage a shift in favour of an 'ecumenical tribe'? This essay explores such questions in four movements: (1) Catholic identity, between the universal and the particular; (2) receptive ecumenical learning: the overcoming of tribal prejudice; (3) irreducible difference: the limits of receptive ecumenical learning; and (4) discerning the conditions for receptive ecumenical learning.

CATHOLIC IDENTITY, BETWEEN THE UNIVERSAL AND THE PARTICULAR

The fundamental issue is a familiar one, the universal and the particular, and it lies at the heart of Christianity as a faith imbued with a universal vision yet sunk in the contingency of history, with a belief in the God who is One and transcendent and yet revealed in the man Jesus. The practice of this faith involves paradox. We must respect the necessary boundaries of the human while impelled to break out beyond them. Seemingly of two minds, this actually exhibits the elusive paradox of Christianity itself. Put concretely, the open community has its boundaries; and not simply as a concession to human frailty, but because the drive to oneness and universality will dissipate unless it is held and channelled in the visible, sacramental community of the faithful.[5]

The 'tribe' has its place. Too easy a move beyond the tribal frontier spells danger. Boundaries must first be marked before they can be transgressed; borders are breached only if previously guarded. This being so, it means that forces of both attraction and repulsion are in play in relations between churches and communities. The central question is identity, a dominant concern today not only for ecumenism but in social life and politics more generally in our complex and pluralist world, where identity politics have come to the fore. In any concern for Receptive Ecumenism, we have, therefore, to reckon with the social psychology of identity formation.

Historic identities are forged in a dynamic process set in train by the determining events in the life of a people—a revolution, a victory, a conversion, a persecution. These set a fundamental pattern of orienting beliefs and motivations, a 'frame' within which group life moves and which determines reactions, alliances, hostilities. Identity is laid down as group life moves repeatedly within the frame and the group carves out its own specificity from the range of social possibilities. The process is not simply self-referential because groups (nations, communities, churches) have to engage with others. Selfhood is acquired by repeated engagement from within the determined frame which reinforces communal beliefs and values. In David Martin's apt phrase: 'societies, like human beings, need to repeat themselves'.[6] As new generations pass through the frame, repetition becomes reproduction, while, at the same time, variations are explored renewing and extending the frame, and in this way learning occurs. 'Steady state' is a balance between stability and openness, neither over-determined by the frame nor destabilized by external influences.

The 'fortress church' and the 'ghetto parish' can be understood as examples of frame. A secular historic example would be the Cold War frame of East–West politics between 1945 and 1989 which held until the internal contradictions of Communism and the contradictions between the frame and the pressures for globalization forced collapse. Closer to the ecumenical agenda, the Reformation and Counter-Reformation set the frame of routinized transactions between the Catholic and Protestant peoples of Europe for four centuries, until it began to unravel in the social upheavals of the Second World War and collapsed (except in Northern Ireland) in the cultural revolution of the 1960s.

In fact, of course, the equilibrium of 'steady state' is unusual and frequently disrupted. We see this in current crises in the church. Celibacy, for example, is central to the established frame of the Catholic priesthood which has, over the centuries, consolidated in a specific priestly identity. But this is put to the test by the drop in vocations in the West and the exposure of failures on the part of some priests to live up to celibacy's requirements. It is always possible—natural even—to cling to received identities and meanings, but such efforts must eventually face the test of realism. The attempt to manage the crisis within the current frame may ultimately result in a new flowering of priestly vocations, but this cannot be taken for granted.

What triggers thinking 'outside the box'? Are there moments when, in Martin's phrase nodding to Marx, we are 'nearly ready'? What might drive a community, a historic tradition, a 'tribe' to look outside its established frame for what it needs to renew, or to recover its self-understanding? I suggest that one condition is some systemic contradiction disturbing the collective consciousness, spurring self-awareness that the 'tribe' does not have within itself the answers to the challenges its faces. Then the impetus to self-transcendence may erupt. Of course, systems may simply react defensively to such cultural crises, but they can also be moments of creative breakthrough.

We might imagine, then, that Catholicism, engulfed in multiple cultural crises, is poised for just this sort of breakthrough: the crisis of transmission of the faith to the next generations; the crisis of vocations; the crisis over collegiality; over the participation of the laity; over sexual ethics; the crisis of confidence because of clerical sexual abuse. Can all this be met by the Catholic Church in sovereign independence? Equally, the crisis of Anglicanism over homosexuality and over admitting women to the priesthood (and, more pointedly, to the episcopate) is driving the Communion to the edge of self-destruction. Is it a spur to look beyond Anglican boundaries for solutions?

RECEPTIVE ECUMENICAL LEARNING: THE OVERCOMING OF TRIBAL PREJUDICE

Ecumenical learning from 'the other' clearly involves very complex transactions when 'the other' represents those with whom one has been locked in conflict and over against whom one's ecclesial identity has been forged. Prejudices, myths, and ingrained views of Catholics about Anglicans and Anglicans about Catholics abound (to say nothing about the mutual views of Anglicans and Methodists), and there are historic resentments, sometimes unacknowledged, sometimes repressed. It is hardly surprising if the praxis and spiritual attitude of ecumenical learning are rare. An eirenic willingness to learn from the other may be an easy habit for the academic mind, but it is not the norm of everyday life.

Even so, it has to be acknowledged that grassroots ecumenism has had its successes in terms of new learning, drawing on the experience of different denominational traditions and their accumulated wisdom and practice in such fields as action for justice, mission, and liturgy. Ecumenical progress has been driven just as much by new levels of cooperation between ordinary churchgoers as by theological investigation. One example among many would be the evangelization group in a Roman Catholic parish in the centre of Southampton which grew out of their enthusiastic involvement in a city-wide mission organized by the Evangelical Alliance.[7] One group member, an elderly married lady from a traditional Catholic background, told of a further event in Devon where she was part of the ecumenical team delivering a comprehensive programme of street and community evangelism to the whole town. Here is a person and a parish group whose vision of faith, mission, and ecumenism has clearly transcended what might be expected from fortress Catholicism.

This is one instance of a small but growing number of groups and agencies dedicated to evangelization.[8] Taking their cue from the Alpha programme and the new religious communities, they emphasize explicit proclamation—not quite 'furious religion', but certainly enthusiastic religion. They tend to have rather warm ecumenical relations. The denominational allegiance of potential converts (or 'reverts') is not an issue, but Catholic agencies do have a feeling for the distinctiveness of their own tradition, especially its sacramental emphasis. CaFE (Catholic Faith Exploration), for example, was founded as the Catholic counterpart to Alpha—although not by any hierarchical agency but by a voluntary group. The movement has its own distinctive sense of mission, rather different from groups devoted to social and political issues (e.g. Justice and Peace) but, like them, ecumenically attuned.

Such convergences of Christians of different stripes come about in face of the challenge a secular society poses to religion itself, and as a result of now widely shared modes of spiritual expression such as Charismatic renewal. The 'tribes' have made peace. At the same time, there are areas where historic conflicts are engaged, when the churches' identity dynamics drive them apart, even re-locking them in conflict. It is then that forces of repulsion rather than attraction are in play.

IRREDUCIBLE DIFFERENCE: THE LIMITS OF RECEPTIVE ECUMENICAL LEARNING?

The Catholic and Anglican crises mentioned above would appear to be instances counter-indicative of ecumenical learning. Many Catholics—including those in the hierarchy—are likely to say 'Whatever we do about our internal crises, let's not do what the Anglicans do. Look where it's got them!' And the prospect of the Church of England entering a self-denying ordinance on women in the episcopate because Rome has not given the green light runs clean contrary to the process hitherto followed, not to say to the Reformation claim of national church self-determination.

It would appear, then, that we are faced with some irreducible differences. On this range of issues—overtly, issues of sexuality and ministry, but, more fundamentally, their ecclesiological ramifications—there seems little foreseeable capacity for receptive ecumenical learning. This is not to say that intelligent conversation does not go on. Rather, it is that neither can receive from the other their respective distinctive insights or practices, because their ecclesial identities and the dynamics by which these are expressed remain, as they historically always have been, in conflict. The Protestant principle and the Catholic principle do not converge.

This is not yet to say anything about the theological case for or against women's ordination or about sexuality, but is simply an analysis of the dialogical relationship that is ecumenism. The particularities of historic identities, pushing churches in different directions, have consequences at the level of decision-making and practice. Even though these are questions of high ecclesiastical policy, the dynamics are not so different from the grass-roots level of the tribe where, despite their warmer relations, Catholics and Protestants still cherish their different symbols of identity, rubbing against each other rather awkwardly when corralled at ecumenical events. Socio-logic can be more powerful than theo-logic.

The attempt may be made to resolve the differences in such cases by reaching an 'agreed position', which can be either a shallow compromise ('Let's agree to be different') or the triumph of one position over the other (Anglicans getting Catholics to acknowledge the validity of women's ordination, or Catholics having Anglicans accept their Communion's limited authority to alter traditional practice). Facile unity schemes, however, are not only unstable but may actually damage the ecumenical cause by hardening theological stances and stoking grass-roots resistance. The 'tribes' can hit back. Ecumenism is best served by openly acknowledging the depth of the differences. Far from being a misfortune, the current impasse could actually be the start of 'real' ecumenism.

What is encouraging is that despite the new obstacles none of the churches has closed down on ecumenism.[9] Even the Anglican decision on ordaining women, which changes the terrain by 'putting new facts on the ground', while it has knock-on effects in terms of Roman recognition of Anglican Orders and the possibility of establishing inter-communion, has not derailed the process of growing together.[10] Equally, the steely stance of the Vatican on what it sees as weaknesses in the ARCIC agreements has not undermined further theological effort. What is frankly acknowledged on all sides is that unity is not to be expected as the fruit of ecclesiastical diplomacy but as a gift from the Lord. This is what keeps the process on track. Moreover, the globalizing world—globally integrated as well as in global conflict—heightens the anomaly of religious disunity and encourages renewed effort.

If, then, the mere fact of disturbance in a church community's collective consciousness because of systemic limitations may not be enough to spur it to ecumenical openness and learning from the other, what else needs to come into play? Here, we are operating at the very limits of social experience, but some clues may be garnered from historic instances.

DISCERNING THE CONDITIONS FOR RECEPTIVE ECUMENICAL LEARNING

Among Catholicism's many new openings to 'the other' in recent decades, its revaluation of relations with Judaism is perhaps the most far-reaching theologically. A deeply embedded antagonism going back to the very origins of Christianity has, in principle, been set aside with the recognition that God's covenant with the Jewish people is not revoked or simply superseded in the Christian dispensation. Thus, there has dawned a fresh perception of them as

'our elder brothers (and sisters) in the faith'. Of course it took the tragedy of
the Shoah and the soul-searching this forced upon Catholicism about being
implicated historically in loading the role of scapegoat upon the Jewish people to
trigger the change. The church was *shocked into* transforming its stance.

The Second Vatican Council itself, the major event in twentieth-century
Catholicism, was driven in part by a recognition that the church needed to learn
from modern secular society. The clearest examples are in *Gaudium et Spes* and
Dignitatis Humanae, where there is a frank admission of the church's indebted-
ness to the world on such matters as religious freedom.[11] After centuries of bitter
conflict with the hostile forces of modernity, the church had to be rescued from
its own (partially understandable) social and cultural blindness. At a certain point
after the Second World War, a feeling emerged in significant quarters, especially
the theological community, that an era dating from the Reformation and the
Enlightenment was ending, and in the council this acquired critical mass.

In another field, the South African Truth and Reconciliation process is rightly
hailed as a major breakthrough in the operation of political processes. The whole
society, its various parties and agencies, including the churches, have had to face
the fact of being implicated in the deep oppressions of apartheid. The Dutch
Reformed Church in particular was led to the painful recognition of its lapse
into heresy by giving the system biblical and theological justification. A similar
challenge arises with the Rwandan genocide. In a Catholic country neighbour fell
upon neighbour simply because of different ethnic origins, and Christian faith
neither restrained the evil nor apparently prevented some priests and nuns from
taking part. The humiliation of all too obvious moral failings spurs recognition
of one's need of forgiveness—one's need of the other.

A common thread here is the making of a new beginning and an orientation to
the future. Dealing with the past is necessary, but for the sake of the future. This,
I would suggest, is a key factor in effective ecumenical dynamics. Ecumenism
has to have eyes for 'the shape of the church to come'.[12] If we compare the
South African political settlement (and more recently Northern Ireland) with
Israel/Palestine, we see that in South Africa the road to the future is open and
building that future can galvanize the energies of the whole society (even if there
is continuing discontent among blacks, and only grudging acquiescence on the
part of some whites, and they have to deal with the huge setback of the HIV-
AIDS epidemic), while the peace process between Israel and Palestine is stalled,
as neither side seems convinced of a two-state solution, suspecting that the other
side would only implement it to their disadvantage. In Northern Ireland a truce
has been called between Catholic and Protestant tribes; it is likely to last, and
a resurgence of ancient enmities avoided, just as long as there is an effective
commitment to building a new future.

When it comes to the future for religion, there are deep problems. Christians
in the West have a hard time coming to terms with the secularization of their

societies. In fact, the modern ecumenical movement arose when secularization was already triggering the long institutional decline of the churches and awareness dawned that in a post-religious age competitive antagonisms were ridiculous. This came about earlier for Protestants than Catholics, because in general their institutional decline started earlier, but Catholicism's entry into the movement in the 1960s coincided with the downturn in its fortunes (in the West). However, an ecumenical 'circling of the wagons'—with atheistic secularism replacing the religiously 'heretical other' as the new enemy—is not a compelling image of the future, and may indeed trigger further secularization.[13] The Christian 'tribes' coming together in coalition to combat the wider world would still be mere tribalism. Moreover, it runs the risk of a reductionist lowest common denominator type of ecumenism which would supersede the 'tribe' by ironing out historic identities and repressing the identity dynamics of particular Christian traditions. This finds little resonance in the religious imagination.

Very few, of course, espouse lowest common denominator ecumenism, but on the other hand robust declarations of individuality are discomforting. To be too Catholic—or too Anglican or Methodist—is seen as a problem. Here lies the challenge.

Church communities are socio-cultural creations as well as faith responses to the Word, and faith and culture cannot simply be separated out; faith must find cultural expression. In this sense, the 'tribe'—the particular and distinct community—is not antipathetic but belongs to the Gospel, in the same way that in the Divine dispensation *one* chosen people, the Jews, and *one* man, Jesus, constitute the offer of *universal* salvation.[14] The implication is that the ecumenical goal in discerning the shape of the church to come should be to enhance particularity, to cherish the maximum diversity of expression of authentic church order, not permit the minimum. Such idealism is also, paradoxically, the most realistic path to take since it respects actual church communities.

This is a special challenge to Catholicism, because, while it is not as monolithic as it sometimes seems, but a real communion of local churches, its dynamics are universalist. In fact, one could say that the role of Catholicism within Christianity is to represent universality. While Anglicanism or Methodism or Lutheranism or Orthodoxy also have universal and international dimensions, their bias is to the local and the particular. In that sense, ecumenical relationships are asymmetrical. But, if the Catholic Church accepts the integrity of other Christian traditions, as it has done since the Second Vatican Council,[15] what are the implications in terms of church order?

What is now becoming clear is that new issues along the ecumenical way arise, inevitably, because individual churches not only have different practices but run on different lines. It is part of the particular identity of Anglicanism stemming from its Reformation origins to reach decisions, even about matters of church order, in its own synodical way, quite different from the Catholic way in which the role of the magisterium is entrenched. This is even more the case with, for example, Presbyterian church order. While the Anglican controversies over women bishops and homosexuality are critical in themselves—for the Anglican communion as well as ecumenically—they are symptomatic of the broader ecumenical challenge: how to respect and accommodate different ecclesial dynamics and the *emerging* practices that arise from different understandings of authority and ways it is exercised? How to live between the particular and the universal, the 'tribe' and the 'oikumene'? How to respect the expression of historic identities while maintaining unity?

Ecumenism has not only to resolve but also accommodate differences in ecclesial practice. George Lindbeck explores a related issue with the thesis that previously polarized theological traditions can achieve consensus while maintaining continuity with their previous historical positions because doctrine is essentially the 'grammar' rather than the 'content' of belief, and so can deliver different, even convergent, readings in changed contexts.[16] Agreement is won without denying difference.

Can something similar hold for practice? This is more speculative. Unlike the dialogue about doctrine where the goal is to supersede past differences, the issue here is of practice that is becoming newly divergent. To what extent could practices that apparently stand in contradiction—permitting and forbidding the ordination of women, for example—be seen as legitimate diversity? Can the circle be squared? The traditional dictum is: 'in essentials, unity; in the doubtful, liberty; in all things, charity'.[17] That, however, is a somewhat static formula, and it runs into the difficulties of how to define the essentials, and of who, prior to unity, gets to define them? Many more issues could be brought into play here—whether, for example, the Pope's *jurisdiction* as codified in Roman Catholic law is essential, or whether different ways of acknowledging the Petrine office would be legitimate.

There are basic theological questions about the nature of ordination and authority which clearly cannot be circumvented, but which are not our concern here. Our issue is the dynamics of institutional relationships and where they lead. High matters of ecclesiastical politics and negotiation are involved. The similarities with secular affairs are worth noting. International bodies such as the European Union also have to accommodate diversity in unity and are in the business of inventing new kinds of structure to meet the realities of a globalized world. The lessons from ecclesiastical experience would be a valid contribution to these debates. On the other hand, the church could learn from political peace processes and conflict resolution. For example, in Northern Ireland it was the recognition of the need to take account of the respective integrity of both communities and their legitimate aspirations that laid the groundwork for the Good Friday Agreement. A global and comprehensive view of the issues is necessary to avoid becoming blocked by immediate dilemmas. Ecumenism has to take issues in the round.

CONCLUSION

Where, then, are the 'tribes' in all this? What hope is there of an 'ecumenical tribe'? Church communities, from parishes to whole denominations, are fiercely protective of their individuality. They resent it if they feel their beliefs and symbols and hallowed practices are being tampered with, and in circumstances of political or cultural threat militant religion is always apt to revive. Yet, religious communities also have a generosity of spirit, and as long as their traditions and spiritual ways are respected they are open to learning from others. The particularity of the religious 'tribe' can be a trap, but it is also a strength if wise leadership keeps the community's perspectives open. In today's circumstances, where historic identities are under threat from so many corrosive influences, these are difficult balances to strike.

It might be thought that only rarely are churches open to external sources of learning. The Catholic Church in particular often seems stubbornly to refuse to face up to the need for new ways. It has a track record of resisting change and it certainly will not be forced to change. However, matters are not so simple. As the Second Vatican Council demonstrated, Catholicism has its own way of changing: it absorbs historical change, eventually transforming itself in the process. This has something to do with the deep logic of Christianity, described as the paradoxical 'tradition of the critique of tradition'.[18] It is not an unyielding, immutable world, as it is often portrayed, but has its own dynamism. From its inception in the life and example of Jesus, Christianity is in contest with 'mere' traditions.

Its genuine spirit is, in fact, as a force for change. Christianity's deep energizing vision is 'the new heavens and the new earth'. Its language of 'analogy, paradox, oxymoron, inversion, conversion' is, according to Martin, 'set in the active-passive voice . . . (to) mount an attack on the frontier of social possibility'.[19] The church's mission, moreover, directs it to the renewal and reshaping of society, not to dwell in its own enclave. The challenge, then, is to see Christianity 'not as a set of propositions but as a repertoire of transforming signs in historic engagement with the deep structures of power and violence'.[20]

In this perspective, the churches will only re-establish their role in late modern society if they succeed in cultivating a reflexive and self-critical identity, humble enough and secure enough to engage in dialogue.[21] As such, the ecclesial virtues at issue in Receptive Ecumenism and Catholic Learning are not simply of intra- and inter-ecclesial significance but of profound extra-ecclesial significance, bearing directly on the authentic mission of the Church. In this context, the role of the leader, the thinker, the theologian is to persist in the patient and imaginative search for ways through present dilemmas in service of the 'new thing' God is always doing.

NOTES

1. Turner, *The Ritual Process: Structure and Anti-structure* (Chicago, Ill.: Aldine, 1970).
2. See Berger, *A Far Glory: The Quest for Faith in an Age of Credulity* (New York: Free Press, 1992), 32.
3. See Michael P. Hornsby-Smith, *Roman Catholic Beliefs in England: Customary Catholicism and Transformations of Religious Authority* (Cambridge: Cambridge University Press, 1991).
4. See Anthony Archer, *The Two Catholic Churches: A Study in Oppression* (London: SCM, 1986).
5. Cf. 'The Church is a dam and builds up enormous potentiality inside it. Unless the divine is held back in sacred space, inside churches, or behind altar rails under priestly control, there will be no build-up. Without quiescence, latency and passivity there is no power, only wastage. So the institutional church is a channel of power and also a temporary but necessary barrier against the premature realization of power. In any case, as Marx pointed out, mankind only takes up those problems for which it is nearly ready.' David Martin, *The Breaking of the Image* (Oxford: Blackwell, 1980), 13.
6. Id., *A General Theory of Secularisation* (Oxford: Blackwell, 1978), 15.
7. Research interviews for a project on evangelization and renewal initiatives in the Roman Catholic Church in England and Wales (research report: *Going Forth*), Von Hügel Institute and Margaret Beaufort Institute, Cambridge, Nov. 2006.
8. See the Catholic Agency for the Service of Evangelization (CASE), an agency of the Catholic Bishops' Conference.
9. In the internal Anglican crisis such openness is under threat with the possibility of a formal schism.
10. The recent warnings by Cardinal Kasper about the consequences of the Church of England ordaining women bishops do, however, indicate the significance of this development for the traditional ecumenical goal of working towards full structural unity; see Chapter 2, n. 23, above.
11. See esp. Vatican II, '*Dignitatis Humanae*: Declaration on Religious Liberty' (7 Dec. 1965), in Austin Flannery (ed.), 799–812 (§ 12) and *GS*, § 44; also Sweeney, 'Catholicism and Freedom: *Dignitatis Humanae*— The Text and its Reception', in E. Arweck and P. Collins (eds.), *Reading Religion in Text and Context* (Aldershot: Ashgate, 2006), 17–33.
12. Cf. Karl Rahner's future-looking pastoral ecclesiological work of this title, *The Shape of the Church to Come*, trans. Edward Quinn (London: SPCK, 1974).
13. See Alan Gilbert, *The Making of Post-Christian Britain: A History of the Secularization of Modern Society* (London: Longman, 1980), 125–30, interpreting ecumenism as further evidence of secularization.

14. See William T. Cavanaugh, 'Church', in P. Scott and W. T. Cavanaugh (eds.), *The Blackwell Companion to Political Theology* (Oxford: Blackwell, 2003), 393–406.

15. Even allowing for all sorts of qualifications and the subsequent austerity of *Dominus Iesus* about the terminology of 'Church'.

16. See Lindbeck, *The Nature of Doctrine: Religion and Theology in a Postliberal Age* (London: SPCK, 1984).

17. Quoted by John XXIII in his first encyclical, '*Ad Petri Cathedram*: Encyclical Letter on Truth, Unity and Peace in a Spirit of Charity' (29 June 1959), § 72, available at <http://www.vatican.va/holy_father/john_xxiii/encyclicals/documents/hf_j-xxiii_enc_29061959_ad-petri_en.html>.

18. Henri-J. Gagey, 'The Need for a Political Theology in Post-modern Times', unpub. paper, presented to the International Association of Catholic Social Thought, Leuven, 2002.

19. Martin, *The Breaking of the Image*, 129.

20. Id., 'Personal Reflections', in Richard K. Fenn (ed.), *The Blackwell Companion to Sociology of Religion* (Oxford: Blackwell, 2001), 23.

21. See Anthony Giddens, *Modernity and Self-Identity* (Cambridge: Polity Press, 1991); also Paul D. Murray, *Reason, Truth and Theology in Pragmatist Perspective* (Leuven: Peeters, 2004).

24

Organizational Factors Inhibiting Receptive Catholic Learning

Thomas J. Reese, SJ

INTRODUCTION

In the context of this volume of essays by distinguished theologians and ecumenists, my task is not a pleasant one. I have been asked to identify and reflect upon the organizational factors militating against receptive ecumenical learning within Roman Catholicism. In other words, I have been asked to throw cold water in the face of ecumenical hope and optimism. Perhaps I have been given this job because I am a social scientist and a former journalist rather than strictly a theologian. As a social scientist and journalist I am a congenital cynic and pessimist, even though as a Christian one has to be a born-again optimist.

I am reminded of a parent–teacher night at a Jesuit high school in California where the concerned parents asked the physics teacher why their son was not doing well in his class. The teacher's response was, 'Your son is either lazy or stupid. Which of you does he take after?' We Catholics might ask the same question about our failure as receptive learners: are we stupid or lazy?

In politics and religion in the United States, journalists are always trying to divide the world into two camps: liberals and conservatives. Conservatives believe that people are basically immoral—that is why we need police, prisons, and a big military so that conservatives can scare everyone into acting like conservatives. Liberals, on the hand, believe that people are basically stupid—that is why we need better schools, more education, and dialogue, so that liberals can persuade everyone to think like liberals. The Catholic Church, on the other hand, has always taught that people are both immoral and stupid—we call that original sin, the only doctrine for which we have empirical evidence.[1]

Bernard Lonergan would, of course, have put this more elegantly. The human project, he maintained, requires intellectual, moral, and religious conversion, and such conversion is not easy.[2] To be attentive, to be intelligent, to be reasonable, to be responsible, and to be loving require hard work. It is easier to be inattentive, thoughtless, unreasonable, irresponsible, and selfish. Our personal, group, and cultural biases keep us from adopting a higher viewpoint from which to see new solutions to our problems.

In the synopsis presented here of what I consider to be the political and organizational factors militating against receptive ecumenical learning within contemporary Roman Catholicism I will be very un-Catholic and begin at the bottom, with the parish and the people in the pews. I will focus mainly on the United States since that is the context I know best. Because of the wide variety of churches present there, the United States has more ecumenical dialogues going on than any other country in the world. We have got everybody in significant numbers, and they are spread in various proportions throughout the country.

PEOPLE IN THE PEWS

Roman Catholics in the United States have accepted the ecumenical direction of the Catholic Church since the Second Vatican Council. If anything, the Catholic laity is more at ease with ecumenism than the hierarchy. Even before the council, Roman Catholics began moving out of the urban ethnic ghettos into the more diversified suburbs as they became better educated and upwardly mobile. In the suburbs, at school, and in the workplace Roman Catholics met Protestants with whom they became friends and colleagues. Most American Roman Catholics do not feel threatened by Protestants. While there are still pockets of anti-Catholicism in the States (primarily in the South), it has significantly declined.[3] Most of what passes for anti-Catholicism in the States today is motivated not by the legacy of the Reformation but by liberal opposition to the bishops' positions on abortion, gay rights, and condoms. The first two issues have in fact made political bedfellows out of the Roman Catholic bishops and historically anti-Catholic Evangelical leaders.

Although American Roman Catholics generally favour ecumenism, most have little patience with the complex theological discussions that theologians and the hierarchy consider the heart of the ecumenical dialogue. They have already made up their minds that these doctrinal issues do not really matter; they do not understand what the fuss is all about. This indifference to theology is fuelled by the widespread ignorance of the laity on religious issues.

While in the past, most non-Catholics converted to Roman Catholicism when they married a Roman Catholic, this is no longer true. Roman Catholics are now just as likely to jump ship. It depends on which partner takes his or her faith more seriously. It also depends on where they feel most welcome. There are also a growing number of ecumenical couples who rotate between churches. This ecclesial fluidity has not just affected those in ecumenical marriages. About 56 percent of Roman Catholics under 40 years of age say that they 'could be happy in another church', a position taken by only 37 percent of those aged 63 or older.[4] In short, many of the people in the pews believe that they are way ahead of the clergy in terms of ecumenism, especially when it comes to things like intercommunion.

On the other hand, many in the hierarchy accuse the laity of relativism or cafeteria Catholicism. This concern has merit since conservative Roman Catholics frequently reject Catholic social teaching whilst liberal Roman Catholics reject Catholic teaching on sexual issues. While many theologians subconsciously use political models in describing the church (members are citizens with right and responsibilities), most Americans subconsciously see religion as a consumer product to which they apply a cost–benefit analysis: 'What's in it for me? What good does it do? Is it worth the time and effort?' In this sense, we are seeing a weakening of 'brand loyalty' among Roman Catholics.

As organized groups, lay people are attempting to flex their muscles but with very limited results. *Call to Action*, one of the oldest groups on the left, has been unsuccessful in recruiting new members, especially among the under-fifties. *Voice of the Faithful*, which began in Boston in response to the sex abuse crisis, has found bishops unwilling to dialogue with it. Meanwhile, groups on the right see their role as spies for Vatican officials, whom they flood with letters and emails of horror stories (some true, some not, and most exaggerated) about what is going on in the American Roman Catholic Church. All these groups are attempting to use websites, e-newsletters, blogs, and other Internet technologies to promote their cause and communicate with members. This is extremely important because while people might become discouraged when they find only a couple of likeminded people in their parish, the Internet allows them to be connected to thousands of people who think as they do. Whether this will lead to anything in the future remains to be seen.

PRIESTS

American Catholic priests are also generally very supportive of ecumenism. They have supported pulpit exchanges, ecumenical covenants, and joint social projects on the parish level. But priests are so overworked that they can hardly keep up with their normal parish duties, let alone have time for ecumenical activities. The Roman Catholic clergy are getting older and fewer. They will support ecumenism as long as it does not mean they have any more meetings to attend.

Most older priests will not enforce the rules against intercommunion if a non-Catholic spouse comes up to Communion. They feel frustrated in promoting pulpit exchanges because the Vatican and the bishops are telling them that the Protestant minister has to preach at the end of Mass, not after the Gospel. Many priests feel that this is so insulting that they are embarrassed to ask the ministers from other traditions to preach under these conditions. In one Roman Catholic diocese where a liberal parish allowed a Protestant minister to preach after the Gospel and help give out Communion, the vicar general used it as an excuse to launch an inquisition that included making the parish staff answer questions under oath.

With regards to younger priests and seminarians, one wonders how interested they will be in ecumenism. Very few American diocesan seminarians are trained in an ecumenical setting where they would take courses with Protestant seminarians. Many of them see their role as re-establishing orthodoxy in the Roman Catholic Church rather than reaching out to ecumenical partners. Their standard of orthodoxy is not the Scriptures, nor the Second Vatican Council; it is the 1992 *Catechism of the Catholic Church*. As a group, their academic credentials are not stellar. Many would not meet the entrance requirements for the better Catholic universities in the United States. This will cause friction. While in the past the pastor may have been the best educated person in the parish, today that is not the case. An educated faithful will not tolerate clerical arrogance. More Roman Catholics who leave the church do so because of clericalism rather than because of theological disagreements.

THEOLOGIANS

The Roman Catholic theological community enthusiastically embraced ecumenism after the Second Vatican Council. Hundreds of Roman Catholic theologians generously give time and effort to ecumenical dialogues. Roman Catholic theologians and their students read Protestant theologians; a number got their degrees under Protestant mentors in Protestant or secular universities; many Catholic universities have hired Protestant theologians. Theological conventions and conferences normally have ecumenical input, and Roman Catholics and Protestants meet together in conventions such as that held by the American Academy of Religion. In addition, some Catholic schools of theology (especially Jesuit and other religious orders) are in ecumenical consortiums.

But while they were dialoguing with other churches, Roman Catholic theologians found dialogue and conversation within their own communion became more and more restricted. Bishops, who gladly meet with a Protestant cleric or theologian, generally shy away from meeting with any Roman Catholic theologian who is under a cloud of suspicion. Scores of theologians, especially priests and religious, were reprimanded, silenced, or removed as a result of Roman intervention, some publicly, others privately. As a result, most theologians practise self-censorship because they do not want their orthodoxy questioned. They avoid topics that would get them in trouble. While tenure and academic freedom can protect lay theologians, Rome uses ecclesial channels to control clerical and religious theologians through their bishops and religious superiors. There were even attempts to control lay theologians through the 'mandatum docendi' of *Ex Corde Ecclesiae.*[5]

The result is a huge chasm between the magisterium of the hierarchy and the magisterium of the academy. In secular terms, this would be the equivalent of a conflict between management and the research division of a multinational corporation. No one in their right mind would invest in such a company since it would have lost it ability to be innovative and respond to its environment.

DIOCESAN BISHOPS

Moving up the ladder, we come to the diocesan bishops.[6] Again in the United States, bishops have been supportive of ecumenism. Many dioceses established covenants with local Protestant churches; many bishops meet on a regular basis with other local Protestant leaders; and churches often work together on charitable and justice issues; larger dioceses, until they got in financial trouble, had ecumenical offices. In general, however, the American bishops are managers before they are theologians. Practically none of them was a prominent academic before becoming a bishop. Again, none of the current American bishops attended the Second Vatican Council, and most were trained in seminaries that had not been influenced by it. In other words, they were neither converted by the experience of the council (unlike their predecessors), nor educated by professors who were imbued with its spirit.

But is this a uniquely American problem? I think not. It is shocking, for example, that one of the leaders of the 2005 Synod on the Eucharist opined that 'No one has a right to the Eucharist', and had to be corrected by the head of the Signatura.[7] Likewise, it is telling that the Pope had to intervene and explain to the bishops that the Eucharist is both a sacrifice and a meal.[8]

Despite all of this, the American bishops generally support ecumenism even though they are not sure what they are supposed to do. Like their pastors, they are pressed for time, and while some bishops make ecumenism a priority, others do not, depending on their interests and the ecumenical make-up of their diocese. Some bishops have been extraordinarily active in dialogues for many years. They are all happy to pray with Protestants and make common cause for social justice. When it comes to doctrine and the Eucharist, however, they defer to the Vatican.

Finally, as everyone knows, the US bishops as a group are under siege because of the sexual abuse crisis. This could have been avoided if early on some of them had been willing to take responsibility for their mistakes and resigned. Their credibility is at a low point, and they have little time to think about ecumenism when they must spend their time strategizing with lawyers, responding to victims, giving depositions, suspending priests, and being sued. Three dioceses have gone into bankruptcy, and the Archdiocese of Los Angeles may face a bill of one billion dollars in lawsuits. Under these circumstances ecumenism is placed on the back burner. Sadly, there is little evidence to show that the community of Roman Catholic bishops outside the United States has learned from the mistakes of the American bishops.

It may be a generation before the bishops regain their credibility, and that will only take place if bishops are appointed who have pastoral skills. But, as long as unquestioning loyalty is the principal quality looked for in episcopal candidates, the quality of episcopal leadership will be challenged.

BISHOPS' CONFERENCES

After the Second Vatican Council, bishops' conferences were revitalized and became important institutions in the church, but during the papacy of John Paul II they came under suspicion and attack.[9] No one symbolized this ecclesiastical flip-flop better than Joseph Ratzinger, who as a priest was a strong supporter of episcopal conferences, but switched his views as Prefect of the Congregation for the Doctrine of the Faith. Once, meetings of the United States Conference of Catholic Bishops were exciting and hopeful; today they are boring and tedious.[10] There has been a tendency in the conference to promote clerics over more competent lay staff. Many of the staff are demoralized, and some, including those with ecumenical expertise, have left for the greener pastures of academia.

Despite the downgrading of episcopal conferences, the USCCB continues to support important official dialogues with the Orthodox, the Polish National Catholic Church, Anglicans, Lutherans, Reformed, Methodists, Southern Baptists, and the Faith and Order Commission, as well as other relationships with African American churches, Pentecostal, Holiness and Evangelical churches, Mennonites, Brethren churches, the Society of Friends, Disciples of Christ, and the National Council of Churches.[11] These dialogues have received strong support and significant time commitments from prominent bishops such as Cardinals Lawrence Shehan, William Baum, Bernard Law, William Keeler, James Francis Stafford, and Archbishops Rembert G. Weakland, and Oscar H. Lipscomb. Other bishops and numerous theologians have also been involved.

The reports coming from these dialogues have often led the way for international dialogues. But one wonders if anyone except the participants is paying much attention.

The USCCB has good relations with the National Council of Churches. It is not a member for a number of reasons, including the fact that, because of its size, it could control the organization if it joined. In November 2004, the Roman Catholic bishops agreed to help form and join Christian Churches Together, a less bureaucratic and more inclusive organization than the National Council of Churches, that will operate under consensus rules. Whether this experiment goes anywhere remains to be seen.

THE VATICAN

I have no doubts about the commitment of the Pope and the Vatican to ecumenism. The transformation of the Vatican's views on ecumenism from before the Council to now has to be listed as one of the greatest examples of organizational conversion in the history of the world. We have come a long way from the days of sneaking the episcopal primate in the back door of the Vatican so that his picture could not be taken (let alone from the days of rabid condemnations).

But these successes are in fact part of the problem. All of the easy things have been done. Apart from recent notable highpoints such as the signing in 1999 of the *Joint Declaration on the Doctrine of Justification* with the Lutheran World Federation,[12] ecumenism today largely seems to be a series of papal photo opportunities with visiting Protestant or Orthodox leaders, or the release of another dialogue report, which no one will read, or another ecumenical prayer service.

The Pontifical Council for the Promotion of Christian Unity and the Council for Interreligious Dialogue are two of the best run and competently staffed dicasteries in the Vatican.[13] They are among the few dicasteries that have, in recent years, been headed by people (Walter Kasper and Michael L. Fitzgerald) who are actually experts in the fields for which they are responsible.[14]

On the other hand, these offices clearly played second fiddle to the CDF during the papacy of John Paul II. The CDF is primarily concerned about doctrinal orthodoxy. It fears creativity because this might lead to error despite the fact that only through creativity can doctrine develop and obstacles be overcome. This problem is exacerbated by the fact that the heavy screening of its consultors for loyalty and orthodoxy means that input into the congregation's discussions is severely limited.

The staffing of the Vatican more generally is a serious issue that will have ramifications for ecumenism in the future. In the past, the best and the brightest of the Italian clergy were recruited into the curia. This is no longer true. Today,

Italy has a severe vocations crisis. Only a handful of Italians are students at the Pontifical Ecclesiastical Academy. Whilst there are exceptions, in general it is only the more conservative of American and European priests who are attracted to the curia or recruited to it. For most First World priests who are creative and pastoral, the Vatican is a place to avoid.

The European hold on the curia is also slipping. For a conservative Third World priest, the Vatican is extremely attractive not only theologically but also as a step-up in lifestyle. If you visit nunciatures around the world, the nuncio will often be Italian, but his secretary and staff will usually be from the Third World. These Third World priests will run the Vatican in the future. This future can be seen in the Congregation for Divine Worship, where the prefect is from Nigeria and the secretary is from Sir Lanka. What this will mean for ecumenism is unclear. Will it be the 'revenge of the colonies', where the Third World enforces its view of Christianity on the First? Or, will a Third World vision find a way beyond what they consider irrelevant European Reformation disputes? The power of Third World bishops in the Anglican Communion may have some lessons for Catholics.

For the immediate future, we will probably see more continuity than change between the papacies of John Paul II and Benedict XVI. It is difficult to think that the concerns of Cardinal Joseph Ratzinger as prefect of the CDF will disappear with his election as Benedict XVI. We will continue to see a Vatican very concerned about the wording of ecumenical agreements. Anything that departs from traditional formulations of doctrine will be carefully scrutinized. Clarity that divides will be preferred to any ambiguity that might unite (e.g. his concern over which Christian communities can be called 'churches').[15] His often articulated concern about the dangers of 'relativism' shows where he puts his priorities.[16] The radical nature of the Second Vatican Council will be played down, and continuity with the past will be stressed.[17]

Perhaps this is one of the problems of electing a very bright theologian as Pope? He knows too much; before he was elected, he had already made up his mind on most issues. Prior to the 2005 conclave, I suggested that rather than electing the brightest man in the room, it would be preferable for the cardinals to elect the man who was willing to listen to all the other bright people in the room and in the church.[18]

The cardinals certainly elected one of the brightest men in the room, and his meeting in the summer of 2005 with Hans Küng was seen as a hopeful indication that he might be able to listen to other bright people. Pope John Paul II would never have met with Küng. On the other hand, the Vatican made a point of stressing that the two had not discussed areas of disagreement. The 2005 appointment of William Levada as Prefect of the CDF is also a hopeful sign, but granted Benedict's earlier track record as Prefect of the Congregation, it is not likely that the breach between theologians and the Vatican will be mended easily.

In addition, unlike Pope John Paul II, the then Cardinal Ratzinger expressed some dissatisfaction with the Second Vatican Council documents, especially *Gaudium et Spes*, which he believed 'took insufficient notice of sin and its consequences, and was too optimistic about human progress'.[19] And if Benedict truly believes in a smaller, purer, more orthodox church, then both ecumenists and Roman Catholic theologians will have rough going. The Roman Catholic Church will move in the direction of becoming a sect rather than the big umbrella church of the past.[20] This is most disconcerting for American Roman Catholics. Vatican policies lost European males during the nineteenth century. Today, Vatican policies are alienating educated Roman Catholics in the United States, especially women, who are most responsible for passing on the faith to the next generation.

CONCLUSION

As I said at the beginning, as a social scientist and journalist I have a pessimistic view of the future of the Roman Catholic Church. My chapter makes it sound as if the church is on a course of self-destruction. I hope and pray that I am wrong and would be delighted to be so. Do not, however, misunderstand me; I do not predict a collapse of the church. Throughout history, those who have predicted the demise of the church have underestimated its resilience. Rather, I think that Roman Catholicism has reached a plateau on which it will be stuck for some time into the future. This may have been all right in the days when the world changed at a glacial rate, but today political, cultural, and social changes occur at light speed. The church can no longer take decades or centuries to respond to change.

The impact of church policy may in fact be exactly the opposite of what the hierarchy desires. For example, if the number of priests continues to decline, then the opposition to married priests and celibate gay priests will help complete what the Reformation began: the declericalization and desacramentalization of the Roman Catholic Church. If this dire forecast comes true, then various Protestant churches may in the future have to pick up the slack and serve the Roman Catholic people. Already, inroads are being made in Latin America by evangelicals because there are too few priests to minister to the people.

In the past, we used to see reform of the Roman Catholic Church as essential to ecumenical progress. Today, the reverse is also true: ecumenism is an essential path to church reform. With the Vatican and much of the hierarchy refusing to talk to Roman Catholic reformers and 'dissident' theologians, it will be up to our ecumenical partners to point out to the hierarchy the importance of reform for ecumenism. Today, Protestant theologians have an easier time getting a hearing from the bishops and the Vatican than do many Roman Catholic theologians.

Church history teaches that there are periods of progress when the church responds with intelligence, reason, and responsibility to new situations. Periods of decline have also marked the church, when individual and group biases blinded people to reality, hindered good judgment, and limited true freedom. Although this is true of any organization or community, what distinguishes the church is its openness to redemption, which can repair and renew Christians as individuals and as a community. Despite their weakness and sinfulness, Christians have faith in the word of God that shows them the way; Christians have hope, based on Christ's victory over sin and death and his promise of the Spirit; and Christians have love that impels them to forgiveness and companionship at the Lord's table. As a Christian, I have to believe that the future of the church and any programme of Receptive Ecumenism and Catholic Learning must be based on such faith, hope, and love.[21]

NOTES

1. Cf. Bernard Lonergan, 'Healing and Creating in History', *A Third Collection: Papers by Bernard J. F. Lonergan, S.J.*, ed. Frederick E. Crowe (London and New York: Geoffrey Chapman/Paulist Press, 1985), 101–2.
2. See Lonergan, *Method in Theology* (London: Darton, Longman & Todd, 1972), esp. 130–2, 237–44, and 267–9.
3. See Philip Jenkins, *The New Anti Catholicism: The Last Acceptable Prejudice* (Oxford: Oxford University Press, 2003).
4. See William V. D'Antonio, et al., *American Catholics: Today* (Lanham, Md.: Rowman & Littlefield, 2007), 32.
5. Pope John Paul II, '*Ex Corde Ecclesiae*: Apostolic Constitution on Catholic Universities' (15 Aug. 1990) (Vatican City: Libreria Editrice Vaticana, 1990); available at <http://www.vatican.va/holy_father/john_paul_ii/apost_constitutions/documents/hf_jp-ii_apc_15081990_ex-corde-ecclesiae_en.html>.
6. See Reese, *Archbishop: Inside the Power Structure of the American Catholic Church* (San Francisco, Calif.: Harper & Row, 1989).
7. 'Top Church Law Expert Says Catholics Have Right to Receive Eucharist', *Catholic News Service* (11 Oct. 2005), available at <http://www.catholicnews.com/data/briefs/cns/20051011.htm#head10>.
8. 'Synod Members Seek Balance: Eucharist as Sacrifice, Communal Meal', *Catholic News Service* (10 Oct. 2005), available at <http://www.catholicnews.com/data/briefs/cns/20051010.htm>.
9. Reese (ed.), *Episcopal Conference: Historical, Canonical and Theological Studies* (Washington, DC: Georgetown University Press, 1989).
10. See id., *A Flock of Shepherds: The National Conference of Catholic Bishops* (Kansas City, Miss.: Sheed & Ward, 1992).
11. For a list and brief history of these dialogues, see <http://www.usccb.org/seia/> and http://www.usccb.org/seia/history.shtml>.
12. Since also signed by the Methodist World Conference at Seoul in July 2006.

13. For a detailed look at Roman dicasteries, see Reese, *Inside the Vatican: The Politics and Organization of the Catholic Church* (Cambridge, Mass.: Harvard University Press, 1996); also John L. Allen Jr., *All The Pope's Men: The Inside Story of How the Vatican Really Thinks* (New York: Doubleday, 2004).

14. In 2006, the Council for Interreligious Dialogue was merged with the Council for Culture and Archbishop Fitzgerald was appointed Apostolic Nuncio to Egypt. If he had still been in the Vatican and read the Pope's 12 Sept. 2006 Regensburg address, he would doubtless have been able to offer invaluable prior advice.

15. See the CDF's 'Note on the Expression "Sister Churches"' (30 June 2000), available at <http://www.vatican.va/roman_curia/congregations/cfaith/documents/rc_con_cfaith_doc_20000630_chiese-sorelle_en.html>.

16. See Joseph Komonchak, 'The Church in Crisis: Pope Benedict's Theological Vision', *Commonweal* (3 June 2005), 11–14.

17. Benedict XVI, 'Address to the Roman Curia' (22 Dec. 2005), available at <http://www.vatican.va/holy_father/benedict_xvi/speeches/2005/december/documents/hf_ben_xvi_spe_20051222_roman-curia_en.html>.

18. Cf. here John Courtney Murray, 'Good Pope John: A Theologian's Tribute', *America* (15 June 1963), 844–5, where Courtney Murray noted that whilst John XXIII was no great scholar, he would go down in history as the 'theologian's Pope', as opposed to Pius XII who tried to be the 'theologian's theologian'. The point being that John raised questions and encouraged discussion rather than giving definitive answers.

19. Avery Cardinal Dulles, 'From Ratzinger to Benedict', *First Things*, 160 (Feb. 2006), 25.

20. One area where there may be progress is with the Orthodox. In addition, Benedict may be able to find common ground with Lutherans in their mutual love for Augustine.

21. Reese, '2001 and Beyond: Preparing the Church for the Next Millennium', *America* (21–28 June 1997), 10–18.

PART V

RETROSPECT AND PROSPECT

Prologue to Part V
Revelation 1: 9–18

Philip Endean, SJ

I, John, your brother, who share with you in Jesus the persecution and the kingdom and the patient endurance, was on the island called Patmos because of the word of God and the testimony of Jesus. I was in the spirit on the Lord's day, and I heard behind me a loud voice like a trumpet saying, 'Write in a book what you see and send it to the seven churches, to Ephesus, to Smyrna, to Pergamum, to Thyatira, to Sardis, to Philadelphia, and to Laodicea.'

Then I turned to see whose voice it was that spoke to me, and on turning I saw seven golden lampstands, and in the midst of the lampstands I saw one like the Son of Man, clothed with a long robe and with a golden sash across his chest. His head and his hair were white as white wool, white as snow; his eyes were like a flame of fire, his feet were like burnished bronze, refined as in a furnace, and his voice was like the sound of many waters. In his right hand he held seven stars, and from his mouth came a sharp, two-edged sword, and his face was like the sun shining with full force.

When I saw him, I fell at his feet as though dead. But he placed his right hand on me, saying, 'Do not be afraid; I am the first and the last, and the living one. I was dead, and see, I am alive for ever and ever; and I have the keys of Death and of Hades.'

The Word is sent to seven churches; it nourishes communion; it exists only in communion. Hence our sacred words, our sacred values, are always dynamic. The Word establishes us in ever new forms of community, generates ever new expressions. The one church subsists always in plurality, multiplicity. Catholic identity is thus something constantly to be discovered, through the kind of ongoing cyclical process that the pioneers of ecumenical dialogue found themselves engaged in. By sharing the Word, we develop new relationships; by developing new relationships, we are led back anew to the Word, and challenged to let it permeate us more deeply.

The Word's power can be terrifying, consuming, destabilizing; all too easily we are tempted to regress to less demanding, static travesties. Yet at its heart is an assurance from the One who is the first and the last, who was dead and is now alive for ever and ever, who holds the keys of Death and Hades.

Thus there is always more to fidelity than mere repetition; more to obedience than conformity; more to tradition than doing things the way we have always done them. It is in and through our relationships, in and though our mutual resonances before the mystery of God, that the Word transforms. St Augustine expressed the principle well in a sentence quoted in Andrew Louth's chapter. Augustine is writing about Christian teaching, and speaking of the affective power released when two spirits are somehow in real communication: '[W]hen people are affected by us as we speak and we by them as they learn, we dwell each in the other, and thus both they, as it were, speak in us what they hear, while we, after a fashion, learn in them what we teach.' Such has been the experience to which this volume bears witness. May we not be deaf to the call which that richness contains, but rather prompt and ready to carry forth God's Word, in the sure hope that yet more light and truth will ever break out from it, until that day when Christ's most holy will for unity is perfectly fulfilled.

25

Receptive Ecumenism and Catholic Learning—an Orthodox Perspective

Andrew Louth

INTRODUCTION

It is an enormous privilege to be asked to take part, as an Orthodox priest and theologian, in this exercise in Receptive Ecumenism. The primary focus is on what Roman Catholics can learn from other Christian confessions but we are all clear, I think, that the process of listening—critical and reflective listening—must always be a two-way process: it is not a matter of one group listening to another group, or other groups, but rather mutual listening, and mutual reflection on a process of learning in which we all share. St Augustine, as usual, has valuable thoughts on the process in which we are engaged, when reflecting on another learning process, that of catechesis. There, he says, sympathy—the ability to suffer or endure with another is crucial; as he puts it: 'For so great is the power of sympathy, that when people are affected by us as we speak and we by them as they learn, we dwell each in the other and thus both they, as it were, speak in us what they hear, while we, after a fashion, learn in them what we teach.' (*Tantum enim valet animi compatientis affectus, ut cum illi afficiuntur nobis loquentibus, et nos illis discentibus, habitemus in invicem; atque ita et illi quae audiunt quasi loquantur in nobis, et nos in illis discamus quodam modo quae docemus.*)[1]

There is a problem about seeking to learn from Orthodoxy, and I think it would be honest to mention this to begin with, and that is that Orthodoxy sees itself as a seamless unity of faith, worship, and practice: you cannot pick and choose, the very essence of Orthodoxy is immersion in a way of life. One of the abbots of the Holy Mountain of Athos has said that Orthodoxy is contained, par excellence, 'in the *Paraklitiki*, the *Triodion* and the *Pentecostarion*'[2]—the three basic service books containing the liturgical poetry used in Orthodox services throughout the year: Orthodox theology is not neatly summarized, it is something prayed and sung. Orthodoxy also emphasizes the role of the spiritual father—the elder, or the *starets*. Here, again, one simply accepts initiation into a way of life; one does not choose what to listen to from one's spiritual father. One of the greatest Orthodox theologians of the last century, who died in Stalin's Gulag, Pavel Florensky, expressed this aspect of Orthodoxy well in the first letter of his remarkable work, *The Pillar and Ground of the Truth*:

The indefinability of Orthodox ecclesiality . . . is the best proof of its vitality . . . What is ecclesiality? It is a new life, life in the Spirit. What is the criterion of the rightness of this life? Beauty? Yes, there is a special beauty of the spirit, and, ungraspable by logical formulas, it is at the same time the only true path to the definition of what is Orthodox and what is not Orthodox. The connoisseurs of this beauty are the spiritual elders, the *startsy*, the masters of the 'art of arts', as the holy fathers call asceticism . . . The Orthodox taste, the Orthodox temper, is felt but it is not subject to arithmetical calculation. Orthodoxy is shown, not proved. That is why there is only one way to understand Orthodoxy: through direct Orthodox experience . . . to become Orthodox, it is necessary to immerse oneself all at once in the very element of Orthodoxy, to begin living in an Orthodox way. There is no other way.[3]

My task has, however, been made easier by Paul McPartlan's chapter here on eucharistic ecclesiology and its development by Metropolitan John of Pergamon (John Zizioulas). Fr Paul expounds with great learning one aspect of Orthodox theology from which he shows us the Roman Catholic Church has already learnt, since the germs of a eucharistic ecclesiology, as found in Nikolai Afanasíev,[4] had a genuine influence on the doctrine of the church expressed in the Second Vatican Council's Dogmatic Constitution on the Church, *Lumen Gentium*.[5] In his chapter, Fr Paul shows how such a eucharistic ecclesiology has been developed by Metropolitan John, and how this development holds out prospects for further Receptive Ecumenism on the part of the Roman Catholic Church, especially over the question of primacy.

My remarks that follow are primarily critical, but they are not properly speaking critical of Fr Paul's exposition of Metropolitan John's ecclesiology, nor are they critical of his emphasis on eucharistic ecclesiology, for such an approach to the doctrine of the church seems to me profoundly Orthodox. My remarks are primarily *self*-critical, that is critical of the way such a eucharistic ecclesiology is worked out in the life of the Orthodox Church, for it seems to me that there is a real danger when reading Metropolitan John, or appreciative expositions of his thought, of being lulled into a sense that this is how we Orthodox live our ecclesiology. The reality is, I fear, rather different.

EUCHARISTIC ECCLESIOLOGY AND RECEPTIVE ORTHODOX LEARNING

Fr Paul makes reference to Henri (later Cardinal) de Lubac and his great work *Corpus Mysticum*.[6] In that book de Lubac explored the way in which in the

West the term *corpus mysticum*, 'mystical body', changed its reference between the ninth and the eleventh centuries. Originally it referred to the eucharistic body of Christ—*mysticus* meant 'sacramental', one of the usual meanings of the Greek word *mystikos*—but over the turn of the millennium it came to refer to the church, the 'mystical body of Christ', while the eucharistic body came to be called *verum corpus*, 'true body', identical with the historical body of Christ. This shift of signification broke the link between the church and the Eucharist, for instead of the 'mystical body' of the Eucharist constituting the church, the eucharistic body came to be seen as the making present of the historical, 'true' body by the power of the priest, and the reality of the church came to be seen as the 'mystical body', the 'hidden body', distinct from the historical reality of the actual community of the church.

Once the inner reality of the church was thought of as the 'mystical body', the actual church was simply thought of as a historical institution, founded by Christ, preserved by the apostolic succession, and ruled by the successor of St Peter, the Pope. The 'mystical body' itself, being hidden, soon came to be identified with the 'elect' predestined to salvation, and western ecclesiology found itself trapped between an all-too-visible institution and an all-too-invisible community of the elect. This account is, of course, hugely oversimplified, but will do as a sketch. De Lubac's book, *Corpus Mysticum*, was published in 1944 (though the Preface was dated 1939), a year after Pope Pius XII's encyclical on the church, *Mystici Corporis Christi*, which made the notion of the church as the 'mystical body of Christ' central to its exposition.

Quite why the Eastern Orthodox Church did not go down the route of the western church in its understanding of the 'mystical body' I am not sure, but the Orthodox Church did preserve a sense that the eucharistic body was both 'true' and 'mystical' and constitutive of the community of the church; the prayers read before communion seem to me to affirm this clearly—in the 'mysteries' we participate in what is 'itself' Christ's 'pure body' and 'precious blood'. It is also the case that as the Orthodox reflected on the meaning of the eucharistic sacrifice, instead of starting from the link between the eucharistic sacrifice and the sacrifice of Christ on the cross, something the West tended to do, it started from the link between the eucharistic sacrifice and Christ's eternal self-offering in heaven.[7] This also had the effect of underlining the Eucharist as a cosmic liturgy—something, too, that Fr Paul rightly asserts is entailed by a eucharistic ecclesiology.

This sense of the celebration of the Divine Liturgy constituting the church is something, too, that has been brought home to the Orthodox Church by centuries of living under harassment and persecution, in which periods the faithful celebration of the Mysteries has been *the* act that affirmed and preserved the church. In the second millennium there has scarcely been a century in which some Orthodox Christians have not been persecuted by the civil powers under which they have lived. This is not to say, however, that we Orthodox have not understood—and experienced—the church as a hierarchical institution. We have indeed—but more of that later.

For such reasons, I would argue that eucharistic ecclesiology is indeed fundamental to the Orthodox Church's sense of itself as the church. However, it was not until the last century that this eucharistic ecclesiology found explicit theological expression. Fr Paul points to that aspect of eucharistic ecclesiology he calls communal—expressing *communio* or *koinonia*. But such an emphasis in Orthodox theology was originally expressed without any reference to the Eucharist itself. For an ecclesiology focused on the idea of *communio, koinonia*, or *sobornost'* was popular in nineteenth-century Russia. The most famous proponent of such an ecclesiology was the Russian nobleman and thinker, Alexei Khomiakov. But Khomiakov's ecclesiology made virtually no reference to the Eucharist. The Eucharist is, of course, an expression of *sobornost'* (a term, incidentally, that Khomiakov does not appear to use),[8] but for the most part Khomiakov discusses his *soborny* ecclesiology by talking of the church simply as communion.

This idea of the church became part of a dispute over the nature of the church in nineteenth-century Russia, between those who saw the church in terms of communion or *sobornost'*, expressed first of all at the local level, and those who saw it more in terms of hierarchy, understood in a mostly quite strident top-down way. This dispute continued through the nineteenth century into the twentieth, as Vera Shevzov has recently demonstrated in her splendid book, *Russian Orthodoxy on the Eve of Revolution*,[9] and lay behind the famous 1917–18 synod (*sobor*) of the church that was cut short by the Revolution. Many of the émigrés shared the ideals expressed by the reforming party at the synod. What we see in Afanasíev, I think, is an attempt to find a deeper justification for the reforming ecclesiology of *sobornost'*. For, in exile, there was no longer anything corresponding to the *symphonia* between church and State with which the Orthodox had lived for centuries (even under the Ottomans, the principle was preserved): the émigrés had to rethink what they were as a 'church' in exile and as exiles.

Fr Paul has mentioned how these émigrés were conscious of the difference between the Orthodoxy they brought with them and the Catholicism they encountered in Paris, and there is no question that they were conscious of a manifold difference—it is manifest in the works of Sergei Bulgakov, for instance. But it was not just difference they encountered; they also encountered a renewed interest in the Fathers in the French Catholic Church, the revival associated with the names of de Lubac, Daniélou, and others—something that they found very congenial. There was regular and friendly contact between Catholics, Orthodox (and Protestants) at the so-called Berdyaev Colloquium, hosted by the émigré philosopher, Nikolai Berdyaev. It was not just a matter of Catholics like Daniélou learning from Orthodox like Myrrha Lot-Borodine a sense of the creative importance of the Fathers;[10] the émigrés themselves found a lively interest in the Fathers among their Catholic and Protestant friends.

It is significant that the principal Father appealed to by Afanasíev in his 'eucharistic ecclesiology' is St Ignatius of Antioch, one of the so-called 'Apostolic Fathers', who is also the inspiration for the Greek theologians, John Romanides[11] and Metropolitan John.[12] For we should recall that this designation—'Apostolic Fathers'—is not a traditional ecclesiastical one, but one invented by the scholars of the seventeenth century, the intellectual heirs of Renaissance scholarship. The prominence of the Apostolic Fathers in our sense of who the Fathers are is a result of western scholarship of the Renaissance and later—the texts of many of the Apostolic Fathers were discovered by such scholars, after centuries of loss or neglect, as in the case of Ignatius himself, the authentic text of whose epistles was discovered in the seventeenth century by the scholars Archbishop Ussher and Gerhard Jan Voss. Afanasíev probably already knew about the Apostolic Fathers from nineteenth-century Russian translations, for there had been a veritable patristic revival in nineteenth-century Russia, but that revival had drawn on western scholarship too.

The point of recalling all this is that the patristic witnesses to which Afanasíev and other Orthodox have recourse is not just a matter of tradition; it is also a matter of western patristic scholarship. The revival of Patristics in the western Catholic world in the twentieth century—and the making available of a host of texts and translations—has helped shape what is meant by 'the Fathers' in twentieth-century Orthodox theology. It is not as if we are opening for you a great treasure that we possess, it is rather than we Orthodox owe a great debt to western scholarship for access to the Fathers, who assume such an important role in our tradition. Our sense of the Fathers has been enriched by western— mainly, but not only, Catholic—patristic scholarship, and with that enrichment our sense of what is meant by the 'mind of the Fathers' has changed and developed. Our sense of the 'mind of the Fathers', and in particular the development of eucharistic ecclesiology, is really an example of Receptive Ecumenism on our part.[13]

EUCHARISTIC ECCLESIOLOGY: RHETORIC AND REALITY

My other reflections concern a point raised by Fr Paul in a rather different context, when he refers to 'the mystery of the one Eucharist celebrated by local churches spread over the face of the world', and adds: 'and I stress *this* world'. When I hear Fr Paul and other western Christians waxing eloquent about Orthodox ecclesiology, I find myself recalling the words of our Lord: 'The scribes and the Pharisees sit on Moses' seat; therefore, do whatever they teach you and follow it; but do not do as they do, for they do not practise what they teach' (Matt. 23: 2–3). I am afraid the same applies to us Orthodox. We are eloquent about our wonderful eucharistic ecclesiology: but what sign is there of it in our practice?

The traditional Orthodox countries are organized on the basis of a system that goes back to the Byzantine or Roman Empire, where the organization of the church reflected the organization of the Empire: bishops in cities, metropolitans in provinces, and what later came to be called patriarchs corresponding very roughly to the areas governed by Praetorian Prefects (now, they tend to correspond to nations). It is institutional: the very word we Orthodox use with such horror when we look to the West! Outside the traditional Orthodox countries, we have what we still call the 'diaspora', where there is a tangle of, if not actually competing jurisdictions (though in some countries, Estonia, for example, it has seemed like that), at any rate different jurisdictions, very far from anything that might be in accord with a 'eucharistic ecclesiology', with one bishop in each place, around whom all the Orthodox gather (the only place in the diaspora I can think of where this ideal is realized is Wichita!). It is, indeed, worse than that. 'Diaspora' Orthodox are mostly organized into exarchates, with an archbishop appointed by the relevant patriarch (the only exceptions I can think of are the Orthodox Church of America, granted autocephaly by the Moscow Patriarchate in 1970, and the Archdiocese of the Antiochene Patriarchate in the United States, granted autonomy in 2003); under these archbishops/exarchs are suffragan bishops with no kind of episcopal independence.

The great Orthodox proponent of eucharistic ecclesiology, Metropolitan John of Pergamon, is himself simply a suffragan to the Patriarch of Constantinople, with no community over which he could preside: Pergamon is a rather fine archaeological site in Turkey, and Metropolitan John lives in Greece. The Ecumenical patriarch claims jurisdiction over such Diaspora Christians, in accordance with canon 28 of the Council of Chalcedon, on the grounds that they are 'barbarians' (though this argument is quite recent); such a claim is, not surprisingly, disputed by other patriarchates.

In practice, not only is there little trace of any kind of 'eucharistic' ecclesiology, there is often enough little trace of the *communio* or *koinonia*, that Fr Paul remarked on as characteristic of the ecclesiology of the first millennium and still of the Orthodox. *Koinonia* implies at least communication, and there is often little of that between patriarchates, especially between the patriarchates of Constantinople and Moscow. The remarks so ripely expressed by the great Jesuit scholar of the Byzantine liturgy, Father Robert Taft, a year or so back, about the Orthodox presence in the West, may have been undiplomatic, but they were hardly inaccurate.[14] I fear there is plenty more such dirty linen that could be washed in public.

There is, however, a more serious point to be made in this connection. For, in expositions of eucharistic ecclesiology (it is true of Afanasíev, Romanides, Zizioulas) there is tendency to demonize what is called an 'institutional' view of the church—to contrast the 'institution' unfavourably with the 'mystery' of the church. But this side of heaven the church is always going to have an institutional expression; what we need are institutions that express what we believe about the church, rather than frustrate it.

EUCHARISTIC ECCLESIOLOGY AND EUCHARISTIC PRACTICE

My other criticism or query asks, in another way, how far this 'eucharistic ecclesiology' corresponds to reality. What I have in mind is that in the Orthodox theologians who have put forward this ecclesiology (Afanasíev, Romanides, Zizioulas), it is always the eucharistic community gathered together with its bishop that is taken to be the norm or ideal, in this following the teaching of St Ignatius. My point is not to question the role of the bishop as the one in whom the fullness of Christian ministerial priesthood is found, but simply to query how far this picture of the church corresponds to reality.[15] In practice, the local eucharistic community gathers round a priest, not a bishop, and yet we would still want to say that 'the Eucharist makes the church' in that case, too.

In some ways, concentrating on the actual situation might solve some of the problems that have been raised about eucharistic ecclesiology, for no one of the Orthodox or Roman Catholic communions would want to abstract the bishop from the presbyteral Eucharist. The presbyter has not only to have been ordained by a bishop, but he has to have the bishop's permission to celebrate—conveyed symbolically in Orthodox practice by the use of an antimension provided by the bishop—and must mention the bishop's name in the eucharistic prayer (and also in the proskomide, along with the name of the bishop who ordained him). All of this prevents any understanding of the Eucharist as 'making the church' in any isolated way; so the problem of the 'one and the many' is already being faced. None the less, the Eucharist, thus celebrated, does make the church in the place where it is celebrated.

Let us push this a little further. It is not really the case that the norm for Orthodox and Catholic is the episcopal Eucharist, the presbyteral Eucharist being a permitted variant. I grant that it would be possible to argue this, especially in the Orthodox case, where the ceremonial of the episcopal liturgy is both different from and more primitive than the presbyteral Eucharist. None the less, it seems to me that there is no getting round the fact that the norm is, and has been for centuries, a presbyteral Eucharist: it is this that makes the actual ecclesial community to which Christians belong. A diocesan Eucharist, celebrated by the bishop with his clergy, is only a reality in small dioceses (like the one I belong to: the Diocese of Sourozh), but even then to see the diocesan Eucharist as the norm from which the parish Eucharist is a permitted variant seems to me to ignore the reality of the situation. The diocesan liturgy, even if possible, is cake to the parish liturgy's bread: and we consecrate bread, not cake.

I have no answer to this problem as to how 'eucharistic ecclesiology' relates to the practical reality of the presbyteral Eucharist, though one can think of several ways of pursuing it. Perhaps parish priests ought really to be bishops, grouped under a metropolitan; but this might, it could be argued, damage the bishop's role as articulating the unity of the church (though it would reflect the reality of the earliest experience of episcopacy). But if we are to start from where we are now, we need to give some consideration to the role of the presbyteral priest, and in doing that we may find ourselves impelled to give more concrete attention to the various ministries performed by the laypeople, who in the discussion of 'eucharistic ecclesiology' tend to be simply those, rather anonymously, gathered round the bishop.

RECEPTIVE ECUMENISM, SYNODALITY, AND *SOBORNOST'*

Another of the chapters in this volume, that by Joseph Famerée, seeks to find lessons for Catholic ecclesiology from the Orthodox, by reflecting on the closely related notion of 'synodality', which might well be translated in Russian as *sobornost'*. Again, like Paul McPartlan, Joseph Famerée gives an accurate picture of the dominant strand in much recent Orthodox reflection on the subject, in particular bringing out how many contemporary Orthodox theologians see in the Trinitarian life of the Godhead some kind of model for the *koinonia* that constitutes the church (appealing to John 17: 21–2 and, more dubiously, to the 34th Apostolic canon), and relating this to the emphasis, again characteristic of much recent Orthodox theology, on the apophatic. What Joseph Famerée does not take into account are the voices of not a few Orthodox theologians who are unhappy with what one might call such 'Being and Communion' ecclesiology, not least because its claims to be rooted in the theology of the (Greek) Fathers are demonstrably shaky.[16] But the kind of 'synodal' ecclesiology Famerée expounds so carefully is one that all Orthodox theologians would want to embrace, even if they traced its roots in rather different ways: by which I mean that his emphasis on mutuality—both horizontally, as it were, between bishop and bishop, and vertically, between bishop and synod (and patriarch and episcopal synod)—and his refusal to allow the local to be absorbed by the universal, or vice versa, are points that any Orthodox ecclesiology would want to emphasize.

However, as with Paul McPartlan's presentation of eucharistic ecclesiology, so with Joseph Famerée's presentation of synodal ecclesiology, I would beg that we attend to what happens, and not just to theory. Orthodox are just as good as Catholics at paying synodality little more than lip service. Some parts of the Orthodox world have a functioning synodal system—Romania, I am told (I have no direct experience). In other parts of the Orthodox world, the question of synodality has been a matter of careful consideration. I have already mentioned the Russian *sobor* of 1917–18, with its attempt to reform the structure of the Russian Church, in which there was a serious attempt to promote a thoroughly synodal understanding of the church—overtaken, alas, by the events of the Bolshevik revolution.[17] Since the Russian Orthodox Church regained its freedom in the years following *glasnost'*, however, there has, been little attempt to put the vision of this *sobor* into practice. In the Russian Diaspora there have, nevertheless, been attempts to model the life of the church on the vision of the *sobor*, in both the Diocese of Sourozh in Great Britain,[18] and the Exarchate for Orthodox of the Russian Tradition in Europe under the Ecumenical Patriarchate (which broke away from the jurisdiction of the Moscow Patriarchate in 1930), but these are rather small-scale experiments. The Orthodox Church of America has also a synodal structure modelled on the principles of the 1917–18 *sobor*. In the rest of the Diaspora synodal government is not much in evidence. As with eucharistic ecclesiology, we Orthodox need to address the correspondence of theory and reality.

During 2006, events in the Diocese of Sourozh, the Russian Orthodox diocese into which I was ordained and still belong, have demonstrated dramatically the chasm between theory and reality in Orthodox ecclesiology. Bishop Basil of Sergievo (the administrator of the diocese since the resignation of Metropolitan Anthony of Sourozh was accepted by Moscow, weeks before his death) sought release from the Moscow Patriarchate for himself, his clergy, and the parishes, and on being refused such release by Moscow appealed to the Ecumenical Patriarchate who accepted him under the authority claimed by the dubious interpretation of canon 28 of Chalcedon mentioned above. This action split the diocese, and had repercussions for the other Orthodox jurisdictions in Britain, and indeed worldwide.

Here is not the place, nor is the time ripe, to discuss this sequence of events, save, perhaps, to mention that it bears out my warning that Orthodox ecclesiology is not all it seems! However, during this period, some people said to me, as an Orthodox priest, and indeed a priest of Sourozh—and others refrained from commenting, out of a deeply appreciated kindness towards me—that what you Orthodox need is a pope! That would certainly be a help in such circumstances, and indeed it could be argued that the grounds cited by the synod of the Ecumenical Patriarchate for receiving Bishop Basil—canons 9, 17, and 28 of the Fourth Ecumenical Synod of Chalcedon—amount to a claim on the part of the Ecumenical Patriarchate to exercise a universal appellate jurisdiction, which is what the papacy claimed for itself (and exercised) in the first millennium!

It might be useful to conclude my contribution to this volume in a personal way by trying to explain why, despite the ecclesiological disarray manifest in the events of 2006, it has never occurred to me to think that Rome might provide a more secure harbour. For me, ultimately, it is not Authority that I see as constituting the church, but rather Tradition—tradition through which authority is mediated, tradition nourished by the prayer of Christians down the ages, and encountered most fully in the Divine Liturgy of the Eucharist.

I find myself in deep sympathy with what Pope Benedict XVI said in a book published while he was still Cardinal Ratzinger: *The Spirit of the Liturgy*.[19] From that densely argued book, there is one theme that seems to me of fundamental importance: what Pope Benedict has to say about the eucharistic liturgy as an apostolic tradition. This, explains the Pope, is meant in no vague sense that the Eucharist goes back to apostolic times, but in a more precise sense that the various forms of the eucharistic prayer—the *anaphora* or the *canon*—are associated with particular apostles: the Syrian rites with the apostles James and Thomas, the Egyptian with St Mark, the Armenian with the Apostles Bartholomew and Thaddeus. The 'two greatest families of rites', as the Pope puts it, the Byzantine and the Roman, draw on various of these traditions. From these observations, the Pope draws several conclusions, most strikingly the importance of respecting the organic growth of these liturgies: the various forms of the Divine Liturgy, and especially of the eucharistic prayer, are not human confections, but forms of prayer with a long history, so that we may think of them as part of the apostolic tradition.

The West seems to me to have fractured this sense of tradition. To put it bluntly, the various eucharistic prayers that emerged from the reforms occasioned by the Second Vatican Council, if apostolic at all, are scholarly reconstructions— that is, reconstructions based on scholarly (and not so scholarly) theories of apostolic traditions—they are not organic developments of a living tradition. If I am asked why I am Orthodox, it is because in the Orthodox Liturgy I have the overwhelming conviction of standing within the people of God before the face of God. We may make a terrible mess of representing that in appropriate structures, but of that central conviction I have no doubt.

CONCLUSION

To return to my original brief—to provide an Orthodox response to the sug- gestions by Paul McPartlan and Joseph Famerée as to what Catholics might learn from the Orthodox—I want to stress that such learning is not a one-way process, and I would suggest that 'eucharistic ecclesiology', in particular, should be seen as a striking example of Receptive Ecumenism on the part of both Roman Catholics and Orthodox. We might well have something to learn by looking at how this took place, and what effect such Receptive Ecumenism had. But I would add that if this is to lead us very far, we need to see how our ecclesiology both affects and addresses our actual ecclesial situations, and that involves paying some serious attention to how ecclesial institutions are to express our ecclesiology, rather than thwart it.

NOTES

1. Augustine, *De Catechizandis Rudibus*, trans. J. P. Christopher (Washington, DC: Catholic University of America, 1926), § 12 (p. 55).
2. Personal communication from Archimandrite Fr Ephrem (Lash), speaking of his own Athonite abbot.
3. Pavel Florensky, *The Pillar and Ground of the Truth*, trans. Boris Jakim (Princeton, NJ: Princeton University Press, 1997), 8–9.
4. Most easily available in English in his brief paper, 'The Church which Presides in Love', in Nicolas Afanasíev, et al. (eds.), *The Primacy of Peter in the Orthodox Church*, trans. Katherine Farrer (London: Faith Press, 1963), 57–110, repr. John Meyendorff (ed.), *The Primacy of Peter: Essays in Ecclesiology and the Early Church* (St Vladimir's Seminary Press, 1992), 91–143. See also, Afanasíev, *The Church of the Holy Spirit*, trans. Vitaly Permiakov (Notre Dame, IN: University of Notre Dame Press, 2007).
5. So Aidan Nichols, *Theology in the Russian Diaspora: Church, Fathers, Eucharist in Nikolai Afanasiev, 1893–1966* (Cambridge: Cambridge University Press, 1989), p. x.
6. De Lubac, *Corpus Mysticum: The Eucharist and the Church in the Middle Ages*, trans. Gemma Simmonds with Richard Price (London: SCM, 2006).
7. See, e.g., Bishop Kallistos (Ware) of Diokleia, 'St Nicolas Cabasilas on the Eucharistic Sacrifice', in Archimandrite Job Getcha and Michel Stavrou (eds.), *Le Feu sur la terre: mélanges offerts au Père Boris Bobrinskoy pour son 80ᵉ anniversaire* (Paris: Presses Saint-Serge, 2005), 141–53—an earnest of his eagerly- and long-awaited treatment of the Byzantine understanding of the eucharistic sacrifice.
8. So Robert Bird, 'General Introduction', in Alexei S. Khomiakov, Ivan Vasilevich Kireevskii, Boris Jakim, and Robert Bird (eds.), *On Spiritual Unity: A Slavophile Reader* (Hudson NY: Lindisfarne Books, 1998), 8, with refs.
9. Vera Shevzov, *Russian Orthodoxy on the Eve of Revolution* (New York: Oxford University Press, 2004), 12–53.
10. See the generous introduction by Cardinal Daniélou to the reprint of Lot-Borodine's articles on deification in M. Lot-Borodine, *Le Déification de l'homme selon la doctrine des pères grecs* (Paris: Cerf, 1970).
11. See John S. Romanides, 'The Ecclesiology of St Ignatius of Antioch', *Greek Orthodox Theological Review*, 7 (1961–2), 53–77.
12. See, at last, in English translation, Metropolitan John's influential doctoral thesis, *Eucharist, Bishop, Church: The Unity of the Church in the Divine Eucharist and the Bishop During the First Three Centuries*, trans. Elizabeth Theokritoff (Brookline, Mass.: Holy Cross Orthodox Press, 2001).
13. I should perhaps point out that some Orthodox theologians would take the above argument that the term 'Apostolic Fathers' is not traditional to demonstrate that such

Fathers are *not* among those who form the *phronema ton pateron* ('the mind of the Fathers'). My point is the opposite.

14. John J. Allen Jr., 'Interview with Robert J. Taft, SJ', *National Catholic Reporter* (6 Feb. 2004), available at <http://ncronline.org/mainpage/specialdocuments/taft.htm>.

15. Some of these reflections I owe to Fr Demetrios Bathrellos, who showed me his contribution to a Festschrift for Metropolitan John: Demetrios Bathrellos, 'Church, Eucharist, Bishop: The Early Church in the Ecclesiology of John Zizioulas', in Douglas H. Knight (ed.), *The Theology of John Zizioulas: Personhood and the Church* (London: Ashgate, 2007), 133–46. He is not responsible for the way I have used points that he made; his points are part of a larger appraisal of Metropolitan John's ecclesiology. I am grateful to him for his allowing me to develop them in my own way here.

16. See, e.g., John Behr, 'The Trinitarian Being of the Church', *St Vladimir's Theological Quarterly*, 48 (2004), 67–88; and J. H. Erickson, 'Baptism and the Church's Faith', in C. E. Braaten and R. W. Jenson (eds.), *Marks of the Body of Christ* (Grand Rapids, Mich.: Eerdmans, 1999), 44–58.

17. Shevzov, *Russian Orthodoxy*, is good on the background of the 1917–18 *sobor*. For a brief account of the *sobor*, see the pamphlet by Alexei Svetozarsky, *The 1917–18 Council of the Russian Orthodox Church* (Oxford: St Stephen's Press, 2003). Also, on the background to the *sobor*, see James W. Cunningham, *A Vanquished Hope: The Movement for Church Renewal in Russia, 1905–1906* (Crestwood, NY: St Vladimir's Seminary Press, 1981), and on the *sobor* itself, most recently, Hyacinthe Destivelle, *Le Concile de Moscou (1917–1918): la création des institutions conciliaires de l'Église orthodoxe russe* (Paris: Cerf, 2006).

18. See Russian Orthodox Patriarchal Church in Great Britain and Ireland, Diocese of Sourozh, *Diocesan Statutes*, rev. edn. (Oxford: St Stephen's Press, 2001).

19. Ratzinger, *The Spirit of the Liturgy*, trans. John Saward (San Francisco, Calif.: Ignatius Press, 2000).

26

Anglicanism and the Conditions for Communion—A Response to Cardinal Kasper

Nicholas Sagovsky

INTRODUCTION

As I write, the parallels between the stresses and strains in the Anglican Communion and the disunity that Paul encountered in the infant church of Corinth are uncomfortably close (cf. 1 Cor. 1: 12). However, precisely because the struggle to maintain communion within the Anglican Communion is at this moment so intense, it may be that Anglicans can ask in a fresh way, 'What are the conditions for communion?' and in so doing discover fresh gifts of patience, mutual understanding, and theological insight which can be shared with the whole church. As Anglicans, we know that our difficulties in resolving issues, which are in one way or another resolved by other traditions as a condition of communion, often causes puzzlement. My aim in this chapter is to answer a question in which I hear an expression of that puzzlement. It is put very sharply by Cardinal Kasper in his contribution to this volume.

CARDINAL KASPER'S QUESTION TO ANGLICANS

'How is it possible', Kasper asks, 'to designate Scripture and the Apostles' and Niceno-Constantinopolitan Creeds as normative in the Chicago–Lambeth Quadrilateral, but to disregard the binding force of the subsequent living tradition?' This is the nub of his question to Anglicans, a question which Anglicans must face in a spirit of Receptive Ecumenism.

First, though, it is important to note how Kasper comes to his question. Adopting an approach 'akin to fundamental theology', he sets out to reflect 'upon the relationship between Catholicism and Protestantism, understood as two principles' and in this context suggests that 'what lies behind the Anglican principle of comprehensiveness is this: the endeavour somehow—and 'somehow' is the operative word—to achieve a harmonious balance between the positions of Catholicism and Protestantism; between Catholic and Protestant principles.' Cardinal Kasper thus aligns himself with Cardinal Cassidy, who argued at the Lambeth Conference of 1998 'that the principle of comprehensiveness was doubtless helpful and good, but should not be overdone'. For Kasper, this principle of comprehensiveness is adequate neither to Catholicism nor to Protestantism, and certainly not to both. In the present situation, 'We have been thrown back to the beginnings of the ecumenical movement. It is understandable that the Anglican Communion, which hopes somehow to hold the two together, suffers particularly under this polarization.'[1] Kasper's method, then, is to show how 'the Catholic and Protestant principles' are not to be stitched together by some overarching, but inadequate 'comprehensiveness'. He asks how they may be brought together in a properly ecumenical unity: 'It is not a matter of juxtaposition, or of merely external mediation, but of an internal mediation, a fusion of the Catholic sacramental and the Protestant prophetic principles.' His question to Anglicans can perhaps be rephrased: 'Do you not try, through the principle of comprehensiveness, to make an "external mediation" do the work of an "internal mediation": and so it must inevitably fail?' The answer to this question must lie in an adequate theological account of the 'mediation' of unity as understood by Anglicans.

KASPER AND THE 'MEDIATION' OF UNITY

Kasper posits the unity of the church as 'fundamental': 'Church division is...antithetical to the essential nature of the Church...Unity in the New Testament is unity in the diversity of charisms, offices, local churches and cultures; unity is symphonic.' The church does not contain the ground of its existence and its unity within itself. The unity of the church 'ex-ists' (comes from without) in 'the external mediation of the Spirit through word and sacrament'. Unity comes through a shared participation in the holy.

Kasper argues that '[u]nderstood correctly, the sacramental Catholic view of the church is not necessarily antithetical to the self-critical Protestant principle': they can be complementary and achieve 'a state of balance' in an 'evangelical Catholicity'. This, he says, was Martin Luther's original intention, and it has been taken up in the twentieth century by Catholics such as Heiler and Küng.[2] He then takes three specific examples (we might say, perspectives) to illustrate his thinking about the 'internal mediation' of unity.

The first is that of 'synchronic unity' in the simultaneous existence of the universal church and the local churches. He has no space to go into this question in detail (for instance, to discuss what is meant by 'the universal church') but he does relate it to the discussion in the *Windsor Report*,[3] showing how this brings into play the question of 'Rome's ministry of unity' and 'the question for Rome of how the relationship between primacy and collegiality or synodality can be better realized'.

Cardinal Kasper then turns to the diachronic unity of the church and the way in which the local church must strive for consensus not only with the other local churches 'as well as' (*sic*) the universal church, but must also be in consensus with the apostolic church and the church of the preceding centuries. It is here that '[i]n so far as tradition [is] understood as a living thing' . . . the 'self-critical prophetic principle' comes into play. It is at this point that he specifically questions Anglicans, whom he sees as accepting Scripture and the creeds of the early councils but denying 'the binding force of the subsequent living tradition'.

Kasper's third example is to look at these questions in the light of doxology. Here he sketches the 'spiritual ecumenism' which binds Anglicans and Catholics together and which is described in rich detail in Keith Pecklers's contribution to this volume.

Cardinal Kasper's conclusion is that all three examples confront us with the fundamental question of ecumenical theology, which is 'the task of reflecting the living tradition'. His question to Anglicans is whether we have missed the challenge of unity by opting for 'comprehensiveness' rather than by striving for the 'internal mediation' of unity in the struggle to hold together unity and holiness. This question, put to us by a friend and a shrewd observer of the life of our churches, is one we cannot ignore.

ANGLICAN COMPREHENSIVENESS AND THE MEDIATION OF UNITY

Cardinal Kasper develops his argument about the unity of the church with reference to its codependent catholicity and holiness. In so doing, he follows the Apostles' Creed ('I believe in the holy catholic church') as the baptismal symbol. It is, however, the Niceno-Constantinopolitan Creed, the eucharistic symbol, which helps us more at this point, as it speaks of the fourfold marks of the church: 'We believe in . . . one, holy catholic *and apostolic* church'. This question of the apostolicity of the church captures precisely the dilemma which Kasper puts before us, for within the New Testament the apostles are responsible both for authentic historic witness to Christ and for the mediation of the message of Christ to new peoples (the Gentiles) in new ways. The question of an 'evangelical Catholicity' is also the question of an 'eschatological apostolicity'.

Though the term 'comprehensiveness' is often used of the Anglican approach to ecclesiology, it is important to see this primarily as a term which describes a political or even pragmatic strategy, adopted by some Anglicans at a precise historical juncture. It is not, strictly, a theological principle. There has never been an Anglican 'principle' of comprehensiveness as such[4] and it would be dangerous to define the boundaries of Anglicanism by any principle other than one of *theological* inclusion, that is to say in terms of apostolicity or catholicity rather than comprehensiveness.

The distinctive Anglican use of the term 'comprehension' was current from the 1660s after the Restoration of the monarchy and the Act of Uniformity, which incorporated the publication of the revised Book of Common Prayer (1662). At that time there were various schools of thought in the Church of England, one arguing for 'comprehension' which would allow dissenters who had not been episcopally ordained to be included within the national church, and another arguing for 'toleration' or 'indulgence', which would preserve the current requirement for episcopal ordination but would remove the disabilities suffered by Protestant dissenters.[5] In 1688, a Committee was set up to revise the Book of Common Prayer in a comprehensive direction[6] and in 1689, after the accession of William III, though no revised ('comprehensive') Prayer Book was introduced, a Toleration Act was passed which was intended to unite the nation against the deposed Roman Catholic James II by removing all criminal penalties from dissenters who took the Oaths of Allegiance and Supremacy. The advocacy of comprehension by divines like Edward Stillingfleet subsequently found expression in Thomas Arnold's proposals for an inclusive national church.[7]

There was in the eighteenth century an important shift in the understanding of Anglican comprehensiveness: from a Protestant inclusiveness, which carried no suggestion of doctrinal liberalism, towards the Lockean liberalism associated first with eighteenth-century deists. This was followed by a further shift towards the Erastian liberalism of Thomas Arnold and his pupil A. P. Stanley.[8] The concern was always, however, for an inclusive *national* church; the mediating principle for such inclusiveness was that of the Church of England as an expression of national identity. Underlying this was an unexpressed theological principle, which ran contrary both to Enlightenment universalism and to Roman Catholic centralism: that nationhood is a God-given matrix within which the identity of the church is to be realized.

The idea that 'comprehensiveness' could be a theological principle, and still more one that is distinctive of Anglicanism, has been powerfully attacked by Stephen Sykes. Sykes does not go into the political history of Anglican ideas of comprehensiveness. For him, the prime culprit in promoting sloppy thinking about comprehensiveness is F. D. Maurice. He is disturbed to find 'Mauricean tones' in a report of the 1948 Lambeth Conference, discussing the tensions set up by differing views of episcopacy. Sykes quotes from the report:

We recognise the inconveniences caused by these tensions, but we acknowledge them to be part of the will of God for us, since we believe it is only through a comprehensiveness which makes it possible to hold together in the Anglican Communion understandings of truth which are held in separation in other churches, that the Anglican Communion is able to reach out in different directions and so to fulfil its special vocation as one of God's instruments for the restoration of the visible unity of His whole church.[9]

When these words were written, the tension in view was that which had existed for 400 years between those who thought that the historical episcopate was of the *esse* of the church and those who thought it of the *bene esse*. On this point, Anglicanism, though it has always remained committed to episcopal order, has maintained a studied ambiguity. The Preface to the episcopal ordinal of the 1552 (and 1662) Book of Common Prayer, which was almost certainly drafted by Cranmer himself, famously begins: 'It is evident unto all men diligently reading holy Scripture and ancient Authors, that from the Apostles' time there have been these Orders of Ministers in Christ's Church: Bishops, Priests, and Deacons.' Again, Hooker is well known to have argued that, though episcopacy was of apostolic origin, 'there may be sometimes very just and sufficient reason to allow ordination made without a bishop',[10] and Stillingfleet, in his *Irenicum* (1659), argued that no one form of church government, not even episcopacy, was of 'divine right' and immutable.[11] The Tractarians of the nineteenth century, however, following the 'high church' tradition of divines who were conscientiously opposed to 'comprehension' because they believed that an episcopally ordered church had been founded by the will of Christ (by 'divine law'), argued passionately against 'liberals' like Thomas Arnold that episcopacy was of the 'essence' of the church.

The question that faces Anglicans today is whether this studied ambiguity about the nature of episcopacy can be extended to undergird the acceptance of women bishops. Walter Kasper and Stephen Sykes are right to reject any appeal to Anglican 'comprehensiveness' as a way of resolving this question, judging it to be little more than a papering over of the cracks. There has to be (and there is) a better theological rationale if such a momentous change is not to bring about a terrible rent in communion.

For Anglicans, one important strand, which relates to 'comprehensiveness', is what we might appropriately call the principle of 'nationality': that the Church of England has an obligation to serve the national structures which maintain the peace and good order from which all members of the nation benefit. From the time of the Reformation and the Elizabethan settlement, the Church of England has seen itself as having an obligation to promote obedience to those in authority, the payment of taxes, loyal citizenship[12]—subject always to the proviso that conscience comes before citizenship. In a contemporary context of increasing social and religious pluralism the Anglican appeal to comprehensiveness translates itself into an appeal for an inclusive society, that is to say an appeal for justice, but not into an appeal for an inherently contradictory church order.

This traditional Anglican concern does, however, have implications for the internal life and ordering of the church: it should be such as enables the church to fulfil its national duty and vocation.[13] More than that, its experience of ministry within British communities may suggest to it ways in which it could be reformed better to fulfil its national vocation, though its experience in specific, local situations can never be coercive over and above the norms indicated by apostolic tradition. An appeal to Anglican comprehensiveness is not the way to circumvent those norms, though it may be one way indirectly to make the case that Anglicans should take seriously their obligation to the 'living tradition' of the Christian churches. If the church 'ex-ists', that is comes to itself in a way that is mediated from outside itself, it would be authentically Anglican to see such ex-istence in the cultural forms it has taken within particular polities. The problem for Anglicans has, however, been that all too often within the Anglican Communion those cultural forms have not represented a realization of the authentic life of the church in specific local situations, but the uncritical and hegemonic transfer of English Christianity to various parts of the world.

ANGLICANISM AND LIVING TRADITION

How is it possible, asks Cardinal Kasper, 'to designate Scripture and the Apostles' and Niceno-Constantinopolitan Creeds as normative in the Chicago–Lambeth Quadrilateral, but to disregard the binding force of the subsequent living tradition?' This raises two questions: first, that of the understanding of the Chicago–Lambeth Quadrilateral within Anglicanism, and, secondly, the understanding of 'the subsequent living tradition' within both Roman Catholicism and Anglicanism.

The Chicago–Lambeth Quadrilateral[14] identifies four characteristics of the church as the indispensable basis for reunion, that is to say as the basis on which participation in a common tradition can already be discerned. These are: the Holy Scriptures of the Old and New Testament as 'containing all things necessary to salvation' and as being the rule and ultimate standard of faith; the Apostles' Creed as the Baptismal Symbol and the Nicene Creed as 'the sufficient statement of the Christian faith'; the two Sacraments ordained by Christ himself—Baptism and the Supper of the Lord; and 'the historic Episcopate, locally adapted in the methods of its administration to the varying needs of the nations and peoples called of God into the Unity of His Church'.

What Anglicans have always recognized is that, even within the common practice of the Christian faith identified by these four characteristics of historic Christianity, there may well be sufficient diversity for Christians to regard one another as not in the fullest sense Christian. The quadrilateral does not, for instance, distinguish between adult and infant baptism; nor between views of the eucharistic presence; nor does it take a position on whether episcopal ministry is distinct from or a function of presbyteral ministry; nor on the origins of episcopal ministry. On each of these Reformation cruces it embraces diversity. This is not to say that Anglican teaching and practice have remained open to all possible views in these areas; merely, that in the search for reunion they have sought to remain open to the diversity that was present in the early church and can be expected to be present within an inclusive national church.

In all four areas of the Lambeth Quadrilateral Anglicans have had to recognize that there is instability: the precise Canon of the Scriptures is diversely identified; Anglicans have accepted the Filioque as an addition to the Nicene Creed,[15] which the Orthodox reject; there remains a question as to whether foot-washing, increasingly accepted amongst Anglicans as a Maundy Thursday devotion, can be regarded as a dominical sacrament; the question as to whether 'the historic Episcopate, locally adapted' could include women remains open amongst Anglicans and Orthodox, though officially closed amongst Roman Catholics. Thus, if the Lambeth Quadrilateral is to be of use as a means of recognizing fellow-Christians, and, indeed, as a means of recognizing fellow-Anglicans, it must be seen as a rough matrix through which there passes a variegated stream of common tradition, but a matrix in which all the constituent elements of that tradition are, practically speaking, in need of further definition.

It is this further definition which, for Anglicans, continues to take place within the stream of living tradition. For Roman Catholics, the instruments of such definition are very clear: the magisterium of the church is exercised through the college of bishops meeting in ecumenical and other representative synods, and (as defined since 1870) through the Bishop of Rome speaking *ex cathedra*, even outside the conciliar context. For Anglicans, the question of magisterium is interpreted as one of communion. There is no role for the Archbishop of Canterbury in the discerning of doctrine analogous to that of the Pope, nor for the Anglican bishops analogous to the magisterial role of Roman Catholic bishops. At root, this is because of the split (since 1054) between West and East and the conviction that for an authoritative exercise of magisterium on an issue that touches all (such as a doctrinal definition) there would have to be unanimity amongst all. The condition of authentic universal magisterium is thus authentic universal communion, and whilst in affirming the Lambeth Quadrilateral Anglicans affirm that the conditions for such communion exist, they have to recognize how far the 'living tradition' that has developed within specific Christian Communions has carried their adherents apart.

Anglicans are now faced with two putative developments of the living tradition on which there can be no adjudication by appeal to the Lambeth Quadrilateral: the acceptance of practising homosexuals in positions of ministerial authority and the ordination of women bishops. At root, the theological issue is one of the hermeneutics of tradition (of 'the living tradition'). Can there be a responsible development of the Christian tradition, both of the interpretation of the moral teaching of Scripture and of the exercise of the Historic Episcopate, which can accommodate these developments?

WHAT BINDS ANGLICANS? COMMUNION AND MAGISTERIUM

Cardinal Kasper's concern is for the 'binding force of the living tradition'. Anglicans have a strong sense of 'the living tradition' and seek to place themselves within a tradition that can demonstrably be traced back to the common life of the early church. The question for Anglicans is what each of the points that define the Lambeth Quadrilateral means for us now. Certainly, this is a question which can only be approached in the confidence that there is in the life of the early church a 'classical' matrix in which we can see how they all intermesh cohesively to give a structure for Christian life, but the emphasis is on the present: what can we accept within the living tradition now?

A distinct concern for Anglicans to put to Roman Catholics is the way in which definitions that have taken place after the division of West and East have for them constrained the development of 'the living tradition' within the understanding of one particular historic epoch. One such case would be the definition of transubstantiation (1215); another would be the definition of the Immaculate Conception (1854); another the bodily Assumption of Mary (1950).[16] In each case, the Orthodox have refrained from making similar definitions. The Orthodox would undoubtedly press the question of the role of the Bishop of Rome in doctrinal definitions such as those of 1854 and 1950, neither of which was made in the conciliar context but only after consultation within the Roman Catholic Church.[17] Yet the Roman Catholic faithful are bound to accept such definitions. Kasper's question to Anglicans about their failure to accept 'the binding power of the living tradition' becomes in reverse a question to Roman Catholics about the premature binding of the living tradition.[18]

For Anglicans, as for Orthodox and Catholics, there is an integral link between tradition and communion. The limits of communion are defined by the reception of tradition and the reception of tradition is what sustains a living communion. Anglicans have from the time of the Reformation experienced the church at local level as a communion. This has been true at provincial and national levels, and has been extended worldwide with the growth of the Anglican Communion. Just as with the notion of 'comprehensiveness', there have been some very hazy notions of provincial autonomy to be found amongst Anglicans. It has all too often been thought that is possible to live as a Communion but to affirm provincial autonomy. This is the international version of sloppy accounts of 'comprehensiveness'.

What has become ever more clear with the challenges to the Anglican churches in the second half of the twentieth century is that there is a choice to be made between provincial autonomy and the demands of communion. The opposite of autonomy in this context is not heteronomy but communion. Without a willingness truly to respect the ways in which Christian and Anglican tradition are appropriated in other provinces there may be a federation of churches but not a communion. This is the nub of the recommendations in the *Windsor Report* and of the subsequent comments by the Archbishop of Canterbury. If communion means 'participation', then the participation of all the churches in the life of each, through the instruments of unity (the ministry of the Archbishop of Canterbury; the Lambeth Conference; the Anglican Consultative Council; the Primates' Meeting), must be respected.

The danger is that this becomes a force for inertia: that change cannot be implemented until all are agreed upon it—though the situations of the churches are so various that what is for one an appropriate, even urgent, development of the living tradition will for another be a distortion, or even a betrayal, of the tradition they have inherited. It remains to be seen how this tension can be handled within Anglicanism. What is clear, though, is that if there is to be a continuing communion between the churches, the demands of communion must be kept to a minimum (which is what the Chicago–Lambeth Quadrilateral affirms). This is a sound Anglican instinct, which can contribute to the reunion of the churches well beyond the tradition of Anglicanism. Anglicans do not want to be bound by any more written statements of church doctrine, any more church practices or structures, than are absolutely necessary to maintain the integrity of the living tradition.

CONCLUSION

I hope that in this essay I have been able to give an answer to Cardinal Kasper's question How it is possible 'to designate Scripture and the Apostles' and Niceno-Constantinopolitan Creeds as normative in the Chicago–Lambeth Quadrilateral, but to disregard the binding force of the subsequent living tradition?' Anglicans do not see themselves as disregarding the binding force of this living tradition. But to explain how this is possible is not simple: it requires a careful account of what the Chicago–Lambeth Quadrilateral is for Anglicans (a matrix through which the 'living tradition' passes); it requires a careful account of how Scripture and the Creeds are seen as normative (as bearing witness to conditions for communion, not as classicist proof-texts); it requires attention to the exercise of the ministry of the historic episcopate (as a continuing medium through which apostolic tradition lives and grows); it requires critical discussion of how the 'living tradition' can have binding force without itself being prematurely or unnecessarily bound to particular historical understandings and interpretations; and it requires an understanding of the historical commitment of the Anglican churches to the life of nations. In each of these areas there is a distinctively Anglican approach, within each there are gifts to be given and received between the various Christian traditions. Taken together, they show how Cardinal Kasper's question may be answered: Anglicans, though they do not define, or make explicit, 'the binding force of the . . . living tradition' as Roman Catholics do, by no means disregard it. At the moment we are far from united on how that 'binding force' may be discerned, but we cannot see in other Christian traditions the specific gift or gifts that can resolve this crisis in communion. It strikes many Anglicans that this is not merely a crisis for Anglicans but for all Christians, and in our weakness (cf. 1 Cor. 2: 3–4) we may yet 're-receive'[19] gifts that the Holy Spirit has for all the churches. Whether and to what extent the Anglican churches can come through the current crisis to a stronger experience of communion, and the part that Receptive Ecumenism has to play in that process, remain to be seen.

NOTES

1. Cardinal Kasper also made this point in his address to the Anglican House of Bishops, 5 June 2006: 'Where and on what side does the Anglican Communion stand, where will it stand in the future. Which orientation does it claim as its own: the Latin, Greek, Protestant, Liberal or Evangelical? It may retreat to the Anglican principle of comprehensiveness and answer: We are a little of everything. Such comprehensiveness is doubtless a good principle to a certain degree, but it should not be overdone, as my predecessor Cardinal Edward Cassidy once told you: one arrives at limits where one must decide one way or the other', 'The Mission of Bishops in the Mystery of the Church', available at <http://www.vatican.va/roman_curia/pontifical_councils/chrstuni/card-kasper-docs/rc_pc_chrstuni_doc_20060605_kasper-bishops_en.html>.
2. For an Anglican classic in this vein, see A. M. Ramsey, *The Gospel and the Catholic Church* (London: Longmans, 1936).
3. The Lambeth Commission on Communion, *The Windsor Report 2004* (London: Anglican Communion Office, 2004), available at <http://www.aco.org/windsor2004/downloads/windsor2004full.pdf>.
4. Contra, e.g., William L. Sachs, *The Transformation of Anglicanism* (Cambridge: Cambridge University Press, 1993), 10.

5. See J. Spurr, 'The Church of England, Comprehension and the Toleration Act of 1689', *English Historical Review*, 54 (1989), 927–46.

6. See T. J. Fawcett (ed.), *The Liturgy of Comprehension 1689: An Abortive Attempt to Revise the Book of Common Prayer* (Southend: Alcuin Club, 1973).

7. See Arnold, *Principles of Church Reform*, with an introductory essay by M. J. Jackson and J. Rogan (London: SPCK, 1962); cf. Paul Avis, *Anglicanism and the Christian Church*, 2nd edn. (Edinburgh: T. & T. Clark, 2002), 271–8.

8. As Dean of Westminster, Stanley found in Westminster Abbey 'the material embodiment of his ideal of a comprehensive national church'; quoted by Edward Carpenter from R. E. Prothero's biography of Stanley, *Westminster Abbey* (London: Weidenfeld & Nicolson, 1989), 118.

9. *The Lambeth Conference 1948* (London: SPCK, 1948), 50 ff., in Sykes, *The Integrity of Anglicanism* (London: Mowbray, 1978), 18.

10. 'The Laws of Ecclesiastical Polity' (1593), VII. xiv. 11, *The Works of Richard Hooker*, ed. John Keble (Oxford: Clarendon Press, 1875), ii. 403.

11. See Avis, *Anglicanism and the Christian Church*, 117–21.

12. See the successive forms of the Prayer for the Church Militant in the 1549, 1552, and 1662 editions of the Book of Common Prayer: the concern for 'Christian Kings, Princes and Governors' is complemented by a concern for a Christian people who are 'godly and quietly governed'.

13. Cf. 'Nevertheless, by reason of new occasions still arising which the Church having care of souls must take order for as need requireth, hereby it cometh to pass, that there is and ever will be great use even of human laws and ordinances, deducted by way of discourse as conclusions from the former divine and natural, serving for principles thereunto', Hooker, 'Laws of Ecclesiastical Polity', VIII. vi. 5, *The Works of Richard Hooker*, ii. 541; also 'The Church being a body which dieth not hath always power, as occasion requireth, no less to ordain that which never was, than to ratify what hath been before', ibid., V. viii. 1; i. 445.

14. See Stephen W. Sykes and J. Booty (eds.), *The Study of Anglicanism* (London: SPCK, 1988), 209–10.

15. A clear example of Anglican acceptance of the 'living tradition' of the West; see Paul Elmer More and Frank Leslie Cross (eds.), *Anglicanism: The Thought and Practice of the Church of England, Illustrated from the Religious Literature of the Seventeenth Century* (London: SPCK, 1962), 76–7.

16. On the difficulties caused by the 'precise formulations' of the Marian definitions, see ARCIC II, *Mary: Grace and Hope in Christ*, ed. Donald Bolen and Gregory Cameron (London: Continuum, 2005), § 61, available at <http://www.vatican.va/roman-curia/pontifical_councils/chrstuni/angl-comm-docs/rc_pc_chrstuni_doc_20050516_mary-grace-hope-christ_en.html>.

17. Cf. the argument that infallibility properly functions in a grammatical, or regulative, way by serving to articulate and maintain the identifying grammar of Christian faith and that which pertains to it. See Paul D. Murray, 'On Valuing Truth in Practice: Rome's Postmodern Challenge', *International Journal of Systematic Theology*, 8 (2006), 163–83 (168–70), also in Laurence Paul Hemming and Susan Frank Parsons (eds.), *Redeeming Truth: Considering Faith and Reason* (London: SCM, 2007), 184–206.

18. See ARCIC II, 'Issues Facing Roman Catholics', and 'Issues Facing Anglicans', *The Gift of Authority: Authority in the Church III* (London: Church House Publishing/CTS, 1999), §§ 56–7, available at <http://www.vatican.va/roman_curia/pontifical_councils/chrstuni/documents/rc_pc_chrstuni_doc_12051999_gift-of-autority_en.html>.

19. For the term 're-reception', see Y. Congar, *Diversity and Communion*, trans. J. Bowden (London: SCM, 1984), 171–2; also ARCIC II, *The Gift of Authority*, §§ 24–5.

27

Receptive Ecumenism and the Future of Ecumenical Dialogues—Privileging Differentiated Consensus and Drawing its Institutional Consequences[1]

Hervé Legrand, OP

INTRODUCTION

As with the January 2006 Durham Colloquium that preceded it, evaluating this exceptionally rich, interdisciplinary volume in a short chapter is impossible. Here I will simply present some reflections on the future of ecumenism that have been aroused or confirmed in me by the conversations that lie behind this volume.

First, as a continental Roman Catholic theologian, I would like to say how much I admire the face of the English Roman Catholic Church that is evident in this project: it appears as a minority church overflowing with intellectual and theological talents, and demonstrating greater vitality than many of its majority sisters on the Continent.

More generally, I would like to say that this project strikes me as the living denial of any supposed ecumenical winter. Let us think about it, only forty-five years ago Catholic theologians still stood under Pope Pius XII's prohibition of Catholic participation in 'so-called "ecumenical" meetings...without the prior consent of the Holy See'.[2] In contrast, at the Durham colloquium we witnessed a Roman cardinal preaching in the context of a Eucharist presided over by the local Anglican bishop and, then, receiving a blessing from that same bishop during the rite of Communion. Again, we saw this same Anglican bishop preaching at a Eucharist presided over by the local Roman Catholic bishop in the chapel of the provincial seminary. Those of us fortunate enough to be at Ushaw College in January 2006 experienced there something completely different from an ecumenical winter. The climate that we experienced does not itself solve any fundamental problems, but without it can one even hope to be able to learn from others?

This volume inspires me to make three specific comments concerning the possible future directions of ecumenism. With great intellectual honesty, we were reminded in Durham of the serious problems confronting the Anglican communion, the Orthodox Church, and the Roman Catholic Church. These problems mean that the dream of structural union, born in the wake of the Second Vatican Council, will not be realized in the foreseeable future. The path towards reunion will, therefore, be longer than some had foreseen. But the duration of the process is not, in itself, an issue.

What is, arguably, first at issue is the model according to which our bilateral dialogues have hitherto been conducted. Equally at issue is the reception of these agreements in the day-to-day life of the churches: the somewhat detached intellectual adhesion generally afforded them does not lead to concrete reforms without which desired unity remains out of reach. Finally, I will briefly comment on the specific responsibility of theologians in this regard.

FROM HOMOGENEOUS UNIVOCAL CONSENSUS
TO DIFFERENTIATED CONSENSUS

Until now, most bilateral dialogues have deemed that ecumenical consensus must be demonstrated even to the point of identity of doctrinal expression. Mary Tanner recalls here how the Congregation for the Doctrine of the Faith failed to recognize a 'substantial agreement' in ARCIC I's *Final Report*. The charges were that the *Report*'s language was not univocal[3] and did not reflect a literal agreement with Catholic dogmatic definitions.[4] ARCIC I experienced the misfortune of arriving too early. Since then, the CDF has reviewed its position.

Recall the fact that no less a thinker than Karl Rahner categorically refused the formula 'Simul iustus et peccator' as being impossible both at theoretical and dogmatic levels.[5] But now the CDF has formally recognized the legitimacy of the once rejected paradigm through the signing of the 1999 *Joint Declaration on the Doctrine of Justification*, which adopted a 'differentiated consensus'; that is to say, an agreement where there remains acceptable differences 'of language, theological elaboration, and emphasis' (§ 40).[6] Henceforth, *JDDJ* represents an official commentary on the Council of Trent.

One has every reason to think that this new model represents a very significant step forward for bilateral dialogues which will in future be increasingly led to this method of expressing the same faith with differing emphases, differing conceptual frameworks, differing thought forms. The adoption of such a methodology would entail numerous benefits.

1. It would do justice, in line with what George Lindbeck has suggested, to the great theological syntheses which must be considered as a whole, and cannot be compared word for word.[7] This was also Yves Congar's insight when he wrote: 'In the East and the West the essentials of faith are both identical and different. It is the identical which is different; the differences which must be recognized and respected, are differences that belong, in fact, to our common Christian identity at its most profound.'[8] The perception which is, therefore, increasingly gaining ground is that of the legitimacy of such differences even within full unity. In an oft-quoted formulation, Joseph Ratzinger affirmed: 'Rome must not require more from the East with respect to the doctrine of primacy than had been formulated and was expressed in the first millennium.'[9]

2. It would lead the bilateral dialogues to a rigorous hermeneutic of difference, identifying those differences that are truly church-dividing. It requires the art of translation and a greater attention to the structures of enunciation. Such a hermeneutic has a better chance of succeeding today, in the Catholic Church of Benedict XVI, than in the past. There are numerous indications confirming the plausibility of such an evolution. We owe to Cardinal Ratzinger the signing of the aforementioned Augsburg declaration (*JDDJ*), the eucharistic sharing with the East Syrian Orthodox Church, whose eucharistic anaphora does not include the words of institution,[10] and the nuanced identification of papal teaching on the non-ordination of women as 'a teaching of the ordinary, non-infallible, papal magisterium'.[11] A final example of such new hermeneutics, put forward in Rome itself, is to be found in a recent paper by Cardinal Kasper, 'Petrine Ministry and Synodality', representing a sustained exploration of the hermeneutical principles for the rereading of the First Vatican Council dogmas.[12]

3. The adoption of such a methodology would allow us to arrive together at a true catholicity of thought. Christian history passes on as a legacy to us a diversity of languages of the faith, each of which has claimed for itself exclusive truth. Through their definitions and associated anathemas, the ecumenical councils of the first millennium elaborated a propositional approach to the truths of faith, striving to delimit orthodoxy within speculative formulations. This pattern was taken up again at the time of the Reformation conflicts. One can thus see with no surprise Catholics and Protestants enunciating anathemas which have remained in force until our day. In the modern Catholic Church, the Congregation of the Holy Office, founded in 1588, undertook to protect the true faith using the same technique, consisting in attributing 'notes' to theological propositions on the basis of their greater or lesser deviation from orthodoxy; a custom which would last until the Second Vatican Council.[13] With this, the role played by the Denzinger compendium in the teaching of theology is well known.[14]

The resources of contemporary culture have shown the numerous inadequacies of such a propositional approach. For example, the simple recourse to linguistics permits exposure of the semantic substratum in the Filioque controversy, for *ekporeusthai* and *procedere* are not equivalent. Or, again, it sheds light on Monophysism having taken root within the Coptic, Syriac, and Armenian churches. This schism still continues even if today it is recognized that the controversy was largely verbal.[15]

In the contemporary intellectual atmosphere, the legitimation of a pluriformity of expressions of the faith, such as those articulated in so-called 'differentiated consensus', is very far from, even opposed to, the doctrinal liberalism of the beginning of the last century.[16] Quite the contrary, it is an approach to catholicity that ecclesial authorities are able to take, even if a similar step is not within the reach of the individual believer. To the extent that this path of catholicity will prove capable of combining diversity within unity at the level of doctrinal expression, it will also facilitate unity at the structural ecclesial level.

4. If differentiated consensus were to be the normal form of doctrinal agreement, then the deep resistance of many Protestants, who fear that unity might be a uniform yoke, would be dispelled. But once it is shown that the unity of faith can be translated into a variety of formulations, it will be clear that the unity sought does not require the sacrifice of confessional identity, but simply its correction. The motto of Malines, 'united but not absorbed', will be heard more widely than the Orthodox and the Anglicans, if a consensus were to be achieved.

5. A final consequence of the adoption of the method of differentiated consensus can be indicated. In the Roman Catholic Church, the evaluation and reception of dialogues should follow a more balanced course. In order to judge the possibility of receiving these dialogues, the local Roman Catholic churches of the same geographical area as their dialogue partners should be more involved than is currently the case. For example, might it not be advisable that, in the evaluation of a bilateral agreement between the Roman Catholic Church and the World Lutheran Federation, the bishops of the German-speaking episcopal conferences and their theology schools be more active than, say, their counterparts in Sicily? In fact, in the preparations for the signing of the Augsburg agreement, only the Holy See was actively involved on the Catholic side while, in contrast, on the Lutheran side all the local Lutheran synods had a say. To hope for a greater involvement of local churches certainly does not mean calling into question the Holy See's right to have the last word; rather it suggests a way in which one could probably obtain more precise evaluations as well as a deeper reception of these agreements.

In summary, the bilateral dialogues remain absolutely necessary, but their future depends on a clear emphasis upon the method of differentiated consensus. The same applies at the level of speculative theology. But I retain a second conviction from the Receptive Ecumenism and Catholic Learning project concerning the reception of the achievements of bilateral processes. This is that such processes will remain theoretical and will fail to convince our dialogue partners if they do not result in institutional reforms consistent with the common faith expressed in the doctrinal agreements. I will present this conviction in relation to the situation in the Roman Catholic Church, for is not the best ecumenical work that which is done at home?[17]

BEYOND DOCTRINAL AGREEMENT TO ECCLESIOLOGICAL CONVERSION

Here I might be allowed to apply a well-known phrase from St John's Gospel: 'those who do what is true come to the light' (John 3: 21). The truth conveyed by bilateral statements is not really received until it shapes new Christian attitudes. This contradicts the idealism and banal intellectualism that still often dominate Christian life, but which can also be found elsewhere; as when it is imagined that society can develop morally through the teaching of moral knowledge. In fact, a society only advances morally by changing its social behaviour.

Let us attempt to draw out the consequences of this insight for the reception of ecumenical documents. One can rely here on the aforementioned hermeneutical principles proposed by Cardinal Kasper to interpret the First Vatican Council.

Let us recall his hermeneutical rules. In the joint *relecture* he proposes, and in accordance with which he hopes for a new reception of the First Vatican Council within the Roman Catholic Church, he sets out as the first rule the need to integrate the statements on primacy within the global context of the theology of the church; furthermore, as the second rule specifies, to situate this council within the whole of tradition; and, third, to historicize its assertions in the particular context of Rome in 1870. He states as the fourth and last rule the need to assess the Petrine ministry against the gospel. In brief, this proposal concerns the appropriate rules for textual and conceptual hermeneutics. In the light of this, it is hoped that Catholics and Orthodox might be able to agree that the 1870 dogmas thus interpreted are not heretical.

However, as can easily be foreseen, the success merely at the doctrinal level of this rereading and re-reception of the First Vatican Council's doctrine on primacy—which Walter Kasper views as 'the only way forward'[18]—will be insufficient for the Orthodox Church to receive the ministry of Peter as it is actually exercised, with its immediate and universal jurisdiction over the whole church and over all the faithful, as well as the potential infallibility of its magisterium. Reception has no chance of taking place unless the Roman Catholic Church first clarifies those dogmas for herself, reaching in this way, with the Orthodox, a renewed understanding of them. What is required is an institutional reception of those dogmas, the implementation of which is first and foremost the Roman Catholic Church's responsibility.

In the official statements such a need is hardly ever evoked,[19] nor does it arouse much interest among theologians either, apart from the moments in which they bemoan the weight of institutions. With great acuity Yves Congar noted that the reception of the ideas of the Second Vatican Council had run up against the reality of the institutions resulting from the First. In his own terms:

> At the Council, and with Paul VI, there was the reception of new ideas ... of ressourcement, of collegiality or coresponsibility, an opening to ecumenism, an opening to the world ... of synodality, and the relative autonomy of local churches ... But neither the Council nor Paul VI really changed the structures of the Church in terms of its juridical organizations and procedures. For example, take the *plenitudo potestatis* [fullness of power/supreme authority] ... the concept of sovereignty which Hermann J. Pottmeyer has shown to have conditioned Vatican I ... the same concept of right, in its account of the sacramental foundations and the theological–Trinitarian status of the People of God, was reconsidered only by some rare spirits and was not renewed.[20]

The topics of the present volume testify to the accuracy of Congar's diagnosis. In spite of the good ideas of the Second Vatican Council, many Catholics are still talking of 'Episcopal Acountability', 'Lay Participation in Decision-making', 'Collegiality', 'Episcopal Conferences', etc. The reason is clear: in all these cases, the theological legacy of the Second Vatican Council has been forced into the procrustean bed of canonical practice inherited from the First. The 1917 Code, barely revised in 1983, operates with secularized categories borrowed from Roman law: the law here is the expression of the will of the universal legislator, the Pope, who alone has the fullness of capacities. Such right cannot provide the structures necessary for communion between the churches and within each church.[21]

The reception of the First Vatican Council is, therefore, a key to the reception of the Second Vatican Council. As such, we cannot avoid the question of whether the dogma of universal jurisdiction justifies the discretionary character—which does not mean arbitrary or despotic—with which papal authority has since been invested? Having all power within the church,[22] restrained only by natural and divine right (i.e. the existence of the episcopate), the Pope is a true monarch. He exercises all his powers according to his personal judgement, as confirmed by the Second Vatican Council.[23] In terms of political science, the Pope enjoys absolute power,[24] in so far as he is not accountable to any other authority.[25] This is also illustrated by the fact that the recognition of the authority of bishops over the universal church by the Second Vatican Council is not translated into any legal determination which would be exterior to papal authority: canonically, episcopal conferences are themselves emanations of the papacy[26] and they can exercise no authentic magisterium by themselves unless they reach unanimity.[27]

The fact that the Pope is accountable to no one but God[28] has represented, in the West, a major bone of contention since the beginning of the Reformation. Melanchthon expressed it with clarity: '*non est transferendum ad pontifices quod dicitur de ecclesia.*'[29] That is: what can be said of the church cannot be exclusively transferred to the papacy. This is also a fundamental Orthodox conviction, as expressed in the twelfth century by Nicetas of Nicomedia in his dialogue with Anselm of Havelberg,[30] and again in the encyclical of the Eastern patriarchs addressed to Blessed Pius IX in 1848.[31]

This sufficiently describes the ecclesiological frame of reference being experienced within the Catholic Church, for the new hermeneutic of the First Vatican Council not to appear unrealistic. The hermeneutics of these dogmas cannot avoid facing the issues coming from canon law, nor from the ecclesial ethos to which it leads. In order to appraise the seriousness of the question, it is enough to note that the Second Vatican Council, often critical of juridicism, pronounced only five times on canon law, while the word 'church' appears 1,135 times in its documents. This is what has caused such an unsatisfactory result.

It is known that the Second Vatican Council's vote in favour of collegiality was greeted quite unanimously as 'the backbone of the entire Council' and 'the centre of gravity of Vatican II'.[32] At the time even Congar wrote that with this vote 'one gained the feeling that that was it: Vatican II had balanced Vatican I... with a majority which never went below 87%'.[33] For Congar, with the adoption of collegiality, the Second Vatican Council had attained its goal: 'to restore to the episcopate a greater importance and initiative in the concrete government of the church, currently dominated by a certain exercise of papal primacy, one requiring the curial system and Roman centralization',[34] and against which 'stumble all the other churches which understand papal power as absolutist and monarchical'.[35] Yet, forty years later, according to current canon law, the bishop has technically become a 'functionary of the pope'.[36] In the wake of the First Vatican Council, Pius IX had himself forcefully protested against this consequence being drawn by Bismarck from the council.[37] What a paradox!

This paradox shows clearly that the future of ecumenism lies in much greater attention to the institutional dimension of the church's life. Thus, for instance, the Roman Catholic Church is a full member of the Faith and Order Commission of the WCC and its representatives have approved *Baptism, Eucharist and Ministry*, which, notably in §§ 26–27 of the third section, forcefully urges each church to seek a better balance between everybody's responsibilities and the responsibilities of a few, even of one person alone. It is a question here of a general ecumenical requirement. One can hardly say that the Roman Catholic Church has sought to progress in this direction during the last twenty years. This example well illustrates the importance of improving the reception of ecumenical agreements at an institutional level.[38]

To add one last important observation: in western societies, at least, ecumenical attitudes are those which appear to be pastorally most fruitful. Let us return to the previous example about the link between corporate and personal responsibility. Given the widespread situation of passive believers, taught, governed, and content to assist at celebrations that are simply done for them, how might the laity ever be able to bear witness to the gospel in the midst of contemporary cultural turmoil? If the hierarchy encourages people to believe that it has an exclusive monopoly on the interpretation of God's word and that the faithful's only task is to interiorize and repeat it, then neither their cultural experience nor their intellectual capacities are of significance in the act of interpretation. As a result, many believers will feel lost and estranged from their faith.[39] Whilst such a system may have suited the rural societies of the nineteenth century, to seek to reinstate it now is to depart from the teaching of *LG*, § 37, according to which bishops are 'helped by the experience of the laity, are in a position to judge more clearly and more appropriately (*distinctius et aptius*) in spiritual as well as in temporal matters'. However one interprets 'secularization', it remains an undeniable fact which raises the question: is it not the poor quality of the intra-ecclesial dialogue between bishops and faithful and, in the same way, of the inter-ecclesial dialogue between the Christian churches, that explains, in large part, the poor quality of the dialogue between the church and contemporary culture, which is, in turn, one of the undeniable sources of secularization? Indeed, the latter can in fact be interpreted as a failure of inculturation. From this particular angle, one can also see how ecumenical attitudes and evangelization are manifestly interdependent in the West.

THE RESPONSIBILITY OF THEOLOGIANS

The future of ecumenism demands of theologians a long-term, persevering commitment. As theologians, we already know that our personal duration and that of the church do not coincide: we are but relays in a long history of meaning, which has preceded us and which will continue after us. Notwithstanding this knowledge, we need encouragement and need, therefore, to identify the positive signs in the present situation.

Firstly: until the 1960s, as with many other innovative movements (notably the biblical, patristic, and liturgical renewals), Catholic ecumenism was the preserve of a very small minority. There were probably only thirty really competent people in France, fifty in Germany, about twenty in Belgium, Holland, England, and Switzerland. Nowadays, the theological community has been won over to the ecumenical cause, which is a guarantee against any turning back.

This leads to a second equally encouraging finding: theologians have some real ability to act in favour of ecumenism. In their universities, while remaining faithful to their specialities, all are able to make ecumenism a dimension of their teaching. In the life of the church, theologians can now be partners with other different actors such as bishops, pastors, social scientists, and canonists, as this volume exemplifies.

Of the two areas which I have indicated as most important for the future of the ecumenical dialogue—that of the search for differentiated consensuses and of research into the institutional implications of the agreements—it is the latter, as already indicated, which demands the most attention. Paradoxically, Roman Catholic theology is especially weak here despite the Roman Catholic Church being regarded, quite rightly, as the most juridical church possible! The remarkable insights of Paul VI in favour of a theological treatment of canon law have, unfortunately, all but remained a dead letter in the edition of the Code promulgated in 1983.[40] If everybody refers to the groundbreaking work of Klaus Mörsdorf[41] on the theology of canon law, the matter has not got beyond, as the following references show, the diagnosis of a lack as formulated by Remigiusz Sobanski, of Warsaw University;[42] the late Mgr Eugenio Corecco, of Fribourg University (and later Bishop of Lugano);[43] and by Professors René Metz[44] and Joseph Hoffmann,[45] of Strasbourg University, who would all agree with the deplorable finding by A. M. Rouco-Varela, Professor Emeritus at Salamanca University and currently Cardinal Archbishop of Madrid: 'There is no Catholic theology of canon law systematically constructed as a specific discipline.'[46] Pleading for 'an historical and theological study of the canonical tradition', with a view to the methodological deficiencies of Roman Catholic canon law as a discipline, Louis Bouyer voiced a warning thirty-five years ago which still stands. He underlined that 'To suppose that we could build a satisfactory ecclesiology in the Catholic Church today, and particularly one that has an ecumenical orientation, without engaging in such research, is an idle, catastrophic dream'.[47] I am of the same opinion.[48] Although institutionalism can be intimidating, and perhaps even alienating, the fact remains that Christian life has to be ordered not simply on an empirical basis. It requires that grace find expressions in institutions.[49] In this perspective, the law of the church does not arise from a law that the founder has given to certain responsible parties. Rather, this law appears to be intrinsic to the rationale of Christianity. It takes it source, as Congar pointed out, in the processes inherent in the profession of faith and celebration of the sacraments. By baptism, Eucharist, ordination, and also marriage, Christians see themselves as being granted a status of citizenship in the church, or as being entrusted with a ministry. All are subjects with rights and responsibilities, as each and all the local churches.

NOTES

1. Translated by Luca Badini-Confalonieri with Paul D. Murray. Those elements of this chapter that featured in the short closing reflection that Hervé Legrand offered at the Jan. 2006 colloquium were originally translated by Catherine E Clifford. Some traces of this earlier translation work remain in the translation offered here and the translators are grateful to Catherine Clifford for her work in this regard.

2. '*Monitum* of the Holy Office' (5 June 1948), *AAS*, 40 (1948), 257.

3. 'Certain formulations in the Report are not sufficiently explicit and hence can lend themselves to a twofold interpretation, in which both parties can find unchanged the expression of their own position', CDF, *Observations on The Final Report of the Anglican–Roman Catholic International Commission* (London: CTS, 1982), § A. 2. iii also available in *AAS*, 74 (1982), 1062–74; cf. Daphne Hampson, *Christian Contradictions: The Structure of Lutheran and Catholic Thought* (Cambridge: Cambridge University Press, 2001), for whom also identity of language is required for identity of faith. Contrast here the remarkable work by Otto H. Pesch, *Die Theologie der Rechtfertigung bei Martin Luther und Thomas von Aquin* (Mainz: Matthias Grünewald Verlag, 1985), which demonstrated the non-contradiction of Luther's and Aquinas' respective theologies of justification. See also Legrand, 'La Légitimité d'une pluralité de "formes de pensée" (Denkformen) en dogmatique catholique: retour sur la thèse d'un précurseur, O. H. Pesch', in François Bousquet, Henri-Jérôme Gagey, and Geneviève Médevielle (eds.), *La Responsabilité des théologiens: Mélanges en l'honneur de Joseph Doré* (Paris: Desclée, 2002), 685–704.

4. To cite two examples: (a) the refusal of 'the possibility of a divergence not only in the practice of adoration of Christ in the reserved sacrament but also in the theological judgements relating to it...the adoration rendered to the Blessed Sacrament is the object of a dogmatic definition in the Catholic Church', CDF, *Observations on the Final Report*, § B. I. 3; (b) 'what ARCIC writes about the role of Peter...does not satisfy the requirements of the dogmatic statement of Vatican Council I: "The apostle Peter...received immediately and directly from Jesus Christ Our Lord a true and proper primacy of jurisdiction"', ibid. § B. III. 1.

5. Rahner, 'Justified and Sinner at the Same Time' (1963), *Theological Investigations*, vol. vi., trans. Karl-H. and Boniface Kruger (London: Darton, Longman & Todd, 1969), 218–30.

6. Available at: < http:// www.vatican.va / roman_curia / pontifical_councils / chrstuni / documents / rc_ pc_ chrstuni_ doc_ 31101999_ cath-luth-joint-declaration_en.html>; also see Chapter 11: William G. Rusch, 'The International Lutheran–Roman Catholic Dialogue—An Example of Ecclesial Learning and Ecumenical Reception'.

7. See Lindbeck, *The Nature of Doctrine: Religion and Theology in a Postliberal Age* (London: SPCK, 1984).

8. Congar, *Une passion: l'unité. Réflexions et souvenirs, 1929–1973* (Paris: Cerf, 1974), 108.

9. Ratzinger, 'General Orientation with Regard to the Ecumenical Dispute about the Formal Principles of Faith' (1976), *Principles of Catholic Theology. Building Stones for a Fundamental Theology*, trans. Mary Frances McCarthy (San Francisco, Calif.: Ignatius Press, 1987), 199. But cf. id., *Church, Ecumenism and Politics: New*

Essays in Ecclesiology, trans. Robert Nowell (Slough: St Paul, 1988), 82–3, where he nuances his position, without renouncing it, by regarding it as an 'artificial withdrawal into the past beyond recall' to exclude from dialogue 'decisions since the separation'.

10. This decision has provoked reservations in the conservative circles of the Roman Curia, as witnessed by the special issue of *Divinitas, Sull'Anafora dei Santi Apostoli Addai e Mari*, ns 47 (2004), most notably the contribution of the editor, Mgr Brunero Gherardini, 'Le parole della consacrazione eucaristica', 141–69.

11. See *L'Osservatore Romano* (19 Nov. 1995). The statement was never published in the *Acta Apostolicæ Sedis*.

12. Kasper, 'Petrine Ministry and Synodality', *The Jurist*, 66 (2006), 298–309, originally presented at a symposium, 'The Relation Between the Bishop and the Local Church: Old and New Questions in Ecumenical Perspective', organized by the Centro Pro Unione at the Pontifical University St Thomas Aquinas, Rome, 3–5 Dec. 2005.

13. Bruno Neveu, *L'Erreur et son juge. Remarques sur les censures doctrinales à l'époque moderne* (Naples: Bibliopolis, 1993).

14. See Congar, 'Du bon usage du Denzinger', in *Situation et tâches présentes de la théologie* (Paris: Cerf, 1967), 111–33.

15. As Pius XII had already acknowledged in his 1951 encyclical *'Sempiternus Rex Christus. On the Council of Chalcedon'* (8 Sept. 1951), *AAS*, 43 (1951), 625–44; also available at <http://www.vatican.va/holy_father/pius_xii/encyclicals/documents/hf_p-xii_enc_08091951_sempiternus-rex-christus_en.html>.

16. See here the analysis of Harding Meyer, who coined the term: 'Grundkonsensus und Kirchegemeinschaft: Eine lutherische Perspektive', in André Birmelé and Harding Meyer (eds.), *Grundkonsens—Grunddifferenz: Studie des Straßburger Instituts für Ökumenische Forschung: Ergebnisse und Dokumente* (Frankfurt: Verlag Otto Lembeck, 1992), 126; also id., 'Die Prägung einer Formel. Ursprung und Intention', in Harald Wagner (ed.), *Einheit aber Wie? Zur Tragfähigkeit der ökumenischen Formels 'differenzierten Konsens'* (Freiburg: Herder, 2000), 36–58; and M. Striet, 'Denkformgenese und analyse in der Überlieferungsgeschichte des Glaubens. Theologisch-hermeneutische Überlegungen zum Begriff des differenzierten Konsenses', ibid. 59–80; also Chapter 20: Geraldine Smyth, 'Jerusalem, Athens, and Zurich: Psychoanalytic Perspectives on Factors Inhibiting Receptive Ecumenism', n. 15.

17. See here *UR*, § 4: '[T]heir [i.e. Catholics'] primary duty is to make a careful and honest appraisal of whatever needs to be renewed and done in the Catholic household itself...'

18. Kasper, 'Petrine Ministry and Synodality', 301.

19. An exception is John Paul II's *Ut Unum Sint*, § 95, where he hopes that 'we may seek—together, of course—the forms in which this ministry may accomplish a service of love recognized by all concerned'.

20. Congar, 'Remarques générales', *Paul VI et la modernité dans l'Église: actes du colloque organisé par l'École française de Rome* (2–4 June 1983) (Rome: École française de Rome, 1984), 851–2.

21. See Legrand, 'Grâce et institution dans l'Église: les fondements théologiques du droit canonique', in Jean-Louis Monneron, et al. (eds.), *L'Église, institution et foi*, 2nd edn. (Brussels: Facultés universitaires St Louis, 1985), 139–72.

22. Thus the Orthodox could be surprised to read in canon 412, § 1, of the Code of the eastern Churches that 'All religious are subject to the Roman Pontiff as their supreme superior, being bound by the obligation to obey him also in virtue of the vow of obedience', and that in canon 1,008, § 1, the Pope is declared 'supreme administrator and steward of all ecclesiastical goods', available at <http://www.intratext.com/IXT/ENG1199/_INDEX.HTM>.

23. Such are the terms of the *Nota Praevia* ('Preliminary Explanatory Note') to ch. 3 of the 'Dogmatic Constitution on the Church', (*LG*): whilst the college can never exercise its power without its head, 'The Roman Pontiff undertakes the regulation, encouragement, and approval of the exercise of collegiality as he sees fit'. Indeed, 'The Pope, as supreme pastor of the Church, may exercise his power at any time, as he sees fit, by reason of the demands of his office (*omni tempore, ad placitum*)' *LG*, 425–6. These two expressions (*ad placitum*, 'as he sees fit') were qualified by Joseph Ratzinger as 'not very felicitous' and 'never having been expressed under this form in a document of the Church', adding: 'moreover, we must be clear that the notion of a collegiality exclusively centred on the whole Church leads to an impasse', 'La Collégialité épiscopale, développement théologique', in G. Baraúna (ed.), *L'Église de Vatican II. Études autour de la constitution conciliaire sur l'Église*, vol. iii (Paris: Cerf, 1966), 785–6.

24. Cf. Henri Morel, 'Absolutisme', in Philippe Raynaud and S. Rials (eds.), *Dictionnaire de philosophie politique* (Paris: Presses Universitaires de France, 1996), 1.

25. See canon 333, § 3: 'No appeal or recourse is permitted against a sentence or decree of the Roman Pontiff.' This immunity from appeal has been expanded after the Second Vatican Council; where the First forbade appeal to a council as the supreme authority, and the 1917 Code (canon 228, § 2) excluded such appeal without further qualifications, the 1983 Code forbids any appeal whatsoever. A similar prohibition has more recently been extended so as to cover the decisions of the CDF; see '*Ratio Agendi*: Regulations for Doctrinal Examination' (30 May 1997), § 27, *AAS*, 89 (1997), 834, also available at <http://www.vatican.va/roman_curia/congregations/cfaith/documents/rc_con_cfaith_doc_19970629_ratio-agendi_en.html>.

26. John Paul II's 1998 motu proprio, *Apostolos Suos*, is clear on this point: 'The binding effect of the acts of the episcopal ministry jointly exercised within Conferences of Bishops and in communion with the Apostolic See derives from the fact that the latter has constituted the former and has entrusted to them...specific areas of competence', '*Apostolos Suos*. Apostolic Letter Issued Motu Proprio on the Theological and Juridical Nature of Episcopal Conferences' (21 May 1998), § 13, *AAS*, 90 (1998), 650–1; also available at <http://www.vatican.va/holy_father/john_paul_ii/motu_proprio/documents/hf_jp-ii_motu-proprio_22071998_apostolos-suos_en.html>.

27. 'In order that the doctrinal declarations of the Conference of Bishops...may constitute authentic magisterium and be published in the name of the Conference itself, they must be unanimously approved by the Bishops who are members, or receive the *recognitio* of the Apostolic See if approved in plenary assembly by at least two-thirds of the Bishops belonging to the Conference and having a deliberative vote'. *Apostolos*

Suos § 22, 655–6. In the current canon law, this is the only requirement of unanimity in force.

28. There is no need to make too much of a quip of the late Cardinal Schotte, Secretary of the Synod of Bishops, to some journalists: 'Bishops are accountable to no one but the pope. And the pope is accountable to no one but Jesus', *The Tablet* (24 Nov. 2001), 1658. On the other hand, altogether more serious matters are the anger and disappointment felt among the faithful, particularly in the US and in Ireland, by the way in which bishops have handled their responsibility vis-à-vis Catholic families and priests in the paedophile crisis.

29. 'Apologia', §188, in André Birmelé and Marc Lienhard (eds.), *La Foi des églises luthériennes: confessions et catéchismes* (Paris and Geneva: Cerf/Labor et Fides, 1991), 159. The immediately preceding sentence runs: 'Our adversaries would perhaps like the Church to be defined thus: it is an external monarchy whose supremacy extends over the entire earth, and in which the Roman Pontiff must have a power which no one has the right to question or judge. Of his own accord, he can establish the articles of faith, abolish the Scriptures, establish modes of worship and liturgy; promulgate laws as he wills and similarly dispense with any law whatsoever according to his will, whether divine, canonical, or civil.'

30. *PL*, 188, cols. 1218–19.

31. See J. D. Mansi, *Sacrorum conciliorum nova et amplissima collectio* (Paris and Leipzig: 1901–27), xl. 408C, where is to be found, 'For us the security of religion resides in the whole body of the Church'; English trans. available as Eastern Orthodox Patriarchs, 'Encyclical of the Eastern Patriarchs (1848): A Reply to the Epistle of Pope Pius IX', at <http://www.fordham.edu/halsall/mod/1848orthodoxencyclical.html>.

32. See Pierre Eyt, 'La Collégialité épiscopale', in Philippe Levillain (ed.), *Le deuxième concile du Vatican, 1959–1965* (Rome: École Française de Rome, 1989), 541, citing Umberto Betti and Antoine Wenger.

33. Congar, *Le Concile au jour le jour: troisième session* (Paris, Cerf, 1964), 44.

34. Ibid. 37.

35. Id., *Le Concile au jour le jour* (Paris: Cerf, 1963), 18.

36. Such is Georg Bier's conclusion in his recent *Habilitationschrift* at the University of Freiburg: 'In summary: the general determinations of the Code concerning the episcopate and the diocesan bishop, as well as the standard understanding of this ministry in the determinations of the Code, describe the diocesan bishop as being juridically a functionary of the Pope', *Die Rechtsstellung des Diözesanbischofs nach dem Codex Iuris Canonici von 1983* (Würzburg: Echter Verlag, 2001), 376.

37. Bismarck's remark, published in 1874, prompted the reaction of the German episcopate in the form of a Feb. 1875 statement specifically stating both that the decrees of the First Vatican Council offer no basis for the position that the Pope has become an absolute sovereign and that 'we can decisively refute the statement that the bishops have become by reason of the Vatican decrees mere papal functionaries with no personal responsibility'. For this statement and Pius IX's official endorsement of it, see *DS*, §§ 3112–17; also F. D. Logan, 'The 1875 Statement of the German Bishops on Episcopal Powers', *The Jurist*, 21 (1961), 286.

38. See Legrand, Personal, Collegial and Synodal Responsibility in The Roman Catholic Church: What Convergences Are There Between the Reception of Vatican II and

BEM?', in Thomas F. Best and Tamara Grdzelidze (eds.), *BEM at 25: Critical Insights into a Continuing Legacy* (Faith and Order Paper, No. 205) (Geneva: WCC, 2007), 105–29.

39. This diagnosis parallels that of Antonio Rosmini in *The Five Wounds of the Church* (1848), where the laity's indifference towards religion, against which he repeatedly warned, was in his view caused precisely by the dominant clerical attitude of leaving the laity completely passive: excluded from episcopal elections, the administration of the Church's temporal goods, and especially liturgical worship, see *The Five Wounds of the Church*, trans. Denis Cleary (Leominster: Fowler Wright, 1987), §§ 77 and 22 (pp. 68–9 and 17–18 respectively).

40. See Eugenio Corecco, 'Paul VI et le statut du droit canonique', in *Paul VI et les réformes institutionnelles dans l'Église, Journée d'Études* (Fribourg, Switzerland; 9 Nov. 1985) (Brescia: Istituto Paolo VI/Edizioni Studium, 1987), 13–29.

41. See A. Cattaneo, *Grundfragen des Kirchenrechts bei Klaus Mörsdorf: Synthese und Ansätze einer Wertung* (Amsterdam: Grüner, 1991).

42. See Sobanski, *Grundlagenproblematik des katholischen Kirchenrechts* (Vienna and Cologne: Böhlau Verlag, 1987).

43. See, in particular, Corecco, *Théologie et droit canon. écrits pour une nouvelle théorie générale du droit canonique* (Fribourg: Éditions universitaires, 1990) and id., 'La Réception de Vatican II dans le code de droit canonique', in Giuseppe Alberigo and J-P. Jossua (eds.), *La Réception de Vatican II* (Paris: Cerf, 1985), 327–91.

44. See Metz, 'Le Problème d'un droit de l'Église dans les milieux catholiques de la seconde moitié du XIX⁰ siècle à la période post-conciliaire (1870–1983)', *Revue de droit canonique*, 35 (1985), 222–44.

45. See Hoffmann, 'L'Horizon œcuménique de la réforme du droit canonique: à propos de deux ouvrages de H. Dombois', *Revue des sciences philosophiques et théologiques*, 57 (1973), 228–50; id., 'Statut et pratique du droit canonique dans l'Église', *Revue de droit canonique*, 27 (1977), 5–37.

46. See Rouco-Varela, Antonio María, 'Grundfragen einer katholischen Theologie des Kirchenrechts: Überlegungen zum Aufbau einer katholischen Theologie des Kirchenrechts', *Archiv für katholisches Kirchenrecht*, 148 (1979), 341; cf. also his latest publication, *Schriften zur Theologie des Kirchenrechts und zur Kirchenverfassung* (Paderborn: Schöning Verlag, 2000).

47. Bouyer, *L'Église de Dieu* (Paris: Cerf, 1970), 208–9; English trans. (Charles Underhill Quinn) *The Church of God: Body of Christ and Temple of the Spirit* (Chicago, Ill.: Franciscan Herald, 1982), 172.

48. See Legrand, 'Grâce et institution dans l'Église'.

49. For some decisive intuitions in this direction, see the work of the Lutheran Hans Dombois, *Das Recht der Gnade: Oekumenisches Kirkenrecht*, vols. i–ii (Witten, Bielefeld: Luther, 1961 and 1969).

28

Receptive Ecumenism and Catholic Learning—Reflections in Dialogue with Yves Congar and B. C. Butler[1]

Gabriel Flynn

INTRODUCTION

Cardinal Yves Congar (1904–95) and Bishop Basil Christopher Butler (1902–86) were both dedicated to the renewal of Catholic Learning and to the promotion of Christian unity. Butler, a convert to Catholicism, followed a more 'conservative' line than Congar. For his part, Congar, the leading figure of the Catholic ecumenical movement in France and a member of the Catholic–Lutheran Commission of Dialogue since 1965, was profoundly influenced by Lutheran theology in the formulation of his later 'progressive' stance on ecumenism. Each served tirelessly at all four sessions of the Second Vatican Council (1962–5): one as a prominent *peritus* (expert), the other as President of the English Benedictine Congregation, and their respective theological visions are enshrined in its principal documents.[2]

This essay explores the themes of Receptive Ecumenism and Catholic Learning as they relate to the thought of Congar and Butler respectively. A related concern is to seek to extrapolate ethical implications for the present-day ecumenical movement. Specifically, I shall attempt to draw Congar and Butler into dialogue on the central doctrine of the incarnation, regarded by the former as 'the key to the whole mystery of the Church'.[3] By relating that dialogue to their ecumenical visions, an effort is made to contribute to a renewed commitment to the original goals of the modern ecumenical movement, as defined at its apex in the mid-twentieth century.[4]

In this regard, the chapter considers whether a return to the incarnate Christ, the primordial source of unity, provides new impetus for receptive ecumenical learning in the postmodern context; a hypothesis that will be tested by reference to the urgent challenges to the ecumenical movement in Northern Ireland. It is precisely in such situations of politico–religious conflict that ecumenism becomes an ethical imperative.[5] Without an effective praxis-orientation, all ecumenical ethics is destined to fail in situations of violent hostility that result from political and/or religious polarization. It must be said, however, that over and above political, intellectual, and psychological factors in the vocation and mission of ecumenists and peacemakers, prayer is foremost. This is a point of fundamental importance and one familiar to Paul Couturier (1881–1953), the renowned French priest who developed the 'Week of Universal Prayer' for church unity. Congar too knew the power of prayer in ecumenical efforts and his remarks in this regard are germane: 'Prayer by common intention and even, where possible, prayer together, constitutes the culminating point of ecumenical experience and activity.'[6]

THE SECOND VATICAN COUNCIL AND THE ARCHITECTS OF CATHOLIC ECUMENISM

Cardinal Augustin Bea (1881–1968), one-time President of the Secretariat for Christian Unity, provided a succinct account of the goals of the ecumenical movement born of the Second Vatican Council. His comments are rooted in Christ's vision of unity, while also taking account of the difficulties in so great a work:

In the Decree on Ecumenism the Council itself declared: 'The restoration of unity among all Christians is one of the principal concerns of the Second Vatican Council.' (§ 1) ... The Council has been able to make a great contribution to the cause of the union of all baptised people. For this reason, since the closing of the Council, every ecumenical movement, in order to be opportune and in accordance with actual reality, must also take into account the ecumenical situation now created by the Council.[7]

It is now almost fifty years since Pope John XXIII (1881–1963) proposed his grand plan of campaign for Christian unity. There are those who claim that in the intervening period the church has garnered little from its myriad endeavours, while the original fervour and optimism of the ecumenical movement now appear almost to be dormant. At the same time it seems that there are signs of renewed hope for the cause of ecumenism.

As explored in greater detail in other chapters in this volume, the dream of unity was revivified by Pope John Paul II (1920–2004) through his papal ministry and, in particular, his 1995 encyclical *Ut Unum Sint*. Again, Pope Benedict XVI's inaugural homily, with its 'explicit call to unity';[8] his subsequent overtures to Eastern Christians;[9] his meeting with Bartholomew I, Ecumenical Patriarch of Constantinople in 2006;[10] the recent document on Mary from the Anglican–Roman Catholic International Commission (ARCIC);[11] and the indispensable contribution of the Christian churches to the peace in Northern Ireland, all provide evidence of new vitality in the otherwise flagging ecumenical movement.

In plotting a course for the third millennium, ecumenists will either operate in the light of Christ's cross so as to unite with and reach out in peace to other religions or be consigned to the graveyard of irrelevance in a world dominated by rampant materialism, secularism, incredulity, and the occult. This is a point of considerable importance since inter-church dialogue in many respects provides a template for inter-religious dialogue. In reflecting on church unity, a difficult question arises. Is the vision for unity presented in John 17, the source and foundation of all ecumenical endeavours, to be taken seriously at the present time? By way of response, I shall consider how the mutual concern for the incarnation in the thought of Congar and Butler has helped to advance the goals of receptive ecumenical learning with integrity across denominational differences.

REAWAKENING ECUMENISM: 'THE QUEST FOR CATHOLICITY'

Consideration of Congar's ecumenism, already documented by theologians,[12] shows that his long life was a veritable school of receptive learning. In the years 1928–9, he experienced the first great interior appeal to dedicate himself particularly to the church and to ecumenism. He always viewed the renewal of ecclesiology in conjunction with 'wide participation in unitive activities'.[13] The decisive point that set his course was his retreat in preparation for ordination:

To prepare for ordination I made a special study both of John's Gospel and Thomas Aquinas' commentary on it. I was completely overwhelmed, deeply moved, by chapter 17, sometimes called the priestly prayer, but which I prefer to call Jesus' apostolic prayer on Christian unity: 'That they may be one as we are one.' My ecumenical vocation can be directly traced to this study of 1929.[14]

Congar argues unambiguously that ecumenism 'presupposes a movement of conversion and reform co-extensive with the whole life of all communions'.[15] The foregoing remarks indicate that without personal conversion of life and institutional reform in all the churches, the entire process of Receptive Ecumenism is necessarily impeded.

I shall now comment briefly on the evolution in Congar's ecumenical thought viewed in the context of his 'total ecclesiology'. He sums up that evolution as follows: 'My confrère and friend J.-P. Jossua finally analysed a change in the key concept from 1937, *Chrétiens désunis* and this book [*Essais œcuméniques*]: i.e. the passage from "Catholicity" to "diversities" and "pluralism".'[16] In *Chrétiens désunis: principes d'un 'œcuménisme' catholique* (1937), the first contribution in French to Roman Catholic ecumenism, catholicity is viewed in dialectical terms as the universal capacity for the unity of the church and the guarantee of respect for what is finest and most authentic in the diversity of languages, nations and religious experiences.[17] Congar argues that while there may be a non-Roman

ecumenism, since no other exists, 'there cannot be a "non-Roman Catholicity".'[18]
This is an indication of how ecumenism has changed since 1937. In *Diversités et
communion: dossier historique et conclusion théologique* (1982),[19] the focus is no
longer on catholicity, but on the necessity of diversity at the heart of communion:
'It was the idea of Catholicity which at the time seemed to me to encompass the
diversities; today I am more aware of the diversities, as is evident from my recent
book *Diversity and Communion*'.[20]

Congar goes even further to give a qualified acceptance to the expression
'reconciled diversities'.[21] The controversial term 'reconciled diversity' (*Versöhnte
Verschiedenheit*) was proposed by the Concord of Leuenberg and adopted by the
assembly of the World Lutheran Federation in 1977.[22] The question must be
asked whether the shift in his ecumenism from catholicity to pluralism/diversities
entails the recognition of the division of Christendom as permanent and irre-
versible. *Diversités et communion* actually endorses an ecumenism which Congar
warned against in *Chrétiens désunis*, namely: the recognition of a certain unity in
diversity. His caveat is stated unambiguously in *Chrétiens désunis*: 'What is today
called "ecumenism" is the introduction of a certain unitedness into an already
existing diversity—oneness in multiplicity.... As Archbishop Söderblom called
it: it is but a mirage of Catholicity (*catholicité*) for those who cannot recognise
among "the Churches" *the* Church of Jesus Christ, visibly one.'[23] This ecumenism, reduced to a common denominator without unity, lacks catholicity.[24] It
is noteworthy that J-P. Jossua views the evolution from '*Catholicity*' to '*diversity
or pluralism*' in positive terms but without denying the inherent tensions therein:
'An all embracing model [catholicity], or an image of unfolding, is followed
by one of openness [diversity], a figure of the tensions existing between two
terms.'[25] From what has been said, it is evident that Congar's evolving ecumenical
perspectives have important implications for those presently engaged in the work
of ecumenism, a question to which I shall return later. For now, I wish briefly to
outline Butler's contribution.

BUTLER ON INCARNATION, REDEMPTION, AND THE
UNITY OF THE CHURCH

Christopher Butler, received into the Catholic Church in 1928, became in turn
a Benedictine monk, then Abbot of Downside Abbey, and, in 1966, Auxiliary
Bishop of Westminster. A trained historian and a foundation member of ARCIC,
he was one of the principal theologians of the Second Vatican Council, engaged
on the creation of its 'Dogmatic Constitution on the Church', which laid the
foundation for the movement towards Christian unity, as well as the 'Pastoral
Constitution on the Church in the Modern World' and the 'Dogmatic Constitution on Divine Revelation'. In his book *The Church and Unity*, he rejected the

view that Christianity is one among many of the versions of the human quest for God, and argues instead that the Christian religion springs from a divine initiative that is disclosed primarily and uniquely in the incarnation. As he writes: 'Christianity is not, fundamentally, nothing more than a human quest for God. At a deeper level, it is God's quest for man. It springs from a divine initiative that is disclosed primarily in the utterly unprecedented, unpredictable, unique fact of the incarnation of the Word of God in Jesus Christ.'[26] Like Congar, Butler places the incarnation, seen as an intensely powerful reality, at the centre of the Christian religion.

The most complete self disclosure is in an act of self-giving love which 'speaks' the very heart of the lover. Such a word is claimed by Christianity to be its core and essence: 'the word became man and dwelt among us'; 'he died for our sins and rose again for our justification.' Nothing like this is found in either Judaism or Islam (nor, to the best of my knowledge, in any other religion; most religions have failed to grasp the gulf between Absolute Mystery and polytheism). Hence, if we are concerned with the question: 'Has God spoken?', it seems reasonable to concentrate, at least in the first instance, on Christianity.[27]

Butler holds that the unity of the church is part of the divine datum of salvation and argues, on the basis of his assertion of the uniqueness of Christianity, that the church and its unity are integral to the divine economy of redemption: 'If the historical and visible unity of the Church is a precarious thing, subject to the fallibility and peccability of the Church's members, and capable of disappearing for a time, or permanently, from among the realities of history, then this unity is not part of the divine *datum* of redemption.'[28] Butler further develops his understanding of unity by arguing that the church is essentially in the stage of probation, a historical reality and not a mere Platonic idea or an eschatological Utopia. But a reality that is essentially and 'visibly' historical, that is, 'concrete and recognizable', must have its own historical and visible unity. Following this line of argument, he arrives at an important conclusion: 'God's fidelity guarantees to our faith that the Church will never fail to be at least adequately holy, catholic, and apostolic. Similarly, it will never cease to be visibly one, with a unity that is not intrinsic to its nature but comes as a gift from God, a gift continually bestowed afresh.'[29] But if the unity of the church is guaranteed, why is the work of ecumenism so important? Butler provides a precise response to this difficulty:

The visible unity of the Church, while certain, is not a magic fact. It does, in a sense, depend on the faithful perseverance of the Church's members—or at least of some of them... The mystery of redemption is a single mystery, including both Jesus Christ and his Church... But schism and the threat of schism are recurrent phenomena in Christian history.[30]

By making church unity, in a sense, dependent on mere mortals, Butler also makes plain the great challenge of ecumenism. If the baton of unity is not successfully passed from generation to generation, the church of Christ is in danger of being reduced to a vast accumulation of tarnished fragments. Ecumenism is, of course, part of the noble call to holiness in the church. Butler argues that as the church grows in holiness it will also grow in unity. By placing unity in eternal, eschatological relief, his thesis on 'the Church and its unity' reaches its zenith:

As the Church grows in holiness, so it will grow towards unity...In this world, the Church will never be perfectly holy...The visible unity of the Church will always be precarious, and may have to be conceived not so much as an attainable and permanent goal but as an unrealizable eschatological hope or a Kantian regulative idea.[31]

Butler was at pains to point out to his 'ecumenical friends' that his 'essay' on ecumenism does not call into question the principle underlying the ecumenical movement or betray its integrity. He, nonetheless, adheres tenaciously to the principle of catholicity as a defence against the delusion of 'false hopes' in ecumenical dialogue. As Butler writes: 'Christianity is meant for everyone, and so the Church is meant for everyone; it is "catholic", universal of right, even when it is not yet universal in fact.'[32] Furthermore, in his vision for the nascent ecumenical movement, Butler calls for the reform of 'extreme centralization' in the church but without departing from the principle of catholicity:[33]

Is it possible to say that the Catholic Church must 'die' in order to live? This essay has been devoted to arguing that there is a limit to such a suggestion: the Catholic Church, in loyalty to itself, its mission and commission, and to Christianity itself and the world to which Christianity is sent, cannot barter away the principle that God's Church 'subsists' in the Roman Catholic Communion.[34]

It is perhaps ironic that Butler's perception of the important role of catholicity is echoed by the American Methodist theologian Stanley Hauerwas. He identifies an obvious weakness in the ecumenical endeavours of some Catholic theologians. As he writes poignantly:

I want you to be Catholics. I also believe that there is nothing more important for the future of the unity of the Church than for you to be Catholic...You have been so anxious to be like us that you have failed in your ecumenical task to help us to see what it means for any of us to be faithful to the Gospel on which our unity depends.[35]

CONGAR AND BUTLER: DIFFERING VOICES

In Butler, then, we hear the clear, decisive voice of the convert. Whereas in Congar it is possible to decipher the evolving, hesitant voice of the ecumenist; a voice that reflects the ecumenical influences of his youth and adolescence, through childhood relations with Protestants and Jews, contact with a Russian seminary at Lille, and a lecture given by his old master Marie-Dominique Chenu on the *Faith and Order* movement of Lausanne.

Careful analysis of Congar's later ecumenical writings reveals the potent influence of his Lutheran and Protestant friends. He was willing to sacrifice his life for a deeper understanding of Luther on the part of Catholics. As he remarks: 'I know that nothing really worthwhile with regard to Protestantism will be achieved so long as we take no steps truly to understand Luther, instead of simply condemning him, and to do him historical justice. For this conviction which is mine I would gladly give my life.'[36]

In some respects, the ambitious ecumenical vision that this suggests is more appealing than Butler's pressing of the thesis of catholicity. Equally, it can legitimately be claimed that the latter, by his adherence to catholicity as the standard for ecumenical dialogue, has contributed more to the preservation of the Christian heritage in its entirety than his erstwhile friend and former colleague from the French Ardennes. Congar, on the other hand, by abandoning catholicity in favour of diversity, has contributed to a diminution of his own theological tradition while the coveted goal of unity, much less reunion, remains unrealized. This point can be made clearer by drawing attention to the present decline in the popular ecumenical movement, a decline that is perhaps nowhere more evident than in the fate of the annual Octave of Prayer for the unity of all baptized Christians. This observance, for which Congar and others had such high hopes,[37] has become little more than polite and powerless exchanges between the few, deprived of universality: an important element in the psychology of the Octave.[38] It seems to me, therefore, that Butler's insistence on the visible unity of the church as part of the divine datum of salvation, as well as on the church's holiness, may well prove more lasting than Congar's more daring but risky embrace of the Lutheran notion of *Versöhnte Verschiedenheit*. At the same time it should be easy to understand how Congar, a lifelong practitioner of 'friendship in the service of unity' (F. Portal) and a master of the psychology of ecumenism, both encapsulates and enhances the whole programme of Receptive Ecumenism. As he wrote:

Ecumenism demands a profound moral and even religious conversion...Ecumenism seeks also a reform within ourselves, for we are full of aggressiveness, clannishness and arrogance, of distrust and rivalry...Ecumenism is an effort to rediscover a unity amongst Christians in keeping at once with the unity of its beginnings in the Upper Room of the Last Supper and of Pentecost, and with that of its eschatological culmination.[39]

In the penultimate part of this chapter, I shall examine how the respective contributions of Congar and Butler can contribute, if at all, to the new science of politics and to the praxis of Receptive Ecumenism currently unfolding in the post-war context of Northern Ireland.

RECEPTIVE ECUMENISM IN NORTHERN IRELAND:
'A WINTER'S JOURNEY'

The politics of prejudice in Northern Ireland, with its familiar garb of mutual intolerance and antipathy, emanating ultimately from a presumed superiority of ascendancy, eventually gave way to the terrible tumult of war and the seemingly endless, bloody, fist and fang of revenge in a brutal, complicated, civil and territorial conflict that spanned almost three decades. The violence was often so extreme that it spilled out over Northern Ireland's borders into England and the Republic of Ireland. The signing of the Good Friday Agreement on 10 April 1998 heralded the end of that bitter, unrelenting winter of war (1969–98). The cessation of hostilities has not, however, resulted in the end of the querulous spirit that for centuries divided the northern counties of Ireland. It is perhaps still too early and too painful for the people of Northern Ireland to peer into that province's looking glass, to acknowledge as their own image and likeness the simulacrum of themselves which lies in the disinterested onlooker's possession. What emerges from behind the shattered shards of the veiled figures in the Anglo–Irish looking glass is the spectre of individuals and families, as well as communities and churches, disfigured by long years of mistrust, violence, and sectarianism; those wild, gnarled shoots springing from the deep roots of an ancient enmity. One such jagged, bloodstained shard that needs to be examined at the propitious moment is the coercive apparatus of the Northern Ireland state, from its foundation in 1920 to the commencement of war in the late 1960s. It is incontrovertible that wars do not just happen; they are caused by people and what they do to their neighbours. In any sovereign democratic state, respect for the human and civil rights of all its citizens demands accountability for the actions of the state, notably, its security services and judiciary.

Happily, a new dispensation has begun to emerge in the realm of Anglo–Irish politics, one that may eventually lead to renewed prosperity and economic independence for Northern Ireland. But politics, like education, works slowly, normally very slowly. While importunate questions of rights and liberties properly belong in the domain of politics, all religious expressions of prejudice, regardless of the denominational affiliations of those who propagate them, are also the concern of the churches. In Northern Ireland's complex web of politics and religion, intimately and intricately interwoven of sharply contrasting colours and antediluvian allegiances, ecumenism cannot be seen as optional or occasional. It is rather an ethical imperative, not so much for the sake of the church and its unity, as for the world and its salvation.

It must be acknowledged, without dissimulation, that Congar's mature ecumenism, replete with the Lutheran *Versöhnte Verschiedenheit* is, in the context of Northern Ireland, untenable, unacceptable, and, it would appear, unworkable in both short- and long-term perspectives. What appears to be lacking in Congar's grand theory of ecumenism is the acceptance that the divisions among Christians are not always necessarily resoluble. In the process of reconciliation in Ireland, respect for the other, for his or her unique political loyalties and religious beliefs, is much more likely to receive a favourable and successful reception than any naïve aspirations for reconciliation of opposing religious and/or political allegiances.

In the final analysis, the greatest contribution of the long-suffering people of Northern Ireland to democratic politics and to Christian ecumenism will undoubtedly be in the sphere of receptive learning with due regard for the integrity of the other. The difficult process of cultivating and then inculcating such respect involves parents, educators, and leaders of state and church; it necessitates fortitude and resilience on the part of its architects, whose painstaking work is, in general, secluded from the mainstream of history. Their efforts at local and national levels may in time become as a plinth crowned with mutual, peaceful acceptance of the respective loyalties of a previously deeply divided community. Less than a generation ago, such sentiments would have seemed illusory. In the context of the present long-awaited peace, carefully nurtured at its most critical stage by the highest office in American politics, it is easy to see how Butler's ecumenism, with its respectful adherence to particular ecclesial loyalties in peaceful coexistence with the other, constitutes a more realistic, robust model of unity than that proposed by Congar.

A renewed ecumenical engagement by the churches on both social and doctrinal matters, thus avoiding the danger of a false and sterile dialectic, is also important for the political process. Such a renewal in ecumenism could contribute towards a more expeditious commencement of the appropriate exercise of the offices of government by the elected representatives of Northern Ireland.

THE INCARNATION OF CHRIST: THE BIRTH OF PEACE

We come finally to discussion of the incarnation. The mystery of the incarnation is the mystery of love and incarnational theology is ever-affective theology, a notable point in the context of ecumenism. Study of the history of the modern ecumenical movement, in fact, reveals that the realization of its original goals is closely linked to that movement's effectiveness in affectivity. Congar, the model par excellence, formulated a rich theology of 'the other' based on mutual esteem and respect. His outstanding contribution spans the most innovative period in Catholic ecumenical activity and one of the most creative periods in the history of Catholic theology. Destined to fail in the realization of his high aspirations for unity and reunion, formulated at the beginning of his dual vocation to ecumenism and ecclesiology, Congar none the less pursued his ambitious plan with determination, as he reached out to embrace a fragmented and bitterly divided former Christendom. His approach to the praxis of ecumenism testifies eloquently to the beauty of charity, and to the pre-eminence of love and sacrifice. As he remarks:

Where ecumenism is concerned, intellectual forces are not the only ones encountered. Each original reality has its order of existence, its laws, and so, when situated within its order, it asserts its value when experienced in accordance with its laws . . . Ecumenism too has its 'order' and it is felt as an authentic Christian value in the original experience which brings it its own light and power. It is difficult to analyse an experience; one makes it. It entails a second birth; or rather it is itself a process of rebirth. One becomes thereby a different person. It is what takes place at, say, the beginning of love or when one has undergone the blessed experience of sacrifice, of the Cross, of humiliation or poverty accepted lovingly for God's sake.[40]

The challenge of ecumenism may be compared to that of a tired but determined pilgrim journeying towards the eternal mystery of the incarnation, walking bravely, falteringly towards the light in the shrouded darkness of a winter epiphany. It is only when the ecumenist enters fully into the mystery of the incarnation, participating in the Lord's *kenosis*, that reception of the other, reform of self, and movement towards the common good become possible.

   The creative genius of artists and poets assists theologians in the articulation of divine mysteries. The sentiments expressed by the English poet Henry Vaughan (1622–95) in his inspiring poem 'The Night' are relevant to our discussion of Receptive Ecumenism in the context of the incarnation:

> Through that pure *Virgin shrine*,
> That sacred vail drawn o'r thy glorious noon,
> That men might look and live, as Glow-worms shine,
>
> . . .
>
> There is in God (some say)
> A deep but dazzling darkness; As men here
> Say it is late and dusky, because they
>   See not all clear.
> Oh for that night! where I in Him
> Might live invisible and dim.[41]

Ecumenism has been for a short time a bright, iridescent light for the churches and a source of hope for a near-naked world clad in the tattered apparel of disunity and the blood-red flags of wars executed with startling brutality in the name of religion, across the 'Christian' centuries, to the present. Still, the 'dazzling darkness' of the light emanating from the 'virgin shrine' reveals the incarnation to a disinterested, rootless world. It is that same 'dusky' light, now illuminating the shadowlands of unbelief, where anxious peoples patiently await the rebirth of untimely hope; hope as may yet trumpet a muffled nocturnal renaissance of faith in a normally 'silent' God.

Returning briefly to the vexatious question of Northern Ireland, I think I can indicate briefly how the incarnation can contribute to the advancement of peace and ecumenism in that troubled province, as well as in the wider wounded world. The mystery of the incarnation is the mystery of childhood, the mystery of love. As Butler remarks:

Love's impulse is to help the beloved by identification with his concerns, and with himself. Christianity teaches us that God so loves us that not only *would* he, if necessary, identify himself with our destiny and our fate in order to lead us to a triumph beyond that fate, but that he *has actually* done so. This is the meaning of the 'incarnation'.[42]

If we do not recapture the unique capacity of children for peace and love, the peace process in Northern Ireland and elsewhere will be further obstructed by the apparently endless accretions of history.

The original lofty goals of the ecumenical movement will only ever be realized in part, and to the extent to which they are pursued in a spirit of fidelity to the gospel, with due regard to the integrity of the other, and with essential realism. The most important lesson of Congar and Butler for the architects of Catholic Learning in the post 9/11 world, characterized by the radicalization of Islam and an ever-increasing fragmentation of Christianity, stripped of catholicity in all its denominations,[43] is to formulate an ecumenical concept of catholicity that is capable of sustaining differences while also withstanding the movement towards reductionism. It is a sacred duty incumbent upon all Christians to work for the unity of the church and the peace of the world, by openness to the Spirit and faithful adherence to Christ, the abiding norm for renewal (*UR*, § 6). I advocate the approach of the French ecumenist, Paul Couturier whose eloquent prayer for unity resonates with unmistakable eschatological overtones: 'That the unity of all Christians may come, such as Christ wills, and by the means that He wills.'

NOTES

1. This chapter draws on elements of an earlier paper published in *Louvaib Studies* 31 (2006), 196–213.
2. See Congar, *Mon journal du concile*, vol. ii. ed. Éric Mahieu (Paris: Cerf, 2002), 511 and 598; also Xavier Rynne, *Letters From Vatican City: Vatican Council II (First Session), Background and Debates* (London: Faber & Faber, 1963), 132, 154, 155, 159, 171, 173, 233, and 238; id., *The Second Session: The Debates and Decrees of Vatican*

Council II, September 29 to December 4, 1963 (London: Faber & Faber, 1964), 60, 66, 137, 157, 247, 276, 290; Giuseppe Alberigo and Joseph Komonchak (eds.), *History of Vatican II*, vol. iii., *The Mature Council: Second Period and Intersession September 1963–September 1964* (Louvain and Maryknoll, NY: Peeters/Orbis, 2000), 108, 115, 130, 264 n. 35, 272 n. 53.

3. Congar, *Divided Christendom: A Catholic Study of the Problem of Reunion*, trans. M. A. Bousfield (London: Geoffrey Bles, 1939), 274; also id., *Chrétiens désunis: principes d'un 'œcuménisme' catholique*, Unam Sanctam, 1 (Paris: Cerf, 1937), 344.

4. See Marc Boegner, *The Long Road to Unity: Memories and Anticipations*, trans. René Hague (London: Collins, 1970); Michael Kinnamon and Brian E. Cope (eds.), *The Ecumenical Movement: An Anthology of Key Texts and Voices* (Geneva and Grand Rapids, Mich: WCC/Eerdmans, 1997).

5. See Flynn, 'Cardinal Congar's Ecumenism: An "Ecumenical Ethics" for Reconciliation?', *Louvain Studies*, 28 (2003), 311–25.

6. Congar, 'Ecumenical Experience and Conversion: A Personal Testimony', in Robert C. Mackie and Charles C. West (eds.), *The Sufficiency of God: Essays on the Ecumenical Hope in Honour of W. A. Visser 't Hooft* (London: SCM, 1963), 81; also id., 'Expérience et conversion œcuméniques', *Chrétiens en dialogue: contributions catholiques à l'œcuménisme*, Unam Sanctam, 50 (Paris: Cerf, 1964), 133.

7. Augustin Bea, *The Way to Unity After the Council: A Study of the Implications of the Council for the Unity of Mankind* (London: Geoffry Chapman, 1967), 7.

8. 'Mass, Imposition of the Pallium and Conferral of the Fisherman's Ring for the Beginning of the Petrine Ministry of the Bishop of Rome: Homily of His Holiness Benedict XVI' (24 Apr. 2005), available at <http://www.va/holy_father/ Benedict_xvi/homilies/2005>.

9. See 'Solemnity of Sts Peter and Paul: Homily of His Holiness Benedict XVI' (29 June 2005), available at <http:/www.vatican.va/holy_father/benedict_xvi/ homilies/2005/documents/hf_ben-xvi_hom_20050629_sts-peter-paul_en.html>.

10. See 'Meeting with His Holiness Bartholomew I Ecumenical Patriarch of Constantinople: Address of the Holy Father' (29 Nov. 2006), available at <http://www. vatican.va/holy_father/benedict_xvi/speeches/2006/november/documents/hf_ben-xvi_spe_20061129_bartholomew-i_en.html>.

11. See ARCIC II, *Mary: Grace and Hope in Christ*, ed. Donald Bolen and Gregory Cameron (London: Continuum, 2006).

12. See Jean-Pierre Jossua, 'L'Œuvre œcuménique du Père Congar', *Études*, 357 (1982), 543–55; Joseph Famerée, ' "Chrétiens désunis" du P. Congar 50 ans après', *Nouvelle revue théologique*, 110 (1988), 666–86; Alberic Stacpoole, 'Early Ecumenism, Early Yves Congar, 1904–1940', *The Month*, 21 (1988), 502–10; id., 'Early Ecumenism, Early Yves Congar, 1904–1940, Part II', ibid. 623–31; Flynn, *Yves Congar's Vision of the Church in a World of Unbelief* (Aldershot: Ashgate, 2004).

13. Congar, *Dialogue Between Christians*, (1966), 9; id., *Chrétiens en dialogue*, p. xviii.

14. Id., 'Letter from Father Yves Congar, O. P.', trans. Ronald John Zawilla, *Theology Digest*, 32 (1985), 213.

15. Id., *Dialogue Between Christians*, 21; id., *Chrétiens en dialogue*, p. xxxi.

16. Id., *Essais œcuméniques: le mouvement, les hommes, les problèmes* (Paris: Centurion, 1984), 6.

17. Id., *Divided Christendom*, 108, 114; id., *Chrétiens désunis*, 137, 148; cf. Étienne Fouilloux, 'Frère Yves, Cardinal Congar, Dominicain: itinéraire d'un théologien', *Revue des sciences philosophiques et théologiques*, 79 (1995), 388.

18. Id., *Divided Christendom*, 101; id., *Chrétiens désunis*, 126.

19. Id., *Diversités et communion: dossier historique et conclusion théologique*, Cogitatio Fidei, 112 (Paris: Cerf, 1982); id., *Diversity and Communion*, trans. John Bowden (London: SCM, 1984).

20. Id., *Fifty Years of Catholic Theology: Conversations with Yves Congar*, ed. Bernard Lauret, trans. John Bowden (London: SCM, 1988), 81; also id., *Entretiens d'automne*, 2nd edn. (Paris: Cerf, 1987), 104.

21. See id., *Diversity and Communion*, 149; id., *Diversités et communion*, 221.

22. See Ulrich Duchrow, *Conflict over the Ecumenical Movement: Confessing Christ Today in the Universal Church*, trans. David Lewis (Geneva: WCC, 1981), 183–204. Duchrow's critique of 'reconciled diversity' as an 'ambiguous concept' subject to 'perilous theological error' is set in the context of a challenge to WCC to remain faithful to the model of unity developed in that body since Uppsala in 1968, namely: that of 'conciliar fellowship'. The crux is whether 'reconciled diversity' evades institutional/structural transformation in favour of the harmonious coexistence of separate confessional churches.

23. Congar, *Divided Christendom*, 101; id., *Chrétiens désunis*, 125; also, Joseph Ratzinger, 'Catholicism after the Council', *The Furrow*, 18 (1967), 21.

24. Congar, *Divided Christendom*, 101; id., *Chrétiens désunis*, 126.

25. Jossua, 'In Hope of Unity', trans. Barbara Estelle Beaumont in Gabriel Flynn (ed.), *Yves Congar: Theologian of the Church* (Louvain: Peeters, 2005), 179.

26. Basil Christopher Butler, *The Church and Unity* (London: Geoffrey Chapman, 1979), 24.

27. Id., *An Approach to Christianity* (London: Collins, 1981), 150.

28. Id., *The Church and Unity*, 25.

29. Ibid. 27–8.

30. Ibid. 27, 31.

31. Ibid. 23.

32. Ibid. 221.

33. Ibid. 4.

34. Ibid. 228.

35. Hauerwas, 'The Importance of Being Catholic: A Protestant View', *First Things*, 1 (1990), 25.

36. Congar, 'Ecumenical Experience and Conversion', 74; id., 'Expérience et conversion Œcuméniques', 126.

37. Id., 'Review of Maurice Villain, *L'Abbé*, *Revue des sciences philosophiques et théologiques*,' 41 (1957), 590.

38. See Geoffrey Curtis, *Paul Couturier and Unity in Christ* (London: SCM, 1964), 63–8.

39. Congar, 'Ecumenical Experience and Conversion', 82–3; id., 'Expérience et conversion Œcuméniques', 134–5.

40. Id., 'Ecumenical Experience and Conversion', 79; id., 'Expérience et conversion Œcuméniques', 131.

41. Henry Vaughan, 'The Night' in *The Metaphysical Poets*, ed. Helen Gordner, 13th edn. (Harmondsworth: Penguin, 1973), 280–1.

42. Butler, 'Jesus and Later Orthodoxy', in Michael Green (ed.), *The Truth of God Incarnate* (London: Hodder & Stoughton, 1977), 100.

43. See Avery Dulles, *The Catholicity of the Church*, 2nd edn. (Oxford: Clarendon Press, 1987), 171–4.

29

Receptive Ecumenism and the Hermeneutics of Catholic Learning—The Promise of Comparative Ecclesiology[1]

Gerard Mannion

INTRODUCTION

This chapter reflects on the actuality of the aspirations evident throughout the other chapters in this volume. The aim is to elucidate common points of reference, areas for further exploration and possible remaining significant differences. The chapter utilizes the methodology of comparative ecclesiology towards the end of eliciting further the enormous potential of the proposed strategy of Receptive Ecumenism.

If other contributors to this volume have focused more upon what Receptive Ecumenism and Catholic Learning entail, here I will explore a little further what form they might take. I begin with some hermeneutical, ecclesiological, and ecumenical reflections before turning to consider the emerging sub-discipline of comparative ecclesiology. I will suggest that, viewed methodologically, Receptive Ecumenism represents one notable and promising form of comparative ecclesiology. With this, in terms of the end goal of improved ecumenical relations, comparative ecclesiology will be commended here as the best way for Catholic Learning to be achieved and for Receptive Ecumenism to bear fruit. The key question is: what sort of ecclesiological methodology will allow its practitioners to respect and celebrate the other as other, whilst remaining comfortable in the celebration of the fundamentals of their own tradition?

This chapter affirms that the notion of the church as a hermeneutical community is of fundamental importance to any understanding of Receptive Ecumenism. A case is traced here for the necessity both of dialogue within the church and of an openness to the world that is inevitably and properly pluralist, or polycentric, in character. If, in contrast, we were to follow the recent trends, across various denominations, towards a renewed ecclesial insularity, then no Receptive Ecumenism and no learning that is truly catholic would be possible.

So the chapter proceeds as follows. I identify postmodern ecclesial polemics as a major obstacle to such dialogue and openness flourishing today. I explore ways in which such polemics might be transcended with a view to developing a 'wider' or 'macro-' ecumenism. I go on to suggest that the fledgling sub-discipline of comparative ecclesiology offers the most promising starting-point for churches wishing to embrace dialogue, openness, and pluralism, as opposed to retreating inwards. Here the work of Roger Haight looms large. Finally, the chapter offers some reflections on how exactly the church might and should be a hermeneutical community.

RE-ENVISIONING THE 'OPEN CHURCH'

In the opening chapter to this volume, Paul Murray speaks about the creative potential for generating a renewed ecumenical optimism for our times. He speaks of an ad hoc process which should, nonetheless, be 'systematically tested' towards the end of preserving the integrity of differing traditions whilst facilitating true ecumenical encounters, where learning as opposed to teaching is the primary focus. Here I would suggest that every act of receptive learning will naturally lead to a situation whereby teaching is likewise offered. Thus, the value of embracing a comparative approach guided by hermeneutical principles towards the end of Catholic Learning. For such can help ensure one enters into enriching encounters with other traditions where one receives and gives in substantial measure alike.

Of course, we must also be mindful of potential pitfalls. Geraldine Smyth here warns us that ecumenical reception can be conceived in terms of loss, just as much as gain. Indeed 'denominational attachments' are perhaps growing all the more rigid in some quarters. But Smyth wisely points us in the direction of hermeneutics (a path explored also by Riccardo Larini), reflecting a sensitivity borne of decades of ecumenical service. And, as she also reminds us, different churches have 'chosen different ecumenical keys'. Whilst some of these can serve dialogue, others work against it. In some ways, this chapter seeks to explore further the implications of such observations.

Here we are also mindful to explicate further Margaret O'Gara's powerful reminder that 'ecumenism is a gift exchange as well'. It is, then, 'a kind of mutual reception'. Here I seek to offer some further modest thoughts as to why such receiving and giving is desirable today, along with suggesting how, in terms of ecclesiological methodology, it might actually unfold. Thomas Reese also tempers any overly enthusiastic expectations that Receptive Ecumenism and Catholic Learning will proceed with ease. So we are aware of the need for realism. But realism and optimism are certainly not incompatible. Indeed, they can prove, as I hope to illustrate, to be complementary.

One of the main questions I wish to explore here is what form of dialogue is best suited to contemporary ecclesiological debates and to Receptive Ecumenism and Catholic Learning? Catholic Learning begins, I believe, *within* one's own tradition; the dialogical imperative it depends upon needs to spread throughout one's own tradition and beyond, embracing the entire human family. But that first step, of trying to transcend divisions within one's own church, demands a return to the source of many such divisions, namely: differing understandings of and responses to contemporary reality and its challenges. As Roger Haight has said, 'Looking back [over the course of church history] it becomes plain that positive constructive dialogue and comparison are a better way to forge communion than polemics or claims to juridical authority.'[2] But how exactly might such ecclesial polemics be transcended?

DAVID TRACY: A PRECURSOR OF RECEPTIVE ECUMENISM?

In many ways such polemics are, in themselves, of a postmodern character and the task of transcending them is, therefore, as much methodological (even epistemological) as it is ecclesiological. Quite often the differences in ecclesiology stem from divisions in these other areas. So there is a need, as David Tracy amongst numerous others suggests, to move beyond foundationalism on the one hand, and relativism on the other.[3] Here, in relation to the idea of a 'wider ecumenism' in general, note how Tracy charts the shift in epistemology in the 'new' Europe, where Christianity's superiority is no longer an assumption taken for granted.

Tracy was writing at the beginning of the 1990s and perhaps his optimism here was soon to be dented—witness, for example, the emergence and, in some quarters, triumph of neo-exclusivism in the years since. Back then, the full impact of works such as John Milbank's *Theology and Social Theory*[4] was yet to be felt. Polemics have not disappeared in our times; rather they have intensified. Much work remains to be done. But Tracy was, perhaps, anticipating the great potential offered to all branches of theology, ecclesiology included, by the emerging discipline of comparative theology. Tracy also offered the insightful warning that, in the postmodern world, we can no longer live enclosed within a tradition in the way we once did. The stark choices are: to go the way of retrenchment (foundationalism), to take flight (the path towards relativism), or to seek to progress via a third route:

What Paul Ricoeur nicely named a 'second naiveté' toward one's tradition (enter critical philosophy and revisionary theology) allied to a genuine openness to otherness and difference... The only serious question becomes: is a second naiveté possible? If so how?

Many of us may rediscover our traditions...in and through discovering others, their difference, and their truth. But is it possible to honour the truth of one's own religious tradition while being genuinely open to other great ways as other? Clearly the answer must be yes or we are all lost in a Hobbesian state of the war of all against all.[5]

We hear in Tracy's words here echoes of the sentiments expressed in many of the Second Vatican Council speeches, humbly expressing appreciation for the debt which the Roman Catholic Church owes to other Christians, to people of other faiths, and, indeed, to people of no faith.[6] In contrast, our polarized relations of more recent times wound the very heart of the Church itself. It seems that in our times it is becoming more difficult even to accept and embrace our own ecclesial sisters and brothers *as* others. We move closer, then, towards identifying key priorities.

TOWARDS A COMPARATIVE AND DIALOGICAL ECCLESIOLOGY

In underlining the inescapable need for a 'new ecumenism', David Tracy also highlighted the path comparative theology might take in its effort to 'find new ways to learn from the other traditions'.[7] This is a path between conservative retreats into foundationalism and utter relativism, and perhaps allows us further to appreciate just why any form of ecclesiological neo-exclusivism cannot serve the church well in our times. In this approach one will begin close to home and cherish what is of value there but also venture out to learn from what may enhance that homestead:

The new search is likely to become that of more and more religious persons: stay faithful to your own tradition; go deeper and deeper into its particularities; defend and clarify its identity. At the same time, wander, Ulysses-like, willingly, even eagerly, among other great traditions and ways; try to learn something of their beauty and truth; concentrate on their otherness and differences as the new route to communality.[8]

Comparative ecclesiology is simply the ecclesiological *application* of such insights to reflection upon the church. I wish also to suggest that it offers a key to the way forward in these debates concerning polarization. The comparative method is what facilitates the possibility of reception and also what revivifies our understanding of catholicity so that all our ecclesial learning is towards the end of greater ecumenism throughout the church and wider human family alike.

EMBRACING A COMPARATIVE ECCLESIOLOGY

As I have suggested, we find Roger Haight addressing similar problems but for a new age. He excels in addressing where the churches find themselves at in the contemporary world and in suggesting ways forward vis-à-vis: (a) their engagement with each other, (b) with those across other religions, and (c) with those beyond the confines of either. He champions the need for the church to embrace a *dialogical* mission. His most extensive work to date in ecclesiology is itself a monumental and pioneering three-volume study in comparative ecclesiology.[9]

In brief, he defines this methodology, thus: 'Comparative ecclesiology consists in analyzing and portraying in an organized or systematic way two or more different ecclesiologies so that they can be compared.'[10] It is characterized by: first, utilizing social and historical science in its study of ecclesiologies; second, attention to representative and/or authoritative sources of particular ecclesiologies; third, organizing the different ecclesiologies under comparison according to a common pattern or template. It acknowledges that 'it is no longer possible to think that a single church could carry the full flow of Christian life in a single organizational form'.[11]

In one of his most recent essays on the theme, Haight clarifies his definition of comparative ecclesiology further, stating that: 'Comparative ecclesiology studies the church in a way that takes into account the various levels of pluralism which mark its existence today ... The thematic that constitutes an ecclesiology as comparative is precisely the various ways ecclesiology explicitly interacts with pluralism.'[12]

In seeking to integrate aspects of these positive ecclesiological developments in our efforts to provide the church with a renewed and continued relevance today, to enable the gospel to be put into practice all the more, and to resist the rise of neo-exclusivism, we might especially gain from adapting and building upon four theses 'against sectarianism' offered by Haight in an earlier essay. These are formulated vis-à-vis certain radical transformations which our age has witnessed in our understanding of *place* and of *church* and of the *idea* and *focus* of theology.[13]

By the 'Idea of *Place*', Haight refers to the way in which the complexification and explosion of knowledge have transformed our very understanding of what a 'place' actually is. Contrary, however, to what some have advocated in a reaction to the developments of postmodernity, he argues against any compartmentalization and localization of theology: 'The localization and compartmentalization of theology is a temptation for many today. Some theologians have become seduced by the very systems of modernity and postmodernity which they attack. That is, they try to escape them by isolating the church from culture and conceiving of theology as a purely confessional and fideist discipline.'[14] For Haight, the significant point needing to be grasped here is that theology transcends church and addresses all reality. The reality of human life is one and so the remit of theology must embrace all human life and reach out into the wider world.

Second, Haight turns to 'the Idea of *Church*', itself. Echoing our earlier discussions, Haight here addresses the rise of historical consciousness and the ecumenical movement. The church cannot be restricted to one confessional movement. Similarly, any genuine ecumenical theology must transcend particular authorities and particular magisteria. The entire Christian church is theology's primary context.[15]

In fastening upon these questions of ecumenism, ecclesial identity, magisterium, and authority in general, Haight draws together many of the issues earlier identified here as priorities for the church in our times and which demonstrate the ecclesiological necessity of dialogue. He continues:

> Again, by extension to the discipline, ecumenical theology must consider a variety of authoritative witnesses from many churches. It must also employ various comparative and dialectical procedures to frame a more general statement of the issue than will be reflected in the particular view of only one church. Theology that is ecumenically conscious is led by a logic other than reliance on the magisterium of a single church and is forced to consult the authorities of all churches in a reverent and critical manner.[16]

Indeed, far from any of this serving to dismiss the need for teaching authority altogether, Haight's analysis allows us to appreciate that such magisterium must be shaped by dialogue and an ecumenical spirit, rather than being driven by entrenched fear of dissent and the other. As he suggests: 'What the internalization of the ecumenical imperative by the churches has done, then, is to moderate the absolutistic or universalistic claims of certain structures of authority in particular churches.'[17] But, as we have sought to suggest, this 'internalization of the ecumenical imperative' is currently under threat from a new dogmatic and exclusivist imperative that is in the ascendancy. It is the fear of postmodernity which drives this on. Haight's alternative vision embraces ecumenism, the world we find ourselves in, and turns towards a truly pluralistic agenda: one that is neither fearful nor suspicious of the pluralistic reality of the world and the human family within it. So, what does this mean within the Christian church? Well, as Haight suggests, it is a call to acknowledge the plurality of teaching authorities that are at work in the service of the gospel today, and hence to dialogue with and learn from each of these:

> Let me summarize this point in the form of a thesis. It is directed against another form of sectarianism. The church is the place for theology. But the church at the end of the twentieth century as a result of the ecumenical movement is recognized to be the whole or total church, despite its disunity and divisions. This means, negatively, that the church in the sense of a particular communion cannot by itself be a final or exclusive limit or constraint or criterion or norm for Christian theology today. Rather, positively, the many magisteria of various churches are witnesses to Christian truth and sources for data for Christian theology.[18]

The third consideration in Haight's analysis is of the '*Idea* of Theology' itself in the light of the reality of pluralism. Here Haight addresses the encounter of Christian theology and the church with world religions. Theology has much to learn and gain from its dialogue with other faiths, which establishes new horizons for its sources and norms. Again echoing our earlier discussion, he reminds us that we now live in a 'dialogical situation' that calls for unending conversing *and* learning from such encounters. Haight's sentiments help provide further grounding for suggestions offered elsewhere[19] concerning the need for ecclesiologies that are both dialogical and prophetic and the inseparability of such from the task of evangelization itself. Thus, we return to our central theme of dialogue. Haight has a particularly well-developed and empowering understanding of the concept, and one which perhaps also encapsulates in a most vivid fashion the aspirations of Receptive Ecumenism:

Dialogue means entering into a respectful and attentive exchange with people, their cultures and their religions. The metaphor of a dialogue or conversation supplies the rules for how the church should encounter the people of other religions at all levels. In other words, a phenomenology of authentic dialogue reveals the characteristics that should qualify the unfolding of the church's mission.[20]

Haight speaks of such dialogue complementing the mission of church, with the sources and data for theology correlatively greatly expanded. Echoing the insights of Gregory Baum,[21] Haight goes on to offer what could serve as a summary of the key concerns and aims of this chapter concerning the transformative nature of encounter and dialogue. Once again, he could just as easily be speaking about the concept of Receptive Ecumenism:

Secondly...in a situation that can be characterized as dialogical in nature...Christian theology is attentive to the voice of dialogue partners. Christian theology is open to learning. The experience of non-Christians becomes in some sense data for Christian theology. The consequences of this have been clearly described by theologians who have engaged in inter-religious dialogues: the understanding of their own faith has been changed. The dialogue, the passing over and entering into the world of the other religion, to whatever extent this is possible, and the return, transform Christian self-understanding.[22]

So, our considerations thus far would support the suggestion of the visionary Vietnamese–American priest-scholar Peter Phan who argues that something of a 'Copernican ecclesiological revolution' is called for in our times. Something similar is echoed in different ways in many of the chapters in this volume—for example, those of Paul Murray, Geraldine Smyth, and Margaret O'Gara. It also resonates with the sentiments expressed throughout Brand Hinze's recent study on *Practices of Dialogue Within the Roman Catholic Church*.[23] These, along with Haight's painstaking work in developing a comparative method in ecclesiology, help contribute towards the emergence of a vision and a call to charity—to dialogue in love and to encounter the other *as* other.

In our ecclesiological investigations today we are called to such dialogue as the most positive and enduring possible response to postmodernity. Our interpretative considerations lead us, logically, to this place. Here, Rahner seems remarkably ahead of his time in the apparent foresight he displayed with regard to the challenges faced by the Church in our times: '[I]f the Church of today is to conduct a dialogue with the world, then it must not be overlooked that this "world" is not simply "outside", but is rather present in the Church herself. This means that the first, and perhaps the decisive dialogue with the world is that which takes place precisely within the Church.'[24]

To summarize thus far, this dialogue and embracing of pluralism is not only necessitated on theological (doctrinal), ecclesiological, and moral grounds, but also upon hermeneutical grounds, relating to the discerning of the signs of the times.

Pluralism is not an ideology, rather it is, in the first instance, a descriptive term for the ways things are, for reality. At the same time it is also the name for the most healthy and appropriate response to the way things are, as opposed to turning away from and attempting to deny that reality in various modes of self-delusion. But why would anyone seek to escape the riches of the diverse gifts God bestows upon humanity? Unless, of course, they have allowed themselves to become fearful of the vast wonders of postmodern existence and to retreat from the world into the perceived 'comfort-zone' of 'certainties' that, in the final analysis, prove to be quite the reverse on both counts?

Embracing pluralism[25] allows us to put the gospel into practice all the more effectively in our times—the parable of the Last Judgement clearly indicates that at its heart the gospel is itself a call both to embrace pluralism and to praxis: 'Truly I tell you, just as you did it to one of the least of these who are members of my family, you did it to me' (Matt. 25: 40). Thus, in our account of Haight's 'comparative ecclesiology', essentially a charter for pluralism and macro-ecumenism, we finally turn to 'the *Focus* of Theology'. Here Haight reflects upon the population explosion and the attendant massive suffering which the world has witnessed through this and other global developments.[26] This is most appropriate for addressing the questions that confront the church in our times. The methodological lesson to be learned here is that theology must address real lives and it must always bear in mind the fundamental social and public dimensions of human existence, as well as the interpersonal and transcendent. In other words, theology should never be a purely individualistic discipline, with regard to its chief areas of concern.

Essentially, Haight is seeking to move theology and, in particular, ecclesiology, beyond all narrow, sectarian, absolutist, and universalizing stances. Is this not also the intention behind any venture in genuinely Receptive Ecumenism? Is this not, indeed, perhaps a definition of the outcome of a truly Catholic Learning?

COMPARATIVE ECCLESIOLOGY: A PATH TOWARDS ECCLESIAL VIRTUE?

We have thus explored and commended the promise of comparative ecclesiology, perceiving it to offer the church in a postmodern world the hope and resources necessary both to meet the challenges of this new historical context and to transcend the competing ecclesiologies that have blighted inter- and intra-ecclesial relations in recent decades. Instead, comparative ecclesiology would allow genuine merits to be shared, differences to be openly acknowledged, and less-profitable ecclesial approaches to be discerned.[27]

The wider project out of which this chapter has developed attempts to sketch a form of ecclesiology which weds ethics closer to ecclesiology and ecclesial life in general, which embraces and celebrates the pluralistic realities in which the church will always find itself, which celebrates the world as God's creation and the scene of God's self-communication, and, finally, weds ecclesial vision (and ecclesiological theory and rhetoric) to ecclesial praxis. Such reflections lead to the conclusion that comparative ecclesiology *is* a virtuous ecclesiology. Trinitarian theology itself can be viewed as a comparative attempt to understand the differing aspects of the being and salvific (economic) activity of God.

In pursuing this path, we are mindful to accord with all five of Haight's 'premises' for a comparative ecclesiology, namely: (1) to immerse our explorations in historical consciousness, thereby inculcating the disposition of humility, both methodologically and in terms of the lived quality of ecclesial life and practice; (2) a positive appreciation of the fact of pluralism; (3) a whole-part conception of church, placing universal neither over and above local nor vice versa; (4) embracing, in practice, the gifts and challenges of religious pluralism; (5) 'Retaining a confessional or particular ecclesial identity'.[28] My concerns here and in the broader project of which it is part have been appropriately addressed first and foremost to issues within my own Roman Catholic context. As Haight states:

[C]omparative ecclesiology consists not in overcoming denominational Christianity or Christianity itself, but in transcending the limits of individual churches by expanding the sources brought to bear on the task of understanding the Christian faith, in this case, the church. What is learned from these sources is brought back as further light on the particularities of any given church. The concern for the truth contained in one's own community guarantees that the discipline remains Christian theology.[29]

I suggest that this is what Catholic Learning ultimately means. Not, then 'resident aliens', but citizens of God's creation. Pluralism (or, if one prefers, 'polycentrism') is here explicitly commended as a further ecclesiological virtue— sectarianism and insularity as ecclesiological vices.

For our contemporary times, the church has still to harmonize adequately its mission to humanity with its evangelical mission. Comparative theology and the sub-discipline of comparative ecclesiology offer a better methodology to take the church forward here than any neo-exclusivistic outlook. And the comparisons can prove fruitful whether across a variety of 'synchronic' or 'diachronic' forms. They can be across history, across communion and denominations (or even within denominations), or, indeed, between differing ecclesiological method-ologies or between the visions of the ecclesial authorities and the local church realities. Haight has shown us examples of so many varieties here as well as, of course, demonstrating the insights that can issue forth from a comparison of ecclesiology 'from above' and 'from below'.[30]

COMMENDING THE HERMENEUTICAL IMPERATIVE OF CONTEMPORARY ECUMENISM

At the outset, we echoed the other chapters here, mindful of the dangers of undue optimism and the potential pitfalls of which to be wary in efforts towards fostering receptivity and the catholicity of our ecclesial learning. So this final section offers some thoughts about how we might move forward even if our comparative ecclesiology endeavours to shed light upon differences that remain problematic and present further obstacles to greater ecumenical charity.

Any comparative approach will bring home to us the somewhat obvious, if none the less disappointing, fact that differing theologies and competing, even conflicting, ecclesiologies often arise from or give rise to contending hermeneutics.[31] Hence, an acceptance of the reality and value of pluralism would appear to be the only positive way forward, and this must bear fruit in ecclesiological and ethical thinking alike. Werner Jeanrond has suggested that:

> In such a state of confusion it must be the task of theologians to serve the Christian com-munity by attempting to clarify the issues as far as possible and to develop an adequate method which will allow them to offer possible criteria for a critical and constructive examination of our common Christian heritage. The simple appeal to tradition in favour of or against a particular ecclesial or theological position can never replace critical and faithful argumentation. The Christian faith must be appropriated, and not just repeated, by all Christians and in every generation anew.[32]

Jeanrond, therefore, espouses the need for a critical theology today which would not only help us understand the Christian message in our contemporary world but would also allow us better to 'understand the multi-dimensional context in which we are trying to grasp the heart of this Christian project'.[33] He continues,

'If the Christian tradition is not to end soon altogether, a critical theology and a critical faith-praxis are urgently demanded'.

Likewise, he calls for a critical hermeneutics where the theologian views appropriation not as the means by which texts are made to accord with one's own pre-understanding but, rather, 'by adopting a critical and self-critical method of text interpretation theologians will always be prepared to challenge and transform their own preunderstandings and interpretative horizons'.[34] In this task, Jeanrond particularly commends Tracy's methodology for its taking of 'plurality and ambiguity' as being 'at the heart of the Christian message'.[35] As Tracy, himself, suggests:

As greater ecumenical self-exposure takes firmer hold on all Christian theologies, the present conflict of interpretations may yet become a genuine conversation. As all theologies—whether focused proximately upon manifestation, proclamation or prophetic action—focus ultimately upon the reality of the event of Jesus Christ, the full scope of the grace released by that event upon the world in its entirety will follow. What unites these conflicting understandings of the world will prove none other than the singular clue which informs their different understandings of God and self. That clue remains the grace which is agapic love disclosed in and by the proleptic event of Jesus Christ. That love as healing gives and demands an opening of every Christian understanding of world to the full scope of the always-already presence of that grace, that love in the worlds of history and nature alike.[36]

As the World Council of Churches' own study in ecclesial hermeneutics, *A Treasure in Earthen Vessels* (*TEV*), states (citing 1 Cor. 10: 23–4): ' "All things are lawful", but not all things build up. Do not seek your own advantage, but that of the other.'[37] In one sense, *all* ecclesiology is hermeneutics. Our aim today should be to build upon those who have fused the most valuable and pioneering insights of those such as Gadamer and Ricœur in order to shape not one overall and overarching ecclesiology, but to allow a healthy and developed hermeneutics of suspicion in the service of a praxis-oriented pluralism guided by true conversation.

Whether we are concerned with intra- and inter-Christian ecclesial and ecclesiological questions, questions of inter-faith dialogue, or quests for global means of conversation, solidarity, and community alike, our hermeneutical endeavours are geared towards reconciling the conflicts (or potential conflicts) between differing horizons—towards finding common ground in order to facilitate peaceful, meaningful, and fruitful coexistence.[38] Perhaps, in relation to this, the passage in *TEV* which contains most promise for ecumenical hermeneutics and hermeneutical ecclesiology and ecumenism is that which seems to embrace the need for humility, and which contains what I have called the ecumenical *necessity* of acknowledging and embracing pluralism, albeit in pregnant form:

[N]o interpretation can claim to be absolute. All must be aware of the limitations of any perspective or position. The catholicity that binds communities together makes possible this awareness of limitation as well as a mutual acknowledgment of contribution to one another's interpretation. In this way, catholicity enables communities to free one another from one-sidedness or from over-emphasis on only one aspect of the Gospel. Catholicity enables communities to liberate one another from being blinded or bound by any one context and so to embody across and among diverse contexts the solidarity that is a special mark of Christian *koinonia*. (*TEV*, § 48)

Dynamic tradition is nothing other than the acceptance of multiplicity and of the inevitability of differing horizons of meaning and interpretation emerging out of differing contexts. Hence the very concept of tradition itself and the sense of the development of doctrine each affirm the hermeneutical exercise.[39]

In all then, we should be aware of the fundamental importance and value of pluralism, dialogue, and encounter. Thus the promise of comparative theology and, in particular, of comparative ecclesiology here prove vital. The potential fruits of those debates we have considered offer great scope also for dialogue beyond the churches and beyond religious faiths altogether. In particular, they offer scope for how people of faith and/or goodwill may today, in unison, confront the most pressing ethical and social challenges, most notably globalization which, as a universal (i.e. ecumenical) problem, requires just such an answer.

The nature and purpose of the church is to be an interpretative community and so, in its mission, the church performs a ministry of interpretation. In its ecumenical endeavours, the church offers great promise for the wider human family, for such ecumenism provides a very real example of what it means to be an interpretive community and, therefore, offers something to the wider world that is redemptively created.[40]

Like Ricœur, I believe we can and must learn from many methods of hermeneutical engagement but be slaves to none. The same, indeed, might also be said for ecclesiology. In *TEV* we see the Trinitarian aspect of Christian community celebrated: 'The Church is a communion of persons in relation; thus active participation and dialogue between communities, and within each community at all levels, is one expression of the Church's nature. The divine being of the Triune God is the source and the exemplar of communion' (*TEV*, § 64). If, for Tracy, the life and work of Jesus Christ is the analogical 'classic' for Christians, i.e. the primary analogate for our hermeneutical way of being human selves,[41] then the Trinity, we may conclude, is the primary analogate for the church and Christians seeking to discern their mode of societal and communitarian existence in general.[42] Hence it is so for our ecclesiological and ecumenical endeavours, also.[43] If one sought to offer a shorter formula for what Receptive Ecumenism and Catholic Learning entail, one might do no better than simply to offer that onomatopoeic concept from the East: *perichoresis*.

NOTES

1. This chapter draws upon themes discussed at greater length in my *Ecclesiology and Postmodernity: Questions for the Church in our Times* (Collegeville, Minn.: Liturgical Press, 2007), esp. 151–72. Cf. also a collection of related essays, Mannion (ed.), *Comparative Ecclesiology: Critical Investigations* (London and New York: T. and T. Clark, 2008) and id., 'Constructive Comparative Ecclesiology: The Pioneering Work of Roger Haight', *Ecclesiology*, 4 (forthcoming, 2008).
2. Haight, 'Comparative Ecclesiology', in Mannion and Lewis Mudge (eds.), *The Routledge Companion to the Christian Church* (London: Routledge, 2007), 388.
3. Tracy, 'Beyond Foundationalism and Relativism: Hermeneutics and the New Ecumenism', *On Naming the Present: God, Hermeneutics, and Church* (Maryknoll, NY: Orbis Books, 1994), 131–9.
4. Milbank, *Theology and Social Theory* (Oxford, Blackwell, 1990).
5. Tracy, 'Beyond Foundationalism and Relativism', 138.
6. See Hans Küng, Yves Congar, and Daniel O'Hanlon (eds.), *Council Speeches of Vatican II* (Glen Rock, NJ: Paulist, 1964), esp. those contained in Part III, 'Reunion of All Christians' (pp. 95–191).
7. Tracy, 'Beyond Foundationalism and Relativism', 137.
8. Ibid.; also 'On the one hand, the new ecumenism agrees with the heart of all the classic religious journeys: the universal is to be found by embracing the particular . . . Surely this route through the particular is a wiser way to find truth than seeking that ever-elusive goal, a common denominator among the religions' (p. 137).
9. See Haight, *Christian Community in History*, vol. i., *Historical Ecclesiology* (New York and London: Continuum, 2004); id., *Christian Community in History*, vol. ii., *Comparative Ecclesiology* (Continuum, 2007); id., *Christian Community in History*, vol. iii., *Ecclesial Existence* (Continuum, 2008); also id., 'Comparative Ecclesiology', *Routledge Companion to the Christian Church*.
10. Id., *Christian Community in History*, ii., 4.
11. Ibid., ii. 7.
12. Id., 'Comparative Ecclesiology', 387.
13. See id., 'Church as Locus of Theology', *Why Theology?, Concilium*, 6 (1994), 22.
14. Ibid. 15.
15. Ibid. 16.
16. Ibid. 16–17.
17. Ibid. 17–18.
18. Ibid. 18. Cf. Richard Gaillardetz: 'It is difficult to imagine a formalized unity among the Churches that does not include some shared understanding of doctrinal teaching authority. Even so, Roman Catholics cannot afford the hubris of thinking that their structures and understandings of authority *in toto* and as presently constituted provide the only viable possibility', *Teaching with Authority: A Theology of the Magisterium in the Church* (Collegeville, Minn.: Liturgical Press, 1997), 276.
19. See the discussions in Mannion, *Ecclesiology and Postmodernity*, 124–74.
20. Haight, 'Church as Locus of Theology', 19.

21. Numerous works by Baum are of relevance here. See, most recently, *Amazing Church: A Catholic Theologian Remembers a Half-Century of Change* (New York: Orbis, 2005).
22. Haight, 'Church as Locus of Theology', 19–20.
23. Bradford Hinze, *Practices of Dialogue Within the Roman Catholic Church: Aims and Obstacles, Lessons and Laments* (New York: Continuum, 2006).
24. Karl Rahner, 'Dialogue in the Church' (1967), *Theological Investigations*, vol. x., trans. David Bourke (London: Darton, Longman & Todd, 1973), 106.
25. I believe the term can still be employed, despite the valid challenges put to certain uses of it by Johann Baptist Metz, who prefers the term 'polycentric', see Metz, 'Theology in the Modern Age, and Before its End', in Claude Geffré, Gustavo Gutiérrez, and Virgil Elizondo (eds.), *Different Theologies, Common Responsibility* (Edinburgh: T. & T. Clark, 1984), 13–17.
26. Haight, 'Church as Locus of Theology', 22; c.f. also Janet Crawford, 'Women and Ecclesiology: Two Ecumenical Streams', *Ecumenical Review*, 53 (2002), 14–24.
27. Here we may draw parallels between Haight's work in ecclesiology and the broader systematic focus of Tracy, in particular his emphasis on the need for reflection 'upon the pluralism *within* the Christian tradition in order to reflect upon the pluralism *among* the religious traditions ... The recognition that no classic tradition should abandon its particular genius in its entry into conversation with the others is a central key for enhancing a genuinely ecumenical theology', *The Analogical Imagination: Christian Theology and the Culture of Pluralism* (London: SCM Press, 1981), 447–8. Haight further develops his own thoughts on intra-Christian pluralism throughout his recently published *Ecclesial Existence*.
28. See Haight, 'Comparative Theology', *Routledge Companion to the Christian Church*, 390–92.
29. See ibid. 391–92; also Tracy, *The Analogical Imagination*, 448.
30. Cf. Haight, *Christian Community in History*, i., 17–68.
31. See, e.g., Werner G. Jeanrond, *Theological Hermeneutics: Development and Significance* (London: SCM Press, 1994); also Francis Schüssler Fiorenza, 'The Conflict of Hermeneutical Traditions and Christian Theology', *Journal of Chinese Philosophy*, 27 (2003), 3–31; Nicholas M. Healy, 'Practices and the New Ecclesiology: Misplaced Concreteness?', *International Journal of Systematic Theology*, 5 (2003), 287–308.
32. Jeanrond, *Theological Hermeneutics*, 166.
33. Ibid. 173.
34. Ibid. 174.
35. See ibid., 174–7. Tracy's primary works of relevance here include: *The Analogical Imagination*; *Dialogue with the Other: The Inter-Religious Dialogue* (Leuven: Peeters, 1990); *On Naming the Present: God, Hermeneutics, and Church* (Maryknoll, NY: Orbis Books, 1994); also 'The Uneasy Alliance Reconceived: Catholic Theological Method, Modernity and Postmodernity', *Theological Studies*, 50 (1989), 548–70.
36. Id., *The Analogical Imagination*, 437–8.
37. For discussion of this document, see Chapter 7: Riccardo Larini, 'Text and Contexts—Hermeneutical Reflections on Receptive Ecumenism'.
38. See Mannion, 'What's in a Name? Hermeneutical Questions on "Globalisation", Catholicity and Ecumenism', *New Blackfriars*, 86 (2005), 204–15.

39. See Congar's seminal study, *Tradition and Traditions: An Historical and a Theological Essay*, trans. Michael Naseby and Thomas Rainborough (London: Burns & Oates, 1966).

40. I am indebted to Kenneth Wilson for suggestions concerning these elements of Church and ecumenical life. On the wider implications of Christian ecumenism, see also Mannion, 'What's In a Name?'

41. See Tracy, *The Analogical Imagination*, particularly those discussions found at 21–135, 339–64, 372–98, and 405–35.

42. But not in the hierarchical sense that we see in some more conservative ecclesiologies based upon Trinitarian thinking. Anton Houtepen suggests the churches require two differing ecumenical endeavours: one, a hermeneutics of Tradition; the other, of Communion—that is, a hermeneutics of the faith in relation to the former and of the Church in relation to the latter; see 'The Faith of the Church Through the Ages: Ecumenism and Hermeneutics', *Bulletin Centro Pro Unione*, 44 (1993), 3–15.

43. See *TEV*, § 68.

30

Receptive Ecumenism—Learning by Engagement

Daniel W. Hardy

INTRODUCTION

The twentieth century appeared to be a time of significant progress in ecumenical relations: there were both collective efforts—most notably in the World Council of Churches—and many bilateral attempts between churches to address the divisions between them. As much advance as these have brought, however, there is still a sense in which ecumenicity—when measured by its highest possibilities—is sadly lacking. That is a sobering statement, but it is borne out by the state of the churches vis-à-vis each other when measured by the high expectations applicable to those who look forward to the kingdom of God.

Our ecumenical situation today is traceable to what has happened over the past millennium both within and outside church life. For complex religious and social reasons, not only theological differences, the one church has become many, a church related even in multiplicity has been replaced by disconnected ecclesial units, and the churches have been displaced from the public domain, especially in modern times. When measured by the expectations applicable to those who in Christ look forward to the kingdom of God, the relations between these units, as well as their efficacy separately and collectively in the world at large, have usually been much less than might be expected to be the case. Often the rationales offered for the churches have disallowed mutual understanding and respect except where imposed by other parties (a state, for example) or—more important—have failed to bring structured co-presence, mutual support, and mutual compassion, and even love, between them. All of this publicly discredits the churches and diminishes their mission in the world. Despite this, the churches have been sanguine: they now tend to accept both their difference and their separation as inevitable, or at least not worth worrying about; they often lapse, if not into self-justifying superiority, into passive disregard for each other; and their witness in the world is less than it might be. This takes many forms.

I recall a number of occasions some years ago when a Serbian Orthodox parish in Birmingham offered the Divine Liturgy for an Anglican–Orthodox society, and the priest usually concluded with a brief address in which he told a story of the great Altar of God. Of the two candlesticks on the altar, one had fallen to the ground and smashed into many fragments, while the other remained in its place. The only possible solution to the division of the church, he said, was for the smashed candlestick to be restored in the image of the other, that is for the divided western churches (Roman Catholic and others) to be reunited in the image of the Orthodox churches.

There are many reasons for these things which we cannot review here, but two are especially important for our purposes, one internal to the churches and the other more circumstantial. On the one hand, from the start, the church marked its identity in Christ through linear continuity in doctrine, ecclesial forms and practices which were taken as necessary to authentic Christianity. It was within these continuities that—like a tree trunk forking into two—differentiations and separations occurred, between eastern and western churches, or with the Reformations in Europe and England. On the other hand, these divisions had important connections with the position of the church vis-à-vis society more widely, both resulting—at least in part—from the emergence of new social entities, and also stimulating them, perhaps even fuelling the rise of secularity itself. This made social change—the increase of multiplicity and complexity within and outside the churches, and the philosophical positions developed from them—a problem for the church. The effect was for change to outstrip existing continuities in doctrine, ecclesial forms, and practices, leaving the churches in the position of bastions of continuity detached from the complexities of modern life. And, as fragmentation in the institutions of ordinary life increases they appear to have little to contribute.

Receptive Ecumenism promises to be a welcome move in addressing such issues as they now affect the church: 'what it means for the church—both the church collectively and for Christians personally—to be called to discern together the living truth of God's ways with the world' in a postmodern situation.[1] It is distinctive in two ways at least. First, it opens the Roman Catholic Church to what may be learned through encounter with other Christian traditions, which denotes a readiness to place that church amongst the churches in a fashion parallel to the Second Vatican Council's renewal of catholicism's engagement with history. Secondly, it engages with the ecclesiological and theological questions which arise for and from the church as it confronts secular counterparts and postmodern critique. What we must do here is to explore what this might mean, and what the fuller implications of such encounter might be, in the hope of making Receptive Ecumenism not only more effective for the Roman Catholic Church, but also beneficial for all the churches.

THE NEED FOR ECCLESIAL MAPPING

There is a prima facie problem with how the churches meet in ecumenical relations. It appears to have three sources.

One has to do with the 'thinkability' of any church in theory and practice. It is striking how difficult it is 'to think' any church—its many aspects, relations, and dynamics—and how much more so 'to think' the ecumenical scene, with many churches which vary in all these respects and yet relate to each other in a variety of ways. How does any church cohere in its self-understanding, life, and witness? In fact, it is no easy thing for any church to understand its own fullness.

A second has to do with whether any church can discover the truth of the Church by itself. While the churches are separate, it is intrinsically difficult for them by themselves to uncover what are the crucial dimensions of the life of the people who are the Body of Christ, and still more difficult to grasp the dynamic of their life in the Holy Spirit for the world. The truth of any church relies on the whole church coming to its truth. As the Archbishop of Canterbury said in 2006: 'only the whole Church knows the whole truth'; and 'If the Good News of Jesus Christ is to be fully proclaimed to a needy world, then the reconciliation of all Christians in the truth and love of God is a vital element for our witness.'[2] These remarks apply to the churches as such, not only to their witness and beliefs: only the whole church (which may include more than those who are acknowledged or acknowledge themselves to be the church) knows the whole truth of the church; and reconciliation is for the churches and not only 'for all Christians'. And if today the Body of Christ is not only divided but also fragmented in its several parts, its full dimensions and dynamic are still more difficult to identify. Reference to the whole church is necessary for finding the full dimensions and dynamics of the church. Without this, attempts to learn from each other easily drift into lesser preoccupations.

A third difficulty arises from the tendency of churches to predefine themselves as normative, as 'the whole church', making their own internal 'map' normative for all the dimensions and dynamics of the Body of Christ. For one who studies ecclesiology, the closely defined character of Roman Catholic ecclesiology is striking. It is an impressively dense, closely articulated whole, comprising an ecclesio-political system in which the very being and life of the church is seen as sacramental of the salvific work of the Trinitarian God. That already raises questions about Receptive Ecumenism: can such a comprehensive and closely articulated ecclesiology engage with others, perhaps especially those which are doctrinally or ecclesially less well defined? Will it not be likely to dictate the terms of engagement? Will the outcome be other than self-reinforcing, with insights from elsewhere seen as capable only of introducing minor caveats in such a close-knit ecclesiology? Of course, the same questions will arise for any church which insists upon its own ways as normative.

If these difficulties are to be surmounted, it will be very important to find a 'map' which will locate the dimensions and dynamics of all the churches about which they need to engage with each other. How they should engage with each other is strongly conditioned by what they are, which makes it difficult for each to see beyond its own 'what' and to engage fully with others with differently construed aspects and dynamics; but that must be the goal of ecumenical relations. Such a map would tell us what are the aspects and dynamics of the churches about which they should engage in Receptive Ecumenism. It would need to be complex enough to identify modalities of church life which are (1) convergent as a whole, (2) contingent in execution, and (3) dynamic in relation to the end towards which they move. Furthermore, it would need to be applicable not only to particular churches, but also to the relations between them, and—above all—to the actualization of the church they may become.

Such an ecumenical 'map' would be more open to the varieties of ecclesiology found amongst all the churches, and—indeed—more open to the secular alternatives with which the churches must deal in the world as it now is. Perhaps such a map would enable us to discern the discussions which will be needed in Receptive Ecumenism. It would need to be able to identify principal areas in accepted ecclesiologies, and locate their elements and dynamics in a common grid of open categories. If this is attempted, it would be tantamount to saying that we need a theory of ecumenical relations for what we do. (To my knowledge, no such thing has ever emerged from ecumenical discussions heretofore, although there have been approximations within some discussions.) It would plot the areas—the dimensions and dynamics—in which ecumenical discussion needs to take place.

UNDERSTANDING THE DEVELOPMENT OF DIFFERENCES

Ironically, some of the considerations necessary for such a map would appear with better logical explanations of the genesis and development of the pluriformity of the churches. To be sure, there are good historical accounts of how the churches divided over doctrinal or moral issues, as one party introduced (substituted) some revised or new emphasis for what had formerly been accepted. What is less well understood is what effect this had on the continuing health of the churches. Did it, as some would now claim, enhance their health by bringing greater pluriformity? Did it sow the seeds of repeated divisiveness, by providing precedents for further schism, encouraging people to substitute still other emphases, in what some call 'the Protestant principle', and thereby promote still further disunity?[3] Did it encourage competing churches to emphasize their distinctive 'proprietary' characteristics, thereby hardening their differences? With their progressive embedding in the continuing life of the churches, how could such divisions be overcome? In the course of time, ecumenical discussion might make the original intentions underlying these substitutions better understood, but that would not bring further church unity. Or a strengthened secular environment might make even long-term religious differences seem less serious, make churches seem similar despite superficial differences, and allow people to transition more easily into other churches; but rarely has ecumenical or secular understanding displaced the division between churches. The point is that the substitution which begets division brings a competitive rivalry which has its own effects, which develop progressively. What began simply becomes ever more complex and intractable. What is most important ecumenically is how such a dynamic, in which relations between the churches are progressively reconfigured, can be turned into a healing one.

This introduces important considerations for our plan to plot the areas—the dimensions and dynamics—in which ecumenical discussion needs to take place. By taking the genesis and development of the pluriformity of churches seriously, we see that even understanding the reasons for different emphases in these areas will be insufficient to heal the church divisions which they involve, for it does not acknowledge—much less overcome—the history of the reconfigurations of the divisions. Whatever map—or theory—we develop for ecumenical relations will need to identify the areas in which progressive reconfigurations have occurred in different churches. The map will need to identify the ways in which the differences between hitherto separate churches—with their progressive 'ornamentation' (in the musical sense of elaborating them) of their original differences—may be attracted to unity. More than a static map of areas will be needed: it will have to be one extended towards a future unity in which 'all will be one' and 'All shall be well, and all shall be well, and all manner of things shall be well' (Mother Julian of Norwich).

ELEMENTALS

It is no easy thing for the churches to seek unity, and any mapping must attend to the primary theological content intrinsic to such unity, and how this shapes the church in its life and witness in the world; that is to the intensity of the identity of the Lord *in* the extensity of the world (see below).

If there is any guiding insight for ecclesial mapping, it is attention to primary theological content. By this I do not mean doctrinal content, except in the most basic sense of the word, but something still more elemental. I mean to suggest that the Lord as found in lived relationship to the Lord is what makes the church. This may be stated as (a) the Lord speaking in the Holy Scriptures, (b) more particularly in the encounter of the Lord with Moses in which the infinitely intense—or concentrated—identity of the Lord is shown in declaring 'I am that I am', or (c) the 'I am the God of Abraham, Isaac and Jacob' and the 'I will be with you', by which are shaped the spatio-temporal covenantal life of the people of

Israel, or (d) the 'Word' which was with the Lord and was the Lord God through whom all that was made was made and all that was redeemed was redeemed, which became flesh, was born, lived, suffered, died, and was resurrected, and (e) the Spirit with and from the Lord in Christ who constituted the church to witness to the world its true purpose and destiny. It is this elemental relationship between the Lord and the Lord's people that is lived by the church.

This, however, does not suggest either that the Lord is exhaustively known, or that the church (or Israel as the people of the Lord) is finally known thereby. There is a sense in which the completeness of such knowledge in each is disallowed by two things: (1) the infinitely intense identification of the Lord in the 'I am that I am', and (2) the promise of the Lord to be with the people, calling them—directing them—to the coming kingdom of the Lord. To say that they are not complete or final is not to say that they are not full in their own right: for the same Lord is known 'relative to them'. The identification of this Lord as 'God' who is 'God of your ancestors' and 'will be with you'; the correlative identification of this spatio-temporally constituted people; and their eschatological anticipation of the kingdom: all three comprise the fullness of these people as the church.

By stating how this Lord is infinitely and intensively 'Lord', and yet calls a people into being (and, without finally completing them as such, calls and accompanies them towards their true eschatological end), we only begin to specify how and where this happens within their real historical existence. For there to be a people materially and spatio-temporally interdependent with the world as it is, for them to be socially and politically ordered for the common good (while having ways of growing to their full stature and promise, and throughout being attracted by the Lord where they are and toward the kingdom of God), all these require the delineation of the most significant ways by which this happens and will continue to happen. Such matters underlie the socio-ecclesial 'maps' below (Figs. 30.1 and 30.2).

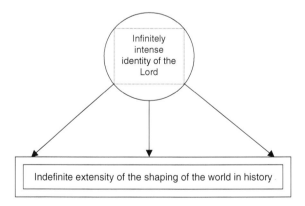

Figure 30.1. *The Lord and the world*

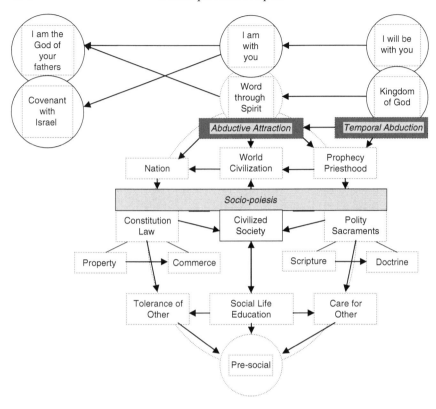

Figure 30.2. *Social and ecclesial dynamics: abductive socio-poiesis*

A SOCIO-ECCLESIAL MAP

Figure 30.1 depicts the content of the Divine in relation to the world: the infinitely intense (maximally concentrated) identity of the Lord is seen as fully engaged—by creation, redemption, and perfection—with the complex and indefinite parameters of the world in history.[4]

Figure 30.2 delineates the ways in which the Divine is present to, and operative in, the affairs of the world, antecedently in Moses and Israel, and retroactively and proactively in the Word of God in Jesus Christ and by the Holy Spirit. Pervasive in these is the way in which the Lord attracts—both in and through history—the self-making of society (socio-poiesis). This attraction is distributed through the socio-poietic modalities shown. The 'map' attempts to show what are the main aspects of the relationship of the Divine to human social life in the world, what are the institutions and practices of human life, and how they are ordered within this dynamic relationship. It is best understood within the context of a still more primary 'map' (not presented here) indicating the engagement of the Divine with the world as such, by which the material world is created and constituted as it is.

The circles and boxes Fig. 30.2 show, in a very preliminary way, the main modalities of society and church in the West, and the arrows show the ways in which they are—directly or mediately—attracted. The content of the circles and boxes is minimally specified, since it will be differently particularized in different nations, societies, and churches. (It is worth noting that there is some difference between nations and churches: a nation incorporates differences (for example, those of factions and localities), but churches—by contrast—are frequently divided.)

For reasons to be explained below, Fig. 30.2 needs to be read as the attraction of socio-poiesis by the Divine. The chart needs to be read along three trajectories.

1. At the left there is: a nation 'made' through its constitution and political process, incorporating citizens who are (through education) socialized, in such a way as (at the minimum) to tolerate each other and care for basic needs.

2. In the middle there is: a global society which arises from the construction of civilized society, incorporating people socialized in appropriate ways for responsibility towards each other, thereby raising people from pre-social, self-preoccupied ways to providing for each other.

3. At the right there is: church formed through its constitution and polity, including the interanimation[5] of the faithful with those ordained to guide them, thereby socializing its people, with a purpose of learning the truth of others through the deepest care for them, by which the church moves civilization by prophecy and priesthood towards the kingdom of God.

All of this is what is termed here socio-poiesis, through which in different ways people are raised or—if they think self-referentially—raise themselves to flourishing as a society. Properly speaking, the trajectories traced are mutually implicated in many ways, even strongly inter-penetrating, although this is frequently discounted if not denied: modern society is often defined in contradistinction to the church (secularism), just as some suggest that the purity of the church and its witness requires its separation from the state (sectarianism).

Many—but by no means all—of these mutual implications are shown by arrows in the chart. The head of each arrow shows the direction from which pressure comes. Hence, ← indicates that the effect comes from a source shown to the right; and → indicates the reverse, while ↔ indicates two-way pressure. Furthermore, where socio-poiesis occurs, its making of society involves attention to certain preconditions; this is indicated by downward arrows (↓). Itself, however, socio-poiesis as a whole may be brought about by other influences not so much outside it as intrinsic to its movement; the arrow ↑ denotes this.

There is more to this than simply ordering the relations between items on the chart. Wherever there is an arrow (e.g. ← or ↓), this suggests that the item to which it points has its own 'content', but also that this is properly to be read by reference to that from which the arrow comes. Conversely, the item from which the arrow comes needs to be seen as mediated by the content of the item pointed to. For example, looking at the middle and right-hand trajectories, 'global civilization' needs to be seen by reference to 'prophecy and priesthood', while they derive their material content from 'global civilization': prophecy speaks into—or within—a civilization to call it to something better; priesthood stands with a civilization to relate it to that by which it is perfected. By their close engagement with it, 'prophecy and priesthood' transform global civilization, while they are best described in terms of their transformation of it. In other words, their meaning (prophecy and priesthood) are to be understood indirectly through their transformative effect on it (global civilization): neither apart from it nor collapsed into it.

The chart reveals that there is much more to socio-poiesis than simply the interaction of human institutions, as if a secular explanation was sufficient, explaining society, social processes, and goals—even those of civil society and ecclesial formation—in terms of human agency, interest, or culture. A more appropriate reading of these trajectories shows the infinitely intense (concentrated) identity of the Lord in the action of the Lord for spatio-temporal humanity in creation, redemption, and eschatological fulfilment. This occurs in particular ways, for Israel, for the world at large, and for Christians, that is in the trajectories seen before. And the effects are seen throughout the socio-poiesis, as it is drawn higher by what is here termed 'abduction'.

ATTRACTIVE PRESSURE

Before discussing abduction, it is important to understand the character of this 'attractive pressure'. As we might suppose, those concerned only with the trajectories at the left and centre of the chart will tend to see the highest points of socio-poiesis in terms of aspiration or desire for the well-being of nation and globe, although they *do* acknowledge how such 'higher ends' are intrinsic to what they do; more rarely, they will measure such well-being in terms of the environment for future generations. There is reference neither to a fuller source from which the attraction might come nor its association with future well-being. This places serious limitations on their capacity to think that which they desire for the present and the future, and therefore on the quality of their desiring. Strangely enough, reason and passions require a fullest source—the Word through the Spirit—if they are to be capable of thinking what they most desire.

Typically, in addition to Jews and Muslims (represented in truncated form at the top left of the chart), the Christian church recognizes the Lord in the most intimate relation to the poiesis of the people (socio-poiesis). This, however, is the

Word which was with and in God from the beginning and in creation, the Word which became flesh in Jesus Christ, constituted a people by his self-giving, and in the Holy Spirit is continuously present as his people are drawn forward to the kingdom of God. The 'abductive attraction' of this incarnate Word, attracting nation, globe, and church to their fullest, and temporally attracting them to the kingdom of God, is what is present in, and intrinsic to, the trajectory (at the right of the chart) through which the church becomes itself in the purposes of God.

ABDUCTION

Why call this 'abductive attraction'? As distinct from the two forms of reasoning most commonly used in theology, deduction and induction, abduction is frequently described as 'thinking to the best explanation'. As used in pragmatist philosophy, it is often seen as the discovery of a 'third' which transcends the polarizations of thought and life by which enmities are constructed and perpetuated.[6] Here, however, we use it in the sense of being given—or 'being found' by—the primary source and goal of reason, passion, and integrity. This use is taken from Coleridge's *Opus Maximum*.[7] Where)(designates continuity in distinction, he describes a 'being drawn towards the true center' from within the self-referential tendencies of the human self which lead to 'the false and fantastic center in the opposite direction':

I. Abduction from the Self, as manifesting the being drawn toward the true center [*sic*], as)(, the self-seeking or tendency to the false and fantastic center [*sic*] in the opposite direction. Attraction ad extra. Appropriative Attraction . . . as)(separative Self-projection, or Volatility.

II. The influx from the Light, with the Spirit[,] as)(by the creaturely: Conjunction: Offspring or realized Poles, Particularization, Contraction as

III. Omneity, Dilation.[8]

Here we find a distinctive conception of abduction, 'the being drawn towards the true center' of all, the Logos and the Spirit, in distinction from but in continuity with self-seeking or self-reference. Extending this into the social sphere, we find that abduction does not extinguish the self-reference of the activities by which socio-poiesis occurs, but draws them to their 'true center' in the 'influx of Light, with the Spirit'. And, recalling the discussion of arrows above, the Word and the Spirit attract socio-poiesis and are best seen through their transformative effects on it. They engage fully with socio-poiesis from within, transforming it and all the activities by which it proceeds. Like prophecy and priesthood, by their close engagement with socio-poiesis, the Word and the Spirit transform it, and are to be understood indirectly through their transformative effect on it, neither apart from it nor collapsed into it. As the chart suggests, furthermore, abduction operates not only to draw all human institutions to a higher condition but also to draw them forward to the kingdom of God.

A most important feature of this abductive attraction is that, while acknowledging the self-referentiality ('self-seeking') of societies as in continuity with it, it recognizes that in abductive socio-poiesis societies are drawn beyond the self-referentiality by which they are usually confined, thereby giving them much fuller possibilities—and hope—than otherwise available. It is tantamount to saying that in their efforts to make themselves, societies are also drawn transformatively beyond themselves. Hence, all aspects of society, whether nation, global, or ecclesial, are open to transformation by the 'influx of Light, with the Spirit'. If we see this in the terms used in the chart, we see that this provides a higher horizon and direction for the constitution and law of nations, for the conditions for civilized society, and for the sacraments and polity of the church, and through these for all other institutions which they attract.

The transformation brought through this abductive attraction is of the most profound kind, entering into and permeating the spheres through which socio-poiesis occurs. It establishes the actuality by which societies are raised to their fullness. By virtue of the attraction of the One who says 'I am with you' in the Word and by the Spirit, and by being drawn in their temporality to the kingdom of God, we see the movement by which societies are drawn to their fullness. Thus are they drawn towards the true centre of all, the Logos and the Spirit, which also draws them to the kingdom of God.

CONCLUSION: INTERACTIVELY PARTICULAR ECUMENICITY

We began by recognizing that only the whole church—reaching out also to those who do not acknowledge themselves to be the church—will know the whole truth of the church. Yet, to avoid the tendency of churches to predefine this 'whole truth' in isolation from each other, we have attempted to map what are the aspects and dynamics of the churches about which they need to engage with each other. Now that we have seen, first the 'context' of the infinitely intense identity of the Lord engaging comprehensively with indefinitely extensive world history, and within it a 'chart' of nation, society, and church, we have a set of areas in which churches may seek to engage with each other, and also engage with societies which in the West are increasingly secular.[9] An outline 'map' of these areas, as well as the relations between them and the directionality of these relations, is all that we can attempt now, although much remains to be said. We must now locate some further implications for ecumenism.

In the history of ecumenism, much like the history of inter-faith relations, there have tended to be two strategies. One is to focus on particular items of church belief and life, especially those of polity, sacraments, scripture, and doctrine, where there is evident disagreement between the parties involved. The other is to generalize about the tradition of others without engaging with them. In the first case, the consequence is that these particularities are isolated from the web of interconnections in which they are implicated, and thus oversimplified. In the second case, a set of externally imposed categories is privileged at the expense of the other tradition.

The way forward in ecumenical discussion needs to be different. With regard to the first, we need to concentrate on particular 'deposits'—of the elements found on the right side of the chart in Fig. 30.2—and to read them in relation to those from which they are drawn and to which they contribute. In effect, therefore, we need to view them with their interconnections and within the dynamics of Divine attraction. With regard to the second, we need to learn not to speak for the traditions of others (and synthesize them by reference to our own), but instead to speak with the others and to indwell their traditions. These two movements can be summarized as interactively particular ecumenicity within the dynamics of the elemental life of the Trinitarian God in the world.

It needs to be emphasized that such ecumenicity is not disengaged from the life of nations and societies. On the contrary, it is profoundly connected with the purposes of God for the whole world. Social reality in the world involves all of the areas and relations identified in the whole chart. They are interdependent, and each trajectory—that of nation, society, or church—requires the others. Furthermore, some form of each is implicit in the others. At one extreme, we might find that, in a theocracy of the sort now advocated in some parts of the Muslim world, all of the areas in the chart are strongly coordinated with each other within one set of overall coordinates. In the Muslim case, the overall coordinates derive from the Quran and must be reflected in every aspect of government, society, and religious observance and their relations, each specified in somewhat different terms than those in the chart. This, however, is not what we find in the modern West, where in a liberal democracy these areas are distinguished much as they are in the chart presented here. None the less, nation, society, and church are co-present, and to varying degrees mirror each other. To take just one example, there are often affinities between the constitutions and laws of nations, and the polities and sacraments of churches; indeed, the assimilation of churches to the hierarchical or democratic processes found in the governments of particular periods and nations is both understandable and dangerous.

The implications for ecumenicity are very demanding. The areas of special interest on which ecumenical discussions often concentrate should not be isolated from the trajectory and dynamics within which they figure, but there must also be greater concern for the interconnections—and dynamics—by which they are related to other trajectories. For instance, we should not expect to be able to consider the constitution of a church by polity and sacraments without reference to the prophecy and priesthood by which they contribute to the emergence of civilized society. To do so would be to practise a particular kind of sectarianism. No more should we expect to consider issues of social justice in different traditions without tracing them to the abductive attraction by Word and Spirit by which we are called to higher kinds of responsibility towards others.

We conclude, however, by noting that the argument presented in this chapter suggests a certain agenda for Receptive Ecumenism, that it should:

1. observe the complex modalities in which differences between the churches are likely to appear;

2. seek to develop abductive socio-poiesis through fostering in ecumenical discussion (a) *interactive* consideration of the complex modalities of church life as they are expressed in *particular* churches and (b) kindred prophetic/priestly responsibility towards nations and civilization;

3. seek to develop temporally abductive socio-poiesis in ecumenical responsibility towards nations and the world, by which all may move towards the kingdom of God;

4. thereby following the Divine movement identified as 'elemental' theology.

It cannot be emphasized too strongly that ecumenical relations are a call to renew all the churches and to contribute to a world in which 'All shall be well, and all shall be well, and all manner of things shall be well' (Mother Julian of Norwich).

NOTES

1. Paul D. Murray, 'On Valuing Truth in Practice: Rome's Postmodern Challenge', *International Journal of Systematic Theology*, 8 (2006), 164, also in Laurence Paul Hemming and Susan Frank Parsons (eds.), *Redeeming Truth: Considering Faith and Reason* (Aldershot: Ashgate, 2007), 184–206 (185).

2. Rowan Williams, the Archbishop of Canterbury, 'Greetings to Pope Benedict' (23 Nov. 2006), available at <http://www.archbishopofcanterbury.org/652>; id., 'The Challenge and Hope of Being an Anglican Today' (27 June 2006), available at <http://www.archbishopofcanterbury.org/640>.

3. See Paul Tillich, *Systematic Theology*, vol. i. (Chicago, Ill.: Chicago University Press, 1951), 42 and 252; and Chapter 15, *The Protestant Era*, trans. and ed. James Luther Adams (London: Nisbet, 1951); also Chapter 6: Walter Kasper, 'Credo Unam Sanctam Ecclesiam'—The Relationship Between the Catholic and the Protestant Principles in Fundamental Ecclesiology'.

4. See Daniel W. Hardy, *God's Ways with the World: Thinking and Practising Christian Faith* (Edinburgh: T. & T. Clark, 1996); and id., *Finding the Church* (London: SCM Press, 2001).

5. See Church of England Working Party, *Education for the Church's Ministry: The Report of the Working Party on Assessment* (London: Church House, 1987).

6. See Peter Ochs, *Peirce, Pragmatism and the Logic of Scripture* (Cambridge: Cambridge University Press, 1998); also David F. Ford and Chad Pecknold (eds.), *The Promise of Scriptural Reasoning* (Oxford: Blackwell, 2006).

7. Coleridge, well known to the pragmatist philosophers, was a likely source for the notion of abduction.

8. Coleridge, *Opus Maximum*, ed. Thomas McFarland (Princeton, NJ: Princeton University Press, 2002), 327.

9. Current decisions in France, and debates in the UK, about the acceptability of religious dress for Muslim women and the elimination of Christian celebrations and symbols from public places in the UK and the USA seem to provide evidence for the growth of self-consciously secular societies.

31

Learning the Ways of Receptive Ecumenism—Formational and Catechetical Considerations

Jeffrey Gros, FSC

INTRODUCTION

Handing on a robust faith within a secure identity is a prerequisite for developing within Roman Catholicism a spirituality and horizon supportive of Receptive Ecumenism. Commitment to the ecumenical goal and humble engagement in the pilgrim journey towards its realization should now be central to this Catholic identity. The challenge, then, for Roman Catholicism at this still early moment in the ecumenical pilgrimage is to develop among believers the receptive attitude that will draw them into ecumenical engagement and motivate them to hand on the relations that have been initiated since the Second Vatican Council. This 'handing on' includes personal relations with people and their churches, the results of the dialogues, and increased understanding of the inner lives, structures, beliefs, and spiritualities of fellow pilgrims. There are three good texts that emanated from the Holy See during the 1990s which emphasize the educational component of Receptive Ecumenism.[1]

If ours is an interim period, ecumenically speaking—a flattened plateau after the hope-filled heights of earlier decades—it also provides a welcome breather for those engaged in the arduous task of taking the results of forty years of dialogue, codifying them in reference volumes, providing study guides, and translating them into accessible formational materials for use at every level of Roman Catholic life.

The 1990s also saw the production of the *Catechism of the Catholic Church* and the *General Directory for Catechesis*,[2] each of which has stimulated significant catechetical initiatives, sometimes informed by forty years of ecumenical dialogue and magisterial ecumenical developments, but also sometimes independent of these developments. Likewise, developments in communication, media trends, and educational thinking have provided further rich resources and difficult challenges for handing on the faith, including its ecumenical component.

In this context, this chapter probes the specifically pedagogical and formational dimension to receptive Catholic Learning in three movements. Following a review of the principles proposed for Roman Catholic ecumenical formation in official teaching, the chapter explores some of the various target audiences for this formation before reflecting on how some specific challenges might best be negotiated.

PRINCIPLES OF ECUMENICAL FORMATION

The aforementioned *Ecumenical Dimension in the Formation of Those Engaged in Pastoral Work* is a brief text that does not attempt a fully developed ecumenical catechesis. It does, however, provide some helpful outlines in three particular regards: (1) hermeneutics; (2) the 'hierarchy of truths'; and (3) communicating the fruits of ecumenical dialogues (§ 11). I will attempt to elaborate on these themes as they touch on Receptive Ecumenism.

Hermeneutics

The argument of *Formation*, § 11 is that Roman Catholics need to learn an interpretive perspective that enables them to distinguish the deposit of faith from its formulations. The believer is challenged to develop a world view that recognizes the historical character of sacred texts and magisterial formulations and that understands the development of doctrine, sacramental practice, and the structures of the church. Above all, it is essential to learn to interpret the other churches and ecclesial communities in the most positive light and in the context of the real, if imperfect, communion that already exists. In turn, this developing hermeneutical sensitivity is an element in the important debate on the intent and implications of the Second Vatican Council's ecumenical principles and ecclesiology.[3]

A prime example of such hermeneutics is the salutary public debate among members and organs of the Roman Curia as to how the '*subsistit*' phrase in *LG*, § 8 is to be understood, and which fixes in the Roman Catholic community the firm recollection that the Council fathers rejected '*est*/is' in favour of '*subsistit*/subsists in'.[4] This change in interpretation opened the way for a new hermeneutic of other churches and ecclesial communities, the specifics of which are inevitably going to be controverted, since the Council did not attempt to provide an exact definition, but left that to post-conciliar theological development and dialogue.[5]

Another example of this hermeneutical formation is the development in evaluating the sacramental life of the churches of the Reformation. The statement of the Council's Decree on Ecumenism (*UR*) was itself quite remarkable at a time when Roman Catholics regarded Protestant celebrations of the Eucharist as inefficacious: 'The brethren divided from us also use many liturgical actions of the Christian religion. These most certainly can truly engender a life of grace in ways that vary according to the condition of each church or community. These liturgical actions must be regarded as capable of giving access to the community of salvation' (*UR*, § 3). Such an affirmation requires a total recasting of standard Catholic interpretations of Protestant sacramental life.

With this, even more important for the development of a receptive ecumenical hermeneutics, is the re-evaluation of Protestant orders themselves and, so, of the Eucharist over which the ordained preside. For example, the United States Lutheran–Catholic dialogue has suggested that the Roman Catholic conviction of real, if imperfect, communion with partner churches also be recognized as applying to their ordained ministries. Therefore, our interpretive approach to ecumenical partners moves beyond the juridical categories used before the dialogues, as was suggested by Joseph Ratzinger before his election as Pope Benedict XVI: 'I count among the most important results of the ecumenical dialogues the insight that the issue of the Eucharist cannot be narrowed to the problem of "validity." Even a theology oriented to the concept of succession . . . need not in any way deny the salvation-granting presence of the Lord in a Lutheran Lord's Supper.'[6] Again, the same dialogue urges that *defectus*, when applied to the ordained ministries of Reformation churches, no longer be rendered *lack* but, more accurately, as *defect* or *deficiency*.[7]

More generally, the ecumenical movement has now progressed so far that it has been necessary to institute a study in this task of ecumenical hermeneutics.[8] Such ecumenical hermeneutics entails a re-reception together of the ancient councils of the church and the later general synods of the West. In this vein, Pope John Paul II famously called for a joint re-examination of the Petrine office itself, entailing a re-evaluation of both the first and the second millennia.[9] Such acts of reinterpretation inevitably provoke concerns regarding the potential for distortion, reduction, and manipulation and need to be discerned carefully against the demands of a rich and responsible *ressourcement*.

The Hierarchy of Truths

Formation, § 12 suggests that the principle of the hierarchy of truths entails a rereading of Christian history and the way it has been taught in order to place the truths of revelation at the centre and then relate the church's history, formulations, and piety to the fundamentals.

A classic ecumenical example of how the hierarchy of truths will reshape Roman Catholic teaching is the explanation of Mary, the Marian dogmas, and

Marian piety in their appropriate relationship to Roman Catholic liturgical life. This will be particularly challenging for those who have hoped to introduce new dogmas (e.g. Mary as co-redemptrix) which the Council fathers explicitly excluded from the Marian chapter of the 'Dogmatic Constitution on the Church'.

All Christians now accept Mary's role as the Mother of God. The divisions of the Council of Ephesus (431) between Assyrian/Chaldean Christians and the rest of Christendom have been laid to rest after the 1994 Common Declaration.[10] The Virgin birth is a widely accepted tradition, though interpreted differently in some churches.

However, the challenge for the Roman Catholic Church is to interpret the more recent Marian dogmas in the light of the whole tradition and to work together so that they can be re-received together in the context of a common doctrine of Christocentric grace and hope. The most recent ARCIC and some of the national English-speaking dialogues have made a major contribution to this process, which provides an important receptive ecumenical resource of Roman Catholic Marian education and piety giving full clarity to the hierarchy of truths.[11]

There is always a danger of making popular pietistic traditions of western Latin Catholics identity-markers for a hardened sense of identity over against fellow Christians. Private practices, like the Rosary or devotion to the reserved Blessed Sacrament, can be given a higher place in the hierarchy of values than the common apostolic faith and the common baptism which are central to the Catholic hierarchy of truths.

Communicating the Truths of Ecumenical Dialogue

Finally, this current interim period provides an opportunity to further the reception of existing ecumenical work into Roman Catholic educational processes and resources (cf. *Formation*, § 13). For this, religious educators need a process of ecumenical conversion combined with simplified materials introducing the ecumenical project and its progress thus far.[12]

In this regard, the *Directory* has excellent principles for enabling seminaries, schools, and parishes to take the lead in ecumenical formation. However, resources need to be provided in each cultural context that relates these principles to the lived reality of the local churches.[13] It is notable that Pope John Paul II encouraged such receptive educational ecumenism over ten years ago:

While dialogue continues . . . a new task lies before us: that of receiving the results already achieved. These cannot remain the statements of bilateral commissions but *must become a common heritage*. For this to come about . . . a serious examination needs to be made, which . . . *must involve the whole People of God*. We are in fact dealing with issues which frequently are matters of faith, and these require universal consent, extending from the Bishops to the lay faithful, all of whom have received the anointing of the Holy Spirit. It is the same Spirit who assists the Magisterium and awakens the *sensus fidei*. (*UUS*, § 80)

Ecumenical formation is about conversion, touching people's hearts so they have a zeal for Receptive Ecumenism. However, it also entails informing their minds so that Roman Catholics and their ecumenical partners know one another and one another's churches better and, likewise, the results of the dialogues. The argument here is that if these somewhat specialized texts are to become a 'common heritage', then teacher-friendly resources need to be provided, correlating the dialogue results to the catechetical programmes of the churches.[14]

In this way, the focus of Receptive Ecumenism must move beyond the institutional and theological specialists to the whole people of God, in accordance with the Holy Spirit moving the minds and hearts of the entire church towards the unity that is central to Roman Catholic identity. To achieve this, attention to hermeneutics, the hierarchy of truths, and making the results of forty years of dialogue a common heritage will all be essential.

TARGET AUDIENCES FOR FORMATION IN RECEPTIVE CATHOLIC LEARNING

The whole people of God, in response to the call of the Holy Spirit, are on a journey towards the unity of the church for which Christ prayed. Fundamental, then, to Catholic Christian identity should be an experience of the pain of separation, the scandal of division, and the call to pray, study, and work for Christian unity in such a fashion as contrasts with the relative ecumenical complacency and passivity that too often characterizes a Catholicism secure in its size and truth claims.

Recognizing this universal call to ecumenical receptivity, there is nevertheless a variety of specific groups in the church with their particular calling, responsibilities, and challenges, and correspondingly diverse formational needs. Attention could usefully be given here to the developmental stages in the education of Catholic youth. Likewise, the specific contexts of clergy and adult lay formation are deserving of fuller treatment. Again, as attended to here, there are the specific formational needs of (1) the theological community and (2) the bishops in their pastoral role as leaders.

Catholic Theologians

In general, Roman Catholic theologians are not well advanced in seeing the results of theological dialogue, the heritage of other churches (beyond their most illustrious scholars), and the horizon of Christian unity as intrinsic to their methodology. The academic culture of many institutions, even Catholic ones, often encourages isolation, specialization, and competitive research that militate against collaboration, ecumenical research, and the interdisciplinary methodology necessary for building the basis for the unity of the church.[15] Indeed, ecumenical research entails not only interdisciplinary and inter-confessional research and dialogue but a corporate type of scholarship untypical of the modern research university, in the humanities at least.

Can we, for example, adequately reflect on Roman Catholic collegiality without attention to the dialogues on connexionalism within Methodism, or penetrating more deeply into the history of provincial development in the Anglican Communion and Orthodox synodality? Similarly, can we talk about Episcopal conferences without attention to ARCIC's *The Gift of Authority* or, even more specifically, to how United Methodist bishops are evaluated and itinerated?[16] Again, can we adequately attend to lay ministry without building on the core agreements in the ministry section of *Baptism, Eucharist and Ministry*, or more specific learning through dialogues with the Lutheran and Reformed Churches?[17] In such ways, the Roman Catholic theological community needs to find ways of holding itself accountable—not least by peer critique—to the methods, results of ecclesial dialogue, and to the common history we now inherit.

Indeed, beyond the substantive specifics of ecumenical theological dialogue, the reclamation of the properly corporate, dialogic, ecclesial character of theological research might be the single most significant contribution of forty years of ecumenical dialogue to theological formation. For example, the biblical scholar who has to move beyond an excellence in peer-evaluated historical–critical research, into an arena in which confessional, historical, and polemical uses of scripture are at play, as well as the pastoral and ecclesial horizons of the research, is both immeasurably enriched and challenged in his or her work. More generally, Michael Root, citing Robert Jenson, recommends that Christian theologians view themselves as working under a double contradiction whereby: (a) they confess the scandal of a divided Christian church, whilst (b) recognizing that 'by every churchly act we contradict that contradiction'.[18]

The Formation of Bishops

The ecumenical formation of bishops and senior church leaders, like the training of other busy, adult populations, has its own set of principles. If, for busy clergy, ecumenical learning is often like my computer learning—on a 'need-to-know' basis, with the theology becoming relevant for them in response to specific pastoral needs—things are even more challenging for bishops, with their busy schedules and multiple responsibilities.

That said, some bishops meet weekly with their ecumenical counterparts. Others have annual retreats, or invite them and their spouses over for social evenings. Still others have well-developed commissions and ecumenical officers who process the magisterial developments and the results of the dialogues and local relations on the ground for them. Again, an affective collegiality develops among some bishops so that they and their partners can provide ecumenically formed and enunciated witness for their communities.[19] Likewise, some bishops counsel, support, and advise one another. A Roman Catholic bishop supports a candidate for the Lutheran episcopacy as she discerns whether to stand for election. An African American Methodist bishop calls on his Roman Catholic counterpart when there is a scandal with a presiding elder. The bishops and church leaders of an area support their Roman Catholic colleague during an investigation and intervention by the Holy See. In all such instances a Receptive Ecumenism has provided the learning about one another—spiritually, institutionally, and theologically—that makes the affective collegiality effective.

Often leaders learn through goal-oriented projects, where knowledge becomes a resource for action. For example, celebrations of the Lutheran–Catholic *Joint Declaration on the Doctrine of Justification* in cathedrals and parishes were occasions of ecumenical reception for bishops and their collaborators. Many caught up with thirty years of dialogue in order to speak intelligently to this great occasion.

Similarly, the production of the British and Irish Roman Catholic episcopal teaching document *One Bread One Body* was an exemplary model of Catholic bishops processing forty years of dialogue on the Eucharist in order to bring their own people up to date on ecumenical developments.[20] In turn, the response of the bishops of the Church of England, *The Eucharist, Sacrament of Unity*, was an admirable exercise in ecumenical etiquette and 'magisterial mutuality'.[21] Of course, one looks forward to the day when just one document would be produced, with the remaining differences of faith, interpretation, and practice duly noted at the end. Short of this, *One Bread One Body* is remarkable for the ability it demonstrated amongst the English, Welsh, Scottish, and Irish Roman Catholic Bishops to come to a common expressed mind on contentious issues that left the US Roman Catholic Bishops unable to agree on anything beyond the briefest of references to the relevant section of the 1983 Code of Canon Law (canon 844, §§ 3–4). With this, is the high level of effective reception of recent ecumenical dialogues on the Eucharist evidenced by *One Bread One Body*. This is particularly marked when compared to Pope John Paul II's last encyclical on this very same subject.[22] So, teaching on the Eucharist illustrates both some of the possibilities of episcopal ecumenical formation and some of the challenges and limitations.

CHALLENGES IN FORMATION FOR RECEPTIVE ECUMENICAL LEARNING WITHIN CATHOLICISM

Among the many challenges facing formation for Receptive Ecumenism within Roman Catholicism, five are particularly significant: (1) preparing a corps of able dialoguers; (2) penetrating a more universal Catholic community; (3) deepening the dialogue to deal with the more difficult issues; (4) rewriting our common history to reflect present ecumenical research and hopes; and (5) providing competent leadership as we move from dialogue to decision in receiving existing ecumenical results.

Formation for Dialogue

Academic specialization often inhibits the formation of leaders who can take up the pioneering challenge of these first four decades of dialogue. Consequently, the church needs to identify theology graduates who, taking, for example, the case of scriptural specialists, not only know their biblical languages, but who also know the councils of the church, and the ecclesiological context of these historical debates. Similarly, historians may have the best patristic or conciliar research at their fingertips, but being able to integrate such learning with the sacramental and ecclesiological contexts of contemporary ecumenical partners generally moves beyond their own horizons. Without settling for generalists, we need to have Roman Catholic scholars willing to enter into dialogue to serve the unity of the church, skilled in dealing with the type of interdisciplinary and inter-confessional research that can produce the quality of texts that have blessed the ecumenical movement to date.

Furthermore, we need genuinely theologically formed educational specialists who can help our communities develop ecumenically competent catechetical programmes. Such programmes would aim not only at making the texts a common heritage but at providing educational models that will bring all Roman Catholics into the experience of the real, if yet imperfect, communion we share with our ecumenical partners.

Universalizing the Call to Receptive Catholic Learning

Whereas the period since the Second Vatican Council has seen many rich developments in ecumenism, particularly so within the North Atlantic community, for many other sectors of Catholicism it has been a time of isolation, as in Eastern Europe where, since 1989, new inter-church tensions have emerged before the reception of the Second Vatican Council has even begun. There the challenges of Receptive Ecumenism in both Catholic and Orthodox worlds are enormous. Likewise, in the Spanish-speaking world, the fruits of ecumenical dialogue are only gradually becoming known. Indeed, it has only been with the post-Franco transition that religious liberty has been possible in Spain.[23] Again, the struggles in Latin America, and the mythology that identifies all non-Catholics with a CIA-inspired invasion of Pentecostal and Evangelical sects from the United States, makes ecumenical initiatives and receptivity among Roman Catholics especially difficult. With this, though many of the Latin American states have religious liberty in their legislation, there is still a variety of privileges accorded to the Roman Catholic Church—in relation, for example, to marriage legislation— that do not give fellow Christians the feeling of living as free and equal citizens in a Catholic cultural society. As I have elsewhere noted, Catholics may formally affirm religious liberty, but the development of a culture of pluralism, respect, and dialogue is still in the early stages of reception.[24]

In short, the universal promotion of Receptive Ecumenism throughout Catholicism will need to be especially sensitive to the context in which texts, churches, and ecumenical initiatives are to be received and how they influence the ongoing life of the church. As a counter-example, whilst there was, as far as I know, no special Latin American edition of the ARCIC *Final Report*,[25] the bulletin of the Council of Latin American Episcopal Conferences did circulate the 1991 response of the Holy See in Spanish.

Dealing with Difficult Issues

Catholic ecumenical partners find it difficult to understand, sometimes, how willing the leadership of the church is to enter into serious dialogue on sensitive issues. For example, the question of women's ordination and certain areas of sexual morality are clearly perceived, in Catholic teaching, as matters of authority. The consequent inability to dialogue as freely about these issues as has been possible with more central sacramental, Christological, and soteriological themes has been marked. If the dialogue of love is to mature into a dialogue of truth, as the late Pope John Paul II has urged, then ways need to be found to face these issues squarely and dispassionately.[26]

Likewise, mutual learning about the use of the sources of authority and the organs for articulating the truth of the Gospel challenges us to deepen our understanding. Sources, criteria, and organs for authoritative teaching must continue to be learned from one another, evaluated, and common ground sought for reconciling these differences. Notably, here, the very process of producing the Lutheran–Roman Catholic statement on justification enabled the identification of future required work on criteriology and ecclesiology in authoritative teaching. For example, the churches of the Lutheran World Federation had to act formally on the text for it to become authoritative, while the Holy See produced one decision, while consulting appropriate episcopal conferences. Similarly, subsequent clarifications from the Holy See indicated the learning about Lutheran authority that had occurred and the further challenges that lay open. As the then Cardinal

Ratzinger noted, reflecting on his work as Cardinal Prefect of the Congregation for the Doctrine of the Faith:

The ecumenical dialogues...have here created a new situation, for this dialogue consists not merely in scholars talking to other scholars...but is a conversation between...Church communities. As a result of the inner commission of the Church and the necessities of the Church's life there has developed...even within Protestantism, something like the teaching authority of the Church...The Catholic Church will continue to reflect self-critically on its perception of the magisterium; conversely...Protestant Christianity is directed to the search for the proper form of ecclesial teaching authority.[27]

Re-writing our Common History

We also need to begin to re-receive the councils and general synods of the West in light of the ecumenical dialogues and subsequent conciliar developments. Just as the Second Vatican Council's collegiality is the appropriate context for understanding the First Vatican Council's treatment of the prerogatives of the papal office, so the dialogues initiated by the Second provide us with the resources for re-receiving the councils of Trent, Lateran IV, Lyons, and Florence.

Beyond this, as we approach the jubilee of the Reformation, 2017, we are challenged to produce works that place ourselves solidly together with one voice, one hope, and one set of differentiated interpretations of the variety of characters, events, and texts that witness how the sixteenth century helped us all refocus on the grace of Christ and the sacramental and biblical richness of the church, in spite of its tragic ecclesial, political, and military consequences.

More urgently and less technically, we are challenged to begin to tell in healing ways the stories of the respective alienations of East and West, of the sixteenth century and of the eighteenth century, based on the hermeneutical tools available to us from the dialogues. This must take place on at least three levels.[28]

First, we need to tell the schism, Reformation, and other alienating moments in light of present ecumenical agreement and accompanying research in both accurate and religiously clarifying ways that focus on the common religious motivation giving rise to such tragic polarizing results. Second, we need to take adequate account of the cultural, political, economic, and psychological factors on both sides of the disputes to make the reconciling prospects come alive as authentic responses to the Christian religious bonds that were never completely lost. Third, we need to use the contemporary methods and historical records of popular religion, devotion, piety, and the authentic faith of all involved in each period, so that the results of theological reconciliation do not obscure the fundamental Christian reality in the minds and hearts of those who carried on their faith in the midst of conflict, polarization, and persecution by fellow Christians. Exemplary here is the work of Eamon Duffy which has both revised the one-sided treatments of history that favoured a partisan sectarian agenda and disclosed to us the rich popular piety infrequently reflected in the systematic or polemic treatments that have survived.[29] In short, we need an authentic hermeneutics of piety for our ecumenical task, both as scholars but also in the educational ministry of the churches.[30]

Leadership

The pilgrimage is long but its early markers are relatively positive. Roman Catholicism has been able to negotiate the move from dialogue to decision with some grace, whilst acknowledging some stumbles in the official, Roman reception process.[31]

For instance, the 1987 Roman Catholic response to *BEM*, the first such response to an ecumenical text since Florence (1439), was basically positive.[32] There was much appreciation from ecumenical colleagues and sacramental theologians for the contribution to moving the discussion forward and providing concrete suggestions where remaining issues linger.[33] In contrast, the response in 1991 to the ARCIC *Final Report* was somewhat more challenging.[34]

Most recently, the 1998 clarifications presented with the decision to sign the *JDDJ* produced a delay in the process.[35] That said, the working together of the Roman Curia, with the input of episcopal conferences around the world, seems to have been much more satisfactory than the evaluating of the two earlier texts independently of the drafting process itself.[36] Whereas the Catholic evaluations of ARCIC and *BEM* can appear as academic exercises external to the inner life of the church, the involvement of the Congregation for the Doctrine of the Faith in the drafting of the *JDDJ*, and its formal approval by the Holy See, with strong papal affirmation, makes clear the more intimate degree of engagement in this process.

Further, what may be perceived as negative evaluations or the articulation of needs for clarification are important incentives for both deeper common reflection, clearer mutual understanding of our respective reception processes and the identifying of necessary work.[37] Of course, for the student of Nicaea or Chalcedon, such continued debate and discussion come as no surprise. The question for the Christian educator and those exploring receptive ecumenical learning is what is to be done, communicated, and pursued further as a result of this dissatisfaction? It is important that these stages in reception be communicated positively to the churches concerned and to their members at large who will not have the resources or inclination to read either the original texts or the responses formulated by the churches.

The Catholic Church is itself in the process of receiving its own return to more collegial structures, renewing its own methods of handing on the faith, and attempting to recruit quality leadership into its episcopacy and Roman Curia to implement the Second Vatican Council. It should, then, be no surprise that learning the ways of Receptive Ecumenism is a gradual process.[38] The fact that we have begun this slow process of reconciliation and growth, however gradually, is a testimony to the Holy Spirit's guidance in a very human church, with its great burdens of history.

CONCLUSION

The ecumenical journey is a hope-filled and gradual one. I often say that ecumenism would be a great project if it did not have to be done ecumenically. That is, we move forward as a whole people of God, all of the baptized; as an ecumenical community, with each partner according to their own ecclesial tradition, methods of dialogue, and ecumenical capacity; and with the structures of Catholic leadership as they evolve in response to the renewing grace of the Holy Spirit. It is easy to be trapped into evaluating the ecumenical pilgrimage as a Pelagian 'good work', graded according to the successes or failure of a particular text, project, or relationship. Receptive Ecumenism is first of all a matter of spirituality, but that spirituality cannot be nurtured without careful attention to mind and heart, to prayer and study, to grace and the good works that flow from the Spirit's gift.

NOTES

1. See PCPCU, *Directory for the Application of Principles and Norms on Ecumenism* (London: Catholic Truth Society, 1993) (*Directory*) available at <http://www.vatican. va/roman_curia/pontifical_councils/chrstuni/general-documents/rc_pc_chrstuni_doc_ 19930325_directory_en.html>; Pope John Paul II, *Ut Unum Sint. Encyclical Letter on Commitment to Ecumenism* (25 May 1995) (London: Catholic Truth Society, 1995) (*UUS*), also available at <http://www.vatican.va/holy_father/john_paul_ii/ encyclicals/documents/hf_jp-ii_enc_25051995_ut-unum-sint_en.html>; PCPCU, *The Ecumenical Dimension in the Formation of Those Engaged in Pastoral Work* (1995) (*Formation*), available at <http://www.vatican.va/roman_curia/pontifical_councils/ chrstuni/general-docs/rc_pc_chrstuni_doc_19950316_ecumenical-dimension_en. html>.
2. Congregation for the Clergy, *General Directory for Catechesis* (London: CTS, 1997), available at <http://www.vatican.va/roman_curia/congregations/cclergy/ documents/rc_con_ccatheduc_doc_17041998_directory-for-catechesis_en.html>.
3. Ormond Rush, *Still Interpreting Vatican II: Some Hermeneutical Principles* (New York: Paulist Press, 2004).
4. 'This Church [of Christ]...subsists in the Catholic Church...', *LG*, § 8; see Chapter 6: Walter Kasper, '"Credo Unam Sanctam Ecclesiam"—The

Relationship Between the Catholic and the Protestant Principles in Fundamental Ecclesiology', n. 8. For the most recent official Roman Catholic contribution to this discussion, see CDF, 'Responses to Some Questions Regarding Certain Aspects of the Doctrine of the Church' (29 June 2007), available at <http://www.vatican.va/roman_curia/congregations/cfaith/documents/rc_con_cfaith_doc_20070629_ responsa-quaestiones_en.html>.

5. Reception, however, is made more complex when a particular interpretation is put forward, by a selective editing of the Conciliar text, and is used by a bishops' conference for evaluating religion textbooks, implying that the more authentic interpretation might lead to indifferentism; see Gros, 'The Reception in the US Catholic Context', in K. Bloomquist and W. Greive (eds.), *The Doctrine of Justification: Its Reception and Meaning Today* (Geneva: Lutheran World Federation, 2003), 25–34.

6. Ratzinger, 'Briefwechsel von Landesbischof Johannes Hanselmann und Joseph Kardinal Ratzinger über das Communio-Schreiben der Römischen Glaubenskongregation', *Una Sancta*, 48 (1993), 348, cited in Randall Lee and Jeffrey Gros (eds.), *The Church as Koinonia of Salvation: Its Structures and Ministries* (Washington, DC: USCCB, 2005) (§ 107), 49, also available at <http://www.usccb.org/seia/koinonia.shtml>.

7. Ibid., §§ 108–9.

8. Faith and Order Commission of the World Council of Churches, *A Treasure in Earthen Vessels: An Instrument for an Ecumenical Reflection on Hermeneutics* (Faith and Order Paper, No. 182) (Geneva: WCC, 1998), available at <http://wcc-coe.org/wcc/what/faith/treasure.html>; also id., *Interpreting Together: Essays in Hermeneutics*, ed. Peter Bouteneff and Dagmar Heller (Geneva: WCC, 2001); Chapter 7: Riccardo Larini, 'Texts and Contexts: Hermeneutical Reflections on Receptive Ecumenism'.

9. See Kasper, 'Introduction of the Theme and Catholic Hermeneutics of the Dogmas of the First Vatican Council', *The Petrine Ministry: Catholics and Orthodox in Dialogue* (New York: Newman Press, 2006), 7–23; also id., 'A Discussion on the Petrine Ministry', *TTMABO*, 136–54.

10. See *Common Christological Declaration of Pope John Paul II and Catholicos–Patriarch Mar Dinkha IV* (11 Nov. 1994), available at <http://www.prounione.urbe.it/dia-int/ac-rc/i_ac-rc-info.html>.

11. See ARCIC II, *Mary: Grace and Hope in Christ*, ed. Donald Bolen and Gregory Cameron (London and New York: Continuum, 2006); British Methodist–Roman Catholic Committee, *Mary, Mother of the Lord: Sign of Grace, Faith and Holiness* (London and Peterborough: CTS/Methodist Publishing House, 1995).

12. See Gros, *That All May Be One: Ecumenism* (Chicago, Ill.: Loyola University Press, 2000).

13. Id., *Handing on the Faith in an Ecumenical World: Resources for Catholic Administrators and Religious Educators in Serving Christian Unity in School and Parish* (Washington, DC: National Catholic Educational Association, 2005).

14. e.g. see Jeffrey Gros and Daniel Mulhall (eds.), *The Ecumenical Christian Dialogues and the Catechism of the Catholic Church* (New York: Paulist Press, 2006).

15. An issue identified as early as 1976 by veteran American ecumenist Paul Minear, see 'Ecumenical Theology—Profession or Vocation?', in Frederick Trost and Barbara Brown Zikmund (eds.), *United and Uniting*, vol. vii. (Cleveland, Ohio Pilgrim Press, 2005), 573.

16. See ARCIC II, *The Gift of Authority: Authority in the Church III* (London: Church House Publishing/CTS, 1999), available at <http://www.vatican.va/roman_curia/pontifical_councils/chrstuni/documents/rc_pc_chrstuni_doc_12051999_gift-of-autority_en.html>; also United Methodist–Roman Catholic Dialogue, *Through Divine Love: The Church in Each Place and All Places* (Washington, DC: USCCB, 2005), available at <http://www.usccb.org/seia/finalUMC-RC5-13masterintro.pdf>.

17. For the latter, see Roman Catholic–Presbyterian/Reformed Consultation, *Laity in the Church and the World: Resources for Ecumenical Dialogue* (Washington, DC: USCCB, 1998).

18. Root, 'Catholic and Evangelical Theology', *Pro Ecclesia*, 15 (2006), 16, citing Jenson, *Systematic Theology*, vol. i. (New York: Oxford University Press, 1997), p. vii.

19. e.g. see David Sheppard and Derek Worlock, *Better Together: Christian Partnership in a Hurt City* (Harmondsworth: Penguin, 1989).

20. Catholic Bishops' Conferences of England and Wales, Ireland, and Scotland, *One Bread One Body: A Teaching Document on the Eucharist in the Life of the Church, and the Establishment of General Norms on Sacramental Sharing* (London and Dublin: CTS/Veritas, 1998).

21. Bishops of the Church of England, *The Eucharist: Sacrament of Unity. An Occasional Paper of the House of Bishops of the Church of England* (London: Church House Publishing, 2001).

22. See *Ecclesia de Eucharistia*: Encyclical Letter on the Eucharist in its Relationship to the Church (London: CTS, 2003), available at <http://www.vatican.va/holy_father/john_paul_ii/encyclicals/documents/hf_jp-ii_enc_17042003_ecclesia-de-eucharistia_en.html>.

23. See Olegario González de Cardedal, *La iglesia en España*, 1950–2000 (Madrid: Promoción Popular Cristiana, 1999).

24. See 'The Reception in the US Catholic Context', 25.

25. ARCIC, *The Final Report* (London: CTS/SPCK, 1982).

26. Relevant here is the argument in Murray, 'On Valuing Truth in Practice: Rome's Postmodern Challenge', *International Journal of Systematic Theology*, 8 (2006), 163–83; also id., *Reason, Truth and Theology in Pragmatist Perspective* (Leuven: Peeters, 2004).

27. Ratzinger, 'The Augsburg Concord on Justification: How Far Does it Take Us?', trans. David Law, *International Journal for the Study of the Christian Church*, 1 (2002), 20.

28. See Gros, 'Toward a Reconciliation of Memory: Seeking a Truly Catholic Hermeneutics of History', *Journal of Latino/Hispanic Theology*, 7 (1999), 56–75; also id., 'Building a Common Heritage: Teaching the Reformation in an Ecumenical Perspective', *Ecumenical Trends*, 35 (May 2006), 11–15.

29. See Duffy, *The Stripping of the Altars: Traditional Religion in England, 1400–1580* (New Haven, Conn. and London: Yale University Press, 1992).

30. See Gros, 'Episcopal–Roman Catholic Bishops Pilgrimage Witnesses Commitment and Realism', *Ecumenical Trends*, 24 (Jan. 1995), 1–14; id., 'Towards a Hermeneutics of Piety for the Ecumenical Movement', ibid. 22 (Jan. 1993), 1–12.

31. John Hotchkin, 'The Ecumenical Movement's Third Stage', *Origins*, 25 (9 Nov. 1995), 353–61.

32. Roman Catholic Church, '*Baptism, Eucharist and Ministry*: An Appraisal. Vatican Response to WCC Document', *Origins*, 17 (19 Nov. 1987); also Max Thurian, (ed.), *Churches Respond to BEM: Official Responses to the Baptism, Eucharist and Ministry Text*, vols. i–vi. (Geneva: WCC, 1986–8).

33. See George Vandervelde, 'Vatican Ecumenism at the Crossroads? The Vatican Approach to Differences with *BEM*', *Gregorianum*, 69 (1988), 689–711.

34. See Christopher Hill and Edward Yarnold (eds.), *Anglicans and Roman Catholics: The Search for Unity* (London: SPCK/CTS, 1994).

35. 'Official Catholic Response to the Joint Declaration: Cardinal Edward Cassidy Press Conference Statement', *Origins*, 28 (16 July 1998), 120–32; cf. Ratzinger, 'The Augsburg Concord on Justification'.

36. See George Tavard, 'Overcoming the Anathemas: A Catholic View', in J. Burgess and M. Kolden (eds.), *By Faith Alone* (Grand Rapids, Mich.: Eerdmans, 2004), 140–66.

37. For two challenging analyses, see Avery Dulles, 'Justification: The Joint Declaration', *Josephinum Journal of Theology*, 9 (2002), 117–19; also Aidan Nichols, 'The Lutheran–Catholic Agreement on Justification: Botch or Breakthrough?', *New Blackfriars*, 82 (2001), 377–8.

38. See Gros, 'Reception of the Ecumenical Movement in the Roman Catholic Church, with Special Reference to *Baptism, Eucharist and Ministry*', *American Baptist Quarterly*, 7 (1988), 38–49.

32

Receiving the Experience of Eucharistic Celebration

Peter Phillips

INTRODUCTION

Robert Frost's 'Masque of Mercy' presents a powerful picture of Jonah, the religious person par excellence, confronted with the challenge of the other. Like many of us, his encounter with another religious tradition leads to the painful discovery that he has to confront and question the boundaries which his own tradition projects onto the unbounded mercy of God. We are rightly pulled up short by Jonah's unsettling discovery that, in the words of Frost, he could no longer 'trust God to be unmerciful'. A wide range of ecumenical encounters, not only on the formal level of inter-church dialogue, but, perhaps more significantly, as local Christians come to worship together, pose similar challenges. We have to ask questions about the boundaries that have served us well in the past and move on to explore the possibilities of judging our current practices from a different perspective.

Ecumenism is facing a critical moment. The heady days of convergence statements seem to be behind us. Problems loom larger than possibilities; some are talking of an ecumenical winter. Frustration and impatience abound. A lot of Christians, faced with serious crises in their churches, are simply losing interest in what might seem an impossible quest, and are falling back into a new confessionalism. Some clergy, as well as laypeople, are beginning to think the strict rules of ecumenical practice are less and less relevant to living out their lives and are simply doing their own thing. It may be that such breaking of the rules might bear fruit, might indeed challenge the churches into a new self-understanding. Be that as it may, it is important that, working patiently within the norms rather than seeking cavalierly to ignore them, we seek out ways in which we can appropriately move forward.

EUCHARISTIC SHARING

Eucharistic sharing is central to this discussion. The relationship between Eucharist and ecumenism is raised in § 30 of Pope John Paul II's 2003 encyclical on 'The Eucharist and the Church', *Ecclesia de Eucharistia*, and the Pope returns to the theme again in §§ 43–6.[1] That ecumenism is raised at all here is, I think, particularly significant because it appears to introduce a point of extreme tension which could understandably have been left out of an internal church discussion of eucharistic adoration (and in a previous generation it would have been). There is no doubt that this was something close to John Paul II's heart and we are meant to take with utmost seriousness the repetition of his statement from *Ut Unum Sint*: 'It is a source of joy to note that Catholic ministers are able, in certain particular cases, to administer the sacraments of the Eucharist, Penance and Anointing of the Sick to Christians who are not in full communion with the Catholic Church but who greatly desire to receive these sacraments . . . ' (*EE*, § 46; cf. *UUS*, § 46).

These are warm and welcoming words but they clash with the context within which they are found. The Pope has already insisted the reception of the Eucharist counters 'the seeds of disunity, which daily experience shows to be so deeply rooted in humanity as a result of sin': the body of Christ has a 'unifying power' (*EE*, § 24) which is particularly effective in promoting communion in a situation like the local church of Corinth where the community is divided (*EE*, §§ 40–1). I am sure that many Roman Catholics attending their parish Eucharist each Sunday fall short of 'full communion in the bonds of the profession of faith' (*EE*, § 44), but they remain open to God's graceful call that this goal be realized in the pattern of their living. In the context of ecumenical relations, however, Eucharist ceases to be a valid path to unity and, indeed, 'might well prove instead to be *an obstacle to the attainment of full communion*' (*EE*, § 44, italics original).

Here is a position with which we are all too familiar. Jeffrey Vanderwilt usefully teases out the question in an article published the year before this encyclical:

I would note that non-Catholic dialogue partners may draw comfort from the realization that Catholic resistance is far more indicative of unresolved dilemmas and controversies among Catholics. At the end of the day, official resistance to eucharistic sharing seems to be premised on unstated fears about the loss of papal authority, a crisis in the understanding of episcopacy, and serious, unresolved questions about the power and the person of the presbyter.[2]

I find these comments illuminating. As Vanderwilt argues, we are going to have to face up to the contradiction that for those baptized and in communion with the Bishop of Rome (who in practice might fall short of a full appreciation of the meaning of the sacrament) Eucharist is a means to the fullness of unity, but for those who share the same baptism but are not in communion with the Bishop of Rome (who in practice might have a much fuller understanding of the meaning of the Eucharist) the sacrament can only express the goal of unity. These are not easy questions, but we cannot indefinitely lay them to one side.

Writing as a Roman Catholic, I am beginning to think that we must move more quickly towards recognizing the possibility of eucharistic sharing as a step on the path to unity, rather than simply as an event celebrating the eventual achieving of unity. To claim that eucharistic hospitality must be understood as a sign of unity achieved is to a certain extent an exercise in studied naivety, for we all come to the Eucharist falteringly as sinners turning to Christ in our need for healing and reconciliation. In practice there are perhaps as many views about the Real Presence within the Catholic community as there are among other Christians. ARCIC was able to reduce the term 'transubstantiation' to a footnote as expressing a highly appropriate, but not exclusive, way of pointing to the reality of Christ's presence in the Eucharist.[3] With this, the 1982 *Final Report* already attests to a substantial agreement regarding eucharistic doctrine between the Anglican and Roman Catholic churches and there is little doubt that many Anglicans, Methodists, and Reformed Christians would affirm the reality of Christ's presence in the Eucharist in the same way as Roman Catholics do, though not using the same formula, in a manner that some Evangelicals and, as we must acknowledge, some Roman Catholics would not. If we could only move some way here it would represent a huge enrichment and ecumenical advance.

EUCHARISTIC HOSPITALITY

A Roman Catholic would argue that there are, of course, two sides to the question of eucharistic hospitality, and that these are asymmetrical. It might seem far easier to invite others to participate in a Roman Catholic celebration of the Eucharist than to accept the validity of a Eucharist celebrated by what is carefully defined in official terms as an ecclesial community. In certain circumstances it is now possible to invite those not in full communion with the Catholic Church to receive Holy Communion. This permission, spelt out in the Catholic Bishops' Conferences of England and Wales, Ireland, and Scotland's teaching document, *One Bread One Body*,[4] should be more widely used, being invoked whenever it is appropriate and as often as possible.

One Bread One Body has much to recommend it, but it remains cautious in tone: it falls short of the joy John Paul finds in the possibility of eucharistic sharing (*UUS*, § 46). Christopher Lightbound, in a 2002 article, 'A More Generous Hospitality?', suggests that it is a principle of Canon Law that favoures are to be interpreted broadly, negative prohibitions strictly: *favores sunt ampliandi et odiosa, restringenda*.[5] The article points out that the norms for occasional eucharistic sharing as interpreted in *One Bread, One Body* allowed admission to Holy Communion for those not in full communion with the church when in danger of death, and in other grave or pressing need, listing the non-Catholic partner celebrating a marriage, or attending a funeral of a close relative, or a child's baptism, or first Holy Communion. Mgr Lightbound argues that the norms for eucharistic sharing could be interpreted much more generously:

> I would maintain that there are other special occasions of 'grave and pressing need', beyond the sacramental events already listed...when a bishop may give generous and correct interpretation of the norms. Special occasions might be, for example, joint retreats, days of recollection, pilgrimages, ecumenical conferences, and so on 'when a temporary community is formed'...Another obvious example is that of 'inter-church' marriages, when the spouses are practicing members of the Catholic Church and of another Christian communion. They are already one in Christ by the sacrament of baptism and matrimony. I believe that a legitimate 'grave and pressing need' for such couples to be one in Christ in the sacrament of the Eucharist arises with great frequency...[6]

Such a statement represents a considerable move forward. The question remains, however, whether there might be any way of exploring the possibility of participating in a eucharistic celebration in a community not yet in full communion with the Roman Catholic Church.

EUCHARISTIC RECEPTIVITY

Just as church establishment is a little discussed, yet central, problem in ecumenical dialogue, so too is a theological discourse, associated particularly with Roman Catholicism, worked out in terms of the language of validity. The tendency to articulate sacramental realities in categories determined by law is used almost without reflection in the life of Catholic communities. Roman Catholics set great store by the concept of the valid Eucharist, narrowing it to an understanding of a celebration by a validly ordained priest who celebrates in communion with his bishop who is in turn in communion with the Bishop of Rome.[7] Such language allows us to accept that a person celebrating the Eucharist within a body not in full communion with Rome may encounter in the Eucharist a subjective occasion of grace. The question remains as to whether we can go further: if we accept the faithfulness of God, could we not argue that this may even imply recognition of God's faithfulness to the sacramental order inherent in churches whose orders have hitherto been considered canonically dubious (see Matt. 7: 9–11)? Ecumenical dialogue demands that we search out other ways of talking about sacramental realities. We need the courage to fashion a language that is subtle enough to respond to the nuances of our lived-out experience.

The careful wording of the Second Vatican Council's Decree on Ecumenism, *Unitatis Redintegratio*, should be invoked here as it offers a much more nuanced understanding of *communio*, which moves away from a merely juridical interpretation of the word. The draft text initially presented for discussion talked merely of ecclesial bodies separated from the communion of the Catholic Church, a statement revised in the final decree (*UR*, § 22) to 'separated from full communion with the Catholic Church' (*a plena communione Ecclesiae catholicae seiunctae*). This allows us to recognize, as Johannes Feiner insists, 'that unity is not radically destroyed'.[8] At the same time the decree enjoins a more comprehensive understanding of the mystery of the Eucharist: it is not merely a question of Real Presence, but 'a commemoration of the Lord's death and resurrection, a sign of life in communion with Christ, and an expectation and anticipation of the parousia of Christ',[9] elements all to be recognized in the celebration of the Eucharist in western churches not in full communion with Rome.

THE AUTHORITY OF EXPERIENCE

If we take the authority of experience as our starting-point we are sometimes led to a rather different conclusion about what is happening than that achieved by the rigorous application of carefully honed and abstract legal norms. How do we affirm such a reality, as surely we must? As far back as 1973, Bishop Christopher Butler suggested in an article in *The Tablet* that we often demand too much of the word 'valid'.[10] It is one thing to be uncertain about offering a guarantee of effectiveness, quite another to give a guarantee of ineffectiveness. This is something inappropriate. Bishop Butler argued that the church's primary task is not to say when an alleged sacrament is invalid, but rather to tell us when it is valid: the church conveys God's assurance that God remains faithful to God's promises. *UR*, § 22, which I have already examined, suggests a much more agnostic, and therefore affirming, attitude towards the celebration of Eucharist in an ecclesial community not in full communion with Rome, which appears to veer away from the earlier certainties of *Apostolicae Curae*'s 'absolutely null and void':[11] we find here no longer a matter of total rejection.[12] Significant also is Cardinal Walter Kasper's discussion of *defectus*, when applied in recent Catholic teaching to the status of orders and the Eucharist in other Christian traditions, as correctly implying not a 'total lack but...a simple defect...a defect in the full form...'[13]

An example might serve to illustrate the point I am making. Isobel Macdonald, in a moving account of her childhood in Portree in the days before the First World War, tells of her grandmother's preparation for Holy Communion as a member of the Free Presbyterian community in Skye.[14] Communion was held but twice a year and to prepare worshippers long services were held for a period of several days beforehand. Even then some of the community felt that they were unworthy and refrained from communicating on particular occasions. The Scottish theologian John Baillie makes exactly the same point in his own autobiographical reflections:

In recent days and in certain other parts of the world to which Scottish influence has penetrated, Presbyterianism has on occasion become a markedly unsacramental religion, the 'coming to the Lord's table' being sometimes regarded as not very much more than a pleasant piece of old-fashioned sentiment and therefore an optional addition to one's central religious duties. Nothing, however, could be a greater departure from *original Scottish religion* as I knew it in my youth. The whole year's religion then seemed to me to revolve round the two half-yearly celebrations, together with their attendant special services stretching from the 'Fast Day' on Thursday...until the following Monday evening. The Scottish sacramental doctrine is a very 'high' one, though not in the sense of conformity to the too crude theory that developed within the Latin countries...[15]

Luther, like Baillie, argued that the Thomist position on the Eucharist was too crude, for Luther's rejection of the language of transubstantiation should be understood similarly as a matter of safeguarding eucharistic devotion. There is no doubt that Luther was anxious to maintain that Christ's true flesh and blood are present in the sacrament. Like Irenaeus, in another context, Luther refused 'to play midwife to the Word'. Luther's astute logical and metaphysical objections to Aquinas' language of eucharistic presence were made precisely to safeguard this insight, arguing that we cannot know or articulate that manner of eucharistic presence and its relation to the elements: all that the person of faith can do is humbly to profess belief.[16]

I labour the point because, especially in Roman Catholic circles, the common perception of the Reformed and Lutheran positions is of holding a very low eucharistic doctrine. We have no vocabulary to express it otherwise. As Baillie makes clear, he cannot express Catholic views of the Eucharist in any other language but as that of 'too crude [a] theory'. We face each other, in the lapidary phrase applied to the two opposing parties represented by the Christological conflict of the fifth century, across a 'chasm of mutually omitted contexts'.[17] But it is not only the omission of contexts that prevent understanding of another's position; we all too often project onto others the position we think they hold and argue strongly against our own false creations, all the more ignorant of the actual beliefs of our brothers and sisters in Christ.

One of the first tasks of ecumenism at a local level as well as at an international level is to engage in a rigorous process of listening to the other, not only to what is said, how belief is formulated, but perhaps even more importantly how belief is enacted, how it is lived out. By the normal criteria of validity, churches which hold to a threefold pattern of ordained ministry might find it hard to recognize the reality of the Scottish Highland eucharistic celebration.

Generations of Roman Catholics have been taught to believe that Reformed theology does not accept the Real Presence. Yet the Eucharist which this small community celebrated so infrequently, coming before its Lord in fear and trembling, hints at a reality that offers a challenge to our broken attempts at theological formulation.

A TWO-WAY PROCESS OF LEARNING

Learning from the other is a two-way process. Reformed theologians such as John Baillie invite Roman Catholics to look again at popular approaches to eucharistic practice in the Roman Catholic Church which have all too often been interpreted as tending towards an over-objectified, even physicalist, interpretation of the eucharistic elements. This was far from Aquinas' intention.[18] Recent scholarly explorations of the often criticized late mediaeval emphasis on gazing upon the Eucharist have revealed a much more complex understanding at work: 'gazing upon' reflects not a superstitious objectification of the Eucharist but marks an intense spiritual experience of reception which not only links temporal sight with eschatological vision, but also seeing with a genuine receiving.[19] In a very different context we should perhaps take to heart Heidegger's insistence that the word 'nature' has a subjective as well as objective reference: '*Physis* is not the essence of things but the essence of things (as process).'[20] As the former Cardinal Joseph Ratzinger, now Pope Benedict XVI, could argue: 'This Body is not the ever-dead corpse of a dead man, nor is the Blood the life-element rendered lifeless. No, sacrifice has become gift, for the Body given in love and the Blood given in love have entered, through the Resurrection into the eternity of love, which is stronger than death.'[21]

The ability to celebrate a sacrament and the experience of living a life sealed by a sacrament brings with it its own experience and its own authority. This was something made clear by Archbishop Worlock and Cardinal Hume at the Synod on the Family held in Rome in 1980: the lived experience of the sacrament of marriage gives a gracious authority and insight into the married state that the unmarried do not possess.[22] Recent reflection on *Apostolicae Curae*, for example, suggests that its argument is determined by far too narrow an understanding of priesthood, an understanding which fails to do justice to the fullness of priestly ministry as it is experienced not only within the Anglican Communion but within the Roman Catholic Church as well.[23] This is a point noted by Cardinal Kasper in his address to the May 2003 St Albans Cathedral conference,[24] contrasting somewhat in tone with the earlier, disappointingly negative, publication of *Dominus Jesus* by the CDF in 2000. Again, this is a point also taken up in a paper by the Bishops of Durham and Salisbury in response to Cardinal Kasper's address to the Church of England House of Bishops on 5 June 2006.[25]

The Roman Catholic understanding of validity in relation to sacramental celebration, though having served well the church in the past, cannot embrace the other in order to provide a coherent language to articulate the reality of sacramental celebration in the Reformation churches of the West. Reflection on the experience of celebrating the Eucharist might allow us to say rather more. In our celebration of the sacraments, we intend to do what the church does, and that intention is grounded in and affirmed by the reality of the Spirit. This was something argued in the joint letter, *Saepius Officio*, of the Archbishops of Canterbury and York in response to *Apostolicae Curae*,[26] and by many others deemed not to be in full communion with Rome. That Rome herself in recent years has begun to move away from a narrow interpretation of validity can be recognized in the fact that the Vatican has come to accept that the ancient eucharistic Anaphora of Addai and Mari, which does not include the words of institution, should be accepted as a genuine celebration of Eucharist, giving approval in July 2001 to intercommunion with the Assyrian Church of the East.[27]

The Roman Catholic Church has always appeared to emphasize the central role of the presbyter in confecting the Eucharist and the careful recitation of the correct formula. In contrast, for example, the Methodist Church emphasizes that it is:

[T]he whole community of the church which 'celebrates the Eucharist' through the offering of thanksgiving. Presbyters have to preside at that celebration not because the *'ordained minister contributes to the eucharist in his/her own person some essential element'* which makes the eucharist into an *'offering of the people ... specifically activated by the minister's presence'* or by some special priestly powers, but because presidency at the Eucharist is the point at which local and universal most intensely meet and where pastoral charge is most powerfully focussed.[28]

We need to ask whether these two positions are utterly irreconcilable. The acceptance of the Anaphora of Addai and Mari suggests a movement towards a more liberal interpretation. I wonder whether this might be taken further in arguing tentatively towards a theology which gives greater prominence to Christ's presence in the community confecting the Eucharist, presided over by the bishop or presbyter, rather than focusing on Christ's presence in the bishop or presbyter confecting the Eucharist before the gathered community. Recent reflection certainly hints at such a possibility. The Second Vatican Council's 'Dogmatic Constitution on the Church', *Lumen Gentium*, carefully distinguishing between sacerdotal language applied to the whole people of God and ministerial language (pastor, presbyter), which applies to the specific order of service, reminds us that the community's role at the Eucharist is not a simply passive one:

Though they differ essentially and not only in degree, the common priesthood of the faithful and the ministerial or hierarchical priesthood are nonetheless ordered to one another; each in its own proper way shares in the one priesthood of Christ. The ministerial priest, by the sacred power that he has, forms and rules the priestly people; in the person of Christ he effects the eucharistic sacrifice and offers it to God in the name of all the people. The faithful indeed, by virtue of their royal priesthood, participate in the offering of the Eucharist. They exercise their priesthood too, by the reception of the sacraments, prayer and thanksgiving, the witness of a holy life, abnegation and active charity. (*LG*, § 10)

The 'Constitution on the Liturgy', *Sacrosanctum Concilium*, appears to go even further in its insistence that it is the community that is 'the subject of the divine liturgy' (*SC*, § 26). These are only hints, but I suspect there might be possibilities for growth here. If such hints were to be developed, Christians might be able to move, slowly perhaps, towards recognizing a eucharistic sharing in a way which focuses not on the presiding presbyter but on the gathered community and its desire to be at one with the universal church, both diachronically and synchronically, in its intention to do what the church does in realizing the presence of Christ in the breaking of bread and pouring of wine. Such a discourse allows us also to explore the possibility of eucharistic sharing which avoids a painful confrontation regarding women's ministry.

The American Roman Catholic Scripture scholar Raymond Brown makes a somewhat similar point in arguing that the New Testament evidence 'does not attribute much eucharistic functioning'[29] to those who are accorded the role of disciple, apostle, or presbyter–bishop, and notes that Paul himself never writes of his own presiding at the Eucharist. All we can reasonably argue is that someone must have presided at the Eucharist:

How one got the right to preside and whether it endured beyond a single instance we do not know; but a more plausible substitute for the chain theory is the thesis that sacramental 'powers' were part of the mission of the Church and that there were diverse ways in which the Church (or the communities) designated individuals to exercise those powers—the essential element always being Church or community consent . . .[30]

Brown goes on to argue that the diversity of practice which must have been present in the earliest church, with churches with no bishop living in communion with churches presided over by a bishop, allows the present possibility of mutual recognition between churches, which acknowledge agreement on '*doctrine, sacraments, and other essentials of Christian life*', without necessarily demanding re-ordination of clergy.[31] Brown's argument needs to be teased out carefully, but his analysis of the situation in the New Testament period certainly adds weight to our acceptance of the possibility of the propriety of eucharistic sharing without previously demanding the recognition of one another's ministries.

CONCLUSION

Augustine's trenchant criticism of the Donatist churches of North Africa regarding their refusal to recognize Catholic baptism, might challenge us to a new recognition that, in the words of Wesley's hymn, it is 'His presence makes the feast': 'So they, by not recognizing our baptism, deny that we are their brethren, but we, by not repeating theirs but recognizing it as ours, say to them, "You are our brethren." Let them ask, if they will, "Why are you seeking us? Why do you want us?" and let us reply, "You are our brethren." '[32] And earlier: 'Let them ask, if they will, "Why are you seeking us? Why do you want us?" and let us reply, "You are our brethren." Let them say, "Get away, we are not interested in you." "Maybe not, but we are very interested in you. We confess one Christ, and we ought to be in one body under one Head." '[33]

The church was able to learn from Augustine that Christ is the true minister of baptism. Perhaps we could also come to accept that Christ, too, acting in the heart of his community, remains the true minister of the Eucharist, calling all Christians, broken and divided as we are by sin, to the same table fellowship of our risen Lord.

NOTES

1. John Paul II, *EE*; also at <http://www.vatican.va/holy_father/john_paul_ii/encyclicals/documents/hf_jp-ii_enc_17042003_ecclesia-de-eucharistia_en.html>.
2. Vanderwilt, 'Eucharistic Sharing: Revising the Question', *Theological Studies*, 63 (2002), 837.
3. 'Eucharistic Doctrine' (1971), *The Final Report* (London: SPCK/CTS, 1982), 14, n. 2.
4. Catholic Bishops' Conferences of England and Wales, Ireland, and Scotland, *One Bread One Body: A Teaching Document on the Eucharist in the Life of the Church, and the Establishment of General Norms on Sacramental Sharing* (London and Dublin: CTS/Veritas, 1998).
5. Lightbound, 'A More Generous Hospitality?', *Priests and People* (Jan. 2002), 18–21.
6. Ibid. 20. It should also be noted that those in inter-church marriages form, in virtue of their joint participation in the two sacraments of baptism and marriage, a *domestic church*, a point constantly urged by the Association of Interchurch Families; see Ruth Reardon, '*One Bread One Body*: A Commentary from an Interchurch Family Point of View', *One in Christ*, 35 (1999), 109–30.
7. Of course, Rome continues to recognize the orders of the eastern Churches tragically divided from the West after the mutual excommunication of 1054. It was this excommunication that was lifted by Pope Paul VI and Patriarch Athenagoras in a moving ceremony in 1965.
8. Johannes Feiner, 'Commentary on the Decree on Ecumenism', trans. R. A. Wilson, in Herbert Vorgrimler (ed.), *Commentary on the Documents of Vatican II*, vol. ii.

(London: Burns & Oates, 1968), 70. The careful use of *seiunctae* in the final text, rather than *separatae*, strengthens this interpretation.

9. Ibid. 155.

10. Basil Christopher Butler, 'Valid Sacraments', *The Tablet* (17 Feb. 1973), 148–9.

11. Leo XIII, '*Apostolicae Curae*: Encyclical Letter on English Ordinations' (13 Sept. 1896), § 10, available in R. William Franklin (ed.), *Anglican Orders: Essays on the Centenary of* Apostolicae Curae, *1896–1996* (London: Mowbray, 1996), 136.

12. But, in stark contrast, see the negative interpretation of CDF, *Doctrinal Commentary on John Paul II's Apostolic Letter* Ad Tuendam Fidem, § 11 (*AAS*, 90 (1998), 542–51); available at <http://www.Vatican.va/roman_curia/congregations/cfaith/documents/rc_con_cfaith_doc_1998_professio-fidei_ge.html>.

13. e.g. Kasper, 'Apostolic Succession: An Ecumenical Problem' (1990), *LIC*, 135–6.

14. Isobel Macdonald, *A Family in Skye, 1908–1916* (Portree: Acair, 1980), 24.

15. Cited in Alec C. Cheyne, 'The Baillie Brothers: A Biographical Introduction', in David Fergusson (ed.), *Christ, Church and Society: Essays on John Baillie and Donald Baillie* (Edinburgh: T. & T. Clark, 1993), 8.

16. See the thought-provoking article by John Heywood Thomas, 'Logic and Metaphysics in Luther's Eucharistic Theology', *Renaissance and Modern Studies*, 23 (1979), 147–59.

17. Henry Ernest William Turner, *The Pattern of Christian Truth* (London: Mowbray, 1954), 477.

18. See Peter Phillips, 'Necessary Fictions, Real Presences', in Geoffrey Turner and John Sullivan (eds.), *Explorations in Catholic Theology* (Dublin: Lindisfarne Books, 1999), 195–207.

19. Ann Eljenholm Nichols, 'The Bread of Heaven: Foretaste or Foresight?', in Clifford Davidson (ed.), *The Iconography of Heaven* (Kalamazoo, Mich.: Medieval Institute Publications, 1994), 40–68; Eamon Duffy, *The Stripping of the Altars* (New Haven, Conn. and London: Yale University Press, 1992), 95–102. See also the fascinating analysis of sight in relation to the annunciation in Fra Filippo Lippi's *Annunciation*, in John Drury, *Painting the Word* (New Haven, Conn. and London: Yale University Press, 1999), 48–54. Alister McGrath perpetuates the older interpretation in his claim that 'for medieval Catholicism, the Mass made Christ physically present for believers, as an object of adoration and devotion', *The Twilight of Atheism* (London: Rider, 2004), 203.

20. Heidegger, 'Aletheia (Heraklit, Fragment 16)', *Vortrage und Aufsätze* (Pfullingen: G. Neske, 1954), 271, cited in Heywood Thomas, *Models in Theology* (St Andrews: Theology in Scotland, 2003), 12.

21. Ratzinger, *The Spirit of the Liturgy*, trans. John Saward (San Francisco, Calif.: Ignatius, 2000), 55.

22. 'Lay Voice on HV', *The Tablet* (4 Oct. 1980), 978–9.

23. e.g. see Franklin, *Anglican Orders*, particularly the essays by Stephen Sykes, Edward Yarnold, and Christopher Hill.

24. Kasper, Keynote Address, *May They All Be One . . . But How? A Vision of Christian Unity for the Next Generation. Proceedings of the Conference Held in St Albans Cathedral on 17 May 2003* (St Albans: Christian Study Centre, 2003), 26–7; also available at <http://www.ecumenicalstudies.org.uk>.

25. N. T. Wright and David Stancliffe, *Women and Episcopacy: A Response to Cardinal Kasper* (Nottingham: Grove Books, 2006); available at <http://www.fulcrumanglican.org.uk/news/2006/20060721kasper.cfm?doc=126>.

26. The Archbishop of Canterbury and the Archbishop of York, '*Saepius Officio*: Answer of the Archbishops of England to the Apostolic Letter of Pope Leo XIII on English Ordinations' (19 Feb. 1897), in Franklin, *Anglican Orders*, 138–49.

27. *The Tablet* (13 Nov. 2005), 32; see PCPCU, 'Guidelines for Admission to the Eucharist between the Chaldean Church and the Assyrian Church of the East' (25 Oct. 2001), available at <http://www.vatican.va/roman_curia/pontifical_councils/chrstuni/documents/rc_pc_chrstuni_doc_20011025_chiesa_caldea-assira_en.html>; also Kasper, *May They All Be One . . . But How?*

28. Ministerial Training Policy Working Group to the Methodist Council, *The Making of Ministry: The Report of the Ministerial Training Policy Working Group to the Methodist Council* (Peterborough: Methodist Publishing House, 1996), 14–15.

29. Raymond Brown, *Priest and Bishop: Biblical Reflections* (London: Geoffrey Chapman, 1970), 40.

30. Ibid. 41.

31. Ibid. 82–6.

32. Augustine, *Expositions of the Psalms*, vol. i., ed. John E. Rotelle, trans. Maria Boulding (New York: Faithworks, 2000), 423–4 (§ 32).

33. Ibid. (§ 29).

Bibliography

Books and Articles

Acerbi, Antonio (ed.), *Il ministero del Papa in prospettiva ecumenica* (Milan: Vita e Pensiero, 1999).

Adams, Nicholas, 'Argument', in David F. Ford, Ben Quash, and Janet Martin Soskice (eds.), *Fields of Faith. Theology and Religious Studies for the Twenty-first Century* (Cambridge: Cambridge University Press, 2005), 137–51.

——, *Habermas and Theology* (Cambridge: Cambridge University Press, 2006).

Afanasiev, Nicolas, et al. (eds.), *La primauté de Pierre dans l'Église orthodoxe* (Neuchâtel: Delachaux & Niestle, 1960); English translation *The Primacy of Peter in the Orthodox Church*, trans; Katherine Farrer (London: Faith Press, 1963).

—— 'Una Sancta', *Irenikon*, 36 (1963), 436–75.

—— 'L'Église qui préside dans l'amour', English translation in N. Afanasiev, et al. (eds.), *The Primacy of Peter in the Orthodox Church*, trans. Katherine Farrer (London: Faith Press, 1963 [1960]), 57–110, repr. John Meyendorff (ed.), *The Primacy of Peter: Essays in Ecclesiology and the Early Church* (St Vladimir's Seminary Press, 1992), 91–143.

—— *The Church of the Holy Spirit*, trans. Vitaly Permiakov (Notre Dame, IN: University of Notre Dame Press, 2007).

Ainsworth, M. D., Blehar, M. C., Waters, E., and Wall, S., *Patterns of Attachment: Assessed in the Strange Situation and at Home* (Hillsdale, NJ: Lawrence Erlbaum, 1978).

—— 'Attachments Beyond Infancy', *American Psychologist*, 44 (1989), 709–16.

Alberigo, Giuseppe, and Jossua, J-P. (eds.), *La Réception de Vatican II* (Paris: Cerf, 1985).

—— and Komonchak, Joseph (eds.), *History of Vatican II*, vol. iii. *The Mature Council: Second Period and Intersession September 1963–September 1964* (Louvain & Maryknoll, NY: Peeters/Orbis, 2000).

Alexander, J. Neil (ed.), *Time and Community: in Honor of Thomas J. Talley* (Washington, DC: Pastoral Press, 1990).

Alfeyev, Hilarion, 'La primauté et la conciliarité dans la tradition orthodoxe', *Irénikon*, 76 (2005), 24–36.

Allen Jr., John L., *All The Pope's Men: The Inside Story of How the Vatican Really Thinks* (New York: Doubleday, 2004).

Anglican Consultative Council, *Women in the Anglican Episcopate* (London: Church House Publishing, 1998).

Anglican–Lutheran International Commission, 'The Pullach Report', repr. Harding Meyer and Lukas Vischer (eds.), *Growth in Agreement: Reports and Agreed Statements of Ecumenical Conversations on a World Level* (Mahwah, NY and Geneva: Paulist Press/WCC, 1984), 14–34.

An Anglican–Methodist Covenant: Common Statement of the Formal Conversations Between the Methodist Church of Great Britain and the Church of England (London: Methodist Publishing House and Church House Publishing, 2001).

Anglican–Roman Catholic Bishops, 'Communion in Mission. The Report of the Meeting of Anglican–Roman Catholic Bishops, Mississauga, May 2000', *Information Service*, 104 (2000), 138–9.

Anscombe, G. E. M., *The Collected Philosophical Papers of G. E. M. Anscombe. Vol. III. Ethics, Religion and Politics* (Oxford: Basil Blackwell, 1981).

——'Modern Moral Philosophy' (1958), in Anscombe, *The Collected Philosophical Papers of G. E. M. Anscombe. Vol. III. Ethics, Religion and Politics* (Oxford: Basil Blackwell, 1981), 26–42.

Anton, Ángel, 'La "recepción" en la Iglesia y eclesiología, I. Noción teológico-eclesiológica y sus procesos históricos en acción', *Gregorianum*, 77 (1996), 57–96.

——'La "recepción" en la Iglesia y eclesiología, II. Fundamentos teológico-eclesiológicos de la "recepción" desde la eclesiología sistemática', *Gregorianum*, 77 (1996), 437–69.

Aquinas, St Thomas, *Summa Theologiæ*, vol. xxxi (2a2æ. 1–7): *Faith*, ed. T. C. O'Brien (London: Eyre & Spottiswoode, 1974).

Archer, Anthony, *The Two Catholic Churches: A Study in Oppression* (London: SCM, 1986).

ARCIC, *The Final Report* (London: CTS/SPCK, 1982).

ARCIC II, *Salvation and the Church* (London: Church House Publishing/CTS, 1987 [1986]).

—— *The Church as Communion: An Agreed Statement by the Second Anglican–Roman Catholic International Commission* (London: Church House Publishing/CTS, 1991 [1990]).

—— *The Gift of Authority: Authority in the Church III* (London: Church House Publishing/CTS, 1999 [1998]).

—— *Mary: Grace and Hope in Christ*, ed. Donald Bolen and Gregory Cameron (London and New York: Continuum, 2006 [2004]).

Armstrong, Regis, and Brady, Ignatius (eds.), *Francis and Clare: The Complete Works* (Mahwah, NY: Paulist Press, 1982).

Arnold, Thomas, *Principles of Church Reform*, with introductory essay by M. J. Jackson and J. Rogan (London: SPCK, 1962).

Arweck, E., and Collins, P. (eds.), *Reading Religion in Text and Context* (Aldershot: Ashgate, 2006).

Ashworth, Pat, 'Unity Is Symphonic, Says Cardinal', *The Church Times* (20 January 2006), 5.

Assagioli, Roberto, *Psychosynthesis* (Harmondsworth and New York: Penguin, 1971).

Assisi, Sts Francis and Clare of, *Francis and Clare: The Complete Works*, ed. Regis Armstrong and Ignatius Brady (Mahwah, NY: Paulist Press, 1982).

Augustine of Hippo, St, *De Catechizandis Rudibus*, trans. J. P. Christopher (Washington, DC: Catholic University of America, 1926).

—— *The Works of Saint Augustine: A Translation for the 21st Century, Part III, Sermons*, vol. vii. *Sermons (230–272B), On the Liturgical Seasons*, trans. Edmund Hill, ed. John E. Rotelle (New York: New City Press, 1993).

—— *Expositions of the Psalms*, vol. i., ed. John E. Rotelle, trans. Maria Boulding (New York: Faithworks, 2000).

Avis, Paul, *Anglicanism and the Christian Church*, 2nd edn. (Edinburgh: T. & T. Clark, 2002).

Baraúna, G. (ed.), *L'Église de Vatican II. Études autour de la constitution conciliaire sur l'Église*, vol. iii. (Paris: Cerf, 1966).

Barker, David G., *Change, Communication and Relationships in the Catholic Church* (Chelmsford: Matthew James, 2002).

Barth, Fredrik (ed.), 'Introduction', *Ethnic Groups and Boundaries: The Social Organisation of Culture Difference* (London and Bergen-Oslo: Allen & Unwin/University of Forlaget, 1969), 9–38.

Barton, S. C. (ed.), *Idolatry: False Worship in the Bible, Early Judaism and Christianity* (London and New York: T. and T. Clark, 2007).

Bathrellos, Demetrios, 'Church, Eucharist, Bishop: The Early Church in the Ecclesiology of John Zizioulas', in Douglas Knight (ed.), *The Theology of John Zizioulas: Personhood and the Church* (London: Ashgate, 2007), 133–46.

Bauberot, Jean, et al. (eds.), *Démocratie dans les Églises: Anglicanisme, Catholicisme, Orthodoxie, Protestantisme* (Brussels: Lumen Vitae, 1999).

Baum, Gregory, *Amazing Church: A Catholic Theologian Remembers a Half-Century of Change* (New York: Orbis, 2005).

Bauman, Zygmunt, *Liquid Modernity* (Cambridge: Polity Press, 2000).

—— *The Individualized Society* (Cambridge: Polity Press, 2001).

—— *Liquid Love: On the Frailty of Human Bonds* (Cambridge: Polity Press, 2003).

—— *Identity* (Cambridge: Polity Press, 2004).

Bea, Augustin, *The Way to Unity After the Council: A Study of the Implications of the Council for the Unity of Mankind* (London: Geoffrey Chapman, 1967).

Beal, John P., 'The Apostolic Visitation of a Diocese: A Canonico-Historical Investigation', *The Jurist*, 49 (1989), 347–98.

Behr, John, 'The Trinitarian Being of the Church', *St Vladimir's Theological Quarterly*, 48 (2004), 67–88.

Beinert, W. (ed.), *Glaube als Zustimmung: Zur Interpretation kirchlicher Rezeptionsvorgange* (Freiburg: Herder, 1991).

Belchem, John (ed.), *Popular Politics, Riot and Labour: Essays in Liverpool History, 1790–1940* (Liverpool: Liverpool University Press, 1992).

Berdiaev, N., *Freedom and the Spirit*, trans. D. Fielding (London: G. Bless/Century Press, 1935 [1927]).

Berger, Peter L., *A Far Glory: The Quest for Faith in an Age of Credulity* (New York: Free Press, 1992).

—— and Luckmann, Thomas, *The Social Construction of Reality. A Treatise in the Sociology of Knowledge* (New York: Doubleday, 1967).

Bier, Georg, *Die Rechtsstellung des Diözesanbischofs nach dem Codex Iuris Canonici von 1983* (Würzburg: Echter Verlag, 2001).

Bilheimer, Robert S., *A Spirituality for the Long Haul: Biblical Risk and Moral Stand* (Philadelphia, Pa.: Fortress Press, 1984).

Bird, Robert, 'General Introduction', in Alexei S. Khomiakov, et al. (eds.) *On Spiritual Unity: A Slavophile Reader* (Hudson, NY: Lindisfarne Books, 1998), 7–25.

Birmelé, André, and Lienhard, Marc (eds.), *La Foi des églises luthériennes: confessions et catéchismes* (Paris and Geneva: Cerf/Labor et Fides, 1991).

—— and Meyer, Harding (eds.), *Grundkonsens—Grunddifferenz: Studien des Straßburger Instituts für Ökumenische Forschung: Ergebnisse und Dokumente* (Frankfurt: Verlag Otto Lembeck, 1992).

Bishops of the Church of England, *The Eucharist: Sacrament of Unity. An Occasional Paper of the House of Bishops of the Church of England* (London: Church House Publishing, 2001).

Bliss, Frederick M., *Understanding Reception: A Backdrop to its Ecumenical Use* (Milwaukee, Wis.: Marquette University Press, 1993).

Bloomquist, K., and Greive, W. (eds.), *The Doctrine of Justification: Its Reception and Meaning Today* (Geneva: Lutheran World Federation, 2003).

Boegner, Marc, *The Long Road to Unity: Memories and Anticipations*, trans. René Hague (London: Collins, 1970).

Bohstedt, John, 'More than One Working Class: Protestant–Catholic Riots in Edwardian Liverpool', in John Belchem (ed.), *Popular Politics, Riot and Labour: Essays in Liverpool History, 1790–1940* (Liverpool: Liverpool University Press, 1992), 173–216.

Bonhoeffer, Dietrich, *The Cost of Discipleship*, ed. R. H. Fuller (London: SCM, 1948 [1937]).

Boone Porter, H., 'Hispanic Influences on Worship in the English Tongue', in J. Neil Alexander (ed.), *Time and Community: in Honor of Thomas J. Talley* (Washington, DC: Pastoral Press, 1990), 171–84.

Borras, A., 'Considérations corrélatives sur l'exercice de la primauté romaine', in P. Tihon (ed.), *Changer la papauté?* (Paris: Cerf, 2000), 85–120.

Bousquet, François, Gagey, Henri-Jérôme, and Médevielle, Geneviève (eds.), *La Responsabilité des théologiens: mélanges en l'honneur de Joseph Doré* (Paris: Desclée, 2002).

Bouteneff, Peter, and Heller, Dagmar (eds.), *Interpreting Together: Essays in Hermeneutics* (Geneva: WCC, 2001).

Bouyer, Louis, *L'Église de Dieu* (Paris: Cerf, 1970).

—— *The Church of God: Body of Christ and Temple of the Spirit*, trans. Charles Underhill Quinn (Chicago, Ill.: Franciscan Herald, 1982 [1970]).

Bowlby, John, *Attachment* (New York: Basic Books, 1969).

—— *Separation: Anxiety and Anger* (New York: Basic Books, 1973).

—— *Loss: Sadness and Depression* (London: Pimlico Press, 1998).

Braaten, Carl E., and Jenson, Robert W. (eds.), *Marks of the Body of Christ* (Grand Rapids, Mich.: Eerdmans, 1999).

—— —— *In One Body Through the Cross: The Princeton Proposal for Christian Unity. A Call to the Churches from an Ecumenical Study Group* (Grand Rapids, Mich.: Eerdmans, 2003).

—— —— (eds.), *The Ecumenical Future: Background Papers for 'In One Body Through the Cross: The Princeton Proposal for Christian Unity'* (Grand Rapids, Mich. and Cambridge: Eerdmans, 2004).

British Methodist Conference, *Hymns and Psalms* (London: Methodist Publishing House, 1983).

—— *A Lamp to My Feet and a Light to My Path: The Nature of Authority and the Place of the Bible in the Methodist Church* (Peterborough: Methodist Publishing House, 1998).

—— *Called to Love and Praise: The Nature of the Christian Church in Methodist Experience and Practice* (Peterborough: Methodist Publishing House, 1999).

—— *Methodist Worship Book* (Peterborough: Methodist Publishing House, 1999).

British Methodist–Roman Catholic Committee, *Mary, Mother of the Lord: Sign of Grace, Faith and Holiness* (London and Peterborough: CTS/Methodist Publishing House, 1995).

Brown, Peter, *Augustine of Hippo* (London: Faber & Faber, 1967).

Brown, Raymond, *Priest and Bishop: Biblical Reflections* (London: Geoffrey Chapman, 1970).

Bruce, Steve, *Religion in Modern Britain* (Oxford: Oxford University Press, 1995).

—— *God is Dead: Secularization in the West* (Oxford: Blackwell, 2002).

—— 'Praying Alone? Church-going in Britain and the Putnam Thesis', *Journal of Contemporary Religion*, 17 (2002), 317–28.

Brueggemann, Walter, *Theology of the Old Testament: Testimony, Dispute, Advocacy* (Minneapolis: Fortress Press, 1997).

Buckley, Michael J., *Papal Primacy and the Episcopate: Towards a Relational Understanding* (New York: Crossroad, 1998).

—— 'Resources for Reform from the First Millennium', in Stephen J. Pope (ed.), *Common Calling: The Laity and Governance of the Catholic Church* (Washington, DC: Georgetown, 2004), 71–86.

Bulgakov, Sergius, *The Orthodox Church*, trans. Lydia Kesich (Crestwood, NY: St Vladimir's, 1988 [1932]).

Burgess, J., and Kolden, M. (eds.), *By Faith Alone* (Grand Rapids, Mich.: Eerdmans, 2004).

Burkhard, John J., *Apostolicity Then and Now: An Ecumenical Church in a Postmodern World* (Collegeville, Minn.: Liturgical Press, 2004).

Burkhardt, Frederick H., Bowers, Fredson, and Skrupskelis, Ignas K. (eds.), *The Works of William James*, vol. i. *Pragmatism* (Cambridge, Mass.: Harvard University Press, 1975).

Butler, Basil Christopher, 'Valid Sacraments', *The Tablet* (17 Feb. 1973), 148–9.

—— 'Jesus and Later Orthodoxy', in Michael Green (ed.), *The Truth of God Incarnate* (London: Hodder & Stoughton, 1977), 89–100.

—— *The Church and Unity* (London: Geoffrey Chapman, 1979).

—— *An Approach to Christianity* (London: Collins, 1981).

—— 'J. M. R. Tillard', in G. R. Evans, Lorelei F. Fuchs, and Diane C. Kessler (eds.), *Encounters for Unity: Sharing Faith, Prayer and Life* (Norwich: Canterbury Press, 1995), 196–202.

Cameron, Averil, *Christianity and the Rhetoric of Empire: The Development of Christian Discourse* (Berkeley, Calif.: University of California Press, 1991).

Canon Law Society of Great Britain and Ireland, *The Canon Law: Letter and Spirit. A Practical Guide to the Code of Canon Law* (London: Geoffrey Chapman, 1995).

Caparros, E., and Aubé, H. (eds.), with J. I. Arrieta, et al. *Code of Canon Law Annotated, Prepared Under the Responsibility of the Instituto Martín de Azpilcueta*, 2nd English edn. (rev. and updated) of the 6th Spanish edn. (Montreal: Wilson & Lafleur, 2004).

Carpenter, Edward, *Westminster Abbey* (London: Weidenfeld & Nicolson, 1989).

Cassidy, Edward, 'Official Catholic Response to the Joint Declaration: Cardinal Edward Cassidy Press Conference Statement', *Origins*, 28 (16 July 1998), 120–32.

—— 'Homily at Lambeth Ecumenical Vespers Service' (20 July 1998), *Information Service*, 98 (1998), 155–7.

Catholic Bishops of England and Wales and of Scotland, *The Gift of Scripture* (London: CTS, 2005).

Catholic Bishops' Conferences of England and Wales, Ireland, and Scotland, *One Bread One Body: A Teaching Document on the Eucharist in the Life of the Church, and the Establishment of General Norms on Sacramental Sharing* (London and Dublin: CTS/Veritas, 1998).

Cattaneo, A., *Grundfragen des Kirchenrechts bei Klaus Mörsdorf: Synthese und Ansätze einer Wertung* (Amsterdam: Grüner, 1991).

Cavanaugh, William T., 'Church', in P. Scott and Cavanaugh (eds.), *The Blackwell Companion to Political Theology* (Oxford: Blackwell, 2003), 393–406.

Chadwick, Henry, 'The Status of Ecumenical Councils in Anglican Thought' (1974), preparatory document for the Anglican–Orthodox Dialogue Commission and, subsequently, for ARCIC, held within the ARCIC archives, Centro Pro Unione, Rome.

—— 'Canterbury and Rome', *The Month*, 5 (1983), 149–54.

—— 'Reception', in G. R. Evans and Michel Gourgues (eds.), *Communion et réunion: mélanges Jean-Marie Roger Tillard* (Leuven: Peeters, 1995), 95–107.

Chapman, David M., *In Search of the Catholic Spirit: Methodists and Roman Catholics in Dialogue* (Peterborough: Epworth, 2004).

Chapman, Mark D. (ed.), *The Future of Liberal Theology* (Aldershot: Ashgate, 2002).

Cheyne, Alec C., 'The Baillie Brothers: A Biographical Introduction', in David Fergusson (ed.), *Christ Church and Society* (Edinburgh: T. & T. Clark, 1993), 3–37.

Chomsky, Noam, *Current Issues in Linguistic Theory* (The Hague: Mouton, 1964).

—— *Cartesian Linguistics: A Chapter in the History of Rationalist Thought*, ed. James McGilvray, 2nd edn. (Christchurch, New Zealand: Cybereditions, 2002 [1966]).

Church of England, *Common Worship: Services and Prayers for the Church of England* (London: Church House Publishing, 2000).

—— 'Eucharistic Prayer G', *Common Worship: Services and Prayers for the Church of England* (London: Church House Publishing, 2000), 201–3.

Church of England Working Party, *Education for the Church's Ministry: The Report of the Working Party on Assessment* (London: Church House, 1987).

Clark, Alan, 'Address to General Synod' (7 Nov. 1974), *One in Christ*, 11 (1975), 182–93.

Clément, Olivier, *L'Église orthodoxe*, 4th edn. (Paris: Presses Universitaires de France, 1991).

Clifford, Catherine E., *The Groupe des Dombes. A Dialogue of Conversion* (New York and Oxford: Peter Lang, 2005).

Coakley, Sarah, *Powers and Submissions: Spirituality, Philosophy and Gender* (Oxford: Blackwell, 2002).

Coleridge, S. T., *Opus Maximum*, ed. Thomas McFarland (Princeton, NJ: Princeton University Press, 2002).

Comité Mixte Catholique–Orthodoxe en France, *La Primauté romaine dans la communion des églises* (Paris: Cerf, 1991).

Congar, Yves, *Chrétiens désunis: principes d'un 'œcuménisme' catholique*, Unam Sanctam, 1 (Paris: Cerf, 1937).

—— *Divided Christendom: A Catholic Study of the Problem of Reunion*, trans. M. A. Bousfield (London: Geoffrey Bles, 1939).

—— 'Review of Maurice Villain, *L'Abbé*', *Revue des sciences philosophiques et théologiques*, 41 (1957), 590.

—— *Le Concile au jour le jour* (Paris: Cerf, 1963).

—— 'Ecumenical Experience and Conversion: A Personal Testimony', in Robert C. Mackie and Charles C. West (eds.), *The Sufficiency of God: Essays on the Ecumenical Hope in Honour of W. A. Visser 't Hooft* (London: SCM, 1963), 71–87.

—— *Le Concile au jour le jour: troisième session* (Paris: Cerf, 1964).

—— 'Expérience et conversion œcuméniques', *Chrétiens en dialogue: contributions catholiques à l'œcuménisme*, Unam Sanctam, 50 (Paris: Cerf, 1964), 123–39.

—— 'Ministères et laicat dans les recherches actuelles de la théologie catholique romaine', *Verbum Caro*, 18 (1964), 127–48.

—— 'The Church: The People of God', *Concilium*, 1 (1965), 7–19.

—— *Lay People in the Church: A Study for a Theology of the Laity*, trans. Donald Attwater, rev. edn. (Westminster, Md.: Newman, 1965 [1953]).

—— *The Mystery of the Church*, rev. trans. (London: Geoffrey Chapman, 1965 [1956, 1960]).

—— *Le Concile au jour le jour. quatrième session* (Paris: Cerf, 1966).

—— *Dialogue Between Christians: Catholic Contributions to Ecumenism*, trans. Philip Loretz (Westminster, Md. Newman, 1966 [1964]).

—— 'The Human Person and Human Liberty' (1952), *Dialogue Between Christians: Catholic Contributions to Ecumenism*, trans. Philip Loretz (Westminster, Md.: Newman, 1966 [1964]), 232–45.

—— *Tradition and Traditions: An Historical and a Theological Essay*, trans. Michael Naseby and Thomas Rainborough (London: Burns & Oates, 1966 [1963]).

—— 'L' ≪Ecclesia≫ ou communauté chrétienne, sujet intégral de l'action liturgique', in J.-P. Jossua and Congar (eds.), *La liturgie après Vatican II* (Paris: Cerf, 1967), 241–82.

—— *Situation et tâches présentes de la théologie* (Paris: Cerf, 1967).

—— *L'Ecclésiologie du haut moyen-âge* (Paris: Cerf, 1968).

—— *Vraie et fausse réforme dans l'Église*, 2nd edn. (Paris: Cerf, 1969 [1950]).

—— 'Ministères et structuration de l'Église', *La Maison Dieu*, 102 (1970), 7–20.

—— 'Quelques problèmes touchant les ministères', *Nouvelle revue théologique*, 93 (1971), 785–800.

—— 'My Pathfindings in the Theology of Laity and Ministries', *The Jurist*, 2 (1972), 169–88.

—— 'Reception as an Ecclesiological Reality', trans. John Griffiths, in Giuseppe Alberigo and Anton Weiler (eds.), *Church History: Election–Consensus–Reception*, *Concilium*, 77 (1972), 43–68.

—— 'La "Réception" comme réalité ecclésiologique', *Revue des sciences philosophiques et théologiques*, 56 (1972), 369–403.

—— *Une Passion: l'unité. Réflexions et souvenirs, 1929–1973* (Paris: Cerf, 1974).

—— *Diversités et communion: dossier historique et conclusion théologique*, Cogitatio Fidei, 112 (Paris: Cerf, 1982).

—— *Diversity and Communion*, trans. John Bowden (London: SCM, 1984 [1982]).

—— *Essais œcuméniques: le mouvement, les hommes, les problèmes* (Paris: Centurion, 1984).

Congar, Yves, 'Remarques générales', in *Paul VI et la modernité dans l'Église: actes du colloque organisé par l'École française de Rome* (2–4 June 1983) (Rome: École française de Rome, 1984), 851–3.

—— 'Letter from Father Yves Congar, O.P.', trans. Ronald John Zawilla, *Theology Digest*, 32 (1985), 213–16.

—— *The Word and the Spirit*, trans. David Smith (London: Geoffrey Chapman, 1986 [1984]).

—— *Entretiens d'automne*, 2nd edn. (Paris: Cerf, 1987).

—— *Fifty Years of Catholic Theology: Conversations with Yves Congar*, ed. Bernard Lauret, trans. John Bowden (London: SCM, 1988).

—— *Mon journal du concile*, vol. ii., ed. Éric Mahieu (Paris: Cerf, 2002).

Congregation for Bishops, *Apostolorum Successores. Directory for the Pastoral Ministry of Bishops* (Vatican: Libreria Editrice Vaticana, 2004).

Congregation for Clergy, *General Directory for Catechesis* (London: CTS, 1997).

Congregation for the Doctrine of the Faith, '*Inter Insigniores*: Declaration on the Question of the Admission of Women to the Ministerial Priesthood' (15 Oct. 1976), *Origins*, 6 (1977–8), 519–20.

—— *Observations on The Final Report of the Anglican–Roman Catholic International Commission* (London: CTS, 1982) (also available in *AAS*, 74 (1982), 1062–74).

—— '*Communionis Notio*: A Letter to the Bishops of the Catholic Church on Some Aspects of the Church Understood as Communion' (28 May 1992) (London and New York: Catholic Truth Society/St Paul Books and Media, 1992).

—— '*Ratio Agendi*: Regulations for Doctrinal Examination' (30 May 1997), *AAS*, 89, (1997), 830–5.

—— *Doctrinal Commentary on John Paul II's Apostolic Letter* Ad Tuendam Fidem, *AAS*, 90 (1998), 542–51.

—— '*Dominus Iesus*: On the Unicity and Salvific Universality of Jesus Christ and the Church' (6 Aug. 2000) (London: CTS, 2000).

Conn, James, Doe, Norman, and Fox, Joseph (eds.), *Initiation, Membership and Authority in Anglican and Roman Catholic Canon Law* (Rome and Cardiff: Pontifical Gregorian University and Pontifical University of St Thomas Aquinas/University of Wales Cardiff, 2005).

Connolly, Patrick, 'Priest and Bishop: Implications of the Abuse Crisis', *The Furrow* 57 (2006), 129–43.

—— 'Contrasts in the Western and Eastern Approaches to Marriage', *Studia Canonica* 35 (2001), 357–402.

Conversi, Daniele, 'Nationalism, Boundaries and Violence', *Millennium Journal of International Relations: Territorialities, Identities and Movement in International Relations*, 28 (1999), 553–84.

Conway, Eamonn, *The Anonymous Christian—A Relativised Christianity? An Evaluation of Hans Urs von Balthasar's Criticisms of Karl Rahner's Theory of the Anonymous Christian* (Bern: Peter Lang, 1993).

—— (ed.), *The Courage to Risk Everything, Essays Marking the Centenary of Karl Rahner's Birth* (Leuven: Peeters, 2004).

—— 'Operative Theologies of Priesthood: Have They Played a Part in Child Sexual Abuse?', *Concilium*, 3 (2004), 72–86.

—— 'A Long Way to Go', *The Furrow*, 57 (2006), 643–51.

Corecco, Eugenio, 'La Réception de Vatican II dans le code de droit canonique', in Giuseppe Alberigo and J.-P. Jossua (eds.), *La Réception de Vatican II* (Paris: Cerf, 1985), 327–91.

—— 'Paul VI et le statut du droit canonique', in *Paul VI et les réformes institutionnelles dans l'Église, Journée d'Études* (Fribourg, Switzerland, 9 Nov. 1985) (Brescia: Istituto Paolo VI/Edizioni Studium, 1987), 13–29.

—— *Théologie et droit canon: écrits pour une nouvelle théorie générale du droit canonique* (Fribourg: Éditions universitaires, 1990).

Cornwell, John (ed.), *Consciousness and Human Identity* (Oxford: Oxford University Press, 1998).

Council for Christian Unity, *The Meissen Agreement*, Council for Christian Unity, Occasional Paper, 2 (London: Church House Publishing, 1992).

Council of Trent, 'Decree on Justification' (13 Jan. 1547), in Norman P. Tanner (ed.), *Decrees of the Ecumenical Councils*, vol. ii., *Trent to Vatican II* (London: Sheed & Ward, 1990 [1972]), 671–81.

Courtney Murray, John, 'Good Pope John: A Theologian's Tribute', *America* (15 June 1963), 844–5.

Crawford, Janet, 'Women and Ecclesiology: Two Ecumenical Streams', *Ecumenical Review*, 53 (2002), 14–24.

Cunningham, James W., *A Vanquished Hope: The Movement for Church Renewal in Russia, 1905–1906* (Crestwood NY: St Vladimir's Seminary Press, 1981).

Cunningham, Lawrence S. (ed.), *Ecumenism: Present Realities and Future Prospects: Papers Read at the Tantur Ecumenical Center, Jerusalem, 1997* (Notre Dame, Ind.: University of Notre Dame Press, 1998).

Curti, Elena, and Hirst, Michael, 'Amid the Cold, Signs of a Thaw', *The Tablet* (21 Jan. 2006), 12–13.

Curtis, Geoffrey, *Paul Couturier and Unity in Christ* (London: SCM, 1964).

Cyprian of Carthage, St, *The Letters of St Cyprian of Carthage*, vols. i–ii, trans. G. W. Clark (New York: Newman, 1984), 52–3.

Daly, Gabriel, *One Church: Two Indispensable Values—Protestant Principle and Catholic Substance* (Dublin: ISE Publications, 1998).

—— 'Catholic Fundamentalism', in Angela Hanley and David Smith (eds.), *Quench Not the Spirit: Theology and Prophecy for the Church in the Modern World* (Dublin: Columba Press, 2005), 125–36.

D'Antonio, William V. et al. *American Catholics Today* (Lanham, Md.: Rowman & Littlefield, 2007).

Davidson, Clifford (ed.), *The Iconography of Heaven* (Kalamazoo, Mich.: Medieval Institute Publications, 1994).

Davie, Grace, *Religion in Britain Since 1945: Believing Without Belonging* (Oxford: Blackwell, 1994).

—— *Europe the Exceptional Case: Parameters of Faith in the Modern World* (London: Darton, Longman & Todd, 2002).

—— 'Praying Alone? Church-going in Britain and Social Capital: A Reply to Steve Bruce', *Journal of Contemporary Religion*, 17 (2002), 329–34.

—— Heelas, Paul, and Woodhead, Linda (eds.), *Predicting Religion: Christian, Secular and Alternative Futures* (Aldershot: Ashgate, 2003).

Dawes, Stephen, 'Revelation in Methodist Practice and Belief', in Clive Marsh, et al. (eds.), *Unmasking Methodist Theology* (London: Continuum, 2004), 109–17.

Dawson, Christopher, *The Spirit of the Oxford Movement* (London: Saint Austin Press, 2001 [1933]).

D'Costa, Gavin, *Theology in the Public Square: Church, Academy and Nation* (Oxford: Blackwell, 2005).

Denaux, Albert (ed.), *From Malines to ARCIC: The Malines Conversations Commemorated* (Leuven: Leuven University Press, 1997).

Denzinger, Henricus (ed.), *Enchiridion Symbolorum Definitionum et Declarationum de Rebus Fidei et Morum*, rev. Adolfus Schönmetzer, 34th edn. (Freiburg and Rome: Herder, 1967).

Destivelle, Hyacinthe, *Le Concile de Moscou (1917–1918): la création des institutions conciliaires de l'Église orthodoxe russe* (Paris: Cerf, 2006).

Dickens, Peter, *Society and Nature* (Cambridge: Polity Press, 2004).

Doe, Norman, *The Legal Framework of the Church of England* (Oxford: Clarendon Press, 1996).

—— *Canon Law in the Anglican Communion: A Worldwide Perspective* (Oxford: Oxford University Press, 1998).

—— 'Canonical Dimensions of ARCIC on Authority: An Anglican Perspective', in James Conn, Norman Doe, and Joseph Fox (eds.), *Initiation, Membership and Authority in Anglican and Roman Catholic Canon Law* (Rome and Cardiff: Pontifical Gregorian University and Pontifical University of St Thomas Aquinas/University of Wales Cardiff, 2005), 213–27.

Dombois, Hans, *Das Recht der Gnade: Oekumenisches Kirchenrecht*, vols. i–ii. (Witten, Bielefeld: Luther, 1961 and 1969).

Douglas, Mary, *Natural Symbols: Explorations in Cosmology* (London: Routledge, 2003 [1970]).

Drury, John, *Painting the Word* (New Haven, Conn. and London: Yale University Press, 1999).

Duchrow, Ulrich, *Conflict over the Ecumenical Movement: Confessing Christ Today in the Universal Church*, trans. David Lewis (Geneva: WCC, 1981).

Duffy, Eamon, *The Stripping of the Altars: Traditional Religion in England, 1400–1580* (New Haven, Conn. and London: Yale University Press, 1992).

Duffy, Eugene, 'On Proclaiming Sound Doctrine: Theology of Method', *The Furrow*, 50 (1999), 77–89.

Dulles, Avery, *The Catholicity of the Church* (Oxford: Clarendon Press, 1985); 2nd edn. (Oxford: Clarendon Press, 1987).

—— *The Craft of Theology: From Symbol to System* (New York: Crossroad, 1995).

—— 'Justification: The Joint Declaration', *Josephinum Journal of Theology*, 9 (2002), 108–19.

—— 'Justification and the Unity of the Church', in Wayne C. Stumme (ed.), *The Gospel of Justification in Christ: Where Does the Church Stand Today?* (Grand Rapids, Mich.: Eerdmans, 2006), 125–40.

—— 'From Ratzinger to Benedict', *First Things*, 160 (Feb. 2006), 24–9.

Duprey, Pierre, 'Anglican/Roman Catholic Dialogue: Some Reflections', *One in Christ*, 10 (1974), 358–68.

Dupuy, B.-D., 'La Succession apostolique dans la discussion œcuménique', *Istina*, 12 (1967), 390–401.

Duquoc, Christian, *Provisional Churches: An Essay in Ecumenical Ecclesiology*, trans. John Bowden (London: SCM, 1986 [1985]).

Durkheim, Émile, *Suicide: A Study in Sociology*, trans. John A. Spaulding and George Simpson, (London: Routledge & Kegan Paul, 1952).

Dyer, Mark J., et al. (eds.), *The Official Report of the Lambeth Conference, 1998* (Harrisburg, Penn.: Morehouse Publishing, 1998).

Edwards, Denis, *Breath of Life: A Theology of the Creator Spirit* (Maryknoll, NY: Orbis, 2004).

Eljenholm Nichols, Ann, 'The Bread of Heaven: Foretaste or Foresight?', in Clifford Davidson (ed.), *The Iconography of Heaven* (Kalamazoo, Mich.: Medieval Institute Publications, 1994), 40–68.

Endean, Philip, *Karl Rahner and Ignatian Spirituality* (Oxford: Clarendon Press, 2001).

Erickson, J. H., 'The "Autocephalous Church"', *The Challenge of Our Past. Studies in Orthodox Canon Law and Church History* (Crestwood, NY: St Vladimir's Seminary Press, 1991), 91–113.

—— 'Baptism and the Church's Faith', in C. E. Braaten and R. W. Jenson (eds.), *Marks of the Body of Christ* (Grand Rapids, Mich.: Eerdmans, 1999), 44–58.

Ernst, Harold E., 'The Theological Notes and the Interpretation of Doctrine', *Theological Studies* 63 (2002), 813–25.

Euart, Sharon, 'Clergy Sexual Abuse Crisis: Reflections on Restoring the Credibility of Church Leadership', *The Jurist*, 63 (2003), 125–38.

Evans, G. R., *Method in Ecumenical Theology: The Lessons So Far* (Cambridge: Cambridge University Press, 1996).

—— *The Reception of the Faith: Reinterpreting the Gospel for Today* (London: SPCK, 1997).

—— Fuchs, Lorelei F., and Kessler, Diane C. (eds.), *Encounters for Unity: Sharing Faith, Prayer and Life* (Norwich: Canterbury Press, 1995).

—— and Gourgues, Michel (eds.), *Communion et Réunion: Mélanges Jean-Marie Roger Tillard* (Leuven: Peeters, 1995).

Evans, G. R., and Percy, Martyn (eds.), *Managing the Church? Order and Organization in a Secular Age* (Sheffield: Sheffield University Press, 2000).

Evdokimov, Paul, *L'Orthodoxie* (Paris-Neuchâtel: Delachaux et Niestlé, 1959).

—— 'Nature', *Scottish Journal of Theology*, 18 (1965), 1–22.

Extraordinary Synod of Bishops, 'Final Report', *L'Osservatore Romano* (English edn.) (16 Dec. 1985), 6–9.

Eyt, Pierre, 'La Collégialité épiscopale', in Philippe Levillain (ed.), *Le deuxième concile du Vatican, 1959–1965* (Rome: École Française de Rome, 1989), 539–48.

Faith and Order Commission of the World Council of Churches, *Baptism, Eucharist and Ministry* (Faith and Order Paper, No. 111) (Geneva: WCC, 1982).

—— *A Treasure in Earthen Vessels: An Instrument for an Ecumenical Reflection on Hermeneutics* (Faith and Order Paper, No. 182) (Geneva: WCC, 1998).

—— *Interpreting Together: Essays in Hermeneutics*, ed. Peter Bouteneff and Dagmar Heller (Geneva: WCC, 2001).

—— *Christian Perspectives on Theological Anthropology* (Faith and Order Paper, No. 199) (Geneva: WCC, 2005).

Falconer, Alan D., 'The Reconciling Power of Forgiveness', in Alan D. Falconer and Joseph Liechty (eds.), *Reconciling Memories*, 2nd edn. (Blackrock, Co. Dublin: Columba Press, 1998), 179–86.

—— and Liechty, Joseph (eds.), *Reconciling Memories*, 2nd edn. (Blackrock, Co. Dublin: Columba Press, 1998 [1988]).

Famerée, Joseph, ' "Chrétiens désunis" du P. Congar 50 ans après', *Nouvelle revue théologique*, 110 (1988), 666–86.

—— 'Bishops and Dioceses and the Communications Media (5–25 Nov. 1963)', in G. Alberigo and J. Komonchak (eds.), *History of Vatican II*, vol. iii. (Louvain and Maryknoll, NY: Peeters/Orbis, 2000 [1998]), 117–88.

—— 'La Fonction du pape: éléments d'une problématique', in P. Tihon (ed.), *Changer la papauté?* (Paris: Cerf, 2000), 63–84.

—— ' "Responsabilisation" des conférences épiscopales et concession de "facultés" aux évêques: signes de décentralisation?', in J. Doré and A. Melloni (eds.), *Volti di fine concilio: Studi di storia e teologia sulla conclusione del Vaticano II* (Bologna: il Mulino, 2000), 27–52.

Fawcett, Timothy J. (ed.), *The Liturgy of Comprehension 1689: An Abortive Attempt to Revise the Book of Common Prayer* (Southend: Alcuin Club, 1973).

Feiner, Johannes, 'Commentary on the Decree on Ecumenism', trans. R. A. Wilson, in Herbert Vorgrimler (ed.), *Commentary on the Documents of Vatican II*, vol. ii. (London: Burns & Oates, 1968 [1967]), 57–164.

Fenn, Richard K. (ed.), *The Blackwell Companion to Sociology of Religion* (Oxford: Blackwell, 2001).

Fergusson, David (ed.), *Christ, Church and Society: Essays on John Baillie and Donald Baillie* (Edinburgh: T. & T. Clark, 1993).

First General Assembly of the World Council of Churches, 'Report of Section I: The Universal Church in God's Design', in W. A. Visser 't Hooft (ed.), *The First Assembly of the World Council of Churches Held at Amsterdam, August 22 to September 4, 1948* (London: SCM, 1949), 51–6.

Fitzgerald, Constance, 'Desolation as Dark Night: The Transformative Influence of Wisdom in John of the Cross', *The Way Supplement*, 82 (1995), 96–108.

Flannery, Austin (ed.), *Vatican Council II: The Conciliar and Post Conciliar Documents* (Leominster: Fowler Wright, 1980 [1975]).

Florensky, Pavel, *The Pillar and Ground of the Truth*, trans. Boris Jakim, with an introd. by Richard F. Gustafson (Princeton, NJ and Chichester: Princeton University Press, 1997).

Flynn, Gabriel, 'Cardinal Congar's Ecumenism: An "Ecumenical Ethics" for Reconciliation?', *Louvain Studies*, 28 (2003), 311–25.

—— *Yves Congar's Vision of the Church in a World of Unbelief* (Aldershot: Ashgate, 2004).

—— (ed.), *This Church that I Love: Essays Celebrating the Centenary of the Birth of Yves Cardinal Congar* (Leuven: Peeters, 2004).

—— (ed.), *Yves Congar: Theologian of the Church* (Louvain: Peeters, 2005).

—— (ed.), *Yves Congar: théologien de l'Église* (Paris: Cerf, 2007).

Ford, David F., *Self and Salvation: Being Transformed* (Cambridge: Cambridge University Press, 1999).

—— and Pecknold, Chad (eds.), *The Promise of Scriptural Reasoning* (Oxford: Blackwell, 2006).

Foucault, Michel, *An Archaeology of Knowledge and the Discourse on Language* (New York: Harper Colophon, 1972).

Fouilloux, Etienne, 'Frère Yves, Cardinal Congar, Dominicain: itinéraire d'un théologien', *Revue des sciences philosophiques et théologiques*, 79 (1995), 379–404.

—— *Une église en quête de liberté: la pensée catholique française entre modernisme et Vatican II, 1914–1962* (Paris: Desclée de Brouwer, 1998).

Fourth General Assembly of the World Council of Churches, 'The Holy Spirit and the Catholicity of the Church: The Report as Adopted by the Assembly', in Norman Goodall (ed.), *The Uppsala Report 1968: Official Report of the Fourth Assembly of the World Council of Churches, Uppsala, July 4–20, 1968* (Geneva: WCC, 1968), 11–19.

Franklin, R. William (ed.), *Anglican Orders: Essays on the Centenary of* Apostolicae Curae, *1896–1996* (London: Mowbray, 1996).

Frei, Hans Wilhelm, *The Eclipse of Biblical Narrative: A Study in Eighteenth and Nineteenth Century Hermeneutics* (New Haven, Conn. and London: Yale University Press, 1974).

—— *Types of Christian Theology*, ed. George Hunsinger and William C. Placher (New Haven, Conn. and London: Yale University Press, 1992).

—— *Theology and Narrative: Selected Essays*, ed. George Hunsinger and William C. Placher (New York and Oxford: Oxford University Press, 1993).

Freud, Sigmund, The Standard Edition of the Complete Psychological Works of Sigmund Freud, vol. xi. (1911), *Five Lectures on Psycho-analysis; Leonardo da Vinci; and Other Works*, ed. James Strachey (London: Hogarth Press, 1957).

—— The Standard Edition of the Complete Psychological Works of Sigmund Freud, vol. xiv. (1914–16), *The History of the Psycho-Analytic Movement: Papers on Metapsychology and Other Works*, ed. James Strachey (London: Hogarth Press, 1957).

—— The Standard Edition of the Complete Psychological Works of Sigmund Freud, vol. xix. (1923–5), *The Ego, the Id; and Other Works*, ed. James Strachey (London: Hogarth Press, 1961).

—— The Standard Edition of the Complete Psychological Works of Sigmund Freud, vol. xxi. (1927–31). *The Future of an Illusion; Civilization and its Discontent; and Other Works*, ed. James Strachey (London: Hogarth Press, 1961).

Füllenbach, J., *Ecclesiastical Office and the Primacy of Rome: An Evaluation of Recent Theological Discussion of First Clement* (Washington, DC: Catholic University of America Press, 1980).

Gadamer, Hans-Georg, *Truth and Method*, trans. Joel Weinsheimer and Donald G. Marshall, 2nd edn. (New York: Crossroad, 1989).

Gagey, Henri-J., 'The Need for a Political Theology in Post-modern Times', unpub. paper, International Association of Catholic Social Thought, Leuven, 2002.

Gaillardetz, Richard, *Teaching with Authority: A Theology of the Magisterium in the Church* (Collegeville, Minn.: Liturgical Press, 1997).

—— 'The Ecclesiological Foundations of Ministry Within an Ordered Communion', in Susan Wood (ed.), *Ordering the Baptismal Priesthood* (Collegeville, Minn.: Liturgical Press, 2003), 26–51.

Gallagher, Tom, 'A Tale of Two Cities: Communal Strife in Glasgow and Liverpool before 1914', in Roger Swift and Sheridan Gilley (eds.), *The Irish in Victorian Britain: The Local Dimension* (Dublin: Four Courts Press, 1999), 106–29.

Gardner, Helen (ed.), *The Metaphysical Poets*, 13th edn. (Harmondsworth: Penguin, 1973).

Garnett, Jane, et al. (eds.), *Redefining Christian Britain: Post 1945 Perspectives* (London: SCM, 2007).

Gassmann, Günther, 'Rezeption im ökumenischen Kontext', *Ökumenische Rundschau*, 26 (1977), 314–27.

—— (ed.), *Documentary History of Faith and Order, 1968–1993* (Geneva: WCC, 1993).

—— (ed.), *Report: International Bilateral Dialogues, 1992–1994* (Faith and Order Paper, No. 168) (Geneva: WCC, 1995).

—— 'From Reception to Unity: The Historical and Ecumenical Significance of the Concept of Reception', in Colin Podmore (ed.), *Community—Unity—Communion: Essays in Honour of Mary Tanner* (London: Church House Publishing, 1998), 117–29.

Geertz, Clifford J., 'Religion as a Cultural System', *The Interpretation of Cultures* (New York: Basic Books, 1973), 87–125.

Geffré, Claude, Gutiérrez, Gustavo, and Elizondo, Virgil (eds.), *Different Theologies, Common Responsibility: Babel or Pentecost?*, *Concilium*, 171 (1984).

General Synod of the Church of England, *Report of Proceedings*, 36 (2005).

Geremek, Bronislaw, 'The Marginal Man', in Jacques Le Goff (ed.), *The Medieval World*, trans. Lydia G. Cochrane (London: Collins & Brown, 1991), 346–71.

Getcha, Job, and Stavrou, Michel (eds.), *Le Feu sur la terre: mélanges offerts au Père Boris Bobrinskoy pour son 80e anniversaire* (Paris: Presses Saint-Serge, 2005).

Gherardini, Brunero, 'Le parole della consacrazione eucaristica', in Gherardini (ed.), *Sull'Anafora dei Santi Apostoli Addai e Mari*, *Divinitas*, ns, 47 (2004), 141–69.

Giddens, Anthony, *Modernity and Self-identity* (Cambridge: Polity Press, 1991).

Gilbert, Alan, *The Making of Post-Christian Britain: A History of the Secularization of Modern Society* (London: Longman, 1980).

Gil Hellín, Francisco, *Concilii Vaticani II Synopsis. Constitutio Dogmatica de Ecclesia: Lumen Gentium* (Vatican City: Libreria Editrice Vaticana, 1995).

Glazer, Nathan, and Moynihan, Daniel P. (eds.), *Ethnicity: Theory and Experience* (Cambridge, Mass.: Harvard University Press 1975).

González de Cardedal, Olegario, 'Development of a Theology of the Local Church From the First to the Second Vatican Council', *The Jurist*, 52 (1992), 11–43.

—— *La iglesia en España*, 1950–2000 (Madrid: Promoción Popular Cristiana, 1999).

Goodall, Norman (ed.), *The Uppsala Report 1968: Official Report of the Fourth Assembly of the World Council of Churches, Uppsala, July 4–20, 1968* (Geneva: WCC, 1968).

Gray, Donald, 'Ecumenical Liturgical Cooperation—Past, Present and Future', *Studia Liturgica*, 28 (1998), 232–43.

Grdzelidze, Tamara (ed.), *One, Holy, Catholic and Apostolic. Ecumenical Reflections on the Church* (Geneva: WCC, 2005).

Green, Michael (ed.), *The Truth of God Incarnate* (London: Hodder & Stoughton, 1977).

Green, Thomas J., 'Subsidiarity During the Code Revision Process', *The Jurist*, 48 (1988), 771–99.

—— 'The Normative Role of Episcopal Conferences in the 1983 Code', in Thomas J. Reese (ed.), *Episcopal Conferences: Historical, Canonical and Theological Studies* (Washington, DC: Georgetown University Press, 1989), 137–76.

Grillmeier, Aloys, 'Konzil und Rezeption: Methodische Bemerkungen zu einem Thema der ökumenischen Diskussion der Gegenwart', *Theologie und Philosophie*, 45 (1970), 321–52.

—— 'The Reception of Church Councils', in Philip McShane (ed.), *Foundations of Theology: Papers from the International Lonergan Congress, 1970* (Dublin: Gill & Macmillan, 1971), 102–14.

Gros, Jeffrey, 'Reception of the Ecumenical Movement in the Roman Catholic Church, with Special Reference to Baptism, Eucharist and Ministry', *American Baptist Quarterly*, 7 (1988), 38–49.

—— 'Towards a Hermeneutics of Piety for the Ecumenical Movement', *Ecumenical Trends*, 22 (Jan. 1993), 1–12.

—— 'Episcopal–Roman Catholic Bishops Pilgrimage Witnesses Commitment and Realism', *Ecumenical Trends*, 24 (Jan. 1995), 1–14.

—— 'Toward a Reconciliation of Memory: Seeking a Truly Catholic Hermeneutics of History', *Journal of Latino/Hispanic Theology*, 7 (1999), 56–75.

—— *That All May Be One: Ecumenism* (Chicago, Ill.: Loyola University Press, 2000).

—— 'The Reception in the US Catholic Context', in K. Bloomquist and W. Greive (eds.), *The Doctrine of Justification: Its Reception and Meaning Today* (Geneva: Lutheran World Federation, 2003), 25–34.

—— *Handing on the Faith in an Ecumenical World: Resources for Catholic Administrators and Religious Educators in Serving Christian Unity in School and Parish* (Washington, DC: National Catholic Educational Association, 2005).

—— 'Building a Common Heritage: Teaching the Reformation in an Ecumenical Perspective', *Ecumenical Trends*, 35 (May 2006), 11–15.

—— and Mulhall, Daniel (eds.), *The Ecumenical Christian Dialogues and the Catechism of the Catholic Church* (New York: Paulist Press, 2006).

—— Meyer, Harding, and Rusch, William G. (eds.), *Growth in Agreement II: Reports and Agreed Statements of Ecumenical Conversations on a World Level, 1982–1998* (Geneva and Grand Rapids, Mich.: WCC/Eerdmans, 2000).

Groupe des Dombes, *For the Conversion of the Churches*, trans. James Greig (Geneva: WCC, 1993 [1991]).

Gruchy, John de, *Reconciliation: Restoring Justice* (London: SCM, 2002).

Gueit, Jean, 'Démocratie dans les Églises: le cas de l'"orthodoxie" ', in Jean Bauberot, Joseph Famerée, Roger T. Greenacre, and Jean Gueit (eds.), *Démocratie dans les Églises. Anglicanisme, Catholicisme, Orthodoxie, Protestantisme* (Brussels: Lumen Vitae, 1999), 63–81.

Guest, Mathew, 'Reconceiving the Congregation as a Source of Authenticity', in Jane Garnett, et al. (eds.), *Redefining Christian Britain: Post 1945 Perspectives* (London: SCM, 2007), 63–72.

—— Tusting, Karin, and Woodhead, Linda (eds.), *Congregational Studies in the UK: Christianity in a Post-Christian Context* (Aldershot: Ashgate, 2004).

Gunton, Colin, *The One, The Three and The Many* (Cambridge: Cambridge University Press, 1995).

—— *The Promise of Trinitarian Theology* (Edinburgh: T. & T. Clark, 1997).

Hagen, Kenneth (ed.), *The Quadrilog: Tradition and the Future of Ecumenism. Essays in Honor of George H. Tavard* (Collegeville, Minn.: Liturgical Press, 1994).

Haight, Roger, 'Church as Locus of Theology', *Why Theology?*, *Concilium*, 6 (1994), 13–22.

Haight, Roger, *Christian Community in History*, vol. i. *Historical Ecclesiology* (New York and London: Continuum, 2004).

—— *Christian Community in History*, vol. ii. *Comparative Ecclesiology* (New York and London: Continuum, 2007).

—— 'Comparative Ecclesiology', in Gerard Mannion and Lewis Mudge (eds.), *The Routledge Companion to the Christian Church* (London: Routledge, 2007), 387–401.

—— *Christian Community in History*, vol. iii. *Ecclesial Existence* (New York and London: Continuum, 2008).

Halleux, André de, 'Le Décret chalcédonien sur les prérogatives de la Nouvelle Rome', *Patrologie et œcuménisme: recueil d'études* (Louvain: Peeters, 1990), 520–35.

—— 'Les deux Rome dans la définition de Chalcédoine sur les prérogatives du siège de Constantinople', in De Halleux, *Patrologie et œcuménisme: recueil d'études* (Louvain: Peeters, 1990), 504–19.

—— 'La Collégialité dans l'Église ancienne', *Revue théologique de Louvain*, 24 (1993), 433–54.

Hamel, Ronald, and Himes, Kenneth (eds.), *Introduction to Christian Ethics: A Reader* (Mahwah, NY: Paulist Press, 1989).

Hampson, Daphne, *Christian Contradictions: The Structure of Lutheran and Catholic Thought* (Cambridge: Cambridge University Press, 2001).

Hanley, Angela, and Smith, David (eds.), *Quench Not the Spirit: Theology and Prophecy for the Church in the Modern World* (Dublin: Columba Press, 2005).

Hardy, Daniel W., *God's Ways with the World: Thinking and Practising Christian Faith* (Edinburgh: T. & T. Clark, 1996).

—— *Finding the Church* (London: SCM, 2001).

Harnack, Adolf von, *Das Wesen des Christentums* (Leipzig: J. C. Hinrichs, 1900).

—— *What is Christianity?*, trans. T. B. Saunders (London: Williams and Norgate, 1904).

Harrington, Wilfred, 'Scribalism in the Church', in Angela Hanley and David Smith (eds.), *Quench Not the Spirit: Theology and Prophecy for the Church in the Modern World* (Dublin: Columba Press, 2005), 44–55.

Hauerwas, Stanley, 'The Importance of Being Catholic: A Protestant View', *First Things*, 1 (1990), 23–30.

Healey, Thomas J., 'A Blueprint for Change', *America*, 193 (26 Sept. 2005), 14–17.

Healy, Nicholas M., *Church, World and the Christian Life: Practical–Prophetic Ecclesiology* (Cambridge: Cambridge University Press, 2000).

—— 'Practices and the New Ecclesiology: Misplaced Concreteness?', *International Journal of Systematic Theology*, 5 (2003), 287–308.

Hebert, Arthur G., *Liturgy and Society: The Function of the Church in the Modern World* (London: Faber & Faber, 1935).

Heidegger, Martin, 'Aletheia (Heraklit, Fragment 16)', *Vortrage und Aufsätze* (Pfullingen: G. Neske, 1954), 257–82.

Hemming, Laurence Paul, and Parsons, Susan Frank (eds.), *Redeeming Truth: Considering Faith and Reason* (London: SCM, 2007).

Hession, Anne, and Kieran, Patricia (eds.), *Exploring Theology: Making Sense of the Catholic Tradition* (Dublin: Veritas, 2007).

Heythrop Institute for Religion, Ethics and Public Life, *On the Way to Life: Contemporary Culture and Theological Development as a Framework for Catholic Education, Catechesis and Formation* (London: Catholic Education Service, 2005).

Heywood Thomas, John, 'Logic and Metaphysics in Luther's Eucharistic Theology', *Renaissance and Modern Studies*, 23 (1979), 147–59.

—— *Models in Theology* (St Andrews: Theology in Scotland, 2003).

Hill, Christopher, 'ARCIC-I and II: An Anglican Perspective', in Albert Denaux (ed.), *From Malines to ARCIC: The Malines Conversations Commemorated* (Leuven: Leuven University Press, 1997), 133–48.

—— and Yarnold, Edward (eds.), *Anglicans and Roman Catholics: The Search for Unity* (London: SPCK/CTS, 1994).

Hill, Mark, 'Authority in the Church of England', in James Conn, Norman Doe, and Joseph Fox (eds.), *Initiation, Membership and Authority in Anglican and Roman Catholic Canon Law* (Rome and Cardiff: Pontifical Gregorian University and Pontifical University of St Thomas Aquinas/University of Wales, Cardiff, 2005), 263–75.

Hinze, Bradford, *Practices of Dialogue Within the Roman Catholic Church: Aims and Obstacles, Lessons and Laments* (New York: Continuum, 2006).

Hiscock, Nigel, *The Wise Master Builder: Platonic Geometry in Plans of Medieval Abbeys and Cathedrals* (Aldershot: Ashgate, 1999).

Hoffmann, Joseph, 'L'Horizon œcuménique de la réforme du droit canonique: à propos de deux ouvrages de H. Dombois', *Revue des sciences philosophiques et théologiques*, 57 (1973), 228–50.

—— 'Statut et pratique du droit canonique dans l'Église', *Revue de droit canonique* 27 (1977), 5–37.

Holc, Pawel, *Un ampio consenso sulla dottrina della giustificazione: Studio sul dialogo teologico cattolico-luterano* (Rome: Editrice Pontificia Università Gregoriana, 1999).

Holmes, Jeremy, *John Bowlby and Attachment Theory* (Hove: Brunner-Routledge, 1993).

—— 'Attachment Theory: A Secure Base for Policy?', in Sebastian Kraemer and Jane Roberts (eds.), *The Politics of Attachment: Towards a Secure Society* (London: Free Association Books, 1996), 27–42.

—— *The Search for the Secure Base: Attachment Theory and Psychotherapy* (Hove: Brunner-Routledge, 2001).

Holy Office, '*Monitum* of the Holy Office' (5 June 1948), *AAS*, 40 (1948), 257.

Hooker, Richard, 'The Laws of Ecclesiastical Polity', *The Works of Richard Hooker*, ed. John Keble, vol. ii. (Oxford: Clarendon Press, 1875 [1593]).

Hoose, Bernard (ed.), *Authority in the Roman Catholic Church. Theory and Practice* (Aldershot: Ashgate, 2002).

Hornsby-Smith, Michael P., *Roman Catholics in England: Studies in Social Structure Since the Second World War* (Cambridge: Cambridge University Press, 1987).

—— *Roman Catholic Beliefs in England: Customary Catholicism and Transformations of Religious Authority* (Cambridge: Cambridge University Press, 1991).

Hotchkin, John, 'The Ecumenical Movement's Third Stage', *Origins*, 25 (9 Nov. 1995), 353–61.

Houtepen, Anton W. J., 'The Faith of the Church Through the Ages: Ecumenism and Hermeneutics', *Bulletin of the Centro Pro Unione*, 44 (1993).

Huber, Wolfgang, *Kirche in der Zeitenwende* (Gütersloh: Gütersloher Verlagshaus, 1999).

Huels, John, 'The Correction and Punishment of a Diocesan Bishop', *The Jurist*, 49 (1989), 507–42.

Hunsinger, George, and Placher, William C. (eds.), *Theology and Narrative: Selected Essays* (New York and Oxford: Oxford University Press, 1993).

Inter-Anglican Theological and Doctrinal Commission, *The Virginia Report* (Harrisburg, Pa.: Morehouse, 1999).

International Anglican–Roman Catholic Commission for Unity and Mission, 'Ecclesiological Reflections on the Current Situation in the Anglican Communion in the Light of ARCIC', *Information Service*, 119 (2005), 102–15.

—— *Growing Together in Unity and Mission: Building on 40 Years of Anglican-Roman Catholic Dialogue* (London: SPCK, 2007).

International Dialogue Between the Roman Catholic Church and the Mennonite World Conference, 'Called Together to Be Peacemakers' (2003), *Information Service*, 113 (2003), 111–48.

International Theological Commission, 'The Apostolic Continuity of the Church and Apostolic Succession', in Michael Sharkey (ed.), *International Theological Commission: Texts and Documents, 1969–1985* (San Francisco, Calif.: Ignatius Press, 1989).

Ipgrave, Michael (ed.), *Scriptures in Dialogue: Christians and Muslims Studying the Bible and the Qur'an Together* (London: Church House Publishing, 2004).

Irenaeus of Lyons, St, 'Against Heresies', in *The Ante-Nicene Fathers*, ed. and trans. Alexander Roberts and James Donaldson, rev. A. Cleveland Coxe (Grand Rapids, MI: Eerdmans, 1996 [1885]), 315–567.

Irish Interchurch Meeting, *Sectarianism: A Discussion Document* (Belfast: Irish Interchurch Meeting, 1993).

Isaacs, Harold R., 'Basic Group Identity: The Idols of the Tribe', in Nathan Glazer and Daniel P. Moynihan (eds.), *Ethnicity: Theory and Experience* (Cambridge, Mass.: Harvard University Press, 1975), 29–52.

James, William, *The Works of William James*, vol. i., *Pragmatism*, ed. Frederick H. Burkhardt, Fredson Bowers, and Ignas K. Skrupskelis (Cambridge, Mass.: Harvard University Press, 1975).

Jauss, Hans Robert, *Toward an Aesthetic of Reception* (Minneapolis, Minn.: University of Minnesota Press, 1995).

Jeanrond, Werner G., *Theological Hermeneutics: Development and Significance* (London: SCM, 1994 [1991]).

Jenkins, Philip, *The New Anti Catholicism: The Last Acceptable Prejudice* (Oxford: Oxford University Press, 2003).

Jenson, Robert W., *Systematic Theology*, vol. i. (New York: Oxford University Press, 1997).

John, Jeffrey (ed.), *Living the Mystery: Affirming Catholicism and the Future of Anglicanism* (London: Darton, Longman & Todd, 1994).

John of the Cross, St, *The Ascent of Mount Carmel*, in Kevin Kavanaugh (ed.), *John of the Cross: Selected Writings* (Mahwah, NY: Paulist Press, 1987), 55–153.

John Paul II, Pope, '*Ex Corde Ecclesiae*: Apostolic Constitution on Catholic Universities' (15 Aug. 1990) (Vatican City: Libreria Editrice Vaticana, 1990).

—— '*Centesimus Annus*: On the Hundredth Anniversary of *Rerum Novarum*' (1 May 1991) (London: CTS, 1991).

—— *Crossing the Threshold of Hope*, ed. Vittorio Messori, trans. Jenny McPhee and Martha McPhee (London: Jonathan Cape, 1994).

—— '*Ordinatio Sacerdotalis*: Apostolic Letter on Reserving Priestly Ordination to Men Alone' (22 May 1994) (London: CTS, 1994).

—— *Ut Unum Sint*: Encyclical Letter on Commitment to Ecumenism (25 May 1995), (London: CTS, 1995).

——'*Apostolos Suos*: Apostolic Letter Issued Motu Proprio on the Theological and Juridical Nature of Episcopal Conferences' (21 May 1998), *AAS*, 90 (1998), 650–1.

—— '*Ecclesia de Eucharistia*: Encyclical Letter on the Eucharist in its Relationship to the Church' (17 Apr. 2003) (London: CTS, 2003).

—— '*Pastores Gregis*: Apostolic Exhortation on the Bishop, Servant of the Gospel of Jesus Christ for the Hope of the World' (16 Oct. 2003) (Vatican City: Libreria Editrice Vaticana, 2003).

—— 'Homily, 13th November 2004, St Peter's Basilica, Rome', *Information Service*, 118 (2005), 29–31.

—— and Carey, Archbishop George, 'The Common Declaration of 5th December, 1996', *Information Service*, 94 (1997), 20–1.

—— and Runcie, Archbishop Robert, 'Common Declaration' (2 Oct. 1989), *Origins*, 19 (1989–90), 316–17 also in *Information Service*, 71 (1989), 122–3.

John VIII, Pope, 'Letter to Anspertus', *Epistola 223*, in J-P. Migne (ed.), *Patrologiæ Cursus Completus*, Series Latina, 126, col. 837.

Joint International Commission for Dialogue Between the Roman Catholic Church and the World Methodist Council, *Growth in Understanding—The Dublin Report* (Dublin: World Methodist Council, 1976).

—— *Towards an Agreed Statement on the Holy Spirit* (Lake Junaluska, NC: World Methodist Council, 1981).

—— *Towards a Statement on the Church* (Nairobi: World Methodist Council, 1986); reprinted in Jeffrey Gros F.S.C., Harding Meyer, and William G. Rusch, (eds.), *Growth in Agreement II. Reports and Agreed Statements of Ecumenical Conversations on a World Level, 1982–1998* (Geneva/Grand Rapids, MI: WCC/Eerdmans, 2000), 583–96.

—— *The Apostolic Tradition* (Singapore: World Methodist Council, 1991), reprinted in Gros, Meyer and Rusch (eds.), *Growth in Agreement II*, 597–617.

—— *The Word of Life* (Rio de Janeiro: World Methodist Council, 1996), reprinted in Gros, Meyer and Rusch (eds.), *Growth in Agreement II*, 618–46.

—— *Speaking the Truth in Love: Teaching Authority Among Catholics and Methodists* (Brighton, 2001).

—— *The Grace Given You in Christ: Catholics and Methodists Reflect Further on the Church* (Lake Junaluska, NC: World Methodist Council, 2006).

Joint International Roman Catholic–Orthodox Theological Commission, 'The Mystery of the Church and the Eucharist in the Light of the Mystery of the Holy Trinity' (1982), in Jeffrey Gros F.S.C., Harding Meyer, and William G. Rusch (eds.), *Growth in Agreement II. Reports and Agreed Statements of Ecumenical Conversations on a World Level, 1982–1998* (Geneva/Grand Rapids, MI: WCC/Eerdmans, 2000), 652–9.

—— 'The Sacrament of Order in the Sacramental Structure of the Church' (1988), in Gros, Meyer, and Rusch (eds.), *Growth in Agreement II*, 671–9.

Joint Lutheran–Roman Catholic Study Commission, 'The Gospel and the Church—The Malta Report' (1972), in Harding Meyer and Lukas Vischer (eds.), *Growth in Agreement: Reports and Agreed Statements of Ecumenical Conversations on a World Level* (Mahwah, NY/Geneva: Paulist Press/WCC, 1984), 168–89.

Joint Lutheran–Roman Catholic Study Commission, 'The Eucharist' (1978), in Meyer and Vischer (eds.), *Growth in Agreement*, 190–214.

—— 'Ways to Community' (1980), in Meyer and Vischer (eds.), *Growth in Agreement*, 215–40.

—— 'All Under One Christ' (1980), in Meyer and Vischer (eds.), *Growth in Agreement*, 241–7.

—— 'The Ministry in the Church' (1981), in Meyer and Vischer (eds.), *Growth in Agreement*, 248–75.

—— 'Martin Luther—Witness to Jesus Christ' (1983), in Gros, Meyer, and Rusch (eds.), *Growth in Agreement II*, 438–42.

—— 'Facing Unity' (1984), in Gros, Meyer, and Rusch (eds.), *Growth in Agreement II*, 443–84.

—— 'Church and Justification' (1993), in Gros, Meyer, and Rusch (eds.), *Growth in Agreement II*, 485–565.

Joint Reformed-Roman Catholic Dialogue, 'The Presence of Christ in Church and World', in Meyer and Vischer (eds.), *Growth in Agreement*, 434–63.

—— 'Toward a Common Understanding of the Church', in Gros, Meyer, and Rusch (eds.), *Growth in Agreement II*, 780–818.

Joint Working Group Between the Roman Catholic Church and the World Council of Churches, 'The Nature and Purpose of Ecumenical Dialogue: A JWG Study', *Eighth Report, 1999–2005* (Geneva and Rome: WCC, 2005), 73–89.

Joint Working Group Between the World Council of Churches and the Secretariat for the Promotion of Christian Unity, 'Study Document on Catholicity and Apostolicity' (1968), *One in Christ*, 4 (1970), 452–83.

Jossua, Jean-Pierre, 'L'Œuvre œcuménique du Père Congar', *Études*, 357 (1982), 543–55.

—— 'In Hope of Unity', trans. Barbara Estelle Beaumont, in Gabriel Flynn (ed.), *Yves Congar: Theologian of the Church* (Louvain: Peeters, 2005), 167–81.

—— and Congar, Yves (eds.), *La liturgie après Vatican II* (Paris: Cerf, 1967).

Kardong, Terrence (ed.), *Benedict's Rule: A Translation and Commentary* (Collegeville, Minn.: Liturgical Press, 1996).

Karras, Valerie A., 'Beyond Justification: An Orthodox Perspective', in William G. Rusch (ed.), *Justification and the Future of the Ecumenical Movement: The Joint Declaration on the Doctrine of Justification* (Collegeville, Minn.: Liturgical Press, 2003), 99–131.

Kasper, Walter, 'Die Funktion des Priesters in der Kirche', *Geist und Leben*, 42 (1969), 102–16.

—— *Glaube und Geschichte* (Mainz: M. Grünewald, 1970).

—— *Jesus the Christ*, trans. V. Green (London and New York: Burns & Oates/Paulist Press, 1976 [1974]).

—— *An Introduction to Christian Faith*, trans. V. Green (London: Burns & Oates, 1980 [1972]).

—— *The God of Jesus Christ*, trans. Matthew J. O'Connell (London: SCM, 1984 [1982]).

—— 'Church as *Communio*', *Communio*, 13 (1986), 100–17.

—— *Theology and Church*, trans. Margaret Kohl (London: SCM, 1989 [1987]).

—— *Apostolic Succession in Episcopacy in an Ecumenical Context* (Baltimore, Md.: St Mary's Seminary and University, 1992).

—— 'The Church as Communio', *New Blackfriars*, 74 (1993), 232–44.

—— 'The 300th Anniversary of the Birth of John Wesley: Cardinal Kasper's Statements', *Information Service*, 114 (2003), 183–6.

—— 'Keynote Address', *May They All Be One . . . But How? A Vision of Christian Unity for the Next Generation: Proceedings of the Conference Held in St Albans Cathedral on 17th May 2003* (St Albans: Christian Study Centre, 2003), 21–30.

—— *Leadership in the Church: How Traditional Roles Can Serve the Christian Community Today*, trans. Brian McNeil (New York: Crossroad, 2003).

—— *That They May All Be One: The Call to Unity Today* (London and New York: Burns & Oates, 2004).

—— 'The Current Situation in Ecumenical Theology', in Kasper, *That They May All Be One: The Call To Unity Today* (London: Burns & Oates, 2004), 14–32.

—— 'The Nature and Purpose of Ecumenical Dialogue', in Kasper, *That They May All Be One: The Call To Unity Today* (London: Burns & Oates, 2004), 33–49.

—— '*Communio*: The Guiding Concept of Catholic Ecumenical Theology', in Kasper, *That They May All Be One: The Call To Unity Today* (London: Burns & Oates, 2004), 50–74.

—— 'Cardinal Walter Kasper's Message to the 13th Anglican Consultative Council Meeting' (18 June 2005), *Information Service*, 119 (2005), 101–2.

—— 'Letter of His Eminence Cardinal Walter Kasper to His Grace Dr Rowan Williams Archbishop of Canterbury' (17 Dec. 2004), *Information Service*, 118 (2005), 38–9.

—— *Sacrament of Unity: The Eucharist and the Church*, trans. Brian McNeil (New York: Crossroad, 2005 [2004]).

—— (ed.), *The Petrine Ministry: Catholics and Orthodox in Dialogue*, trans. Staff of the Pontifical Council for Promoting Christian Unity (Mahwah, NY: Newman Press, 2006).

—— 'Petrine Ministry and Synodality', *The Jurist*, 66 (2006), 298–309.

Kavanaugh, Kevin (ed.), *John of the Cross: Selected Writings* (Mahwah, NY: Paulist Press, 1987).

Kegan, Robert, *The Evolving Self: Problem and Process in Human Development* (Cambridge, Mass.: Harvard University Press, 1982).

Kerkhofs, Jan (ed.), *Europe Without Priests?* (London: SCM, 1995).

Kerr, Madeleine, *The People of Ship Street* (London: Routledge & Kegan Paul, 1958).

Khomiakov, Alexei S., Kireevskii, Ivan Vasilevich, Jakim, Boris, and Bird, Robert (eds.), *On Spiritual Unity: A Slavophile Reader* (Hudson, NY: Lindisfarne Books, 1998).

Kilmartin, E. J., 'Reception in History: An Ecclesiological Phenomenon and its Significance', *Journal of Ecumenical Studies*, 21 (1984), 34–54.

Kinnamon, Michael, and Cope, Brian E. (eds.), *The Ecumenical Movement: An Anthology of Key Texts and Voices* (Geneva and Grand Rapids, Mich.: WCC/Eerdmans, 1997).

Knight, Douglas H. (ed.), *The Theology of John Zizioulas: Personhood and the Church* (London: Ashgate, 2007).

Kolb, Robert, and Wingert, Timothy J. (eds.), *The Book of Concord: The Confessions of the Evangelical Lutheran Church* (Minneapolis, Minn.: Fortress Press, 2000).

Komonchak, Joseph, 'The Church in Crisis: Pope Benedict's Theological Vision', *Commonweal* (3 June 2005), 11–14.

König, Franz, *Open to God, Open to the World*, ed. Christa Pongratz-Lippitt (London and New York: Continuum, 2005).

Kraemer, Sebastian, and Roberts, Jane (eds.), *The Politics of Attachment: Towards a Secure Society* (London: Free Association Books, 1996).

Kuhn, Thomas, *The Structure of Scientific Revolutions* (Chicago, Ill.: University of Chicago Press, 1970).

Küng, Hans, *Justification: The Doctrine of Karl Barth and a Catholic Reflection*, trans. Thomas Collins, Edmund E. Tolk, and David Granskou (London: Burns & Oates, 1964 [1957]).

—— Congar, Yves, and O'Hanlon, Daniel (eds.), *Council Speeches of Vatican II* (Glen Rock, NJ: Paulist Press, 1964).

Küppers, W., 'Reception, Prolegomena to a Systematic Study', in Lukas Vischer (ed.), *Councils and the Ecumenical Movement* (Geneva: WCC, 1968), 76–98.

Lakeland, Paul, *The Liberation of the Laity: In Search of an Accountable Church* (New York: Continuum, 2003).

Lambeth Commission on Communion, *The Windsor Report, 2004* (London: Anglican Communion Office, 2004).

Lambeth Conference of Bishops of the Anglican Communion, *The Lambeth Conference, 1948* (London: SPCK, 1948).

—— *The Official Report of the Lambeth Conference, 1998*, ed. Mark J. Dyer, et al. (Harrisburg, Penn.: Morehouse Publishing, 1998).

Lanne, E., 'Pluralism and Unity: The Possibility of a Variety of Typologies Within the Same Ecclesial Allegiance', *One in Christ*, 6 (1970), 430–51.

Larini, Riccardo, 'The Birth of Christian Identity: Criteria for Unity and Room for Diversity in the New Testament and Apostolic Fathers' Time', unpub. MPhil diss., Univ. of Cambridge, 2005.

Lash, Nicholas, *Newman on Development: The Search for an Explanation in History* (London: Sheed & Ward, 1975).

—— *Theology on Dover Beach* (London: Darton, Longman and Todd, 1979).

—— *A Matter of Hope: A Theologian's Reflections on the Thought of Karl Marx* (London: Darton, Longman & Todd, 1981).

—— *Theology on the Way to Emmaus* (London: SCM, 1986).

—— *Easter in Ordinary: Reflections on Human Experience and the Knowledge of God* (London: SCM, 1988).

—— ' "A Seat of Wisdom, a Light of the World": Considering the University', in Terrence Merrigan (ed.), *John Henry Cardinal Newman, 1801–1890. A Special Issue of Louvain Studies* (Louvain: Peeters, 1990), 188–202.

—— *The Beginning and the End of 'Religion'* (Cambridge: Cambridge University Press, 1996).

—— 'Recovering Contingency', in John Cornwell (ed.), *Consciousness and Human Identity* (Oxford: Oxford University Press, 1998), 197–211.

—— 'The Laboratory We Need', *The Tablet* (15 April 2000), 514.

—— 'Authors, Authority and Authorization', in Bernard Hoose (ed.), *Authority in the Roman Catholic Church. Theory and Practice* (Aldershot: Ashgate, 2002), 59–71.

—— *Holiness, Speech and Silence: Reflections on the Question of God* (Aldershot: Ashgate, 2004).

—— 'Introduction', *New Blackfriars* 87 (2006), 109.

—— 'Churches, Proper and Otherwise', *The Tablet* (21 July 2007), 13–14.

—— *Theology for Pilgrims* (London: Darton, Longman & Todd, 2008).

—— 'What Happened at Vatican II?', in Lash, *Theology for Pilgrims* (London: Darton, Longman & Todd, 2008), 240–8.

Lauret, Bernard (ed.), *Fifty Years of Catholic Theology: Conversations with Yves Congar*, trans. John Bowden (London: SCM, 1988).

Lee, Randall, and Gros, Jeffrey (eds.), *The Church as Koinonia of Salvation: Its Structures and Ministries, Lutherans and Catholics in Dialogue*, vol. x., *Agreed Statement of the Tenth Round of the U.S. Lutheran–Roman Catholic Dialogue with Background Papers* (Washington, DC: USCCB, 2005).

Le Goff, Jacques (ed.), *The Medieval World*, trans. Lydia G. Cochrane (London: Collins & Brown, 1991).

Legrand, Hervé, 'Grâce et institution dans l'Église: les fondements théologiques du droit canonique', in Jean-Louis Monneron, et al. (eds.), *L'Église, institution et foi*, 2nd edn. (Brussels: Facultés universitaires St Louis, 1985 [1979]), 139–72.

—— 'Brève note sur le synode de Sardique et sur sa réception: Rome, instance d'appel ou de cassation', in *La Primauté romaine dans la communion des Églises*, Comité Mixte Catholique–Orthodoxe en France (Paris: Cerf, 1991), 47–60.

—— 'Conclusions du comité mixte', in *La Primauté romaine dans la communion des Églises*, Comité Mixte Catholique–Orthodoxe en France (Paris: Cerf, 1991), 113–25.

—— 'La légitimité d'une pluralité de "formes de pensée" (Denkformen) en dogmatique catholique: retour sur la thèse d'un précurseur, O. H. Pesch', in François Bousquet, Henri-Jérôme Gagey, and Geneviève Médevielle (eds.), *La Responsabilité des théologiens: mélanges en l'honneur de Joseph Doré* (Paris: Desclée, 2002), 685–704.

—— 'The Bishop is in the Church and the Church is in the Bishop', *The Jurist*, 66 (2006), 70–92.

—— 'Personal, Collegial and Synodal Responsibility in the Roman Catholic Church: What Convergences Are There Between the Reception of Vatican II and *BEM*?', in Thomas F. Best and Tamara Grdzelidze (eds.), *BEM at 25: Critical Insights into a Continuing Legacy* (Faith and Order Paper, No. 205) (Geneva: WCC, 2007), 105–29.

—— Manzanares, J., and García y García, A. (eds.), *The Nature and Future of Episcopal Conferences*, trans. Thomas J. Green, Joseph A. Komonchak, and James H. Provost (Washington, DC: Catholic University of America Press, 1988).

Lehmann, Karl, and Pannenberg, Wolfhart (eds.), *The Condemnations of the Reformation Era: Do They Still Divide?*, trans. Margaret Kohl (Minneapolis, Minn.: Fortress Press, 1999 [1988]).

Leo XIII, Pope, '*Apostolicae Curae*: Encyclical Letter on English Ordinations' (13 Sept. 1896), in R. William Franklin (ed.), *Anglican Orders: Essays on the Centenary of Apostolicae Curae, 1896–1996* (London: Mowbray, 1996), 127–37.

Levinas, Emmanuel, *Collected Philosophical Papers*, trans. Alphonso Lingis (Dordrecht, Boston, and London: Kluwer, 1987).

Lieu, Judith, *Christian Identity in the Graeco–Roman World* (Oxford: Oxford University Press, 2004).

Lightbound, Christopher, 'A More Generous Hospitality?', *Priests and People* (Jan. 2002), 18–21.

Lindbeck, George A., *The Nature of Doctrine: Religion and Theology in a Postliberal Age* (London: SPCK, 1984).

Logan, F. D., 'The 1875 Statement of the German Bishops on Episcopal Powers', *The Jurist*, 21 (1961), 285–95.

Lonergan, Bernard, *Method in Theology* (London: Darton, Longman & Todd, 1972).

——*A Third Collection: Papers by Bernard J. F. Lonergan, SJ*, ed. Frederick E. Crowe (London and New York: Geoffrey Chapman/Paulist Press, 1985).

Longley, Clifford, 'Methodism: Distinctive, or just Catholic?', in Clive Marsh, et al. (ed.), *Unmasking Methodist Theology* (London: Continuum, 2004), 198–203.

Lossky, Nicholas, et al. (eds.), *Dictionary of the Ecumenical Movement*, 2nd edn. (Geneva: WCC, 2002).

Lossky, Vladimir, *The Mystical Theology of the Eastern Church* (London: James Clarke, 1957 [1944]).

Lot-Borodine, Myrrha, *Le Déification de l'homme selon la doctrine des pères grecs* (Paris: Cerf, 1970 [1932–50]).

Lubac, Henri de, *Les Églises particulières dans l'Église universelle* (Paris: Aubier-Montaigne, 1971).

——*The Splendour of the Church*, trans. Michael Mason (San Francisco, Calif.: Ignatius, 1986 [1953]).

——*Catholicism: Christ and the Common Destiny of Man*, trans. Lancelot C. Sheppard, 4th edn. (San Francisco, Calif.: Ignatius, 1988 [1947, 1938]).

——*Corpus Mysticum: The Eucharist and the Church in the Middle Ages*, trans. Gemma Simmonds with Richard Price (London: SCM, 2006 [1944, 1949]).

Lutheran World Federation and the Roman Catholic Church, *Joint Declaration on the Doctrine of Justification* (Grand Rapids, Mich. and London: Eerdmans/CTS, 2000/2001).

McCaughey, Terence P., *Memory and Redemption: Church, Politics and Prophetic Theology in Ireland* (Dublin: Gill & Macmillan, 1993).

Macchia, Frank D., 'Justification and the Spirit of Life: A Pentecostal Response to the Joint Declaration', in William G. Rusch (ed.), *Justification and the Future of the Ecumenical Movement: The Joint Declaration on the Doctrine of Justification* (Collegeville, Minn.: Liturgical Press, 2003), 133–49.

Macdonald, Isobel, *A Family in Skye, 1908–1916* (Portree: Acair, 1980).

McGrail, Peter, *First Communion: Ritual, Church and Popular Religious Identity* (Aldershot: Ashgate, 2006).

McGrath, Alister, *The Twilight of Atheism* (London: Rider, 2004).

MacIntyre, Alasdair, *Three Rival Versions of Moral Enquiry* (London: Duckworth, 1990).

——'Review of Herbert McCabe, *The Good Life: Ethics and the Pursuit of Happiness*, (London: Continuum, 2005)', *The Tablet* (10 September 2005), 22.

Mackie, Robert C., and West, Charles (eds.), *The Sufficiency of God* (London: SCM, 1963).

Macmurray, John, *The Form of the Personal*, vol. ii., *Persons in Relation* (London: Faber & Faber, 1961).

MacNamara, Vincent, *New Life for Old: On Desire and Becoming Human* (Dublin: Columba Press, 2004).

McPartlan, Paul, 'Eucharistic Ecclesiology', *One in Christ*, 22 (1986), 314–31.

——*The Eucharist Makes the Church: Henri de Lubac and John Zizioulas in Dialogue*, 2nd edn. (Fairfax, VA: Eastern Christian Publications, 2006 [1993]).

—— 'The *Catechism* and Catholic–Orthodox Dialogue', *One in Christ*, 30 (1994), 229–44.

—— *Sacrament of Salvation: An Introduction to Eucharistic Ecclesiology* (London: Continuum, 2005 [1995]).

—— 'The Local Church and the Universal Church: Zizioulas and the Ratzinger–Kasper Debate', *International Journal for the Study of the Christian Church*, 4 (2004), 21–33.

—— 'Liturgy, Church and Society', *Studia Liturgica*, 34 (2004), 147–64.

—— (ed.), *One in 2000? Towards Catholic–Orthodox Unity: Agreed Statements and Parish Papers* (Slough: St Paul's, 1993).

Mahieu, Éric (ed.), *Yves Congar: mon journal du concile*, vol. ii. (Paris: Cerf, 2002).

Malloy, Christopher J., *Engrafted into Christ: A Critique of the Joint Declaration* (New York: Peter Lang, 2005).

Mannion, Gerard, 'What's in a Name? Hermeneutical Questions on "Globalisation", Catholicity and Ecumenism', *New Blackfriars*, 86 (2005), 204–15.

—— *Ecclesiology and Postmodernity: Questions for the Church in our Times* (Collegeville, Minn.: Liturgical Press, 2007).

—— 'Constructive Comparative Ecclesiology: The Pioneering Work of Roger Haight', *Ecclesiology*, 4 (forthcoming, 2008).

—— (ed.), *Comparative Ecclesiology: Critical Investigations* (London and New York: T. & T. Clark, forthcoming 2008).

—— and Mudge, Lewis (eds.), *The Routledge Companion to the Christian Church* (London: Routledge, 2007).

Mansi, J. D., *Sacrorum conciliorum nova et amplissima collectio*, vol. xl. (Paris and Leipzig: 1901–27).

Markham, Donna J., *Spiritlinking Leadership: Working Through Resistance to Organizational Change* (Mahwah, NY: Paulist Press, 1999).

Marris, Peter, *The Politics of Uncertainty: Attachment in Private and Public Life* (London/New York: Routledge, 1996).

Marsh, Clive, et al. (eds.), *Unmasking Methodist Theology* (London: Continuum, 2004).

Martin, David, *A General Theory of Secularisation* (Oxford: Blackwell, 1978).

—— *The Breaking of the Image* (Oxford: Blackwell, 1980).

—— 'Personal Reflections', in Richard K. Fenn (ed.), *The Blackwell Companion to Sociology of Religion* (Oxford: Blackwell, 2001), 23–38.

—— *On Secularization: Towards a Revised General Theory* (Aldershot: Ashgate, 2005).

Maximos IV, 'Intervention', *Acta Synodalia Sacrosancti Concilii Oecumenici Vaticani II*, vol. ii. (Vatican City: Typis polyglottis Vaticanis, 1972), 516–19.

Mayer, Annemarie C., 'Language Serving Unity? Linguistic–Hermeneutical Considerations of a Basic Ecumenical Problem', *Pro Ecclesia*, 15 (2006), 205–22.

Merrigan, Terrence (ed.), *John Henry Cardinal Newman, 1801–1890. A Special Issue of Louvain Studies* (Louvain: Peeters, 1990).

Methodist Church of Great Britain and the Church of England, *An Anglican–Methodist Covenant: Common Statement of the Formal Conversations between the Methodist Church of Great Britain and the Church of England* (London: Methodist Publishing House and Church House Publishing, 2001).

Metz, Johann-Baptist, *Faith in History and Society: Toward a Practical Fundamental Theology*, trans. David Smith (London: Burns & Oates, 1980).

—— 'Theology in the Modern Age, and Before its End', in Claude Geffré, Gustavo Gutiérrez, and Virgil Elizondo (eds.), *Different Theologies, Common Responsibility* (Edinburgh: T. & T. Clark, 1984).

Metz, René, 'Le Problème d'un droit de l'Église dans les milieux catholiques de la seconde moitié du XIXe siècle à la période post-conciliaire (1870–1983)', *Revue de droit canonique*, 35 (1985), 222–44.

Metzger, Marcel (ed. and trans.), *Les Constitutions apostoliques*, vol. iii., Sources chrétiennes, 336 (Paris: Cerf, 1987).

Meyendorff, John, *Orthodoxy and Catholicity* (New York: Sheed & Ward, 1966).

—— *Byzantine Theology: Historical Trends and Doctrinal Themes* (New York: Fordham University Press, 1983 [1974]).

—— (ed.), *The Primacy of Peter: Essays in Ecclesiology and the Early Church* (St Vladimir's Seminary Press, 1992).

Meyer, Harding, 'Grundkonsensus und Kirchengemeinschaft: Eine lutherische Perspektive', in André Birmelé and Harding Meyer (eds.), *Grundkonsens—Grunddifferenz: Studie des Straßburger Instituts für Ökumenische Forschung: Ergebnisse und Dokumente* (Frankfurt: Verlag Otto Lembeck, 1992), 126.

—— 'Die Prägung einer Formel: Ursprung und Intention', in Harald Wagner (ed.), *Einheit aber Wie? Zur Tragfähigkeit der ökumenischen Formels 'differenzierten Konsens'* (Freiburg: Herder, 2000), 36–58.

—— 'Differentiated Participation: The Possibility of Protestant Sharing in the Historic Office of Bishop', *Ecumenical Trends*, 34 (2005), 10–14.

—— and Vischer, Lukas (eds.), *Growth in Agreement: Reports and Agreed Statements of Ecumenical Conversations on a World Level* (Mahwah, NY and Geneva: Paulist Press/WCC, 1984).

Milbank, John, *Theology and Social Theory* (Oxford: Blackwell, 1990).

Minear, Paul, 'Ecumenical Theology—Profession or Vocation?', in Frederick Trost and Barbara Brown Zikmund (eds.), *United and Uniting*, vol. vii. (Cleveland, Ohio: Pilgrim Press, 2005), 572–5.

Ministerial Training Policy Working Group to the Methodist Council, *The Making of Ministry: The Report of the Ministerial Training Policy Working Group to the Methodist Council* (Peterborough: Methodist Publishing House, 1996).

Möhler, Johann Adam, *Unity in the Church, or, The Principle of Catholicism: Presented in the Spirit of the Church Fathers of the First Three Centuries*, trans. Peter C. Erb (Washington, DC: Catholic University of America Press, 1996 [1825]).

—— *Symbolism: Exposition of the Doctrinal Differences Between Catholics and Protestants as Evidenced by their Symbolical Writings*, trans. James Burton Robertson (New York: Crossroad, 1997 [1832]).

Moltmann, Jürgen, *A Theology of Hope: On the Ground and the Implications of a Christian Eschatology*, trans. James W. Leitch (London: SCM, 1967 [1965]).

Monneron, Jean-Louis, et al. (eds.), *L'Église, institution et foi*, 2nd edn. (Brussels: Facultés universitaires St Louis, 1985 [1979]).

Moore, Robert Ian, *The Formation of a Persecuting Society: Power and Deviance in Western Europe, 950–1250* (Oxford: Blackwell, 1994).

More, Paul Elmer, and Cross, Frank Leslie (eds.), *Anglicanism: The Thought and Practice of the Church of England, Illustrated from the Religious Literature of the Seventeenth Century* (London: SPCK, 1962 [1935]).

Morel, Henri, 'Absolutisme', in Philippe Raynaud and S. Rials (eds.), *Dictionnaire de philosophie politique* (Paris: Presses Universitaires de France, 1996), 1–9.

Morris, Jeremy, and Sagovsky, Nicholas (eds.), *The Unity We Have and the Unity We Seek: Ecumenical Prospects for the Third Millennium* (London and New York: T. & T. Clark, 2003).

Murray, Paul D., 'A Liberal Helping of Postliberalism Please', in Mark D. Chapman (ed.), *The Future of Liberal Theology* (Aldershot: Ashgate, 2002), 208–18.

—— *Reason, Truth and Theology in Pragmatist Perspective* (Leuven: Peeters, 2004).

—— 'On Valuing Truth in Practice: Rome's Postmodern Challenge', *International Journal of Systematic Theology*, 8 (2006), 163–83; also in Laurence Paul Hemming and Susan Frank Parsons (eds.), *Redeeming Truth: Considering Faith and Reason* (London: SCM, 2007), 184–206.

—— 'Catholicism and Ecumenism', in Anne Hession and Patricia Kieran (eds.), *Exploring Theology: Making Sense of the Catholic Tradition* (Dublin: Veritas, 2007), 305–16.

—— 'Theology "Under the Lash": Theology as Idolatry-Critique in the work of Nicholas Lash', in Stephen C. Barton (ed.), *Idolatry: False Worship in the Bible, Early Judaism and Christianity* (London: T. & T. Clark, 2007), 246–66.

National Review Board for the Protection of Children and Young People, *A Report on the Crisis in the Catholic Church in the United States* (Washington, DC: USCCB, 2004).

Nethoefel, Wolfgang, and Grunwald, Klaus-Dieter (eds.), *Kirchenreform Jetzt! Projekte—Analysen—Perspektiven* (Schenefeld: EB-Verlag, 2005).

Neveu, Bruno, *L'Erreur et son juge: Remarques sur les censures doctrinales à l'époque moderne* (Naples: Bibliopolis, 1993).

Newman, John Henry, *The Via Media of the Anglican Church*, 3rd edn. (London: Longmans, Green, & Co., 1877).

—— *Sermons Preached on Various Occasions* (London: Longmans, Green, & Co., 1900).

—— *Newman's University Sermons: Fifteen Sermons Preached Before the University of Oxford, 1826–43*, 3rd edn., introductions by D. M. MacKinnon and J. D. Holmes, (London: SPCK, 1970 [1871]).

—— *The Letters and Diaries of John Henry Newman*, ed. Charles Stephen Dessain, vol. xx., *Standing Firm amid Trials: July 1861 to December 1863* (London: Thomas Nelson, 1970).

—— *An Essay on the Development of Christian Doctrine* (1845), ed. J. M. Cameron (Harmondsworth: Penguin, 1974) (also rev. edn. (London: Pickering, 1878)).

—— *The Via Media of the Anglican Church*, ed. H. D. Widner, 3rd edn. (Oxford: Clarendon Press, 1990 [1877]).

Nichols, Aidan, *Theology in the Russian Diaspora: Church, Fathers, Eucharist in Nikolai Afanas'ev, 1893–1966* (Cambridge: Cambridge University Press, 1989).

—— 'The Lutheran–Catholic Agreement on Justification: Botch or Breakthrough?', *New Blackfriars*, 82 (2001), 375–86.

Nissiotis, Nikos A., 'The Main Ecclesiological Problem of the Second Vatican Council', *Journal of Ecumenical Studies*, 2 (1965), 31–62.

Nissiotis, Nikos A., 'Pneumatological Christology as a Presupposition of Ecclesiology', *Oecumenica*, 2 (1967), 235–51.

Norgren, William A., and Rusch, William G. (eds.), *'Towards Full Communion' and 'Concordat of Agreement'. Lutheran-Epislopal Dialogue USA*; 3rd Series, 1983–1991 (Cincinnati, Ind. and Minneapolis, Minn.: Augsburg & Forward Movement Publications, 1991).

—— *Called to Common Mission: A Lutheran Proposal for a Revision of the 'Concordat of Agreement'* (Chicago, Ill.: Evangelical Lutheran Church in America, 1999).

Oakley, Francis, and Russett, Bruce (eds.), *Governance, Accountability and the Future of the Catholic Church* (New York and London: Continuum, 2004).

Ochs, Peter, *Peirce, Pragmatism and the Logic of Scripture* (Cambridge: Cambridge University Press, 1998).

O'Gara, Margaret, *Triumph in Defeat: Infallibility, Vatican I, and the French Minority Bishops* (Catholic University of America Press, 1988).

—— *The Ecumenical Gift Exchange* (The Liturgical Press, 1998).

—— 'Apostolicity in Ecumenical Dialogue', *Mid-Stream*, 37 (1998), 174–212.

O'Malley, John W., 'The Scandal: A Historian's Perspective', *America*, 186 (27 May 2002), 14–17.

Örsy, Ladislas, *The Church, Learning and Teaching: Magisterium, Assent, Dissent, Academic Freedom* (Wilmington, Del.: Michael Glazier, 1987).

—— *Theology and Canon Law* (Collegeville, Minn.: Liturgical Press, 1992).

—— 'Stability and Development in Canon Law and the Case of Definitive Teaching', *Notre Dame Law Review*, 76 (2001), 863–79.

Outler, A. C. (ed.), *The Works of John Wesley*, vol. i., *Sermons I (1–33)* (Nashville, Tenn.: Abingdon Press, 1984).

Paul VI, Pope, '*Ecclesiam Suam*: Encyclical Letter on the Church in the Modern World' (6 Aug. 1964) (London: CTS, 1979 [1965]).

—— '*Apostolica Sollicitudo*: Apostolic Letter Issued Motu Proprio on Establishing the Synod of Bishops for the Universal Church' (15 Sept. 1965), *AAS*, 57 (1965), 775–80.

—— and Ramsey, Michael, 'The Common Declaration by Pope Paul VI and the Archbishop of Canterbury in 1966', in Alan C. Clark and Colin Davey (eds.), *Anglican–Roman Catholic Dialogue: The Work of the Preparatory Commission* (Oxford: Oxford University Press, 1974), 1–4.

Paulson, Steven P., 'The Augustinian Imperfection: Faith, Christ, and Imputation and Its Role in the Ecumenical Discussion of Justification', in Wayne C. Stumme (ed.), *The Gospel of Justification in Christ: Where Does the Church Stand Today?* (Grand Rapids, Mich.: Eerdmans, 2006), 104–24.

Pecklers, Keith, 'Il pellegrinaggio cristiano: ritorno alle sorgenti della grazia', *Ecclesia Orans*, 16 (1999), 101–7.

—— *Dynamic Equivalence: The Living Language of Christian Worship* (Collegeville, Min.: Liturgical Press, 2003).

Pellew, Mark (ed.), *Anglicanism and the Western Christian Tradition: Continuity and Change* (Norwich: Jarrold Publishing, 2002).

Pesch, Otto H., *Die Theologie der Rechtfertigung bei Martin Luther und Thomas von Aquin* (Mainz: Matthias Grünewald Verlag, 1985 [1967]).

Phillips, Peter, 'Necessary Fictions, Real Presences', in Geoffrey Turner and John Sullivan (eds.), *Explorations in Catholic Theology* (Dublin: Lindisfarne Books, 1999), 195–207.

Pius XII, Pope, '*Sempiternus Rex Christus*: Encyclical Letter on the Council of Chalcedon' (8 Sept. 1951), *AAS*, 43 (1951), 625–44.

Podmore, Colin (ed.), *Together in Mission and Ministry: The Porvoo Common Statement with Essays on Church and Ministry in Northern Europe (Conversations Between the British and Irish Anglican Churches and the Nordic and Baltic Lutheran Churches)* (London: Church House Publishing, 1993).

——*Anglican–Moravian Conversations: The Fetter Lane Common Statement with Essays in Moravian and Anglican History*, Council for Christian Unity, Occasional Paper, 5 (London: Church House Publishing, 1996).

——*Community—Unity—Communion: Essays in Honour of Mary Tanner* (London: Church House Publishing, 1998).

——*Called to Witness and Service: The Reuilly Common Statement with Essays* (London: Church House Publishing, 1999).

Pöhlmann, Horst Georg (ed.), *Unser Glaube: Die Bekenntnisschriften der evangelisch-lutherischen Kirche* (Gütersloh: Gütersloher Verlagshau, 2000).

Pontifical Council for Promoting Christian Unity, *Directory for the Application of Principles and Norms on Ecumenism* (London: CTS, 1993).

——'Reports to the PCPCU Plenary: Petrine Ministry', *Information Service*, 109 (2002), 29–42.

——'Visit to Rome of the Archbishop of Canterbury Dr Rowan Williams', *Information Service*, 114 (2003), 173–80.

——'Visit to Rome by Representatives of the World Methodist Council', *Information Service*, 120 (2005), 163–4.

Pottmeyer, Hermann, 'The Reception Process: The Challenge at the Threshold of a New Phase of the Ecumenical Movement', in Lawrence S. Cunningham (ed.), *Ecumenism: Present Realities and Future Prospects, Papers Read at the Tantur Ecumenical Center, Jerusalem, 1997* (Notre Dame, Ind.: University of Notre Dame Press, 1998), 149–68.

Provost, James H., 'Towards Some Operative Principles for Apostolic Visitations', *The Jurist*, 49 (1989), 543–67.

Pseftongas, B., 'L'unità nella Chiesa e le istituzioni che l'esprimono', in Antonio Acerbi (ed.), *Il ministero del Papa in prospettiva ecumenica* (Milan: Vita e Pensiero, 1999), 33–50.

Puglisi, James F., *The Process of Admission to the Ordained Ministry: A Comparative Study*, vols. i–iii. (Collegeville, Minn.: Liturgical Press, 1996–2001).

——'Ecumenical Developments in Ordination Rites', in Tamara Grdzelidze (ed.), *One, Holy, Catholic and Apostolic. Ecumenical Reflections on the Church* (Geneva: WCC, 2005), 226–41.

——(ed.), *Petrine Ministry and the Unity of the Church* (Collegeville, Minn.: Liturgical Press, 1999).

——(ed.), *Liturgical Renewal as a Way to Christian Unity* (Collegeville, Minn.: Liturgical Press, 2005).

Purcell, Michael, *Lévinas and Theology* (Cambridge: Cambridge University Press, 2006).

Putney, Michael E., 'The Holy Trinity and Ecumenism', in Winifred Wing, Han Lamb and Ian Barns (eds.), *God Down Under: Theology in the Antipodes* (Adelaide: Australian Theological Forum, 2003), 23–39.

—— 'A Roman Catholic Understanding of Ecumenical Dialogue', *Ecclesiology 2* (2005), 179–194.

Quinn, John R., *The Reform of the Papacy: The Costly Call to Christian Unity* (New York: Crossroad, 1999).

Rahner, Karl, 'The Hermeneutics of Eschatological Assertions' (1960), *Theological Investigations*, vol. iv., trans. Kevin Smyth (London: Darton, Longman & Todd, 1966), 323–46.

—— 'The Church of Sinners' (1947), *Theological Investigations*, vol. vi., trans. Karl-Heinz Kruger and Boniface Kruger (London: Darton, Longman & Todd, 1969), 253–69.

—— 'Justified and Sinner at the Same Time' (1963), *Theological Investigations*, vol. vi., trans. Karl-H. Kruger and Boniface Kruger (London: Darton, Longman & Todd, 1969), 218–30.

—— 'The Sinful Church in the Decrees of Vatican II' (1965), *Theological Investigations*, vol. vi., trans. Karl-H. Kruger and Boniface Kruger (London: Darton, Longman & Todd, 1969), 270–94.

—— 'Dialogue in the Church' (1967), *Theological Investigations*, vol. x., trans. David Bourke (London: Darton, Longman & Todd, 1973), 103–21.

—— 'On the Theology of Hope' (1968), *Theological Investigations*, vol. x., trans. David Bourke (London: Darton, Longman & Todd, 1973), 242–59.

—— *The Shape of the Church to Come*, trans. Edward Quinn (London: SPCK, 1974 [1972]).

Raiser, Konrad, *Ecumenism in Transition: A Paradigm Shift in the Ecumenical Movement?*, trans. Tony Coates (Geneva: WCC, 1991 [1989]).

Ramsey, A. M., *The Gospel and the Catholic Church* (London: Longmans, 1936).

Ratzinger, Joseph, 'The Pastoral Implications of Episcopal Collegiality', *Concilium*, 1 (1965), 20–34.

—— 'La Collégialité épiscopale, développement théologique', in G. Baraúna (ed.), *L'Eglise de Vatican II. Études autour de la constitution conciliaire sur l'Église*, vol. iii. (Paris: Cerf, 1966), 763–90.

—— 'Catholicism after the Council', *The Furrow*, 18 (1967), 3–23.

—— *Introduction to Christianity*, trans. J. R. Foster (London: Burns & Oates, 1969 [1968]).

—— 'Pastoral Constitution on the Church in the Modern World', Herbert Vorgrimler (ed.), *Commentary on the Documents of Vatican II*, vol. v., trans. W. J. O'Hara (London: Burns & Oates, 1969), 115–63.

—— *Principles of Catholic Theology: Building Stones for a Fundamental Theology*, trans. Mary Frances McCarthy (San Francisco, Calif.: Ignatius Press, 1987 [1982]).

—— *Church, Ecumenism and Politics: New Essays in Ecclesiology*, trans. Robert Nowell (Slough: St Paul, 1988 [1987]).

—— 'Briefwechsel von Landesbischof Johannes Hanselmann und Joseph Kardinal Ratzinger über das Communio-Schreiben der Römischen Glaubenskongregation', *Una Sancta*, 48 (1993), 347–52.

—— *The Spirit of the Liturgy*, trans. John Saward (San Francisco, Calif.: Ignatius Press, 2000).

—— 'The Augsburg Concord on Justification: How Far Does it Take Us?', trans. David Law, *International Journal for the Study of the Christian Church*, 1 (2002), 5–20 (20).

Rausch, Thomas P., 'Reception Past and Present', *Theological Studies*, 47 (1986), 497–508.

Raynaud, Philippe, and Rials, S. (eds.), *Dictionnaire de philosophie politique* (Paris: Presses Universitaires de France, 1996).

Reardon, Ruth, '*One Bread One Body:* A Commentary from an Interchurch Family Point of View', *One in Christ*, 35 (1999), 109–30.

Reese, Thomas J., *Archbishop: Inside the Power Structure of the American Catholic Church* (San Francisco, Calif.: Harper & Row, 1989).

—— (ed.), *Episcopal Conference: Historical, Canonical and Theological Studies* (Washington, DC: Georgetown University Press, 1989).

—— *A Flock of Shepherds: The National Conference of Catholic Bishops* (Kansas City, Miss.: Sheed & Ward, 1992).

—— *Inside the Vatican: The Politics and Organization of the Catholic Church* (Cambridge, Mass.: Harvard University Press, 1996).

—— '2001 and Beyond: Preparing the Church for the Next Millennium,' *America* (21–28 June 1997), 10–18.

Reno, Rusty R., 'The Debilitation of the Churches', in Carl E. Braaten and Robert W. Jenson (eds.), *The Ecumenical Future: Background Papers for* In One Body Through the Cross: The Princeton Proposal for Christian Unity (Grand Rapids, Mich. and Cambridge: Eerdmans, 2004), 46–72.

Rescher, Nicholas, *A System of Pragmatic Idealism*, vol. i., *Human Knowledge in Idealistic Perspective* (Princeton, NJ: Princeton University Press, 1992).

—— *A System of Pragmatic Idealism*, vol. ii., *The Validity of Values* (Princeton, NJ: Princeton University Press, 1993).

—— 'Précis of *A System of Pragmatic Idealism*', *Philosophy and Phenomenological Research*, 54 (1994), 377–90.

—— *A System of Pragmatic Idealism*, vol. iii., *Metaphilosophical Inquiries* (Princeton, NJ: Princeton University Press, 1994).

Richter, Philip, 'Denominational Cultures: The Cinderella of Congregational Studies?', in Mathew Guest, Karin Tusting, and Linda Woodhead (eds.), *Congregational Studies in the UK: Christianity in a Post-Christian Context* (Aldershot: Ashgate, 2004), 169–84.

Ricœur, Paul, *History and Truth* (Evanston, Ill.: Northwestern University Press, 1965).

—— *The Conflict of Interpretations: Essays in Hermeneutics* (Evanston, Ill.: Northwestern University Press, 1974).

—— *The Rule of Metaphor: Multi-Disciplinary Studies of the Creation of Meaning in Language* (London: Routledge & Kegan Paul, 1978), 9–13.

—— *Oneself as Another*, trans. Kathleen Blamey (Chicago, Ill.: Chicago University Press, 1992 [1990]).

—— *Figuring the Sacred: Religion, Narrative and Imagination*, ed. Mark I. Wallace, trans. David Pellauer (Minneapolis, Minn.: Fortress Press, 1995).

—— *Totality and Infinity: An Essay on Exteriority*, trans. Alphonso Lingis (Pittsburgh, Penn.: Duquesne University Press, 1998 [1961]).

Ritschl, Dietrich, *The Logic of Theology: A Brief Account of the Relationship Between Basic Concepts in Theology*, trans. John Bowden (London: SCM, 1986 [1984]).

Roberts, Alexander, and Donaldson, James (ed. and trans.), *The Ante-Nicene Fathers*, rev. A. Cleveland Coxe (Grand Rapids, MI: Eerdmans, 1996 [1885]).

Rodger, P. C., and Vischer, L. (eds.), *Scripture, Tradition and Traditions: The Fourth World Conference on Faith and Order, Montreal 1963* (Faith and Order Paper, No. 42) (London: SCM, 1994 [1964]).

Roman Catholic Church, *The Divine Office: Liturgy of the Hours According to the Roman Rite, Approved for Use in Australia, England & Wales, Ireland, New Zealand, Scotland*, vol. ii. (London and Glasgow: Collins, 1974).

—— *Codex iuris canonici auctoritate Ioannis Pauli PP. II promulgatus* (Vatican City: Libreria Editrice Vaticana, 1983).

—— '*Baptism, Eucharist and Ministry*: An Appraisal. Vatican Response to WCC Document', *Origins*, 17 (19 Nov. 1987).

—— *Catechism of the Catholic Church* (1992) (London: Geoffrey Chapman, 1994).

—— *Code of Canon Law Annotated, Prepared Under the Responsibility of the Instituto Martín de Azpilcueta*, 2nd English edn. (rev. and updated) of the 6th Spanish edn., ed. E. Caparros and H. Aubé, with J. I. Arrieta, et al. (Montreal: Wilson and Lafleur, 2004).

Roman Catholic–Presbyterian/Reformed Consultation, *Laity in the Church and the World: Resources for Ecumenical Dialogue* (Washington, DC: US Catholic Bishops' Conference, 1998).

Romanides, John S., 'The Ecclesiology of St Ignatius of Antioch', *Greek Orthodox Theological Review*, 7 (1961–2), 53–77.

Root, Michael, 'Catholic and Evangelical Theology', *Pro Ecclesia*, 15 (2006), 9–16.

Rosmini, Antonio, *The Five Wounds of the Church*, trans. Denis Cleary (Leominster: Fowler Wright, 1987 [1848]).

Rotelle, John E. (ed.), *The Works of Saint Augustine: A Translation for the 21st Century. Part III, Sermons*, vol. vii., *Sermons (230–272B) On the Liturgical Seasons*, trans. Edmund Hill (New York: New City Press, 1993).

Rouco Varela, A. M., 'Grundfragen einer katholischen Theologie des Kirchenrechts: Überlegungen zum Aufbau einer katholischen Theologie des Kirchenrechts', *Archiv für katholisches Kirchenrecht*, 148 (1979), 341–52.

—— *Schriften zur Theologie des Kirchenrechts und zur Kirchenverfassung* (Paderborn: Schöning Verlag, 2000).

Rowell, Geoffrey, Stevenson, Kenneth, and Williams, Rowan, *Love's Redeeming Work: The Anglican Quest for Holiness* (Oxford: Oxford University Press, 2001).

Runcie, Robert, 'Archbishop Robert Runcie to Cardinal Jan Willebrands' (22 Nov. 1985), *Origins*, 16 (1986–7), 156–8 (also in *Information Service*) 61 (1986), 107–9.

Rusch, William G., *Reception: An Ecumenical Opportunity* (Philadelphia, Penn.: Fortress Press, 1988).

—— 'The History and Methodology of the *Joint Declaration on Justification*: A Case Study in Ecumenical Reception', in Jean-Marie Tillard (ed.), *Agapè. Études en l'honneur de Mgr Pierre Duprey M. Afr.* (Chambésy and Geneva: Centre orthodoxe du Patriarcat œcuménique, 2000), 169–84.

—— (ed.), *Justification and the Future of the Ecumenical Movement: The Joint Declaration on the Doctrine of Justification* (Collegeville, Minn.: Liturgical Press, 2003).

—— 'Structures of Unity: The Next Ecumenical Challenge—A Possible Way Forward', *Ecumenical Trends*, 34 (2005), 1–8.

—— *Ecumenical Reception: Its Challenge and Opportunity* (Grand Rapids, Mich.: and Cambridge: Eerdmans, 2007).

Rush, Ormond, *The Reception of Doctrine: An Appropriation of Hans Robert Jauss' Reception Aesthetics and Literary Hermeneutics* (Rome: Pontificia Università Gregoriana, 1997).

—— *Still Interpreting Vatican II: Some Hermeneutical Principles* (New York: Paulist Press, 2004).

Russian Orthodox Patriarchal Church in Great Britain and Ireland, Diocese of Sourozh, *Diocesan Statutes*, rev. edn. (Oxford: St Stephen's Press, 2001 [1998]).

Ryan, Desmond, *The Catholic Parish: Institutional Discipline, Tribal Identity and Religious Development in the English Church* (London: Sheed & Ward, 1996).

Ryan, Thomas, *A Survival Guide for Ecumenically Minded Christians* (Collegeville, Minn.: Liturgical Press, 1989).

Rynne, Xavier, *Letters From Vatican City: Vatican Council II (First Session), Background and Debates* (London: Faber & Faber, 1963).

—— *The Second Session: The Debates and Decrees of Vatican Council II, September 29 to December 4, 1963* (London: Faber & Faber, 1964).

Sachs, William L., *The Transformation of Anglicanism* (Cambridge: Cambridge University Press, 1993).

Sagovsky, Nicholas, *Ecumenism, Christian Origins and the Practice of Communion* (Cambridge: Cambridge University Press, 2000).

—— and Morris, Jeremy (ed.), *The Unity We Have and the Unity We Seek: Ecumenical Prospects for the Third Millennium* (London and New York: Continuum, 2003).

Saliers, Donald E., 'Liturgy and Ethics: Some New Beginnings', in Ronald Hamel and Kenneth Himes (eds.), *Introduction to Christian Ethics: A Reader* (Mahwah, NY: Paulist Press, 1989), 175–86.

Schatz, Klaus, *Papal Primacy: From its Origins to the Present*, trans. John A. Otto and Linda M. Maloney (Collegeville, Minn.: Liturgical Press, 1996 [1990]).

Schein, Edgar H., *The Corporate Culture Survival Guide* (San Francisco, Calif.: Jossey-Bass, 1999).

Scherle, Peter, 'Nachhaltige Kirchenentwicklung', in Wolfgang Nethoefel and Klaus-Dieter Grunwald (eds.), *Kirchenreform Jetzt! Projekte—Analysen—Perspektiven* (Schenefeld: EB-Verlag, 2005), 39–60.

Schlink, Edmund, *The Coming Christ and the Coming Church*, trans. I. H. Neilson (Edinburgh and London: Oliver & Boyd, 1967).

Schmemann, Alexander, *For the Life of the World* (Crestwood, NY: St Vladimir's, 1973).

—— *The Eucharist* (Crestwood, NY: St Vladimir's, 1988).

Schmidt, Peter, 'Ministries in the New Testament and the Early Church', in Jan Kerkhofs (ed.), *Europe Without Priests?* (London: SCM, 1995), 41–88.

Schüssler Fiorenza, Francis, 'The Conflict of Hermeneutical Traditions and Christian Theology', *Journal of Chinese Philosophy*, 27 (2003), 3–31.

Secretariat for Promoting Christian Unity, 'Reflections and Suggestions Concerning Dialogue' (15 Aug. 1970), in Austin Flannery (ed.), *Vatican Council II: The Conciliar and Post Conciliar Documents* (Leominster: Fowler Wright, 1980 [1975]), 535–53.

Selfridge, Richard L., and Sokolik, Stanley L., 'A Comprehensive View of Organization Management', *MSU Business Topics*, 23 (1975), 46–61.

Sennett, Richard, *The Uses of Disorder: Personal Identity and City Life* (London: Faber & Faber, 1996).

Sesboüé, Bernard, 'Groupe des Dombes', in Nicholas Lossky, et al. (eds.), *Dictionary of the Ecumenical Movement*, 2nd edn. (Geneva: WCC, 2002), 503–5.

Sheldrake, Philip, 'Practising Catholic "Place"—The Eucharist', *Horizons: The Journal of the College Theology Society*, 28 (2001), 163–82.

Sheppard, David, and Worlock, Derek, *Better Together: Christian Partnership in a Hurt City* (Harmondsworth: Penguin, 1989).

Shevzov, Vera, *Russian Orthodoxy on the Eve of Revolution* (New York: Oxford University Press, 2004).

Sharkey, Michael (ed.), *International Theological Commission: Texts and Documents, 1969–1985* (San Francisco, Calif.: Ignatius Press, 1989).

Shortt, Rupert, *God's Advocates. Christian Thinkers in Conversation* (London: Darton, Longman & Todd, 2005).

Smith, Jonathan Z., *Map is Not Territory: Studies in the History of Religions* (Leiden: Brill, 1978).

Smyth, Geraldine, *A Way of Transformation: A Theological Evaluation of the Conciliar Process of Mutual Commitment to Justice, Peace and the Integrity of Creation, World Council of Churches, 1983–1991* (Berne: Peter Lang, 1995).

—— 'Envisaging a New Identity and a Common Home: Seeking Peace on our Borders', *Milltown Studies*, 46 (2000), 58–84.

—— 'Churches in Ireland—Journeys in Identity and Communion', *Ecumenical Review*, 53 (2001), 155–66.

—— 'A Habitable Grief: Forgiveness and Reconciliation for a People Divided', *Milltown Studies*, 53 (2004), 94–130.

Smyth, Geraldine and Pierce, Andrew (eds.), *The Critical Spirit: Theology at the Crossroads of Faith and Culture* (Dublin: Columba Press, 2003).

Sobanski, Remigiusz, *Grundlagenproblematik des katholischen Kirchenrechts* (Vienna and Cologne: Böhlau Verlag, 1987).

Spohn, William, *Go and Do Likewise: Jesus and Ethics* (New York: Continuum, 1999).

Spurr, J., 'The Church of England, Comprehension and the Toleration Act of 1689', *English Historical Review*, 54 (1989), 927–46.

Stacpoole, Alberic, 'Early Ecumenism, Early Yves Congar, 1904–1940', *The Month*, 21 (1988), 502–10.

—— 'Early Ecumenism, Early Yves Congar, 1904–1940, Part II', *The Month*, 21 (1988), 623–31.

Staples, Peter, 'Apostolicity', in Nicholas Lossky, et al. (eds.), *Dictionary of the Ecumenical Movement*, 2nd edn. (Geneva: WCC, 2002), 49–53.

Stolz, Fritz, *Grundzüge der Religionswissenschaft* (Göttingen: Vandenhoeck & Ruprecht, 1988).

Strachey, James (ed.), *The Standard Edition of the Complete Psychological Works of Sigmund Freud*, vol. xi. (1911), *Five Lectures on Psycho-analysis; Leonardo da Vinci; and Other Works* (London: Hogarth Press, 1957).

—— *The Standard Edition of the Complete Psychological Works of Sigmund Freud*, vol. xiv. *(1914–16)*, *The History of the Psycho-Analytic Movement: Papers on Metapsychology and Other Works* (London: Hogarth Press, 1957).

—— *The Standard Edition of the Complete Psychological Works of Sigmund Freud*, vol. xix. (1923–5), *The Ego, the Id and Other Works* (London: Hogarth Press, 1961).

—— *The Standard Edition of the Complete Psychological Works of Sigmund Freud*, vol. xxi. *(1927–31)*, *The Future of an Illusion; Civilization and its Discontents, and Other Works* (London: Hogarth Press, 1961).

Striet, M., 'Denkformgenese und analyse in der Überlieferungsgeschichte des Glaubens. Theologisch-hermeneutische Überlegungen zum Begriff des differenzierten Konsenses', in Harald Wagner (ed.), *Einheit aber Wie? Zur Tragfähigkeit der ökumenischen Formels 'differenzierten Konsens'* (Freiburg: Herder, 2000), 59–80.

Stumme, Wayne C. (ed.), *The Gospel of Justification in Christ: Where Does the Church Stand Today?* (Grand Rapids, Mich.: Eerdmans, 2006).

Sullivan, Francis A., 'The Impact of *Dominus Iesus* on Ecumenism', *America*, 183 (28 Oct. 2000), 8–11.

—— *From Apostles to Bishops: The Development of the Episcopacy in the Early Church* (Mahwah, NY: Newman Press, 2001).

—— 'St Cyprian on the Role of the Laity in Decision Making in the Early Church', in Stephen J. Pope (ed.), *Common Calling: The Laity and Governance of the Catholic Church* (Washington, DC: Georgetown, 2004), 39–49.

Svetozarsky, Alexei, *The 1917–18 Council of the Russian Orthodox Church* (Oxford: St Stephen's Press, 2003).

Swan, Darlis J., 'The Impact of the Bilateral Dialogues on Selected Religious Education Materials Published by the Lutheran Church in America', PhD thesis, Catholic University of America, 1988.

Swatos Jr., William H., and Olson, Daniel V. (eds.), *The Secularization Debate* (Lanham Md., Boulder Colo., New York and Oxford: Rowman & Littlefield, 2000).

Sweeney, James, 'Catholicism and Freedom: *Dignitatis Humanae*—The Text and its Reception', in E. Arweck and P. Collins (eds.), *Reading Religion in Text and Context* (Aldershot: Ashgate, 2006), 17–33.

Swift, Roger, and Gilley, Sheridan (eds.), *The Irish in Victorian Britain: The Local Dimension* (Dublin: Four Courts Press, 1999).

Sykes, Stephen W., *The Integrity of Anglicanism* (London: Mowbray, 1978).

—— and Booty, J. (eds.), *The Study of Anglicanism* (London: SPCK, 1988).

Tabart, Jill, *Coming to Consensus: A Case Study for the Churches* (Geneva: WCC, 2003).

Taft, Robert F., 'Mass Without the Consecration? The Historic Agreement on the Eucharist Between the Catholic Church and the Assyrian Church of the East, Promulgated 26th October 2001', in James F. Puglisi (ed.), *Liturgical Renewal as a Way to Christian Unity* (Collegeville, Minn.: Liturgical Press, 2005), 199–226.

Tanner, Mary, 'A Unique Meeting in Mississauga', *One in Christ*, 39 (2004), 3–6.

Tanner, Norman P. (ed.), *Decrees of the Ecumenical Councils*, vol. ii., Trent to Vatican II (London: Sheed & Ward, 1990 [1972]).

Tavard, George, 'For a Theology of Dialogue', *One in Christ*, 15 (1979), 11–20.

—— *The Church, Community of Salvation: An Ecumenical Ecclesiology* (Collegeville, Minn.: Liturgical Press, 1992).

—— '*The Final Report*: Witness to Tradition', *One in Christ*, 32 (1996), 118–29.

—— 'Overcoming the Anathemas: A Catholic View,' in J. Burgess and M. Kolden (eds.), *By Faith Alone* (Grand Rapids, Mich.: Eerdmans, 2004), 140–66.

—— 'Hospitality as an Ecumenical Paradigm', *Bulletin of the Centro Pro Unione*, 69 (2006), 9–19.

Telford, John, *The Life of John Wesley*, 4th edn. (London: Epworth, 1924 [1906]).

—— (ed.), *The Letters of the Rev. John Wesley*, vol. viii., *July 24, 1787 to February 24, 1791* (London: Epworth, 1931).

Temple (Archbishop of Canterbury), Frederick, and Maclagan (Archbishop of York), William, '*Saepius Officio*: Answer of the Archbishops of England to the Apostolic Letter of Pope Leo XIII on English Ordinations' (19 Feb. 1897), in William R. Franklin (ed.), *Anglican Orders: Essays on the Centenary of* Apostolicae Curae, 1896–1996 (London: Mowbray, 1996), 138–49.

Theissen, Gerd, *A Theory of Primitive Christian Religion* (London: SCM, 1999).

Thiel, John E., *Senses of Tradition: Continuity and Development in Catholic Faith* (Oxford: Oxford University Press, 2000).

Thurian, Max. (ed.), *Churches Respond to BEM: Official Responses to the Baptism, Eucharist and Ministry Text*, vols. i–vi. (Geneva: WCC, 1986–8).

Tillard, Jean-Marie R., *The Bishop of Rome*, trans. John de Satgé (London: SPCK, 1983 [1982]).

—— 'Tradition, Reception', in Kenneth Hagen (ed.), *The Quadrilog: Tradition and the Future of Ecumenism. Essays in Honor of George H. Tavard* (Collegeville, Minn: Liturgical Press, 1994), 328–43.

—— 'La Réception comme exigence œcuménique', in G. R. Evans and M. Gourgues (eds.), *Communion et réunion. Mélanges J.-M. R. Tillard* (Leuven: Leuven University Press, 1995), 75–94.

—— 'Authentic *Koinonia*, Confessional Diversity', in Colin Podmore (ed.), *Community—Unity—Communion: Essays in Honour of Mary Tanner* (London: Church House Publishing, 1998), 262–73.

Tilley, Terrence W., *Inventing Catholic Tradition* (Maryknoll, NY: Orbis, 2000).

Tillich, Paul, *The Protestant Era*, trans. and ed. James Luther Adams (London: Nisbet, 1951).

—— *Systematic Theology*, vol. i. (Chicago: Chicago University Press, 1951).

Tjørhom, Ola, *Visible Church—Visible Unity: Ecumenical Ecclesiology and 'The Great Tradition of the Church'* (Collegeville, MN: Liturgical Press, 2004).

Tracy, David, *The Analogical Imagination: Christian Theology and the Culture of Pluralism* (London: SCM, 1981).

—— 'The Uneasy Alliance Reconceived: Catholic Theological Method, Modernity and Postmodernity', *Theological Studies*, 50 (1989), 548–70.

—— *Dialogue with the Other: The Inter-Religious Dialogue* (Leuven: Peeters, 1990).

—— *On Naming the Present: God, Hermeneutics, and Church* (Maryknoll, NY: Orbis Books, 1994).

Trost, Frederick, and Brown Zikmund, Barbara (eds.), *United and Uniting*, vol. vii. (Cleveland, Ohio: Pilgrim Press, 2005).

Turner, Geoffrey, and Sullivan, John (eds.), *Explorations in Catholic Theology* (Dublin: Lindisfarne Books, 1999).

Turner, Henry Ernest William, *The Pattern of Christian Truth* (London: Mowbray, 1954).

Turner, Victor, *The Ritual Process: Structure and Anti-structure* (Chicago, Ill.: Aldine, 1970).

United Methodist–Roman Catholic Dialogue, *Through Divine Love: The Church in Each Place and All Places* (Washington, DC: USCCB, 2005).

United States Conference of Catholic Bishops, *Co-workers in the Vineyard of the Lord: A Resource for Guiding the Development of Lay Ecclesial Ministry* (Washington, DC: USCCB, 2005).

US Lutheran–Roman Catholic Dialogue, in Randall Lee and Jeffrey Gros (eds.), *The Church as Koinonia of Salvation: Its Structures and Ministries. Lutherans and Catholics in Dialogue*, vol. x., *Agreed Statement of the Tenth Round of the US Lutheran–Roman Catholic Dialogue with Background Papers* (Washington, DC: USCCB, 2005).

Vandervelde, George, 'Vatican Ecumenism at the Crossroads? The Vatican Approach to Differences with BEM', *Gregorianum*, 69 (1988), 689–711.

Vanderwilt, Jeffrey T., *A Church Without Borders: The Eucharist and the Church in Ecumenical Perspective* (Collegeville, Minn.: Michael Glazier, 1998).

—— 'Eucharistic Sharing: Revising the Question', *Theological Studies*, 63 (2002), 826–39 (837).

Vatican I., '*Dei Filius*: Dogmatic Constitution on the Catholic Faith' (24 Apr. 1870), in Norman P. Tanner (ed.), *Decrees of the Ecumenical Councils*, vol. ii. (London: Sheed & Ward, 1990 [1972]), 804–11.

Vatican II: '*Dignitatis Humanae*: Declaration on Religious Liberty' (7 Dec. 1965), in Austin Flannery (ed.), *Vatican Council II: The Conciliar and Post-Conciliar Documents* (Leominster: Fowler Wright, 1980 [1975]), 799–812.

—— '*Gaudium et Spes*: Pastoral Constitution on the Church in the Modern World' (7 Dec. 1965), in Austin Flannery (ed.), *Vatican Council II: The Conciliar and Post-Conciliar Documents* (Leominster: Fowler Wright, 1980 [1975]), 903–1001.

—— '*Lumen Gentium*: Dogmatic Constitution on the Church' (21 Nov. 1964), in Austin Flannery (ed.), *Vatican Council II: The Conciliar and Post-Conciliar Documents* (Leominster: Fowler Wright, 1980 [1975]), 305–423.

—— '*Unitatis Redintegratio*: The Decree on Ecumenism' (21 Nov. 1964), in Austin Flannery (ed.), *Vatican Council II: The Conciliar and Post-Conciliar Documents* (Leominster: Fowler Wright, 1980 [1975]), 452–70.

Vaughan, Henry, 'The Night', in *The Metaphysical Poets*, ed. Helen Gardner, 13th edn. (Harmondsworth: Penguin, 1973), 280–1.

Visser 't Hooft, Willelm Adolph (ed.), *The First Assembly of the World Council of Churches Held at Amsterdam August 22nd to September 4th, 1948* (London: SCM, 1949).

Volkan, Vamik, *Bloodlines: From Ethnic Pride to Ethnic Terrorism* (Boulder, Colo.: Westview Press, 1997).

Vorgrimler, Herbert (ed.), *Commentary on the Documents of Vatican II*, vol. ii. (London: Burns & Oates, 1968 [1967]).

Wainwright, Geoffrey, *Is the Reformation Over? Catholics and Protestants at the Turn of the Millennia* (Milwaukee, Wis.: Marquette University Press, 2000).

—— 'The Global Structures of Ecumenism', in Carl E. Braaten and Robert W. Jenson (eds.), *The Ecumenical Future. Background Papers for In One Body Through the Cross: The Princeton Proposal for Christian Unity* (Grand Rapids, Mich. and Cambridge: Eerdmans, 2004), 11–28.

Wagner, Harald (ed.), *Einheit aber Wie? Zur Tragfähigkeit der ökumenischen Formels 'differenzierten Konsens'* (Freiburg: Herder, 2000).

Waldgogel, S., Coolidge, J., and Hahn, P., 'The Development, Meaning and Management of School Phobia', *American Journal of Ortho-Psychiatry*, 27 (1957), 754–80.

Wallace, Mark I. (ed.), *Figuring the Sacred: Religion, Narrative and Imagination*, trans. David Pellauer (Minneapolis, Minn.: Fortress Press, 1995).

Ware, Kallistos, 'Through the Creation to the Creator', *Ecotheology*, 2 (1997), 8–30.

—— 'St Nicolas Cabasilas on the Eucharistic Sacrifice', in Archimandrite Job Getcha and Michel Stavrou (eds.), *Le Feu sur la terre: mélanges offerts au Père Boris Bobrinskoy pour son 80ᵉ anniversaire* (Paris: Presses Saint-Serge, 2005), 141–53.

Weigel, George, *The Truth of Catholicism: Inside the Essential Teachings and Controversies of the Church Today* (New York: HarperCollins, 2001).

Wesley, John, 'To Frances Godfrey' (2 Aug. 1789), in John Telford (ed.), *The Letters of the Rev. John Wesley*, vol. viii., *July 24, 1787 to February 24, 1791* (London: Epworth, 1931), 158.

—— The Means of Grace' (Sermon 16), in A. C. Outler (ed.), *The Works of John Wesley*, vol. i., *Sermons I (1–33)* (Nashville Tenn.: Abingdon Press, 1984), 376–97.

—— 'Advice to the People called Methodists' (1745), in R. E. Davies (ed.), *The Works of John Wesley*, vol. ix., *The Methodist Societies—History, Nature and Design* (Nashville, Tenn.: Abingdon Press, 1989), 123–31.

—— 'Hymns for Christian Friends', in Franz Hildebrandt and Oliver A. Beckerlegge (eds.), with the Assistance of James Dale, *The Works of John Wesley*, vol. vii., *A Collection of Hymns for the Use of the People Called Methodists* (Nashville, Tenn.: Abingdon Press, 1989), 685.

—— 'The Nature, Design and General Rules of the United Societies in London, Bristol, Kingswood, and Newcastle upon Tyne' (1743), in R. E. Davies (ed.), *The Works of John Wesley*, vol. ix., *The Methodist Societies—History, Nature and Design* (Nashville, Tenn.: Abingdon Press, 1989), 67–75.

—— 'A Plain Account of the People Called Methodists' (1749), in R. E. Davies (ed.), *The Works of John Wesley*, vol. ix., *The Methodist Societies—History, Nature and Design* (Nashville, Tenn.: Abingdon Press, 1989), 254–80.

Wesleyan Methodist Church, *Minutes of the Methodist Conferences*, vol. i. (1744–98) (London: John Mason, 1862 [1812]).

Wilber, Ken, *A Sociable God: A Brief Introduction to a Transcendental Sociology* (New York: McGraw-Hill, 1983).

—— *The Eye of Spirit: An Integral Vision for a World Gone Slightly Mad* (Boston, Mass. and London: Shambhala Publications, 1997).

Willebrands, Jan, 'Anglican–Roman Catholic Dialogue', *One in Christ*, 15 (1979), 290–304.

Williams, Rowan, 'Does it Make Sense to Speak of Pre-Nicene Orthodoxy?', in Williams (ed.), *The Making of Orthodoxy: Essays in Honour of Henry Chadwick* (Cambridge: Cambridge University Press, 1989), 1–23.

—— and Sheldrake, Philip, 'Catholic Persons: Images of Holiness. A Dialogue', in Jeffrey John (ed.), *Living the Mystery: Affirming Catholicism and the Future of Anglicanism* (London: Darton, Longman & Todd, 1994), 76–89.

—— *On Christian Theology* (Oxford: Blackwell, 2000).

—— *Lost Icons: Reflections on Cultural Bereavement* (Edinburgh: T. & T. Clark, 2000).

—— 'Keynote Address', in *May They All Be One...But How?, Proceedings of the Conference Held in St Albans Cathedral on 17 May 2003* (St Albans: St Albans Centre for Christian Studies, 2003), 5–10.

—— 'Christian Theology and Other Faiths', in Michael Ipgrave (ed.), *Scriptures in Dialogue: Christians and Muslims Studying the Bible and Qur'an Together* (London: Church House Publishing, 2004), 131–43.

—— 'Saint Benedict and the Future of Europe: Speech Given at St Anselmo in Rome' (21 Nov. 2006), *The Tablet* (25 Nov. 2006), 8–11.

Wood, Susan K. (ed.), *Ordering the Baptismal Priesthood* (Collegeville, Minn.: Liturgical Press, 2003).

World Council of Churches, 'Scripture, Tradition and Traditions: Report of Section II', in P. C. Rodger and Lukas Vischer (eds.), *The Fourth World Conference on Faith and Order: The Report from Montreal 1963* (New York: Association Press, 1964).

World Council of Churches, 'Towards Unity in Tension', in Günther Gassmann (ed.), *Documentary History of Faith and Order, 1968–1993* (Geneva: WCC, 1993), 144–7.

Wright, Frank, 'Reconciling the Histories of Protestant and Catholic in Northern Ireland', in Alan D. Falconer and Joseph Liechty (eds.), *Reconciling Memories*, 2nd edn. (Blackrock, Co. Dublin: Columba Press, 1998 [1988]), 128–48.

Wright, N. T., and Stancliffe, David, *Women and Episcopacy: A Response to Cardinal Kasper* (Nottingham: Grove Books, 2006).

Wuerl, Donald W., 'Reflections on Governance and Accountability in the Church', in Francis Oakley and Bruce Russett (eds.), *Governance, Accountability, and the Future of the Catholic Church* (London & New York: Continuum, 2004), 13–24.

Yarnold, Edward, 'Tradition in the Agreed Statements of the Anglican–Roman Catholic International Commission', in Kenneth Hagen (ed.), *The Quadrilog: Tradition and the Future of Ecumenism. Essays in Honor of George H. Tavard* (Collegeville, Minn.: Liturgical Press, 1994), 239–54.

Young, Frances, *Biblical Exegesis and the Formation of Christian Culture* (Cambridge: Cambridge University Press, 1997).

Zizioulas, John D., 'Ortodossia', in *Enciclopedia del Novecento*, vol. v. (Rome: Istituto della Enciclopedia Italiana, 1980), 1–18.

—— *L'Être ecclésial* (Geneva: Labor et Fides, 1981).

—— 'The Ecclesial Presuppositions of the Holy Eucharist', *Nicolaus*, 10 (1982), 333–49.

—— *Being as Communion: Studies in Personhood and the Church* (London: Darton, Longman & Todd, 1985).

—— 'The Theological Problem of Reception', *One in Christ*, 21 (1985), 187–93.

—— 'The Mystery of the Church in Orthodox Tradition', *One in Christ*, 24 (1988), 294–303.

Zizioulas, John D., 'Preserving God's Creation: Lecture One', *King's Theological Review*, 12 (1989), 1–5.

—— 'Apostolic Continuity of the Church and Apostolic Succession in the First Five Centuries', *Louvain Studies*, 21 (1996), 153–68.

—— 'Primacy in the Church: An Orthodox Approach', in James F. Puglisi (ed.), *Petrine Ministry and the Unity of the Church* (Collegeville, Minn: Liturgical Press, 1999), 115–25.

—— *Eucharist, Bishop, Church: The Unity of the Church in the Divine Eucharist and the Bishop During the First Three Centuries*, trans. Elizabeth Theokritoff (Brookline, Mass.: Holy Cross Orthodox Press, 2001 [1994]).

—— *L'Osservatore Romano* (English edn.) (2 Nov. 2005), 13.

—— 'Where the Eucharist is, There is the Catholic Church' (Interview with Gianni Valente), *30 Days*, 8 (2005), 8–12.

—— 'Recent Discussions on Primacy in Orthodox Theology', in Walter Kasper (ed.), *The Petrine Ministry: Catholics and Orthodox in Dialogue* (Mahwah, NY: Newman Press, 2006), 231–46.

Zoghby, Elias, 'Eastern and Western Tradition in the One Church', in Hans Küng, Yves Congar, and Daniel O'Hanlon (eds.), *Council Speeches of Vatican II* (Glen Rock, NJ: Paulist Press, 1964), 32–5.

Zohar, Danah, and Marshall, Ian, *Spiritual Capital: Wealth We Can Live By* (London: Bloomsbury, 2004).

Zulehner, P. M., and Hennersperger, A., *'Sie gehen und werden nicht matt' (Jes 40: 31), Priester in heutiger Kultur* (Ostfildern: Schwabenverlag, 2001).

Web References

Allen J., John L., 'Pastoral ideas nixed as curia holds the line', *National Catholic Reporter* (29 Oct. 1999) <http://ncronline.org/NCR_Online/archives/102999/102999h.htm>.

—— 'Interview with Robert J. Taft, SJ', *National Catholic Reporter* (6 Feb. 2004) <http://ncronline.org/mainpage/specialdocuments/taft.htm>.

Anglican Communion News Service, 3314, 'Statement from the Archbishop of Canterbury and the Cardinal Archbishop of Westminster' (20 Feb. 2003) <http://www.anglicancommunion.org/acns/news.cfm/2003/2/20/ACNS3314>.

Anglican–Roman Catholic Bishops, 'Communion in Mission: The Report of the Meeting of Anglican–Roman Catholic Bishops, Mississauga, May 2000' <http://www.vatican.va/roman_curia/pontifical_councils/chrstuni/angl-comm-docs/rc_pc_chrstuni_doc_20000519_iarccum-mississauga_en.html>.

ARCIC, *The Final Report* (1982) <http://www.prounione.urbe.it/dia-int/arcic/doc/e_arcic_final.html>.

ARCIC II, *Salvation and the Church* (1987) <http://www.prounione.urbe.it/dia-int/arcic/doc/e_arcicII_salvation.html>.

—— *The Church as Communion: An Agreed Statement by the Second Anglican–Roman Catholic International Commission* (1991) <http://www.prounione.urbe.it/dia-int/arcic/doc/e_arcicII_communion.html>.

—— *The Gift of Authority: Authority in the Church III* (1999) <http://www.vatican.va/roman_curia/pontifical_councils/chrstuni/documents/rc_pc_chrstuni_doc_12051999_gift-of-autority_en.html>.

——*Mary: Grace and Hope in Christ* (2004) <http://www.vatican.va/roman_curia/pontifical_councils/chrstuni/angl-comm-docs/rc_pc_chrstuni_doc_20050516_mary-grace-hope-christ_en.html>.

Benedict XVI, Pope, 'First Message of His Holiness Benedict XVI at the End of the Eucharistic Concelebration with the Members of the College of Cardinals in the Sistine Chapel' (20 Apr. 2005)<http://www.vatican.va/holy_father/benedict_xvi/messages/pont-messages/2005/documents/hf_ben-xvi_mes_20050420_missa-pro-ecclesia_en.html>.

——'Mass, Imposition of the Pallium and Conferral of the Fisherman's Ring for the Beginning of the Petrine Ministry of the Bishop of Rome: Homily of His Holiness Benedict XVI' (24 Apr. 2005) <http://www.va/holy_father/Benedict_xvi/homilies/2005>.

——'Address of His Holiness Benedict XVI to the Delegates of Other Churches and Ecclesial Communities and of Other Religious Traditions' (25 Apr. 2005)<http://www.vatican.va/holy_father/benedict_xvi/speeches/2005/april/documents/hf_ben-xvi_spe_20050425_rappresentanti-religiosi_en.html>.

——'Solemnity of Sts Peter and Paul: Homily of His Holiness Benedict XVI' (29 June 2005) <http://www.vatican.va/holy_father/benedict_xvi/homilies/ 2005/documents/hf_ben-xvi_hom_20050629_sts-peter-paul_en.html>.

——'Address to the Roman Curia' (22 Dec. 2005) <http://www.vatican.va/holy_father/benedict_xvi/speeches/2005/december/documents/hf_ben_xvi_spe_20051222_roman-curia_en.html>.

——'Meeting with His Holiness Bartholomew I Ecumenical Patriarch of Constantinople: Address of the Holy Father' (29 Nov. 2006) <http://www.vatican.va/holy_father/benedict_xvi/speeches/2006/november/documents/hf_ben-xvi_spe_20061129_bartholomew-i_en.html>.

Bishops of the Church of England, 'Civil Partnerships—A Pastoral Statement from the House of Bishops of the Church of England' (25 July 2005) <http://www.cofe.anglican.org/news/pr5605.html>.

British United Reformed Church, *Conversations on the Way to Unity*—Conciliarity <http://www.urc.org.uk/conversations/conciliarity.htm>.

Carey, Archbishop George, and John Paul II, Pope, 'The Common Declaration of 5 Dec. 1996' <http://www.vatican.va/roman_curia/pontifical_councils/chrstuni/angl-comm-docs/rc_pc_chrstuni_doc_19961205_jp-ii-carey_en.html>.

Cassidy, Edward, 'Homily at Lambeth Ecumenical Vespers Service' (20 July 1998) <http://www.lambethconference.org/1998/news/lc034.cfm>.

Congregation for Bishops, and Congregation for the Evangelisation of Peoples, *Instruction on Diocesan Synods* (8 July 1997) <http://www.vatican.va/roman_curia/congregations/cbishops/documents/rc_con_cbishops_doc_20041118_diocesan-synods-1997_en.html>.

Congregation for Clergy, *General Directory for Catechesis* (1997) <http://www.vatican.va/roman_curia/congregations/cclergy/documents/rc_con_ccatheduc_doc_17041998_directory-for-catechesis_en.html>.

Congregation for the Doctrine of the Faith, '*Inter Insigniores*: Declaration on the Question of the Admission of Women to the Ministerial Priesthood' (15 Oct. 1976) <http://www.newadvent.org/library/docs_df76ii.htm>.

Congregation for the Doctrine of the Faith, '*Communionis Notio*: A Letter to the Bishops of the Catholic Church on Some Aspects of the Church Understood as Communion' (28 May 1992)<http://www.vatican.va/roman_curia/congregations/cfaith/documents/rc_con_cfaith_doc_28051992_communionis-notio_en.html>.

—— '*Ratio Agendi*: Regulations for Doctrinal Examination' (30 May 1997) <http://www.vatican.va/roman_curia/congregations/cfaith/documents/rc_con_cfaith_doc_19970629_ratio-agendi_en.html>.

—— *Doctrinal Commentary on John Paul II's Apostolic Letter* Ad Tuendam Fidem (1998) <http://www.Vatican.va/roman_curia/congregations/cfaith/documents/rc_con_cfaith_ doc_ 1998_ professio-fidei_ ge. html>.

—— '*Dominus Iesus*: On the Unicity and Salvific Universality of Jesus Christ and the Church' (6 Aug. 2000) <http://www.vatican.va/roman_curia/congregations/cfaith/documents/ rc_con_cfaith_doc_20000806_dominus-iesus_en.html>.

—— 'Note on the Expression "Sister Churches"' (30 June 2000) <http://www.vatican.va/roman_curia/congregations/cfaith/documents/rc_con_cfaith_doc_ 20000630_chiese-sorelle _en.html>.

—— 'Responses to Some Questions Regarding Certain Aspects of the Doctrine of the Church' (29 June 2007) <http://www.vatican.va/roman_curia/congregations/cfaith/documents/rc_con_cfaith_doc_20070629_responsa-quaestiones_en.html>.

Eastern Orthodox Patriarchs, 'Encyclical of the Eastern Patriarchs (1848). A Reply to the Epistle of Pope Pius IX' <http://www.fordham.edu/halsall/mod/1848orthodoxencyclical.html>.

Faith and Order Commission, *A Treasure in Earthen Vessels: An Instrument for an Ecumenical Reflection on Hermeneutics* (Faith and Order Paper, No. 182; 1998) <http://wcc-coe.org/wcc/what/faith/treasure.html>.

Harries, Richard, 'The Female Mitre', *The Tablet* (15 July 2006) <http://www.thetablet.co.uk/articles/8235/>.

House of Bishops of the Church of England, 'Civil Partnerships—A Pastoral Statement' (25 July 2005) <http://www.cofe.anglican.org/news/pr5605.html>.

Inter-Anglican Theological and Doctrinal Commission, *Virginia Report* (Harrisburg, Pa.: Morehouse, 1999) <http://www.lambethconference.org/1998/documents/report-1.pdf>.

International Anglican–Roman Catholic Commission for Unity and Mission, 'Ecclesiological Reflections on the Current Situation in the Anglican Communion in the Light of ARCIC' (2004) <http://www.prounione.urbe.it/dia-int/iarccum/doc/e_iarccum_2004.html>.

—— *Growing Together in Unity and Mission: Building on 40 Years of Anglican-Roman Catholic Dialogue* <http://www.vatican.va/roman_curia/pontifical_councils/chrstuni/angl-comm-docs/rc_pc_chrstuni_doc_20070914_growing-together_en.html>.

International Dialogue Between the Roman Catholic Church and the Mennonite World Conference, 'Called Together to Be Peacemakers' (2003) <http://www.prounione.urbe.it/dia-int/mn-rc/doc/e_mn-rc_fr2003.html>; also at <http://www.bridgefolk.net/calledtogether.htm>.

John XXIII, Pope, '*Ad Petri Cathedram*: Encyclical Letter on Truth, Unity and Peace in a Spirit of Charity' (29 June 1959) <http://www.vatican.va/holy_father/john_xxiii/encyclicals/documents/hf_j-xxiii_enc_29061959_ad-petri_en.html>.

John Paul II, Pope, '*Ex Corde Ecclesiae*: Apostolic Constitution on Catholic Universities' (15 Aug. 1990) <http://www.vatican.va/holy_father/john_paul_ii/apost_constitutions/documents/hf_jp-ii_apc_15081990_ex-corde-ecclesiae_en.html>.

—— '*Centesimus Annus*: On the Hundredth Anniversary of *Rerum Novarum*' (1 May 1991) <http://www.vatican.va/holy_father/john_paul_ii/encyclicals/documents/hf_jpii_enc_01051991_centesimus-annus_en.html>.

—— '*Ordinatio Sacerdotalis*: Apostolic Letter on Reserving Priestly Ordination to Men Alone' (22 May 1994) <http://www.vatican.va/holy_father/john_paul_ii/apost_letters/documents/hf_jp-ii_apl_22051994_ordinatio-sacerdotalis_en.html>.

—— and Mar Dinkha IV, *Common Christological Declaration of Pope John Paul II and Catholicos-Patriarch Mar Dinkha IV* (11 Nov. 1994) <http://www.prounione.urbe.it/dia-int/ac-rc/i_ac-rc-info.html>.

—— *Ut Unum Sint. Encyclical Letter on Commitment to Ecumenism* (25 May 1995) <http://www.vatican.va/holy_father/john_paul_ii/encyclicals/documents/hf_jp-ii_enc_25051995_ut-unum-sint_en.html>.

—— and Carey, Archbishop George, 'The Common Declaration' (5 Dec. 1996) <http://www.vatican.va/roman_curia/pontifical_councils/chrstuni/angl-comm-docs/rc_pc_chrstuni_doc_19961205_jp-ii-carey_en.html>.

—— '*Apostolos Suos*: Apostolic Letter Issued Motu Proprio on the Theological and Juridical Nature of Episcopal Conferences' (21 May 1998) <http://www.vatican.va/holy_father/john_paul_ii/motu_proprio/documents/hf_jp-ii_motu-proprio_22071998_apostolos-suos_en.html>.

—— and Bartholomew I, 'Common Declaration on Environmental Ethics' (10 June 2002) <http://www.vatican.va/holy_father/john_paul_ii/speeches/2002/june/documents/hf_jp-ii_spe_20020610_venice-declaration_en.html>.

—— '*Ecclesia de Eucharistia*: Encyclical Letter on the Eucharist in its Relationship to the Church' (17 Apr. 2003) <http://www.vatican.va/holy_father/john_paul_ii/encyclicals/documents/hf_jp-ii_enc_17042003_ecclesia-de-eucharistia_en.html>.

—— 'Address to the Bishops of the Ecclesiastical Region of Pennsylvania and New Jersey (USA) on their "Ad Limina" Visit' (11 Sept. 2004) <http://www.vatican.va/holy_father/john_paul_ii/speeches/2004/september/documents/hf_jp-ii_spe_20040911_ad-limina-usa_en.html>.

—— 'Homily, 13th November 2004, St Peter's Basilica, Rome' <http://www.vatican.va/holy_father/john_paul_ii/homilies/2004/documents/hf_jp-ii_hom_20041113_unitatis-redintegratio_en.html>.

Joint International Commission for Theological Dialogue Between the Roman Catholic Church and the Orthodox Church, 'The Mystery of the Church and of the Eucharist in the Light of the Mystery of the Holy Trinity' (1982) <http://www.prounione.urbe.it/dia-int/o-rc/doc/e_o-rc_03_munich.html>.

—— 'The Sacrament of Order in the Sacramental Structure of the Church' (1988) <http://www.prounione.urbe.it/dia-int/o-rc/doc/e_o-rc_05_valamo.html>.

Joint International Commission for Dialogue Between the Roman Catholic Church and the World Methodist Council, *The Grace Given You in Christ: Catholics and Methodists Reflect Further on the Church* (2006) <http://www.vatican.va/roman_curia/pontifical_councils/chrstuni/meth-council-docs/rc_pc_chrstuni_doc_20060604_seoul-report_en.html>.

Kasper, Walter, 'Keynote Address', in *May They All Be One...But How? Proceedings of the Conference Held in St Albans Cathedral on 17 May 2003* (2003) <http://www.ecumenicalstudies.org.uk>.

—— 'Letter of His Eminence Cardinal Walter Kasper to His Grace Dr Rowan Williams Archbishop of Canterbury' (17 Dec. 2004) <http://www.vatican.va/roman_curia/pontifical_councils/chrstuni/card-kasper-docs/rc_pc_chrstuni_doc_20041217_kasper-arch-canterbury_en.html>.

—— 'The Mission of Bishops in the Mystery of the Church: Reflections on the Question of Ordaining Women to Episcopal Office in the Church of England' (5 June 2006) <http://www.vatican.va/roman_curia/pontifical_councils/chrstuni/card-kasper-docs/rc_pc_chrstuni_doc_20060605_kasper-bishops_en.html>.

Lambeth Commission on Communion, *The Windsor Report 2004* (2004) <http://www.aco.org/windsor2004/downloads/windsor2004full.pdf>.

Lash, Nicholas, 'Churches, Proper and Otherwise', *The Tablet* (21 July 2007), 13–14 <http://www.thetablet.co.uk/articles/10084/>.

Lutheran World Federation and the Roman Catholic Church, *Joint Declaration on the Doctrine of Justification* (2000–1) <http://www.vatican.va/roman_curia/pontifical_councils/chrstuni/documents/rc_pc_chrstuni_doc_31101999_cath-luth-joint-declaration_en.html>.

Martin, Diarmuid, 'Will Ireland be Christian in 2030?', Twenty-fifth Patrick MacGill Summer School (18 July 2005) <http://www.dublindiocese.ie/index.php?option=com_contentandtask=viewandid=89andItemid=21>.

National Review Board for the Protection of Children and Young People, *A Report on the Crisis in the Catholic Church in the United States* (2004) <htpp://www.nccbuscc.org/nrb/nrbstudy/nrbreport.pdf>.

O'Brien, Keith Michael Patrick, 'Archbishop Reveals that Curial Bishops Blocked Reforms', *National Catholic Reporter* (29 Oct. 1999) <http://ncronline.org/NCR_Online/documents/JA10–22.htm>.

Paul VI, Pope, '*Ecclesiam Suam*: Encyclical Letter on the Church in the Modern World' (6 Aug. 1964) <http://www.vatican.va/holy_father/paul_vi/encyclicals/documents/hf_p-vi_enc_06081964_ecclesiam_en.html>.

—— '*Apostolica Sollicitudo*: Apostolic Letter Issued Motu Proprio on Establishing the Synod of Bishops for the Universal Church' (15 Sept. 1965) <http://www.vatican.va/holy_father/paul_vi/motu_proprio/documents/hf_p-vi_motu-proprio_19650915_apostolica-sollicitudo_en.html>.

—— '*Marialis Cultus*: Apostolic Exhortation for the Right Ordering and Development of Devotion to the Blessed Virgin Mary' (2 Feb. 1974) <http://www.vatican.va/holy_father/paul_vi/apost_exhortations/documents/hf_p-vi_exh_19740202_marialis-cultus_en.html>.

Pius X, Pope, '*Vehementer Nos*: Encyclical Letter on the French Law of Separation' (11 Feb. 1906) <http://www.vatican.va/holy_father/pius_x/encyclicals/documents/hf_p-x_enc_11021906_vehementer-nos_en.html>.

Pius XI, Pope, '*Mortalium Animos*: On Religious Unity' (6 Jan. 1928) <http://www.vatican.va/holy_father/pius_xi/encyclicals/documents/hf_p-xi_enc_19280106_mortalium-animos_en.html>.

—— '*Quadragesimo Anno*: On Reconstruction of the Social Order' (15 May 1931) <http://www.vatican.va/holy_father/pius_xi/encyclicals/documents/hf_p-xi_enc_19310515_quadragesimoanno_en.html>.

Pius XII, Pope, '*Sempiternus Rex Christus*: Encyclical Letter on the Council of Chalcedon' (8 Sept. 1951) <http://www.vatican.va/holy_father/pius_xii/encyclicals/documents/hf_p-xii_enc_08091951_sempiternus-rex-christus_en.html>.

Pontifical Council for Promoting Christian Unity, *Directory for the Application of Principles and Norms on Ecumenism* (1993) <http://www.vatican.va/roman_curia/pontifical_councils/chrstuni/general-documents/rc_pc_chrstuni_doc_19930325_directory_en.html>.

—— *The Ecumenical Dimension in the Formation of Those Engaged in Pastoral Work* (1995) <http://www.vatican.va/roman_curia/pontifical_councils/chrstuni/general-docs/rc_pc_chrstuni_doc_19950316_ecumenical-dimension_en.html>.

—— 'Guidelines for Admission to the Eucharist between the Chaldean Church and the Assyrian Church of the East' (25 Oct. 2001) <http://www.vatican.va/roman_curia/pontifical_councils/chrstuni/documents/rc_pc_chrstuni_doc_20011025_chiesa-caldea-assira_en.html>.

Prendergast, Martin, 'Compatible Not Competing—Pastoral Practice and Civil Partnerships' (2003) <http://www.titipu.demon.co.uk/samesexunions/compatcompete.htm>.

Sullivan, Francis A., 'The Impact of *Dominus Iesus* on Ecumenism', *America*, 183 (28 Oct. 2000), 8–11 <http://www.americamagazine.org/content/article.cfm?article_id=2266>.

United Methodist–Roman Catholic Dialogue, *Through Divine Love: The Church in Each Place and All Places* (2005) <http://www.usccb.org/seia/finalUMC-RC5-13masterintro.pdf>.

United States Conference of Catholic Bishops, *Charter for the Protection of Young People* (2002) <http://www.usccb.org/ocyp/norms.shtml>.

—— *Co-workers in the Vineyard of the Lord: A Resource for Guiding the Development of Lay Ecclesial Ministry* (2005) <http://www.usccb.org/laity/laymin/co-workers.pdf>.

US Lutheran–Roman Catholic Dialogue, *The Church as Koinonia of Salvation: Its Structures and Ministries. Lutherans and Catholics in Dialogue*, vol. x. (2005) <http://www.usccb.org/seia/koinonia.shtml>.

Williams, Rowan, 'Shaping Holy Lives: A Conference on Benedictine Spirituality' (29 Apr. 2003) n.p.

—— 'One Holy Catholic and Apostolic Church' (23 October 2005) <http://www.archbishopofcanterbury.org/965>.

—— 'The Challenge and Hope of Being an Anglican Today' (27 June 2006) <http://www.archbishopofcanterbury.org/640>.

—— 'Saint Benedict and the Future of Europe: Speech given at St Anselmo in Rome' (21 Nov. 2006) <http://www.archbishopofcanterbury.org/657>.

—— 'Archbishop's Greetings to Pope Benedict' (23 Nov. 2006) <http://www.archbishopofcanterbury.org/652>.

Wright, N. T., and Stancliffe, David, *Women and Episcopacy: A Response to Cardinal Kasper* (2006) <http://www.fulcrum-anglican.org.uk/news/2006/20060721kasper.cfm?doc=126>.

Name Index

Subject Index